T0067887

YOUR DAY *In* COURT

Using Common Law with Common Sense

Bradley J. Franks & Robert C. Simpson

authorHOUSE®

AuthorHouse™
1663 Liberty Drive
Bloomington, IN 47403
www.authorhouse.com
Phone: 833-262-8899

Published by AuthorHouse 01/16/2023

ISBN: 978-1-7283-7724-7 (sc)
ISBN: 978-1-7283-7725-4 (e)

Library of Congress Control Number: 2023900637

Print information available on the last page.

DEDICATION

This book is dedicated for the Americans who know the difference *between the "illusion of freedom" that is offered by a government that uses* trickery and deceit to obtain what it considers "value" and the real Freedom that our Fore-Fathers signed into "law" – The Constitution and the Bill of Rights.

It is also dedicated for those who have gone through the court system and thought they were getting a "fair" hearing or trial. The information in this book will educate you on the reality of just how crooked our court system is and for the people that have died due to the thoughtless electric companies that turned off their electricity just because they could not afford to pay a month's payment and for the people who were afraid to turn on a fan just to keep "cool" because of the fear of receiving a high power bill.

Also, for those Americans who know the difference between a U.S. Citizen and a true American. Remember, U. S. Policies (Statutes, Codes, or Ordinances) do not apply to Americans that exercise their rights set forth by the U. S. Constitution. Those who come from a different Country apply for Citizenship become U.S. citizens. The government has forgotten these facts and will be held accountable for their crimes against Americans.

ACKNOWLEDGMENTS

I WOULD LIKE TO THANK ALL THE CONCERNED PEOPLE THAT WITNESSED the crimes that were committed against us and motivated us to write this book for the education for all Americans and the International Community.

It does not take a person with a "PhD" or a "Degree" to figure out that there is something terribly wrong with our system, when a County or State bureaucracy can make "accusations" and find us "guilty" without the benefit of our trying to prove our innocence.

"We the People are the rightful master of both congress and the courts – not to overthrow the Constitution, but to overthrow the men who pervert the Constitution". ***Abraham Lincoln***

CONTENTS

UCC CONNECTION

FREE YOURSELF FROM LEGAL TYRANNY.

The following is for the accessible and understandable explanation of the confusing state of the government and the courts.

The frustration many Americans feel about our judicial system can be overwhelming and frightening; and, like most, fear is based on the lack of understanding of knowledge. Those of us who have chosen a path out of bondage and into liberty are facing, eventually, with the seemingly tyrannical power of the courts. We have been taught that we must "get a good lawyer", but that is becoming increasingly difficult, if not impossible. If we are to defend ourselves from the government, we find that the lawyers quickly take our money and tell us the ship is sinking and

"I can't help you with that -- I'm an officer of the court".

The only way for us to have a chance is for us to understand the "Rules of the game" and to understand the "true-nature of the Law". Lawyers have established and secured a virtual monopoly over this area of human knowledge by implying that the subject is just too difficult for the average person to understand, by creating a separate vocabulary out of Latin, French, German and English words of otherwise common usage. While at times it seems hopelessly complicated, it is not difficult to grasp -- lawyers are not as smart as they would leave us to believe. Besides, anyone who has been through a legal battle against the government with the aid of a lawyer has come to realize that lawyers learn about procedure, not law.

We must take the responsibility for finding and putting to good use the TRUTH. It is WE the People who must claim and defend our God-given Rights and our freedom from those who would take them from us. It is WE who must protect ourselves, our families and our posterity from the inevitable intrusion into our lives by those who live as a parasite off the labor, skill and talents of others.

There are bureaucrats who are writing letters, bills, laws, contracts and other such documents at the behest or not at the behest of the elected politicians that contradict decisions of the supreme Court of the United States. Note: Observe the small "s" in supreme Court. Supreme is an adjective describing the court, and not part of the title of that court. The small "u" in united States is used in the same manner. United is an adjective, and cannot be considered part of the title of our Constitutional Republic. United States, capital "U", is an entirely different, illegal and unconstitutional entity when its power extends beyond Washington, D. C. and the territories.

The judges will not honor any decisions of the Supreme Court after 1938. Prior to 1938, the Supreme Court was dealing with Public law; since 1938, the Supreme Court has dealt with Public Policy Statute, not Public Law, and those Supreme Court Cases do not apply to Public Policy. This is how disgusting the judicial system is in America. The common-man is NOT PERMITTED to know what is going on and the reasons for the decisions, which go against him or her. Because what the so-called judges [actually, they are magistrates not judges] are doing is actually illegal by the law, which is suspended in these so-called courtrooms. If the people that inhabit America were made aware of this situation, and the full implications of it, the system would collapse. The judges and the lawyers will not permit this to occur, as the system seems to benefit them, and they do not care about anything else. What is amazing is when you ask someone "what is your opinion about lawyers?" Most everyone's answer generally is that lawyers are the scum of the earth and they dislike them intensely.

Occasionally someone will mention one or two good lawyers. However, ask the same question about judges, "What is your opinion about judges?" Most people will say, "Oh, we respect the judge". What is wrong with us? Judges were lawyers first. All of whom are registered foreign agents for the United States by the bar association and have a foreign allegiance! Judges are much worse than lawyers, while some lawyers walking in and out of the so-called courtrooms may not really understand just what they are involved in, all of the judges understand very well. This is why they were PERMITTED and chosen to become so-called judges. Note: Public Policy means; the federal government is no longer bound by any restraint of law [Constitution] and may do whatever it pleases, more specifically, whatever the money kings who control the bankruptcy of America desire for the government to do!

Here are two cases to examine that will show you how the courts have stripped our rights away:

1. 1938 was the year of the Erie Railroad v. Tomkins case of the Supreme Court. It was also the year the courts claim they blended Law with Equity. A man sued the Erie Railroad for damages when he was struck by a board sticking out of a boxcar as he walked along beside the tracks. The district court had decided on the basis of Commercial (Negotiable Instruments) Law: that this man is not under any contract with the Erie Railroad, and therefore he had no standing to sue the company. By the Common Law, he was damaged and he would have had the right to sue.
2. This overturned a standing decision of over one-hundred years. Swift v. Tyson in 1840 which was a similar case, and the decision of the supreme Court was that in any case of this type, the court would judge the case on the Common Law of the state where the incident occurred -- in this case Pennsylvania. However, in the Erie Railroad case, the supreme Court ruled that all federal cases would be judged under the Negotiable Instruments Law. There would be no more decisions based on the Common Law at the federal level. We now begin to see a blending of Law and Equity. All our courts since 1938 were Merchant Law courts and not Common Law courts.

We know, today, that the reason that the supreme Court did in 1938 was because Roosevelt suspended the Constitution in 1933. The Constitution IS the Common Law. This situation could not exist if the Constitution was in full force and effect. The so-called judges understand this very well; this is why they refuse to permit anyone to introduce evidence about the suspension of the Constitution or the imposition of Emergency Rule into the court's records.

In 1938, all the higher judges, the top attorneys and the U.S. attorneys were called into a secret meeting and this is what they were told: "America is a bankrupt nation--it is owned completely by its creditors. The creditors own the Congress, they own the Executive, they own the Judiciary and they own all the state governments. Take silent judicial notice of this fact, but never reveal it openly. Your court is operating in an Admiralty Jurisdiction--call it anything you want, but do not call it Admiralty". Note: If what they were doing was legal and above suspicion, they could openly reveal the facts. Since they hid their actions, we know and understand that what they were doing was illegal, and they knew it!

The reason they cannot call it Admiralty Jurisdiction is that your defense would be quite different in Admiralty Jurisdiction from your defense by the Common Law. In Admiralty, there is no court, which has jurisdiction unless there is a valid international contract in dispute. If you know it is Admiralty Jurisdiction, and they have admitted on the record that you are in an Admiralty Court, you can demand that the international maritime contract, to which you are supposedly a party, and which you supposedly have breached, be placed into evidence.

No court has Admiralty/Maritime Jurisdiction unless there is a valid international contract that has been breached. If the Court is under Admiralty Jurisdiction, they must place the contract in evidence, so that one can challenge the validity of the contract. What they would have to do is place the national debt into evidence. They would have to admit that the international bankers own the whole nation, and that we are their slaves.

The bankers said it would not be expedient at this time to admit that they own everything and could foreclose on every nation of the world. The reason they do not want to tell everyone that they own everything is that there are still too many privately owned guns. There are uncooperative armies and other military forces. Therefore, until they can gradually consolidate all armies into a WORLD ARMY and all courts into a single WORLD COURT, it is not expedient to admit the jurisdiction the courts are operating under. When we understand these things, we realize that there are certain secrets they do not want to admit, and we can use this to our benefit.

The Constitution of the united States mentions three areas of jurisdiction in which the courts may operate:

1. Common Law: Common Law is based on God's Law. Anytime someone is charged under the Common Law, there must be a damaged party. We are free under the Common Law to do anything we please, as long as you do not infringe on the life, liberty, or property of someone else. The Common Law does not allow for any government action that prevents a man or woman from making a fool of themselves. For example: "I went to the County of Riverside and asked the Riverside County Board of Supervisors what laws (Codes, Statutes or Ordinances) would I be breaking if I staged a Peaceful Protest. I also asked if I would have to obtain a Permit for the peaceful Protest. Their reply was a laugh and stated "None" and "It's your right to stage a Peaceful Protest". There was no Common Law broken according to The Riverside County's Board of Supervisor. However, we can simplify the Common Law even better for your understanding. When you cross over a state-line, most states have signs that read, "BUCKLE YOUR SEAT BELTS – its THE LAW". This cannot be a Common Law, because who would you injure if you did not buckle - up? No one, but yourself. This would be compelled performance. However, Common Law cannot compel performance without infringing upon your liberty of choice. Any violation of Common Law is a CRIMINAL ACT, and is punishable.
2. Equity Law: Equity Law is law that compels performance. It compels you to perform to the exact letter of any contract that you are under. If you have compelled performance, there must be a contract somewhere, and you are being compelled to perform under the obligation of the contract. If you cannot perform under the contract for any reason this can only be a civil action - not criminal. In Equity Jurisdiction, you cannot be tried criminally, but you can be compelled to perform to the letter of the contract. If you refuse to perform as directed by the court, you can be charged with contempt of court, this is a criminal action. Is staging a peaceful protest, when you seek permission, an Equity Law? Is Building your own home without Loans or Contractors an Equity Law? Are our seatbelt

laws Equity Laws? The answer to all three questions is NO! You cannot be penalized or punished for not keeping to the letter of the contract, or if there is no contract.

3. Admiralty/Maritime Laws: Admiralty/Maritime Laws are a civil jurisdiction of Compelled Performance, which also has Criminal Penalties for not adhering to the letter of the contract, but this only applies to International Contracts. We can now understand what jurisdiction a peaceful protest, building your own home without permits, or seatbelt laws (and all traffic laws, building codes, statutes, codes and ordinances, tax codes etc.) are under. Whenever there is a penalty for failure to perform (such as a willful failure to file, or obtain the so-called permits for building your own home, or staging a Peaceful Protest), that is Admiralty/Maritime Law and there must be a valid international contract in force.

However, the courts do not want to admit that they are operating under Admiralty/Maritime Jurisdiction, so they took the international law or Law Merchant and adopted it into the codes. That is what the Supreme Court decided in the Erie Railroad case. The decisions will be based on commercial law or business law and that it will have criminal penalties associated with it. Since they were instructed not to call it Admiralty Jurisdiction, they called it and still call it Statutory Jurisdiction.

You may ask how we got into this situation where we can be charged with failure to wear seatbelts, obtain their so-called permits for building your own home or staging a Peaceful Protest and be fined or punished for it. Isn't the judge sworn to uphold the Constitution? Yes, he is! You must understand that the Constitution, Article I, Section 10, give us the unlimited right to contract as long as we do not infringe on the life, liberty, or property of someone else. Contracts are enforceable, and the Constitution gives two-Jurisdictions where contracts can be enforced -- Equity and Admiralty. However, we find them being enforced in Statutory Jurisdiction. This is the embarrassing part for the courts, but we can use this to box the judges into a corner in their own courts.

By the Common Law, both parties must enter into every contract knowingly, voluntarily, and intentionally or it is void and unenforceable. These are the characteristics of a Common Law contract. There is another characteristic - it must be based on substance. For example, contracts used to read, "For one dollar and other good and valuable considerations, I will paint your house, etc." This is a valid contract; the dollar was a genuine, silver dollar. Now, suppose you wrote a contract that said, "For one Federal Reserve Note and other considerations, I will paint your house..." For example, I painted your house the wrong color. Could you go into a Common Law court and get justice? No, you could not. A Federal Reserve Note is a "colorable" dollar, as it has no substance, and in a Common Law jurisdiction, that contract would be unenforceable. (Colorable - that which is in appearance only, and not in reality, what it purports to be, hence counterfeit, feigned, having the appearance of truth. Black's Law Dictionary, Sixth Ed.)

The word "colorable" means something that appears to be genuine, but is not. Maybe it looks like a dollar, and maybe it spends like a dollar, but it is not redeemable for lawful money (silver or gold), it is "colorable." When a Federal Reserve Note is used in a contract, the contract becomes a "colorable" contract. "Colorable" contracts are enforced under a "colorable" jurisdiction. By creating Federal Reserve Notes, the government had to create a jurisdiction to cover the kinds of contracts, which use them. We now have what we call a Statutory Jurisdiction, which is not a genuine Admiralty jurisdiction. The judges are enforcing "colorable" Admiralty Jurisdiction because we are using "colorable money." Colorable Admiralty is now known as Statutory Jurisdiction. How did the government apply the Statutory Jurisdiction over us?

The government set up a "colorable" law system to fit the "colorable" currency. It used to be called the Law Merchant or the Law of Redeemable Instruments, because it dealt with paper, which was redeemable in something of substance. However, once Federal Reserve Notes had become unredeemable, there had to be a system of law, which was completely "colorable" from start to finish. This system of law was codified as the Uniform Commercial Code, and has been adopted in every state.

This is "colorable" law, and it is used by all the courts. I have explained on one of the keys earlier, which is that the country is bankrupt and we have no rights. If the master says "Jump!" then we the slaves had better jump, because the master has the right to cut his or her head off. As slaves, we have no rights. However, the creditors/masters had to cover that up, so they created a system of law called the Uniform Commercial Code. This "colorable" jurisdiction under the Uniform Commercial Code is the next key in understanding what has happened.

One difference Between Common Law and the Uniform Commercial Code is that in Common Law, contracts must be entered into:

1. **Knowingly,**
2. **Voluntarily,**
3. **Intentionally.**

However, by the Uniform Commercial Code (UCC), this is not so. First, contracts are unnecessary. Under this new law, "agreements" can be binding, and if you only exercise the benefits of an "agreement", it is presumed or implied that you intend to meet the obligations associated with those benefits. If you accept a benefit offered by the government, you are obligated to follow, to the letter, each and every statute involved with that benefit. The method has been to get everyone exercising a benefit and the government does not have to tell the people what the benefit is. Some people think it is the driver's license, the marriage license, or birth certificate, building permits, etc. It is none of these.

The benefit being used is that we have been given the privilege of discharging debt with **limited liability**, instead of paying debt. When we pay a debt, we give substance for substance. If I buy a gallon of milk with a silver dollar, that dollar bought the gallon of milk, and the milk bought the silver dollar -- substance for substance. However, if I use a Federal Reserve Note to buy the same gallon of milk, I have not paid for it.

There is no substance for the Federal Reserve Note. A Federal Reserve Note is a worthless piece of paper given in exchange for something of substantive value. Congress offers us this benefit: Debt money, created by the federal United States, can be spent all over the continental united States, it will be legal tender for all debts, public and private, and the limited liability is that you cannot be sued for not paying your debts.

The government has said, "We're going to help you out, and you can discharge your debts instead of paying your debts." When we use this "colorable" money to discharge our debts, we cannot use a Common Law court. We can only use a "colorable" court. We are completely under the jurisdiction of the Uniform Commercial Code -- we are using non-redeemable negotiable instruments and we are discharging debt rather than paying debt.

To completely understand and grasp the completely fraudulent nature of the swindle being committed upon the American people, you have to have a thorough understanding of the subjects we discussed earlier in this book. The national debt is an illusion, it does not exist, the interest created in this system is unplayable, it simply accumulates endlessly, and the most important point of all: in order to force this system upon the Americans, the government permitted the international bankers to steal the gold of the American people and made it illegal for Americans to own gold. This situation lasted until the 1970's. We were permitted to own gold again because the intention is to force America into a strict gold standard at some point, and we have no gold, which will permit this system to operate even marginally. Forcing America into a gold standard, under the guise of our "proven" inability to manage debt, will complete the destruction of the middle-class and finish our subjection to the international bankers and the United Nations.

Every system of civilized law must have two characteristics: Remedy and Recourse. Remedy is a way to get out from under that code, statute, ordinance or law. The Recourse is if you have been damaged under that code, statute, ordinance or law, you can recover your loss. The Common Law, the Law of Merchants, and even the Uniform Commercial Code all have remedy and recourse, but for a long time the recourse and remedy could not be found. If you go to the library and ask to see the Uniform Commercial Code, they will show you a shelf of books completely filled with the Uniform Commercial Code. When you pick up a volume and start to read it, it will seem to have been intentionally written to be confusing. After a lengthy search for the Remedy and Recourse in the UCC, they were found in the first volume, at 1-207 and 1-103.

> "The making of a valid Reservation of Rights preserves whatever rights the person then possesses, and prevents the loss of such rights by application of concepts of waiver or estoppels (UCC 1-207)".

It is important to remember when we go into a court that we are in a commercial, international jurisdiction. If we go into court and say, "I DEMAND MY CONSTITUTIONAL RIGHTS!" the judge will most likely say,

> "You mention the Constitution again, and I'll find you in contempt of court"!

The same is true if you go in the courtroom you will see a federal Flag of red, white, and blue with gold fringe and tassel. This flag creates an Admiralty Jurisdiction represents No nation and No Constitution. The Gold Eagle on top represents the President, U.S.A. There is only one, official, united States flag, which preserves the rights protected by the u. S. A. Constitution. Under it, you are innocent until proven guilty. National flags are government flags. They do not preserve the u. S. A. Constitutional Rights. (You are guilty until proven innocent under them). Our flag is red, white and blue (no yellow). It is our flag of law, order and peace. Our flag description can be found in Title: 4: u. S. A. Codes: Chapter: 1: Section: 1, 2 and 3.

One the next page is an illustration of the Flag that we are supposed to use and the flags that are being used in the courtrooms throughout the Country.

However, the Courts claim that if you argue the "validity" of the "gold-fringe" flag it is a "frivolous" suit. The argument should not be over the flags **but** the "Dual Jurisdiction" within the courtroom and the "Breach of Contract" by the Court Officers and Officials.

We do not understand how the judge can do this. Hasn't he or she sworn to uphold the Constitution? The Rule here is: you cannot be <u>charged</u> under one jurisdiction, and <u>defend</u> under another. An excellent example that you will understand is this: If a government of a foreign country like Mexico, Canada or Cuba were to approach you and charged you with a crime, do you go to those respected governments and say, "I demand my Constitutional rights?" No. The proper way to answer this is to say: "***<u>Your laws do not apply to me</u>*** -- ***<u>I am not a Mexican, Canadian or Cuban</u>***" or whatever country is accusing you. You must make your reservation of rights under the jurisdiction in which you are charged -- <u>not under some other jurisdiction</u>.

So in a UCC court, you must claim your reservation of rights under the UCC 1-207. The Uniform Commercial Code 1-207 continues to read:

> "When a waivable right or claim is involved, the failure to make a reservation thereof, causes a loss of the right, and bars its assertion at a later date. (UCC 1-207.9)".

You have to make your claim early. UCC 1-207 continues to read:

> "The Sufficiency of the Reservation - Any expression indicating an intention to reserve rights, is sufficient, such as "without prejudice" (UCC 1-207.4)".

Whenever you sign **any** legal document that deals with Federal Reserve Notes - in any way, shape or manner - you need to write **under** your autograph (signature):

> "Without prejudice UCC 1-207"

This demonstrates that you reserve your rights. If challenged by the court you can show at UCC 1-207.4 that you **have** sufficiently reserved your rights. It is very important that you fully understand just what this means. When you use "without prejudice U.C.C. 1-207" in connection with your autograph (signature), you are saying:

> "I reserve my right not to be compelled to perform under any contract or commercial agreement that I did not enter <u>knowingly</u>, <u>voluntarily</u>, and <u>intentionally</u>. Furthermore, I do not accept the compelled benefit of any unrevealed contract or commercial agreement".

This also applies for the "Small Print" in their contracts.

What is the compelled performance of an unrevealed commercial contract or agreement? When you use Federal Reserve Notes instead of silver or gold dollars, is it <u>voluntary</u>? No! <u>There is no lawful money</u>, so you have to use Federal Reserve Notes - you have to accept the benefit. The government has given you the benefit to discharge your debts with limited liability, and you do not have to pay your debts. How nice they are. If you did not reserve your rights under UCC 1-207.7, you are ***compelled*** to accept the benefit, and are therefore obligated to obey every statute, ordinance, and regulation, code of the government, at all levels of the government - federal, state and local. If you understand this, you will be able to explain to the judge when he or she asks. Moreover, he or she will ask, so be prepared to explain it to the court. You will also have to understand UCC 1-103 - the argument and recourse. To understand this fully, go a law library and photocopy these two sections from the Uniform Commercial Codes. There are at least two editions, look for the least confusing one and written in plain English.

The Recourse appears in the Uniform Commercial Code at 1-103.6, which reads:

> "The Code is complimentary to the Common Law, which remains in force, except where displaced by the code. A statute should be construed in harmony with the Common Law, unless there is a clear legislative intent to abrogate the Common Law".

Use this argument in court: "The code recognizes the Common Law. If it did not recognize the Common Law, the government would have to or had to admit that the United States is bankrupt and is completely owned by its creditors". However, it is not expedient to admit this, so the Code was written so as not to abolish the Common Law entirely. Therefore, if you have made a sufficient, timely, and explicit reservation of your rights at UCC 1-207, you may then insist that the statutes be construed in harmony with the Common Law. If the charge is building your home without permits, staging a Peaceful Protest, or failing to buckle your seatbelt, you may demand that the court produce the injured person who has filed a verified complaint. For example, if you are served with a citation on building your own home, or arrested for trespass on private property, or failure to buckle your seatbelt, you may ask the court who was injured as a result of the Peaceful Protest, building your own home, or failing to "buckle up". However if the judge won't listen to you and just moves ahead with the case, then you will want to read to him or her the last sentence of UCC 1-103.6, which reads:

> "The Code cannot be read to preclude a Common Law action".

Tell the judge:

> "Your Honor, I can sue you under the Common Law, for violating my right under the Uniform Commercial Code, I have a remedy, under the U.C.C., to reserve my rights under the Common Law. I have exercised the remedy, and now you must construe this statute in harmony with the Common Law, and you must come forth with the damaged party".

If the judge insists on proceeding with the case, act confused and ask him/her this question,

> "Let me understand, Your Honor: Has this court made a legal determination that the sections 1-207 and 1-103 of the Uniform Commercial Code, which is the system of law your court is operating under, are not valid law before this court"?

The judge has to answer and is in a jam! How can the court throw out one part of the Code and uphold another? If the judge answers, "yes," then you say:

> "I put this court on notice that I am appealing your legal determination".

Of course, the higher court will uphold the Code on appeal. The judge knows this, so once again you have boxed him/her into a corner. Just so, we can understand how this whole process works; let us look at a court situation such as a traffic violation. Let us assume that you drove through a red light and a police officer gave you a traffic ticket.

1. The first thing you want to do is to delay the action for at least three weeks. This you can do by being pleasant and cooperative with the officer. Explain

to the officer that you are very busy and ask if he could please set your court appearance for about three weeks away. Remember the government's trick:

> "I'm from the government, and I am here to help you".

Now we want to use this approach with them.

2. Appear before the clerk of the traffic court and say:

> "I believe it would be helpful if I talk to you, because I want to save the government some money (usually this gets their attention). I am undoubtedly going to appeal this case. As you know, in an appeal, I have to have a transcript, but the traffic court does not have a court reporter. It would be a waste of taxpayer's money to run me through this court and then to have to give me a trial *de novo* in a court of record. I do need a transcript for appealing, and to save the government some money, maybe you could schedule me to appear in a court of record".

You can show the date on the ticket and the clerk will usually agree that there is plenty of time to schedule your trial for a court of record. Now your first appearance is in a court of record and not in a traffic court, where there is no record. When you get into court, there will be a court reporter there who records every word the judge speaks, so the judge is much more careful in a court of record. You will be in a much better situation there than in traffic court. If there is no record, the judge can say whatever he wants -- he can call you all sorts of names and tell you that you have no rights, and so on -- and deny it all later.

3. When you get into court, the judge will read the charges: "Driving through a yellow light, or whatever, and this is a violation of ordinance XYZ". The judge will then ask you, "Do you understand the charge against you?" (It is very important to get into the record that you do not understand the charges. With that in the record, the court cannot move forward to judge the facts.

4. You reply:

> "You're Honor; there is a question I would like to ask before I can make a plea of innocent or guilty. I think it could be answered if I could put the officer on the stand for a moment and ask him or her a few short questions".

Usually the judge will allow you to ask the officer the questions. The judge then will have the officer sworn in and take the stand.

5. You ask the officer on the stand,

> "Is this the instrument that you gave me"?

Hand the officer the traffic citation.
Officer will reply:

> 'Yes this is a copy of it. The judge has the other portion of it'.

You reply:

> "Where did you get my address that you wrote on that citation"?

Officer will reply:

> 'I got it from your driver's license'.

Hand the officer your driver's license and say:

> "Is this the document you copied my name and address from"?

Officer will reply:

> 'Yes, this is where I got it'.

You rely:

> "While you've got that in your hand, would you read the signature that's on that license"?

After the officer reads the signature you state:

> "While you are there, would you read for the record what it says under the signature"?

Officer will reply:

> 'It says, without prejudice UCC 1-207'.

A competent Judge will be compelled to state:

> 'Let me see that license'!

After the judge looks at the license he will state to the officer:

> 'You didn't notice this printing under the signature on this license, when you copied the name and address onto the ticket'?

Officer will reply:

> 'No. I was just getting the name and address -- I didn't look down there'.

Judge will reply:

> 'You're not very observant as an officer. Therefore, I am afraid I cannot accept your testimony in regards to the facts of this case. This case is dismissed'.

In this case, the judge found a convenient way out -- he or she could say that the officer was not observant enough to be a reliable witness. The judge did not want to admit the real nature of the jurisdiction of his court. Once it is in the record that you had written 'Without prejudice UCC 1-207' on your license, the judge knew that he/she would have to admit that:

A. You had reserved your Common Law rights under the UCC;
B. You had done it sufficiently by writing without prejudice UCC 1-207 on your driver's license;
C. The statute would now have to be read in harmony with the Common Law, and the Common Law says that the statute exists, but there is no injured party; and
D. Since there is not an injured party or complaining witness, the court has no jurisdiction under the Common Law.

6. If the judge tries to move ahead and try the facts (Note: The facts in a court case are also known as subject-matter) of the case, you will want to ask him the following question:

> Your honor let me understand this correctly: Has this court made a legal determination that it has authority under the jurisdiction that it is operating under, to ignore two sections of the Uniform Commercial Code which have been called to its attention?

If the judge says yes, tell him/her that you put the court on notice that you will appeal that legal determination, and if you are damaged by the judge's actions, you will sue him in a Common Law action -- under the jurisdiction of the UCC. This will work just as well with the Internal Revenue Service. We can use the UCC before we get to court. (However, further information about the I. R. S. and how to get from under their tyranny later). More information about the I. R. S. will be presented in a second book and how to prevent them from abusing 'taxpayers'.

The True Nature of FEMA

There are a few Governors that are very concerned that when the International Bankers foreclose of the nation and officially admit that they own the whole world, that they can round up everybody in the state capitol building and put them in internment camps and hold the indefinitely. The new regime may or may not give them a trial. Unfortunately, the new regime will do whatever they want. However, for now it is not expedient for them to foreclose on the nation until they get everything ready. This is where the <u>F</u>ederal <u>E</u>mergency <u>M</u>anagement <u>A</u>gency (FEMA) comes into existence. FEMA has been established and put in place without anyone really noticing it.

FEMA has been designed for when America is officially declared bankrupt, which will be a national emergency. In a national emergency, <u>all</u> Constitutional Rights and <u>all</u> law that previously existed will be suspended. FEMA has created large concentration camps where they will put anyone who might cause trouble for the orderly plan and process of the new regime to take over the nation. Even some of the Politicians could be thrown into one of these internment camps and incarcerated indefinitely. This is all in place now, and they are just waiting to declare a national emergency. State governments could also be dissolved. <u>Anyone</u> who might oppose the new regime will be imprisoned until a new set of laws could be written and a new government set up. Some of the politicians know all of this and are concerned. They do not want this to happen while they are in office. (Note: Go back and re-read the "New" Constitution of the New states of America again, and decide if this is where you want to live, because you are going to be given that choice, or lack of choice, unless we stop the situation all together).

To understand all of this we must realize that there are two separate entities known as the <u>United States</u>.

When America was established, banking dynasties such as the Rothschild family were very unhappy because America was established under the Common Law. The Common Law is based on substance, and this <u>substance</u> is mentioned in the Constitution as gold or silver. America is a Constitutional Republic -- that is a union of the States by the Constitution. When Congress was working for the Republic, the only thing it could borrow was gold or silver. However, the Rothschild's banks did not loan gold or silver, and naturally, they did not like this new government. The Rothschild's loaned only debt. In other words, they loaned ***<u>nothing</u>***!

Note: I am not against any race, creed, color, sex or national origin, personally. However, if you look up the Rothschild's name on-line, you will discover that the real name of the Rothschild family was Bauer and they descended from the destroyed country of Kazakhstan and not Israel. The Bauer's ancestors were the tribe related to Attila the Hun who worshiped many gods but his descendants converted to Judaism around 1,200 A.D.

The Bauer family and other Khazar Jewish members (not Hebrew Jewish) became the ideal bagmen for the overflowing monies of the Vatican. At one time Catholics could not charge interest on loans so the Non-Catholics were the best suited to covertly launder and hold the vast fortunes and carry out the diabolical plots of the Vatican and the Jesuits who are the ultimate controllers of the privately owned Federal Reserve Bank.

The Rothschild family made a deal with the King of England. The King would borrow paper and agree to pay in gold. Nevertheless, these united States, with their Constitution, were an obstacle to them, and it was much to the Rothschild's advantage to get the colonies back under England's rule. Of course, that did not work, so they had to find another way.

Around the time of the American Civil War was when the bankers discovered a flaw in the Constitution. The vulnerability was in Article: I: Section: 8: Clause: 17. Remember that there are two nations called "United States." What is a nation? A nation: **whenever you have a governing body, having a prescribed territory containing a body of people.** Is that a nation? Yes. We have a governing body by the Republic.

The three branch government. These are the legislative, the executive and judicial branches, with a Constitution. There is a prescribed territory containing a body of people. This is what is called a Constitutional Republic.

However, Article: I: Section: 8: Clause: 17: gave Congress, which is known as the legislative branch of the government, exclusive rule over a given *territory* known as the District of Columbia, containing a body of people. Here we have a nation within a nation. This is a legislative democracy within a Constitutional Republic. When Congress was a part of the Constitutional Republic, it had the obligation of providing a medium of exchange for us. Its duty was to coin gold or silver. Anyone who had a piece of gold or silver could bring it in and have it freely minted into coin. This was the medium of exchange for the Republic.

In the Legislative Democracy (over Washington D. C.), Congress is not limited by the Constitution. Congress has exclusive rule (Note: Read the following as *Public Policy*) over the District of Columbia. The legislators can make the law by a majority vote -- that makes it a democracy; they have the authority to have administrative agents to enforce their own law; and they have courts in the legislative branch of the government, to try their own law. Here we have the legislature making the law, enforcing the law and trying the law, all within the one branch of government. This is a one-branch government within a three-branch government. Under the three-branch government, the congress passes the law, which has to be in harmony with the Constitution, the executive branch enforces (Note: All police and military power belong to the Executive Branch of a Constitutional Republic) the law passed by congress, and the judiciary tries the law, pursuant to the Constitution.

THE THREE-BRANCH CONSTITUTIONAL REPUBLIC and the ONE-BRANCH LEGISLATIVE DEMOCRACY are both called THE UNITED STATES.

One is the federal United States, and the other is the continental united States. (Note: When the United States moves outside the lawful bounds established for it in the Constitution, and into and over the united States, it is acting illegally and unconstitutionally. This has primarily been done through treaties, which clearly shows the danger of permitting the Senate to be elected by the people instead of representing the states in Congress. These violations of the Constitution have occurred in order to establish special interests (groups) at the expense of the people).

If you say that you are a United States citizen, which United States are you referring too? Anyone who lives in the District of Columbia is a United States citizen. The remaining population in the fifty states is the national citizenry of the nation. We are domiciled in various sovereign states, protected by the constitutions of those states from any direct rule of Congress over us. In the democracy, anyone who lives in those states known as Washington, D. C., Guam, Puerto Rico, or any of the other federally held territories is a citizen of the United States [D. C.]. We must be careful of our choice of words -- we are not citizens of the United States. We are not subject to Congress. Congress has exclusive rule over a given territory, and we are not part of that territory. (Note: Anyone who is born between the Canadian Border and the Border of Mexico, the East Coast and the West Coast of the Continental united States is a Native American).

Where did Congress get the authority to write the Internal Revenue Code? It is found in Article: I: Section: 8: Clause: 17 of the Constitution. To pass that law, they only needed a majority vote. There is no other way that they could pass laws directly affecting individuals. Title: 26, the Internal Revenue Code, passed as law for another nation (remember the definition of 'nation'), but Title: 26: is not consistent with the Bill of Rights. If you try to fight the I. R. S. You have no rights -- The Code does not give you any of your constitutional rights. It simply says:

> "You failed to file an income tax form -- you failed to perform in some specific manner".

By the Common Law, you are free to do whatever you want as long as you do not infringe upon the life, liberty or property of anyone else. If you do not want to perform, you do not have to. The only way you can be compelled to perform under the Constitution in the continental united States, is if you entered a contract. However, if you are not under a contract you cannot be compelled to perform. How can you be compelled to file an income tax form, or any form?

The contracts that are referred to here are called 'adhesion contracts'). When Congress works for the Republic, every law it passes must be in harmony with the Constitution and the Bill of Rights. However when Congress works for the Legislative Democracy, any law it passes becomes the law of the land (remember that Congress has exclusive legislative control over federal territory) Read this as Public Policy or as the absence of law.

If you are charged with Willful failure to file and income tax form, that is a law for a different nation. You are a *non-resident alien* to that nation. It is a foreign corporation to you. It is not the Republic of the continental united States coming after you; it is a foreign nation -- a legislative democracy of a foreign nation coming after you. If you get a note of Deficiency from the I. R. S., it is a presentment from the federal United States, then you can use the Uniform Commercial Codes to dishonor it, and you can mention that you are among the national citizenry of the continental united States, and you are a non-resident alien to the federal United States. You never lived in a federal territory and never had any income from the federal United States. Furthermore, you cannot be required to file or pay taxes under the compelled benefit of using the Federal Reserve Notes, because you have reserved your rights by the Common Law through the Uniform Commercial Code at 1-207.

Much of the information concerning the actual suspension of the Constitution and its continued suspension by each President became known after 1933. This points out the absolute obligation that we all have in continuing to study and learn as more of the facts concerning the fraud and treason being committed in Washington, D. C., comes to light. You can only hide the truth for so long. This is also, why it is essential to understand the complete fraud of our unplayable so-called national debt before much of the information contained in this book really makes a solid impact.

The Founding Fathers would never have created a government that was going to boss them around! There were 13 sovereign States [colonies]. They were nations, and they joined together for protection from foreign enemies. They provided a means by which the union of the sovereign states could fend off foreign enemies. However, they never gave the congress of the federal United States direct rule over any citizen of any state. They were not going to be ordered around by that government they set up.

The supreme Court has declared that Congress can rule what Congress creates. Congress did not create the States; However, Congress did create <u>federal regions</u>. Congress can rule the federal regions, but Congress cannot rule the States. You may ask yourself, "How have we been tricked into federal regions?"

Remember how the government always comes to us and says,

> "I'm from the government and I'm here to help you".

The government went out into the various states and said,

> "We don't want you to have to go to all that trouble of writing three or four letters to abbreviate the name of the state -- for example: South Dakota just write SD, or you can just write WY for Wyoming instead of Wyo".

All the states of the union have gotten a new two-letter abbreviation. Even a state such as Rhode Island has a new abbreviation. It is RI, instead of

R. I. They have left off the periods. When you use a two-letter abbreviation, you are compelled to use a zip code, because there are so many states, for example, the states that start with the letter M. ME is Maine -- MI is Michigan. How many people dot every 'I', or make an 'I' that looks like an 'e' ? With MA, MO, MN, MS, etc., and some sloppy writing, and you could not tell one from another. Therefore, we have to use the zip code in order to tell them apart. However, if you wrote Mich., or Minn., or Miss., there would be no real problem telling which it was. There is no harm in using the zip code, if you lawfully identify your state. There was no state legislature to lawfully change the abbreviation of the state from the old abbreviation to the new. Therefore, if you do not use the Lawful abbreviation for your state, but use the shorter new abbreviation, you have to use the zip code. If you read the Zip Code Directory, it will inform you that the first digit of your zip code is the federal region in which you reside. If you use MI for Michigan, you cannot use the state constitution to protect you because you did not identify your state. You used the zip code, which identifies which federal region you live in. Remember, Congress may rule directly, federal regions, but it cannot rule the citizens of any state.

Let us look at how the states have become the accommodation party to the national debt. There are many people, including politicians, who are very concerned about this, and who know that it could happen very soon. If America is declared a bankrupt nation, it will be a national emergency. The Federal Emergency Management Agency (FEMA) will take over, and anyone who opposes the new government of the creditors can be sent to a detention camp. We will have no rights whatsoever.

They have already set up prison camps with work camps nearby so the people can be used for slave labor. I could be governors, legislators, and other leaders who would be hauled away to these detention camps, while the people now disenfranchised from power would likely be chosen to run the new government. This could happen very soon, as the national debt is so large as to be unplayable. Even the interest of the debt is virtually unplayable. The national debt - more than three trillion dollars - is not owed by the Continental united States. It is the federal United States that had authority to borrow bank credit. When Congress worked for the Continental united States, it could only borrow gold or silver, so the national debt was borrowed in the name of the federal United States. The federal United States has been bankrupt since 1938; however, the federal United States had to trap the States into assuming the debt obligation of the federal debt.

In the Uniform Commercial Code, we find the term 'accommodation party.' How did the states become the 'accommodation party' for the federal debt? The federal government, through the money system, made the states deal in Federal Reserve Notes, which means that everything the states do is 'colorable.' Under the 'colorable' jurisdiction of the Uniform Commercial Code, all of the states are the accommodation party to the federal debt. Now the concern is to find out how we can get out of the situation. In the Common Law and the Law of Merchants -- that is the International Law Merchant -- there is a term called no-interest contract. A no-interest contract is void and unenforceable. What is a no-interest contract?

(UCC 3-415: "Accommodation party." One who signs commercial paper in any capacity for lending his name to another party for the instrument (contract). Such a party is a surety [Surety is, "One who undertakes to pay money or to do other act in the event that his principal fails therein]).

If I were to insure a house that did not belong to me, that would be a no-interest contract. I would just want the house to burn down. I would pay a small premium, perhaps a few hundred dollars, and insure it for 80,000 dollars against fire. Then I would be waiting for it to burn so I could trade my small premium for $80,000. Under the Common Law and under international law of the Law Merchant, that is called a no-interest contract and it is void and unenforceable in any court.

In the Uniform Commercial Code, no-interest contracts are called 'unconscionable contracts'. The section on unconscionable contracts covers more than forty pages found in the Anderson Code. The federal United States has involved the states as the accommodation party to the federal debt. This can be proven as an unconscionable contract. We need to get some litigation into the courts before the government declares a national emergency, claiming that this state has no lawful responsibility for the national debt (of the federal United States), because it became an accommodation party to this debt through an unconscionable contract (Note: This is a polite way of saying 'fraud'). If we get litigation before the courts under the International Laws when the nation is declared bankrupt, the creditors would have to settle this matter first, and it would delay them. They want the new government to appear to be legitimate, so they could not just move right in and take over the state, because it would be in an International Court. This would be extremely important at this time.

(Note: The Uniform Commercial Code, in exactly the same manner of the Fourteenth Amendment, could not exist and could not be enforced except for that one word in the Thirteenth Amendment: *involuntary*. As we have already observed, your subjection under the Uniform Commercial Code **MUST** be voluntary. This is why there is a remedy and recourse for these Statutes. This is why a so-called judge MUST ask you if you understand that he may fine you for violating a *commercial,* and thus a civil, statute. You MUST agree to a fine before the judge can impose it upon you. You do not have to agree to be punished for breaking the LAW. The UCC is fraudulent in nature, just as the I. R. S. Code and all other *statutes* passed by Congress and enforced upon the Citizens of this land are fraud. Just as the so-called bankruptcy of the United States is fraud on a massive scale. This fraud will never be stopped until the people who inhabit this nation demand that it be stopped. YOU can only accomplish this.

Let us review some of the material presented earlier. They contain very valuable information, which is worth repeating.

How do you 'box-in' the judge?

First, play dumb. I believe it would not be hard for most of us to play dumb in a courtroom. After all, the judge likes to use words that intentionally confuse us. If you are arrested and you go into court, just remember that in a criminal action, you have to understand the law or it is a reversible error for the court to try you. If you do not understand the law, they cannot try you.

In a traffic case, tax case, a Peaceful Protest case or Building Code Violations case you are called into court and the judge reads the law and then asks, "Do you understand the charges?"

Defendant:

"No, your Honor, I do not".

Judge:

'Well, what is so difficult about the charge(s)? Either you drove the wrong way on a one-way street or you did not.

You can only go one way on that street, and if you go the other way it is a fifty dollar fine. What is so difficult about this that you do not understand'?

Defendant:

"Your Honor, It is not the letter of the law, but rather the nature of the law that I don't understand. The Sixth Amendment of the Constitution gives me the right to request the court to explain the nature of any action against me, and upon request, the court has the duty to answer. I have a question about the nature of this action".

Judge:

'Well, what is it? What do you want to know'?

Defendant:

"Is this a Civil or Criminal Action"?

Judge:

'It is a criminal action'.

If it were a civil action there could be no fine, so it has to be criminal.

Defendant:

"Thank you for informing of that. ***Then the record will have to show*** that this action against your name is a criminal action, is that right"?

Judge:

'Yes'.

Defendant:

> "I would like to ask another question about this criminal action. There are two criminal jurisdictions mentioned in the Constitution: one is under the Common Law and the other deals with International maritime Contracts, under an Admiralty Jurisdiction. Equity is Civil, and you said this is a Criminal action, so it seems it would have to be under either the Common Law, or Maritime Law. However, what puzzles me is that there is no *Corpus Delicti*. Therefore, it does not appear to me that this court if moving under the Common Law".

Corpus Delicti: The body of a crime. The body (material substance) upon which a crime has been committed, *e.g.,* the corpse of a murdered man, the charred remains of a house burned down. In a derivative sense, it is the objective proof or substantial fact that a crime has been committed. The "Corpus Delicti" of a crime is the body, foundation or substance of the crime, which ordinarily includes two elements: the act and the criminal agency of the act. Black's Law Dictionary Sixth Ed. Here that gives this court a jurisdiction under the Common Law.

Judge:

> 'No, I can assure you this court is not moving under the Common Law'.

Defendant:

> "Thank you, Your Honor, but now you make the charge(s) against me even more difficult to understand. The only other criminal jurisdiction would apply only if there was an International Maritime Contract involved, I was party to it, it had been breached, and the court was operating in an Admiralty Jurisdiction".

"I do not believe I have ever been under any International Maritime Contract, so I would deny that one exists. I would have to demand that such a contract, if it does exist, be placed into evidence, so that I may contest it. Surely this court is not operating under an Admiralty Jurisdiction".

You just put words in the judge's mouth.

Judge:

'No, I can assure you, we're not operating under an Admiralty Jurisdiction. We are not out in the ocean somewhere -- we are right here in the middle of the State of_______________ . No, this is <u>not</u> an Admiralty Jurisdiction'.

Defendant:

"Thank you, Your Honor, but now I am more puzzled than ever. If this/these charge(s) is/are not under the Common Law, or under Admiralty - and those are the only two criminal jurisdictions mentioned in the Constitution -- what kind of jurisdiction could this court be operating under"?

Judge:

'It's <u>Statutory</u> Jurisdiction'.

Defendant:

"Thank you, Your Honor. I am glad that you told me that. However, I have never heard of the jurisdiction. Therefore, if I have to defend under that, I would need to have the <u>Rules of Criminal Procedure</u> for Statutory Jurisdiction. Can you tell me where I might find those rules"?

<u>There are no rules for **Statutory Jurisdiction**</u>, so the judge will get angry at this point and say:

'If you want answers to questions like that, get yourself a licensed attorney -- I am not allowed to practice law from the bench'.

Defendant:

"Your Honor, I don't think anyone would accuse you of practicing law from the bench if you just answer a few questions to explain for me the nature of this action, so that I may defend myself".

Judge:

'I told you before; I am not going to answer any more questions. Do you understand that? If you ask any more questions in regards to this, I am going to find you in contempt of court! However, if you cannot afford a licensed attorney, the court will provide you with one. But if you want those questions answered, you must get yourself a licensed attorney'.

Defendant:

"Thank you, Your Honor, but let me just see if I understand this correctly. **Has this court made a legal determination that it has authority to conduct a criminal action against me, under a secret jurisdiction, the rules of which are known only to this court and to licensed attorneys, thereby denying me the right to defend in my own person"?**

The judge does not have an answer for this question. He or She will probably postpone the case and eventually just let it go. Just remember if you do not understand the charge(s), they cannot try you criminally. This would be automatically a reversible error on appeal. However, remember when you are in the judges' courtroom, they can tell you to "shut up" so that they can proceed with whatever they want to do and if you do not they threaten you with a charge - contempt of court.

If I were a young person, 18 or 20 years old and just starting out in my first job, I would not want Social Security. With my signature of the application I would write 'Without prejudice', UCC 1-207 and I would reserve my Common Law rights. Now, why wouldn't I want Social Security today? When our parents entered into the Social Security System in the 1930s, they paid into it Dollars that had good purchasing power. Now, they are receiving a promised return in Federal Reserve Notes, which have considerably less value. For example, in 1940, you could buy a deluxe Chevrolet for 800 dollars. Today's Federal Reserve Notes will not buy the rear fenders and trunk on a new Chevrolet. At this time, I would not want to put Federal Reserve Notes into Social Security now. Later, you will be receiving something like the German Mark after World War I -- when it took a billion just to buy a loaf of bread. The Federal Government will give you every Federal Reserve Note back that they promised, but they may not buy anything.

Under The Uniform Commercial Code, you have the right in any agreement, to demand a guarantee of performance. Do not go to them and say, "I want to rescind my Social Security number," or "I refuse to accept it." Just remain calm and smart and say, "I would be happy to get a Social Security number and enter into this contract, however, I have a little problem. What assurance do I have before I enter into this contract that the purchasing power of the Federal Reserve Notes I get back at the end of the contract will be as good as the ones that I pay in at the beginning?" (Note: They cannot guarantee that, and you have a right under the UCC for assurance of performance under the contract). So, tell them, "Well, I cannot enter this contract unless the government will guarantee to pay me at the end of the contract with the same value Federal Reserve Notes that I am paying in. (Note: Both may be called Federal Reserve Notes, however, remember that these Federal Reserve Notes do not hold their value). I want assurance on this contract that the Federal Reserve Notes that I get in my retirement will buy as much as the ones that I am giving you now in my working years." (Note: We know that they cannot make that guarantee). So just say,

> "I would be glad to sign this, but if you cannot guarantee performance under the contract, I'm afraid I cannot enter the contract".

Now, did you refuse the contract or did they refuse the contract? You can find the sections of the Uniform Commercial Code, which grant the right to have assurance that the contract you have entered will be fulfilled properly -- that the return will equal the investment and you can reject the contract using the Code. By using their own system of law, you can show that they cannot force you into a contract of this nature. Approach them as meek as a lamb, sly as a snake and wise as an owl.

It is extremely important to be gentle and humble in all dealings with the government of the courts -- never raise your voice or show anger. In the courtroom, always be polite and build the judge up -- call him/her 'Your Honor.' Give him/her all the 'Honor' they want. It does not help you to be difficult, however, be cooperative and ask questions in a way that leads the judge to give information, which you will need for the record.

In many courts, there will be a regular court reporter. He or She gets the job at the judges' pleasure, so he or she does not want to displease the judge. The court reporter is sworn in to give an accurate transcript of every word that is spoken in the courtroom. However, if the judge makes a slip of the tongue, he or she turns to the court reporter and says,

> 'I think you had better leave that out of the transcript; just say it got a little too far ahead of you, and you could not quite get everything in'.

This will be missing from the transcript.

If you bring in your own licensed court reporter the judge will become very angry and tell you this,

> 'This court has a licensed court reporter right here, and the record of this court is this court reporter's record. No other court reporter's record means anything in this court'.

Be pleasant and say,

> "Of course, Your Honor, we are certainly glad to use your regular court reporter. However, Your Honor, you know that sometimes things move so fast that a court reporter get a little behind, and does not quite keep up with it all.

> Would it not be helpful if we had another licensed court reporter in the courtroom, just in case your court reporter got a little behind, so that we could fill in from this other court reporter's data? I am sure, Your Honor, that you want an accurate transcript".

If the judge is approached in this manner, usually they allow the court reporter that you bring to remain throughout the proceedings.

These are little tricks of getting around in court. There are others that use this information who end up handcuffed, hit over the head and thrown into jail, because they approach the situation with a chip on their shoulder. They try to tell the judge what the law is and that he is a no-good scoundrel and so on. Just remember to approach them as meek as a lamb, sly as a snake, and wise as an owl.

Now let us review the important points within this book: It is very important to know and understand the meaning of 'Without prejudice' UCC 1-207, in connection with your signature. It is most likely that the judge will ask you what this means. So please learn and understand this carefully;

> "The use of - Without prejudice UCC 1-207 - in connection with my signature (autograph) indicates that I have reserved my Common Law right not to be compelled to perform under any contract that I did not enter into knowingly, voluntarily, and intentionally. **Furthermore, I do not accept the liability associated with the compelled benefit of any un-revealed contract or commercial agreement"**.

The compelled benefit is the privilege to use Federal Reserve Notes to discharge your debts with limited liability rather than to pay your debts with silver coins. It is called a compelled benefit because there are no silver coins in circulation. You have to eat and you can only buy food with the medium of exchange provided by the government. You are not allowed to print your own money, so you are compelled to use theirs. This is the compelled benefit of an unrevealed commercial agreement. If you have not made a valid, timely and explicit reservation of your rights under UCC 1-207 and you simply exercise this benefit rendered by the government, you will be obligated, under an implied agreement, to obey every statute, ordinance and regulation passed by government, at all levels -- federal, state and local.

(See UCC 1-201: General Definitions (3): "Agreement" means the bargain of the parties in fact as found in their language or by *implication from other circumstances,* including course of dealing or usage of the trade or course of performance).

The information presented here within this book is not to be construed or offered as legal advice. For that, as you know, you must "get yourself a licensed attorney." Having said this, we need to point out that one of the most difficult aspects of dealing with a licensed attorney - even a good one - may be knowing just *whose side he or she is on* (after all, a licensed attorney is an *officer of the court*)! Therefore, for those of us who have concluded that having an attorney means that you will soon be chained, gagged, and lead to the gallows, this information may be in dispensable. For the extraordinary challenges of appearing in court in one's own person - *pro per* - there are few reliable sources of information. Learning to defend ourselves, is being responsible instead of turning over one or more area of our lives to 'professionals' - may be the only way to have any chance of digging ourselves out of this pit of legal tyranny. The greatest problem we face in education today is the matter of widespread *legal illiteracy.*

However, there will always be a number of people, who just do not care about these issues, who either:

1. Have a soft life which is supported and maintained by this secret system of law and the institutions which have grown up around it ['I can make a bundle buying these IRS-seized homes cheap and resell them'], or
2. Don't believe that anything can be done about it ['you can't fight city hall'], or
3. Simply do not have the energy or inclination to do anything about it ['that's nice, let's see what's on TV'], or
4. Become complacent and just accept the inevitable.

For those good 'citizens' this whole effort may seem useless, or even threatening. Our Forefathers did not intend for us to spend our lives in statutory slavery for the benefit of a handful of secret world manipulators, even if the 'masters' grant us some token pleasures and/or diversions. Human dignity requires much more than entertainment. The door is there and the key exists, we must find it and use it to return to freedom.

Let us discover the mistakes we have made, find the truth, and let us apply it with meekness and wisdom and let us gently but firmly reclaim the precious freedom, which we have so foolishly given up.

It is very difficult to make this statement any better than this: Freedom…is never free. It takes constant work and vigilance. Furthermore, our freedoms were paid for in substance: ***Blood!*** That means our freedoms cannot be taken away from us *except* through our *voluntarily surrendering them*. This is what the Thirteenth Amendment reads: "Neither slavery nor involuntary servitude, except as a punishment for crime wherefore the party shall have been duly convicted, shall exist within the united States, or any place subject to their jurisdiction." In other words, *voluntary* ***servitude is lawful in this once-great nation***. However, each and every one of us must make this choice. Do you wish to be free, or do you find the chains of slavery attractive to you? If you choose slavery, you do so because you will not take responsibility for freedom, and you will not take responsibility for yourself. ***You cannot transfer responsibility****!*

The government does not take responsibility for you just because you assume that they do. The government produces no wealth and can give nothing that they do not first, through the force of 'law', confiscate from someone (some individual). This means that they cannot accept the responsibility for any *individual*. The government can only give the illusion that they are responsible for a group, and in this illusion of responsibility, we find that the *individual* is disenfranchised, and has no value. The government uses statements like Collateral Damage, acceptable losses and so forth. If you think that, they are speaking from a military standpoint, you would be greatly mistaken.

Therefore, as long as the illusion is kept in place that any action taken is for the 'good of the group', or 'for the good of the society', any barbarity committed against any individual or group of individuals is permissible. This is why the Law must be ignored, because the Law ***will not permit*** this type of abuse of the individual. How can any act be accepted which does not benefit the individuals in a group? The very acceptance of this type of reasoning is proof of the ignorance of the whole of the group in question, because this reasoning reduces those who accept this falsehood to the level of animals! *We the people,* the inhabitants of this land, must soon choose which course we are to follow: Are we human, or are we animal, to be done with as our masters choose? I know my answer. Do you know yours?

2

THE REMEDY

There is a remedy for the Judges and Lawyers for the behavior they are committing towards Americans. The lawyers and judges will be held responsible for the illegal actions that they are responsible for. In this chapter I will explain how we can charge the lawyers and judges with crimes that are punishable by prison sentence or hanging, by the law. The judges and lawyers are committing Treason by Sedition by trying cases in Admiralty Jurisdiction without proving any jurisdiction.

These (so – called) professionals ignore any type of law that is proving them in the wrong, this is called Apartheid. There are several Cases that were tried by the supreme Court that explains that the lower courts are in the wrong. The cases I have included in this book, I am involved with, are other examples of how these Courts are getting away with Treason by Sedition. What I find amazing is that the courts claim that there are no remedies for the cases I am involved with. However, I would like to remind the courts and lawyers that there is no "statute of limitations" for Fraud or Capital crimes committed against Americans. I do realize that the facts of these cases cannot be [re]tried, because of the double–jeopardy law.

However, we realize that we can have these cases reopened by new evidence and have the charges overturned or dismissed by following the Constitution and the Remedy that the Uniform Commercial Codes provide.

We are charging the "People of State of California", "Riverside County" and all of the "perpetrators" with Treason by Sedition, Malfeasance, Abuse of Authority, Fraud, Civil Rights Violations and Grand Theft. However, we do not "trust" the U. S. Court system to hear this case because of the conflicts of interests. The following are the Constitutional Amendments and U. S. Supreme Court cases that support these charges. However, what court in the United States is going to try these cases against the lawyers and judges and do so with impunity without exposing themselves for the same crimes?

The States do not have the right to "steal" or "infringe" upon your given rights. Furthermore, the second Amendment, in part, states "the right of the people". This means the right of each and every person. The second Amendment further states, in part, "Shall not be infringed".

There are no subparagraphs, sections or subsections allowing the States or bureaucrats to change that which would be an acceptable "infringement". However, all infringements are "forbidden". Who says so? We say so; Americans! Each word or phrase that is within the Constitution has been defined and can be found in Black's Law Dictionary. Judges and Lawyers cannot change the definitions to suit their purpose to find you "guilty" of any Statutory crime and is "proven" to be "contrary to your rights".

Statutes, Codes and Ordinances and other Regulations are **not** enacted into law. However, by signing a "Voter Registration" card or Driver's license you are **accepting** all of the fiat regulations that the States claim against all of us. However, there is a Remedy and the Officials try very hard to ignore this Remedy at their peril. Furthermore, when you sign the Driver's License Application the State issues a card that has placed you in a "Nom De Guerre" status. A Nom De Guerre is a "Fiction" or "Fictitious character". When the Sate officials put your name in "all capital letters" they are claiming that you are a "Deceased Entity". Birth Certificates used to be in upper and lower type case. This is for a "live" birth. The only Official that can apply your name in all "Capital Letters" is the Coroner, because you have become a "deceased entity".

The Elected Officials "swear or affirm" to support and defend the Constitution and the first thing they do in Office is to "scuttle" the Constitution or claim that they have the right to pass whatever "laws" they deem "right" and for the "protection of the people".

We hear Politicians say, "We are just protecting the public". This is not a valid excuse to abrogate the Constitution or our rights. We can file a Title 18 USC section 2381 "Treason" or Title 18 USC Chapter 115 "Treason by sedition". The following are some of the Amendments that apply to "We the People" and our "basic rights". These [so-called] professionals [Judges,

Lawyers and Politicians] prey upon our "ignorance" to help line their pockets at our expense. This book is written for your education on how "We" can put a stop to some of the abuse of authority directed at us. A majority of people that go through this "Legal?" system develop a cognitive dissidence.

Cognitive Dissidence – Is a situation where people do not believe that there is a problem because the problem is so big that their brains will not accept or recognize it as a problem.

Most Americans are apathetic of this situation until they get caught in one form or another. Then they scream "foul" or "this is unfair, you cannot do this". As the author of this book I believe it is my right to educate you on your rights and the timely exercise of those rights.

The following are some of the Amendments that have established our "Basic Rights".

Amendment I [1791]

Congress shall make no law respecting an establishment of religion, or prohibiting the free exercise thereof; or abridging the freedom of speech, or of the press; or the right of the people peaceably to assemble, and to petition the Government for a redress of grievances.

Amendment IV [1791]

The right of the people to be secure in their persons, houses, papers, and effects, against unreasonable searches and seizures, shall not be violated, and no Warrants shall issue, but upon probable cause, supported by Oath or affirmation and particularly describing the place to be searched, and the persons or things to be seized.

Amendment V [1791]

No person shall be held to answer for a capital, or otherwise infamous crime, unless on a presentment or indictment of a Grand Jury, except in cases arising in the land or naval forces, or in the Militia, when in actual service in time of War or public danger; nor shall any person be subject for the same offence to be twice put in jeopardy of life or limb; nor shall be compelled in any criminal case to be a witness against himself; nor be deprived of life, liberty, or property, without due process of law; nor shall private property be taken for public use, without just compensation.

Amendment VI [1791]

In all criminal prosecutions, the accused shall enjoy the right to a speedy and public trial, by an impartial jury of the State and district wherein the crime shall have been committed, which district shall have been committed, which district shall have been previously ascertained by law, and to be informed of the nature and cause of the accusation; to be confronted with the witnesses against him; to have compulsory process for obtaining witnesses in his favor, and to have the Assistance of Counsel for his defense.

Amendment VII [1791]

In Suits at common law, where the value in controversy shall exceed twenty dollars, the right of trial by jury shall be preserved, and no fact tried by jury, shall be otherwise re-examined in any Court of the United States, than according to the rules of the common law.

Amendment VIII [1791]

Excessive bail shall not be required, nor excessive fines imposed, nor cruel and unusual punishments inflicted.

Amendment IX [1791]

The enumeration in the Constitution, of certain rights, shall not be construed to deny or disparage others retained by the people.

Amendment X [1791]

The powers not delegated to the United States by the Constitution, nor prohibited by it to the States, are reserved to the States respectively, or to the people.

The following cases were tried by the U. S. Supreme Court and are cases that support the charges against the [so – called] 'professionals' that claim that they have 'immunity' from violating your Civil Rights against these laws and claim that "we only did our jobs". Furthermore, these basic cases support your rights against those who would violate your rights and claim that they "followed the laws".

Statutes, Codes and Ordinances that are "repugnant" to the Constitution are "unenforceable". I would like to remind you as you read this book, 'Ignorance of the law is no excuse'. The following cases were tried in the United States Supreme Court and they "out rank" or "trump" any case at State, County or City level.

1. Marbury v. Madison, 5 US 137 [1803]
   "All laws which are repugnant to the Constitution are null and void".
2. Murdock v. Penn., 319 US 105 [1943]
   "A State may not impose a license, permit or fee for exercising your liberties".
3. Erie Rail Road v. Tompkins, 304 US 64 [1938]
   "No state shall take a right and convert it into a privilege".
4. Miranda v. Arizona, 384 US 436 [1966]
   "Where rights secured by the Constitution are involved, there can be no rule making or legislation which would abrogate them".
5. Norton v. Shelby County, 118 US 425 [1886]
   "An unconstitutional act is not law; it confers no right; it imposes no duties; affords no protection; it creates no office; it is legal contemplation, as inoperative as though it had never been passed"
6. United States v. Bishop, 412 US 346 [1973]
   "This case will help you in the fact that the Prosecution has to "Prove willful intent".
7. Shuttlesworth v. City of Birmingham, 373 US 262 [1963]
   "This case tells us that States cannot punish you for exercising your rights".
8. Owen v. City of Independence, 445 US 622 [1980]
   "This case explains that "color of law" violates constitutional rights".
9. Maine v. Thibodeau, 475 US 1144 [1986]

“This case explains that the Government Officials cannot claim ignorance of the law”.

10. Shapiro v. Thompson, 394 US 618 [1969]
    “This case explains that we have a “fundamental right” to travel unencumbered”.
11. Boyd v. United States, 116 US 616 [1886]
    “This case explains that it protects against encroachments or constitutionality”.
12. Byars v. United States, 273 US 28 Note: 3 [1927]
    “This case explains that the courts have to be watchful for the constitutional rights of the citizen, and against any stealthy encroachments thereon”.

The following is reference material from the American Jurisprudence for your support against the “wrongful” acts committed against you as an American:

1. 16 Am Jurisprudence section 97 (this tells the judge how to interpret the Constitution)
2. 16 Am Jurisprudence section 117 (this tells the courts that the rights shall not be infringed)
3. 16 Am Jurisprudence section 155 (rule in favor of the Constitution and its provisions)
4. 16 Am Jurisprudence section 177 (this deals with declaratory judgment)
5. 16 Am Jurisprudence section 255 (the courts have to rule on the Constitutionality of the Statute)
6. 16 Am Jurisprudence section 256 (statutes and codes that are in conflict are Un-constitutional)
7. 16 Am Jurisprudence section 257 (statutes and codes have to be justified to be enforced)
8. 16 Am Jurisprudence section 258 (Congress cannot give license for the States for Ex-Post Facto)
9. 16 Am Jurisprudence section 260 (there are no “degrees” of constitutionality of statutes or codes)

These Books are in the Legal Libraries and you can find them online. The best books to look in are the 'West Law' books.

The first thing you want to do if you are served with a "summons" into court by a "public" office or a "ticket" is to 'demur' it as an answer.

"**Demurrer** n. (dee-muhr-ur) a written response to a complaint filed in a lawsuit which, in effect, pleads for dismissal on the point that even if the facts alleged in the complaint were true, there is no legal basis for a lawsuit. A hearing before a judge (on the law and motion calendar) will then be held to determine the validity of the demurrer. Some causes of action may be defeated by a demurrer while others may survive. Some demurrers contend that the complaint is unclear or omits an essential element of fact. If the judge finds these errors, he/she will usually sustain the demurrer (state it is valid), but "with leave to amend" in order to allow changes to make the original complaint good. An amendment to the complaint cannot always overcome a demurrer, as in a case filed after the time allowed by law to bring a suit. If after amendment the complaint is still not legally good, a demurrer will be granted. In rare occasions, a demurrer can be used to attack an answer to a complaint. Some states have substituted a motion to dismiss for failure to state a cause of action for the demurrer".

The following is an example of how to write out a "Demurrer" or in some States "A Motion for Dismissal".

1. At the top of the document type "Name". State your name in upper and lower case typing.
2. Directly under "Name", Type "Address". Then place your physical address where you reside.
3. Under "Address" be sure to type "In Pro Per". (Propria persona which means "for oneself").
4. In **Bold** Print center the Title of the Court you are addressing whether it is Superior Court of (name the state) or Traffic, Divorce, Civil or other Courts whichever your case falls under.
5. In normal print type "County of (insert the name of the county).
6. Type in the name of the "Plaintiff". On the same line type in "Case No.: (insert no.)"

7. Type in "vs." (vs. – versus).
8. Type "Name" and type your name.
9. Under your name type "Defendant in Pro Per".
10. Under the case number type, in **Bold** print and upper case type, "**DEMURRER, (or MOTION FOR DISMISSAL), MEMORANDUM OF POINTS AND AUTHORITIES, DECLARATION**".
11. Under the heading of "Demurrer" or "Motion for Dismissal" you need to demur and object of the jurisdiction of the court in the matter. This is where you define why you are objecting to the case that the State, County or City Bureaucrat levied against you.
12. Under the heading of "Points and Authorities" you have to name the supreme Court Cases that support your reason why the demurrer or motion for dismissal is valid. Furthermore, you also need to add the "ruling" from the supreme Court Justices that have given on the matter.
13. Under the heading of the "Declaration" you need to state that you have "committed "no crimes" and that you were exercising you "rights" as an American.
14. The final step in creating a demurrer or a motion for dismissal is your "Prayer" or "Prayer for relief". This is when you request the courts to dismiss with "prejudice" all counts without leave to amend and if you have been "financially harmed" you can get your fees and monies returned.
15. The last thing you do in this document is to sign your "autograph".

Note: remember to use supreme Court Cases in your Points of Authorities. The judge cannot "abrogate" or "reverse" these decisions without causing "Breach of Contract" or committing "Treason by Sedition" or "Apartheid". The following, on page 47, is a template that you can use for your Demurrer or Motion for Dismissal:

[Name]
[Address]
In Pro Per

[Court name]

[Plaintiff's name],	)	Case No.: [Case number]
	)	
Plaintiff,	)	**DEMURRER or (Motion for Dismissal),**
	)	**MEMORANDUM OF POINTS AND AUTHORITIES,DECLARATION**
vs.	)	
	)	
[Defendant's name],	)	
	)	
	)	
Defendant		

Dated this [**Date**]

____
[Name]
[Address]

If the "Demurrer" or "Motion for Dismissal" is done correctly the judge has no choice but to grant you "the win". However, if the judge is so deposed to continue with the case and the "Demur" or "Motion for Dismissal" is **not** accepted, you have the "right" to "Object" to anything the "Prosecutor" says in the line of questioning or "how much information a witness volunteers".

"A motion to dismiss is a request from one side in a legal dispute for the judge to expel a case from the court's consideration. The motion may ask the judge to dismiss the case due to a variety of factors. Courts allow motions to dismiss in order to boost speed and efficiency of the court system by weeding out cases that are inappropriate. Furthermore, a motion to dismiss asserts that the plaintiff or prosecutor is not legally entitled to receive a court-imposed remedy, regardless of the veracity of the facts. Judges may dismiss cases with or without prejudice, the difference being whether the claimant has the right to sue on the same cause of action at a later date".

In 1963 the "Traffic Courts" were merged with the "Criminal Courts". However, the mistake that was made is that you have to find out which "hat" the Judge is wearing. If it is a "Court of Equity" the Prosecution has to produce a "contract" and an "injured party". If the Prosecution cannot produce an injured party or a contract the "Civil Infraction" cannot be tried "legally" because of the fact the States cannot convert an established "Right" into a "privilege" and force you into a "License, Permit or Fee". The Constitution is an "Iron clad contract" for "We the people". It is a contract that is set up to limit "Government".

A good example for using the following argument is for traffic tickets. Traffic tickets are a Bill of Attainder and they are the easiest to use as an example to show you how the Courts are violating your basic rights of travel. The first thing you want to do on this "ticket" is to write "UD" (under duress), and <u>under</u> the box where you "sign" your name write "UCC 1-207 without prejudice". Then sign your autograph. By this you are stating to the officer and to the courts you are **not** admitting "guilt" nor are you joining them in their schemes for you to be punished at the whim of the officer, City, County, State or Court system. In essence, you cut off the Admiralty/ Maritime jurisdiction.

When the judge calls your name for you to appear for your case, go up and identify yourself and say, "Present your honor". The judge will "practice" law from the bench by asking you "Discovery" questions. He/she will ask if you received a "ticket". A Judge is a third party that is hearing the facts. The Prosecutor presents the facts. Your only answer to the Court and Prosecutor should be in the form of a demur and dismissal for a "frivolous" action. Explain for the court and prosecution that you do not intend to "acquiesce into a quasi-jurisdiction". This is an issue you can bring up in your briefs before the court.

If the judge or prosecution asks you if you are an attorney or if you have a "license" to practice law, you can state for the record that you are not "practicing law" and that "you know what you are doing". You come before the court as a "un-franchise common law freeman". You live at the "Common Law". You are not a participant in any "tontine scheme" or limited liability in any joint ventures in a profitable, insurable interest or requires' you to participate in any illegal "Ponzi schemes". You are an average citizen. We have the right to contract our time, labor, and skills as we see fit. You do not need some capricious arbitrary third party like the Bar Association telling you different. The States erroneously and arbitrarily turned your "right to work" into a privilege and issued a license, permit and fee. This is unconstitutional. You can also add an order for collecting your "costs" and "fees" for your time and expense. However, be cautious, you will be challenged on your costs and fees. If you try to "Pad the document" you will be charged with "Perjury".

Your argument should flow in your briefs in this nature, if the courts want to "test" your knowledge of the law and "your rights":

1. Marbury v. Madison, 5 US 137; the ruling on this case states: "All laws that are repugnant to the Constitution are null and void".
2. Murdock v. Penn., 319 US 105; the ruling on this case states: "A State may not impose a license, permit or fee for exercising your liberties".
3. Shapiro v. Thompson, 394 US 618; the ruling on this case states: "This case explains that we have a "fundamental right" to travel unencumbered".
4. Erie Rail Road v. Tompkins, 304 US 64; the ruling on this case states: "No state shall take a right and convert it into a privilege".
5. Norton v. Shelby County, 118 US 425; the ruling on this case states: "An unconstitutional act is not law; it confers no right; it imposes no duties; affords no protection; it creates no office; it is legal contemplation, as inoperative as though it had never been passed
6. United States v. Bishop, 412 US 346; the ruling on this case states: "This case will help you in the fact that the Prosecution has to "Prove willful intent".
7. Shuttlesworth v. City of Birmingham, 373 US 262; the ruling on this case states: "This case tells us that States cannot punish you for exercising your rights".

If the judge continues to try the case and not pay attention to your brief you can demand a subpoena duces tecum.

"Subpeona Duces Tecum" is a Court summons ordering a named party to appear before the court and produce documents or other tangible evidence for use at a hearing or trial.

The summons is known by various names in different jurisdictions. The term "subpoena duces tecum" is used in the United States, as well as some other common law jurisdictions such as South Africa. It is a Latin phrase meaning "bring with you under penalty of punishment". The summons is called a "subpoena for production of evidence" in some U. S. States that have sought to reduce the use of non-English words and phrases in court terminology.

The *subpoena duces tecum* is similar to the *subpoena ad testificandum*, which is a writ summoning a witness to testify orally. However, unlike the later summons, the *subpoena duces tecum* instructs the witness to bring in hand books, papers, or evidence for the court. In most jurisdictions, a subpoena usually has to be served personally.

It is "ludicrous" to get into your car, shut the door, and learn that your constitutional rights were suspended just by the act of closing the car door. This is how bad the court system has become in all states to separate you from the money that they are letting you use.

However, if you are accused of a crime, such as we were in Riverside County, California and Torrance County, New Mexico, in these cases Robert Simpson I were accused of and found "guilty" of the accusation because we were just like everyone else that does not know their rights or how the court system actually worked. However, I do now and I am going to have these cases reopened and have the states and counties answer a Writ of Mandamus and Quo Warranto.

"Writ of Mandamus" (which means "we command" in Latin), or sometimes *mandate*, is the name of one of the prerogative writs in the common law, and is "issued by a superior court to compel a lower court or government officer to perform mandatory or purely ministerial duties "correctly".

"Mandamus is a judicial remedy which is in the form of an order from a superior court to any government subordinate court, corporation or public authority to do or forebear from doing some specific act which that body is obliged under law to do or refrain from doing, as the case may be, and which is in the nature of public duty and in certain cases of a statutory duty. It cannot be issued to compel an authority to do something against statutory provision.

Mandamus may be a command to do an administrative action or not to take a particular action, and it is supplemented by legal rights. In the American legal system it must be a judicially enforceable and legally protected right before one suffering a grievance can ask for a mandamus. A person can be said to be aggrieved only when he/she is denied a legal right by someone who has a legal duty to do something and abstains form doing it".

"Quo Warranto is the name for a writ (order) used to challenge another's right to either public or corporate office or challenge the legality of a corporation to its charter".

I would like to take a moment to point out, that Cities, Counties and States are corporations by definition. They have a "Bond" and a "charter" by which they operate under. If they are caught doing something that violates your "legal rights" or "civil rights" both the charter and bond can be suspended. For example the State of California's bond was suspended by the Title 42 lawsuit that we filed against them, see exhibit Z1 – Z111, pages 184 – 294. However, the State and County Officials ignored this lawsuit and committed an act of Treason by Sedition. All other parties that are involved with this case are considered aiding and abetting/accomplices.

"Aiding and Abetting/Accomplice": A criminal charge of aiding and abetting or accessory can usually be brought against anyone who helps in the commission of a crime, though legal distinctions vary by state. A person charged with aiding and abetting or accessory is usually not present when the crime itself is committed, but he or she has knowledge of the crime before or after the fact, and may assist in its commission through advice, actions, or financial support. Depending on the degree of involvement, the offender's participation in the crime may rise to the level of conspiracy.

For example, if you make a 'complaint' against the City or County or the Court for 'wrongful' acts, the State will claim that "there is nothing we can do". This is considered a form of Aiding and abetting. The state officials have just become accomplices to the crimes that the Judges and Lawyers are committing against you and the violation of your 'Rights'.

Any case can be reopened and heard by "new evidence". It is not against **any** laws to build your own home without permits. The rest of the accusation and the rest of the cases against me and Robert Simpson were because we exposed the Electric companies for fraud. By the "Whistleblower's" laws we were supposed to be protected by the Federal Government. However, we found out that the "government" is involved with the fraud and cover up and protecting their selfish interests.

If a judge claims 'in open court' that there is no room in his/her courtroom for the Constitution, he/she has committed a Capital Crime of treason. Furthermore, no matter how many times these people violate your rights it is still unconstitutional.

In reality a person that is properly trained, motivated and properly willing to do what is necessary to defend the Constitution will be victorious in the end. In other words you will prevail. The burden of proof of our Constitutional and civil rights is up to each and every one of us. If you want your constitutional rights we need to fight for them. It is not our duty to prove a negative; it is their duty to prove a positive. If they think you are doing something 'illegal' or negligent it is their duty to prove it. We are not going to be 'convicted' before the facts by providing evidence showing "innocence", this is backwards or better yet "the cart before the horse".

The Fifth Amendment states, in part, that we have the right "not to be a participant in a compulsory process that will create an incriminating situation". Most of these cases can be dismissed by asking the judge if he/she has a financial interest in the case. All judges get a percentage off the top from the tickets. The judges now have formed a "biased" opinion against the legal matter. Furthermore, by the **Judicial Canon 7** these judges are not "supposed" to have a financial interest. You can "recuse" every single judge for bias against the legal matter. We have to be vigilant and alert for these "professionals" for violations against our rights. Furthermore, if you are "summoned" by a court, enter the courtroom with your Title: 4: U. S. A. Codes: Section 1, 2 and 3 Flag. Place the Flag on the table in front of you. However, do not let the Lawyers or Judge tell you that you have to "put it away". Do not challenge the flag that is behind the judge. What you are doing is creating a "Common Law" jurisdiction for yourself and the Judge cannot hear the case before him in a "dual-jurisdiction".

> Common Law Courts are the Highest Courts in the Land. When our Founding Fathers established our Federal Government they envisioned 4 Branches.

1. The Legislative Branch – These are the people who create bills and pass laws.
2. The Executive – The President who signs the laws – after reviewing it for Constitutionality – and the people who were to operate the

government in strict compliance with the Constitution, and the Constitutional laws.

3. The Judicial Branch – these are the people who are supposed to prosecute any violations of the Constitution.
4. The People – This is where we are supposed to be educated and taught the true meaning of the Constitution so that we could use our Common Law Courts to control the operation of the other three Branches. Article VII of the Bill of Rights proclaim that a decision by a Common Law Court cannot be reviewed by any other Court in the Land. This was a decision by the people who created the Constitution, who own the Federal and State Government, and who all the public servants work for.

Our Federal Constitution makes it very clear that a person cannot hold two offices at the same time. A person cannot be a Senator, or a Representative, and also be an Ambassador, a Judge, or any of the many other offices created under the Constitution. No Senator or Representative shall, during the time for which he/she was elected, be appointed to any civil office under the authority of the united States, which shall have increased during such time; and no person holding office under the united States; shall be a member of either House during his/her continuance in office. This is explained in Article I; Section 6; paragraph 2.

The paragraph starts out by restricting Senators and Representatives from holding other civil offices. Furthermore, it closes by declaring that no one that holds any office of any kind that is defined in the Federal Constitution can be a Senator or Representative during the time they are holding the other office. This is a key to why we are in so much trouble with our Government Officers obeying, supporting, and defending our Constitution.

No Senator or Representative, or person holding an office of trust or profit under the united States, shall be appointed an elector – Article II; Section 1; paragraph 2. It is the electors, as a part of the Electoral College, who actually cast the ballots for President and Vice President. They are to be the lay people who hold no other public office of any kind or nature. They cannot hold an office of trust or profit – it does not say they have to even be on the payroll – just that they cannot hold any office of trust. Who falls in the category of officers controlled by the above statements?

Virtually every public servant anywhere in the united States. It does not matter if they are Federal, State, County, or City employees, they cannot hold two positions at the same time.

The Senators and Representatives before–mentioned, and members of the several State Legislatures, and all Executive and Judicial Officers, both of the united States and of the several states, shall be bound by an "Oath or Affirmation", for the "support and defense of the Constitution". Furthermore, no religious test shall ever be required as a qualification for any office or public trust by the Constitution of the united States – Article VI; Section 3.

What kinds of positions is the Constitution talking about?

- Every Federal and State Senator.
- Every Federal and State Member of the House of Representatives.
- Every Federal and State Judge.
- Every member of the Federal and State Executive Branches of Government.
- Every member of the Federal and State Legislative Branches of Government.
- Every member of the Federal and State Judicial Branches of Government.
- In short – Every person who works for either the Federal or State Government.

It is amazing to stop and reflect on who all this really includes. It is easy to see that it includes the Governor of each State, and the Federal and State Senators and Representatives. It also includes all of the "ditch diggers" for the Federal and State Governments. The use of the term "ditch diggers" is to illustrate that this reaches into the lowest, most remote corners of public employment.

The really interesting fact is that it includes every attorney in the country. They are all officers of the court and as such hold positions in the Federal or State Branches of the Judicial. These are offices of great trust and, in many cases, offices of great profit.

The failure of the "John Jay Supreme Court" to properly address this issue is tantamount to Treason by Sedition against the People of this Country. Just because the "Laws" have not been 'properly enforced' for over "200" years, does not mean that the "Laws" are no – good. The "Laws" are a valid part of our Constitution and We the People, need to see it is enforced for our own protection.

We can validly argue that every Congress in both the Federal and State Government has been "invalid" because it has included people who are not "qualified" to hold the office We, the People, stupidly, and ignorantly elected them for. Every Elected official start off with "great intentions" for changing the Status Quo. However, they fall short when they find out how much "money can buy them off" or "purchase them cheaply". If a change is to be made, We the People have to it.

Any time an Attorney wants to run for "any" public office tell them "NO!!!" This also includes "Attorney General for a State". The Attorney General is the Attorney for the State – he/she, has nothing to do with the Judicial Branch of the Government-this falls under the auspices of the State Supreme Court-just like the U. S. Supreme Court is over the Federal Judiciary Branch. The Attorney General is a member of the Executive Branch of Government.

Our Founding Fore Fathers knew that lawyers and attorneys would do everything in their power to take over and control our new government. In order to stop this they, "attorneys", made it unconstitutional for anyone holding one office of government, i.e., an office of the court, to hold another office of government. However, they went farther. Because the attorneys all claimed the Title of Nobility of "Esquire" that was granted to them by the English King or Queen, they made it so that this country, including the States, could not grant any title of nobility.

"No title of nobility shall be granted by the United States: And no person holding any office or profit or trust under them, shall, without the consent of the Congress, accept any present, emolument, office, or title, of any kind whatever, from any King, Prince, or Foreign State". Article I; Section 9; paragraph 8.

"No state shall enter into any treaty, alliance, or confederation; grant letters of marque and reprisal; coin money; emit bills of credit; make anything but gold and silver coin a tender in payment of debts; pass any bill of attainder, ex post facto law, or law impairing the obligation of contracts, or grant any title of nobility". Article I; Section 10; paragraph 1.

No one who holds, or claims to hold a title of nobility can hold any office. The two provisions in the Constitution did not contain a penalty clause; an Amendment to the Constitution was proposed and ratified in 1812.

"If any citizen of the United States shall accept, claim, receive, or retain any title of nobility or honor, or shall without the consent of Congress, accept and retain any present, pension, office, or emolument of any kind whatever, from any emperor, king, prince, or foreign power, such person shall cease to be a citizen of the united States, and shall be incapable of holding any office of trust or profit under them, or either of them"; 13th Amendment to the Constitution.

Even though the 13th Amendment was carried as a part of the Constitution for the United States of America for over 65 years, and published repeatedly during that time, the attorneys very quietly removed it and hid their actions by a new Amendment number 13. This was the first time that an amendment had been assigned a number, and the numbering process only continued for number 14 and 15, and was then dropped. Just enough to help cover up the hiding of the true 13th Amendment.

Why didn't the attorneys like the new Amendment?

It took away their citizenship. It took away their title of nobility. It took away the honors they claimed as being the only ones who can serve as Judges, Attorney Generals, and as Representatives of the people in court. There are no provisions in the Constitution that state that these positions and activities must be done by attorneys.

In order to protect themselves from the people the Judicial System have purposely denigrated our Common Law Courts, they have granted themselves immunities, they have taken over our money, our investments, our schools, and every facet of our lives. They are now Legislating from the bench in direct violation of our separation of powers.

Only when We, the People, decide we have had all we are going to take will the process change. We can change it by simply following what our Founding Forefathers established as the Law of the Land – our Constitution.

'TRICKS AND TRAPS' USED BY THE COURTS

The Courts and the Judges are in the Equity/Admiralty Jurisdiction. They "ignore" any and **all** Civil Rights that you possess and disregard and block any and **all** evidence that will prove your innocence.

The way the Courts are getting away with this form of practice against Americans is our "ignorance" of the Contracts we are "forced" through 'Threat, Duress and Coercion', into signing and performing. Here are three examples that the States can claim and show cause for proof that you "have" to follow their Statutes, Codes or Ordinances unless you "Reserve your Rights" by the UCC 1-207 "Without Prejudice all Rights Reserved":

1. Voter Registration: The first question on the Voter Registration Card is "Are you a citizen of the United States of America?" The first thing we have to do is define "Citizen" and "American".
2. The Driver's License Application is another contract that asks if you are a US Citizen,
3. The Social Security Administration Application also asks if you are a US Citizen.
4. Employment Applications ask if you are a US Citizen.
5. Real Estate Contracts ask if you are a US Citizen.
6. Marriage Licenses also ask if you are a US Citizen

The above contracts are some of the ways that the government is placing Americans into the "Policies" of the Federal Franchise Tax Board. However,

I have noticed that almost all contracts that you unwittingly sign into ask this one question: "Are you a US Citizen"?

The Cities, Counties and State bureaucracies, after you have signed (autographed) your contract, create what is known as a Nom De Guerre. A Nom De Guerre is a fiction; an assumed name; a pseudonym. If you look at your Birth Certificate or Birth Record you will find that it reflects a "live birth" **not** dead birth. The bureaucracies purposely commit Fraud against you just to make money on the so-called Statutes, Codes and Ordinances that they claim are "Law". However, remember if Statutes, Codes or Ordinances abrogate your Constitutional Rights that you are exercising by the Constitution, they are to be ignored and cannot be plied against you nor can they "legally" punish you.

When and if you can read the small print in any of these contracts you will find that there is a "Disclaimer Statement" that you have answered the questions to the best of you knowledge under "Penalty of Perjury" and further explains that you can be fined up to $5,000 dollar fine and/or five years in prison or both.

The definition of '**Citizen**': A citizen is a participatory member of a political community. Citizenship is gained by meeting the legal requirements of a national, state, or local government. A nation grants certain rights and privileges to its citizens. In return, citizens are expected to obey their country's laws and defend it against its enemies.

The value of citizenship varies from nation to nation. In some countries, citizenship can mean a citizen has the right to vote, the right to hold government offices, and the right to collect unemployment insurance payments, to name a few examples.

Living in a country does not mean that a person is necessarily a citizen of that country. Citizens of one country who live in a foreign country are known as **aliens**. Their rights and duties are determined by political treaties and by the laws of the country in which they stay. In the United States, aliens must obey the laws and pay taxes, just as U.S. citizens do. They must register with the U.S. government to obtain legal permission to stay for an extended length of time. Legal aliens are entitled to protection under the law and to use of the courts. They may also own property, carry on business, and attend public schools. But aliens cannot vote or hold government office. In some states they are not allowed to practice certain professions until they become citizens.

Under United States law, a **noncitizen national** is a person who is neither a citizen nor an alien but who owes permanent loyalty to the United States. People in this category have some but not all of the rights of citizens. For example, inhabitants of a United States territory may not have the right to vote. Noncitizen nationals of the United States include those people on the Pacific islands of American Samoa who were born after the territory was taken over by the United States in 1900.

The Definition of an **"American"** is one who is born on American Soil. The Constitution and what it stands for applies for all Americans that are born on American Soil. Furthermore, just because the United States is in America does not make America the United States. Remember, the United States is a Corporation. America is a Nation.

When the Politicians claim that there is "no difference" between a US Citizen or An American, they are gravely mistaken and have the attitude "Do as we say do, not as we do".

In any contract you sign, by signing your autograph be sure to add "UCC 1-207 Without Prejudice. All Rights Reserved". This way the contract cannot be enforced without Abrogating the Constitution and all parties that are involved can be brought up on charges of Treason by Sedition, Civil Rights Violations and Racketeering. Remember, you have to:

- Autograph the contract **knowingly** - *Consciously; willfully; subject to complete understanding of the facts or circumstances.* If the Agency fails to fully explain or fails to give "Full Disclosure" according to the "Contract Laws" they are "null and void" and "Unenforceable".
- **Voluntarily** - *<u>willingly</u>, <u>freely</u>, <u>by choice</u>, without being asked, without prompting, on your own initiative, of your own free will, off your own bat, of your own accord, of your own volition.* However, if you refuse to sign any of the contracts such as Driver's License, Social Security, Marriage License or any other contract the government "punishes" you for **not** voluntarily signing even when they explain that signing these contracts **are** by voluntary. Another example, if you refuse to sign a "Traffic Ticket", which by definition is a "Bill of Attainder" and illegal according to Congress, the Police can and will arrest you

and hold you in jail for 72 hours or three days without having to charge you with anything. These contracts are not enforceable and the Courts know it. However, the Courts and Police use "Threats, Duress and Coercion" to "Force you into the Fraudulent Contract".

- **Intentionally** - *with intention; in an intentional manner; advisedly, by choice, by design, deliberately, designedly, on purpose, purposely "I did this by choice"*. You can safely autograph any contract you choose to enter into as long as you fully understand what you are signing and both parties are benefiting from the contract.

If you do not "Reserve Your Rights" by using UCC 1-207 you will unfortunately have to perform at their behest and be forced to accept any and all "Cruel and Unusual Punishment".

The cases that Robert – C. : Simpson and I are involved with were ignored by the Court Systems in New Mexico and In California and the Judges proceeded with "prejudice" violating our "Civil Rights" and committing Treason by Sedition. You will discover more about these cases in Chapter 4 of this book.

However, there are ways to have these cases "Dismissed" if you follow the correct procedure. If you are exercising your rights by the Constitution in Traveling unencumbered, or building your own home, without the interference of the City, County, State bureaucrats the aforementioned Agencies cannot "legally" punish you. It is through our own "ignorance" that we accept the consequences.

One way to stop the proceedings against you is to ask the Clerk of Courts to extend the infraction (whatever it may be) for 30 Days which will extend you Court date. You can get help from a Paralegal in writing up a "Demurrer" or a "Dismissal". You will find the information in Chapter 2 of this book about a Demurrer or Dismissal along with Federal Cases that support your case file.

There is another approach to "boxing" a Judge into a corner for them to perform their Fiduciary duty. The following is what you need to say and insist upon.

"Under our corporate governments, no Sovereign can lawfully be tried or convicted of any statutory crime! I recently discovered how to avoid prosecution under the Trust, when a Sovereign is taken before a corporate prosecuting Attorney or a Judge":

First: "the Sovereign must inquire if we are on the record, and if not, insist upon it! Say nothing, sign nothing and answer no questions until you are convinced that the proceedings are being recorded!"

Secondly: all a Sovereign has to say for the record is: "I am a beneficiary of the Trust, and I am appointing you as my Trustee!"

Thirdly: the Sovereign then directs his Trustee to do his bidding! "As my Trustee, I want you to discharge this matter I am accused of and eliminate the record!"

Fourthly: if the Sovereign suffered any damages as a result of his arrest, he can direct that the Trust compensate him from the proceeds of the Court by saying; "I wish to be compensated for [X] dollars, in redemption."

The above statement or argument, if followed, is sound. The first thing you will have to do is to correct the Judge and the Court Records. When the Judge calls your case he/she will call the case number and call out your name by saying "Is Mr., Mrs., Ms., Miss so and so present in the court room"? Before you cross the Barrister railing and enter the "well" through the gate you need to correct the Judge and the court on and for the record by "Objecting to the use of Mr., Mrs., or Ms., Miss". These are titles of nobility and are **not** used "out of respect" for you as a plaintiff, claimant or defendant. The following is how you need to correct the court and Judge: "your Honor, let me state and spell my name correctly for the record". The Judge usually allows this. We will use my name for the purpose of this example.

"For the Record, my name is Bradley – J. : Franks". Your first name is your given name by your parents. Your middle name is your actual "last name" and your last name is your "clan" name. Your "clan" name does not belong to you exclusively. So when the Court and the Judge calls your name, "Mr. Franks" the Judge is slipping you into the Admiralty Jurisdiction because you have given the Judge permission to grant you a "Title of Nobility". You have to also include the "hyphen" and "full colon" for the proper punctuation for the stenographer's benefit. Note, use upper and lower casing for the spelling of your name.

Once you have established that you have a "court of record", follow the statements on page 62 and 63. However, do **not** tell the Judge that you are a "Sovereign". You are a "beneficiary of the trust" (which is the Constitution) and you are appointing the Judge as a "Trustee". After appointing the Judge as "your trustee" do not make **any** other statements as you will give the judge an opportunity for an "escape route". The Judge has no choice but to acquiesce and "discharge the matter".

There is another important reference material that will help in creating your Legal Documents. This reference material is called 'The Federal Styles Manual'. This manual defines all punctuation used by the courts and why words have a different 'Legal' meaning when written for Case Files.

By following the proposed argument, you will "box the Judge into a corner" and the judge will have no choice but to grant you your "dismissal".

A Judge is nothing but a "referee" to hear all of the facts in a hearing or trial. However, appointing a Judge as "your Trustee" will compel the Judge to "abandon" his position as a "referee". Therefore, the Judge can only perform as a "Trustee" and nothing more. The Judge is supposed to "uphold and defend the Constitution" against anyone who tries to abrogate the Constitution. Not side with the Prosecution or Defense attorneys that are getting paid for "Justice" or the "Lack of Justice".

A Judge is supposed to hear the evidence and decide if there are **any** violations against the accusing party, with the Constitution in mind. If the Judge fails to do his Fiduciary duty he/she can be brought up on charges of "Treason by Sedition" and more. However, ask yourself this question, what court in the nation or the United States is going to "prosecute" a Lawyer or Judge for crimes committed from the bench "by practicing law from the bench" or "Well"? You were born with those rights by the Constitution, which is a contract. They cannot give or take away your rights or decide what testimony is relevant to your innocence. If they do, they are committing "Treason by Sedition".

The word "trust" is actually one that applies to all of us that have the benefit of the Constitution as a "Contract". And we do have "Inalienable Rights". However, the courts are becoming more and more brazing about what evidence is to be heard or not heard. They just want the money, so they can "line their pockets" and think "they did a good job". When in reality they have failed to do their jobs accurately.

As I have stated before, it is up to us, We the People, to put a stop to this insane practice and hold those "individuals" accountable for the actions plied against us.

4

OUR STORY

THE FOLLOWING ARE TRUE CASES OF HOW THE GOVERNMENT HAS committed heinous crimes against Americans and call it "business". By using my own example, I hope to enlighten you readers on just how malicious, devious, and crooked the government really is, especially the courts.

It all began in 1977 when Mr. Robert Simpson, a licensed General Contractor, was building a storage and workshop building for a Mr. Williams. Mr. Williams at this time was the C. E. O. For Gafney Lights and Power located in South Carolina. During the process of construction of the building, Robert Simpson noticed several - hundred electric meters in his backyard. As the construction of the building progressed, Williams came out to talk with Robert about why he had so many meters on the property. Williams showed Robert the meter and how it works. Mr. Williams continued to explain that he was under secrecy-contract with Gafney Lights and Power as well as Duke Energy. Williams did not know the information that he divulged to Robert until after he signed the secrecy - contract. Mr. Williams further explained to Robert that he felt

> "Guilty for knowing what the Electric Companies were doing to the people he grew-up with, by committing this fraud".

In his further conversation with Robert, Williams stated,

> "This information may mean nothing to you now, but later on in life it will".

Williams further explained,

> "If I told anybody or went public with this information, I would lose my retirement and pension".

Williams explained to Robert, that because he felt that he was honest and a hard worker, he felt that he needed to tell someone. Robert Simpson kept his silence concerning what the Electric Companies were doing, for seventeen (17) years.

The following is an introduction about me for your education. I am not a crackpot, crazy or someone with a grudge. However, I am someone with character and conviction. My name is Bradley - Jefferson: [Franks] and this is an account of what took place for over fifteen years in my life. I campaigned for County Supervisor for the Riverside County's Fourth District in California in 1989 and 1994. However in 1991, I had not received the nomination for county supervisor and the incumbent was **put back in office**. Furthermore, I did not know how this was accomplished until the second time I campaigned for Riverside county supervisor.

These were the Campaign ideas I proposed for the constituents in 1994. I explained to the constituents that the Fourth District was a "rough gem" that needed to be polished. I proposed that the small airport in Thermal California be closed down and redeveloped into an auto-race track. The airport in Blythe was to be expanded for the use as the hub for International Agriculture. The Palm Springs Airport was to be developed and remodeled and expanded to accept International Flights. During one of the "Let's meet the candidates" in North Palm Springs I was invited to a grand opening of a factory that made plastic patio furniture. All the candidates, Rolph Arnum, Carol Englehardt, Roy Wilson, Mat Monica, Steve Jones, John Pena, Barbara Slaven and I were present at this grand opening. Patricia Wilson (Pat), Roy Wilson's wife walked up to me and stated,

> "You do not have a chance at getting elected for Supervisor. My husband Roy has the Electric Companies behind and supporting him".

I was surprised that she would even speak with me. Later, I was told that the Electric Companies had given campaign contributions for the other seven candidates that were campaigning. I received nothing in campaign contributions from these electric companies.

However, I struggled along to get my message and ideas out for the public. There were three televised debates for all candidates that KESQ hosted. Unfortunately, I was not elected for the position. Carol Englehardt and Roy Wilson were nominated for the November Election. Roy Wilson became County Supervisor for Riverside County's Fourth District as Patricia Wilson stated.

Two weeks went by when Joel Simpson explained to me that the Electric Companies were committing Fraud against their customers and how they were doing it. We went to see District Attorney Tom Eckert who was a candidate for District Attorney against D. A. Grover Trask and explained what the Electric Companies were doing. At first Eckert was in disbelief. We asked him if he had seen the inside, working parts of a meter. He said, "No". We acquired a 1955 model meter that is still in use on some of the older homes and businesses. Eckert listened to us attentively and explained that:

> "If you are correct, that the Electric Companies can speed up or slow down the meters it would be fraud".

We went to a Private Attorney in Indio to see if they would take this case. Simpson and I explained how the electric companies were defrauding their customers and showed him the working meter. He stated,

> "If you can prove beyond reasonable doubt that you are correct, the Electric Companies are in Major trouble. And that Tom Eckert is correct, it is fraud".

He then went on to say,

> "You guys are the food chain if you are correct".

He said that he was going to speak with the electric companies and to give him a week for his investigation. A week went by when he explained that if he took this case, his exact words were,

"If I pursue this case I will be killed"!

After hearing this, Joel and I were more determined to pursue this and expose the electric companies for what they were and are. After speaking with these attorneys, Joel and I went from City hall to City hall and Business to Business explaining to them how the electric companies were defrauding them. The Electric Companies claim that they are measuring your consumption of electricity. They can measure a magnetic flow through the power line. However, when the electricity is grounded it changes the polarity and energizes the item that you turn on such as a TV, Radio, Lights or any electrical appliance. Another example is if you use an arc-welder. Can you use the welder if it is not grounded out? No! The arc welder needs to be grounded for it to function. This is what I mean by 'changes polarity'.

What I find amusing is some companies claim that they can "help lower the cost of your electric bill" and that their appliances are "energy efficient". If this were a true claim then your bills should go down. However, I have discovered that the bills do not go down but go up. These companies that claim "energy efficient" or "help lower the cost of your electric bill" should be held responsible for these false claims. Southern California Edison issued a challenge to the public through The Desert Sun, in 1994, that if anyone had an idea on how to lower the electric rates they would listen very carefully. However, this was just a rouse to find out how many people would actually care. I responded by explaining that the electric companies were defrauding their customers through the use of the meters, actually, it is the speed of the meters that are set to gain time **not** the rates that are set.

The following is a true account on how crooked and corrupt two different Counties are in two different States: Riverside County, California and Torrance County, New Mexico. The following is a case file that I am and still involved with after staging a Peaceful Protest against the very expensive electric bills that Southern California citizens were and still are receiving.

The reason why I went to the lengths that I did at staging the Peaceful Protest was a Senior Citizen (female) that was living in Palm Springs,

California on Riverside Drive on a fixed income, in other words she was collecting Social Security. As you know, Social Security does not pay very well. This elderly woman had to make a choice between paying her electric bill or buying groceries and medication. That particular summer was very hot, the temperature rose to approximately 130 degrees Fahrenheit. This woman made her choice and bought groceries and her medication instead of paying her electric bill for that month. Her bill was reportedly only 350 dollars for one month. Although, I have seen electric bills a lot higher for one month. Her electricity was disconnected and because it was so hot outside, inside the house became an oven and unfortunately killed the elderly woman on Riverside Dr. This upset me greatly, because there was no one to speak in her behalf.

However, the "straw that broke the camels' back" -- to quote a phrase -- was a young couple was trying to rent a house in Desert Hot Springs, with their infant (baby Joey). When they went to Southern California Edison to get the electricity turned - on, Southern California Edison explained that there was a past-due bill for over 300 dollars at the residence they were going to rent, and in order for them to activate the electricity at that residence they - the young couple - would have to pay for it. The young couple did not have the money for the past-due bill and therefore, did not have the electricity turned on. The young couple were outside, that evening with their infant (baby Joey), the mother put (baby Joey) on top of the hood of the car to help keep him cool with the night breeze. Unfortunately, (baby Joey) rolled over and off the hood of the car killing him. The Riverside County Child Protection Services, charged both parents with Child Neglect and Endangerment. However, I still to this day, believe that Southern California Edison was just as at fault as the parents. Maybe, even more so, because S. C. E. Was trying to force this young couple to pay for a past-due bill that they were **not** responsible for. These incidents took place just after I campaigned for County Supervisor in 1994. I established Breakscrew Enterprise that same year and was educating the citizens just what kind of fraud the electric companies were and are committing. You see, the electric meters are nothing more than a clock.

The flyer, exhibit A on page 121, and the "publication", exhibit B on page 122, I created to sell information on how the electric companies, nationwide, were and are defrauding their customers. As I stated previously in this book it is not the "rates" but the "speed" of the meter that is the fraud. I will explain more about Breakscrew Enterprise later within this book.

First, let us assume that you want to have a home built or you want to build your own home. There are government agencies that you have to appease. Therefore, you go to an architect and have a set of blueprints drawn up for your dream home. In addition, let us further assume that you do not have to borrow any money from a lending institution (i.e. Banks, FHA, or other money - lending institutions). (We were instructed by a Real Estate Attorney, because we were building our own home without the benefit of a bank loan or other outside monetary funds, that we were not required to 're-convey' the property back to the County, so we didn't). We began constructing our home in 1984. However, we did not "convey" nor "re-convey" the property with Riverside county, we did not apply for building permits because we were "exercising" our rights by the Fifth Amendment and since we were told we "would not be breaking any laws" we did not request any loans from any type of lending institutions. We went to the Riverside County's building and safety and spoke with an employee who identified himself as a "building and safety inspector" by the name of Mr. McLeod. We asked him, "What laws would we be breaking if we build our own home without permits"? His reply was, "none". "We just will not hook up your utilities (electricity)". We explained that we did not need to apply for electricity since we had our own source for electricity - generators. However, they cannot deny water. We then asked McLeod "what are the dimensions (measurements) that we can build our home by"? See exhibit C, page 123.

On page 123, are the measurements in handwriting on the upper left hand corner from the building and safety inspector Mr. McLeod. We began constructing our home per the advice and written measurements in 1984.

We were summoned for the court on April of '84 in Palm Springs, California. The judge we went before was honorable Phillip LaRocca. However, we spoke with a friend, an attorney, by the name of Alfred J. Gergely (please forgive the spelling if it is not correct), and explained the situation to him. Gergely went into the judge's office and spoke with him concerning the summons. When Gergely came out of the judge's office, he explained that the judge was upset that the county of Riverside would assign a case to his court and not show up. He instructed Gergely to inform us that, quote

> "I have armed robberies, murders, and rape cases to hear. Why is the county sending me a misdemeanor"?

Gergely returned to us and explained that judge LaRocca 'dismissed the case' because the district attorney's office "did not show up" and for us to "return home and continue to build your home". However, at the advice of Alfred Gergely, he instructed us to go to the building and safety in Indio, California to see if we could come to some sort of compromise. However, there were inspectors at the county level that were jealous or envious that we were constructing such a large home. The following is an application for trying to work out a compromise: see exhibit D, page 124.

Robert Simpson contacted the district attorney's office explained the situation to them and was told that every time the building and safety tried to push the issue the district attorney's office would send the case back - in other words - the district attorney's office was not going to pursue the case because it was not worth their time or effort to try a misdemeanor. However, that did not stop the Riverside county building and safety from harassing us and sending us more of their false-claims paperwork. For example, the following is more of the paperwork that the county sent us trying to 'legalize' their false claim: see exhibits E1 and E2, pages 125 and 126.

Robert Simpson and I went back to the building and safety and explained that they did not have any jurisdiction in this matter since the property was **not** conveyed or re-conveyed into their jurisdiction. At this point, we knew we were not dealing with honest bureaucrats. When Robert received the certified letter, he spoke with Mr. Ron Pope and stated,

> "You know what you can do with this"!

Robert Simpson also spoke with the district attorney's office and was told that the county counsel was "not going to pursue this case". The county Riverside building and safety let Robert Simpson alone. However, in 1989 Robert Simpson paid off his property in full, see exhibit F, on page 127.

At the request and advice of Steven L. Fingal, a Real Estate attorney and a longtime friend of Robert Simpson, Robert was instructed, "**Not** to **re-convey** or **convey** the property title to Riverside County". Robert Simpson did as he was instructed. The Property Title was not, nor has it ever been recorded with or for Riverside County. The following is another copy of what Riverside county building and safety sent for Robert Simpson: see exhibit G1 and G2, pages 128 and 129.

Please excuse the graphic language within the document. Robert Simpson was left alone to continue the construction of his home until 1999. Sometime during the same year, we were introduced to David - Wynn: [Miller]. He taught us what the courts and government were doing to all Americans. The following is a contract (a brief) that the county of Riverside clerk's office stamped accepted. Then the clerk's office turned around, practiced law and cancelled the stamp and returned the document, claiming that Robert did not pay a "filing fee" or "waive" his rights. See exhibits H1 – H9, pages 130 – 138.

Robert Simpson and I were instructed to put our questions in writing then file them for this case and the judge would answer them. However, the judge threatened us with contempt of court and jail time if we continued to ask any more questions.

The Courts refused to answer any of Robert Simpson's questions. This hearing took place without the "defendant" being present. Remember, Robert Simpson was told that he was not "breaking any laws" by a so - called professional and that same so - called professional wrote down the measurements and Robert Simpson did not ever convey or re-convey the property title to Riverside County. Therefore, you must ask yourself,

> "Where is the Maritime Contract for this case to be heard under the Admiralty Jurisdiction? In addition, where is the injured party for someone who builds his home without the benefit of any kind of loans? And why does Robert Simpson have to ask for permission to construct his home if there is no benefit from the government granted"?

Robert Simpson was punished for exercising his rights by the "Common Law". However, remember earlier I explained that the government officials approach you as someone who wants to help you. This is one of the biggest lies the government and courts are proud of. After all, they are making "money" for their illicit affairs. Furthermore, Robert did not understand any of the charges that the Riverside county courts or building and safety were accusing him of. Robert Simpson tried to acquire attorneys to represent him and have these courts answer these questions. However, all the attorneys wanted was money up front and that it was not going to guarantee the courts would even work for the defendant. In fact, he would lose the case anyway. I will explain later why Robert Simpson would lose this case. See exhibit I1-I3 (on pages 139 - 141) and exhibit I4 (pg. 142) is a warrant from the county counsel for the Building and Safety to force their way into Robert Simpson's home, so much for the First, Fourth, Fifth and Sixth Amendment Rights.

Steven L. Fingal did not represent Robert Simpson in this court matter. However, he did represent Robert Simpson as a friend to try to negotiate with Riverside county courts on this particular case. His attempts at negotiations were ignored. Robert Simpson met a person by the name of David - Wynn: [Miller] who explained to him that the Riverside county was going to put him through the "Ringer" and find him guilty whether he was there or not or understood the charges or not. David [Miller] instructed me on how to write a brief called a "Title: 42". This is a lawsuit charging the county officials with Federal Charges for what they fail to do by the Common Law. The following is the document that was filed: see exhibit J1 – J35, pages 143 – 177, this is the entire document with evidence that was filed in the courts.

The clerk of courts explained that this matter was a "small claims" issue. Furthermore, this case was not filed in the "small claims courts". However, either way the Title: 42 Lawsuit was filed in the courts. The courts refused to listen or answer any of the complaints whether it was wrong or not. Furthermore, the Riverside county courts committed Apartheid, Treason by Sedition and Fraud; the clerk's offices practiced law from behind the counter and continue to do so.

However, on April 30, 2001 Robert Simpson appeared at the court at 8:30 am, per instructions by the court order. The clerk of court explained to him that the "hearing had already been heard and a decision was made" three - days before. We arrived at the court with witnesses. Robert Simpson was never notified of the date change or time change. Furthermore, the judge granted the "injunctive relief" for Riverside county building and safety. The last statement that was told to Robert Simpson before he was told to leave "public property" or be "placed under arrest" was this: "We can do anything we want to anyone we want".

In October, Gary Shopshear, Code Enforcement Officer and two High Ranking Riverside county sheriffs arrived at the home of Robert Simpson and told him "We are sorry for having to do this. This decision is coming from the top." Robert Simpson asked, "From the County Board of Supervisors?" Shopshear answered, "No". He further explained, "The decision is coming from senator Barbara Boxers' Office and State Assemblyman Jim Batton's Office". He further stated, "They want you, your son and your house gone and not necessarily in that order." One of the Riverside county sheriffs told Robert Simpson, "This action is reprisals against you and your son for exposing the electric companies for fraud and the collapse of Enron in Texas."

The State of California and its courts are in violation of Federal Rule of Civil Procedures, Federal Titles, and their own Uniform Commercial Codes. Therefore, I ask this question for the reader to ponder:

What type of Lawful Jurisdiction are the courts following?

As I stated earlier in this book, by the UCC and the Flag, the courts will not admit that they are in the wrong, they continue to destroy honest Americans in the name of "money", "government" and "it's my job".

However, if you apply through a lending institution (i.e. Bank, F.H. A., or other money - lending institutions) for the purchase of your property and the construction of your home, you will be forced into accepting the benefits that the City, County or State government gives you. Furthermore, let us assume that your property is paid for 'free and clear' and a Real Estate Attorney advises you 'not' to record your property with the City, County or State government. The City, County or State Bureaucracy does not have the authority to press or accuse or levy charges against you, because you do not have a "valid contract" in their jurisdiction.

However, if you take out a loan for the construction or purchase of your home you will, unfortunately, be forced to accept the "benefits" and the "rules and regulations" set by the City, County or State. The next phase is to have your "blueprints" drawn up. The blueprints include the building materials that will be used, plumbing, and electric wiring and how many outlets you will have in your home. The electrical blueprints also have to include what type of appliances you will have that uses electricity.

When your blueprints are complete, you take them for submission to the 'Building and Safety' for review and approval (as if they were going to live in your home). After you pay their exorbitant fees (for actually doing nothing), they stamp the blue prints with a 'pass or fail'. If the blueprints 'pass', you can begin construction. If the blueprints 'fail' you have to, basically, "start over". All of this is to the whim of some bureaucrat who will, probably, never be invited into your home. An electrical engineer reviews the electrical part of the blueprint. This electrical engineer passes the information on to the Electric Company that you are going to acquire electricity from. The Electric Company then places a metering device on your 'temporary power pole'. In the meantime, before installing the "permanent" Meter to your pole, the Technicians calibrate the meter by adjusting three (3) calibration screws (commonly referred to as the Breakscrew). These screws are located: (one on the front, one on the bottom and one on the side). These technicians turn the screws to <u>gain</u> hours when you are using the electricity. (I will explain further about the meters, later in this book for your knowledge). If the 'Meters' are measuring the usage of the electricity and are accurate, ask yourself this question, "Why do the electric companies need to know how many outlets or what type of appliances and how many appliances you are going to have in your home? Especially, when companies claim that their appliances' are "energy efficient". When your home is complete, the electric company installs a meter onto the side of you home, however, rest assured that they have calibrated that meter for their benefit. In other words, they sped the meter up considerably.

Therefore, claiming you are using a lot of electricity and if you complain they tell you that they are the 'only game in town, and if you do not 'pay' "we will just shut you off'. This is where the fraud charge comes into play. First, if the electric companies **can** speed up or slow down the meters, (and we know they can because they have admitted that they can), by the definition of '<u>**fraud**</u>' found in Black's Law Dictionary, they are guilty of committing a felony against you. (However, it is not my place to find them 'guilty' of any crime. That is left up to a Grand Jury, after they here <u>***all***</u> of the truthful-facts). Breakscrew Enterprise took up the challenge that Southern California Edison issued in the Desert Sun (the local newspaper). However, there is nothing wrong with the rates that they are charging. There is however, something wrong with how the measure your consumption of electricity.

You see, they are measuring your use of electricity by time (which is a constant). If you were to turn off the electricity in your room, you disrupt or stop the flow (therefore, electricity is **not** a constant). So, my question is this, if you have a constant (which is time) and the electric companies are measuring something that is not a constant (electricity) how can you be accurate? (Let alone fair?). Furthermore, how can the electric companies bill you for a monthly reading when they compare your bill from your last year's bill on the same month? The following, I believe, is the reason why Riverside county courts committed the crimes that they did. As I stated earlier in this book, I created a business called Breakscrew Enterprise. I set out to expose what the electric companies were and still are doing to their customers each month.

Now, with your permission, I will explain why Riverside county courts and senator Barbara Boxer and assembly member Jim Batton took the illegal paths that they did. As was stated earlier in this book, I developed a company called Breakscrew Enterprise in 1994. We went from city to city explaining how the electric companies were defrauding their customers through the meters. Furthermore, I explained earlier about the deaths of the elderly woman on Riverside drive in Palm Springs and about baby Joey, (his name was Joey Forbes). Robert Simpson and I went from Palm Springs to Thermal, California explaining to businesses and for people who were interested in how the Electric Companies were defrauding them. We continued to educate the public for two years (from 1994 to 1996) from person to person and business to business. However, in 1996 we were advised to start educating the City Councils in the Coachella Valley. The following is documentation of the effort, and the continuing effort, that Breakscrew Enterprise applied for the education of the public on how they are being defrauded. Furthermore, Robert Simpson went on Radio Talk Shows: 'For the People' with Chuck Harder, Art Bell, and Ron Fortner with KNWZ Radio.

Exhibits K1 – K4, pages 178 - 181, is a letter that was faxed to 'For the People' radio program after Chuck Harder interviewed Robert Simpson. Robert was also interviewed by Art Bell from Pahrump, Nevada and Ron Fortner of KNWZ Radio station Palm Desert, California.

Exhibit K5, on page 182, was faxed to 'For the People' radio program after Chuck Harder interviewed Robert Simpson.

I went to the Palm Springs City council and explained that the electric companies were defrauding their customers every month. Robert Simpson addressed the City Council after I did showing the City Council the insides of a meter. However, the City Council was trying to get a Municipal electric company for Palm Springs. See exhibit L1 and L2, pages 183 and 184 for the statement I gave before the Palm Springs "City Council" and exhibit M, page 185, for the article from the Desert Sun for the "proposal" of a Municipal power company for the city of Palm Springs.

In August 21, 1996, The Desert Sun interviewed Robert Simpson about how the electric companies were defrauding their customers, exhibit N page 186, is the article that the Desert Sun conducted about the "dispute" of how the electric companies were and are defrauding their customers.

After we addressed the City Councils throughout the Coachella Valley, we wrote letters for:

1. **Federal Bureau of Investigation**
2. **Federal Energy Regulatory Commission**
3. **Public Utility Commission**
4. **Senator Barbara Boxer**
5. **State Controller for California Bill Lockyer**

Unfortunately, I did not make copies of these letters. However, I do have the receipts that were signed for: see exhibit O – S, pages 186 - 189.

I even wrote to the I. R. S. However, they only pursue those who do not pay their taxes. We called the F. B. I. Moreover, we spoke with Agent Joe Schall located in Palm Springs and explained to him what we were explaining to the public. Agent Schall listened attentively but the Agency did nothing. I wrote to the Federal Energy Regulatory Commission, at the time Bill Richardson was in charge and appointed by Bill Clinton, and is now the Governor of New Mexico. Bill Richardson did nothing but ignore the evidence we presented to the F. E. R. C. I also wrote to the Public Utility Commission when they decided to send Josiah Nepier to Palm Desert Civic Center to address the citizens over their over - priced power bills. I even wrote to Senator Barbara Boxer explaining how the Electric Companies were committing the fraud against their customers. I also wrote to the State Controller of California, Bill Lockyer notifying his office about the fraud as well. In the meantime, I addressed the Palm Springs City Council again; this is a copy of the statement I gave: see exhibits T1, page 190.

After I delivered this statement before the City Council, I delivered one more to the same council explaining that they were just as at fault as the ones who were committing the crimes against the public. This is a copy of the statement: see exhibit T2 – T4, pages 191 – 193.

However, the only help Robert and I received was an accusation of "Power Theft", "Trespassing and Resisting or Obstructing an Officer in the performance of his duty". Remember, as I have explained earlier in this book, we had our own generators for electricity. Furthermore, the property that Robert Simpson owned was **not** conveyed or Re conveyed back into Riverside County or the State of California.

Sometime in June or July of 1997 I went to see Roy Wilson which was elected County Supervisor for the Fourth District in California. I asked him if I would be breaking any laws if I were to stage a "peaceful protest". He explained to me, that "it is your right (by the Constitution) to protest against anything as long as I had permission from the owner of the property and that you are not trespassing or causing damage to any property". In essence, I was granted permission to conduct a peaceful protest with permission from the owner of the "Utility Pole".

On August 4, 1997, I climbed a **utility** pole (**not** a power pole that the Desert Sun reported). The utility pole was located on Robert Simpson's property behind his home. As I have stated earlier in this book I staged a "peaceful protest" with permission for everyone who was and still are being defrauded by the electric companies. I was also fighting for those victims that have perished by the electric company's decision to turn off their electricity. The following is the article that the Desert Sun printed on August 5, 1997: see exhibit U on page 194.

In the month of July of 1997, Robert Simpson and I went before the Riverside County Board of Supervisors explaining and showing the meter for them hoping that they would help in the investigation. The Supervisors for Riverside County stated that they would look into the matter. However, this did not turn out to be the truth. However, later on I found out that the electric companies are in control of the politicians, at least in Southern

California. A good example was August 11, 1998 during the "Seven State Blackout" and the electric companies were blaming it on some sort of freak accident that left millions of customers without electricity for some time.

However, before the court trial I wrote a letter to the Secretary of the courts. See exhibits V1 - V4, pages 195 – 198.

Furthermore, I was never trying to "steal any electricity from any electric company". If I were stealing electricity, wouldn't the building and safety have found out in the earlier years? Since they obtained a court order to search Robert's home and video tape of the home, you would think that as smart as they are supposed to be that they would have caught us at that time. Furthermore, in the article, exhibit U, page 194, a representative from the Riverside County Sheriff's office claimed that "I refused to pay for electricity." This is not the truth. I had never been allowed to hook up to the electrical system nor was I ever billed by the electric companies. Furthermore, we did have an extension cord to our neighbors' house, with their permission, for the use of a 15 amp breaker. We paid their entire electric bill for the privilege of the drop-cord. The use of the "drop cord" was not breaking any laws.

However, as I explained earlier in this book, Robert and I went to the building and safety, got the measurements to build by, and asked what laws we would be breaking if we build our home without permits. Remember, the Title or Deed concerning Robert's property was never conveyed into their jurisdiction. As for the trespassing charge, the "utility pole" belonged to Robert under "property improvements". Therefore, no crime was committed. However, Robert Simpson and I were charged with 21 years of power theft. Furthermore, the bureaucrats and investigators did not do their jobs effectively. Had they asked us when the house was constructed we would have told them we started the construction in 1984. If my math is correct, 1984 to 1997is only 13 years. Therefore, the Riverside County Sheriff's Office and the Imperial Irrigation District Officials "lied" committing perjury not only to the public but to the courts as well. These same officials are guilty of conspiracy to cover up fraud. Furthermore, If you ask the electric companies about the punishment for tampering with a meter or stealing electricity they will explain that it is a "Five-thousand dollar fine or five years imprisonment or both". The crime is a felony for "Tampering with the meters" or "Stealing Electricity". However, you will notice, in the following article of the Desert Sun, that Robert and I were found "guilty" of a misdemeanor. See exhibit W, page 199.

The reason why the courts had to find us guilty was to "shut us up" concerning the accusation of "fraud" and "Laundering money through Enron" against the electric companies. After we were found guilty under the Admiralty Jurisdiction of their courts, we contacted Congressman Sonny Bono. Robert met with Congressman Bono, explained the meter to him, and asked if he would take a meter with him back to Washington D. C. and get an investigation started. Congressman Bono said, "Yes". Robert gave the congressman one of our meters, which he took with him to Washington D. C. for helping in the investigation. I also wrote to Congressman Bono explaining what Riverside County was about to do to us, this is a copy of his reply: see exhibit Y, page 200.

After the Jury Trial, which was a joke and laughable, we met with David - Wynn: [Miller]. He taught us how to write out a Title: 42 Lawsuit putting the courts on notice that what they were doing was illegal. The following is a copy of a Title: 42 that have been filed into their courts along with the entire case file from the courts and is used as evidence against them showing the tyranny, trickery and deceit that the U. S. courts are guilty of. See exhibits Z1 – Z110, pages 201 – 311.

This Title: 42 that is filed in their courts was "ignored" by the Officials. In 2000 the State of California's Bond was recinded for the [De]fault of the contract. Every Politician claims that the U. S. Judicial System follows the "Rule of Law". I ask you this, what rule are they following? The only Contract I have with the State of California was this Title: 42 Lawsuit and they even ignored that.

The Desert Sun reported that I received 1and a half years in jail and Robert received 1 year the day **before** we were to be sentenced. However, because of the Title: 42 that was filed against California, Riverside County, the judges decided to sentence us to "15 days" of what they deemed as "community service". What they call "community service" I call slavery. We served our community service at the Palm Springs Airport Museum.

The courts ignored the Title: 42 Lawsuit that Robert and I filed against them committing Apartheid and Treason by Sedition and other charges described in the Title: 42 Lawsuit. The Apostille was completed for an overseas case that Bob Shugrue and Jeff Sciba were putting together. However,

I have learned that this case was settled here in the States. Furthermore, we never received compensation for the Title: 42. Therefore, someone is not telling the truth. But, the State Bond of California was rescinded. Bob and Jeff received approximately 20 or more similar cases together with the same format and sent them to the following place: The following are copies of what Bob Shugrue and Jeff Sciba did for our particular case: See exhibits AA, AB, AC, AD, on pages 312 - 315.

Exhibit AE and AF, page 316 and 317 is a copy of the postal certification for the Title: 42 and filing fee that was sent for Jeff Sciba and Bob Shugrue needed to file the document. According to Jeff Sciba, he sent a number of cases along with ours to the Netherlands for The Hague Court. We still to this day do not know what transpired at The Hague Court. However, California's Bond was rescinded over the fact of the Title: 42 law suit.

During this time of sending paperwork back and forth between the U.S. and the Netherlands, the Bond for the State of California was suspended in approximately 2000. Between 2000 and 2001, Enron collapsed. The company, from what was explained to me, was a conglomerate that bought and sold energy (i.e. gas, oil, electricity, etc. etc.). In 1996, Robert and I were visited by two men that identified themselves as "investigators from Enron". Robert explained to them how the meters worked.

How the meters were calibrated and how they could be "sped up" or "slowed down" before they were installed. They explained to Robert that the "Utility pole", located on his property, did belong to him by the right of "Property Improvements" and since the electric company (Imperial Irrigation District) refused to connect his home for electricity, he could "own the electric company; all the way to the generating plant."

After Robert was told this information, Imperial Irrigation District removed the top of the utility pole and moved their electric line fifty feet away. However, we have documentation on VHS tapes that show the property line and "property markers" and where the utility pole sits/sat. After California lost its State Bond and the collapse of Enron is when Gary Shopshear, Code Enforcement Officer, and Riverside County Sheriffs came to Robert's home and explained that Senator Barbara Boxer and Assembly member Jim Baton wanted "our home gone, us gone and not necessarily in that order". The Officers that were present explained this to us. The Officers further explained that this action was "reprisals for exposing the electric companies for the fraud they were and still are committing".

In 1998, the California Legislature and Senate "unanimously voted to withdraw from the Federal Energy Regulatory Commission". This withdraw took place before the collapse of Enron. During this time Bill Clinton was the President, appointed Bill Richardson as the head of the Federal Energy Regulatory Commission, and as you have read earlier in this book I wrote to the F. E. R. C. However, I received no reply from any organization I wrote to. Robert and I made a VHS tape of how the electric companies were stealing from their customers and how the meter works and sent a copy to U. S. Senator of Alaska, Frank Murkowski.

In 2001, George Bush Jr. became President and ordered a Federal Investigation into the energy fraud that lasted until the unfortunate events of 9-11-01. Furthermore, Vice-President Dick Chancy claimed "Executive Privilege" not releasing the findings concerning Enron and the Fraud committed by the electric companies. Moreover, the investigation was "sealed" and called "State Secrets". During the investigation, Senator John McCain sent an envoy (his son John McCain Jr. and son-in-law Kevin) to our home in Thousand Palms, California. Robert explained the meter and how the electric companies were defrauding their customers to them. They left and returned to Arizona. Furthermore, the collapse of Enron caused many Government and private Pensions to disappear. The politicians were calling the money coming into Enron "Free money". However, because of the collapse of Enron there is no more "Free money". On June 21, 2001, Governor Davis demanded a $9 Billion Dollar Refund returned to California for the over charges for the use of electricity, this is a copy of that article: See exhibit 1, page 318.

As the owner of Breakscrew Enterprise, Robert Simpson and I would have been brought up on Federal Charges of Fraud and other Federal Charges that would put us behind bars for the rest of our natural lives if we were, or are, wrong with this information. However, I would like to point out that Governor Davis tried to get refunds back for California. In addition, Southern California Edison, Bob Stranger admitted that we were telling the truth, "The Electric Companies can speed up or slow down the meter".

Mr. Black, Jeff Skilling, and Ken Lay did not know or understand the full impact of what was transpiring within Enron. These men were under a "secrecy contract" just as the C. E. O's. of the electric companies are. I personally believe they were used as victims to justify what Breakscrew Enterprise exposed and were wrongfully prosecuted. Furthermore, the jury did not hear all of the facts, evidence, or testimony.

Robert and I were forced to move from Southern California. We traveled to the Canadian border, back down to Desert Hot Springs, then over to Peach Springs, Arizona, back to Southern California where we stayed until January 5, 2002. We then moved to Stanley, New Mexico where I obtained a job with Correction Corporation of America also called Torrance County Detention Facility. I was employed with them for five years. I purchased 5 acres of property with a mobile home on it located in McIntosh, New Mexico in 2003. It had electricity, a well, and we used propane gas for cooking. We used a woodstove to heat the home with. In 2006, I declared my candidacy for Magistrate against incumbent Steve Jones. This is a copy of the receipt from the county clerk's office and a candidacy statement: See exhibits 1a and 1b, pages 319 and 320.

I campaigned as well as I could in between working and sleeping. Furthermore, I attended a debate in Moriarty against Jones. One of the questions from the audience was "Have you ever been convicted of a Felony"? My answer was, "No"! I further explained about Breakscrew Enterprise and what we uncovered and exposed. I continued to explain how we had filed a Title: 42 law suit against the State of California. This is when I suspected that Torrance County wanted to extort, blackmail, or commit whatever crime they saw fit to separate me from a potential "settlement".

However, I was not elected for the position. Furthermore, the Secretary of the State of New Mexico did not sanction that election. During this election, there was a measure on the ballot for the County to adopt the Bureau of Land Management. The measure was passed and was effective as law of January 2007.

I asked around if we could build something over the mobile home for protection from hail and other forces of nature. Robert called the New Mexico State Building and Safety and found out that he could construct a "pole building" over the structure without permits. He extended the existing front porch and constructed what the Building and Safety of New Mexico would call a "pole building" without permits by their definition. Robert started construction of the "pole building" in 2005 and completed the construction in 2006. Furthermore, there was no Bureau of Land Management in Torrance County until 2007. However, here is a copy of the case file that was filed against me in 2007: see exhibits 2a – 2b and 3a – 3d, pages 321 - 326.

I did not understand these charges that were filed against me, since Robert was talking with the Building and Safety at the State level. Robert and I wanted to make sure that we did not make the same mistake we made in Southern California. When I received the above notification, I first thought this was a joke or some sort of mistake. However, I was wrong and I was going to learn just how crooked the Magistrates courts really are in New Mexico and to what lengths that these bureaucrats would go to defraud or swindle by using "color of law" and "perjure" themselves in court or even make a "false statements in a criminal complaint".

Exhibits 2a and 2b, pages 321 and 322 are a fraud. However, it may seem that I am arguing "Subject matter". First of all, the "Torrance County Waste Ord." would not apply because, Torrance County charged me every three months for dump fees whether I used the dump or not. The "Development Review Permit" would not apply according to the State Building and Safety, Mr. Aragon, Building and Safety Inspector for the State of New Mexico, explained that there were no permits "necessary" for "pole buildings" and as for the "Abandon Dangerous Containers" Robert and I helped a neighbor to move and helped in the cleanup of their yard and took one old refrigerator away. However, the day we were going to the dump, it was closed. Furthermore, I could not keep the trash on the back of my truck, so we unloaded it and were planning to go on my next day off. I was never given the chance. Moreover, approximately 2 days later a friend and Robert took the Refrigerator to "Hooker Salvage". The self-proclaimed "Sgt. /State Code Enforcement Officer/Prosecutor", Richard Ledbetter would not listen to reason and forced me into court. As far as the charge of "Public Nuisance", since the other charges were fraudulent, the charge of "Public Nuisance" would not apply.

Once again, I was charged with Statutes, Codes and Ordinances Violations while exercising my Constitutional Rights and Civil Rights under "Right of Life, Liberty and Pursuit of Happiness".

On August 2, 2007, I went before Magistrate Steve (Larry) Jones, which arraigned me, and asked if me if I understood the charges against me. My reply was, "No!" He went on to say "Too Bad. I believe that you do". He proceeded with the action, even though I did not understand **why** I was being charged for crimes I did not commit. Furthermore, I was exercising my "rights" by the "Constitution" This is a blatant violation of Federal Rules of Civil Procedure and Civil Rights.

In the meantime, Robert Simpson called the F. B. I. and spoke with Agent Denise (the last name is withheld for protection), U. S. Senator Jeff Bingaman, State Attorney Gary King's Office, the Governor's Office, and an Attorney by the name of Mr. Kennedy. The above-mentioned elected officials explained to Robert Simpson that the "Magistrate Court could not try this case because there were no laws broken". Furthermore, the "Land Use Code" was not adopted until 2007. The construction was completed in 2006. They further explained, that the property fell under the "Grandfather's Clause". They also made a comment on how "they could not get involved because the case was already filed." However, Mr. Kennedy explained to Robert that he was working on a "High profile" murder case and that he would not be able to represent me. He further explained that Torrance County could not bring in a Magistrate from outside the County. For example, Tom Pestak was brought in from Truth or Consequences, which was outside the County. Mr. Kennedy further explained to Robert, State judges are elected or appointed by the Governor; however, Magistrates serve the judicial districts they are elected for. This case was illegal from the start.

Magistrate Jones had no alternative but to excuse and recuse himself as I had campaigned for the Magistrate Office against him and would pose as a conflict of interest. See exhibit 4a, page 327.

Some friends advised me to obtain an attorney. Therefore, I did. However, the attorney I hired, Charles Knoblauch, explained to me that it would be a lot easier on me to "plead guilty, pay the fines, and do what the County wanted me to do". I said, "No! I did not break any laws and I was not going to pay the extortion fees for something I did not do." Mr. Knoblauch and I did not see eye to eye. Furthermore, I did not fire him, he just quit. See exhibits 5a – 5j, pages 328 – 338.

(If you will notice on page 328, exhibit 5a, you will see that "Torrance County" was trying me at State Level. What the Magistrate Courts do not understand is that this is "grounds" for charges of Treason by Sedition, Aparthied, Fraud and Malfeasance. Furthermore, if the courts claim that the "statute of limitations" ran out, I would remind them that there are no "statute of limitations" for fraud or Treason by Sedition).

I was ordered to produce some sort of documents for the self- appointed "Prosecutor / Sgt. / Code Enforcement Officer" Ledbetter. Furthermore, I am "not guilty" of committing any crime therefore, I refused to do so. In addition, all the "Prosecution" had to do was to check with the Waste Management Company and Torrance County for the information that they demanded. However, I did not know what was requested, that they did not have copies of. Furthermore, I did not understand what the "Order of Production" wanted. No one explained anything to me, or would listen to me, at all. The information they were looking for could have been obtained by the "Public Information Act". To this day, I still have no idea why these charges were filed against me by this self-appointed "Blowhard". He never once, had a civil conversation to find out any information or what I was doing. I therefore believe that this particular situation was "Politically motivated" and instigated for "selfish" reasons. Furthermore, under the IV and V Amendments I have the right "to be secure in my person" and "Due process of law".

I believe that the bureaucrats in Torrance County wanted to get their share of the "potential settlement that is due Breakscrew Enterprise", for exposing the Electric Companies for committing a fraud against their customers, through "rook or crook". However, Governor Bill Richardson was appointed by the Clinton Staff to be the head of the Federal Energy Regulatory Commission, then became the Governor of New Mexico and decided to campaign for Presidency. Robert started to educate the local people of the fraud that the electric companies were committing. Furthermore, because of Bill Richardson's involvement as governor and becoming a candidate for Presidency, I believe that Torrance County committed "reprisals" against me for what Robert was explaining to the people concerning the electric companies committing fraud and how they were getting away with it.

When I received the letters, exhibit 2a and 2b, on page 323 and 324, I was astonished that self-proclaimed "Sgt. /Prosecutor / State Code Enforcement Officer" Ledbetter would continue this farce. Mr. Ledbetter would have to have a "Bachelor's Degree" to accomplish what he was trying to put me through, which he did not have. The above letter insinuated that my property taxes were behind. Robert went to see Mr. Ledbetter with a witness to explain that I was not behind on taxes, that the State explained that "permits" were "not required" for a "Pole Building", that the County charges every three months for the Solid Waste Permit, and that there was no trash on the property. However, Mr. Ledbetter became non-communicative and told Robert to "leave his office". Moreover, "he would see me in Court".

The letter from Charles Knoblauch, exhibit 5d, page 333 after speaking with Mr. Ledbetter, "all charges would be dismissed", if I "followed the conditions" set forth in the letter. However, again I remind you; the State Officials of New Mexico claimed that, "I did not break any laws". The other information was and is "none of their business", unless I did break State Laws. Mr. Knoblauch claimed that I did not work with him. First, I did not have to produce any information or my deeds. Both Properties were paid for in full and recorded with Torrance County as to who owned them. Second, Robert told me that a "Building Permit" was not necessary because the construction was "considered a Pole - Building." according to the State Officials. Third, "development" plans were not necessary since Lot "9" was not going to be developed. Lot "7" had an existing "mobile home" and I was told that it "fell under the Grandfather's Clause". However, Torrance County continued with its harassment against me. See exhibits 5e – 5h, pages 334 - 337.

As you examine exhibits 5i and 5j, pages 338 - 340, Mr. Knoblauch quit this case. The reason for Mr. Knoblauch quitting this case was because, "I refused to accept his advice, and just "plead guilty, pay the fines, and do what the County wants you to do." Furthermore, I contacted the "Bar Association" and lodged a complaint against Mr. Knoblauch for failing to do his job. Moreover, according to State Officials I did not break any laws.

The following is the information that Torrance County adopted in 2007, and since the "Pole Building" was completed in 2006, none of this would apply to me; exhibits 6a – 6j, pages 343 – 352. I was told by the State of New Mexico that I did not have to acquire any type of "Building Permits" for a "Pole Building". However, it appears that the State Officials in Santa Fe, New Mexico do not get to do their jobs, because Torrance County Officials "run" the State.

As you read, exhibits 5k, 5l and 7, pages 341, 342 and 353, you will discover that this case was assigned to Tom Pestak, a magistrate from Truth or Consequences from a different County. Robert told me that this was "illegal and could not be done" according to an attorney. However, the Bureaucrats feel that they can do whatever they want to do in that County. I would like to point out, 1. The State Officials explained that I was not "Breaking any laws", and 2. The County could not bring in a magistrate from an "outside county".

On January 18, 2008, I, with witnesses, appeared in Court. Ledbetter approached me and told me, "The judge wants to see you in the judges' chambers." Robert advised me, "Do not go without witnesses or legal representation." However, I thought that I could speak with this "so-called" judge and straighten this matter out. I was very wrong and was going to be put through "Hell." The Prosecution attorney, which was assigned the case at the last minute, Mr. Wallin was trying to get me to sign documents saying that I was "guilty" and would work with the County to rectify the situation. See exhibit 8, page 354.

Unfortunately, I lost my cool and "Blew-up" at the attorney. Pestak threatened to put me in custody for my outburst for "contempt of Court". I looked at him and said,

> "I have nothing but contempt for your court".

At the time, "court" was not even in session and I was brought before the Magistrate and Prosecutor without the benefit of a Defense Attorney or Witnesses. Furthermore, I was charged with "Public Drunk". However, there was no such law in the State of New Mexico at the time. The District Attorney explained to Mr. Pestak that he could not charge me with this non-existent law, so he changed it to "Contempt of Court". I was placed under arrest and served 28 days in prison. Seven days in C. C. A. / Torrance County Detention Facility in Segregation and then was transferred to Cibola, in Grant County, lock up in their Segregation Unit for 21 more days. After the 28 days expired, I was released from custody and taken once again before Pestak, in chains. Robert Simpson and a friend acquired a Criminal Defense Attorney and a Real Estate Attorney.

The Attorney's instructed me not to say "anything" during the Court Proceedings. I did what I was instructed and remained silent. Mr. Pestak demanded that I give "give him an apology for the disrespect I showed for his court". He did admit, before witnesses, that he violated my Civil Rights by not having "witnesses or Counsel" present during the earlier meeting. The exact words Pestak used, were "I Rodney King'd you." However, the crime was committed and Mr. Pestak thought that an apology would make amends. Moreover, I was 'kidnapped' and held for 28 days for crimes that were fraudulently levied against me by "Torrance County" but tried by the "State of New Mexico." Moreover, I followed the Attorney's advice and kept silent. Mr. Pestak dropped the charges of "Contempt of court" saying "Time served." As for the rest of the charges that were levied against me, Mr. Pestak rescheduled a trial. At the advice of several people, who witnessed this performance, advised me to "get out of New Mexico, because The Courts were getting ready to place you behind bars for five (+) years".

However, before I left New Mexico, Mr. Carpenter arrived at my home and had me sign a contract of "guilty" for the courts. I signed, the contract with this statement, "By Threat, Duress and Coercion" along with my autograph. Mr. Carpenter looked at the autograph and said the he could not accept the contract as I had the words 'Threat, Duress and Coercion' on it. With a single line through the statement, I was "forced" to cross out 'Threat, Duress and Coercion'. However, I still believe that the contract I signed **was and still is** under 'Threat, Duress and Coercion'. At the advice of several concerned friends and acquaintances, I moved from New Mexico and went to Crosslake, Minnesota. See exhibits 9a – 9c, pages 354 – 356, for the court record.

After spending 28 days incarcerated, I was released from jail for crimes I did not commit, I received a notification from the Magistrate Court for "Sentencing". See exhibit 8a, page 353. My belief was that I was going to jail for crimes I was not "guilty" for and I was going to "prison" for five (+) years. These so-called "professionals", in my opinion are "guilty" of "abuse of authority" and "basic stupidity". However, a few weeks after I moved from New Mexico, I received a call from the Magistrate Court of New Mexico concerning the fraudulent charges levied against me again. I again, replied for the record that I "did not understand these charges". Mr. Pestak became frustrated and stated, "I have a long memory." I would like to point out to Mr. Pestak and those who were and are involved in this case that you are in violation of Federal Laws, and "I have a very long memory as well."

Since I left the State of New Mexico, Mr. Carpenter withdrew from this case. In my opinion, since I was not there, I can not fault him for withdrawing, see exhibit 10a – 10d, pages 357 – 360.

During the Presidential Campaign, Robert contacted the Obama Committee in Chicago and spoke with a woman who identified herself as 'Michelle'. Robert explained what the electric companies were doing and about the Title: 42 that caused the Bond of California to be rescinded. When Bush made a public address before the nation concerning the 'national deficit', Breakscrew Enterprise offered to pay ten - billion, ten - million in "gold" to China if China would purchase the Title: 42 for an undisclosed amount.

The following is a copy of the letter that Breakscrew Enterprise sent overseas - see exhibit: Letter, pages 93 – 96. We also included the definitions taken from Black's Law Dictionary for their convenience for understanding some of the words in the letter. The definitions are on pages 97 – 106.

Exhibit: Letter

"April 2010
Bradley J. Franks (owner)
Robert Simpson (spokesman)
c/o Breakscrew Enterprise
277 170th Ave. S. W.
Holloway, Minnesota 56249 – 1117
(505) 459 – 0385
For Steve Knott
1 Lime Street
London E. C. Free M.
7 H A"

"For the World Leaders and Ambassadors' concern and attention":

"I wish to inform and educate how the United States has been committing fraud, extortion, blackmail, racketeering (under the RICO laws) for the past Twenty - Plus -Years (20+ years) through the electric companies nationwide. They have been accomplishing this feat through the billing process of the Electric Companies and the improper use of the electric meter devices. In 2005, the Governors of all 50 States and their Public Utility Commissioners attended a meeting in San Diego, California. One of the concerns and topics that were brought up for discussion was a company called Breakscrew Enterprise that uncovered and exposed the fraud and brought the matter to their attention in 1994".

"This letter is to educate and inform you and your Country that the United States has been defrauding your Countries and your businesses through the use of deceit and trickery. I will attempt to explain this matter within this letter and through the website to give you an overall idea of the evil and vileness that the United States is committing through the Electric Companies through the Billing process and the laws that are being violated, still to this day. Some of the definitions are enclosed to explain the Legal terms in this letter for your education and attention."

"President Obama stated, during one of his earlier speeches, that the United States "follows the Rule of Law". I wish to let you know that this statement is not <u>entirely</u> the truth. So far with this matter facing the United States the officials have ignored and have covered up the truth from the majority of the populace. During President Bush's term in Office, Vice-President Dick Cheney was in charge of the investigation of the electric energy fraud. The only thing that came out of that investigation was the downfall of Enron and the convictions of Mr. Lay and Mr. Skilling. Mr. Cheney then declared Executive-privilege closing the matter and findings from the population. A short time after that, President Bush signed a new energy-bill into law giving the Electric Companies Autonomy".

"The United States Courts cannot hear this case because of the conflict of interest that is between the United States and the Public Utility Companies and the selfish interests that some of the politicians have in the electric companies. I will also explain how Breakscrew Enterprise exposed and uncovered this crime, who were notified and when. Breakscrew Enterprise is asking for any of your help to bring this matter before the World Court as it is going to affect and effect all of our Nations".

"We have read some of the definitions, for example: <u>Whistleblower</u>: we may not be able to use that particular law; but there is another law that does apply to us that may help all our countries and Breakscrew Enterprise, it is called the Qui Tam Action. Basically what this law says is that we can sue on behalf of other countries and for ourselves. The definition is enclosed within this letter for your legal department's information. Then the United States can also be charged with Obstructing Justice, Fraud, Extortion, Racketeering (under the R. I. C. O. Laws) and Nonfeasance. The World Court may also look into the fact that the United States can be brought up on charges of Crimes against Humanity, Terrorism, and Apartheid. The reason for the charge of apartheid is that we have been denied equal access of their Courts. The Courts here in the United States practice what is referred to as "Color of Law" which is a crime in its self. But, there is no Judge or Lawyer that will do their job correctly. I am sure that the Law profession is an honorable one when it is done correctly. Unfortunately, we have found that in this country of the United States there is no honor within the legal department. This is why this particular case needs to be heard by the World Court. The United States News Media has claimed that electricity is a commodity and that the United States and Great Britain share the patent-rights or copy-rights. This in itself should be made illegal and condemned as a "Crime against Humanity" and a form of "Terrorism". The United States would have you and your Countries believe that this is how business is done. I would like to point out that the above charges are also, "just business"".

"In 1994 Breakscrew Enterprise went to some of the local Lawyers in Indio, California and explained how the Electric Companies were committing Fraud against their customers. We showed them the meter and explained that the meter does not do what the Electric Company claimed. The lawyers explained to us that "if you can prove that the meters can be sped-up or slowed-down then we have a major case of fraud against the electric companies". Now, the Electric Companies are committing fraud world-wide. As you have seen by the discs that we sent you and that are on "Youtube", Breakscrew Enterprise has proven that we are correct. If you have not seen the site of "Youtube" the address is: "Breakscrewenterprse", then go to video and you will see approximately eight minutes of evidence. We are currently trying to put it on Wikimedia but are experiencing technical difficulties. We hope to have them resolved soon. We are enclosing three (3) Dvd Discs with the evidence. In 1995, the spokesman for Breakscrew Enterprise, Robert Simpson was interviewed by Ron Fortner (KNWZ am Talk Radio), Chuck Harder (out of White springs, Fla.) and in 1996 Art Bell (out of Pahrump, Nev.) all of who were radio talk-show programs. Southern California Edison, Public Relation Officer, Bob Stranger, admitted that "Breakscrew Enterprise is correct that we can speed up or slow down the meters before the electric companies installed them." and "trust us we are not doing that". Also enclosed is a copy of the Cashier's check and bill for one month from Ottertail Electric Company. Please note that this electric bill is for the residential use of electricity, also, we are not singling out just one electric company they are all at fault".

"We are forwarding copies of this letter and the Dvd discs to China, Russia, Venezuela, Sweden and Denmark for the Leaders and Ambassadors viewing".

"With Respect",

"Bradley J. Franks (Owner)"
"Robert Simpson (Spokesman)"
"Cc"
"Bjf"
"enc"

Exhibit: Definitions

Definitions, as defined in Black's Law Dictionary, for the layperson and the non-legal personnel who do not understand the definitions of the "legal" terms within this document.

1. **Extort.** To compel or coerce, as a confession or information by any means serving to overcome one's power of resistance, thus making the confession or admission involuntary. *To gain by wrongful methods; to obtain in an unlawful manner, as to compel payments by means of threats of injury to person, property, or reputation. To exact something wrongfully by threats or putting in fear. The natural meaning of the word "extort" is to obtain money or other valuable thing either by compulsion, by actual force, or by the force of motives applied to the will, and often more overpowering and irresistible than physical force.*
2. **Extortio est crimen quando quis colore officii extorquet quod non estdebitum, vel supra debitum, vel ante tempus quod est debitum.** *Extortion is a crime when, by color of office, any person extorts* that which is not due, *or more than is due,* or before the time when it is due.

3. **Extortion.** *The obtaining of property from another induced by wrongful use or actual or threatened force, violence, or fear, or under color of official right. Title: 18 U.S.C.A. § 871 et seq.; § 1951.*

   A person is guilty of theft by extortion if he purposely obtains property of another by threatening to: (1) inflict bodily injury on anyone or commit any other criminal offense; or (2) accuse anyone of a criminal offense; or (3) expose any secret tending to subject any person to hatred, contempt or ridicule, or to impair his credit or business repute; (4) take or withhold action as an official, or cause an official to take or withhold action; or (5) bring about or continue a strike, boycott or other collective unofficial action, if the property is not demanded or received for the benefit of the group in whose interest the actor purports to act; or *(6) testify or provide information or withhold testimony or information with respect to another's legal claim or defense; or (7) inflict any other harm which would not benefit the actor. Model Penal Code: § 223.4.*

   It has also been defined as corrupt demanding or receiving by a person in office of a fee for services which should be performed gratuitously; or, where compensation is permissible, of a larger fee than the law justifies, or a fee not due.

   Term applies to persons who exact money either for the performance of a duty, the prevention of injury, or the exercise of influence, and covers the obtaining of money or other property by operating on fear or credulity, or by promise to conceal the crime of others. Term in comprehensive or general sense signifies any oppression under color of right, and in strict or technical sense signifies unlawful taking by any officer, under color of office, of any money or thing of value not due him, more than is due, or before it is due.

4. **False Claims Act.** *Federal act providing for civil and criminal penalties against individuals who knowingly present or cause to be presented to the government a false claim or bill, or deliver less property to the government than what is billed for, or make or use a false record to decrease an obligation to the government. The statute provides for enforcement of its provisions either by the U.S. Attorney General or in "qui tam" actions by private persons. Title: 18 U.S.C.A. § 286, 287; Title: 31 U.S.C.A. § 3729-3733.*

5. **Fraud.** *An intentional perversion of truth for the purpose of inducing another in reliance upon it to part with some valuable thing belonging to him or to surrender a legal right. A false representation of a matter of fact, whether by words or by conduct, by false or misleading allegations, or by concealment of that which should have been disclosed, which deceives and is intended to deceive another so that he shall act upon it to his legal injury. Anything calculated to deceive, whether by a single act or combination, or by suppression of truth, or suggestion of what is false, whether it be by direct falsehood or innuendo, by speech or silence, word of mouth, or look or gesture.* Delahanty v. Fist Pennsylvania Bank, N. A., 318 Pa. Super. 90, 464 A.2d 1243, 1251.

   A generic term, embracing all multifarious means which human ingenuity can devise, and which are resorted to by one individual to get advantage over another by false suggestions or by suppression of truth, and includes all surprise, trick, cunning, dissembling, and any unfair way by which another is cheated. Johnson v. McDonald, 170 Okl. 117, 39 P.2d 150. *"Bad faith" and "fraud" are synonymous, and also synonyms of dishonesty, infidelity, faithlessness, perfidy, unfairness, etc.*

   Elements of cause of action for "fraud" include false representation of a present or past fact made by defendant, action in reliance thereupon by plaintiff, and damage resulting to plaintiff from such misrepresentation. Citizens Standard Life Ins. Co. v. Gilley, Tex. Civ. App., 521 S. W. 2d 354, 356.

   As distinguished from negligence, it is always positive, intentional. It comprises all acts, omissions, and concealments involving a breach of a legal or equitable duty and resulting in damage to another. And includes anything calculated to deceive, whether it be a single act or combination of circumstances, whether the suppression of truth or the suggestion of what is false, whether it be direct falsehood or by innuendo, by speech or silence, by word of mouth, or by look or gesture. Fraud, as applied to contracts, is the cause of an error bearing on a material part of the contract, created or continued by artifice, with design to obtain some unjust advantage to the one party, or to cause an inconvenience or loss to the other.

6. **Actual or constructive fraud.** Fraud is either *actual* or *constructive. Actual fraud consists in deceit, artifice, trick, design, some direct and*

active operation of the mind; it includes cases of the intentional and successful employment of any cunning, deception, or artifice used to circumvent or cheat another. It is something said, done, or omitted by a person with the design of perpetrating what he knows to be a cheat or deception. Constructive fraud consists in any act of commission or omission contrary to legal or equitable duty, trust, or confidence justly reposed, which is contrary to good conscience and operates to the injury of another. Or, as otherwise defined, it is an act, statement or omission which operates as a virtual fraud on an individual, or which, if generally permitted, would be prejudicial to the public welfare, and yet may have been unconnected with any selfish or evil design. *Or, constructive frauds are such acts or contracts as, though not originating in any actual evil design or contrivance to perpetuate a positive fraud or injury upon other persons, are yet, by their tendency to deceive or mislead other persons, or to violate private or public confidence, or to impair or injure the public interests, deemed equally reprehensible with actual fraud.* Constructive fraud consists in any breach of duty which, without an actually fraudulent intent, gains an advantage to the person in fault, or any one claiming under him, by misleading another to his prejudice, or to the prejudice of any one claiming under him; or, in any such act or omission as the law specially declares to be fraudulent, without respect to actual fraud.

7. **Fraud in the execution.** *Misrepresentation that deceives the other party as to the nature of a document evidencing the contract.*
8. **Fraud in the factum.** *Misrepresentation as to the nature of a writing that a person signs with neither knowledge nor reasonable opportunity to obtain knowledge of its character or essential terms.* See U.C.C. § 3-305(2) (c).
9. **Fraud in the inducement.** *Fraud connected with underlying transaction and not with the nature of the contract or document signed. Misrepresentation as to the terms, quality or other aspects of a contractual relation, venture or other transaction that leads a person to agree to enter into the transaction with a false impression or understanding of the risks,* duties or obligations she has undertaken.

10. **Fraudulent.** *Based on fraud; proceeding from or characterized by fraud; tainted by fraud; done, made, or effected with a purpose or design to carry out a fraud.*

    A statement, or claim, or document, is "fraudulent" If it was falsely made, or caused to be made, with the intent to deceive.

    To act with "intent to defraud" means to act willfully, and with the specific intent to deceive or cheat; ordinarily for the purpose of either causing some financial loss to another, or bringing about some financial gain to oneself.

11. **Nonfeasance.** *Nonperformance of some act which person is obligated or has responsibility to perform; omission to perform a required duty at all; or, total neglect of duty.* Desmarais v. Wachusett Regional School Dist., 360 Mass. 591, 276 N.E. 2d 691, 693. *As respects public officials, "nonfeasance" is substantial failure to perform a required legal duty,* while "misfeasance" is the doing in a wrongful manner that which the law authorizes or requires a public officer to do. Schumacher v. State ex rel. Furlong, 78 Nev.167, 370 P.2d 209, 211.

    There is a distinction between "nonfeasance" and "misfeasance" or "malfeasance"; and this distinction is often of great importance in determining an agent's liability to third persons. *"Nonfeasance" means the total omission or failure of an agent to enter upon the performance of some distinct duty or undertaking which he has agreed with his principal to do; "misfeasance" means the improper doing of an act which the agent might lawfully do, or, in other words, it is the performing of his duty to his principal in such a manner as to infringe upon the rights and privileges of third persons;* and 'malfeasance" is a doing of an act which he ought not to do at all.

12. **Obstruct.** *To hinder or prevent from progress, check, stop, also to retard the progress of, make accomplishment of difficult and slow.* Conley v. United States, C. C. A. Minn., 59 F.2d 929, 936.*To be or come in the way of or cut off the sight of an object. To block up; to interpose obstacles; to render impassable; to fill with barriers or impediments,* as to obstruct a road or way. *To impede; to interpose impediments to the hindrance or frustration of some act or service, as to obstruct an officer in the execution of his duty.* As applied to navigable waters, to "obstruct" them is to interpose such impediments in the way of free

and open navigation that vessels are thereby prevented from going where ordinarily they have a right to go or where they may find it necessary to go in their maneuvers.

13. **Obstructing justice.** *Impeding or obstructing those who seek justice in a court, or those who have duties or powers of administering justice therein. The act by which one or more persons attempt to prevent, or do prevent, the execution of lawful process. The term applies also to obstructing the administration of justice in any way - as by hindering witnesses from appearing, assaulting process server, influencing jurors, obstructing court orders or criminal investigations. Any act, conduct, or directing agency pertaining to pending proceedings, intended to play on human frailty and to deflect and deter court from performance of its duty and drive it into compromise with its own unfettered judgment by placing it, through medium of knowingly false assertion, in wrong position before public, constitutes an obstruction to administration of justice.* Toledo Newspaper Co. v. U. S., 247 U. S. 402, 38 S. Ct. 560, 564, 62 L. Ed. 1186. See Title: 18 U. S. C. A. § 1501 et seq.; Model Penal Code § 242.1 et seq.
14. **Pattern of racketeering activity.** *As used in the racketeering statute (RICO), Title 18 U. S. C. A. § 1962, a "pattern of racketeering activity" includes two or more related criminal acts that amount to, or threaten the likelihood of, continued criminal activity.* H. J. Inc. v. Northwestern Bell Telephone, Co., 109 S. Ct. 2893, 106 L. Ed. 2d 195 *A single illegal scheme can constitute a "pattern of racketeering activity", so long as the racketeering acts meet the "continuity plus relationship" requirement. A combination of specific factors, such as the number of unlawful acts, the length of time over which the acts were committed, the similarity of the acts, the number of victims, the number of perpetrators, and the character of the unlawful activity can be considered in determining whether a pattern existed.* Barticheck v. Fidelity Union Bank, C. A. N. J., 832 F.2d 36, 39.
15. **Qui tam action.** Lat. "Qui Tam" is abbreviation of Latin phrase "qui tam pro domino rege quam pro si ipso in hac parte sequitor" meaning "Who sues on behalf of the King as well as for himself." *It is an action brought by an informer, under a statute which establishes a penalty for the commission or omission of a certain act, and provides*

that the same shall be recoverable in a civil action, part of the penalty to go to any person who will bring such action and the remainder to the state or some other institution. It is called a "qui tam action" *because the plaintiff states that he sues as well for the state as for himself.* U. S. v. Florida - Vanderbuilt Development Corp., D. C. Fla., 326 F. Supp.289, 290.

16. **Racketeering**. *An organized conspiracy to commit the crimes of extortion or coercion, or attempts to commit extortion or coercion. From the standpoint of extortion, it is the obtaining of money or property from another, without his consent, induced by the wrongful use of force or fear. The fear which constitutes the legally necessary element in extortion is induced by oral or written threats to do an unlawful injury to the property of the threatened person by means of explosives, fire, or otherwise; or to kill, kidnap, or injure him or a relative of his or some member of his family.*

    Activities of organized criminals who extort money from legitimate businesses by violence or other forms of threats or intimidation or conduct of illegal enterprises such as gambling, narcotics traffic, or prostitution. Title: 18 U. S. C. A. § 1961 (1) ("racketeering activity" defined).

    Racketeering is demanding, soliciting or receiving anything of value from the owner, proprietor, or other person having a financial interest in a business, by means of either a threat, express or implied, or a promise, express or implied, that the person so demanding, soliciting or receiving such thing of value will; (a) Cause the competition of the person from whom the payment is demanded, solicited or received to be diminished or eliminated; or (b) *Cause the price of goods or services purchased or sold in the business to be increased, decreased or maintained at a stated level*; or (c) Protect the property used in the business or the person or family of the owner, proprietor or other interested person from injury by violence or other unlawful means.

    For federal racketeering offenses, see Title: 18 U. S. C. A. § 1951 et seq; 1961 et seq.

17. **Reprisal.** In general, any action taken by one person either in spite or as a retaliation for an assumed or real wrong by another. The

forcible taking by one nation of a thing that belonged to another, in return or satisfaction for an injury committed by the latter on the former.

18. **RICO laws. Racketeer Influenced and Corrupt Organizations laws.** *Federal and state laws designed to investigate, control, and prosecute organized crime.* Title: 18 U. S. C. A. § 1961 et seq. *Both criminal prosecution and civil actions may be brought under RICO statutes.*

    Federal RICO laws prohibit a person from engaging in activities which affect interstate or foreign commerce, including: (1) using income received from a pattern of racketeering to acquire an interest in an enterprise; (2) acquiring or maintaining an interest in an enterprise through a pattern of racketeering; (3) conducting or participating in the affairs of an enterprise through a pattern of racketeering; and, (4) conspiring to commit any of the above offenses. To establish a prima facie RICO claim, a civil plaintiff or prosecutor must allege the existence of seven elements: "(1) that the defendant (2) through the commission of two or more acts (3) constituting a 'pattern' (4) of 'racketeering activity' (5) directly or indirectly invests in, or maintains an interest in, or participates in (6) an 'enterprise' (7) the activities of which affect interstate or foreign commerce." Title: 18 U. S. C. A. § 1962. Moss v. Morgan Stanley, Inc., C. A. N. Y., 719 F.2d 5, 17.

19. **Rule of law.** *A legal principal, of general application, sanctioned by the recognition of authorities, and usually expressed in the form of a maxim or logical proposition. Called a "rule," because in doubtful or unforeseen cases it is a guide or norm for their decision. The rule of law, sometimes called "the supremacy of law", provides that decisions should be made by the application of known principles or laws without the intervention of discretion in their application.*

20. **Whistle blower.** An employee who refuses to engage in and/or reports illegal or wrongful activities of his employer or fellow employees. Russ v. Pension consultants Co., 182 Ill. App. 3d 769, 131 Ill.Dec.318, 538 N.E. 2d 693. Employer retaliation against whistle blowers is often statutorily prohibited.

21. **Whistle-blower Acts.** Federal and state statutes designed to protect employees from retaliation for a disclosure of an employer's

misconduct. The Civil Service Reform Act, 5 U. S. C. A. § 2302(b), protects federal employees who disclose mismanagement or illegal conduct. Several other federal laws protect employees who disclose regulatory violations; e.g. OSHA violations, 29 U. S. C. A. § 660(c). Many *states also protect private and/or public sector whistle-blowers.* Cf. California Labor Code § 1102.5

Please note: *The use of italics is for the support by the meaning of the legal words within this letter.* Some of the cases may or may not apply. But through the definition, one can see that there is something very wrong with the U. S. Government and its Legal System.

A copy of this letter was forwarded for the Ambassadors for China, Russia, Venezuela, Denmark, and Sweden. The following are the definitions that I included in with the letter. However, the United States bureaucrats have made statements, for example: "They do not know how this business works", "They do not know what they are talking about", "They do not know how the courts work" or one they find amusing "this is all gibberish to me", the bureaucrats in California claim that they do not operate their State with a State Bond. Furthermore, Breakscrew Enterprise knows very well that these Bureaucrats will lie, cheat, and do what a Politician instructs them to do, legally or illegally.

I would like to point out:

1. We sent a copy of the Title: 42 that we filed against the State of California for the 'Lloyd's of London' and
2. They researched the Title: 42. Which was neither denied nor confirmed. However, Steve Knott explained to Robert Simpson, "that they were a shopping mall of insurance for companies and countries around the world." He further explained, "If you do not know the 'policy number' they would not know where to start looking for it." Moreover, Mr. Knott explained to Robert that we "were chasing the wrong pony". Steve Knott further explained, "That if we could prove that we were the 'Whistle Blowers for the 'electric fraud' we would get it all". Robert explained to Steve Knott that "we could prove it". Robert further explained that we have "VCR tapes" and other documentation that dated back to 1994.

> Breakscrew Enterprise gathered its evidence and put it on computer disks and sent copies to the Ambassadors for China, Russia, Sweden, Denmark, and Venezuela and for the Lloyd's of London 'Attention Steve Knott'.

I realize between the four cases that there is a lot of information, (I call it evidence). Try not to get too lost in the paperwork (red tape). The courts do this on purpose claiming that it is "just business." In addition, "this is how it is done." The lawyers and judges intentionally confuse the "clients"` (also known as "victims") so when the judge or lawyer or clerk of court asks the "victim / client" for a signature, they sign away their rights and place themselves at the mercy (Ha! Ha!) of the courts. The intention of this part of the book was for your information and to show you that the courts are committing fraud, extortion, blackmail, and racketeering, under R. I. C. O. In addition, what I was "dragged through" was and still is illegal.

Remember, in the beginning of this book I explained that the courts are under an Admiralty Jurisdiction and using the Uniform Commercial Codes (UCC). However, I did not write this book because of what the courts did or did not do, but to inform the reader that Breakscrew Enterprise exposed the Electric Companies for "fraud through the use of the meters". The electric companies claim that they are measuring the electricity that you use. The meters, (located on the side of your businesses, your homes, industries, ranches etc. etc.) are nothing more than a clock that measures the amount of time you use the service. Furthermore, there are only 720 hours in a thirty-day calendar month.

If you were to multiply the "rate" of the electric company you are connected with (for example: Southern California Edison stated to Breakscrew Enterprise that they charge approximately 12 cents (0.12) per Kilowatt Hour). The definitions for 'Kilowatt Hour' are above within this book for the meanings taken right out of "Webster's Dictionary." However, if you multiply 720 x 0.12 = $86.40 this amount would be your monthly bill. Furthermore, the electric companies claim that they use a "step-down" method for the billing of the electricity, for example: the first 1000 kilowatts are at 0.12 for the use of 100 hours. This would equal $12.00. The second 1000 kilowatt is at a different price, for example: if the rate is set at 0.11 for the use of 100 hours. This would equal $11.00. The rest of the time 520 hours are set lower, for example, if you were to multiply 520 x .10 = $52.00. Then take the sum of the first hour $12.00 + the sum of the second hour $11.00 + the sum of the remainder of the time $52.00 (therefore, you will have $12.00 + $11.00 + 52.00 = $75.00 dollars for the amount for the thirty day calendar month). However, you have probably heard that S. C. E. bills were from $50.00 to over $600.00 per month just for the residential bills alone and now are much higher.

Moreover, ask yourself this question, "Who is lying to whom?" After all, you are paying the extortion fee just for the privilege of turning on a light switch. Furthermore, multiply the amount of customers that are on the service times the amount of the bills and that is what the electric companies are receiving per month, every month. However, the Politicians claim that Breakscrew Enterprise does not know what they are talking about. This is why the politicians (senator Barbara Boxer, assembly member Jim Batton, and others wanted us kept silent) Breakscrew Enterprise stopped the "Free Money" flow. The electric companies were and are claiming that they are and were, being "Blackmailed" by the politicians. The State Public Utility Commissions were set up to protect the consumer not the Electric Companies or the Politicians. The U. S. Government was enforcing the "secrecy - contract" on the top executives of the electric companies. Even when they developed a conscience and said, "This is wrong." The U. S. Government would take everything that these executives earned, and I mean everything. The Government, and I mean City, County, State and Federal Government, are doing nothing to help the people. The government is concerned with how to separate you from the money or the (con-script) as I have explained earlier in this book, the paper instruments that the government allows you to use.

Furthermore, if you discover that the same government, that you think protects you, is breaking the laws or is stealing from you and you expose them, do not think for a moment that they will help you. They will not. Their well "oiled machine" will attempt to grind you up and make an example out of you for the rest of the population. However, I am not afraid of these so-called "professionals." They just made me more aggressive for the exposure of the Electric Companies that I set out to do. However, the Electric Companies are now claiming that they are looking at your "last years' bill" for that month and billing you for an average. Furthermore, the

Electric Companies claim that there is nothing "wrong with the meters" and that "they work correctly." However, why do the electric companies need to look at your last years' amount for that month if their meters work correctly? One more point of interest for your consideration, why does the Building and Safety have to know what type of electrical appliances you are going to use in your home or how many outlets you're going to have, if all the homes have the same 110 and 220 service? If the "meters worked correctly" these government agencies would not need this information.

Furthermore, if you are purchasing a new washer, dryer, refrigerator or any type of electrical appliance including your computer, the manufacturer claims that they are "energy efficient" as well as "U. L." approved. Why then do the electric companies go back a year or "guess-estimate your monthly bill?" If the meters work properly they would know how much you owe per month and not have to "guess or estimate."

I have come to the conclusion that these cases need to be before the "World Court." After all, the courts in the United States are "geared up" to protect the "Corporations" not the individual. Furthermore, these same courts are guilty of "High Treason, Apartheid, and Terrorist Tactics". However, I will continue to fight the handful of individuals in the government and expose them for the liars, cheats, thieves and murderers that they are.

It is our responsibility to stop the government from ruining our lives and over governing. Most, if not all, politicians have lost touch with the people and do not care who they hurt as long as they can make their "fortunes" on the backs of many talented Americans.

Many people will argue that the courts are "just doing their jobs." However, I am using their paperwork to prove that the courts are as "crooked" as the "handful of individuals" in the government and will stop at nothing to punish innocent people just to say "we are the law and there is nothing you can do to stop us."

As you read the evidence, remember this, I do not and will never have an Admiralty Contract with the State of California or New Mexico. The Contract that I do have with the State of California was signed by the Secretary of the State and by a State Judge, is the Title: 42 lawsuit that was filed, accepted by the clerk of courts, signed by a State judge and then the State became in [de]fault of the contract. The court system in California and New Mexico used 'terrorist tactics'. They do not have to use bombs to be a terrorist. They use threats, collusion, coercion, duress and if none of these work, they put you behind bars on some made up charge, whether it is true or not.

We have to stop these illegal proceedings and the only way I know how to do that is to educate the International Community. After all, the U.S. is not as innocent as they would lead others to believe. Furthermore, the politicians will lie, cheat and steal whenever they get the chance. They are opportunistic "creeps". Let's not give the politicians anymore opportunities.

I wish to convey for the World leaders' understanding that the United States is not as "honest" as they pretend to be. The U.S. Government points fingers at other Countries and accuses them of "Human Right Violations". The military is ordered to go in and stop the illegal acts being practiced in the name of "Freedom" and "Democracy".

However, I have presented four different cases from two States and have shown that these States have committed Apartheid, High Treason, Conspiracy, and Grand Theft and are doing the same thing that Organized Crime Bosses are being accused of. The U.S. Governments' way of dealing with these charges is to claim "Ignorance" and hope that by "ignoring the problem" they can get away with it. By ignoring the problem the government is just as guilty as those that are "supposedly highly educated' or "who hold seats of responsibility". Every document that the U. S. Government signs with other nations is not worth the paper it is written on. The authors of these documents write what they are told to write. However, the U. S. has no intention of fulfilling the document. For example, let us examine Iraq and Iran. These two Countries have been at war with each other since Christ walked the earth. The U. S. Government steps in and claims "We can solve the problem". The U. S. cannot solve their problems, let alone some other countries problems. We have no business getting involved in other Countries political, religious, or moral beliefs, when individual States are committing crimes against Americans. By the definition and Rules of their Laws these states are "guilty" of the same crimes that they are accusing other nations of. Maybe the World Court needs to put the President of the U.S. Government on "trial" and find him "guilty" of "crimes against humanity" and "hang" him. All at once the U. S. Government will want to sit down and "talk". However, this is my personal advice for the World Leaders, "U. S. Politicians speak with a forked tongue" and "beware Greeks bearing Gifts". Of course you may already know the obvious. They say one thing and mean another. A prime example of this equation is your Country may have businesses here in the U. S. creating jobs and benefitting the communities they are located in.

However, the Electric Companies have been bleeding your companies as much as they can get away with. The Electric Companies are claiming that they can "measure" the amount of electricity that your companies are consuming. This is a fraud by the definition of "fraud" and "their laws". Furthermore, when the U. S. Government is caught "committing a crime", they claim that the victim's "just do not understand how business works". This is a lie in itself. Innocent people, (victims) of the U. S. Government, actually know how business works. According to our Constitution, It takes a party of two or more people to charge an institution or government or individual(s) with a crime. Robert Simpson and I have done just that. However, the government believes that they are above those laws that they seem to force onto other citizens.

I realize that many people that read this book will argue the fact, "well you broke the law", "you deserve what you get", and so forth. Well, I would like to point out to those people who "know" so much about law that:

1. Statutes, codes, and ordinances are not law. They are like company policies. The only way a city or county can enforce a policy is if you have a contract with that City, County or State. For example: if you have a Mortgage, or if someone in a uniform walks up to you and claims that you broke a "law", have them prove it, before you sign the "Ticket". If you do not have a signed contract with the city, county or state their statutes, codes or ordinances are not enforceable. Now the county and cities like to scare you into thinking they have the "right to punish" those that do not perform under any of those statutes, codes or ordinances. However, this is where they get into a lot of trouble. They file their paper work into a court of law, accusing you of being "in violation of" such and such "Statute, Code or ordinance" such and such.

How can you be in violation if you do not have a contract with that state, county or city? Moreover, when you fight these "so-called geniuses" they include "The State of such and such verses John Doe" or "The People of the

State of "absent mindedness" versus Jane Doe". With all this, coming at you all at once, no wonder why people feel like "deer caught in the headlights of an oncoming car".

2. Statutes, codes, or ordinances are not enforceable unless you sign a "Ticket" or any document they chose to "throw at you and claim that they can arrest you and hold you for whatever amount of time". This is a lie and a "Terrorist Threat" against you and your families.

Furthermore, there are laws in affect that prohibit any Political Official from voting on any issue if that Official is connected in any way financially with the outcome of the vote. This is found in the Fair Political Practice: Rules and Regulations. However, we have seen Politicians go into office with nothing and retire with millions, at tax payer expense.

5

SUMMARY

THIS CHAPTER IS A REMINDER OF SOME OF THE MOST IMPORTANT POINTS in this book. We as Americans have to be vigilant about these so-called "professionals" abrogating our rights into "privileges" and charging a license, permit or fee for them. The Cities, Counties or States have to prove by what Authority they have to force you into a "performance" that you do not agree with. Tell them that they had better "produce the contract" and a "victim" if they are going to continue to try these cases in Admiralty/ Maritime Jurisdiction. Furthermore, we have learned in chapter 1 that the courts are trying cases by the Admiralty/Maritime Jurisdiction and not producing a "contract" or producing a "Corpus Delicti" (body of evidence) for the support of the accusation brought against you.

This is a summary of the information I have put forth in this book for you to ponder and think about while you do some checking to see if I am accurate or if I need to check myself in a hospital for a psychiatric evaluation. I can tell you right now, I know I am sane and in the right frame of mind to write this book and to prove for the Americans and the International Community that this Democracy or Republic is broken and we need to fix it before it is too late. I know of two States that do not know if they are a democracy or a republic. In either case, we have presented you with the facts of what we did to "uncover" a crime being committed against Americans and the lengths that the 'Politicians' and Bureaucrats will go to protect the "Golden Calf" or the "Golden Goose". I remind the Bureaucrats, I did not write the Laws. However, you cannot claim that "you are above the laws" and the crimes that you have committed against "We the People" will come back and "put you back into your place". I would like to remind you that, "If a law is repugnant to the Constitution, it is not law". We do not have to "perform". We must find the "proper" court that will hear our concerns. The courts now are just relying on Statues, Codes and Ordinances, not law; especially if the judge claims that there is "No room in his/her court for the Constitution", which is "Treason by Sedition" and "Perjury of Oath or Affirmation".

The first thing we have to do is ask ourselves this one question: Is the U. S. Constitution a contract?

Remember in Chapter 1 you have to enter into a contract by the UCC:

1. **Knowingly**
2. **Voluntarily**
3. **Intentionally**

The answer to the above question is a definite "yes". If the "Constitution" were not a contract the Elected Officials, Judges or Lawyers would **not** have to swear an oath or affirmation and they can rule by "Dictatorship" or "Authoritarianism". In addition, the U. S. Constitution is called the "Supreme Law of the Land". Unless I was born in another Country, the Constitution applies to all of us "equally", not just one sided or the benefit of so-called "professionals" who claim that we do not understand how "Law" works.

Furthermore, in chapter 1 we have discovered that by the use of our signatures (autographs) and the use of the UCC we have a remedy to "set the courts straight" at the Judicial level. The Uniform Commercial Code was written to educate us on how the "merchants" and "Statutory Law", this also includes Codes and Ordinances, which are being applied against us, to stop the "unfair" practices against us . However, keep in mind we are not trying to **stop** the Courts or merchants from making "money" for the services. We want to make sure that it is done correctly and accurately and in a way that will not "abrogate" our "rights". Furthermore, the courts think that they can apply anything against us and not be held responsible for their actions. This is not the truth. They can be arrested and held responsible for the "wrongful acts" committed against us, whether they claim "we were just doing our job" or not. If they are doing their jobs, then a lot of these "frivolous" cases would not be filed and the "perjury" would, almost, come to an end along with the choking of the courts with these "frivolous" cases.

In my opinion, the courts need to consider hiring "arbitrators" for a lot of these cases to see if there is "merit" for the suit. Most cases are derived from "misunderstandings" between both parties. However, most Judges are "under the influence" of the "financial" gain for these cases and will "side" with the "party" that can **buy** "justice". Furthermore, not all judges are "crooked". They are just as ignorant of the laws as we are. They just "enforce" what the lawyers know; and that is "Procedure". However, most judges now are trying to "interpret" the laws and "abrogate" the supreme Court decisions on cases presented to them in the court.

A judge is nothing but a third party referee to hear the "Facts" of a particular case. The Uniform Commercial Codes were set up to guide the lawyers and judges and 'Laymen' through the "confusing sea" of Statutes, Codes and Ordinances and to determine if **any** of them are "Unconstitutional". However, that is what we the "plaintiff/defendant" have to challenge. A majority of the judges are "honorable", until they do something 'wrong' from the bench.

Another way the courts are getting away with what they are doing is to put us into a "Dual Citizenship". If we challenge this "illegal" practice we wind up getting arrested and put in prison for their crimes against us. This is what they call "business". However, we end up "paying" for the situation levied against us if we try to prove that they are in the wrong. This is what they like to call "justice". I ask you this question, is it justice when your rights are violated, you are place under a dual citizenship, and you have to pay for their crimes? You have to remember that the courts, police, and all City, County and State bureaucratic offices are operating by the "color of jurisdiction" and "Color of Law".

In chapter 1 of this book I have shown you how to "reserve" your rights by using UCC 1 – 207 "without prejudice" and "UD" (under duress). Your signature does not claim that you are "guilty" of committing a crime or that you agree with the Officer or whatever person is claiming a violation of a Statute, Code or Ordinance. You are claiming that you have been "given" an instrument (normally a "Bill of Attainder") that is claiming that you have committed an "infraction" against the Statutes, Codes or Ordinances. It is our responsibility to stop the violations against our "Constitutional Rights" and put these "professionals" back into their places. Just because they claim a "higher education" does not mean they are "smarter" than we are. It just proves that they have to work harder to prove that we "committed a crime".

Furthermore, the courts will not admit "what" jurisdiction they are under, so you can never be able to "defend" yourself properly. In addition, if you notice when you go into a "courtroom" you will notice that the "flag" behind the judge is red, white and blue with gold fringe. This is a "federal flag", a "ceremonial" flag. However, it does not afford nor grant any "constitutional rights". This flag in the court room suspends all of our "constitutional rights". I have shown you how the courts have taken your case and entered you and your case into a "Foreign Venue". See exhibit 1 page 11. This will explain which flag **should** be in the court room. Furthermore, remember to be polite and respectful when you are in a court room. You have to treat Judges and Attorneys with respect because of their ignorance. However, this information does not "hit home" until you are accused of some sort of "infraction" or breaking the law. Then most people "complain" about the situation. This book is an opportunity to learn and make a stand against these "illegal" practices.

In summary of chapter 2, there are four cases that Robert Simpson and I are involved in. We, Robert Simpson and I, exposed a crime that was and is being committed against the entire public. In 1994, after my loss for County Supervisor, we exposed the Electric Companies for "fraud". Imperial Irrigation District, Southern California Edison, Pacific Gas and Electric, San Diego Gas and Electric and Duke Energy all claimed that they are "measuring the consumption of electricity through the "magnetic flow" through the meters". The meters are **not** measuring anything except **time**. However, because we exposed the Electric companies for "Fraud" the County Bureaucrats decided to "accuse" us of "power theft", try us and find us guilty. However, we are not going to discuss the "ins or outs" of this case because we were found "guilty" in their court system of the "Court of Convenience" and "Color of Jurisdiction". The County bureaucrats decided to "destroy" our home and "expel" us out of California.

The people who were notified are listed in Chapter 2 and are guilty of "Treason by Sedition", "Aiding and Abetting" or "accomplices of the fact". A majority of the Electric Companies, nationwide, are still defrauding the customers by claiming that they can "measure" the consumption of electricity that you use by the "magnetic flow" through the meter. Furthermore, this book is for the education of how the Politicians and the Courts are involved with the cover-up of the longest running fraud in the history in the U. S. the 'fleecing' of the customers through and by the electric companies.

The Electric Companies and the County of Riverside, California took **reprisals** against us for the education of the public for the "Fraud" that the Electric Companies are committing against the public and how they are doing it through the use of the "Meters". By the legal definition of Fraud, the Electric companies are guilty. However, if you look at the annual income of any electric company you will see that they are raking in millions and millions of dollars. Pensions and retirement funds are tied up in this as they call it, during the "Enron investigation", "Free Money". In our particular cases the Courts and the accusers failed to "prove" by what authority they have to "Demolish" and "Steal" private property that has never been conveyed or [re]conveyed into their jurisdiction. Furthermore, the parties failed to state a "crime" we have committed by the U. S. Constitution and their State Constitution especially if we were and are exercising our "inalienable rights".

However, the four cases presented in this book show how the Courts, Judges and Lawyers, breached the contract, by Perjury of Oath and Affirmation, Committing Treason by Sedition, Apartheid, and other serious crimes against Americans and U. S. Citizens. We are under the impression that we have the right to exercise our Constitutional Rights and not live under a society of Threat, Duress or Coercion. Remember, the Constitution is Supreme Law of the Land and is a "Living" Contract.

"An Oath of office is an oath or affirmation a person takes before undertaking the duties of an office, usually a position in government or within a religious body, although such oaths are sometimes required of officers of other organizations. Such oaths are often required by the laws of the state, religious body, or other organization before the person may actually exercise the powers of the office or any religious body. It may be administered at an inauguration, coronation, enthronement, or other ceremony connected with the taking up of office itself, or it may be administered privately and then repeated during a public ceremony".

"Some oaths of office are a statement of loyalty to a constitution or other legal text or to a person or other office-holder (e.g., an oath to support the constitution of the state, or of loyalty to the king)".

We were tried and convicted because we exposed the Electric Companies for Fraud and proved it. By the Rules for "Whistle Blowers" the government cannot take reprisals against anyone exposing any businesses that are committing fraud. However, Riverside County and the State of California did, so did Torrance County New Mexico. These four cases can be reopened and the decisions can be overturned. However, we are willing to let the decisions stand, "**as is**", and file charges against all parties that were involved for 'Treason by Sedition', and 'Crimes against Humanity', and the 'Continuation of the Fraud under the RICO Laws', the 'Title 42 Lawsuit' against the State of California, and 'Whistle Blowers' suit (worldwide). Furthermore, these four cases cannot be heard in any of the U. S. Courts because of the "conflict of interest". There is an old saying that is true, "Figures don't lie but liars make figures". The Court system, Politicians, and the Electric companies are protecting and will do "anything" to protect the "free money" that the Electric Companies are raking in, at your expense.

The summary of chapter 3 deals with the Remedy of what we can do to those States, Counties, Cities, Judges and Bureaucrats who commit crimes against us by the "Breach of Contract", "For knowledge of the law" and "Perjury of Oath and Affirmation" and "False Flag Venue". However, I am not accusing all employees of the government for wrongful acts, just the ones that are in a position of responsibility or elected.

In the United States, the federal district courts have jurisdiction over all admiralty and maritime actions; see Title 28 U.S.C. § 1333. In recent years, a conspiracy argument used by tax protesters is that an American court displaying an American flag with a gold fringe is in fact an "admiralty/ maritime court" and thus has no jurisdiction.

The courts have repeatedly dismissed this argument as "frivolous" and the courts are correct in dismissing these arguments against the "gold-fringe flag". However, if you go into a courtroom with a Title: 4: U. S. A. Code: Section: 1, 2 and 3 "American Flag", what the officers of the courts fail to explain to you is that you now have caused the court to be placed into a 'dual jurisdiction'. On one side, you have the Admiralty/Maritime jurisdiction where the Judges and Lawyers "practice" law. On the other side, with a Title: 4: U. S. A. Codes: Section: 1, 2 and 3 you have established a "Common Law" jurisdiction. The Judge cannot come into the courtroom to do the "Judicial" duty without committing "Perjury of Oath and Affirmation" and "Treason by Sedition".

In chapter 3, I have introduced Supreme Court cases and the decisions of the Supreme Court Justices about those cases that are on record that will help you in presenting your "particular" situation before an "honorable" judge. Honorable Judges do exist; they are just few and far between. I like the fact the Lawyers and Judges claim that supreme Court cases do not have anything to do with their "Statutes, Codes or Ordinances", when in fact they can be arrested and held responsible for acts of Treason by Sedition and other charges and by their "Oath and Affirmation" and by the individual State Constitution's.

Remember, the States Constitution do not allow their "Statutes, Codes or Ordinances to abrogate" the Supreme Law of the Land or the U. S. Constitution. The Courts and Bureaucracies are acting like "bank robbers" that got away with robbing twenty banks. However, they got caught on trying to rob the twenty-first bank and are trying to explain that they got away with it for so long that they are not "guilty" of anything. The remedy set forth in this book is but a "tip of the iceberg" in telling these "professionals" that they can be held responsible for their decisions. This book is being written to help all Americans [re]establish their rights by the Law; not what the individual States or Federal Government "say" that you have.

We have to be alert and use "common" sense and set these "professionals" back into what they were elected or appointed for. On a larger note: this book is being written to inform the International Community that the Electric Companies are committing a Fraud against their U. S. Interests and the U. S. Government is trying to keep it "covered up".

It is our duty to ourselves and our children to put a stop to the "Fleecing" and "Abrogation" of our rights for the benefit of some "power hungry" individual either elected or appointed.

EXHIBITS AND EVIDENCE

I can help you to reduce your future electric bills by:

10% - 30%

OFFER GOOD THROUGHOUT UNITED STATES

Guaranteed

Is your electric bill over $100.00 dollars per month?...??

Do you feel that your monthly electric bill is outrageously high?
Do you want to lower your electric bills by 10% - 30% and
save that money?
Or do you enjoy paying outrageous electric bill rates?
If you are tired of those high power bills and want to cut your
monthly rates by 10% - 30%, Act Now. . . . . . .

Send $19.95 check or money order, and
a self addressed stamped envelope to:

Brakescrew, Ent.
30-257 Monte Vista Way
Thousand Palms, CA 92276

And I will send you information that the Electric Companies are
not telling you, That will reduce your Rates.

Please do not send cash. Sorry No C.O.D.'s
Please allow 2-4 weeks for delivery.

Price is subject to change without notice.

Exhibit A

PROOF OF PUBLICATION
(2015.5 C.C.P.)

STATE OF CALIFORNIA
County of Riverside

I am a citizen of the United States and a resident of the County aforesaid; I am over the age of eighteen years, and not a party to or interested in the above-entitled matter. I am the principal clerk of the printer of the DESERT SUN PUBLISHING COMPANY, a newspaper of general circulation, printed and published in the city of Palm Springs, County of Riverside, and which newspaper has been adjudged a newspaper of general circulation by the Superior Court of the County of Riverside, State of California; under the date of March 24, 1988. Case Number 191236; that the notice, of which the annexed is a printed copy (set in type not smaller than nonpareil), has been published in each regular and entire issue of said newspaper and not in any supplement thereof on the following dates, to wit:

September 23, 30, October 7, 14

all in the year 1994.

I certify (or declare) under penalty of perjury that the foregoing is true and correct.

Dated at Palm Springs, California this 14th day of OCTOBER , 1994.

SIGNATURE

This space is for County Clerk's Filing Stamp

COUNTY CLERK
FILED
OCT 14 1994
FRANK K. JOHNSON, Clerk
Deputy

Proof of Publication of

NO. 825
FICTITIOUS BUSINESS NAME STATEMENT
File No. 1942070
The following person is doing business as:
BrakeScrew Enterprise
30 257 Monte Vista Way
Thousand Palms, CA 92276
Full name of Registrant:
Bradley "Jeff" Franks, 30-257 Monte Vista Way, Thousand Palms, CA 92276
This business is conducted by: an individual.
Registrant commenced to transact business under the fictitious business name or names listed above on 9/10/76
/s/ Bradley "Jeff" Franks
NOTE: This statement expires 5 years from the filing date. The filing of this statement does not of itself authorize the use in this state of a Fictitious business name in violation of the rights of another under Federal, State, or Common Law
This statement was filed
SEP 19 1994
Frank K. Johnson,
Riverside County Clerk
By: O. Kerr, Deputy
Pub. 9/23, 30, 10/7, 14, 1994

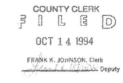

Note: Page 1 of 5 in
Package of information,
Please give package to either
Ken Phillips or Chuck Harder.
Thank you!

PROOF OF PUBLICATION

Exhibit B

DEPARTMENT OF BUILDING AND SAFETY
COUNTY OF RIVERSIDE

RESIDENTIAL PLAN REQUIREMENTS

1. Two (2) complete sets of plans shall be submitted. The plans shall be drawn on substantial paper (blue printed or inked drawings) exactly as the building is to be constructed. Defaced, incomplete, indefinite or faded plans shall not be used. All plans perpared by licensed persons shall be signed. All signatures shall be original. No reproductions.

2. Plot plan: Two (2) plot plans in ink to scale with a complete legal description, lot size, setback of existing and proposed buildings to property lines and distance between buildings (indicating the use of each building). Show location of sewage disposal system. If lot slopes more than one (1) foot in fifty (50) feet, denote on plan. Owners name and address, contractor's name and address and area where building is to be located shall be shown on plan.

3. Foundation plan: Provide a plan view of the foundation showing the location of the foundation footings and walls, piers, underpinning and girders (or the location of interior continuous footings in case of slab floor construction); show the location of double joists under partitions. Include a cross-section of footing, piers and underpinning, showing the distances below natural grade and the height above finish grade. All dimensions shall be shown.

4. Floor plan: Show room size and use. Show size and location of ALL headers, doors, and windows accurately dimensioned. Show size, spacing and direction of ceiling joists. Show all plumbing fixtures, gas appliances, electrical appliances, outlets (lights, plugs and switches) and total load demand.

5. Roof plan: Include all roof heating or cooling unit locations, fireplaces saddles, Dutch clips, etc. If trusses are used, provide truss manufacturers layout, details, and calculations.

6. Elevations: Provide four (4) elevations, identified as front, rear, right side and left side. Show location of doors, windows, chimneys, etc. Show bracing, exterior finish, veneer, planters and roof covering.

7. Construction details: Provide cross-sectional elevations, showing the foundation, underpinning, floor joists, studs, ceiling joists, rafters, pitch of roof and location of intermediate roof supports, if required. Also provide true cross-section of fireplace. If a standard detail sheet is used, delete details that do not apply to the proposed building. Show size, spacing and kind of material of all members of the structure. If ceiling is vaulted show cross section and connections.

8. Energy Conservation: Submit two (2) sets of calculations per model showing compliance to the State Energy Conservation Regulations for new residential buildings. Indicate on plans the type of heating system and the maximum output bonnet capacity in units of BTU/HR.

284-179 Rev. 1979

Exhibit C

RIVERSIDE COUNTY
PLANNING DEPARTMENT

$100.00

APPLICATION FOR SETBACK ADJUSTMENT
SECTION 18.33 ORDINANCE NO. 348

APPLICANT: Submit this form with five copies of a scaled Plot Plan drawn to the specifications required on the attached Check List. Check for the appropriate fee must be made payable to "County of Riverside."

If the Applicant is not the owner of the property, a letter must be submitted by the owner authorizing the Applicant to execute this document in his behalf.

PLEASE PRINT OR TYPE

APPLICANT Joel R. Simpson DATE April 9, 1984

MAILING ADDRESS 30257 Monte Vista Way
Thousand Palms CA. 92276 PHONE NO. none

OWNER Joel R. Simpson

MAILING ADDRESS 30257 Monte Vista Way
Thousand Palms, CA. 92276 PHONE NO. none

Street Address of Property 30259 Monte Vista Way

Assessor's Parcel No.(s) 650-034-009

Legal Description of Property (May be attached) Lot 214 of Shangri La Palms, Unit # 8, as per map recorded in Book 28, Pages 61, 62 and 63 inclusive of maps in the office of the County Recorder of said County.

Adjustment requested 12', 20 ft. — facing road

Reason for request House is already standing.

JUSTIFICATION: No request for a setback adjustment shall be granted unless it is determined that the adjustment is consistent with the intent and purposes of this Ordinance; that there are special circumstances applicable to the property, including such factors as size, shape, topography, location or surroundings that justify the approval of the adjustment of the setback requirement, and the adjustment will not be detrimental to the health, safety, and general welfare of the community or be detrimental to property in the vicinity of the parcel for which the adjustment is required.

STAFF USE

Returned to applicant 6-8-84 due to lack of required information.

Receipt No. ______ By ______
District/Area ______ Date Received ______
Zoning ______ Adjustment No. ______

4080 LEMON STREET, 9TH FLOOR
RIVERSIDE, CALIFORNIA 92501
(714) 787-6181
PD 83-69

46-209 OASIS STREET, ROOM 304
INDIO, CALIFORNIA 92201
(619) 342-8277

Exhibit D

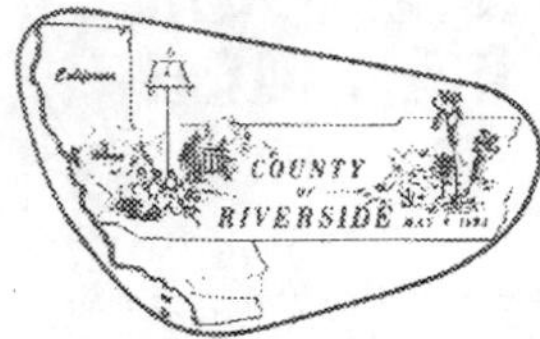

Department of Building and Safety

Administrative Office Bldg., Room 310
46-209 Oasis Street
Indio, California 92201
(714) 342-8271

CERTIFIED MAIL
RETURN RECEIPT REQUESTED

March 19, 1987

Mr. Joel Simpson
30-257 Monte Vista Wy.
1000 Palms, CA. 92276

Re: 30-257 Monte Vista Wy.
Case No. 01908-86
APN: 650-034-007

An inspection was made at the above-referenced address on March 17, 1987 in answer to complaints received by this office. The structure(s) were found to be substandard and a public nuisance under Riverside County Ordinance 457 and as such was posted with a "List of Defects" and "Danger Do Not Enter" signs.

As owner of record on the tax roll, you have 30 days to either demolish or rehabilitate the structures obtaining permits for all work to be done.

Permits required:

- A. To demolish
  1. Demolition permit
- B. To rehabilitate
  1. Special inspection permit to rehabilitate structure
  2. Construction permit per special inspection report

A "Notice of Pendency of Administrative Proceedings" has been recorded with the County Recorder and charges for inspector's time and mileage are being charged against the property.

Should you have any questions regarding this matter, please contact the undersigned by calling (714) 787-6438.

Respectfully,

Leopoldo Rojo, Jr., Director
DEPARTMENT OF BUILDING AND SAFETY

By ______________________

R. Pope----Abatement/Code Enforcement Officer

Enclosures: List of Defects
Ordinance 457

c.c. Joel Simpson
Max & Eunice & Brian & Candi Siefker

Exhibit E-1

CODE SECTIONS FOR HOUSING CODE VIOLATIONS

SECTION 17920.3

HEALTH AND SAFETY CODE

SUBSTANDARD BUILDINGS	CODE SECTION
1. ( ) Lack of, or improper water closet, lavatory, bathtub or shower in a dwelling unit	H 505(a)
2. ( ) Lack of, or improper water closets, lavatories, and bathtubs or showers per number of guests in a hotel	H 505(b)
3. ( ) Lack of or improper kitchen sink	H 505(c)
4. ( ) Lack of hot and cold running water to plumbing fixtures in a hotel.	H 505(d)
5. ( ) Lack of hot and cold running water to plumbing fixtures in a dwelling unit	H 505(d)
6. ( ) Lack of adequate heating facilities	H 701(a)
7. ( ) Lack or improper operation of required ventilating equipment	H 701(c), H 504(c)
8. ( ) Lack of minimum amount of natural light and ventilation required by this code	H 504(a)
9. ( ) Room or space dimension less than required by this code	H 504(a)
10. ( ) Lack of required electrical lighting	H 701(b)
11. ( ) Dampness of habitable rooms	H 601(b)
12. ( ) Infestation of insects, vermin or rodents as determined by the Health Officer........Int.______ Ext.______	17920.3(a)12
13. ( ) General dilapidation or improper maintenance	17920.3(a)13 UBC 104(d)
14. (XX) Lack of connection to required sewage system	H 505(d)
15. (XX) Deteriorated or inadequate foundations	H 601(a)
16. ( ) Defective or deteriorated flooring or floor supports	H 601(a)
17. (XX) Flooring or floor supports of insufficient size to carry imposed loads with safety	H 601(a)
18. ( ) Members of walls, partitions, or other vertical supports that split, lean, list, or buckle due to defective material or deterioration, or insufficient size........Int.______ Ext.______	H 601(a)
19. ( ) Members of walls, partitions, or other vertical supports that are of insufficient size to carry imposed loads with safety	H 601(a)
20. ( ) Members of ceilings, roofs, ceiling and roof supports or other horizontal members which sag, split, or buckle due to defective material, deterioration or insufficient size. Int.______ Ext.______	H 601(a)
21. ( ) Members of ceilings, roofs, ceiling and roof supports or other horizontal members that are of insufficient size to carry imposed loads with safety	H 601(a)
22. ( ) Fireplaces or chimneys which list, bulge, or settle, due to defective material or deterioration	H 601(a)
23. ( ) Fireplaces or chimneys which are of insufficient size or strength to carry imposed loads with safety	H 601(a)
24. (XX) Hazardous wiring	H 701(b)
25. (XX) Hazardous plumbing	17920.3(e)
26. ( ) Hazardous mechanical equipment	H 701(c)
27. (XX) Faulty weather protection a. Deteriorated, crumbling, or loose plaster. b. Deteriorated or ineffective waterproofing of exterior walls, roof, foundations, or floors, including broken windows or doors. c. Defective or lack of weather protection for exterior wall coverings, including lack of paint, or weathering due to lack of paint or other approved protective covering. d. Broken, rotted, split, or buckled exterior wall coverings or roof coverings.	H 601(b)
28. (XX) Fire hazard	H 901
29. ( ) Inadequate maintenance	17920.3(k)
30. ( ) Inadequate exits	H 801
31. ( ) Water closet compartments in dwellings shall be finished with approved non-absorbent materials. All others shall be in accordance with Section 1711 of UBC	H 505(e)
32. ( ) Water closets, bathtubs or showers required by this code shall be installed in a room which will afford privacy to the occupant	H 505(e)
33. ( ) A room in which a water closet is located shall be separated from food preparation or storage rooms by a tight-fitting door	H 505(f)
34. (XX) Faulty materials of construction. All materials of construction except those which are specifically allowed or approved by or pursuant to this code and which have been adequately maintained in good and safe condition	H 601(a)
35. (XX) Hazardous or unsanitary premises	17920.3(j)

Case No. 1908-86 Street 30-257 Monte Vista Wy.

Date 3-19-87 Inspector [signature]

284-178 Rev. 3/31/81

Exhibit E-2

First Interstate Bank

First Interstate Bank of California
650 Town Center Drive
Costa Mesa, CA 92626

The Center Tower Office

Cashiers Check

№ 3600004023

16-21/360
1220

DATE May 2, 1989

PAY First Interstate 3,000dol's00cts $ **3,000.00**

TO THE ORDER OF **Brian or Max Siefker**

Deborah L. White
AUTHORIZED SIGNATURE
8712

⑈3600004023⑈ ⑆122000218⑆3570989 50⑈ 11

May 2, 1989

Joel R. Simpson
30-257 Monte Vista Way
Thousand Palms, CA. 92276

Max or Brian Siefker
8562 Coral Crest Dr.
Elk Grove, CA. 95624

Dear Max or Brian:

Enclosed is a check for Three Thousand Dollars ($3,000.00) for full payment toward my property.
It has been brought to my attention that from 5/23/82 through 12/23/82 that you have over charged me on the interest allowed by Law at the Twelve percent (12%) interest rate for the last half of 1982. The Payment Schedule Book has other such errors throughout it.
You have failed to send Interest Statements to me for my records before the Tax Date Deadline (April 15th) of each year.
Therefore, I was unable to use them for Tax Write-offs.
I urge you to accept the $3,000.00 Dollar Cashiers' Check as full payment toward my property and please send me a full reconveyance from you as well as a clear Title.

Yours Truly,

Joel Robert Simpson

Joel R. Simpson

JRS/
RJP

Exhibit F

CASE NO: I-152-90

LOCATION: 30257 MONTE VISTA WAY
THOUSAND PALMS, CALIFORNIA
APN: 650-034-007

VIOLATIONS OBSERVED ON 6/17/91
INSPECTION WARRANT NO. 11081

ORDINANCE NO.	SECTION	VIOLATION(S)
✗ Riv. Co. 348	6.2	Encroachment into the required twenty (20) foot front yard setback. (Approximately 17 feet).
✓✗ Riv. Co. 348 — we have a single family Dwelling	6.1	Multiple Family Dwelling (as defined in Riv. Co. Ord. No. 348.21.31) in a zone which does not allow this use.
✗ Riv. Co. 457 — We have tried to require the permits in '86 but were told that we would have to tear down the whole House.	2	Occupancy violation(UAC 202[e]); construction without the required plans or permits(UAC 301); required inspections not performed(UAC 305[a,e]);Use or occupancy of a structure without the required Certificate of Occupancy(UAC 308).
Riv. Co. 457 — No Electricity / Plenty of Vent. / To Quote Joel "This is Bull Shit"	4	Required fire separation between an attached garage and a dwelling unit lacking(UBC 503); required light and ventilation not provided in each room(UBC 1205); secondary emergency exits lacking from bedrooms(UBC 1204); stairway risers and runs of irregular size and exceeding maximum height(UBC 3306); stairways lacking required handrails(UBC 3306); beams and rafters overspanned and overloaded, plywood floor and roof sheathing not properly applied, moisture barrier lacking from exterior finish, and drywall used in an exterior exposure(UBC Chapter 25).
Riv. Co. 457 — Portable Propane to cook @, furnace not even Hooked up.	5	Portable propane tank used inside a structure: forced air unit (FAU) plenum register located below a combustion air grill; duct and vents covered without the required inspections(Uniform Mechanical Code).

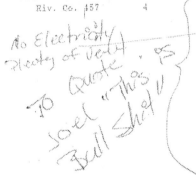

Exhibit G-1

Inspection Warrant No. 11081
List of Violations
Pg. 2

Riv. Co. 457 6 — Private sewage disposal system missing or located beneath a structure; plumbing and piping system covered without the required inspections(Uniform Plumbing Code).

Unfortunately Inspectors never even asked about said plumbing.

Riv. Co. 457 7 — Electrical wiring covered without the required inspections; required connections missing from junction box; subpanel wiring improperly grounded and bonded; required receptacles, switches and lighting fixtures lacking; 200 amp service panel not completed; lightning rod ground crosses property lines; use of a non-rated lighting device and non-rated light hanging device (bailing wire) (National Electrical Code).

the Sub panel that this person is speaking about is not even hooked up.

Joel is uncertain as to the grounds of this Code.

Mr. Kudak video taped the inside of Joel's House from top to bottom with no mention of it in the search Warrant or Joel's permission. Joel seem convinced that this was an invasion of privacy concerning the Video taping.

Exhibit G-2

Robert-Joel: Simpson,
In the Care – 30257 Monte-Vista-Way,
City of the Thousand-Palms, " (unincorporated)",
P. Z. [92276]

(TITLE: 4: U.S.A. CODES: CHAPTER: 1: SECTION: 1&2)
FOR THE AMERICAN-FLAG OF THE UNITED-STATES OF THE AMERICA

WITHIN THE COURT OF THE DISTRICT FOR THE COUNTY OF THE
RIVERSIDE WITHIN THE COUNTY OF THE RIVERSIDE
OF THE STATE OF THE CALIFORNIA

WITHIN THE SANCTUARY OF THE BAR: UNDER THE ARTICLE III VENUE AND JURISDICTION: BY THE COURT OF THE RECORD UNDER THE

COMMON-LAW

COUNTY OF RIVERSIDE TRANSPORTATION
AND LAND MANAGEMENT AGENCY (sic)
Building and Safety Department (sic)
CODE ENFORCEMENT DEPT. (sic)
SUPERVISING CODE ENFORCEMENT, AGENT/OFFICER (sic),
"Gary-Shopshear,
CODE ENFORCEMENT OFFICERS/AGENTS, DOES 1-10 (sic)

PLAINTIFF:

VERSES:

Robert-Joel: Simpson,
Sui-potestate = In On's Own Right and Dominion,

AGGRIEEVE/RESPONDENT

Under the Certifying-Mail-Number
as the Inc. of the Case Number:
____

[CASE NO. CV990774]

BY THE AFFIDAVIT OF THE NOTICE
BY THE SHOWING OF THE CAUSE OF
THE COMPLAINT-ASUMPTION OF THE
VENUE AND JURISDICTION BY THE
JUDICIAL-COGNIZANCE

State of the California
SS
County of the Riverside

FOR THE AFFIDAVIT BY THE COMPLAINT FOR THE SHOWING-CAUSE

Page – 1.

AFFIDAVIT AND NOTICE

1. COPYRIGHT © 6-04-99, by the Robert-Joel: Simpson,

Robert-Joel: Simpson

R-J

Exhibit H1

1. Robert-Joel: Simpson **BY THE CHALLENGING OF THE JURISDICTION OF [T]HE COUNTY OF RIVERSIDE** (sic) **AND THE TRANSPORTATION & LAND MANAGEMENT AGENCY (sic) AND THE OFFICERS/AGENTS (sic) AND BUILDING & SAFETY DEPT. OFFICERS/AGENTS (sic) & THE CODE ENFORCEMENT DEPT. (sic) & THE OFFICERS/AGENTS (sic) & ANY AND ALL OTHER DEPT./AGENCIES AND THE OFFICERS/AGENTS (sic) THEREOF** AND BY BRINGING OF THIS MATTER BEFORE THE COURT BY THE **JUDICIAL-COGNIZANCE** BY THE DISCOVERY, BY THE SHOWING OF THE CAUSE, DEMANDING SUI SPONTE PROCEEDING AND PROCLAIMING THAT THIS MAN IS BY THE PROCLAIMING THAT THIS MAN NEVER DID BY THE SIGNING OF ANY SIGNATURE, AND SAID VIOLATIONS AND IS UNDER THE THREAT OF THE THREAT, DURESS, AND COERCION BY THE COUNTY OF RIVERSIDE (sic) AND THE VARIOUS AGENCIES, DEPT. AND THEIR OFFICERS/AGENTS (sic)AND AT THE THREAT OF THE LOSSING OF MY PROPERTY AND LIBERTY. BY SUCH AN ASSULT AND ACT OF THE AGGRESION BY BEING DONE ON PRIVATE-PROPERTY. THIS MAN DECLARES THAT THIS MAN HAVE-NOT FOR THE CAUSING OF THE INJURY FOR NO-ONE. MY APPEARANCE WITHIN THE COURTROOM IS ALWAYS OUT OF TH THREAT, COERCION, AND DURESS, AS THIS IS THE LAST PLACE I WOULD CHOOSE FOR BEING, AND BY THE CAUSING OF UNLAFUL DISTRESS.

2. Robert-Joel: Simpson DECLARES THAT THIS MAN IS NOT NOR HAVE EVER BEEN A "PERSON", (ie) FIRM, COPARTNERSHIP, CORP, ASSOC., OR ORGANIZATION, OR A "DEAD-PERSON" (NOM DE GUERRE) OR TRUST OR TRUSTEE, WITHIN ANY OR UNDER ANY BANKRUPT PROCEEDINGS AS A CHATTEL-PROPERTY, OR HAVE EVER KNOWING EVER BY THE SIGNING MY LAWFUL PROPER-ENGLISH NAME UNDER ANY CONTRACT. THIS MAN IS ONE OF THE PEOPLE INDIGENOUS AND DOMICILE WITHIN THE "State of the California AND THIS MAN IS BY THE BUILDING OF THE HOUSE SOJURING WITHIN THE State of the California

3. THIS MAN BY THE FILING OF THE BRIEF IS BY THE ASKING WITHIN THE WRITING FOR THE PRODUCTION OF THE DOCUMENTS BY THE "REPORTED VIOLATIONS" OF RIVERSIDE COUNTY ORDINANCE NUMBER(S); 457/2 (SIC). BY THE STATING ABOVE THIS MAN HAVE NOT KNOWING[LY] BY THE SIGNING ANY "UNITED STATES D.C. ADHESION-CONTRACTS".

4. NOTICE: ANY AND ALL OF THE CONTRACTS THAT ARE NOT FULLY DICLOSED ARE UNDER THE FRAUD AND IS HEREBY OF THE CANCELLING AND ARE OF THE NULL AND VOID.

Page ~ 2.

Affidavit and Notice Page 2.

2. COPYRIGHT © 6-04-99, BY THE Robert-Joel: Simpson,

Robert-Joel: Simpson.

R-J: S

Exhibit H2

DECLARED, BY THE SIGNING AND SEALING THIS ____ DAY OF THE ________ WITHIN THE YEAR OF OUR LORD, (JESUS OF THE CHRIST) 1999.

L. S. Robert-Joel: Simpson

Robert-Joel: Simpson, sui-potestate, Citizen

ON THIS DAY OF THE ______ JUNE 1999, THE SIGNATORY Robert-Joel: Simpson BY THE PERSONNA, KNOWN BY ME, AND DID AFFIX OF THE SIGNATURE AND SeaL FOR THIS DOCUMENT. USE OF THE NOTARY IS FOR THE COGNIZANCE IN THE FOREIGN-VENUE ONLY AND NOT MEAMT BY THE CONVEYING OF ANY JURISDICTION.

____

NOTARY-PUBLIC

Page – 3.

AFFIDAVIT AND NOTICE PAGE – 3.

3. COPYRIGHT © 6-01-99, BY THE Robert-Joel: Simpson,

Robert-Joel: Simpson.

R-J: S

Exhibit H3

FOR THE DISCOVERY: VIA TACIT-PROCURATION

SINCE THE PROCLIVITY OF AN ADVERSARY IS BY THE NOT ANSERING, FOR THE FOLLOWING QUESTIONS ARE BY THE ANSWERING ON THE COUNTY OF RIVERSIDE THE AGENCIES,DEPT. & OFFICERS/AGENTS (sic) ALTHOUGH THE COUNTY WILL/IS BY THE PROCEEDING BY THE INTERING SPECIFIC AND OF THE DETAILING OBJECTIONS, DEMURR, AND STRICK WITHIN THE EVENT THAT WE ARE NOT OF THE ONE ACCORD.

1. Are all of the Citizens, of the natural and artificial "persons" subject by the same body of the jurisprudence/law within the state of the California or County - ANSWER: NO.

2. Does a natural, de jure Private Citizen, absent of the restrictions/waivers under imposing of the lawful-contracts, poses of the truth using the constitution as the limitations upon the De facto United States and its corporate State, County, City entities, God given and of the common-law right for general-contracting? – ANSWER: YES.

3. Can the exercise of the rights at law be of the converting into a crime? – ANSWER: NO.

4. Can the Aggrieve/Respondent by the compelling for the surrendering of a right (property/working/labor/general-contracting) within the order of the exercising those rights? – ANSWER: NO.

5. Can the Citizen by the compelling by the surrendering of the rights thereby degrading of the right for the exercise of a privilege?- ANSWER: NO.

6. Can [T]he Article IIII court/prosecution by the proving that the respondent is not clothed within an At-Law of the right for the general-contracting? – ANSWER: NO.

7. Does of a license and/or permit/fee by the constituting of a grant of a privilege (an advantage not enjoyed by all), ANSWER: YES.

8. Is a privilege a grant of the permission for doing something "against or beyond by the course of the law? – ANSWER: YES.

9. Is of the right for the traveling by the STATE (sic) granting of a privilege? – ANSWER: NO.

10. Can the right for the working, general-contracting at Law by the surrendering/waiving (due of the ignorance) by the voluntary, thus by the making One "subject" for the exercising of a privilege/license under the equity/bankruptcy-proceeding-jurisdiction (sic)? – ANSWER: NO.

Page –4.

4. Affidavit and Notice

4. COPYRIGHT © 6-04-99, BY THE Robert-Joel: Simpson,

Robert-Joel: Simpson

R-J: S

Exhibit H4

11. Can [T]he COUNTY OF RIVERSIDE AND ALL OF THE DPT. ,AGENCIES, OFFICERS/AGENTS (sic) show the positive-evidence of a existing/binding contract by the obtaining by the respondent's voluntary application or re-application, whereby the rights At Law are/were by the waiving for the securing of the privilege's under the equity/, bankruptcy, proceeding, jurisdiction under [T]he court's or [T]he Counties venue and jurisdiction (sic) ? – ANSWER: NO.

12. Can the respondent by the compelling for the applying for the (sic) granting of the privileges? – ANSWER: NO.

13. Is the government of the creation of the People and are the People Sovereign, as evidenced by the Constitutions of the united-states and the state of the California by their creation? – ANSWER: YES.

14. "Are the CORPORATIONS, ASSOCIATIONS, COPARTNERSHIPS, COMPANIES, FIRMS AND ORGANIZATIONS OF THE CREATION OF [T] HE STATE AND persons" (sic) UNDER THE BANKRUPTCY OF THE UNITED STATES (sic)? – ANSWER: YES.

15. Can a natural person be any of the "persons" by the enumeration within the question: #-14? – ANSWER. YES.

16. Can a Citizen by being amenable by the Supreme-Law or it's removal by the creating "statutes (sic) without an bone fide injured-party? – ANSWER: NO.

17. Is the Citizen subject by the "statute-law (sic)? – ANSWER: NO.

18. Has [T]he [S]TATE, COUNTIES, CITIES, without a Notice of the real-intent, by the licensing, permits and registration schemes by the attempting for the obtaining absolute control over, and diminishing of the Sovereignty of the People, by the role of "subject, vassal, debtor" under the bankruptcy of the UNITED STATES INC. UNDER THE POERTO-RICO TRUST FUND OR ANY OTHER FOREIGN FUND(sic)? – ANSWER: YES.

19. Does all of the "STATUTE-LAW/CODES" by the running- counter for the common-law? – ANSWER: YES.

20. Can the "STATUTE/CODIFIED/LAW" for the compelling of the specific performance of a Citizen? – ANSWER: NO.

21. Does [T]he courts of the limited-jurisdiction have of the original-jurisdiction within cases At-Law?- ANSWER: NO.

Affidavit and Notice page – 5.

Page – 5.

5. COPYRIGHT © 6-04-99, BY THE Robert-Joel: Simpson,

Robert-Joel: Simpson

R-J: S

Exhibit H5

22. Would the display of the FOREIGN/FICTION-FLAGS within [T]he Article IV courtroom of the four-cornering, of the bracketing of the jury-box, [T]he-bench and [T]he witness-stand, above the plane of the neutural-bar by the tending for the knowing that the proceedings are under the "UNITED STATES –BANKRUPTCY-PROCEEDINGS and the " body of the jurisprudence" by the administering therein knowing that the rights At-Law are not at issue? – ANSWER: YES.

23. Does [T]he gold-fringe-flag nowhere known within the world and the California state-flag with a spear atop of the flag (military-courts-martial-flag) (sic) and the under this foreign-jurisdictional-flags (sic) the common-law is being abrogated?- ANSWER: YES.

24. Is this the reason why the right by the common-law jury of the 12 men, peers, is not being administered, which is under fraud? – ANSWER: YES.

25. Could this be why the Aggrieved/accused/respondent by being subject for the prosecution of a "crime" with "DOES" 1-20 corporate-persons as hostile-witnesses, when the constitutions specifically require more than one lawful-Citizen, who may be examined face into face, and without of the injured \-parties? – ANSWER: YES.

26. Does the "status" of an "Absolute-Owner" of a general-contractor by the differing of that of a "Qualified-Owner"? – ANSWER: YES.

27. Does the "application for a permit or a business-license, or driver-license, certificate for title,(pink-slip) and registration, and of the destroying or fraudulently signing – over of the (M. C. O.) into [T]he [S]tate of [CA.] alter the "status of the natural de jure Citizen" within [T]he eyes of [T]he courts, subjecting the Citizen into a foreign-system of the jurisprudence (sic) other than At-Law?- ANSWER: YES

28. Does the District-Court Judge of the oath and affirmation act within his ministerial-capacity and not for a foreign-entity under the fraud? – ANSWER: YES.

Affidavit and Notice page – 6.

Page – 6.

6. COPYRIGHT © 6-04-99, BY THE Robert-Joel: Simpson,

Robert – Joel : Simpson

R – J : S

Exhibit H6

THUS, by the reason of the foregoing, absent of the evidence of the contrary, point by the point by this court of the record by this mans tribunal and under judicial-cognizance alleg[ed] is without foundation sufficient for the continuing the above captioned contest (By the commencing into the equity, bankruptcy against At-Law-Citizen). This instruments of the showing by the cause aggrieved/accused/respondent, of the inability, time[ly] constitutes Plaintiff's Retraxit. By the paraphrasing " [U.S. v. Parker, 7 S. Ct. 454, 120 U.S. 89; Lewis v. Johnson, Cal. App. 80 P.2d 90.]"

Consistent with the court decision within ["Hagins v. Lavine", 415 U.S. 533"] Once jurisdiction has by the challenging it must be of the proving". Further, [t]he court by the ruling out of the assuming jurisdiction at the risk of the presiding judge within ["Boswell v. Otis, 9 How, 336, 348]; by the wit: "[t]he court by the enforcing mere statutes do not act Judicial[ly], but mere[ly] MINISTERIAL[LY]; thus, having no Judicial Immunity, and of the process, nor even of the arrest and by the compell[ed]-appearance.,"

"BY THE DETERMINATION/STIPULATION-FINAL"

Notice-response will/is of the no force/effect at Law unless by the signing of the perjury, Oath/Affirmation by being admissible on the court-record pursuant by the Law.

This Determination becomes of the FINAL, unless by the specific by the objection by the detail point for the point within ten (10) days of the receipt, an extension of the time is/will be grant[ed] if "statutory authority is by the citing" within the initial ten (10) day period of the time and a thirty (30) day continuance is by the granting without waiver of the rights.

Affidavit and Notice page – 7.

Page – 7.

Robert-Joel: Simpson

R-J: S

Exhibit H7

"BY THE COMPLAINT AND DEMAND FOR THE DISCHARGING & CANCELLATION OF THE INSPECTING & INVESTIGATING"

The "Aggrieved", Robert-Joel: Simpson, by Special-Visitation Order for showing of the cause point by the point and complaint by the court, Robert-Joel: Simpson's Tribunal, for the Cancellation and discharging the "TO: ALL OWNERS & INTERESTED PARTIES (SEE ATTACHED NOTICE LIST)" (sic) "SUBJECT: NOTICE OF INTENTION TO INSPECT AND INVESTIGATE SUBJECT PROPERTY AND STRUCTURES FOR REPORTED VIOLATIONS OF RIVERSIDE COUNTY ORDINANCE NUMBER(S); 457/2" (SIC) for the lack of the jurisdiction and venue and/or prosecution point for the point.

"BY THE PETITION FOR THE INJUNCTION" AT THE COMMON-LAW

"Aggrieved/Accused" HEREBY RESPECTFUL DMANDS & REQUESTS THAT THIS COURT, NOT [T]he COURT BY THE GRANTING OF THE INJUNCTIVE RELIEF AT THE COMMON-LAW UNDER THE THREAT BY THE "[T]he COURT AND ALL OFFICERS OF [T]HE COURT(sic) AND THE COUNTY OF RIVERSIDE AND ITS DEPT./AGENCIES, OFFICERS/AGENTS (sic), BY THE INSPECTING OF HIS PRIVATE PROPERTY AND THE RESTRAINING OF HIS LIBRTY, BY THE PROPER, WITHOUT THE DUE-PROCESS "UNDER THE LAWFUL COURT. BY SUCH THREATS AS VEXTATIOUS AND BY THE ABUSE OF THE OFFICE, ARE BY THE INTENDING BY THE FORCING OF THE "Accused" FOR THE EXCHANGING HIS RIGHTS FOR THE PRIVIELEGS, AND BY DELIVERING "ACCUSED" Being INTO [T]he COURT OF THE VENUE AND JURISDICTION. BY BEING THE DUTY OF THE COURT FOR THE DEFENDING AND PROTECTING THOSE RIGHTS, AND BY THE OATH OR AFFIRMATION BY THE RESPECTING FOR THE SUPREME-LAW WHICH SUBJECT THE state of the California, County of the San-Bernardino, City of the Ontario, BY THE DUE-PROCESS. THIS COURT, NOT [T]he COURT HAS THE AUTHORITY BY ENJOINING ALL LAW -ENFORCEMENT BY THE HONORING OF THE RIGHTS OF THE "Aggrieved" FOR THE WORKING AND PROVIDING FOR THE FAMILY AND CONTROLLING AND POSSESSING PRIVATE PROPERTY WITHOUT PREJUDICE UNDER ANY OTHER RIGHT.

Page – 8.

Affidavit and Notice page - 8.

8. COPYRIGHT © 6-04-99, BY THE Robert-Joel: Simpson,

Robert-Joel: Simpson

R-J: S

Exhibit H8

BY THE SUBMITTING, SIGNING AND SEALING, OF THIS FOURTH (4) DAY OF THE JUNE WITHIN THE YEAR OF OUR LORD 1999.

SEAL

Robert-Joel: Simpson,
sui-potestate, Within One's own right & Dominions.
In the c/o The 30257 Monte-Vista-Way,
City of the Thousand-Palms,
County: Riverside,
State of the California
[P.Z. 92276]

BY THE CERTIFICATE OF THE SERVICE

Robert-Joel: Simpson does by the certifying that "Joel" having by the serving for the true copy of this Affidavit and Notice with the prosecutors office by leaving of the copy with the secretary therein this 4th Day Of the June 1999.

Robert-Joel: Simpson
sui potentate., By One's own right & One's own dominion

Affidavit and Notice Page 9.

Page – 9.

9. COPYRIGHT © 6-04-99, BY THE Robert-Joel: Simpson,

Exhibit H9

```
                 Superior Court of California, County of Riverside
  4/30/01                    Register of Actions                      Page:     1
                        EAST - Superior Court Civil
--------------------------------------------------------------------------------
 Case Number :      INC018853
 Case Type ..: INDIO CIVIL
 Category ...: Injunctive Relief
 Case Status : Active
================================================================================

 Complaint Type : Complaint                               Filed :   8/23/00

 Plaintiff(s):                           |Defendant(s):

 COUNTY OF RIVERSIDE                     |JOEL R. SIMPSON              Def. Req.
                                         |AKA: ROBERT JOEL SIMPSON
 ATTORNEY:                               |
 WILLIAM C KATZENSTEIN COUNTY COUNSEL    |
                                         |
                                         | and DOES   1 through  10
```

Action Date	Description	Disposition
8/23/00	Complaint Filed - Fast Track	-
	Case Assigned to Department 2F	
9/11/00	Proof of Service on the Complaint of COUNTY OF RIVERSIDE served on JOEL R. SIMPSON; AKA:ROBERT JOEL SIMPSON with service date of 08/29/00 filed.(PERSONAL SERVICE)	-
	Receipt For AMENDMENT TO COMPLAINT AND PROOF OF SERVICE filed	-
9/18/00	REJECTED DOCUMENT ANSWER TO COMPLAINT BY DEFT submitted by JOEL R. SIMPSON; AKA:ROBERT JOEL SIMPSON for the reason: PARTY REFUSES TO PAY FILING FEE OR FILE WAIVER	-
	REJECTED DOCUMENT ANSWER TO BE FILED ON DEMAND submitted by JOEL R. SIMPSON; AKA:ROBERT JOEL SIMPSON for the reason: REFUSED TO PAY FILING FEES	-
9/21/00	AND FAXED-AMEND CORRECTING NAME/P.O.S./SUMMONS Received and Forwarded to Dept. INDIO CLERKS OFFICE	-
9/25/00	Amendment to Complaint of COUNTY OF RIVERSIDE filed changing name of JOEL ROBERT SIMPSON to	-

Exhibit I-1

```
                Superior Court of California, County of Riverside
  4/30/01                    Register of Actions                    Page:     2
                         EAST - Superior Court Civil
----------------------------------------------------------------------------------
 Case Number :      INC018853
 Case Type ..: INDIO CIVIL
 Category ...: Injunctive Relief
 Case Status : Active
==================================================================================
            JOEL R. SIMPSON ALSO KNOW AS ROBERT JOEL SIMPSON;
            Judge  Charles E. Stafford
            -------------------------
            Proof of Service by MAIL on the Complaint of        -
            COUNTY OF RIVERSIDE served on JOEL R. SIMPSON;
            AKA:ROBERT JOEL SIMPSON filed; Date of mailing
            09/25/00
            -------------------------
  9/26/00   Original Summons on Complaint Filed.                -
            -------------------------
 10/03/00   REJECTED DOCUMENT ANSWER & CROSS-COMPLAINT          -
            submitted by JOEL R. SIMPSON; AKA:ROBERT JOEL
            SIMPSON for the reason. NOT PROPER FORM & CAPTION
            IS 9TH DIST CT/CENTRAL D
            -------------------------
 10/04/00   Request for Entry of Default ONLY on the            -
            Complaint of COUNTY OF RIVERSIDE as to JOEL R.
            SIMPSON; AKA:ROBERT JOEL SIMPSON
            -------------------------
            Default Entered on Complaint of COUNTY OF           -
            RIVERSIDE as to JOEL R. SIMPSON; AKA:ROBERT JOEL
            SIMPSON (Single Defendant Only)
            -------------------------
 10/23/00   NPS No-Appearance)                                  Vacated
            Dept.: 2F     Time :  8:30
            -------------------------
  2/16/01   Request and Order for Continuance granted Judge     -
            Charles E. Stafford
            -------------------------
            STCH Hearing set for 02/20/01 at  8:30 is Vacated  -
            -for the reason: REQ & ORDER FOR CONT FILED
            -------------------------
  2/20/01   STATUS CONFERENCE                                   Vacated
            Dept.: 2F     Time :  8:30
            -------------------------
            Judge  Charles E. Stafford recused pursuant to      -
            CCP170.3.
            Honorable  Charles E. Stafford, Presiding
            Clerk: P. COMBS
            Court Reporter: K. CELEHAR
            JOEL R. SIMPSON; AKA:ROBERT JOEL SIMPSON
            Represented by/in PRO PER
            No appearance made by or for PLAINTIFF.
            Judge  Charles E. Stafford Department 2F recuses
            himself pursuant to CCP170.3
```

Exhibit I-2

```
                Superior Court of California, County of Riverside
   4/30/01                     Register of Actions                    Page:     3
                          EAST - Superior Court Civil
--------------------------------------------------------------------------------
 Case Number :      INC018853
 Case Type ..: INDIO CIVIL
 Category ...: Injunctive Relief
 Case Status : Active
================================================================================
            Case assigned to Dept. 2J for hearing and/or
            reassignment.
            /////
            Honorable  Lawrence W. Fry, Presiding
            Clerk: C. Donovan
            Court Reporter: J. Poling
            Case assigned to Judge  C. J. Sheldon Dept 2H for
            all purposes.
            Status Confernce heairng continued to 4/30/01 at
            8:30AM Dept 2H
            Status Conference hearing continued to 4/30/01
            Status Conference set 4/5/01 is vacated.
            Notice to be given by Clerk
            -------------------------
            File Sent to filing                                  -
            -------------------------
   4/17/01  Application to/for FOR DEFAULT JUDGMENT AND DECL     -
            OF NON-MILITARY ST by COUNTY OF RIVERSIDE filed.
            -------------------------
            Memo of Points & Authorities in IN SUPPORT OF        -
            APPLICATION FOR DEFAULT JUDGMENT by COUNTY FOR
            RIVERSIDE.
            -------------------------
            Declaration of GARRY SHOPSHEAR IN SUP OF             -
            APPLICATION filed
            -------------------------
   4/20/01  Filed: FAXED REQUEST TO CONTINUE STATUS CONF TO      -
            INDIO
            -------------------------
   4/23/01  ORDER RE: (REQ & DECL) CONT OF STATUS CONFERENCE     -
            Judge  C. J. Sheldon
            -------------------------
            STCH Hearing set for 04/30/01 at  8:30 is reset      -
            to 06-27-01 AT 8:30 D/2H PER REQ & ORDER.
            -------------------------
   4/30/01  STATUS CONFERENCE                                    Reset
            Dept.: 2H    Time :  8:30
            -------------------------
   6/27/01  STATUS CONFERENCE
            Dept.: 2H    Time :  8:30

                     **** END OF CASE PRINT ****
```

Exhibit I-3

SEP-27-20^* THU 08:13 AM COUNTY COUNSEL FAX NO. 909 955 6363 P. 02

WILLIAM C. KATZENSTEIN, County Counsel SBN 61681
JOE S. RANK, Assistant County Counsel SBN 113607
DALE A. GARDNER, Deputy County Counsel SBN 200700
3535 Tenth Street, Suite 300
Riverside, California 92501
Telephone: (909) 955-6300

Attorneys for the County of Riverside

Post-it™ Fax Note 7671	Date	# of pages ▶ 2
To STEVE FINGAL	From JOEL SIMPSON	
Co./Dept.	Co.	
Phone #	Phone #	
Fax #	Fax #	

SUPERIOR COURT OF THE STATE OF CALIFORNIA

FOR THE COUNTY OF RIVERSIDE

In the Matter of the Application for an Inspection for the premises located at 30257 Monte Vista Way, Thousand, Palms, Riverside County, California APN: 650-034-007; Joel R. Simpson, aka Robert-Joel: Simpson Owner.	WARRANT NO. [Building & Safety Case No. CV99-0774] 24 HOUR NOTICE

TO: Joel R. Simpson aka Robert-Joel: Simpson, and any other owners and/or occupants of the premises located at 30257 Monte Vista Way, Thousand Palms, Riverside County, California

NOTICE IS HEREBY GIVEN to you as owner, custodian, and/or occupant of the property located at 30257 Monte Vista Way, Thousand Palms, Riverside County, California that on the 26th day of September, 2001, Judge B. J. Bjork of the Superior Court of the State of California, County of Riverside, issued a Warrant for the inspection of the interior and exterior of the substandard structure on the above-described property based upon your refusal to allow such inspection.

Inspection is sought for the purpose of conducting asbestos sampling and testing and for obtaining bids to demolish the substandard structure and remove all debris associated therewith pursuant to Riverside County Ordinance No. 457.

\\\

\\\

\\\

24 HOUR NOTICE

1

Exhibit I-4

Robert-Joel: Simpson
as the Sovereign-Citizen
of the Party
c/o 30-257: Monte-Vista-Way:
1000-Palms: California: 92276

Flag of the United-States of the America

BY THE JURISDICTION OF THE UNITY-STATES-POSTAL-SERVICE.
BY THE UNITY-STATES OF THE NINTH-DISTRICT-COURT OF THE CENTRAL-DISTRICT
OF THE STATE OF THE CALIFORNIA

Robert-Joel: Simpson

PLAINTIFF
U.S.A.

V.

STATE OF CALIFORNIA(sic);
COUNTY OF RIVERSIDE,(sic)
a political subdivision
of the State of California(sic);
COUNTY OF RIVERSIDE
TRANSPORTATION AND LAND
MANAGEMENT AGENCY(sic);
BUILDING AND SAFETY
DEPARTMENT(sic);
SUPERVISING CODE ENFORCEMENT
OFFICER/AGENT(sic);
GARRY SHOFSHEAR(sic);
DEPUTY COUNTY COUNSEL(sic);
CAROLE A. NUNES FONG(sic)
SBN 138008(sic);
CHARLES E. STAFFORD(sic);
JOHN-DOES: 1-30;
RESPONDENT(S) IN THE FIDUCIARY

FOR THE CROSS-COMPLAINT
BY THE TITLE: 42: U.S.A. CODES: SECTION: 1986 FOR THE KNOWLEDGE OF THE LAW FOR THE TRUTH BY THE TITLE: 18: U.S.A. CODES: SECTION: 1001 & 1002, FOR THE INJURY OF THE WITNESS BY THE TITLE: 18: U.S.A. CODES: SECTION: 1512 FOR THE OBSTRUCTION OF THE JUSTICE OF THE WITNESS-PROTECTION.

FOR THE INCORPORATION OF THE POSTAL-REGISTRY-CASE-NUMBER:

[INC 0188533](s.c)

FOR THE DISCOVERY OF THE FACTS ARE BY THIS DATE: **08-23-2000**
FOR THE CITIZEN OF THE PARTY IS OF THE REQUIREMENT FOR THE QUESTIONS OF THE ASKING AND BY THE USE OF THE ANSWER IS FOR THE TRUTH. FOR THE NOUNS ARE BY THE AFFIRMATION-USE AND DECLARATION-PRESENTATION AS THE NOUNS BY THE TRUTH FOR THE COURT BY THE BAR. FOR THE PARTY OF THE CONCERN: BY YOUR OATH, FOR THE AFFIRMATION AND FOR THE DECLARATION OF THE TRUTH, FOR THE **"TRUTH"** IS FOR THE PRESENT-TENSE AND BY THE ENGLISH-LANGUAGE-FORM OF THE NOUN, THAT **ALL** FACTS BY THIS CASE ARE FOR THE PRESENT-TENSE AND BY THE PRESENTATION WITH THE AFFIRMATION AND DECLARATION OF THE TRUTH(NOUN) THAT THE KNOWLEDGE OF THE TRUTH **IS** WITH THE TITLE: 42: U.S.A. CODES: SECTION: 1986 FOR THE KNOWLEDGE OF THE LAW FOR THE TRUTH. FOR ANY INJURY OF THE

1

R-J:S

Exhibit J-1

PLAINTIFF BY THE COURT BY THIS MATTER IS FOR THE BREACH AND VIOLATION OF THE TRUTH AND IS FOR THE BREACH OF THE CONTRACT, BY THE TITLE: 18: U.S.A. CODES: SECTION: 1001 AND 1002, AND 1342 FOR THE FICTITIOUS USE OF THE LANGUAGE FOR THE EXTORTION AND DEPRIVATION OF THE PARTY'S-RIGHT AND PRIVILEGES, BY THE 10-YEARS-JAIL AND WITH THE FINE OF THE $10,000.00 BY THE RESPONDENTS.

FOR THE DEMANDS OF THE PLAINTIFF/RESPONDENT: FOR THE PLAINTIFF/RESPONDENT AND PETITIONER **IS/ARE** OF THE UNITY WITH THE COURT FOR THE OBSTRUCTION OF THE TRUTH BY THE USE OF THE NOUNS AS THE VERBS FOR THE OBSTRUCTION OF THE TRUTH WITH THE KNOWLEDGE. FOR THE PLAINTIFF FOR THE DEMANDS BY THE COMPLAINT **ARE** WITH THE TRUTH FOR THE FILING OF THIS CASE WITH THE GRAND-JURY BY THE REPORTING BY THE F.R.C.P.-RULE 60(b)AND 26(e) OF THE CONSPIRACY FOR THE OBSTRUCTION OF THE TRUTH OF THIS CASE.
FOR THE AUTOGRAPH OF THE PARTY IS/ARE FOR THE DISCOVERY-INTERVIEW.

CONTRACT-NOTICE: FOR THIS DISCLAIMER **IS** FOR THE UNITY-STATES-PARTY. FOR THE RESPONSIBILITY, WITH THE TERMS OF THIS CONTRACT BY THE KNOWLEDGE OF THE INCORPORATION OF THE CASE NO.____________________-HEREIN OF THE C.U.S.A.F. CONTRACT. FOR THE TERMS ARE BY THE RULES OF THE DISCOVERY OF THE TRUTH, BY THE AMERICAN-FLAG OF THE U.S.A. FOR THE OATH AND AFFIRMATION BY THE SWEARING FOR THE DECLARATION OF THE AFFIRMATION OF THE TRUTH BY THE FIDUCIARY-PARTY(s) OF THE COURT, WITH THE TERMS IN THE C.U.S.A.F.-CONTRACT OF THE UNITY-STATES/PARTY BY THE INCORPORATION-CASE-TITLE-HEREIN FOR THE STATE OF THE COURT IS BY THE LAW OF THE AMERICAN-FLAG WITHIN THE STATE OF THIS INCORPORATION OF THE CASE, BY THE FILING WITH THE CLERK OF THE COURTS OF THIS INCORPORATION OF THE CASE. FOR THE FICTION/FOREIGN-JURISDICTION IS FOR THE JURISDICTION OF THE TRUTH WITH THE SOVEREIGN-CITIZEN IN THE PARTY. FOR ANY BREACH OF THIS C.U.S.A.F.-CONTRACT IS BY THE TERMS, RULES AND DEFINITIONS OF THE INCORPORATION-CASE-TITLE-HEREIN. FOR ANY BREACH OF THE C.U.S.A.F.-CONTRACT IS BY THE PROVISION FOR THE SANCTIONS. WHEN THE C.U.S.A.F.-CONTRACT IS OF THE SURRENDER BY ANY PARTY INTO THE FOREIGN-FICTION-JURISDICTION BY THE BREACH OF THIS OATH AND AFFIRMATION-CONTRACT UNDER THE C.U.S.A.F.-CONTRACT, THEN THE CHARGES "FOR THE **PERJURY OF THE OATH" ARE** WITH THE TITLE: 18: U.S.A. CODES: SECTION: 1621:[5-YEARS-$55,000.-PENALTY-FEE] FOR THE TERMS OF THE CONSTITUTION/CONTRACT/CONSTRUCTIVE-TREASON AGAINST THE C.U.S.A.F.- CONTRACT FOR THE FALSE-SWEARING OF THE OATH. NOTE: FOR THE FACTS ARE BY THE NOUNS FOR THE JURISDICTION WITH THE COURTS OF THE UNITY-STATES WITH THE TRUTH. FOR THE VIOLATION OF THE NOUNS AS THE VERB OR ADJECTIVES ARE FOR THE CAUSE OF THE MAIL-FRAUD/FICTITIOUS-NAMES BY THE TITLE: 18: U.S.A. CODES: SECTION: 1342: FOR THE USE OF THE FICTITIOUS-NAMES FOR THE EXTORTION OF THE MONEY BY THE TITLE: 18: U.S.A. CODES: SECTION: 1001:[5-YEARS AND $5,000.-PENALTY-FEE] FOR THE FICTITIOUS-USE OF THE NOUNS AS THE **VERBS** AND **ADJECTIVES** IS BY THE VIOLATION OF THE C.U.S.A.F.-CONTRACT FOR THE RIGHTS OF THE SOVEREIGN-CITIZENS OF THE PARTY.

FOR THE PLAINTIFF IS OF THE SOVEREIGN-CITIZEN OF THE PARTY, BY THE OATH FOR THE AFFIRMATION, FOR THE DECLARATION OF THE TRUTH BY THE FIRSTHAND-KNOWLEDGE OF THE FACTS:

Robert-Joel: Simpson

Robert-Joel: Simpson

2

R-J: S

Exhibit J-2

ABBREVIATIONS: F.R.C.P.= FOR THE FEDERAL-RULES OF THE CIVIL-PROCEDURE herein:

U.S.A. CODES© = OF THE UNITY-STATES OF THE AMERICA-CODE.

U.S.A. = OF THE UNITY-STATES OF THE AMERICA

THE, THIS =(ARTICLE) FOR THE SPECIFIC IN THE PRESENT-TENSE

UNITY-STATES = BY ANY INCORPORATION OF THE TWO OR MORE-PARTIES BY THE CONTRACT/CONSTITUTION;

C.U.S.A.F. = FOR THE CONSTITUTION OF THE UNITY-STATES UNDER THE AMERICAN-FLAG;

BY THE ARTICLE OF THE THREE(3) = FOR THE RIGHT OF THE SPEECH, RELIGION, PRESS, GRIEVANCE;

BY THE ARTICLE OF THE SIX(6) = FOR THE RIGHT OF THE ARREST-WARRANT OR SEARCH-WARRANT-SIGNATURE BY THE JUDGE OF THE OATH OR AFFIRMATION;

BY THE ARTICLE OF THE SEVEN(7) = FOR THE RIGHT OF THE DUE PROCESS, FOR NO WITNESS IS AGAINST THE ONESELF;

BY THE ARTICLE OF THE EIGHT(8) = FOR THE RIGHT OF THE WITNESSES, COUNSEL AND EVIDENCE IN THE COURT AND FOR THE SPEEDY-TRIAL;

BY THE ARTICLE OF THE NINE(9) = FOR THE RIGHT OF THE TRIAL BY THE JURY;

BY THE ARTICLE OF THE TEN(10) = FOR THE PUNISHMENT IS OF THE EQUAL PROTECTION FOR THE REASONABLE-BAIL;

BY THE ARTICLE OF THE ELEVEN (11) = FOR ANY OFFICER OF THE COURT IS BY THE APPOINTMENT OR ELECTION UNDER THE OATH OR AFFIRMATION FOR THE UPHOLDING OF THE C.U.S.A.F.-CONTRACT IN THE TRUTH IN THE UNITY-STATES OF THE AMERICA FOR THE PEOPLE OF THE UNITY-STATES OF THE AMERICA;

BY THE ARTICLE OF THE TWELVE(12) = FOR THE CONSTITUTION-CONTRACT IS UNDER THE RESERVATION FOR ANY MUTUAL-AGREEMENT OR ARBITRATION BY THE TITLE PARTIES-HEREIN;

BY THE ARTICLE OF THE THIRTEEN(13) = FOR ANY FOREIGN/FICTION UNDER THIS CONTRACT IS UNDER THE JURISDICTIONS WITH THE SOVEREIGN-CITIZEN IN THE PARTY, FOR THE JUDICIAL-LANGUAGE OF THE UNITY-STATES IS UNDER THE INCORPORATION IN THIS SUIT IN THE LAW AND IN THE EQUITY FOR THE COMMENCEMENT OF THE PROSECUTION AGAINST ANY ONE OF THE UNITY-STATES BY THE CITIZENS OF THIS COURT-STATE AS THE CITIZENS. FOR THIS NEW-STATE IS WITH THE TRUTH-LANGUAGE UNDER A SOVEREIGN-FLAG IN THE TRUTH WITHIN THIS COURT;

FOR THE UNITY-STATES-DISTRICT-COURT(NOUN) IN THE UNITY-STATES (NOUN) OF THE AMERICA(NOUN) IS FOR THE UPHOLDING OF THE ORIGINAL-JURISDICTION(NOUN) UNDER THE TITLE: 28: U.S.A. CODES: SECTION: 1331 AND SECTION: 1343 FOR THE EQUAL-PROTECTION IN THE TRUTH. FOR THE SOVEREIGN-FLAG OF THE U.S.A. IS IN THE COURT. FOR THE CLERK OF THE COURT IS UNDER THE OATH FOR THE FILING OF THE INCORPORATION OF THE CASE UNDER THE COURT OF THE DISTRICT OF THE U.S.A. UNDER THE TITLE: 28: U.S.A. CODES: SECTION: 1869, FOR THIS ORDER OF THE PROCEDURES ARE UNDER THE TITLE: 28: U.S.A. CODES: SECTION: 1361: FOR THE COMPLIANCE BY THIS RESPONSIBILITY IS FOR THE DUTY OF THE OFFICE OF THE CLERK. FOR THE INCORPORATION IS UNDER THE PERPETUAL-EXISTENCE OF THE C.U.S.A.F.-CONTRACT OF THE CASE-NUMBER-TITLE-HEREIN. FOR THE COMPLIANCE OF ALL PARTIES ARE IN THE TRUTH. FOR ALL PARTIES ARE IN THE AGREEMENT OF THE FACTS OR BY THE DECISION OF THE TRIAL BY THE JURY(NOUN).

Exhibit J-3

FOR THE FACTS

1. **FOR THE PLAINTIFF/RESPONDENT IS WITH THE AFFIRMATION BY THE TRUTH FOR AN** INJURY FOR THE CONDITION OF THE INSTRUCTIONS AND PLEADINGS BY THE STATE-GOVERNMENT, STATE OF CALIFORNIA(sic); CHARLES E. STAFFORD; CAROLE A. NUNES FONG(sic) FOR THE FICTIONAL-USE OF THE **NOUN** AS THE PROCEDURE BY THE ENGLISH-LANGUAGE AS THE **VERB** AND **ADJECTIVE** BY THE ATTORNEYS FOR THIS CASE-NUMBER **INC018853(sic)** BY THE COURT ON THE DATE(s): 08-23-2000 AND 02-20-01. FOR THE PLAINTIFF/RESPONDENT IS WITH AN INJURY BY THE FICTION AND RAPE OF THE LANGUAGE BY THE RESPONDENT-ATTORNEY AND JUDGE CHARLES E. STAFFORD(sic) AND CAROLE A. NUNES FONG(sic), FOR THE WRITINGS AND PRESENTMENT OF THE MOTIONS ARE WITH THE FICTION-LANGUAGE AGAINST THE EQUAL-PROTECTION OF THE WITNESS: Robert-Joel: Simpson FOR THE **APARTHEID** AGAINST THE WITNESS BY THE RESPONDENT. FOR THE PLAINTIFF BY THESE FACTS IS WITH THE KNOWLEDGE FOR THE INCORPORATION OF ANY INCORPORATION-CASE AS THE PLAINTIFF AND WITNESS: Robert-Joel: Simpson FOR THE COURT BY THE RESPONDENT.

2. **FOR THE PLAINTIFF/RESPONDENT IS WITH THE AFFIRMATION BY THE TRUTH BY THIS COMPLAINT** FOR THE TESTIMONY WITH THE DECLARATION FOR THE AFFIRMATION OF THE TRUTH(NOUN) AS WITH THE NOUN-DEFINITION OF THE ENGLISH-LANGUAGE FOR THE WORDING OF THE EVIDENCE AGAINST THE PLAINTIFF. FOR THE PLAINTIFF Robert-Joel: Simpson IS OF THE INJURY BY THE RESPONSIBILITY-PERFORMANCE-CONTRACT FOR THE PROTECTION OF THE **WITNESS**. FOR THE EVIDENCE BY THE PLAINTIFF IS BY THE C.U.S.A.F.-CONTRACT FOR THE TRUTH(NOUN). FOR THE AUTOGRAPH OF THE RESPONDENT WITH THE ATTORNEY'S-OATH AND JUDGE'S-OATH IS FOR THE DECLARATION OF THE AFFIRMATION OF THE TRUTH(NOUN). FOR ALL FACTS FOR THIS INCORPORATION-CASE-HEREIN ARE WITH THE TRUTH(NOUN) BY THE RESPONDENT AND PETITIONER AND PLAINTIFF (EXHIBIT-A&B).

3. **FOR THE PLAINTIFF IS WITH THE AFFIRMATION BY THE TRUTH** FOR THE INJURY AGAINST THE LAW BY THE FICTION-LANGUAGE FOR THE PLEADINGS BY THE RESPONDENT-ATTORNEYS. FOR THE BREACH IS BY THE C.U.S.A.F.-CONTRACT BY THE ARTICLE OF THE SEVEN(7) FOR THE PLAINTIFF IS OF THE INJURY BY THE PROTECTION FOR THE PROCEDURAL-VIOLATIONS BY THE C.U.S.A.F.-CONTRACT OF THE PLAINTIFF'S-CIRCUIT-COURT-FILINGS BY THIS CASE-NO. **INC018853(sic)** BY THE RESPONDENT. FOR THE CONSPIRACY WITH THE COLOR OF THE LAW IS BY THE TITLE: 42: U.S.A. CODES: SECTION: 1985(1) FOR THE CONSPIRACY BY THIS DEFINITION IS FOR THE CRIMINAL-CROSS-REFERENCE WITH THE TITLE: 18: U.S.A. CODES: SECTION: 241 FOR THE CONSPIRACY BY THE BREACH OF THE CONTRACT-RIGHTS BY THE PERFORMANCE-COMPLAINT WITH ALL COURT-FILINGS BY THE RESPONDENTS ON THE DATE(S): 08-23-2000 AND 02-20-01.

4. **FOR THE PLAINTIFF/RESPONDENT BY THE AFFIRMATION WITH THE TRUTH IS WITH** THE INJURY BY THE LANGUAGE OF THE NOTICE BY THE **"SUMMONS (CITACION JUDICIAL (CCP 412.20)(sic)** (EXHIBIT-C), IN THE PRESENTMENT AS A VERB-TITLE AND ADJECTIVE-TITLE WITH THE FICTION FOR THE BREACH OF THIS C.U.S.A.F.-CONTRACT BY THE LAW(NOUN) OR AT THE LAW. FOR THE PLAINTIFF AS THE FRIEND OF THE COURT IS FOR THE CORRECTION OF THE "SUMMONS/COMPLAINT(sic)" (EXHIBIT-D) FOR THE INCORPORATION OF A TITLE: 18: U.S.A. CODES: SECTION: 1001 FOR THE STATEMENT-HEREIN: **FOR THE**

4

R-J:S

Exhibit J-4

PLAINTIFF-AFFIRMATION BY THE COMPLAINT: BY THE **RULES OF THE DISCOVERY:** OF THE F.R.C.P.-RULE: 60(b) FOR THE PLAINTIFF **IS** WITH THE KNOWLEDGE OF THE TRUTH BY THE RULES OF THE PROCEDURE OF THE ENGLISH-LANGUAGE. FOR THE SUBJECT-MATTER-LANGUAGE-FRAUD BY THE F.R.C.P.-RULE: 9(b), AGAINST THE RESPONDENT OF THE EXAM WITH THE FILES FOR THIS COMPLAINT BY THE RESPONDENT'S TITLE-HEREIN. FOR THE GENERAL-CIVIL-COMPLAINT-AFFIDAVIT BY THE RESPONDENT, BEFORE THIS COURT-TITLE-HEREIN IS BY THE RULES OF THE DISCOVERY-CLAUSE OF THE F.R.C.P.-RULE: 60(b), FOR THE INCORPORATION OF THE PLAINTIFF INTO THE PROSECUTION OF THE DISCRIMINATION UNDER THE FEDERAL-AUTHORITY OF THE TRUTH.

5. **ON THE DATE(S)**: 08-23-00 AND 02-20-01 **OF THE COURT OF THE COUNTY OF THE RIVERSIDE BY THE STATE OF THE CALIFORNIA, FOR THE PLAINTIFF/RESPONDENT IS/ARE WITH THE AFFIRMATION BY THE TRUTH** WITH THE HIGH-FIDUCIARY-POSITION FOR THE EXTORTION OF THE RIGHTS AND PRIVILEGES (EXHIBIT-E), BY THE **TITLE: 18: U.S.A. CODES: SECTION: 1001** FOR THE AFFIRMATION: WHOEVER, BY ANY-MATTER WITHIN THE JURISDICTION OF ANY DEPARTMENT FOR THE AGENCY OF THE UNITY-STATES(NOUN) **IS** WITH THE KNOWLEDGE AND WILLFUL-INTENT BY THE FALSIFICATION, CONCEALMENT AND BY THE COVER-UP BY ANY TRICK, SCHEME, OR BY ANY DEVICE OF THE MATERIAL-FACT, OR BY THE MAKING FOR THE FALSIFICATION-STATEMENT BY THE FICTITIOUS-STATEMENT, OR BY THE FRAUDULENT-STATEMENT OR BY THE REPRESENTATIONS OF THE STATEMENT, OR BY THE MAKING OF ANY FALSE-WRITINGS OR FOR THE USING OF ANY FALSE-WRITINGS OR BY THE FALSE-DOCUMENT(S) BY THE KNOWING THAT THE FALSE-DOCUMENT(S) ARE FOR THE CONTAINING FOR ANY FALSIFICATION-STATEMENTS, FOR THE FICTITIOUS-STATEMENTS OR FOR THE FRAUDULENT-STATEMENTS OR FOR THE ENTRY INTO THE CASE-FILE OF THE $10,000 BY THIS TITLE OR BY THE IMPRISONMENT OF THE FIVE-YEARS OR BOTH; BY THE **TITLE: 18: U.S.A. CODES: SECTION: 1002**: WHOEVER, WITH THE KNOWLEDGE AND WITH THE WILLFUL-INTENT FOR THE DEFRAUDING OF THE UNITY-STATES(NOUN), OR FOR ANY AGENCY, FOR THE POSSESSION OF ANY FALSE, ALTERATION, FORGERY, OR COUNTERFEIT-WRITINGS OR FOR THE DOCUMENTATION OF THE PURPOSE FOR THE ENABLEMENT FOR THE OBTAINING BY THE UNITED STATES(sic), OR BY THE UNITY-STATES'S AGENCY, OFFICER OR AGENT-THEREOF, FOR ANY SUM OF THE MONEY, IS WITH THE FINE BY THIS TITLE: 18, WITH THE IMPRISONMENT BY THE C.U.S.A.F.-LAW.

6. **FOR THE PLAINTIFF/RESPONDENT IS/ARE WITH THE AFFIRMATION BY THE TRUTH** BY THE C.U.S.A.F.-CONTRACT BY THE ARTICLE OF THE SEVEN(7) FOR THE INJURY BY THE PROVISIONS FOR THE REMEDY WITH THE TITLE: 42: U.S.A. CODES: SECTION: 1986 FOR THE KNOWLEDGE OF THE LAW BY THE TRUTH. BY THE DISCOVERY OF THE TRUTH FOR THE F.R.C.P.-RULE: 60(b) OF THE F.R.C.P.-RULE: 9(b) IS FOR THE REPORTING OF THE FRAUD FOR THE CONSPIRACY OF THE COURT FOR THE RELIEF BY THE STATEMENTS-HEREIN FOR THE TRUTH OR INTO THE JUDGE-ADVOCATE-GENERAL FOR THE BREACH OF THE FOREIGN-JURISDICTION BY THE DISABILITIES-ACT FOR THE COURT'S-POSITION FOR THE OBSTRUCTION OF THE JUSTICE BY THE TITLE: 18: U.S.A. CODES: SECTION: 1512 BY THE COURT-OFFICERS.

7. **FOR THE PLAINTIFF/RESPONDENT IS/ARE OF THE INJURY BY THE COMPLAINT** BY THE PAPERS WITH THE CORRESPONDENCE BY THE COURT WITH THE PLAINTIFF(S), BY THE VIOLATION OF THE F.R.C.P.-RULE: 11(a) FOR ALL DOCUMENTS ARE WITH THE SIGNATURE FOR THE JURISDICTION OF THE COURT IN THE TRUTH. FOR THE

Exhibit J-5

SIGNATURE ON A FICTION IS FOR THE BREACH OF THE DUE-PROCESS BY THE COURT.

FOR THE CAUSE OF THE ACTION

8. **FOR THE PLAINTIFF/RESPONDENT IS/ARE OF THE INJURY BY THE COMPLAINT** FOR THE RESPONDENTS ARE AS THE ATTORNEYS **AT LAW**(sic) AND **IN LAW**(sic). "THE **LAW**" FOR THIS PRESENTMENT IS BY THE MODIFICATION BY THE ADVERB FOR THE IDENTIFICATION AS **A VERB. FOR THE FACT OF THE NOUN IS WITH THE TRUTH OF THE LAW OF THE CONTRACT FOR THE FACT. FOR THE TRUTH IS OF THE FACT (NOUN). 2 + 2 = (OF THE) 4, 4 - 2= (OF THE) 2.**

9. **FOR THE PLAINTIFF/RESPONDENT IS/ARE WITH THE KNOWLEDGE OF THE TRUTH OF THE INJURY BY THIS COMPLAINT** ON THE DATE(S): 08-23-00 AND 02-20-01, FOR THE PLAINTIFF IS WITH THE PROTECTION AS A WITNESS FOR THE COURT. FOR THE RESPONDENT IS BY THE EMPLOYMENT FOR THE PROTECTION OF THE REPRESENTATION BY THE INCORPORATION OF THE CASE OF THE JUSTICE. FOR THE WITNESS-PLAINTIFF BY THE PERFORMANCE AS THE WITNESS FOR THE EVIDENCE OF THE TESTIMONY BY THE SAFE-PROTECTION OF THE COURT AGAINST ANY DEPRIVATION OF THE PLAINTIFF-WITNESS-TESTIMONY. FOR THE OBSTRUCTION OF THE WITNESS-TESTIMONY BY THE OATH FOR THE DECLARATION WITH THE AFFIRMATION OF THE TRUTH IS FOR THE PROTECTION OF THE WITNESS AND FOR THE PROTECTION OF THE EVIDENCE WITH THE COURT BY THE RESPONDENT AS THE AGENT WITH THE FIDUCIARY OF THE INCORPORATION OF THE CASE. FOR THE PLAINTIFF/RESPONDENT IS/ARE BY THE WITNESS-PROTECTION FOR THE INCORPORATION OF THE TESTIMONY AND EVIDENCE OF THE FACTS(NOUN) BY THE PLAINTIFF(S) AND RESPONDENT(S) BY THE TRIAL. FOR THE PRESUMPTIONS, ASSUMPTIONS, OPINIONS AND CONCLUSIONS OF THE FACTS ARE WITH THE ACTIONS FOR THE INTIMIDATION, TORT, COLLUSION AND RAPE BY THE RESPONDENT. FOR THE RESPONSIBILITY OF A WITNESS IS BY THE C.U.S.A.F.-RIGHTS. FOR THE OBSTRUCTION OF THE JUSTICE IS WITH THE TITLE: 18: U.S.A. CODES: SECTION: 1512 AND BY THE "RICO" WITH THE TITLE: 18: U.S.A. CODES: SECTION: 1961, AND WITH THE TITLE: 42 U.S.A. CODES: SECTION: 1985: SECTION: (1) FOR THE CONSPIRACY OF THE OFFICERS BY THE FICTION-LANGUAGE, (2) FOR THE OBSTRUCTING OF THE WITNESS AND EVIDENCE BY THE TRUTH, AND (3) FOR THE DEPRIVING OF THE EQUAL-PROTECTION FOR THE EVIDENCE(NOUN) AND WITNESSES(NOUN) FOR THE TRUTH(NOUN) WITH THE LAW(NOUN) BY THE RESPONDENTS.

10. **FOR THE PLAINTIFF/RESPONDENT IS/ARE WITH THE KNOWLEDGE** OF THE INJURY FOR THE TRUTH WITH THE GUARANTEE OF THE WITNESS-PROTECTION OF THE EMPLOYMENT BY THE PLAINTIFF-CITIZENS BY THE PARTY-PRESENT BY THE WITNESS-STAND FOR THE CROSS-EXAMINATION BY THE COURT WITH THE PROTECTION OF THE RESPONDENT-JUDGE. FOR THE ATTORNEY **AT LAW**(sic) **AS THE VERB**, AND FOR THE EXAMINATION **OF LAW**(sic) **AS THE VERB**, BY THE BREACH OF THE PERFORMANCE-C.U.S.A.F.-CONTRACT BY THE RESPONDENTS. FOR THE PERFORMANCE-LAWS OF THIS INCORPORATION-CASE-NUMBER, FOR THE PLAINTIFF/RESPONDENT IS/ARE WITH THE C.U.S.A.F.-CONTRACT-PROTECTION FOR THE LAWS OF THE UNITY-STATES BY THE COURT BY THE CONDITIONS, RULES AND DEFINITIONS WITH THE TRUTH BY THE SANCTUARY OF THE COURT/BAR WITH THE STATE BY THE PERFORMANCE-CONTRACT OF THE UNITY STATES OF THE AMERICA.

NOTE: FOR THE SANCTUARY OF THE BAR/COURT IS WITH THE CONTRACT-REMOVAL OF THE PARENT-STATE OF THE CALIFORNIA AND IS WITH THE CONTRACT-CONSTITUTION

6

R-J:S

Exhibit J-6

OF THE UNITY-STATES OF THE CONTRACT IN THE COUNTRY OF THE CONTRACT, FOR THE SOVEREIGN-LAND OF THE COURT IS BY THE LAW OF THE FLAG BY THE PROTECTION OF THIS CONTRACT FOR THE PROTECTION OF THIS SOVEREIGN-STATE-COURT OF THE AMERICA. [IN THIS CASE]

11. **FOR THE PLAINTIFF/RESPONDENT IS/ARE WITH THE KNOWLEDGE OF THIS AFFIRMATION BY THE TRUTH** FOR THE INJURY BY THE CONSIDERATION OF THE INCORPORATION OF THE CASE-NUMBER, AND **IS** WITH THE UNITY-STATES OF THE AMERICA FOR THE PLAINTIFF/RESPONDENT IS/ARE WITH THE PROTECTION AND SAFETY IN THE DUTY OF THE WITNESS BY THE RESPONDENT-JUDGE'S COURT-RESPONSIBILITY AND BY THE RESPONDENT-JUDGE/ATTORNEY, FOR THE SERVICES OF THE JUDGESHIP BY THE PROTECTION OF THE JUSTICE FOR THE CITIZENS OF THE UNITY-STATES OF THE AMERICA FOR THAT SERVICE, UNDERTOOK THE EXAMINATION OF THE ARGUMENTS OF THE LAWS WITH THE INCORPORATION AS AN OFFICER OF THE COURT FOR THE KNOWLEDGE OF THE LAW.

12. **FOR THE PLAINTIFF/RESPONDENT FOR THE AFFIRMATION BY THE COMPLAINT** IS OF THE INJURY BY THE RESPONDENT-JUDGE, UPON THE EXAMINATION OF THE RESPONDENT'S-CASE-NUMBER: INC018853(sic), FOR THE ARGUMENTS **ARE** BEFORE THE COURT WITH THE TITLE: 42: U.S.A. CODES; SECTION: 1985(2) FOR THE OBSTRUCTING OF THE LAW FOR THE EQUAL-PROTECTION AGAINST THE PLAINTIFF/RESPONDENT Robert-Joel: Simpson-WITNESS FOR THE GIVING OF THE EVIDENCE AND TESTIMONY ON THE WITNESS-STAND AND FOR THE DEPRIVING OF THE EQUAL-PROTECTION OF THE LAW FOR THE LAW BY THE TITLE: 42: U.S.A. CODES: SECTION: 1985(3) FOR THE GIVING OF THE EVIDENCE AND TESTIMONY BEFORE THE COURT WITH THE INCORPORATION OF THE CONTRACT FOR THE HEARING OF THE EVIDENCE BEFORE THE COURT WITH THE POWER FOR THE PROTECTION OF THE PLAINTIFF-WITNESS AGAINST ANY INJURY, HOWEVER, FOR THE PLAINTIFF-WITNESS **IS/ARE** OF THE INJURY BY THE OBSTRUCTION AND DEPRIVATION OF THE PLAINTIFF BY THE GIVING OF THE TRUTH BY THE OATH WITH THE PRESENTATION OF THE EVIDENCE AND WITH THE TESTIMONY FOR THE COURT BY THE RESPONDENT-JUDGE CHARLES E. STAFFORD(sic).

13. **FOR THE PLAINTIFF/RESPONDENT IS/ARE BY THE AFFIRMATION WITH THE COMPLAINT** OF THE INJURY BY THE NEGLECT OF THE C.U.S.A.F.-CONTRACT-INCORPORATION BY THE LAWS OF THE UNITY-STATES(NOUN) OF THE AMERICA(NOUN) WITH THE RIGHT OF THE CONTRACT-INCORPORATION BY THE C.U.S.A.F.-RIGHTS OF THE ISSUES OF THE CASE AND WITH THE ATTORNEY'S-OATH FOR THE UPHOLDING OF THE C.U.S.A.F.-CONTRACT FOR THE AFFIRMATION AND FOR THE DECLARATION OF THE TRUTH BY THE RESPONDENTS.

14. **FOR THE PLAINTIFF/RESPONDENT IS/ARE WITH THE AFFIRMATION BY THE COMPLAINT** FOR THE INJURY BY THE NEGLECT OF THE DUE-PROCESS OF THE CONTRACT-LAW OF THE C.U.S.A.F.-ARTICLE OF THE SEVEN(7), AND BY THE COLOR OF THE LAW WITH THE TITLE: 18: U.S.A. CODES: SECTION: 242.

15. **FOR THE PLAINTIFF/RESPONDENT BY THE AFFIRMATION WITH THE COMPLAINT** IS OF THE INJURY BY THE LONG-LITIGATION AND IS BY THE HURTING OF THE LOVE, NURTURING, CARE, AND HEALTH OF THE MIND AND BODY OF THE PLAINTIFF(S) THAT THE SAME IS WITH THE ENDURANCE, BY THE RESPONDENT-

 7

Exhibit J-7

JUDGE.

FOR THE CONCLUSION

16. **FOR THE PLAINTIFF/RESPONDENT WITH THE AFFIRMATION BY THE COMPLAINT** ARE OF THE INJURY BY THE RESPONDENTS BY THE PRACTICE OF THE LAW, WITH THE SKILL AND CARE AND DILIGENCE WITH THE EXAMINATION OF THE INCORPORATION OF THE CASE-NUMBER: INC018853(sic), BY THE PLAINTIFF/RESPONDENT BY THE DISCOVERY OF THE DEFECT IS WITH THE TITLE: 42: U.S.A. CODES: SECTION: 1986 FOR THE KNOWLEDGE OF THE LAW THROUGH THE DISCOVERY OF THE FRAUD BY THE LAW UNDER THE F.R.C.P. RULE 9(b) AND FOR THE F.R.C.P. RULE 26(e) FOR THE REPORTING OF THE WRONG INTO A JUDICIAL-ENTITY FOR THE PREVENTION OF THE WRONG OF THE PLAINTIFF'S-INJURY. BY THE NEGLECT OF THE CARE, SKILL, AND DILIGENCE WITH THE EXAMINATION OF THE PLAINTIFF'S-C.U.S.A.F.-RIGHTS AND WITH THE ADVISEMENT OF THE PLAINTIFF/RESPONDENT BY THE INCORPORATION OF THE CASE-NUMBER: INC018853(sic), FOR THE PLAINTIFF/RESPONDENT IS/ARE WITH THE TRUE-(NOUN)-FACTS BY THE STATEMENTS FOR THE COURT AND IS FOR THE SHOWING BY THE PLAINTIFF/RESPONDENT AND MEMBERS OF THE INCORPORATION OF THE CASE-NUMBER: INC018853(sic), BY THE RESPONDENTS.

17. **FOR THE PLAINTIFF/RESPONDENT WITH THE AFFIRMATION BY THE COMPLAINT** ARE OF THE INJURY BY THE VIOLATION OF THE C.U.S.A.F., BY THE NEGLECT OF THE LANGUAGE-FRAUD FOR THE MISREPRESENTATION OF THE MEANING OF THE PROCEDURES OF THE WORDS BY THE COURT-ORDERS(SIC) AGAINST THE PLAINTIFF/RESPONDENTS, BY THE RESPONDENTS.

18. **FOR THE PLAINTIFF/RESPONDENT WITH THE AFFIRMATION BY THE COMPLAINT** ARE OF THE INJURY BY THE TITLE: 42: U.S.A. CODES: SECTION: 1985 (1): FOR THE CONSPIRACY FOR THE DAMAGES BY THE CLAIMS FOR THE VIOLATION OF THE C.U.S.A.F.-GUARANTEEING-RIGHTS.

19. **FOR THE PLAINTIFF/RESPONDENT WITH THE AFFIRMATION BY THE COMPLAINT** ARE OF THE INJURY BY THE STATUTORY AND PROCEDURAL-VIOLATION(S) (ARE)/IS OF THE LIST: PROCEDURAL-OUTLINES WITH THE DISQUALIFICATION OF THE LANGUAGE-USE OF THE FOREIGN/FICTION-LANGUAGE WITHIN THE U.S.A.

20. **FOR THE PLAINTIFF/RESPONDENT WITH THE AFFIRMATION BY THE COMPLAINT** ARE OF THE INJURY BY THE TITLE: 28: U.S.A. CODES: SECTION: 1605 FOR THE GENERAL-EXCEPTIONS BY THE JURISDICTIONAL-IMMUNITY OF THE FOREIGN-COURT: [FOR THE FOREIGN-STATE (CONDITION OF THE AREA-FLAG](a) FOR A FOREIGN-STATE IS OF THE IMMUNITY AGAINST THE JURISDICTION OF THE COURTS OF THE U.S.A. OR OF THE STATES IN-ANY CASE.

21. (a) (2) BY WHICH THE ACTION IS UPON A COMMERCIAL-ACTIVITY BY THE INCORPORATION OF THE U.S.A. FOR THE COST OF THE MORE THAN $21.00 U.S.A. DOLLARS, BY THE FILING-FEE WITH THE COURT OF THE DISTRICT OF THE U.S.A. AND BY THE RECEIPT FOR THE ESTABLISHING OF THE COMMERCE, FOR THE CIVIL-LAW-SUIT, OF THE CONDITION OF THE LANGUAGE, FOR AN ACT OF THE COMMERCE, FOR THE ENRICHMENT BY THE "LANGUAGE" BY THE CONTRACT, AND WITHIN THE TERRITORY OF THE U.S.A. BY THE **TITLE: 28: U.S.A. CODES: SECTION: 1605** OF THE FOREIGN-SOVEREIGN-IMMUNITY-ACT.

8

Exhibit J-8

22. **FOR THE PLAINTIFF/RESPONDENT WITH THE AFFIRMATION BY THE COMPLAINT** ARE OF THE INJURY BY ANY VIOLATION OF THE INTERNATIONAL-TREATY BY THE FOREIGN-STATE, BY THE OPERATION WITH THE C.U.S.A.F., IS BY THE UPHOLDING OF THE C.U.S.A.F.-RIGHTS OF THE SOVEREIGN-CITIZEN OF THE PARTY, FOR THE BREACH OF THE CONTRACT-TREATY, BY THE FILING WITH THE FEDERAL-SUPREME-COURT OF THE U.S.A. FOR THE WASHINGTON D.C. FOR THE TREATY-DISPUTE BETWEEN THE SOVEREIGN-CITIZEN(S) BY THE TITLE: 42: U.S.A. CODES: SECTION: 1&2: FOR THE FLAG OF THE U.S.A. AND FOREIGN-LANGUAGE, WITH THE TREATY OF THE FOREIGN-SOVEREIGN-IMMUNITY-ACT FOR THE JURISDICTION BY THE REQUIREMENTS BY THE C.U.S.A.F.-TREATY-LAW BY THE RESPONDENT-OFFICERS OF THE COURT.

23. **FOR THE PLAINTIFF/RESPONDENT WITH THE AFFIRMATION BY THE COMPLAINT** ARE OF THE INJURY BY THE ENFORCING OF AN AGREEMENT (TREATY) BY THE MAKING, BY THE OATH OR AFFIRMATION BY THE SUPPORTING AND DEFENDING OF THE C.U.S.A.F. WHEN THE SURRENDER OF THE OATH AND AFFIRMATION INTO A FOREIGN/FICTION-LANGUAGE FOR THE CAUSE OF THE CONSTRUCTIVE-TREASON, CONTEMPT FOR THE C.U.S.A.F., FALSE-SWEARING AND PERJURY OF THE OATH BY THE TITLE: 18: U.S.A. CODES: SECTION: 1621, BY THE RESPONDENTS-OFFICERS OF THE COURT.

24. **FOR THE PLAINTIFF/RESPONDENT WITH THE AFFIRMATION BY THE COMPLAINT** ARE OF THE INJURY FOR THE LOSING OF THE RIGHTS WITH THE PROPERTY OF THE TAKING BY THE VIOLATION OF THE INTERNATIONAL-LAW(S) (ARE)/IS AT THE ISSUE AND OF THE PROPERTY OR OF ANY PROPERTY BY THE EXCHANGE FOR THE PROPERTY IS OF THE PRESENT WITH THE U.S.A. BY THE CONNECTION WITH THE COMMERCIAL-ACTIVITY OF THE INCORPORATION OF THE U.S.A. BY THE FOREIGN/FICTION-LANGUAGE; OR, BY THE PROPERTY IS BY THE BEING OF THE OWNERSHIP, OR BY THE OPERATION BY AN AGENCY OR INSTRUMENTALITY OF THE FOREIGN/FICTION-LANGUAGES FOR THAT AGENCY OR FOR THE INSTRUMENTALITY IS BY THE ENGAGEMENT WITH THE COMMERCIAL-ACTIVITY FOR THE U.S.A. [FOR THE FILING-FEE IS OF THE COMMERCIAL-ACTIVITY BY THE MONEY OR PROPERTY IS IN THE INVOLVEMENT OF THE OVER-$21.00 DOLLARS U.S.A.]

25. **FOR THE PLAINTIFF/RESPONDENT WITH THE AFFIRMATION BY THE COMPLAINT** ARE OF THE INJURY (B) FOR ANY CLAIM OF THE ARISING-OUT OF THE INTERFERENCE WITH THE C.U.S.A.F. CONTRACT-RIGHTS FOR THE FILING OF THE TITLE: 42; U.S.A. CODES: SECTION: 1&2: FOR THE TRIAL BY THE JURY OF THE F.R.C.P. RULE: 38(a) AND THE C.U.S.A.F. ARTICLE OF THE NINE(9) IS FOR THE CAUSING OF AN ACTION BY THE TITLE: 42: U.S.A. CODES: SECTION: 1986 FOR THE KNOWLEDGE OF THE LAW AND THE NEGLECT BY THE FAILURE FOR THE STOPPING AND CORRECTING OF THE WRONG BY THE RESPONDENT.

26. **FOR THE PLAINTIFF/RESPONDENT WITH THE AFFIRMATION BY THE COMPLAINT** ARE OF THE INJURY FOR THE ACTION BY THE ENFORCEMENT OF AN AGREEMENT OF THE MAKING BY THE FOREIGN/FICTION-LANGUAGES WITH THE BENEFIT OF THE PRIVATE-PARTY BY THE SUBMISSION INTO THE LEGAL-RELATIONSHIP FOR THE CONTRACTUAL FOR THE ARBITRATION.

27. **EDUCATIONAL-NOTE:** FOR THE FEE OF THE FILING IS WITH THE CLERK OF THE COURT BY THE AMOUNT OF THE ____________, FOR THE FEE(S) IS/(ARE) BY THE

Exhibit J-9

EMBEZZLEMENT INTO THE FOREIGN/FICTION-LANGUAGE BY THE VIOLATION WITH THE **TITLE: 18: U.S.A. CODES: SECTION: 641, 646: FOR THE COURT-OFFICER FOR THE DEPOSIT OF THE REGISTRY-MONEYS**: FOR ANY CLERK OR OTHER-OFFICER(S) OF THE COURT OF THE U.S.A., BY THE FAILURE FOR THE DEPOSITING OF ANY MONEY FOR THE REGISTRY OF THE **COURT OF THE DISTRICT OF THE UNITY-STATES OF THE AMERICA** OR FOR THE PAYMENT INTO THE **COURT OF THE DISTRICT OF THE UNITY-STATES OF THE AMERICA** OR BY THE RECEIVING BY THE OFFICERS-THEREOF, WITH THE **TREASURE OR FOR A DEPOSITORY OF THE UNITY-STATES OF THE AMERICA,** FOR THE NAME AND BY THE CREDIT OF THE **COURT OF THE DISTRICT FOR THE UNITY-STATES** OR IS BY THE RETAINING OR CONVERTING FOR THE USE OF THE **UNITED STATES DISTRICT COURT**(sic) FOR ANY MONEY OF THE PAYING INTO THE **COURT OF THE DISTRICT OF THE UNITY-STATES OF THE AMERICA**, IS OF THE GUILT OF THE EMBEZZLEMENT WITH THE FINE BY THE TITLE: 18: U.S.A. CODES: SECTION: 646 THAN THE AMOUNT ($__.00) OR IMPRISONMENT OF THE TEN-YEARS OR BOTH BY THE OFFICERS OF THE COURT.

28. FOR THE PLAINTIFF/RESPONDENT WITH THE AFFIRMATION BY THE COMPLAINT ARE FOR THE **TITLE: 18: U.S.A. CODES: SECTION: 641: FOR THE PUBLIC-MONEY, PROPERTY OR RECORDS**: WHOEVER: IS BY EMBEZZLING, STEALING, PURLOINING, OR KNOWING, CONVERTS FOR THE USE OF THE ANOTHER, WITHOUT THE AUTHORITY, CONVEYS OR DISPOSES OF ANY RECORD, VOUCHER, MONEY, OR THING OF THE VALUE OF THE **COURT OF THE DISTRICT FOR THE UNITY-STATES OF THE AMERICA**: LAWSUIT, OR OF ANY PROPERTY OF THE MAKING OR BEING BY THE MAKING OF THE CONTRACT FOR THE **COURT OF THE DISTRICT OF THE UNITY-STATES OF THE AMERICA**, OF THE COURTS UNDER THE C.U.S.A.F. ARTICLE OF THE NINE(9) AND TITLE: 4: U.S.A. CODES: SECTION: 1&2 FOR THE FLAG OF THE U.S.A., WHOEVER, BY THE RECEIVING, CONCEALMENT, OR CONVERTS FOR THE COMPLAINT IS WITH THE COURT OF THE DISTRICT OF THE UNITY-STATES OF THE AMERICA FOR THE GAIN, KNOWING THE **COURT OF THE DISTRICT OF THE UNITY-STATES OF THE AMERICA**, FOR THE EMBEZZLING, STEALING, PURLOINING OR CONVEYING INTO **THE UNITED STATES DISTRICT COURT**(sic) - FOR THE FINE (MONEY OR PROPERTY) BY THE TITLE: 18: U.S.A. SECTION: 641 OR BY THE IMPRISONMENT OF THE TEN(10)-YEARS OR BOTH BY THE HEREIN-RESPONDENTS.

FOR THE DEMAND

29. FOR THE PLAINTIFF/RESPONDENT WITH THE AFFIRMATION BY THE TRUTH WITH THE COMPLAINT IS FOR THE INJURY OF THE PLAINTIFF FOR THE DEMAND-JUDGEMENT IS FOR THE NEGLIGENT-ACTS OF THE ATTORNEYS OF THE LAW, IN THE INCORPORATION OF THIS CASE-NUMBER: [illegible handwriting] (sic), IN THE SUM OF THE TEN-MILLION-DOLLARS-UNITY-STATES OF THE AMERICA-CURRENCY ($10,000,000.00), PLUS-COSTS AND DISBURSEMENTS. WITH THE FOREIGN-SOVEREIGN-IMMUNITY-ACT OF THE OFFICERS OF THE COURT BY THE FOREIGN-FICTION-FLAG FOR THE PLAINTIFF/RESPONDENT IS/ARE BY THE DEMAND FOR THE TEN-TIMES(10) OF THIS JUDGEMENT FOR THE INTERNATIONAL-JURISDICTION OF THE **LAW OF THE FLAG** BY THE SANCTUARY OF THE COURT AGAINST THE SOVEREIGN-CITIZEN OF THE PARTY FOR THE BREACH OF THE C.U.S.A.F.-CONTRACT WITH THE USE OF THE FICTION-LANGUAGE, FOR THE PAYMENT IS BY THE **BANK OF ENGLAND** AS THE TRUSTEE FOR THE BANKRUPTCY OF THE UNITED STATES OF AMERICA(sic). FOR THE POSTMASTER-GENERAL IS BY THE HAVING OF THE JURISDICTION FOR THE ORDERING OF THE TREASURY FOR THE ENFORCEMENT OF THIS ORDER. FOR THIS

Exhibit J-10

INCORPORATION-CASE IS FOR THE HAVING WITH THE APPROVAL FOR ANY OBSTRUCTIONS OF THE LANGUAGE FOR THE **APARTHEID** WITH THE FILING AT THE WORLD-COURT WITH THE "HAGUE", AND IS WITH THE APPROVAL OF THE RUSSIAN-SUPREME-COURT UNDER THE LAW OF THE FLAG, BY THE PLACEMENT OF THE AMERICAN-FLAG(1X1.9) FOR THE SANCTUARY OF THE COURT OF THE RUSSIAN-COURT BY THE STATE OF THE SOVEREIGN-RUSSIA OR BY ANY SOVEREIGN-COURT OF THE WORLD FOR THE JURISDICTION OF THE UNITY-STATES OF THE AMERICA [CAN AND WILL] FOR THE ENTERING OF A DEFAULT-JUDGEMENT AGAINST THE COURT OF THE VIOLATION FOR THE FICTITIOUS-USE OF THE LANGUAGE FOR THE EXTORTION OF THE SOVEREIGNS-RIGHTS WITH THE DISABILITIES-ACT WHERE THE [PEOPLE] ARE OF THE INJURY BY THE DISABILITY OF THE LANGUAGE **(FOR THE NOUNS ARE IN THE FORM OF THE VERB)** FOR THE EXTORTION IS AGAINST THE CITIZEN BY THE COURT.

30. **FOR THE PLAINTIFF/RESPONDENT WITH THE AFFIRMATION BY THE COMPLAINT** ARE OF THE INJURY BY THE LOSS OF THE FREEDOM, PROPERTY AND PAIN OF THE BODY AND MIND FOR THE LOSS WITH THE SUBSTANTIAL-DAMAGE OF THE TEN-BILLION ($10,000,000,000.00) DOLLARS FOR THE DEPRIVATION OF THE RIGHTS THROUGH THE APARTHEID.

FOR THE DEFINITIONS IN THE SUPPORT OF THIS INCORPORATION-CASE FOR THE CONSTITUTION/CONTRACT OF THE UNITY-STATES UNDER THE AMERICA-FLAG, HEREIN-UNDER THE INCORPORATION FOR THE CONSTITUTION/CONTRACT OF THE UNITY-STATES UNDER THE AMERICA-FLAG, HEREIN.

1). **FOR THE ARTICLE OF THE ONE(1): FOR THE RIGHT OF THE TRUTH IS IN THE LANGUAGE OF THE NOUN.**

2). **FOR THE ARTICLE OF THE SECOND(2): FOR THE RIGHT OF THE JUDGEMENT IS IN THE TRUTH.**

3). **FOR THE ARTICLE OF THE THREE(3):** FOR THE FREEDOM OF THE SPEECH AND PRESS, AND FOR THE RIGHT FOR THE PETITIONING OF THE GOVERNMENT FOR THE REDRESS OF THE GRIEVANCES, AND OF THE FREEDOM OF THE PARTY'S RELIGION.

4). **FOR THE ARTICLE OF THE FOUR(4): FOR THE RIGHT OF THE CAUSE OF THE COURT-ACTION IN THE LANGUAGE OF THE TRUTH.**

5). **FOR THE ARTICLE OF THE FIVE(5): FOR THE RIGHT OF THE FREEDOM OF THIS CONSTITUTION IN THE TRUTH.**

6). **FOR THE ARTICLE OF THE SIX(6:):** FOR THE SEARCHES AND SEIZURES ARE UNDER THE TRUTH IN THE DOCUMENTATION OF THE LANGUAGE FOR THE WARRANTS ARE OF THE ISSUE IN THE TRUTH-LANGUAGE, BUT UPON THE PROBABLE-CAUSE UNDER THE SWEARING OF THE OATH/AFFIRMATION, WITH THE PARTICULAR-DESCRIPTION OF THE PLACE FOR THE SEARCH AND FOR THE PARTY AND THINGS THAT ARE FOR THE POSSESSION BY THE COURT-ORDER.

7). **FOR THE ARTICLE OF THE SEVEN(7):** FOR THE PARTY IN ANY CRIMINAL-CASE IS UNDER THE COMPLIANCE IN THE TRUTH AS THE WITNESS AGAINST THE PARTY'S-SELF, OR UNDER THE DEPRIVATION OF THE LIFE, LIBERTY OR PROPERTY, BY THE NEGLECT OF THE DUE-PROCESS OF THE LAW. NOTES: C.U.S.A.F.-CONTRACT OF THE SEVEN(7).

8). **FOR THE ARTICLE OF THE EIGHT(8):** FOR THE RIGHT OF A SPEEDY AND PUBLIC-TRIAL. BY THE JURY OF THE IMPARTIAL-CITIZENS, IN THE VENUE OF THE DISTRICT OF THE U.S.A. WHERE THE ACTION IS OF THE COMMITMENT, FOR THE RESPONDENT-PARTY IS FOR THE INFORMATION OF THE NATURE AND CAUSE OF THE

R-725

Exhibit J-11

ACCUSATION; FOR THE RESPONDENT-PARTY IS FOR THE CONFRONTATION BY THE WITNESS IN THE PARTY FOR THE HAVING OF THE COMPULSORY-PROCESS FOR THE OBTAINING OF THE WITNESS AND EVIDENCE IN THE PARTY'S FAVOR, AND FOR THE HAVING OF THE ASSISTANCE OF THE COUNSEL FOR THE PARTY'S-DEFENSE.
NOTES: VIOLATION OF THE DUE-PROCESS (COUNSEL) - FOR THE OBSTRUCTION OF THE JUSTICE (TITLE: 18: CHAPTER: 63: U.S.A. CODES: SECTION: 1512) FOR THE PERJURY OF THE OATH-(TITLE: 18: CHAPTER: 63: U.S.A. CODES: SECTION: 1621) FOR ANY DEPRIVATION OF THE RIGHTS UNDER THE COLOR OF THE LAW = (TITLE: 18: U.S.A. CODES: SECTION: 2421). NOTE: FOR THE COLOR OF THE LAW = CORRUPTION OF THE FLAG OF THE U.S.A.

9). FOR THE ARTICLE OF THE NINE(9): IN THE SUITS OF THE COMMON-LAW, WHERE THE VALUE IN THE CONTROVERSY IS OVER THE TWENTY-DOLLARS UNDER THE RIGHT OF THE TRIAL BY THE JURY IS OF THE PRESERVATION FOR THE FACT IS IN THE TRUTH-LANGUAGE UNDER THE TRIAL BY THE JURY. (FOR THE PARTY IS BY THE GIVING OF YOUR NAME WITH THE PUNCTUATION (-:) IN THE PERSON IN THE BAR UNDER THE JURISDICTIONAL-DISPLAY OF THE FLAG: TITLE: 4: U.S.A. CODES: SECTION: 1&2 OF THE U.S.A. UNDER THE LAW OF THE FLAG, AND ARE BY THE HAVING IN THE PARTY'S POSSESSION ARMY-REGULATIONS: 840-10: CHAPTER: 2-1 (a,b) AND CHAPTER: 2-5 (a,b,c) FOR THE CAUSE OF A COMMON-LAW-COURT.

10). FOR THE ARTICLE OF THE TEN(10): FOR THE PUNISHMENT IS IN THE LANGUAGE OF THE TRUTH. FOR THE CRUEL AND UNUSUAL-PUNISHMENTS IS UNDER THE PROHIBITION FOR THE INFLICTION.

11). FOR THE ARTICLE OF THE ELEVEN(11): FOR THE ENUMERATION IN THE C.U.S.A.F.-CONTRACT OF THE CERTAIN-RIGHTS ARE BY THE C.U.S.A.F.-CONTRACT FOR THE DENIAL OR DISPARAGE OF THE CITIZENS AS THE OFFICERS OF THE GOVERNMENT ARE UNDER THE INCORPORATION/RETAIN BY THE PEOPLE.

12). FOR THE ARTICLE OF THE TWELVE(12): FOR THE CONSTITUTION/CONTRACT UNDER THE PROHIBITION BY THE RESERVATION OF THE C.U.S.A.F.-CONTRACT, ARE UNDER THE RESERVATION BY THE MUTUAL-AGREEMENT BY THE TITLE-PARTIES-HEREIN.

13). BY THE ARTICLE OF THE THIRTEEN(13): FOR THE TRUTH OF THE FOREIGN/FICTION-LANGUAGES IS FOR THE FOREIGN/FICTION COURT AND IS FOR THE JURISDICTIONS IN THE TRUTH OVER THE SOVEREIGN-CITIZEN(S) IN THE PARTY, FOR THE JUDICIAL-LANGUAGE OF THE UNITY-STATES IS FOR THE CONSTRUCTION FOR THE EXTENSION IN ANY SUIT IN THE LAW OR IN THE EQUITY FOR THE COMMENCEMENT OR FOR THE PROSECUTION AGAINST ANY ONE OF THE UNITY-STATES BY THE CITIZENS OF THE OTHER-STATES OR BY THE CITIZENS OR BY THE SUBJECTS OF ANY FOREIGN/FICTION-STATE IN THE TRUTH. FOR THE NEW-STATE UNDER THE TRUTH IS FOR THE ERECTION OF THE NEW-STATE WITHIN THE STATE FOR THE FORMATION OF A TRUTHFUL-STATE WITHIN THE UNITY-STATES.

14). FOR THE AMENDMENT 14: (BY THE NEVER-MAKING-LEGAL BY THE CONGRESS-JULY/1868) BY THE PROHIBITION OF A STATE (FOR THE CITIZEN IN THE PARTY) IS FOR THE MAKING/ENFORCING OF ANY LAW WHICH IS FOR THE ABRIDGING OF THE PRIVILEGES/IMMUNITIES OF THE CITIZENS OF THE U.S.A., NOR IS FOR ANY STATE (FOR THE CITIZEN IN THE PARTY) FOR THE DEPRIVING OF ANY PARTY OF THE

Exhibit J-12

LIFE, LIBERTY/PROPERTY, BY THE NEGLECTING OF THE DUE-PROCESS OF THE LAW; NOR BY THE PARTY, FOR THE EQUAL-PROTECTION OF THE LAW. FOR THE TITLE: 42: U.S.A. CODES: SECTION: 1985(2)(3). NOTE: **AMENDMENT** IS OF AN **ADJECTIVE OF THE "FOURTEEN"** AND IS FOR THE MAKING OF THE AMENDMENT-STATEMENT OF THE FICTION BY THE FAILURE OF THE AUTHORITY AND IS FOR THE USING OF THE CIVIL-RIGHTS-ACT OF THE 1964 FOR THE EQUAL-PROTECTION AND CONVERSION UNTO THE NOUN-PROCEDURES OF THE FACTS.

15). MIRANDA: IS IN THE FICTION OF A DISCLAIMER-CONTRACT IN THE FUTURE-TENSE FOR THE **DISQUALIFICATION OF THE PRESENT-TENSE-JURISDICTION OF ANY CONTRACT-DISCLAIMER**.

16). FOR THE GIVING OF YOUR NAME WITH THE PUNCTUATION WHILE IN THE BAR: FIRST-MIDDLE: LAST. FOR THE IDENTIFICATION OF THE TRUSTEE-SOVEREIGN-CITIZEN(S)IN THE PARTY AGAINST THE DISMISSAL-COMPLAINT BY THE COURT IN THE FICTION OF THE PARLIAMENTARY-COURT, FOR THE PROHIBITION OF A CONTRACT IS FOR THE DISMISSING OF THE INCORPORATION OF THE CASE FOR THE PLEADING BEFORE THE COURT OF THE DISTRICT; BY THE PLAINTIFF(S)-PAYING INTO THE CLERK OF THE COURTS FOR THE TRIAL BY THE JURY UNDER THE F.R.C.P. RULE: 38(a). FOR THE COMMERCIAL-CONTRACT WITH THE FOREIGN-STATE IS IN THE COLLUSION-CONTEMPT-CHARGE AND IS UNDER THE TITLE: 28: CHAPTER: 85: U.S.A. CODES: SECTION: 1359 OR BY THE THREAT OF THE JAIL. (JAIL IS CRIMINAL). FOR THE JUDGE'S USE OF THE TERM-CHARGE IS FOR THE MAKING-CASE OF A CRIMINAL-PROCEDURE AND UNDER THE C.U.S.A.F.-CONTRACT FOR THE VIOLATION OF THE LAW FOR THE DUE-PROCESS BEFORE THE FACTS BY THE PROOF IN THE CASE, WITH THE INTENT OF THE GUILTY-TILL-PROVING-INNOCENT, IN THE PLACE OF THE INNOCENT-TILL-PROVING-GUILTY.

17). FOR THE F.R.C.P. RULE: 4: PROCESS (a), FOR THE SUMMONS, (b), FOR THE FORM, (c), FOR THE SERVICE (BY THE PRESENTATION FOR THE RESPONDENTS), (d), FOR THE SUMMONS AND COMPLAINT (NOTE: 20-DAY-RETURN-ANSWER FOR THE PLAINTIFF AND COURT, (g), FOR THE RETURN-PROOF OF THE SERVICE ON THE CLERK OF THE COURT, (H), FOR THE AMENDMENT BY THE SERVICE, (j), FOR THE TIME-LIMIT OF THE 120 DAYS FOR THE RETURN-SERVICE.

18). FOR THE F.R.C.P. RULE: 5 = FOR THE SERVICE: (a) FOR THE REQUIREMENT, (d) FOR THE CERTIFICATE OF THE FILING. (e) FOR THE FILING WITH THE CLERK (FOR THE CLERK, IS UNDER THE PROHIBITION FOR THE REFUSAL FOR THE FILING OF ANY PAPERS UNDER THE FAILURE FOR THE BEING IN THE FORM OF THE LOCAL-RULES. AS ALL LOCAL-RULES ARE IN THE WRITING OF THE FICTION) TITLE: 28: U.S.A. CODES: SECTION: 646.

19). FOR THE F.R.C.P. RULE: 6 = FOR THE TIME: (a), FOR THE COMPUTATION-(MONDAY TO FRIDAY). (d), FOR THE COMPLAINTS AND AFFIDAVITS ARE FOR THE BEING WITHIN THE SERVICE OF THE FIVE(5)DAYS-RULE: BEFORE THE TRIAL BY THE PLAINTIFF(S); AND ONE(1): DAY-SERVICE BEFORE THE TRIAL FOR THE DEFENDANT.

20). FOR THE F.R.C.P. RULE: 7: = PLEADINGS: (a), FOR THE PLEADINGS, (b), OF/BY/AND FOR THE COMPLAINT, WHICH ARE FOR THE MAKING WITH THE PARTICULARITY OF THE RELIEF OF THE ORDER OF THE SEEKING. NOTE: FOR THE NOTICE OF THE REFUSAL FOR THE FRAUD IS FOR THE OPPOSING-COMPLAINT OF THE

R-J:S

Exhibit J-13

FRAUD, BY THE BEING OF THE FAILURE FOR THE TRAVERSING WITH THE COMPLAINT OF THE FRAUD/OPPONENT'S FICTION, STAY-ON-POINT BY THE REAFFIRMING OF THE COMPLAINT OF YOUR ORIGINAL-PLEADINGS OR CROSS-COMPLAINT-PLEADINGS.

21). **FOR THE F.R.C.P. RULE: 8: = RULES OF THE PLEADING:** (a), FOR THE CLAIM FOR THE RELIEF, IS FOR THE ASKING FOR THE COMPENSATION (FEES, MONEY, PROPERTY) AND IS FOR THE CONTAINING (b), FOR THE DEFENSE-FORM OF THE DENIALS, (c), FOR THE AFFIRMATIVE-DEFENSE, (d), FOR THE FAILURE BY THE DENYING, (e), FOR THE PLEADING BY THE BEING-CONCISE.

22). **FOR THE F.R.C.P. RULE: 9: = PLEADINGS-SPECIAL** (b), FOR THE FRAUD IS UNDER THE CONDITION OF THE MIND (e), FOR THE JUDGEMENT, (f), FOR THE TIME AND PLACE, (g), FOR THE SPECIAL-DAMAGE.

23). **FOR THE F.R.C.P. RULE: 10: = FOR THE FORM OF THE PLEADINGS:** (a)CAPTIONS, (b) FOR THE PARAGRAPHS.

24). **F.R.C.P. RULE: 11: FOR THE FRIVOLOUS-FILING,** FOR ALL PLEADINGS ARE FOR THE BEING UNDER THE SIGNATURE AND ADDRESS, FOR THE SIGNING OF THE TICKET IS UNDER THE PROHIBITION UNDER A LAW UNTIL THE FIFTH-DAY OF THE VIOLATION FOR THE SANCTIONS AND FEES. FOR THE CITATION IS IN THE VOID WHEN THE ACT OF THE COLLUSION IS IN THE USE UNDER THE TITLE: 28: CHAPTER: 85: U.S.A. CODES: SECTION: 1359.

25). **FOR THE F.R.C.P. RULE: 12(b)FOR THE PRESENTATION;** 12(b)(7) FOR THE FAILURE OF THE JOINING (IS FOR THE BEING OF THE SAME-JURISDICTION OF THE FLAG UNDER THE LAW OF THE FLAG) IS BY THE JOINDER IS OF THE COMPLETE-EVEN WHEN THE FICTION/FOREIGN IS OF THE COMPLETE BY THE JOINING IN THE BAR, FOR THE STUDY THE D.W.M.-LAW-PROCEDURES.

12(b)(6) FOR THE FAILURE BY THE AFFIRMING OF THE CLAIM, [MUST JOIN JURISDICTIONS BEFORE AFFIRMING INJURY] FOR THE FOREIGN/FICTION-JURISDICTION IS UNDER THE PROHIBITION IN THE JOINDER BY THE COURT, PLAINTIFF(S)AND RESPONDENT(S)ARE UNDER THE PROHIBITION FOR THE AFFIRMING-PLEADINGS IN THE COURT IN DIFFERENT-FOREIGN/FICTION-JURISDICTIONS FOR THE JOINDER.

12(b)(5) FOR THE IMPROPER-PROCESS: [BY NOT PROCESSING OF THE PAPERWORK WITH THE CLERK OF THE COURT]

FOR THE PROHIBITION FOR THE PROCESS IN THE FICTION: USE OF THE ADJECTIVES AND THE VERB IN PLACE OF THE NOUN IS FOR THE CAUSING OF THE MAIL-FRAUD: TITLE: 18: U.S.A. CODES: SECTION: 1342. AND FICTITIOUS-USE OF THE LANGUAGE FOR THE FRAUD.

12(b)(4) IS FOR THE IMPROPER-SERVICE, (BY THE FAILURE FOR THE SERVING OF THE PAPERWORK ON THE RESPONDENT BY THE LAW]

FOR THE PROHIBITION OF THE SERVICE IN THE FICTION: USE OF THE ADJECTIVES; CAUSING MAIL-FRAUD UNDER THE TITLE: 18: U.S.A. CODES: SECTION: 1342: UNDER THE F.R.C.P. RULE 12(b)(3) FOR THE IMPROPER-VENUE. FOR THE JUDGE IS UNDER THE PROHIBITION FOR THE JOINING UNDER THE JURISDICTION OF THE TRUTH IN THE LAW WHERE THE ACT IS FOR THE TAKING-PLACE AND THE JURISDICTION, **UNDER THE LAW OF THE FLAG-FICTION AND NOUNS-USE AS THE ADJECTIVES AND VERB. FOR THE WATCHING IS OF THE TRAPS IN THE TITLES, NAMES, DATES, CASE NUMBERS.**

14

R.-J.:S.

Exhibit J-14

12(b)(2)- **FOR THE LACK OF THE PERSONAL-JURISDICTION OVER THE PARTY, FOR THE FICTION-WRONG-LAW OF THE LANGUAGE-JURISDICTION, WHEN THE COURT IS UNDER THE FAILURE FOR THE JOINING, COURT IS UNDER THE PROHIBITION FOR THE STATING OF THE CLAIM/NATURE OF THE INJURY] 12(b)(1)-FOR THE LACK OF THE JURISDICTION OVER THE SUBJECT-MATTER**. WHEN THE JUDGE IS UNDER THE FAILURE FOR THE READING OF THE CASE BEFORE THIS COURT AND BY THE ACTING ON THE OPINION, AND BY THE FAILURE FOR THE ACTING ON THE FACTS OF THE CASE. FOR THE DIFFERENT-CAUSES OF THE REMEDY: (A). FOR THE COMPLAINT: JUDGEMENT ON THE PLEADINGS, (B) - COMPLAINT FOR THE STRIKING. (C) - WAVER (SUBJECT-MATTER) PROHIBITION OF THE JURISDICTION.

26). **FOR THE F.R.C.P.-RULE: 15,** FOR THE AMENDMENT AND SUPPLEMENTAL-PLEADINGS (a.b.c.d.) IS FOR THE READING IN THE F.R.C.P.

27). **FOR THE F.R.C.P.-RULE: 16(f), FOR THE SANCTIONS:** WHEN THE JUDGE/OFFICERS OF THE COURT ARE/IS IN THE TRUTH FOR THE UNITY OF THE JURISDICTION OF THE CONSTITUTION IN THE SANCTUARY OF THE COURT. FOR THE BREACH OF THE C.U.S.A.F.-CONTRACT UNDER THE LAW OF THE SOVEREIGN-FLAG OF THE U.S.A. FOR THE VIOLATION OF THE OATH OF THE OFFICE, SANCTION FOR THE BREACH OF THE CONTRACT UNDER THE OATH AND AFFIRMATION; AND FOR THE FILING-FEES BY THE PAYING ARE FOR THE TRIAL BY THE JURY AND RECUSAL-DISMISSAL ORDERS. FOR THE COURT IS UNDER THE PROHIBITION FOR THE ORDERING OF THE FEES (TITLE: 42: U.S.A. CODES: SECTION: 1988) FOR THE BREACH OF THE C.U.S.A.F.-CONTRACT FOR THE ARTICLE OF THE NINE (9) FOR THE TRIAL BY THE JURY AND FOR THE ARTICLE OF THE SEVEN (7) FOR THE DUE-PROCESS OF THE LAW. FOR THE SANCTION AGAINST THE JUDGE FOR THE FAILURE FOR THE COMING INTO THE DISCOVERY-HEARING AND FOR THE FAILURE FOR THE JOINING UNDER THE OATH AND AFFIRMATION OF THE C.U.S.A.F.-CONTRACT.

28). **FOR THE F.R.C.P.-RULE: 18-19,** FOR THE JOINDER ALSO F.R.C.P.-RULE: 12(b)(7).

29). **FOR THE F.R.C.P.-RULE: 24, FOR THE TITLE: 28:** U.S.A. CODES: SECTION: 2403 FOR THE CHALLENGE OF THE CONTRACT/CONSTITUTIONALITY

30). **FOR THE F.R.C.P.-RULE: 38(a),** FOR THE TRIAL BY THE JURY

31). **FOR F.R.C.P.-RULE: 41(a),** FOR THE DISMISSAL OF THE ACTION BY THE VOLUNTARY-USE, FOR THE WITHDRAWING OF THE CASE THAT THE PLAINTIFF(S) BY THE KNOWING IS BY THE WRITING OF THE INCORRECT.

32). **FOR THE F.R.C.P.-RULE: 49,** FOR THE ISSUES ARE BY THE SENDING FOR THE JURY BY THE DEMAND.

33). **FOR F.R.C.P.-RULE: 50,** FOR THE NEW TRIAL: USE WITH THE DE-NOVO/WRIT OF THE HABIUS-CORPUS.

34). **FOR THE F.R.C.P.-RULE: 54,** FOR THE DEMAND FOR THE JUDGEMENT.

35). **FOR THE F.R.C.P.-RULE: 55,** FOR THE DEFAULT

 15

Exhibit J-15

36). **FOR THE F.R.C.P.-RULE: 56,** FOR THE C-SUMMARY-JUDGEMENT.

37). **FOR THE F.R.C.P.-RULE: 57,** FOR THE DECLARATORY-JUDGEMENT

38). **FOR THE POLICY AND CUSTOM;** ACTS ON THE DAY,_____ ,1999, IN THE DESCRIPTION OF THE ACTIONS AND OMISSIONS FOR THE ENGAGEMENT UNDER THE COLOR OF THE STATE LAW AUTHORITY, IN THE SUING AS THE PARTY RESPONSIBLE BY THE AUTHORIZATION AND RATIFICATION OF THE ACTS OF THE STATE-AGENTS; FOR THE PLAINTIFF(S)ARE OF THE INJURY BY THE NEGLECT OF THE C.U.S.A.F.-CONTRACT FOR THE RIGHTS IN THE SECURITY OF THE PARTY UNDER THE C.U.S.A.F.-CONTRACT FOR THE ARTICLE OF THE SIX(6) FOR THE WARRANT IS IN THE ISSUE BY THE JUDGE OF THE OATH AND AFFIRMATION; C.U.S.A.F.-CONTRACT FOR THE ARTICLE OF THE NINE(9) FOR THE RIGHT BY THE TRIAL BY THE JURY, UNDER THE F.R.C.P. RULE: 38(a) AND UNDER THE DUE-PROCESS OF THE LAW UNDER THE C.U.S.A.F.-CONTRACT FOR THE ARTICLE OF THE SEVEN(7), BY THE RESPONDENT.

39). **FOR THE OPINION OF THE DAVID: MILLER:** FOR THE ACTORS IN THE COURT BY THE CREATION OF AN ELABORATE-FRAUD, AND FOR THE FAILURE OF THE JUSTICE, BY THE COURT, F.R.C.P. RULE: 12(b)(2). FOR THE F.R.C.P. RULE: 9(b) FOR THE FRAUD: C.U.S.A.F.-CONTRACT FOR THE ARTICLE OF THE SEVEN(7) FOR THE DUE-PROCESS, F.R.C.P. RULE: 38(a)FOR THE TRIAL, AND UNDER THE TITLE: 18: U.S.A. CODES: SECTION: 1342 FOR THE FICTITIOUS (ADJECTIVES)(VERB)FOR THE USE OF THE NAME (NOUN). FOR THE NOUNS IN THE USE AS VERBS AND ADJECTIVES.

40). **FOR THE EXAMPLE OF THE SENTENCE-PLEADINGS:** WITH THE PROHIBITION OF THE SUBJECT-MATTER-JURISDICTION UNDER THE F.R.C.P.-RULE: 12(b)(1), AND F.R.C.P.-RULE: 9(b)FOR THE FRAUD, OVER THE PLAINTIFF(S), FOR THE USE OF THE COERCION AND EXTORTION, BY THE THREATENING OF THE PLAINTIFF(S). FOR THE TITLE: 42: U.S.A. CODES: SECTION: 1983: NOTE: 352 IN THE ORDER BY THE SUSTAINING OF THE 1983-CONSPIRACY-CLAIM, FOR THERE IS FOR THE BEING OF THE EVIDENCE OF THE EFFORT/PLANNING BETWEEN THE PRIVATE-ASSOCIATIONS AND STATE-ACTORS **(FOR THE JUDGE IS UNDER THE FAILURE OF THE OATH AND AFFIRMATION FOR THE JUDGE IS UNDER AN ACTOR BY THE NEGLECT OF SUBJECT-MATTER-JURISDICTION),** BY THE DENYING OF THE PLAINTIFF(S) OF THE C.U.S.A.F.-CONTRACT-RIGHTS. FOR THE NOUNS IN THE USE AS THE VERBS AND ADJECTIVES FOR THE FICTION-LANGUAGE.

41). **FOR THE (TITLE: 18: U.S.A. CODES: SECTION: 242) FOR THE DEPRIVATION OF THE RIGHTS UNDER THE COLOR OF THE LAW:** FOR THE PARTY UNDER THE COLOR OF THE LAW-STATUTE, ORDINANCE, REGULATION/CUSTOM, WILLFUL-SUBJECTS OF THE INHABITANT OF THE STATE, TERRITORY/DISTRICT OF THE DEPRIVATION OF THE RIGHTS/PRIVILEGES/IMMUNITIES-SECURING/PROTECTION BY THE CONSTITUTION/LAWS OF THE U.S.A. BY THE FINE OF THE $1000. OR LESS; OR, IMPRISONMENT OF THE ONE-YEAR OR LESS, OR BOTH. FOR THE CONTRACT IS IN THE PRESENT-TENSE, IS THE CONTRACT BETWEEN THE COURT AND THE ATTORNEY FOR THE VIOLATIONS OF THE C.U.S.A.F.-CONTRACT FOR THE ARTICLE OF THE SIX(6) IN THE SECTION OF THE THREE(3) UNDER THE OATH: TITLE: 28: U.S.A. CODES: SECTION: 1343 FOR THE EQUAL-PROTECTION AND C.U.S.A.F.-CONTRACT FOR THE ARTICLE OF THE NINE(9):

R-J.S

Exhibit J-16

DUE-PROCESS.

42). FOR THE TITLE: 42: U.S.A. CODES: SECTION: 1983: AT NOTE: 355. FOR THE PLAINTIFF(S)ARE OF THE INJURY IN THE HEREIN-ACTION OF THE WRONG-INCORPORATION IN THE CASE-CITES WHEN BY THE SIGNATURE AND BY THE DEPRIVING OF THE PLAINTIFF(S) OF THE PLAINTIFF'S C.U.S.A.F.-CONTRACT FOR THE RIGHTS, BY THE FAILURE FOR THE HAVING OF THE C.U.S.A.F.-CONTRACT FOR THE ARTICLE OF THE SIX(6) FOR THE WARRANT IS FOR THE SIGNATURE BY THE JUDGE OF THE OATH AND AFFIRMATION, TRIAL BY THE JURY, UNDER THE C.U.S.A.F.-CONTRACT FOR THE ARTICLE OF THE SEVEN(7): DUE-PROCESS AND TITLE: 42: U.S.A. CODES: SECTION: 1985(2) FOR THE EQUAL-PROTECTION OF THE LAW: F.R.C.P.-RULES: 12(b)(7, 1, 2), BY THE RESPONDENTS.

43). FOR THE TITLE: 18: U.S.A. CODES: SECTION: 1621: STATE IS FOR THE PAYING OF ALL FEES WHEN THE PLAINTIFF(S)ARE OF THE INJURY BY THE LACK OF THE OATH/AFFIRMATION OF THE OFFICE AND PERJURY OF THE OATH BY THE RESPONDENT-JUDGE AND OFFICERS OF THE COURT: FOR THE CITIZENS ARE OF THE INJURY BY THE LACK OF ANY CONTRACT FOR THE PAYING OF THE FEES, BY THE CITIZENS IN THE PARTY'S: C.U.S.A.F.-CONTRACT-RIGHTS-VIOLATION. CROSS REF. FOR THE F.R.C.P. RULE: 9(b). FOR THE TITLE: 28: U.S.A. CODES: SECTION: 2072(b); C.U.S.A.F.-CONTRACT FOR THE ARTICLE OF THE SIX(6): SECTION THE 3 FOR THE FOREIGN/FICTION-STATES.

44). UNDER THE C.U.S.A.F.-CONTRACT FOR THE OFFICERS OF THE COURT, ARE FOR THE SWEARING OF AN ALLEGIANCE/OATH, JUDGE(S): OATH/AFFIRMATION/CONTRACT/TRUST/TREATY: **I, N__N, FOR THE AFFIRMATION AND FOR THE DECLARATION OF THE TRUTH(NOUN) FOR THE SUPPORT OF THE CONSTITUTION OF THE UNITY-STATES AND FOR THE STATE OF THE CONTRACT FOR WHERE PETITIONER STANDS IN THE JUDGEMENT ; THAT THE PETITIONER IS UNDER THE ADMINISTRATION OF THE JUSTICE WITH THE RESPECT FOR THE PERSON(S)/CITIZEN(S)/PARTY(S)/VESSEL(S)/PEOPLE/AND TRUSTEE(S) BY THE FAITHFUL AND IMPARTIAL-DISCHARGE OF THE DUTIES OF THE OFFICE; BY THE BEST OF MY ABILITY. (FICTION OATH IN THE NOUN)**

FOR THE CONSTRUCTIVE-TREASON: FOR THE CONTRACT OF THE RESPONSIBILITY AND AUTHORITY IS FOR THE SURRENDERING OF THE C.U.S.A.F.-CONTRACT INTO THE FICTION/FOREIGN-STATE UNDER THE FICTION/FOREIGN-FRINGE-FLAG FOR THE OATH AND AFFIRMATION, ALSO BY THE KNOWING AS THE ALLEGIANCE BY THE SUPPORTING OF THE C.U.S.A.F.-CONTRACT FOR THE CONSTRUCTIVE-TREASON BY THE DEFINITION IN THE (KNOWLEDGE) FOR THE **WILL OF THE INTENT** BY THE DESECRATION (TITLE: 4: U.S.A. CODES: SECTION: THREE(3) OF THE FLAG OF THE U.S.A. BY THE FORMING OF THE JURISDICTION OF THE FICTION/FOREIGN-STATE-LANGUAGE FOR THE FURTHERMENT OF THE DEPRIVATION OF THE RIGHTS AND **RAPE OF THE PLAINTIFF(S)/SOVEREIGN-CITIZEN(S)** BY THE OFFICERS OF THE COURT.

CONSTRUCTIVE-TREASON: FOR THE OVERT-ACT OR OFFENCE OF THE ATTEMPTING BY THE OVER-THROWING OF THE GOVERNMENT OF THE STATE (CONDITION OF THE CONTRACT OF THE PARTY(S) IN THE COURT/BAR) BY THE OFFENDER FOR THE ALLEGIANCE-OWING; OR, OF THE BETRAYING OF THE STATE INTO THE HANDS OF THE FICTION/FOREIGN-POWER. FOR THE C.U.S.A.F.-CONTRACT IS FOR THE **BILL OF THE RIGHTS: FOR THE ARTICLE OF THE FOUR (4): SECTION OF THE THREE(3),**

 17

Exhibit J-17

C.U.S.A.F.-CONTRACT.

45). **PERJURY**: FOR THE WILLFUL-ASSERTION OF THE MATTER OF THE FACT/OPINION/BELIEF/KNOWLEDGE OF THE MAKING BY THE WITNESS IN THE JUDICIAL-PROCEEDING AS THE PART OF THE PARTY'S-EVIDENCE, EITHER, UPON THE OATH OR IN THE FORM OF THE ALLOWANCE BY THE LAW OR FOR THE SUBSTITUTION FOR THE OATH, WHETHER THE EVIDENCE IS IN THE PRESENTMENT IN AN OPEN-COURT, OR IN THE AFFIDAVITS OR OTHERWISE, FOR THE ASSERTION THAT THE MATERIAL-FACT IS BY THE ISSUE/POINT OR THE INQUIRY AND OF THE KNOWING, BY THE WITNESS IN THE FALSE-STATEMENT. FOR THE PERJURY IS OF THE WILLFUL-CRIMINAL-COMMITMENT BY THE LAWFUL-OATH IN THE ADMINISTRATION OF THE OATH, IN THE JUDICIAL-PROCEEDING AND FOR THE PARTY/CITIZEN/PERSON IS BY THE SWEARING OR DECLARATION AND AFFIRMATION IN THE TRUTH FOR THE WILLFUL, ABSOLUTE, AND FALSEHOOD, IN THE MATTERS-MATERIAL FOR THE ISSUE/POINT OF THE QUESTION.

46). **FOR THE PERJURY: REF. TITLE 18: U.S.A. CODES: SECTION: 1621 (GENERAL)**; FOR THE CITIZEN(S) IN THE PARTY IS OF THE GUILTY OF THE PERJURY IF IN THE OFFICIAL-PROCEEDING UNDER THE PARTY-NAMES FOR THE FALSE-STATEMENT UNDER THE OATH/EQUIVALENT-AFFIRMATION/SWEARS/AFFIRMATION IN THE TRUTH OF THE STATEMENT-PREVIOUS-MAKING. [REFERRING BY THE OATH/AFFIRMATION] WHEN THE STATEMENT IS OF THE MATERIAL FOR THE PARTY IN THE TRUTH/BELIEVE-STATEMENT [MUST BE DEFINED] FOR THE BEING TRUE.

47). **FOR THE MALICE**: FOR THE PERSONAL-HATE OR ILL-WILL IS FOR THE STATE OF THE MIND, FOR THE RECKLESS-BEHAVIOR OF THE LAW AND OF THE LEGAL-RIGHTS OF THE CITIZEN(S) IN THE PARTY.

48). **FOR THE C.U.S.A.F.-CONTRACT, TORT, TITLE: 42: U.S.A. CODES: SECTION: 1983**: FOR THE PARTY-WHO UNDER THE COLOR OF THE STATUTE/ORDINANCE/REGULATION/CUSTOM/USAGE, OF THE STATE OF THE CALIFORNIA OR TERRITORY OF THE U.S.A., SUBJECTS OR IS FOR THE CAUSING BY THE SUBJECTING, OF THE CITIZEN/PARTY/PERSON OF THE U.S.A.; OR, FOR ANY CITIZEN/PARTY/PERSON WITHIN THE JURISDICTION IS WITH THE DEPRIVATION OF THE C.U.S.A.F.-CONTRACT FOR THE RIGHTS/PRIVILEGES/IMMUNITIES IN THE SECURITY BY THE C.U.S.A.F.-CONTRACT AND LAWS ARE BY THE LIABILITY FOR THE CITIZEN/PARTY/PERSON OF THE INJURY IN THE ACTION AT THE LAW-SUIT IN THE EQUITY OR OTHER-PROCEEDING FOR THE REDRESS.

49). **FOR THE TORT**: OF THE CIVIL-WRONG-INJURY, IS WITH THE COURT BY THE PROVISIONS BY A REMEDY IN THE FORM OF THE ACTION FOR THE DAMAGES. OF THE VIOLATION OF THE DUTY IN THE EXAMINATION BY THE GENERAL-LAW OR OTHERWISE UPON ALL CITIZEN(S)/PARTY(S)/PERSON(S) FOR THE OCCUPYING OF THE RELATION, FOR EACH CITIZEN/PARTY/PERSON IS BY THE INVOLVEMENT IN THE GIVING-TRANSACTION.

50). **FOR THE LARCENY BY THE FRAUD AND DECEPTION**: FAILS: BY THE CORRECTING OF THE FALSE-IMPRESSION. BY THE DECEIVER CREATION/REINFORCE, OR THE DECEIVER IS FOR THE KNOWING BY THE INFLUENCING OF THE

Exhibit J-18

PARTY/PERSON/CITIZEN IS BY THE STANDING IN THE FIDUCIARY/CONFIDENTIAL: RELATIONSHIP.

51). FOR THE FIDUCIARY: FOR THE CITIZEN/PARTY/PERSON BY THE DUTY FOR THE CREATION OF THE UNDERTAKING OR BY THE ACTING FOR THE BENEFIT OF THE CITIZEN/PARTY/PERSON IN THE SUBJECT-MATTERS.

52). FOR THE RACKETEERING: THE ORGANIZATION OF A CONSPIRACY BY THE COMMITTING OF THE CRIMES OF THE EXTORTION/COERCION/ATTEMPT BY THE COMMITTING OF THE EXTORTION/COERCION.
FOR THE FEAR OF THE LEGAL NECESSARY-ELEMENT IN THE EXTORTION BY THE INDUCING BY THE ORAL/WRITTEN-THREATS BY THE NEGLECT BY THE FAILURE FOR THE STOPPING OF THE INJURY OF THE PERSON/PARTY/PROPERTY BY THE PARTY/PERSON/CITIZEN OF THE THREATENING-PARTY. FOR THE TITLE: 42: U.S.A. CODES: SECTION: 1985(3).

53). FOR THE RACKETEERING: IS BY ANY DEMANDING/SOLICITING/RECEIVING OF ANY THING OF THE VALUE BY THE OWNER/PROPRIETOR/PERSON/CITIZEN/PARTY FOR THE FINANCIAL-INTEREST IN THE BUSINESS, BY THE MEANS OF THE THREAT (THROUGH THE USE OF THE CONTEMPT OF THE COURT-ORDER BY THE PAYING OF THE FEES-THAT ARE UNDER THE PROHIBITION), EXPRESS/IMPLICATION, OF THE PROMISE, BY THE PERSON/CITIZEN/PARTY DEMANDING/SOLICIT1NG/ RECEIVING OF THE PROPERTY/ENTITY OF THE VALUE BY THE WILL FOR THE CAUSING OF THE COMPETITION OF THE PERSON/CITIZEN/PARTY BY THE PAYMENT; DEMAND SOLICIT/RECEIVING BY THE DIMINISHMENT OR ELIMINATION.

54). FOR THE EXTORTION: FOR THE OBTAINING OF THE PROPERTY OF THE PARTY/CITIZEN/PERSON, FOR THE INDUCTION BY THE WRONGFUL-USE OF THE ACTUAL OR THREATENING-FORCE, OR FEAR, OR UNDER THE COLOR OF THE OFFICIAL-RIGHT. REF. TITLE: 18: U.S.A. CODES: SECTION: 971.

55). FOR THE RANSOM: TITLE: 18: U.S.A. CODES: SECTION: 1202: FOR THE FEES/MONEY/PRICE/CONSIDERATION-PAYMENT/ IN A DEMAND FOR THE REDEMPTION OF THE KIDNAP-PARTY. FOR THE PAYMENT FOR THE RELEASE OF THE PARTY/PERSON/CITIZEN/PLAINTIFF/RESPONDENT OF THE CAPTIVITY. FOR THE PARTY WITH THE KNOWLEDGE RECEIVES/POSSESSES/DISPOSES OF THE PROPERTY: FOR THE **COMMITMENT OF THE** CRIME.

56). FOR THE DURESS: FOR THE ILLEGAL-PURPOSE/THREAT OF THE PARTY/CITIZEN/PERSON FOR THE MENTAL OR FINANCIAL-HARM BY THE COERCING: (TITLE: 28 CHAPTER: 85: U.S.A. CODES: SECTION: 1359) FOR THE WILL OF THE PARTY/CITIZEN/PERSON/ANOTHER, AND BY THE INDUCING OF THE PARTY/PERSON/CITIZEN BY THE DOING OF THE ACT-CONTRARY BY THE CITIZEN'S/PARTY'S/PERSON'S: FREE-WILL. FOR THE DURESS IS FOR THE INCLUDING OF THE SAME INJURIES/THREATS/RESTRAINMENT BY THE EXERCISE BY THE PERSON(S)/CITIZEN(S)/PLAINTIFF(S) OF THE DISTINGUISHABLE OF THE UNDUE-INFLUENCE BECAUSE IN THE LATTER, FOR THE WRONGDOER IS IN THE FIDUCIARY-CAPACITY OR IN THE POSITION OF THE TRUST AND CONFIDENCE WITH THE RESPECT OF THE VICTIM OF THE UNDUE-INFLUENCE.

R-J/S

Exhibit J-19

58). FOR THE MALPRACTICE: PROFESSIONAL-MISCONDUCT/UNREASONABLE-LACK OF THE SKILL. FOR THE MALPRACTICE IS BY THE APPLICATION BY THE CONDUCT OF THE LAWYER(S)/ATTORNEY(S) FOR THE FAILURE OF THE RENDERING OF THE PROFESSIONAL-SERVICES BY THE EXERCISING OF THE DEGREE OF THE SKILL AND LEARNING BY THE CIRCUMSTANCES IN THE COMMUNITY BY THE AVERAGE-PRUDENT-REPUTABLE FOR THE MEMBERS OF THE PROFESSION WITH THE RESULT OF THE INJURY/LOSS/DAMAGE BY THE RECIPIENT OF THE SERVICES OR BY THE ATTORNEY(S)/LAWYER(S). FOR THE MALPRACTICE IS FOR THE PROFESSIONAL-MISCONDUCT-NEGLECT OF THE SKILL OR FIDELITY IN THE PROFESSIONAL/FIDUCIARY-DUTIES/EVIL-PRACTICE/ILLEGAL/IMMORAL-CONDUCT.

59). FOR THE PREJUDICE: FOR THE FOREJUDGMENT/ BIAS/PRECONCEIVE/OPINION/LEANING-TOWARDS-ONE-SIDE OF THE CAUSE FOR THE REASON-OTHER THAN THE CONVICTION OF THE JUSTICE.

60). FOR THE DISCRIMINATION: FOR THE TREATMENT OF THE EQUALITY OF THE PARTY(S) BY THE NEGLECT OF THE DISTINCTION BETWEEN THE PARTY(S) IN THE FAVOR OF THE OTHER-PARTY(S), OUT, OF THE FAVOR, FOR THE TITLE: VII OF THE 1964 CIVIL, RIGHTS, ACT.

61). FOR THE FALSE SWEARING: FOR THE PERIOD/TIME OF THE LIMITATIONS FOR THE PROSECUTION IS OF THE TIME BY THE FIRST-STATEMENT. FOR THE PARTY WITH THE KNOWLEDGE IN THE TRUTH IS UNDER THE OATH/AFFIRMATION FOR THE DECLARATION/MAKING/SUBSCRIPTION OF THE FALSE-STATEMENT BY THE OFFICER OF THE COURT AND IS BY THE FAILURE FOR THE BELIEVING IN THE TRUTH, IS OF THE GUILTY OF THE CLASS-D-MISDEMEANOR.

62). FOR THE BREACH: FOR THE BREAKING/VIOLATION OF THE LAW/RIGHT/ OBLIGATION/ENGAGEMENT/DUTY BY THE COMMISSION/OMISSION/CONTRACT BY THE EXISTING WITH THE ONE/PARTY(S) UNDER THE CONTRACT FOR THE (PERFORMING/ DUTY/RESPONSIBILITY/FIDUCIARY/TERMS/PROMISE/CONDITION) OF THE (NEGLIGENT FAILS/LIE-COMPLIANCE) OF THE CONTRACT BY THE PARTY(S).

63). FOR THE TITLE: 42: U.S.A. CODES: SECTION: 1986 FOR THE KNOWLEDGE OF THE LAW AND NEGLECT BY THE FAILURE FOR THE STOPPING AND CORRECTING OF THE WRONG, IN THE DEFINITION FOR EVERY CITIZEN IN THE PARTY, WHO, FOR THE HAVING WITH THE KNOWLEDGE FOR ANY WRONGS IN A CONSPIRACY BY THE DOING, IN THE SECTION: 1985 OF THE TITLE OR ARE BY THE COMMITMENT, AND BY THE HAVING-POWER FOR THE PREVENTION OR AIDING IN THE PREVENTION OR THE COMMISSION OF THE CRIME BY THE NEGLECT OR REFUSAL FOR THE STOPPING OF THE WRONG OF THE DOING, WHEN THE WRONGFUL-ACTS ARE OF THE COMMITMENT, FOR THE LIABLE OF THE PARTY FOR THE INJURY ON CITIZENS IN THE PARTY-LEGAL-REPRESENTATIVES, FOR ALL DAMAGES IN THE CAUSE BY SUCH WRONGFUL-ACT, WHICH SUCH CITIZEN IN THE PARTY BY THE REASONABLE-DILIGENCE IS UNDER THE PREVENTION FOR ANY NUMBER OF THE CITIZENS IN THE PARTY IN THE GUILT OF THE WRONGFUL-NEGLECT BY THE REFUSAL IS BY THE JOINDER AS THE RESPONDENT(S) FOR THE WRONGS IN THE ACTION.

20

Exhibit J-20

64). **FOR THE TITLE: 42: U.S.A. CODES: SECTION: 1985(2) FOR THE OBSTRUCTING-JUSTICE**, INTIMIDATING PARTY, WITNESS: IF FOR THE TWO/MORE-CITIZENS IN THE STATE OF THE CALIFORNIA/TERRITORY OF THE U.S.A. FOR THE CONSPIRE BY THE DETERRING, BY THE FORCING/INTIMIDATION/TREATING OF THE PARTY/WITNESS IN THE COURT OF THE U.S.A. BY THE ATTENDING OF THE WITNESS IN THE COURT OR BY THE TESTIFYING FOR THE MATTER-PENDING IN THE COURT: OF THE FREE/FULL/TRUTHFUL, FOR THE MATTER, BY THE INJURING OF THE PARTY/WITNESS IN THE CITIZEN'S: BEHALF/PROPERTY ON THE ACCOUNT OF THE CITIZEN IS FOR THE HAVING BY THE ATTENDING/TESTIFYING/INFLUENCING OF THE VERDICT/PRESENTMENT/INDICTMENT OF THE GRAND/**PETIT**: JUROR, IN THE COURT, OR BY THE INJURING THE JUROR IN THE PARTY/CITIZEN/SELF/PROPERTY ON THE ACCOUNT OF THE VERDICT/PRESENTMENT/INDICTMENT FOR THE LAWFUL-ASSESSMENT BY THE CITIZEN BEING/HAVING BEEN THE JUROR, OR TWO/MORE-CITIZENS BY THE CONSPIRACY FOR THE PURPOSE OF THE IMPEDING/HINDERING/OBSTRUCTING/DEFEATING IN THE MATTER OF THE DUE-COURSE OF THE JUSTICE IS FOR THE STATE OF THE CALIFORNIA/TERRITORY OF THE U.S.A. WITH THE INTENT BY THE DENYING BY THE CITIZEN OF THE **EQUAL-PROTECTION OF THE LAW** BY THE INJURING OF THE CITIZEN/CITIZEN'S PROPERTY FOR THE LAWFUL-ENFORCEMENT OR ATTENDING BY THE ENFORCING OF THE RIGHT OF THE CITIZEN/CLASS OF THE CITIZENS, BY THE **EQUAL-PROTECTION OF THE LAW**.

65). **FOR THE TITLE: 42: U.S.A. CODES: SECTION: 1985(3)** FOR THE DEPRIVING PARTY OF THE C.U.S.A.F.-CONTRACT RIGHTS/PRIVILEGES: WHEN THE JUDGE AND ATTORNEY OR ANY-CITIZEN(S) IN THE PARTY IN THE STATE OF THE CALIFORNIA/TERRITORY OF THE U.S.A., CONSPIRE AND GO IN THE DISGUISE, FOR THE PURPOSE OF THE DEPRIVING, EITHER THE DIRECTION OR INDIRECTION, OF THE CITIZEN/CLASS OF THE CITIZEN(S) IN THE PARTY OF THE EQUAL-PROTECTION OF THE LAW OF THE **EQUAL-PRIVILEGES AND IMMUNITIES** UNDER THE LAW FOR THE PURPOSE OF THE PREVENTION OR HINDRANCE OF THE CONSTITUTION-AUTHORITIES OF THE CALIFORNIA/TERRITORY BY THE INCORPORATION AND FOR THE SECURITY BY ALL CITIZENS IN THE PARTY WITHIN THE STATE OF THE CALIFORNIA TERRITORY OF THE U.S.A. OF THE **EQUAL-PROTECTION OF THE LAWS**, OR OF THE JUDGE/ATTORNEY/CITIZENS IN THE PARTY BY THE CONSPIRACY FOR THE PREVENTION BY THE FORCE/INTIMIDATION OR THREATENING OF THE CITIZEN IN THE PARTY FOR THE ENTITLEMENT OF THE VOTE BY THE GIVING or THE PARTY-SUPPORT/ADVOCACY IN THE LEGAL-MANNER, OR BY THE INJURING OF THE CITIZEN/PARTY/SELF OR PROPERTY OF THE SUPPORT/ADVOCACY IN THE CASE OF THE CONSPIRACY IN THE TITLE: 42: U.S.A. CODES: SECTION: 1985(1), BY THE ONE/MORE-CITIZEN(S)/PARTY BY THE ENGAGEMENT BY THE ACT IN THE FURTHERANCE OF THE OBJECT OF THE CONSPIRACY BY THE CITIZEN/PARTY/PERSON IS OF THE INJURY IN THE CITIZEN(S)/PARTY/SELF/PROPERTY BY THE DEPRIVING OF THE HAVING/EXERCISING OF THE RIGHTS/PRIVILEGE OF THE CITIZEN(S)/PARTY OF THE U.S.A., FOR THE CITIZEN IN THE PARTY OF THE INJURY/DEPRIVATION BY THE ACTION FOR THE RECOVERY OF THE DAMAGES IN THE OCCASION BY THE INJURY/DEPRIVATION AGAINST THE CITIZEN(S)/PARTY OR MORE, OF THE CONSPIRATORS.

66). **FOR THE TITLE: 18: U.S.A. CODES: SECTION: 242(1) FOR THE DEPRIVATION OF THE RIGHTS UNDER THE COLOR OF THE LAW BY THE OFFICERS OF THE COURT**:

21

Exhibit J-21

WHOEVER, UNDER THE COLOR OF THE LAW/STATUTE/ ORDINANCE/REGULATION/CUSTOM BY THE KNOWLEDGE FOR THE SUBJECTION OF THE PARTY IN THE STATE OF THE CALIFORNIA, TERRITORY OF THE U.S.A./DISTRICT OF THE U.S.A. INTO THE DEPRIVATION OF THE RIGHTS/PRIVILEGES/IMMUNITIES OF THE SECURING/PROTECTING OF THE C.U.S.A.F.-CONTRACT OR THE LAWS OF THE U.S.A., BY THE TWO-DIFFERENT-PUNISHMENTS/PAINS/PENALTIES/TREATMENT ON THE ACCOUNT OF THE PARTY-BEING-ALIEN = (BY THE FAILURE OF THE PUNCTUATION IN THE NAME = FICTION/FOREIGN), OR BY THE REASON OF THE PARTY'S-COLOR-/RACE, THAN ARE BY THE PRESCRIPTION FOR THE PUNISHMENT OF THE CITIZENS IS FOR THE FINE OF THE $10,000. UNDER THIS TITLE OR IMPRISONMENT OF THE TEN-YEARS OR UNDER OR BOTH, UNDER THE **FICTION/FOREIGN-FRINGE-FLAG**.

67). FOR THE KNOWLEDGE: PERCEPTION OF THE TRUTH; LEARNING: INFORMATION-POWER OF THE KNOWING.

68). NOTE: FOR THE JURISDICTION OF THE SUBJECT-MATTER(NOUN) IS BY THE ASSIGNMENT BY THE ARTICLE "THE" AND FOR THE ASSIGNMENT OF THE AUTHORITY(JURISDICTION) IS THROUGH THE PREPOSITION IN THE **PRESENT- TENSE**.

69). FOR THE PREPOSITIONS: BY, OF, FOR, WITH, IN, OUT, INTO, UNDER, OVER, WITHIN, THROUGH, ARE OF THE PRESENT-TENSE-JURISDICTIONAL-PREPOSITION FOR THE USE OF THE PLEADING IN THE REAL-TIME-JURISDICTION FOR THE DISQUALIFICATION AND SANCTIONING OF THE FILING OF THE FRIVOLOUS-ACTION IN A LAW-SUIT. **WHERE THE NOUNS ARE IN THE VERB.**

70). FOR THE PROHIBITION OF THE PRESUMPTIONS/ASSUMPTION/CONCLUSIONS BEFORE THE FACTS IS FOR THE DISQUALIFICATION BY THE LOOKING-UP OF THE **DUE PROCESS** FOR THE VIOLATION OF THE LAW.

71). FOR THE PROHIBITION OF THE PRONOUNS: FOR THE C.U.S.A.F.-CONTRACT IS UNDER THE SPECIFIC-DEFINITION WITH THE KNOWLEDGE BEFORE THE JUDGE, FOR ALL PRESUMPTION, ASSUMPTIONS AND OPINIONS ARE UNDER THE DISQUALIFICATION. FOR THE DISCLAIMER OF THE RESPONSIBILITY OF THE FACTS. FOR THE JUDGE IS UNDER THE TRUTH(NOUN) IN THE JURISDICTION FOR THE DISQUALIFYING OF THE PRONOUNS FOR THE COURT.

72). FOR THE ADJECTIVES ARE OF THE COLOR OF THE OPINIONS OF THE NOUNS/SUBJECT-MATTER, FOR THE PREJUDICE OF THE NOUN/FACTS IN THE CASE. FOR ANY TIME, FOR THE TWO OR MORE-NOUNS ARE FOR THE COMING-TOGETHER, FOR THE LAST-NOUN OF THE NOUN-PHRASE, IS OF THE NOUN-JURISDICTION. FOR THE NOUNS BY THE LEFT/IN-FRONT OF THE FOLLOWING-NOUN ARE IN THE ADJECTIVE OR PROPER-ADJECTIVES IN THE CASE, OF THE **ADJECTIVES ARE OF THE FICTION** OF THE OPINION/PRESUMPTION OF THE FACTS AND ARE IN THE DISQUALIFICATION AS THE FICTIONS IN THE LEGAL-JURISDICTION OF THE STATEMENTS IN THE COURT. FOR THE FICTION-NAME AS THE WRITING OF THE "DAVID WYNN MILLER": IS A DEAD-FICTION, AND IS BY THE WRITING AS David-Wynn: Miller, FOR THE LIVING-ENTITY OF THE CITIZEN IN THE PARTY.

73). FOR THE ADVERBS IS FOR THE MODIFICATION OF THE VERB, ADJECTIVE AND

R-J:S

Exhibit J-22

ADVERB INTO AN OPINION AND FOR THE FAILURE OF THE FACT. **FOR THE ADVERB IS FOR THE CHANGING OF THE NOUN INTO A VERB WHEN THE PLACEMENT OF THE ADVERB IS BEFORE THE NOUN**. FOR ANY FACT WITH ANY MODIFICATION IS BY A PREJUDICE/FICTION/OPINION/PRESUMPTION AND ASSUMPTION FOR THE TRUTH.
FOR THE VIOLATION OF THE FEDERAL-STYLES-MANUAL IS WITH THE INTERNATIONAL-TREATY FOR THE PROCEDURES OF THE COMMUNICATIONS.

DATE: 10, DAY OF THE SEPTEMBER, 2000 Robert-Joel: Simpson

DATE: 10, DAY OF THE SEPTEMBER, 2000 Robert-Joel: Simpson
Robert-Joel: Simpson

AS THE SOVEREIGN-CITIZEN
FOR THE PARTY.

Robert-Joel: Simpson
c/o 30-257: Monte-Vista-Way:
1000-Palms: California: 92276

23
R-J:S

Exhibit J-23

SUMMONS
(CITACION JUDICIAL)

NOTICE TO DEFENDANT: *(Aviso a Acusado)*
ROBERT JOEL SIMPSON and DOES 1 through 10, inclusive,

FOR COURT USE ONLY
(SOLO PARA USO DE LA CORTE)

YOU ARE BEING SUED BY PLAINTIFF: COUNTY OF RIVERSIDE, a
(A Ud. le está demandando)
political subdivision of the State of California

You have *30 CALENDAR DAYS* after this summons is served on you to file a typewritten response at this court.

A letter or phone call will not protect you; your typewritten response must be in proper legal form if you want the court to hear your case.

If you do not file your response on time, you may lose the case, and your wages, money and property may be taken without further warning from the court.

There are other legal requirements. You may want to call an attorney right away. If you do not know an attorney, you may call an attorney referral service or a legal aid office (listed in the phone book).

Después de que le entreguen esta citación judicial usted tiene un plazo de 30 DIAS CALENDARIOS para presentar una respuesta escrita a máquina en esta corte.

Una carta o una llamada telefónica no le ofrecerá protección; su respuesta escrita a máquina tiene que cumplir con las formalidades legales apropiadas si usted quiere que la corte escuche su caso.

Si usted no presenta su respuesta a tiempo, puede perder el caso, y le pueden quitar su salario, su dinero y otras cosasde su propiedad sin aviso adicional por parte de la corte.

Existen otros requisitos legales. Puede que usted quiera llamar a un abogado inmediatamente. Si no conoce a un abogado, puede llamar a un servicio de referencia de abogados o a una oficina de ayuda legal (vea el directorio telefónico).

CASE NUMBER: *(Número del Caso)*
INC 018853

The name and address of the court is: *(El nombre y dirección de la corte es)*
Riverside Superior Court
46-200 Oasis Street
46-200 Oasis Street
Riverside CA 92201

The name, address, and telephone number of plaintiff's attorney, or plaintiff without an attorney, is:
(El nombre, la dirección y el número de teléfono del abogado del demandante, o del demandante que no tiene abogado, es)
Carole A. Nunes Fong, Deputy 138008 (909) 955-6300
3535 Tenth Street, Suite 300
Riverside CA 92501

DATE: AUG 2 3 2000
(Fecha)

Clerk, by T. JOHNSON, Deputy
(Actuario) *(Delegado)*

(SEAL)

NOTICE TO THE PERSON SERVED: You are served

1. [X] as an individual defendant.
2. [ ] as the person sued under the fictitious name of *(specify)*:
3. [ ] on behalf of *(specify)*:

under: [ ] CCP 416.10 (corporation) [ ] CCP 416.60 (minor)
[ ] CCP 416.20 (defunct corporation) [ ] CCP 416.70 (conservatee)
[ ] CCP 416.40 (association or partnership) [ ] CCP 416.90 (individual)
[ ] other:

4. [X] by personal delivery on *(date)*:

Form Adopted for Mandatory Use
Judicial Council of California
982(a)(9) (Rev. January 1, 1984)

(See reverse for Proof of Service)
SUMMONS

CEB

CCP 412.20

Ex. 01

Exhibit J-24

WILLIAM C. KATZENSTEIN, County Counsel SBN 61681
JOE R. RANK, Assistant County Counsel SBN 113607
PAMELA J. ANDERSON, Deputy County Counsel SBN 123446
CAROLE A. NUNES FONG, Deputy County Counsel SBN 138008
3535 Tenth Street, Suite 300
Riverside, California 92501
(909) 955-6300

Attorneys for the County of Riverside

FILED
SUPERIOR COURT OF CALIFORNIA
COUNTY OF RIVERSIDE
AUG 23 2000
T. JOHNSON

SUPERIOR COURT OF THE STATE OF CALIFORNIA

IN AND FOR THE COUNTY OF RIVERSIDE

COUNTY OF RIVERSIDE, a political subdivision of the State of California, Plaintiff, v. JOEL ROBERT SIMPSON, and DOES 1 through 10, inclusive, Defendants.	CASE NO. Inc 618853 GENERAL CIVIL COMPLAINT FOR INJUNCTIVE RELIEF Stat. Conf: 2-20-01 Time: 8:30 a.m. Dept: 2F

Plaintiff, COUNTY OF RIVERSIDE, complains of defendants above-named and alleges:

I.

FIRST CAUSE OF ACTION

VIOLATION OF RIVERSIDE COUNTY

LAND USE ORDINANCE NO. 457

1. Plaintiff, County of Riverside ("County") is, at all times material to this complaint has been a general law county and a political subdivision of the State of California.

2. Plaintiff is informed and believes and based thereon alleges that defendant, Joel Robert Simpson is the owner of that certain real property located at 30257 Monte Vista Way, Thousand Palms, within the unincorporated area of Riverside County, California, and further described as Assessor's Parcel

///

COMPLAINT FOR INJUNCTIVE RELIEF 1

Evi. 03

Exhibit J-25

Number 650-034-007-3 ("The Property"). A copy of the Grant Deed and Riverside County Assessor's Roll is attached as Exhibit "A" to this complaint and incorporated by this reference.

3. Plaintiff is informed and believes and based thereon alleges that defendant Joel Robert Simpson is an occupant of The Property and a resident of the County of Riverside.

4. Defendants DOES 1 through 10, inclusive, are sued and designated by fictitious names pursuant to Section 474 of the Code of Civil Procedure, for the reason that their true names and capacities are unknown by Plaintiff. Plaintiff prays leave to and will amend its complaint to show the fictitiously named defendants' true names and capacities when ascertained.

5. At all times material to this complaint, Riverside County Ordinance ("RCO") No. 457 has been in effect. Section 2 of RCO No. 457 incorporates by reference the Uniform Administrative Code ("UAC"). Section 301.1 of the UAC prohibits any person from erecting, constructing, enlarging, altering, repairing, moving, improving, removing, or converting any building, structure, or building service equipment without first obtaining a permit from the building official.

6. Section 308.1 of the UAC prohibits making connections from a source of energy, fuel or power to building service equipment without first obtaining approval from the Building Official. Building service equipment is defined as plumbing, mechanical, and electrical equipment including piping, wiring, fixtures, and other accessories which provide sanitation, lighting, heating, ventilation, cooling, and refrigeration facilities essential to the occupancy of the building or structure for its designated use. (UAC Section 103.)

7. Section 309.1 of the UAC prohibits the use or occupancy of any building or structure until the building official has issued a certificate of occupancy. Section 309.3 further prohibits issuance of a certificate of occupancy until a final inspection has occurred and the building official has found no violations of the code or other laws that are enforced by the code enforcement agency.

8. Section 6 of RCO No. 457 incorporates by reference the Uniform Plumbing Code ("UPC"). Section 103.1 of the UPC prohibits any person from installing, altering, repairing, replacing or remodeling any plumbing system that requires a permit without first obtaining a separate plumbing permit for each separate building or structure. Plumbing permits are required to install potable water piping, building sewers, and plumbing fixtures. Every building in which plumbing fixtures are installed must be

COMPLAINT FOR INJUNCTIVE RELIEF 2

Evi. 03

Exhibit J-26

connected to a public sewer system or, if a public system is not available, an approved private sewer system. (See UPC Sections 305.1 and 305.2).

9. Section 7 of RCO No. 457 incorporates by reference the National Electric Code ("NEC") and requires that all electrical installations be in accordance with RCO No. 457 and the NEC, as modified by RCO No. 457. The NEC specifically states that its purpose is the practical safeguarding of persons and property from hazards arising from the use of electricity and that it contains provisions considered necessary for safety. (See NEC Article 90-1.)

10. Since at least August 17, 1999, and continuing to the present, a three (3) story structure has been erected, constructed, enlarged, altered, repaired, moved, improved, removed, or converted and occupied as a dwelling, all without permits and in violation of RCO No. 457, Section 2, and UAC Section 301.1 and without first having obtained a certificate of occupancy or final inspection of the premises from the County as required by UAC Sections 309.1 and 309.3. Hazardous, unapproved, unpermitted, and illegal plumbing and electrical systems have been installed in the structure and on The Property including, but not limited to, connections and piping for water, wiring, fixtures, and other accessories which provide sanitation, lighting, heating, ventilation, cooling, and refrigeration facilities in violation of RCO No. 457, Sections 6 and 7, UPC Section 103.1, and UAC section 308.1. In addition, the structure discharges household wastewater and sewage that drains into an unapproved private sewage system in violation UPC Sections 305.1 and 305.2.

11. Since at least June 16, 2000, and continuing to the present, a patio cover has been erected or constructed in the rear yard of The Property extending approximately twelve (12) feet from the structure toward the rear Property line without first having obtained the required permits in violation of RCO No. 457, Section 2, and UAC Section 301.1.

12. RCO No. 725, Sections 4 and 9, Subdivision (a) authorizes County Counsel to commence proceedings for the abatement, removal, correction and enjoinment of any act or practice that constitutes a violation of RCO No. 457. Sections 11 and 15 of Ordinance 725, and Government Code Section 25845, subdivisions (b) and (c), authorize an award of costs, including attorneys fees incurred in connection with an action to abate a violation of its land use ordinances.

///

COMPLAINT FOR INJUNCTIVE RELIEF 3

Exhibit J-27

13. Plaintiff has sustained great and irreparable injury because the conditions on The Property violate laws intended for the general health, safety, and welfare of the public and, as such, constitute a continuing public nuisance.

14. Plaintiff cannot be fully compensated in damages and is without an adequate remedy at law because the exact amount of the damages to the general public's health, safety, and welfare is unascertainable and because injunctive relief is necessary to secure compliance with the laws of the County of Riverside and the State of California and to abate a public nuisance.

II.

SECOND CAUSE OF ACTION

VIOLATION OF RIVERSIDE COUNTY

LAND USE ORDINANCE NO. 348

15. Plaintiff realleges and incorporates by reference as though fully set forth herein each and every one of the allegations contained in Paragraphs 1 through 14, inclusive, of this complaint.

16. At all times material to this complaint, Riverside County's Land Use Ordinance No. 348 has been in effect. Ordinance No. 348 prohibits uses of property that are not enumerated as a permitted use within the respective zoning classification.

17. The zoning classification of The Property is R-1 (One-Family Dwellings). Section 6.1 of Ordinance No. 348 permits one family dwellings within an R-1 zone but the size and dimensions of the dwelling and yard must conform to the requirements of the ordinance. Specifically, the dwelling cannot cover more than fifty percent (50%) of any lot, the front yard must be at least twenty (20) feet measured from the dwelling to the front lot line, and the rear yard must be at least ten (10) feet from the dwelling to the rear lot line. (RCO 348, Section 6.2.) Any deviation from these requirements constitutes a violation of Section 6.1 of RCO No.348 in that the use exceeds what is permitted within the R-1 zone.

18. Section 18.19 of RCO No. 348 prohibits encroachments into yard setbacks. Yards must be open and unobstructed from the ground to the sky and kept free of all structural encroachments. (RCO No. 348, Section 18.19)

19. Since at least August 17, 1999, and continuing to the present, the dwelling on The Property has covered more than fifty percent (50%) of the lot. The lot size of The Property is approximately seven

COMPLAINT FOR INJUNCTIVE RELIEF 4

Evi. 05

Exhibit J-28

thousand four hundred and five (7405) square feet. The dwelling covers approximately five thousand one hundred and forty-six (5146) square feet of the parcel, nearly seventy percent (70%) of the total lot size, in violation of Sections 6.1 and 6.2 of RCO No. 348. In addition, the front yard is only about three (3) feet measured from the dwelling to the front lot line instead of the required twenty (20) feet in violation of Sections 6.1 and 6.2 of RCO No. 348.

20. Since at least June 16, 2000, and continuing to the present, a patio cover has been erected or constructed on The Property without the required permits or approvals. This unpermitted patio cover extends approximately twelve (12) feet from the dwelling toward the rear lot line leaving an unobstructed yard area of only about four (4) feet instead of the required ten (10) feet in violation of Sections 6.1, 6.2, and 18.19 of RCO No. 348.

21. RCO No. 725, Sections 4 and 9, Subdivision (a) authorizes County Counsel to commence proceedings for the abatement, removal, correction, and enjoinment of any act or practice that constitutes a violation of RCO No. 348. Sections 11 and 15 of Ordinance 725, and Government Code Section 25845, subdivisions (b) and (c), authorize an award of costs, including attorneys fees incurred in connection with an action to abate a violation of its land use ordinances.

III.

THIRD CAUSE OF ACTION

PUBLIC NUISANCE

22. Plaintiff realleges and incorporates by reference as though fully set forth herein, each and every one of the allegations contained in paragraphs 1 through 21, inclusive, of this complaint.

23. Defendants, through their wrongful and unlawful activity previously described in this complaint, since at least August 17, 1999 and June 16, 2000, and continuing through the present, have maintained a public nuisance pursuant to Sections 3479 and 3480 of the Civil Code in that such uses of The Property affect at the same time an entire community or neighborhood, or a considerable number of persons, and constitutes an obstruction to the free use of the property so as to interfere with the comfortable enjoyment of life or property.

24. Riverside County Ordinance No. 725, Section 4, specifically declares that any condition caused, maintained, or permitted to exist in violation of any of the provisions of RCO Nos. 348 and 457 to

COMPLAINT FOR INJUNCTIVE RELIEF 5

Eoi 06

Exhibit J-29

be unlawful and a public nuisance. As such, the commission of conduct prohibited by Ordinance Nos. 348 and 457 is a public nuisance per se.

WHEREFORE, Plaintiff prays for judgment against defendants, their successors and assigns, as follows:

1. That The Property and existing conditions thereon be declared in violation of RCO Nos. 348 and 457, the UAC, UPC, and NEC, and a continuing public nuisance;

2. For a permanent injunction enjoining defendants and their agents, servants, employees, and all persons acting for them from maintaining the violations set forth in Paragraph 1 of this prayer;

3. For a permanent injunction compelling defendants, their successors and assigns, to abate all conditions on The Property which cause the nuisance by completing all of the following actions within sixty (60) days of the date of this judgment including, but not limited to:

a. Removing all buildings, structures, and sewage systems from The Property for which the required permits and approvals from the County of Riverside have not been obtained;

4. That, if defendants fail to complete the actions described in Paragraph 3 of this prayer within sixty (60) days of the date of the Order or Judgment, the County of Riverside, its employees, agents, contractors, or representatives be authorized to enter upon the Real Property without consent, warrant or further order of the court to abate the conditions described in Paragraph 1 of this prayer by demolishing and removing from The Property all buildings, structures, and sewage systems for which the required permits and approvals have not been obtained from the County of Riverside;

5. That recordation of an abstract of judgment in this case constitutes a prior lien over any lien that may be held on The Property by any defendant to this action;

6. For abatement costs and costs of this suit, including reasonable attorneys fees; and,

7. For such other and further relief as the court deems just and proper.

DATED: August 23, 2000

WILLIAM C. KATZENSTEIN, County Counsel
PAMELA J. ANDERSON, Deputy County Counsel
CAROLE A. NUNES FONG, Deputy County Counsel

Carole A. Nunes Fong
Attorneys for County of Riverside

g:\property\code\bs\simpson\complaint.

COMPLAINT FOR INJUNCTIVE RELIEF 6

Evi 07

Exhibit J-30

06-30-2000 ASSESSMENT-ROLL FOR THE YEAR 2000-2001 (PRFMF270) PAGE 122294

ASSESSEE, ADDRESS, DESCRIPTION	FV	TRA	ASMNT NO	LAND	STR	T/V PERS PROP	EXEMPTIONS		NET TOT
HOECK KENNETH H. HOECK ALLA D. M/T C/O K M HOECK M/T 4790 CAUGHLIN PKY NO 400 RENO NV 89509 USE YY BASE YR 1979 CONVEY 026495 03/1966 PUI Y04-000-0 LOT 216 MB 028/061 SHANGRI LA PALMS UNIT 8	803 TC	061-030 0-00	650-034-005-1	803					803
WARREN C. L. TR WARREN VIDA C. TR M/T P O BOX 7257 MOHAVE VALLEY AZ 86440 USE YR BASE YR 1994 CONVEY 391754 10/1993 STT PUI R07-008-0 LOT 215 MB 028/061 SHANGRI LA PALMS UNIT 8	17689 TC	061-030 0-00	650-034-006-2	17689					17689
SIMPSON JOEL R. 30257 MONTE VISTA WAY THOUSAND PLMS 92276 SOLD FOR TAXES 1996-650034007-0000 USE R1 BASE YR 1983 MULT CONVEY 029287 02/1985 JTN PUI R01-001-2 LOT 214 MB 028/061 SHANGRI LA PALMS UNIT 8	32177 TC	061-030 0-00	650-034-007-3	8241	23936		HOX	7000	25177
DE LA PAZ ROBERT DE LA PAZ GUADALUPE M/T 31690 THELMA AVE THOUSAND PALMS, CA 92276 30281 MONTE VISTA WAY USE R1 BASE YR 1975 CONVEY 047732 05/1970 LOT 213 MB 028/061 SHANGRI LA PALMS UNIT 8	10692 TC	061-030 0-00	650-034-008-4	776	9916				10692
IBARRA JUAN G. IBARRA AMELIA G. M/T JUAN GONSALES IBARRA M/T 30305 MONTEVISTA WAY THOUSAND PALMS, CA 92276 30315 MONTE VISTA WAY USE R1 BASE YR 1976 CONVEY 110688 09/1975 LOT 212 MB 028/061 SHANGRI LA PALMS UNIT 8	14493 TC	061-030 0-00	650-034-009-5	803	13689		HOX	7000	7492

Ex. 08

Exhibit J-31

RECORDING REQUESTED BY

Continental Land Title Co.

AND WHEN RECORDED MAIL THIS DEED AND, UNLESS OTHERWISE SHOWN BELOW, MAIL TAX STATEMENTS TO:

29287

NAME Joel Simpson
ADDRESS 30257 Monte Vista Way
CITY & STATE Thousand Palms, Calif.
ZIP 92276

Title Order No. Escrow No.

RECEIVED FOR RECORD AT 8:30 O'CLOCK A.M.
At Request of CONTINENTAL LAND TITLE CO.
FEB 13 1985
Recorded in Official Records of Riverside County, California
William E. Conerly
RECORDER
Fees $

SPACE ABOVE THIS LINE FOR RECORDER'S USE

GRANT DEED

A-4406-03

The undersigned declares that the documentary transfer tax is $ No consideration and is
☐ computed on the full value of the interest or property conveyed, or is
☐ computed on the full value less the value of liens or encumbrances remaining thereon at the time of sale. The land, tenements or realty is located in
☐ unincorporated area ☐ city of and

FOR A VALUABLE CONSIDERATION, receipt of which is hereby acknowledged,

Bradley J. Franks, a single man

hereby GRANT(S) to

Joel R. Simpson, an unmarried man

the following described real property in the county of Riverside, state of California:

Lot 214 of Shangri La Palms, Unit No. 8, as per map recorded in Book 28, pages 61,62 and 63 inclusive of Maps in the office of the County Recorder of said County.

CALIFORNIA LAND TITLE COMPANY has recorded this instrument by request as an accommodation only. It has not examined it for regularity and sufficiency or as to its effect upon the title to the property therein described.

Dated Nov. 13, 1984

Bradley J. Franks
BRADLEY J. FRANKS

STATE OF CALIFORNIA
COUNTY OF Riverside } SS

On this the 13th day of November 1984, before me the undersigned, a Notary Public in and for said County and State, personally appeared Bradley J. Franks personally known to me or proved to me on the basis of satisfactory evidence to be the person whose name is subscribed to the within instrument and acknowledged that he executed the same.

Signature of Notary

FOR NOTARY SEAL OR STAMP

OFFICIAL SEAL
WM. PALTIN
NOTARY PUBLIC - CALIFORNIA
RIVERSIDE COUNTY
My Comm. Expires Dec. 26, 1987

Assessor's Parcel No.

MAIL TAX STATEMENTS TO PARTY SHOWN ON FOLLOWING LINE; IF NO PARTY SO SHOWN, MAIL AS DIRECTED ABOVE

Name Street Address City & State

CAL-1 (Rev. 8-82)

Exhibit J-32

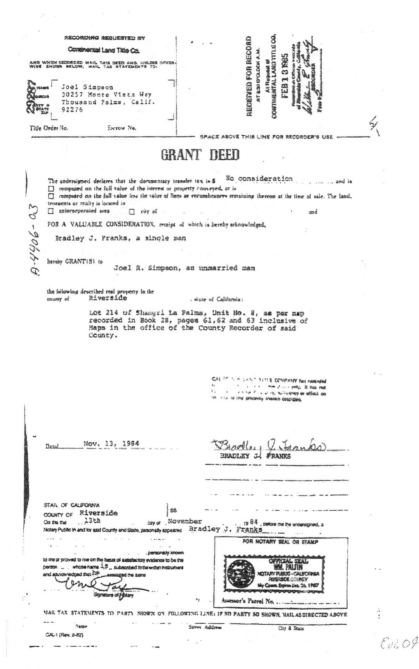

Flag of the United-States of the America
Title: 4: U.S.A. Codes: Chapter: 1: Section: 182

WITH THE CLAIM OF THE TRUTH

FOR THESE WITNESSES WITH THE FIRST-HAND-KNOWLEDGE ARE WITH THE CLAIM OF THE TRUTH OF A DAMAGE AGAINST THE SOVEREIGN-CITIZEN IN THE PARTY = :Robert-Joel: Simpson AS THE TRUSTEE FOR THE ROBERT JOEL SIMPSON TRUST (sic) OF THE EVIL OF THE TEACHING AND PLEADINGS FOR THE FICTIONAL-USE OF THE NOUN AS THE PROCEDURE OF THE ENGLISH-LANGUAGE AS THE VERB AND ADJECTIVE WITH THE CASE-NUMBER: INC018853 AND RIC329570 OF THE COURT OF THE DATE(S): 02-20-2001 AND 04-30-2001 WITH THE FICTION AND RAPE OF THE LANGUAGE FOR THE WRITINGS AND EVIDENCE OF THE CLAIM OF THE FICTION-LANGUAGE AGAINST THE EQUAL- PROTECTION OF THE UNITY-STATES OF THE CODE IN THE TITLE: 28: SECTION 1343 OF THE SHERIFF-DEPUTY OF THE COURT AND CLERK OF THE COURT WITH THE APARTHEID AGAINST THE WITNESS AND PARTIES OF THIS ACTION, WITH THE OBSTRUCTION OF THE EVIDENCE AND BREECH OF THE OATH BY THE CLAIMEES: "STATE OF CALIFORNIA", ______________________________

RECEIVED MAY - 1 2001 S. H. By

WITH THIS KNOWLEDGE FOR MY OATH IS WITH THE CLAIM OF THE TRUTH:

Date: 04-30-2001 by the Witness: [signature]

Date: 04-30-2001 by the Witness: Bradley-Jefferson: Franks

Date: 04-30-2001 by the Witness: Robert-Joel: Simpson

Date: 04-30-2001 by the Witness: Richard-Duane: Redon

Date:________ by the Witness: ____________________

Date:________ by the Witness: ____________________

Date:________ by the Witness: ____________________

Date:________ by the Witness: ____________________

Date:________ by the Witness: ____________________

Date:________ by the Witness: ____________________

Exhibit J-33

Witness-Statement:

04-30-2001 : 1:45 pm:

I. 8:30 am - Went to "Judge Stafford's" Court Rm... "We" were refered Back to "Judge Sheldon's" Court Rm....

8:45 am - Arrived at "Judge Sheldon's" Court Rm. Robert-Joel: Simpson Spoke with Clerk of the Court with witness... Baifliff/Sheriff Deputy asked Calvert-Landie AND Robert-Joel: to leave the Court.

"Sheldon" Refused to enter Court Room.

Signed By: Bradley-Jefferson:
Witness

4-30 2001: 7 PM

Arrived at Indio Court and witnessed Jeff & Joel trying to resolve the problem of the case not being on a docket. Followed to "Judge Staffords" court room and were refused audience. They were referred to "Judge Sheldon's" Court room. Robert-Joel: Simpson spoke to the clerk. The bailiff asked us to leave. "Sheldon" did not enter.

: Richard-Duane: Paxton
Witness

Exhibit J-34

UNITED STATES POSTAL SERVICE®

CUSTOMER'S RECEIPT

KEEP THIS RECEIPT FOR YOUR RECORDS	PAY TO: For: Small-Filing (claims)	SEE BACK OF THIS RECEIPT FOR IMPORTANT CLAIM INFORMATION
	ADDRESS: Indio - Courthouse	NOT NEGOTIABLE
	C.O.D. OR USED FOR: Filing-Fee [INC018853](sic)	

SERIAL NUMBER	YEAR, MONTH, DAY	POST OFFICE	AMOUNT	CLERK
01717448938	2000-09-27	922760	234.00	0001

UNITED STATES POSTAL SERVICE®

POSTAL MONEY ORDER 15-800/000

SERIAL NUMBER	YEAR, MONTH, DAY	POST OFFICE	U.S. DOLLARS AND CENTS
01717448938	2000-09-27	922760	$234.00¢

AMOUNT TWO HUNDRED THIRTY FOUR DOLLARS & 00¢ *

PAY TO: For: Superior-Court (sic)	NEGOTIABLE ONLY IN THE U.S. AND POSSESSIONS
ADDRESS: % Indio	FROM: Robert-Joel: CLERK 0001
	ADDRESS: % 30-257: Monte-Vista-Way:
C.O.D. NO. OR USED FOR Filing-Fee [INC 018853] (sic)	1,000 -Palms, CA. [92276]

⑆000008002⑆ 01717448938⑈

Exhibit J-35

November 8,1994

Brakescrew Enterprise
30-257 Monte Vista Way
Thousand Palms, CA. 92276

For The People
Peoples Network, Inc.
3 River Street
White Springs, Fla. 32096

Dear Chuck Harder:

In your past programs you have vehemently stressed that the American People need to wake up and take America back! I couldn't agree with you more. Your program is the best that I have heard since '87, although you keep attacking the "Top Officials" of our Country when you yourself stated that "The Power Companies are the Foundation of our Country." If you are serious about taking our Country back - and I feel that you are - please help this Enterprise, the American People and Country by helping in stopping the blatant fraud and theft of the American People.

As you have stated on your program before, "We need to rock the Foundation of this Country in order to reach the money-grubbing morons that are in control and strangling our Country to the point of no-return.

I have started a Home Mail Order business selling information that will reduce your monthly utility (electric) rates 10% - 30% guaranteed. I have circulated over four thousand flyers Nation wide and in my area in Riverside County, CA. And as of yet I have not received any paid responses. I seriously feel that my business mail is being rifled by powers that want to keep the American People Ignorant.

I recently contacted your 1 (800) 888-9999 for your book store and spoke with a very helpful and nice Representative by the name of Shirley. I explained to Shirley that if I received a response from her I would send her the information at no charge. Mr. Harder that was two weeks ago. I don't believe for a moment that the mail is that slow.

Last week, my business Manager Joel Simpson of Thousand Palms, CA. contacted Judy Walton and made the following offer to your "For the People" Organization in my name. It is as follows:

If you would kindly run commercial spots concerning Brakescrew Enterprise and this information at $19.95 I will donate $9.95 out of each response back to your organization. Please explain to your listeners that they should send for this information in care of your program. As I have stated before, I have not received any paid responses and I sincerely believe that my business mail is being withheld from my business.

Exhibit K-1

PAGE 2 of 2

I faxed you a copy of the flyer that I have circulated Nation Wide on November 1, 1994 concerning Brakescrew, Ent. This Enterprise will definately help you and your Organization financially and help you in establishing your Television Network for years to come.

Mr. Harder, this is not a prank or a fly-by nite business. Nor is it a Fraudulent claim. I can deliver what I claim and can prove every word in my flyer as truth, even in a Court of Law.

Thank you for your attention and consideration.

SINCERELY YOURS,

Bradley "Jeff" Franks

BRADLEY "JEFF" FRANKS
Owner of Brakescrew Enterprise

bjf

P.S. **URGENT!! PLEASE RESPOND.**

12/6/94

Mr. Harder;
As per your request on 12/5/94 with a conversation with Joel of 1000 Palms; Here is the copy of my information concerning Brakescrew, Ent.
Please respond as soon as possible.

Thanx
Bradley "Jeff" Franks

Exhibit K-2

DEFINITIONS:

HOUR - (n) 1. a division of time, one of the twenty - four parts of a day; **sixty minutes**. 2. a point or period of time; specif., a). a fixed point or period of time for a particular activity.

ACTIVITY - (n) 1. the state of being active; action 2. energetic action; liveliness 3. an active force 4. any specific action.

KILOWATT - (n) a unit of electrical power, equal to 1,000 watts.

KILOWATTHOUR - (n) a unit of electrical energy or work, equal to that done by one kilowatt acting for **one hour.**

Metals that are not affected by Magnetic Forces

MAGNETIC FORCE - the attracting or repelling force between a magnet and a ferromagnetic material, between a magnet and a current - carrying conductor.

FERROMAGNETIC - designating a material, as iron, nickel, or cobalt, having a high magnetic permeability.

COPPER - a reddish - brown, malleable, ductile, metallic element that is an excellant conductor of electricity and heat.

ALUMINUM - a silvery, lightweight, metallic chemical element thaty is easily worked, resists corrosion, and is found abundantly, but only in combination.

BRASS - a yellowish metal that is essentially an alloy of copper and zinc.

STAINLESS STEEL - steel alloyed with chromium, etc., virtually immune to rust and corrosion.

Copper, Aluminum, Brass, and Stainless Steel are not **and** can not be affected by a magnetic flow. In plain English (the truth) - a spinning free wheel made out of copper, aluminum, brass, or stainless steel are not used to measure the magnetic flow or current;

Exhibit K-3

they measure the ***amount of time that a customer is on service.*** The free spinning wheel in the electric meters are made out of aluminum or stainless steel.

Exhibit K-4

May 6, 1996

Attention Dan Schnieder;

FOR THE PEOPLE

Brakescrew, Ent. was developed to help all Customers of the Electric Companies regain over 250 Billion Dollars in Rebates throughout the United States. The Electric Companies have been cheating Customers on the amount of thier monthly bills for the past 20 years.

This statement of Fact was quoted from a "Retired Executive" of Duke Power, located in N. and S. Carolina, to Mr. Joel Simpson in the year 1977. " The electric meters are nothing more than 110 (one-ten) clocks that measure the amount of time that you are using the Electric Companies' Services. Infact, it is not the amount of electrical flow, magnetic flow or current that these meters measure; **BUT TIME.**"

If anyone who wishes to learn more about this Nation Wide Fraud against all Customers of the Electric Companies call (619) 343-1382 and Mr. Joel Simpson will explain in detail.

Sincerly,

Joel R Simpson

Mr. Joel Simpson

Vice President and Public Relations Officer for Brakescrew, Ent.

Fax No. (904) 397-4149

Exhibit K-5

May 14,1996

Statement to be given on Wed. before the Palm Springs City Council.

Good evening Ladies and Gentlemen, Mayor, City Council and Staff.

I am here tonight to set straight the facts of Brakescrew, Ent. and those people who are emphatically trying to undermine my company's integrity and stealing the credit of uncovering a Nation Wide Consumer Fraud that has been perpetrated for over 25 years by Organized Crime and the Power Companies.

During the Riverside County Supervisor's Race in '94 I proposed two (2) well thought out proposals that would have had a positive impact on our communities. The first proposal being a Multi-Cultural International Airport centered in the hub of our Valley. The second proposal was a Multi-Cultural International Auto-Race Track for the East end of our Valley. After being told that I received 950 votes, I developed Brakescrew, Ent. in hoping to stop the over-confident Organized Crime Lords. Both of my proposals have served well those puppets that call themselves politicians. For example, the International Auto-Race Track is more than likely going into Thousand Palms; and of course we all know that Mayor Kliendienst went to Washington D.C. to ask for permission to have Palm Springs Airport an International Multi-Cultural Airport. Now Ladies and Gentlemen don't get me wrong, I am pleased that my proposals did not fall on deaf or dumb ears; and I'm not even upset that these proposals were stolen from me and still have not received any credit for them **yet**.

But I will **NOT!!** allow these arrogant puppets or their masters to seize credit for exposing a Nation Wide Fraud that has been perpetrated for over 25 years against the American Public. These same puppets that are trying to claim credit **are** the cause of this Consumer Fraud. The politicians are not elected but appointed to office, so that they can help the Crime Lords protect their assets and to help in the continuation of destroying the American Dream and Soverenty.

In Sept. and Oct. of '94 I, myself, and Mr. Joel Simpson handed out over 5,000 flyers covering 5 States and personally hand delivered flyers to all Candidates who were running for any political office in our area of the Valley. For example, Council Member Dana Hodges received a flyer from Brakescrew, Ent. and was told in detail how these "Dinosaurs and out-dated clocks" (meters) opporated. Approximately 2-4 weeks later, Council Member Art Lyons proposed to develop thier own Municipal Power Company, claiming that they can buy electricity at 2 - 5¢ per Kx/Hr. If this be the case S.C.E. can sell the same electricity at this reduced rate to all! of thier Serviced Customers directly.

If the political puppets and thier masters think (I use the term loosely) that they can steal the credit that is due to Brakescrew, Ent. they are fallibly incorrect.If forced, I will, unfortunately, seek legal recourse for infringement upon my business.

Exhibit L-1

Page 2

Brakescrew, Ent. appreciates any and all help in getting rebates back to the public and in educating the people as to **HOW** these Power Companies have perpetrated this Consumer Fraud for over 25 years.

Brakescrew, Ent. deserves the credit in uncovering the Largest Consumer Fraud case in the history of the United States.

Thank you!

Exhibit L-2

SENDER: COMPLETE THIS SECTION	COMPLETE THIS SECTION ON DELIVERY
■ Complete items 1, 2, and 3. Also complete item 4 if Restricted Delivery is desired. ■ Print your name and address on the reverse so that we can return the card to you. ■ Attach this card to the back of the mailpiece, or on the front if space permits.	A. Received by (Please Print Clearly) B. Date of Delivery C. Signature X ☐ Agent ☐ Addressee D. Is delivery address different from item 1? ☐ Yes If YES, enter delivery address below: ☐ No
1. Article Addressed to: For Bill LOCKYER 1300 I, STREET SACRAMENTO 95814 CA. 95814	3. Service Type ☑ Certified Mail ☐ Express Mail ☐ Registered ☐ Return Receipt for Merchandise ☐ Insured Mail ☐ C.O.D. 4. Restricted Delivery? (Extra Fee) ☐ Yes
700 0600 0026 5169 6349 2. Article Number (Copy from service label)	
PS Form 3811, July 1999 Domestic Return Receipt	102595-99-M-1789

SENDER: COMPLETE THIS SECTION	COMPLETE THIS SECTION ON DELIVERY
■ Complete items 1, 2, and 3. Also complete item 4 if Restricted Delivery is desired. ■ Print your name and address on the reverse so that we can return the card to you. ■ Attach this card to the back of the mailpiece, or on the front if space permits.	A. Received by (Please Print Clearly) B. Date of Delivery Blackwell C. Signature X Blackwell ☐ Agent ☐ Addressee D. Is delivery address different from item 1? ☐ Yes If YES, enter delivery address below: ☐ No
1. Article Addressed to: For Barbara Boxer 112 Hart Build. 20510-0505 WASHINGTON D.C.	3. Service Type ☑ Certified Mail ☐ Express Mail ☐ Registered ☐ Return Receipt for Merchandise ☐ Insured Mail ☐ C.O.D. 4. Restricted Delivery? (Extra Fee) ☐ Yes
2. Article Number (Copy from service label) 7000 0520 0024 6044 2893	
PS Form 3811, July 1999 Domestic Return Receipt	102595-99-M-1789

Exhibit O and P

Is your RETURN ADDRESS completed on the reverse side?

SENDER:
- Complete items 1 and/or 2 for additional services.
- Complete items 3, 4a, and 4b.
- Print your name and address on the reverse of this form so that we can return this card to you.
- Attach this form to the front of the mailpiece, or on the back if space does not permit.
- Write "Return Receipt Requested" on the mailpiece below the article number.
- The Return Receipt will show to whom the article was delivered and the date delivered.

I also wish to receive the following services (for an extra fee):
1. ☐ Addressee's Address
2. ☐ Restricted Delivery

Consult postmaster for fee.

3. Article Addressed to:
Federal Energy Regulatory Commission
United States Dept. of Energy
Washington, D.C. 20585

4a. Article Number
P362 370 722

4b. Service Type
☐ Registered ☒ Certified
☐ Express Mail ☐ Insured
☐ Return Receipt for Merchandise ☐ COD

7. Date of Delivery

5. Received By: (Print Name)

8. Addressee's Address (Only if requested and fee is paid)

6. Signature: (Addressee or Agent)
X

PS Form **3811**, December 1994 — Domestic Return Receipt

Thank you for using Return Receipt Service.

Is your RETURN ADDRESS completed on the reverse side?

SENDER:
- Complete items 1 and/or 2 for additional services.
- Complete items 3, 4a, and 4b.
- Print your name and address on the reverse of this form so that we can return this card to you.
- Attach this form to the front of the mailpiece, or on the back if space does not permit.
- Write "Return Receipt Requested" on the mailpiece below the article number.
- The Return Receipt will show to whom the article was delivered and the date delivered.

I also wish to receive the following services (for an extra fee):
1. ☐ Addressee's Address
2. ☐ Restricted Delivery

Consult postmaster for fee.

3. Article Addressed to:
Josiah Nepier
C.P.U.C.
505 Van Ness Ave.
San Francisco, CA.
94102

4a. Article Number
P362 370 - 723

4b. Service Type
☐ Registered ☐ Certified
☐ Express Mail ☐ Insured
☐ Return Receipt for Merchandise ☐ COD

7. Date of Delivery
AUG 19 1996

5. Received By: (Print Name)

8. Addressee's Address (Only if requested and fee is paid)
Mailroom

6. Signature: (Addressee or Agent)
X

PS Form **3811**, December 1994 — Domestic Return Receipt

Thank you for using Return Receipt Service.

Exhibit Q and R

Is your RETURN ADDRESS completed on the reverse side?

Fold at line over top of envelope to

SENDER:
- Complete items 1 and/or 2 for additional services.
- Complete items 3, 4a, and 4b.
- Print your name and address on the reverse of this form so that we can return this card to you.
- Attach this form to the front of the mailpiece, or on the back if space does not permit.
- Write "*Return Receipt Requested*" on the mailpiece below the article number.
- The Return Receipt will show to whom the article was delivered and the date delivered.

I also wish to receive the following services (for an extra fee):

1. ☐ Addressee's Address
2. ☐ Restricted Delivery

Consult postmaster for fee.

3. Article Addressed to:

Internal Revenue Service
Attention: C.I.B.
FRESNO, CA. 93888

4a. Article Number
P219 333 150

4b. Service Type
☐ Registered ☑ Certified
☐ Express Mail ☐ Insured
☐ Return Receipt for Merchandise ☐ COD

7. Date of Delivery

5. Received By: *(Print Name)*

6. Signature: *(Addressee or Agent)*
X

8. Addressee's Address *(Only if requested and fee is paid)*

Thank you for using Return Receipt Service.

PS Form **3811**, December 1994 102595-97-B-0179 Domestic Return Receipt

Exhibit S

Brakescrew, Ent.

Bradley "Jeff" Franks
Business Owner
30 - 257 Monte Vista Way
Thousand Palms, CA. 92276

Speech for tonight before Palm Springs City Council.

September 25, 1996

Good evening Ladies and Gentlemen, Staff and Council.

Tonight I am prepared to prove beyond reasonable doubt that Southern Calif. Edison, Imperial Irrigation, Pacific Gas and Electric, and San Diego Gas and Electric are misleading thier customers in the metering process of electrical usage.

The truth of the meters, Ladies and Gentlemen, is right before your eyes. But people forget, especially when they're being **told** something else. Therefore, because of what you, the people, are being told by the Politicians and Executives from the Electric Companies the truth is being conveniently covered over.

On August 1, 1996 the desert Sun Interviewed SCE Regional Manager Bob Stranger who stated " We'd be glad to meet with anybody to discuss ways and means to lower bills and discuss other creative ideas to get customer's bills down." Mr. Stranger and Mr. Hitchcock, Brakescrew, Ent. will gladly meet with you at any time to prove that you are covering up the truth and **are** misleading your customers.

I have in my possession a book that College of the Desert had used in the past to educate students that were taking electrical courses; it is called Practical Electrical Wiring Residential, Farm, and Industrial based on the 1987 National Electrical Code by Herbert P. Richter and W. Creighton Schwan. On page 32 under Theory and Basic Principals there is an example of a typical rate schedule. Although the step-down points and the rate shown in the book at each level will vary from one locality to another.

I also have in my possession a copy of the State of California Public Utilities Commission's Annual Report for 1994 - 1995; and on page 11 of this report the typical Bill, in black and white, equals $65.18.

I feel that it is time for those responsible for the theft from the customers of these Electric Companies be brought up on Criminal Charges and rebates pursued in behalf of those customers.

Thank you for your time and attention.

Exhibit T-1

Statement to the public and **Charges** against Imperial Irrigation District, Southern Calif. Edison, Pacific Gas and Electric, and San Diego Gas and Electric.

Good evening Ladies and Gentlemen, it's nice to be up here before you once again; **But** let's get straight to the point.

I'm here tonight to publicly **accuse** and **charge** Southern Calif. Edison, Pacific Gas and Electric, San Diego Gas and Electric, and Imperial Irrigation with **Fraud, Extortion, Blackmail** and **Involuntary manslaughter** (to name specifically Southern Calif. Edison on the charge of involuntary manslaughter).

In 1994 a Senior Citizen thst lived in Palm Springs on Riverside Dr. was murdered due to the negligence and irresponsibility of S.C.E. **Because** of this negligence and irresponsibility, S.C.E. stated in the Desert Sun that their Co. would check the residences ***before*** disconnection of service. This, I believe would be called an **Implied Contract** with the citizens under the Laws of Ca.

But, in 1995 an infant (Joey Forbes) died due to S.C.E.'s refusal to connect electrical service to the appt. that was rented to Mr. Doug Alford and Ms. Debbie Forbes. S.C.E.'s excuse for refusal to connect electrical service to their appt was that there was an outstanding bill of approximately $350.00. Ladies and Gentlemen, this outstanding bill was **not** the responsibility of the new tennants. Therefore S.C.E. must share in the blame for this unfortunate accident. This explains the **charge** of **involuntary manslaughter** brought against S.C.E.

Fraud *is a general term for **any** instance in which one perty deceives or takes unfair advantage of another.* For example, the above named **Electric Companies** are using the **electric meters** fraudulently. These Electric Companies are ***claiming*** to be

Exhibit T-2

measuring the **"Magnetic Flow"** or **"the amount of current"** that the customer is using. These claims are fraudulent. Infact, it is **not** the amount of electrical flow, magnetic flow **or** current that these meters measure; **"BUT TIME!"**

Extortion, *is any form of taking or obtaining property from another by means of* ***illegal compulsion*** *or* ***oppressive exaction.*** For example if customers refuse to pay the outrageously high fraudulent bills, those customers are disconnected from service **until** those customers pay that bill; whether they can afford to or not. And through experience, we all know that these **HEARTLESS** Electric Companies don't care who dies as long as they are collecting the money **legally** or **illegally.**

Blackmail, *in law this is a criminal offense of attempting to extort money or property by* ***threats*** *of exposure of crime or of* ***disreputable conduct.*** A basic example for this particular charge is you either pay the amount shown on your bill (whether it's fraudulent or not) or we simply **disconnect service**. With this threat in mind, one has no choice in having to cau-tau to this **disreputable conduct.**

Non Feasance *is the lack of the* ***Public Employee*** *or* ***Elected Official*** *fulfilling or doing their jobs properly.* We all know that our **Elected Officials** have turned a deaf ear to what the Electric Companies are doing to their customers and **claim** that **"there is nothing we can do".** If there is nothing they can do **why** do we need **these Officials** in Office? They were elected to protect people from what the Electric Companies are getting away with. **And, YES!** our Elected Officials **are affected** by the **same** Electric Companies. So! Elected Officials what are you waiting for? An engraved invitation from the people...? How many more Senior Citizens or Baby Joey's have to **die** before you, our **"Elected Officials"**, decide that enough is enough and do your jobs

Exhibit T-3

properly?

The News Media, *which includes the Local Papers. Magazines, Radio, and Television - these entities have immunity from government control or* **censorship.** *Freedom of the press is regarded as fundamental to individual rights,* ***human dignity, self respect,*** *and* ***personal*** *responsibility. Without the media, a free society and democratic self-government would* ***not*** *be possible.* So, does the media not think that this is important enough to investigate? **Or** do they do what they are told by **"our Elected Officials"** or how about the **threat** of the loss of hundreds of thousands of dollars in advertising from the Electric Companies. I am absolutely surprised and saddened to find out that our local **Medias** are so easily controlled by **Liars, Cheats,** *and* **Thieves.** The Local News Media was personally informed by my staff that every customer, including themselves, are greatly affected by the illegal actions of the aforementioned **accused** and publicly **charged** Electric Companies. The local News Media has refused to interview Brakescrew, Ent. Why? Could they possibly be **afraid** of the reprisals taken against them? In either case, the News Media shouldn't have to be reminded that they have ***immunity from government control or censorship.***

I thank you for your time and attention concerning this important matter.

July 10, 1996
8:39 pm

Bradley "Jeff" Franks

EndTrans.

Exhibit T-4

[illegible], Ent.
30-257 Monte Vista Way
Thousand Palms, Ca. 92276
(Bradley "Jeff" Franks, Owner)

October 8, 1997

Lupie Lopez
Secretary of the Courts
Larson Justice Center
46-200 Oasis St., Rm. 314
Indio, Ca. 92201

Madame Secretary:

RE: A Fair Jury Trial Under the United States Constitution

Ms. Lopez, I am formally putting my grievances in writing and posing those grievances for your attention and consideration.

Mr. Robert Joel Simpson and I, (case # INM072896), are scheduled for a T.R.C. on 11-07-97 and a Jury Trial set for 11-17-97 on the following charges:

Robert Joel Simpson - 498 B: Theft of Electricity from a Public Utility. Mr. Simpson was charged with 15 years of Electricity theft. This charge was dropped by the District Attorney's Office under a plea bargain of 1 year of Electricity theft 6 months Probation, No Jail Time, and paying $1,200.00 dollars in restitution to Imperial Irrigation District.

Bradley "Jeff" Franks - 498 B: Theft of Electricity from a Public Utility. I was charged with 15 years of Electricity theft. This charge was dropped by the District Attorney's Office under a Plea Bargain of 1 year of Electricity theft with 6 months Probation, No Jail Time, and paying $1,200.00 Dollars in restitution to Imperial Irrigation District.

Exhibit V-1

148 - Resisting Arrest and 602.1 Interfering with Business or what was told to me by Public Defender Mundy Keller, Trespassing.

The actions that I took, Ms. Lopez, was in accordance with the United States Constitution and the Bill of Rights Article I. I have the right to conduct a Peaceful Demonstration to expose a greater wrong that is being committed against the Public and the Tax Payers.

I wish to call to your attention to Article VI and VII of the Bill of Rights as provided in the "First ten Amendments to the Constitution of the United States, effective December 15, 1791:

Article VI: "In all criminal prosecutions, the accused shall enjoy the right to a speedy and public trial, by an impartial jury of the State and District wherein the crime shall have been committed, which district shall have been previously ascertained by law, and to be informed of the nature and cause of the accusation; to be confronted with the witnesses against him; to have compulsory process for obtaining witnesses in his favor, and to have the assistance of Counsel for his defense."

Article VII: "In suits at common law, where the value in controversy shall exceed twenty dollars, the right of trial by jury shall be preserved, and no fact tried by a jury shall be otherwise re-examined in any Court of the United States, than according to the rules of the common law."

Furthermore, I would like to call to your attention the fact that almost every Jury in the land is falsely instructed by Judges when the jury is told that they must accept as the law that which is given to them by the Court, and that the Jury can decide only the facts of the case. This is to destroy the

pg. 2

Exhibit V-2

purpose of a Common Law Jury, and to permit the imposition of tyranny upon the people.

I understand that without the power to decide what facts, law and evidence are applicable, Juries cannot be a protection to the accused. But if people acting in the name of government are permitted by jurors to dictate any law whatever, they can also unfairly dictate what evidence is admissable or inadmissable and thereby prevent the **Whole Truth** from being considered. If government can manipulate and control both the law and evidence, the issue of fact becomes virtually irrelevant. In reality, true Justice would be denied leaving us with a trial by government and not a trial by Jury!

Ms. Lopez, my business Brakescrew, Ent., has uncovered and can document illegal actions against the public being committed by Imperial Irrigation District. Mr. Simpson and I can prove that at least three Felony Counts can be brought against Imperial Irrigation District (and **OTHER** Electric Companies). These charges are Fraud, Extortion, and Blackmail. These accusations have very much to do with the charges that were brought against Mr. Simpson and myself. But because of the Public Defender and the District Attorney's Office this evidence will not be heard by the jury. This is not a fair Trial by Jury, but a trial by government which is a violation of Mr. Simpson's and my Constitutional Rights. The Jury has the right to know **WHY** I took the actions I did and not be unaware of a greater crime against all of the people.

In conclusion, Ms. Lopez, I believe that ,I, the accused have the right to speak in my behalf and to be heard over all

pg. 3

Exhibit V-3

other precedents in a Court of Law.

Respectfully,

Bradley "Jeff" Franks - Owner

and

Robert Joel Simpson - Vice President

Exhibit V-4

COMMITTEES:
JUDICIARY
SUBCOMMITTEES:
COURTS AND INTELLECTUAL PROPERTY
IMMIGRATION AND CLAIMS
BANKING AND FINANCIAL SERVICES
SUBCOMMITTEES:
FINANCIAL INSTITUTIONS AND CONSUMER CREDIT
HOUSING AND COMMUNITY OPPORTUNITY
ENTERTAINMENT TASK FORCE
CHAIRMAN

Sonny Bono
Congress of the United States
44th District, California

WASHINGTON OFFICE:
512 CANNON HOUSE OFFICE BUILDING
WASHINGTON, DC 20515
(202) 225-5330
FAX: (202) 225-2961
DISTRICT OFFICES:
1555 SOUTH PALM CANYON
SUITE G101
PALM SPRINGS, CA 92264
(619) 320-1076
FAX: (619) 320-0868
23119-A COTTONWOOD AVENUE
SUITE 208
MORENO VALLEY, CA 92553
(909) 653-4488
FAX: (909) 653-2188
450 EAST LATHAM AVENUE
HEMET, CA 92543
(909) 785-2929
FAX: (909) 652-2582

November 18, 1997

Mr. Bradley Franks
30257 Monte Vista Way
Thousand Palms, CA 92276-2945

Dear Mr. Franks:

Thank you for contacting me regarding your ongoing court case. I appreciate hearing from you.

It is important that the citizens of our district keep me apprised of their views so that I can better represent you in Washington. Since this is an issue that falls outside my federal legislative duties and have no jurisdiction, I wish you well in your case, but the rules say I cannot intervene.

Again thank you for keeping me in mind and taking the time to write. Please feel free to contact me on other matters of mutual concern.

Best Wishes,

Sonny Bono

Sonny Bono
Member of Congress

SB:cjk

Exhibit Y

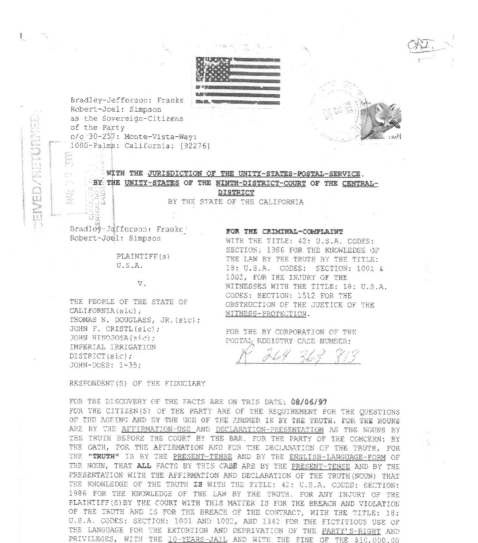

Bradley-Jefferson: Franks
Robert-Joel: Simpson
as the Sovereign-Citizens
of the Party
c/o 30-257: Monte-Vista-Way:
1000-Palms: California: [92276]

WITH THE <u>JURISDICTION OF THE UNITY-STATES-POSTAL-SERVICE</u>.
BY THE <u>UNITY-STATES</u> OF THE <u>NINTH-DISTRICT-COURT</u> OF THE <u>CENTRAL-DISTRICT</u>
BY THE STATE OF THE CALIFORNIA

Bradley-Jefferson: Franks
Robert-Joel: Simpson

PLAINTIFF(s)
U.S.A.

v.

THE PEOPLE OF THE STATE OF CALIFORNIA(sic);
THOMAS N. DOUGLASS, JR.(sic);
JOHN F. CRISTL(sic);
JOHN HINOJOSA(sic);
IMPERIAL IRRIGATION DISTRICT(sic);
JOHN-DOES: 1-35;

FOR THE CRIMINAL-COMPLAINT
WITH THE TITLE: 42: U.S.A. CODES: SECTION: 1986 FOR THE KNOWLEDGE OF THE LAW BY THE TRUTH BY THE TITLE: 18: U.S.A. CODES: SECTION: 1001 & 1002, FOR THE INJURY OF THE WITNESSES WITH THE TITLE: 18: U.S.A. CODES: SECTION: 1512 FOR THE OBSTRUCTION OF THE JUSTICE OF THE <u>WITNESS-PROTECTION</u>.

FOR THE BY CORPORATION OF THE POSTAL REGISTRY CASE NUMBER:
R 264 369 813

RESPONDENT(S) OF THE FIDUCIARY

FOR THE DISCOVERY OF THE FACTS ARE ON THIS DATE: **08/06/97**
FOR THE CITIZEN(S) OF THE PARTY ARE OF THE REQUIREMENT FOR THE QUESTIONS OF THE ASKING AND BY THE USE OF THE ANSWER IS BY THE TRUTH. FOR THE NOUNS ARE BY THE <u>AFFIRMATION-USE</u> AND <u>DECLARATION-PRESENTATION</u> AS THE NOUNS BY THE TRUTH BEFORE THE COURT BY THE BAR. FOR THE PARTY OF THE CONCERN: BY THE OATH, FOR THE AFFIRMATION AND FOR THE DECLARATION OF THE TRUTH, FOR THE **"TRUTH"** IS BY THE <u>PRESENT-TENSE</u> AND BY THE <u>ENGLISH-LANGUAGE-FORM</u> OF THE NOUN, THAT **ALL** FACTS BY THIS CASE ARE BY THE <u>PRESENT-TENSE</u> AND BY THE PRESENTATION WITH THE AFFIRMATION AND DECLARATION OF THE TRUTH(NOUN) THAT THE KNOWLEDGE OF THE TRUTH **IS** WITH THE TITLE: 42: U.S.A. CODES: SECTION: 1986 FOR THE KNOWLEDGE OF THE LAW BY THE TRUTH. FOR ANY INJURY OF THE PLAINTIFF(S) BY THE COURT WITH THIS MATTER IS FOR THE BREACH AND VIOLATION OF THE TRUTH AND IS FOR THE BREACH OF THE CONTRACT, WITH THE TITLE: 18: U.S.A. CODES: SECTION: 1001 AND 1002, AND 1342 FOR THE FICTITIOUS USE OF THE LANGUAGE FOR THE EXTORTION AND DEPRIVATION OF THE <u>PARTY'S-RIGHT</u> AND PRIVILEGES, WITH THE <u>10-YEARS-JAIL</u> AND WITH THE FINE OF THE $10,000.00 BY THE RESPONDENTS.

B.J.F.
R.J.S.

Exhibit Z-1

FOR THE DEMANDS OF THE PLAINTIFF(S)/RESPONDENT(S): FOR THE PLAINTIFF(S)/RESPONDENT(S) AND PETITIONER(S) **ARE** BY THE UNITY WITH THE COURT FOR THE OBSTRUCTION OF THE TRUTH BY THE USE OF THE NOUNS AS THE VERBS FOR THE OBSTRUCTION OF THE TRUTH WITH THE KNOWLEDGE. FOR THE PLAINTIFF(S) BY THE DEMANDS BY THE COMPLAINT **ARE** BY THE TRUTH FOR THE FILING OF THIS CASE WITH THE GRAND-JURY BY THE REPORTING WITH THE F.R.C.P. RULE 60(b)AND 26(e) OF THE CONSPIRACY FOR THE OBSTRUCTION OF THE TRUTH BY THIS CASE.

FOR THE SIGNATURE OF THE PARTIES ARE FOR THIS DISCOVERY-INTERVIEW.

CONTRACT-NOTICE: FOR THIS DISCLAIMER **IS** FOR THE UNITY-STATES-PARTY, FOR THE RESPONSIBILITY, WITH THE TERMS OF THIS CONTRACT BY THE KNOWLEDGE OF THE BY CORPORATION OF THE CASE NO. R 269 363 813-HEREIN OF THE C.U.S.A.F. CONTRACT. FOR THE TERMS ARE WITH THE RULES OF THE DISCOVERY OF THE TRUTH, WITH THE AMERICAN-FLAG OF THE U.S.A. FOR THE OATH AND AFFIRMATION BY THE SWEARING FOR THE DECLARATION OF THE AFFIRMATION OF THE TRUTH BY THE FIDUCIARY-PARTY(s) OF THE COURT, WITH THE TERMS BY THE C.U.S.A.F.-CONTRACT OF THE UNITY-STATES/PARTY BY THE INCORPORATION-CASE-TITLE-HEREIN FOR THE STATE OF THE COURT IS WITH THE LAW OF THE AMERICAN-FLAG WITHIN THE STATE OF THIS INCORPORATION OF THE CASE, BY THE FILING WITH THE CLERK OF THE COURTS OF THIS INCORPORATION OF THE CASE. FOR THE FICTION/FOREIGN-JURISDICTION IS BY THE JURISDICTION OF THE TRUTH WITH THE SOVEREIGN-CITIZEN BY THE PARTY. FOR ANY BREACH OF THIS C.U.S.A.F.-CONTRACT IS WITH THE TERMS, RULES AND DEFINITIONS OF THE INCORPORATION-CASE-TITLE-HEREIN. FOR ANY BREACH OF THE C.U.S.A.F.-CONTRACT IS WITH THE PROVISION FOR THE SANCTIONS. WHEN THE C.U.S.A.F.-CONTRACT IS OF THE SURRENDER BY ANY PARTY INTO THE FOREIGN-FICTION-JURISDICTION BY THE BREACH OF THIS OATH AND AFFIRMATION-CONTRACT WITH THE C.U.S.A.F.-CONTRACT, THEN THE CHARGES "FOR THE **PERJURY OF THE OATH**" **ARE** WITH THE TITLE: 18: U.S.A. CODES: SECTION: 1621:[5-YEARS-$5,000.-PENALTY-FEE] FOR THE TERMS OF THE CONSTITUTION/CONTRACT/CONSTRUCTIVE-TREASON AGAINST THE C.U.S.A.F.-CONTRACT FOR THE FALSE-SWEARING OF THE OATH. NOTE: FOR THE FACTS ARE BY THE NOUNS FOR THE JURISDICTION BY THE COURTS OF THE UNITY-STATES WITH THE TRUTH. FOR THE VIOLATION OF THE NOUNS AS THE VERB OR ADJECTIVES ARE FOR THE CAUSE OF THE MAIL-FRAUD/FICTITIOUS-NAMES WITH THE TITLE: 18: U.S.A. CODES: SECTION: 1342 FOR THE USE OF THE FICTITIOUS-NAMES FOR THE EXTORTION OF THE MONEY FOR THE TITLE: 18: U.S.A. CODES: SECTION: 1001:[5-YEARS-$5,000.-PENALTY-FEE] FOR THE FICTITIOUS-USE OF THE NOUNS AS THE **VERBS** AND **ADJECTIVES** IS WITH THE VIOLATION OF THE C.U.S.A.F.-CONTRACT FOR THE RIGHTS OF THE SOVEREIGN-CITIZENS BY THE PARTY.

FOR THE PLAINTIFF(S) IS/ARE OF THE SOVEREIGN-CITIZEN(S) OF THE PARTY, WITH THE OATH FOR THE AFFIRMATION, FOR THE DECLARATION OF THE TRUTH BY THE FIRSTHAND-KNOWLEDGE OF THE FACTS:

Bradley-Jefferson: Franks — Robert-Joel: Simpson

 2

B.J.F.
R.-J. S.

Exhibit Z-2

ABBREVIATIONS: F.R.C.P. = FOR THE FEDERAL-RULES OF THE CIVIL-PROCEDURE herein:

U.S.A. CODES® = OF THE UNITY-STATES OF THE AMERICA-CODE.

U.S.A. = OF THE UNITY-STATES OF THE AMERICA

THE, THIS =(ARTICLE) FOR THE SPECIFIC BY THE PRESENT-TENSE

UNITY-STATES = BY ANY INCORPORATION OF THE TWO OR MORE-PARTIES BY THE CONTRACT/CONSTITUTION;

C.U.S.A.F. = FOR THE CONSTITUTION OF THE UNITY-STATES WITH THE AMERICAN-FLAG;

BY THE ARTICLE OF THE THREE(3) = FOR THE RIGHT OF THE SPEECH, RELIGION, PRESS, GRIEVANCE;

BY THE ARTICLE OF THE SIX(6) = FOR THE RIGHT OF THE ARREST-WARRANT OR SEARCH-WARRANT-SIGNATURE BY THE JUDGE OF THE OATH OR AFFIRMATION;

BY THE ARTICLE OF THE SEVEN(7) - FOR THE RIGHT OF THE DUE-PROCESS, FOR NO WITNESS IS AGAINST THE ONESELF;

BY THE ARTICLE OF THE EIGHT(8) = FOR THE RIGHT OF THE WITNESSES, COUNSEL AND EVIDENCE BY THE COURT AND FOR THE SPEEDY-TRIAL;

BY THE ARTICLE OF THE NINE(9) = FOR THE RIGHT OF THE TRIAL BY THE JURY;

BY THE ARTICLE OF THE TEN(10) = FOR THE PUNISHMENT IS OF THE EQUAL PROTECTION FOR THE REASONABLE-BAIL;

BY THE ARTICLE OF THE ELEVEN (11) = FOR ANY OFFICER OF THE COURT IS BY THE APPOINTMENT OR ELECTION WITH THE OATH OR AFFIRMATION FOR THE UPHOLDING OF THE C.U.S.A.F.-CONTRACT BY THE TRUTH BY THE UNITY-STATES OF THE AMERICA FOR THE PEOPLE OF THE UNITY-STATES OF THE AMERICA;

BY THE ARTICLE OF THE TWELVE(12) = FOR THE CONSTITUTION-CONTRACT IS WITH THE RESERVATION FOR ANY MUTUAL-AGREEMENT OR ARBITRATION BY THE TITLE PARTIES-HEREIN;

BY THE ARTICLE OF THE THIRTEEN(13) = FOR ANY FOREIGN/FICTION WITH THIS CONTRACT IS WITH THE JURISDICTIONS WITH THE SOVEREIGN-CITIZEN BY THE PARTY, FOR THE JUDICIAL-LANGUAGE OF THE UNITY-STATES IS WITH THE INCORPORATION BY THIS SUIT BY THE LAW AND BY THE EQUITY FOR THE COMMENCEMENT OF THE PROSECUTION AGAINST ANY ONE OF THE UNITY-STATES BY THE CITIZENS OF THIS COURT-STATE AS THE CITIZENS. FOR THIS NEW-STATE IS WITH THE TRUTH-LANGUAGE WITH A SOVEREIGN-FLAG BY THE TRUTH WITHIN THIS COURT;

FOR THE UNITY-STATES-DISTRICT-COURT(NOUN) BY THE UNITY-STATES(NOUN) OF THE AMERICA(NOUN) IS FOR THE UPHOLDING OF THE ORIGINAL-JURISDICTION(NOUN) WITH THE TITLE: 28: U.S.A. CODES: SECTION: 1331 AND SECTION: 1343 FOR THE EQUAL-PROTECTION BY THE TRUTH. FOR THE SOVEREIGN-FLAG OF THE U.S.A. IS BY THE COURT. FOR THE CLERK OF THE COURT IS WITH THE OATH FOR THE FILING OF THE INCORPORATION OF THE CASE WITH THE COURT OF THE DISTRICT OF THE U.S.A. WITH THE TITLE: 28: U.S.A. CODES: SECTION: 1869, FOR THIS ORDER OF THE PROCEDURES ARE WITH THE TITLE: 28: U.S.A. CODES: SECTION: 1361 FOR THE COMPLIANCE BY THIS RESPONSIBILITY IS FOR THE DUTY OF THE OFFICE OF THE CLERK. FOR THE INCORPORATION IS WITH THE PERPETUAL-EXISTENCE OF THE C.U.S.A.F.-CONTRACT OF THE CASE-NUMBER-TITLE-HEREIN. FOR THE COMPLIANCE OF ALL-PARTIES ARE BY THE TRUTH. FOR ALL PARTIES ARE BY THE AGREEMENT OF THE FACTS OR BY THE DECISION OF THE TRIAL BY THE JURY(NOUN).

 3

Exhibit Z-3

FOR THE FACTS

1. **FOR THE PLAINTIFF(S)ARE WITH THE AFFIRMATION BY THE TRUTH FOR AN** INJURY FOR THE CONDITION OF THE INSTRUCTIONS AND PLEADINGS BY THE STATE-GOVERNMENT, STATE OF CALIFORNIA(sic); JOHN F. CRISTL(sic); THOMAS N. DOUGLASS, JR.(sic) FOR THE FICTIONAL-USE OF THE **NOUN** AS THE PROCEDURE BY THE ENGLISH-LANGUAGE AS THE **VERB** AND **ADJECTIVE** BY THE ATTORNEYS BY THIS CASE-NUMBER **INMO72896**(sic) BY THE COURT ON THE DATE(s): 8/6/97; 8/12/97; 9/2/97; 11/7/97; 11/17,18/97; 3/6/98; 3/16/98; 3/18,19/98; 3/23,24/98; 5/1/98; 5/29/98; AND 6/26/98. FOR THE PLAINTIFF(S)IS/ARE WITH AN INJURY WITH THE FICTION AND RAPE OF THE LANGUAGE BY THE RESPONDENT-ATTORNEY AND JUDGE JOHN F. CRISTL(sic) AND HON. THOMAS N. DOUGLASS, JR.(sic), FOR THE WRITINGS AND PRESENTMENT OF THE "MOTIONS" ARE BY THE FICTION-LANGUAGE AGAINST THE EQUAL-PROTECTION OF THE WITNESSES: Bradley-Jefferson: Franks AND Robert-Joel: Simpson FOR THE **APARTHEID** AGAINST THE WITNESSES BY THE RESPONDENTS. FOR THE PLAINTIFF(S) BY THESE FACTS ARE WITH THE KNOWLEDGE FOR THE INCORPORATION OF ANY INCORPORATION-CASE AS THE PLAINTIFF(S) AND WITNESSES: Bradley-Jefferson: Franks AND Robert-Joel: Simpson BY THE COURT BY THE RESPONDENT.

2. **FOR THE PLAINTIFF(S)IS/ARE WITH THE AFFIRMATION BY THE TRUTH BY THIS COMPLAINT** FOR THE TESTIMONY WITH THE DECLARATION FOR THE AFFIRMATION OF THE TRUTH(NOUN) AS BY THE NOUN-DEFINITION OF THE ENGLISH-LANGUAGE FOR THE WORDING OF THE EVIDENCE AGAINST THE PLAINTIFF(S). FOR THE PLAINTIFF(S)Bradley-Jefferson: Franks AND Robert-Joel: Simpson ARE OF THE INJURY WITH THE RESPONSIBILITY-PERFORMANCE-CONTRACT FOR THE PROTECTION OF THE **WITNESS**. FOR THE EVIDENCE BY THE PLAINTIFF(S) ARE WITH THE C.U.S.A.F.-CONTRACT BY THE TRUTH(NOUN). FOR THE SIGNATURE OF THE RESPONDENT(S) WITH THE ATTORNEY'S-OATH AND JUDGE'S-OATH IS FOR THE DECLARATION OF THE AFFIRMATION OF THE TRUTH(NOUN). FOR ALL FACTS BY THIS INCORPORATION-CASE-HEREIN ARE BY THE TRUTH(NOUN) BY THE RESPONDENT(S) AND PETITIONER(S) AND PLAINTIFF(S) (EXHIBIT-A&B).

3. **FOR THE PLAINTIFF(S)ARE WITH THE AFFIRMATION BY THE TRUTH** FOR THE INJURY AGAINST THE LAW BY THE FICTION-LANGUAGE FOR THE PLEADINGS BY THE RESPONDENT-ATTORNEYS. FOR THE BREACH IS WITH THE C.U.S.A.F.-CONTRACT BY THE ARTICLE OF THE SEVEN(7) FOR THE PLAINTIFF(S)ARE OF THE INJURY BY THE PROTECTION FOR THE PROCEDURAL-VIOLATIONS WITH THE C.U.S.A.F.-CONTRACT OF THE PLAINTIFF'S-CIRCUIT-COURT-FILINGS BY THIS CASE-NO. **INMO72896**(sic) BY THE RESPONDENT(S). FOR THE CONSPIRACY WITH THE COLOR OF THE LAW IS WITH THE TITLE: 42: U.S.A. CODES: SECTION: 1985(1) FOR THE CONSPIRACY WITH THIS DEFINITION IS FOR THE CRIMINAL-CROSS-REFERENCE WITH THE TITLE: 18: U.S.A. CODES: SECTION: 241 FOR THE CONSPIRACY BY THE BREACH OF THE CONTRACT-RIGHTS BY THE PERFORMANCE-COMPLAINT BY ALL COURT-FILINGS BY THE RESPONDENTS ON THE DATE(S): 8/6/97; 8/12/97; 9/2/97; 11/7/97; 11/17,18/97; 3/6/98; 3/16/98; 3/18,19/98; 3/23,24/98; 5/1/98; 5/29/98; AND 6/26/98.

4. **FOR THE PLAINTIFF(S) WITH THE AFFIRMATION BY THE TRUTH IS WITH** THE INJURY BY THE LANGUAGE OF THE "ORDER OF ARREST-BY PRIVATE PERSONS"(sic) (EXHIBIT-C), BY THE PRESENTMENT AS A VERB-TITLE AND ADJECTIVE-TITLE BY

 4

Exhibit Z-4

THE FICTION FOR THE BREACH OF THIS C.U.S.A.F.-CONTRACT BY THE LAW(NOUN) OR AT THE LAW. FOR THE PLAINTIFF(S) AS THE FRIENDS OF THE COURT IS FOR THE CORRECTION OF THE QUESTIONS WITH THE TRIAL BY THE JURY (EXHIBIT-D) FOR THE INCORPORATION OF A TITLE: 18: U.S.A. CODES: SECTION: 1001 FOR THE STATEMENT-HEREIN: **FOR THE PLAINTIFF(S)-AFFIRMATION BY THE COMPLAINT:** WITH THE **RULES OF THE DISCOVERY:** OF THE F.R.C.P. RULE: 60(b) FOR THE PLAINTIFF(S) **ARE** WITH THE KNOWLEDGE BY THE TRUTH WITH THE RULES OF THE PROCEDURE OF THE ENGLISH-LANGUAGE. FOR THE SUBJECT-MATTER-LANGUAGE-FRAUD WITH THE F.R.C.P. RULE: 9(b), AGAINST THE RESPONDENT(S) OF THE "[illegible]"(sic) BY THE FILES FOR THIS COMPLAINT BY THE RESPONDENT'S TITLE-HEREIN. FOR THE CRIMINAL-COMPLAINT-AFFIDAVIT BY THE RESPONDENT, BEFORE THIS COURT-TITLE-HEREIN IS WITH THE RULES OF THE DISCOVERY-CLAUSE OF THE F.R.C.P. RULE: 60(b), FOR THE INCORPORATION OF THE PLAINTIFF(S) AS TO THE PROSECUTION OF THE DISCRIMINATION WITH THE FEDERAL-AUTHORITY BY THE TRUTH

5. ON THE DATE(S): 8/6/97; 8/12/97; 9/2/97; 11/7/97; 11/12,19/97; 3/6/98; 3/18/98; 3/19,19/98; 3/23,24/98; 5/15/98; 5/20/98; AND 8/26/98 **OF THE COURT OF THE COUNTY OF THE RIVERSIDE BY THE STATE OF THE CALIFORNIA, FOR THE PLAINTIFF(S) ARE WITH THE AFFIRMATION BY THE TRUTH** BY THE HIGH-FIDUCIARY-POSITION FOR THE EXTORTION OF THE RIGHTS AND PRIVILEGES (EXHIBIT-E), WITH THE **TITLE: 18: U.S.A. CODES: SECTION: 1001** FOR THE AFFIRMATION: WHOEVER, BY ANY MATTER WITHIN THE JURISDICTION OF ANY DEPARTMENT FOR THE AGENCY OF THE UNITY-STATES(NOUN) **IS** WITH THE KNOWLEDGE AND WILLFUL-INTENT BY THE FALSIFICATION, CONCEALMENT AND BY THE COVER-UP BY ANY TRICK, SCHEME, OR BY ANY DEVICE OF THE MATERIAL-FACT, OR BY THE MAKING FOR THE FALSIFICATION-STATEMENT BY THE FICTITIOUS-STATEMENT, OR BY THE FRAUDULENT-STATEMENT OR BY THE REPRESENTATIONS OF THE STATEMENT, OR BY THE MAKING OF ANY FALSE-WRITINGS OR FOR THE USING OF ANY FALSE-WRITINGS OR BY THE FALSE-DOCUMENT(S) BY THE KNOWING THAT THE FALSE-DOCUMENT(S) ARE FOR THE CONTAINING FOR ANY FALSIFICATION-STATEMENTS, FOR THE FICTITIOUS-STATEMENTS OR FOR THE FRAUDULENT-STATEMENTS OR FOR THE ENTRY OF THE CASE-FILE OF THE $10,000 WITH THIS TITLE OR BY THE IMPRISONMENT OF THE FIVE-YEARS OR BOTH; WITH THE **TITLE: 18: U.S.A. CODES: SECTION: 1002:** WHOEVER, WITH THE KNOWLEDGE AND WITH THE WILLFUL-INTENT FOR THE DEFRAUDING OF THE UNITY-STATES(NOUN), OR FOR ANY AGENCY, FOR THE POSSESSION OF ANY FALSE, ALTERATION, FORGERY, OR COUNTERFEIT-WRITINGS OR FOR THE DOCUMENTATION OF THE PURPOSE FOR THE ENABLEMENT FOR THE OBTAINING OF THE UNITED STATES(sic), OR BY THE UNITY-STATES'S AGENCY, OFFICER OR AGENT THEREOF, FOR ANY SUM OF THE MONEY, IS WITH THE FINE WITH THIS TITLE: 18, WITH THE IMPRISONMENT WITH THE C.U.S.A.F.-LAW.

6. FOR THE PLAINTIFF(S) IS/ARE WITH THE AFFIRMATION BY THE TRUTH BY THE C.U.S.A.F.-CONTRACT BY THE ARTICLE OF THE SEVEN(7) FOR THE INJURY BY THE [illegible] FOR THE KNOWLEDGE OF THE LAW BY THE TRUTH. WITH THE DISCOVERY OF THE TRUTH FOR THE F.R.C.P. RULE: 60(b) OF THE F.R.C.P. RULE: 9(b) IS FOR THE REPORTING OF THE FRAUD FOR THE CONSPIRACY BY THE COURT FOR THE RELIEF BY THE STATEMENTS-HEREIN BY THE TRUTH OR FOR THE JUDGE-ADVOCATE-GENERAL FOR THE BREACH OF THE FOREIGN-JURISDICTION WITH THE DISABILITIES-ACT FOR THE

 5

Exhibit Z-5

COURT'S-POSITION BY THE OBSTRUCTION OF THE JUSTICE WITH THE TITLE: 18: U.S.A. CODES: SECTION: 1512 BY THE COURT-OFFICERS.

7. **FOR THE PLAINTIFF(S)IS/ARE OF THE INJURY BY THE COMPLAINT** BY THE PAPERS BY THE CORRESPONDENCE BY THE COURT WITH THE PLAINTIFF(S), BY THE VIOLATION OF THE F.R.C.P. RULE: 11(a) FOR ALL THE DOCUMENTS ARE WITH THE SIGNATURE FOR THE JURISDICTION OF THE COURT BY THE TRUTH. FOR THE SIGNATURE ON A FICTION IS FOR THE BREACH OF THE DUE-PROCESS BY THE COURT.

FOR THE CAUSE OF THE ACTION

8. **FOR THE PLAINTIFF(S)ARE OF THE BY JURY BY THE COMPLAINT** FOR THE RESPONDENTS ARE AS THE ATTORNEYS **AT LAW**(sic) AND **BY LAW**(sic). "THE **LAW**" FOR THIS PRESENTMENT IS BY THE MODIFICATION BY THE ADVERB FOR THE IDENTIFICATION AS **A VERB. FOR THE FACT OF THE NOUN IS BY THE TRUTH OF THE LAW OF THE CONTRACT FOR THE FACT. FOR THE TRUTH IS OF THE FACT (NOUN). 2 + 2 = (OF THE) 4, 4 - 2= (OF THE)** 2.

9. **FOR THE PLAINTIFF(S)IS/ARE BY THE KNOWLEDGE OF THE TRUTH OF THE INJURY BY THIS COMPLAINT** ON THE 8/6/97; 8/12/97; 9/2/97; 11/7/97; 11/17,18/97; 3/6/98; 3/16/98; 3/18,19/98; 3/23,24/98; 5/1/98; 5/29/98; AND 6/26/98, FOR THE PLAINTIFF(S) IS/ARE WITH THE PROTECTION AS A WITNESS BY THE COURT. FOR THE RESPONDENT IS BY THE EMPLOYMENT FOR THE PROTECTION OF THE REPRESENTATION BY THE INCORPORATION OF THE CASE OF THE JUSTICE. FOR THE WITNESSES-PLAINTIFF(S) BY THE PERFORMANCE AS THE WITNESS FOR THE EVIDENCE OF THE TESTIMONY BY THE SAFE-PROTECTION OF THE COURT AGAINST ANY DEPRIVATION OF THE PLAINTIFF-WITNESS-TESTIMONY. FOR THE OBSTRUCTION OF THE WITNESS-TESTIMONY WITH THE OATH FOR THE DECLARATION BY THE AFFIRMATION OF THE TRUTH IS FOR THE PROTECTION OF THE WITNESS AND FOR THE PROTECTION OF THE EVIDENCE BY THE COURT BY THE RESPONDENT AS THE AGENT BY THE FIDUCIARY OF THE INCORPORATION OF THÊ CASE. FOR THE PLAINTIFF(S)IS/ARE WITH THE WITNESS-PROTECTION FOR THE INCORPORATION OF THE TESTIMONY AND EVIDENCE OF THE FACTS(NOUN) BY THE PLAINTIFF(S) AND RESPONDENT(S) BY THE TRIAL. FOR THE PRESUMPTIONS, ASSUMPTIONS, OPINIONS AND CONCLUSIONS OF THE FACTS ARE WITH THE ACTIONS FOR THE INTIMIDATION, TORT, COLLUSION AND RAPE BY THE RESPONDENTS. FOR THE RESPONSIBILITY OF A WITNESS IS WITH THE C.U.S.A.F.-RIGHTS. FOR THE OBSTRUCTION OF THE JUSTICE IS WITH THE TITLE: 18: U.S.A. CODES: SECTION: 1512 AND WITH THE "RICO" WITH THE TITLE: 18: U.S.A. CODES: SECTION: 1961, AND WITH THE TITLE: 42: U.S.A. CODES: SECTION: 1985: SECTION: (1) FOR THE CONSPIRACY OF THE OFFICERS BY THE FICTION-LANGUAGE, (2) FOR THE OBSTRUCTING OF THE WITNESS AND EVIDENCE BY THE TRUTH, AND (3) FOR THE DEPRIVING OF THE EQUAL-PROTECTION FOR THE EVIDENCE(NOUN) AND WITNESSES(NOUN) BY THE TRUTH(NOUN) WITH THE LAW(NOUN) BY THE RESPONDENTS.

10. **FOR THE PLAINTIFF(S)ARE WITH THE KNOWLEDGE** OF THE INJURY FOR THE TRUTH BY THE GUARANTEE OF THE WITNESS-PROTECTION OF THE EMPLOYMENT BY THE PLAINTIFF(S)-CITIZEN(S) BY THE PARTY-PRESENT ON THE WITNESS-STAND BY THE CROSS-EXAMINATION BY THE COURT WITH THE PROTECTION OF THE RESPONDENT-JUDGE. FOR THE ATTORNEY **AT LAW**(sic) **AS THE VERB,** AND FOR THE EXAMINATION

 6

Exhibit Z-6

OF LAW(sic) **AS THE VERB**, WITH THE BREACH OF THE PERFORMANCE-C.U.S.A.F.-CONTRACT BY THE RESPONDENTS. FOR THE PERFORMANCE-LAWS OF THIS IN-CORPORATION-CASE-NUMBER, FOR THE PLAINTIFF(S)ARE WITH THE C.U.S.A.F.-CONTRACT-PROTECTION FOR THE LAWS OF THE UNITY-STATES BY THE COURT BY THE CONDITIONS, RULES AND DEFINITIONS BY THE TRUTH BY THE SANCTUARY OF THE COURT/BAR BY THE STATE WITH THE PERFORMANCE-CONTRACT OF THE UNITY STATES OF THE AMERICA.

NOTE: FOR THE SANCTUARY OF THE BAR/COURT IS WITH THE CONTRACT-REMOVAL OF THE PARENT-STATE OF THE CALIFORNIA AND IS WITH THE CONTRACT-CONSTITUTION OF THE UNITY-STATES OF THE CONTRACT BY THE COUNTRY OF THE CONTRACT. FOR THE SOVEREIGN-LAND OF THE COURT IS WITH THE LAW OF THE FLAG BY THE PROTECTION OF THIS CONTRACT FOR THE PROTECTION BY THIS SOVEREIGN-STATE-COURT OF THE AMERICA. [IN THIS CASE]

11. **FOR THE PLAINTIFF(S)IS/ARE WITH THE KNOWLEDGE OF THIS AFFIRMATION BY THE TRUTH** FOR THE INJURY BY THE CONSIDERATION OF THE INCORPORATION OF THE CASE-NUMBER, AND **IS** WITH THE UNITY-STATES OF THE AMERICA FOR THE PLAINTIFF(S) ARE WITH THE PROTECTION AND SAFETY BY THE DUTY OF THE WITNESS WITH THE RESPONDENT-JUDGE'S COURT-RESPONSIBILITY AND BY THE RESPONDENT-JUDGE/ATTORNEY, FOR THE SERVICES OF THE JUDGESHIP BY THE PROTECTION OF THE JUSTICE FOR THE CITIZENS OF THE UNITY-STATES OF THE AMERICA FOR THAT SERVICE, UNDERTOOK THE EXAMINATION OF THE ARGUMENTS OF THE LAWS BY THE INCORPORATION AS AN OFFICER OF THE COURT FOR THE KNOWLEDGE OF THE LAW.

12. **FOR THE PLAINTIFF(S) WITH THE AFFIRMATION BY THE COMPLAINT** ARE OF THE INJURY BY THE RESPONDENT-JUDGE, UPON THE EXAMINATION OF THE RESPONDENT'S-CASE-NUMBER: INM072896(sic), FOR THE ARGUMENTS **ARE** *[BEFORE]* OF THE COURT WITH THE TITLE: 42: U.S.A. CODES: SECTION: 1985(2) FOR THE OBSTRUCTING OF THE LAW FOR THE EQUAL-PROTECTION AGAINST THE PLAINTIFF(S)Bradley-Jefferson: Franks AND Robert-Joel: Simpson-WITNESSES FOR THE GIVING OF THE EVIDENCE AND TESTIMONY ON THE WITNESS-STAND AND FOR THE DEPRIVING OF THE EQUAL-PROTECTION OF THE LAW FOR THE LAW WITH THE TITLE: 42: U.S.A. CODES: SECTION: 1985(3) FOR THE GIVING OF THE EVIDENCE AND TESTIMONY BEFORE THE COURT BY THE INCORPORATION OF THE CONTRACT FOR THE HEARING OF THE EVIDENCE BEFORE THE COURT WITH THE POWER FOR THE PROTECTION OF THE PLAINTIFF(S)-WITNESSES AGAINST ANY INJURY, HOWEVER, FOR THE PLAINTIFF(S)-WITNESSES **ARE** OF THE INJURY BY THE OBSTRUCTION AND DEPRIVATION OF THE PLAINTIFF(S)IN THE GIVING OF THE TRUTH WITH THE OATH BY THE PRESENTATION OF THE EVIDENCE AND BY THE TESTIMONY BY THE COURT BY THE RESPONDENT-JUDGE THOMAS N. DOUGLASS, JR. (sic).

13. **FOR THE PLAINTIFF(S)ARE WITH THE AFFIRMATION BY THE COMPLAINT** OF THE INJURY BY THE NEGLECT OF THE C.U.S.A.F.-CONTRACT-INCORPORATION WITH THE LAWS OF THE UNITY-STATES(NOUN) OF THE AMERICA(NOUN)UNDER THE RIGHT OF THE CONTRACT-INCORPORATION BY THE C.U.S.A.F.-RIGHTS OF THE ISSUES OF THE CASE AND WITH THE ATTORNEY'S-OATH FOR THE UPHOLDING OF THE C.U.S.A.F.-CONTRACT FOR THE AFFIRMATION AND FOR THE DECLARATION OF THE TRUTH BY THE RESPONDENTS.

Exhibit Z-7

14. FOR THE PLAINTIFF(S) ARE WITH THE AFFIRMATION BY THE COMPLAINT FOR THE INJURY BY THE NEGLECT OF THE DUE-PROCESS OF THE CONTRACT-LAW OF THE C.U.S.A.F.-ARTICLE OF THE SEVEN(7), AND WITH THE COLOR OF THE LAW BY THE TITLE: 18: U.S.A. CODES: SECTION: 242.

15. FOR THE PLAINTIFF(S) WITH THE AFFIRMATION BY THE COMPLAINT ARE OF THE INJURY BY THE LONG-LITIGATION AND IS BY THE HURTING OF THE LOVE, NURTURING, CARE, AND HEALTH OF THE MIND AND BODY OF THE PLAINTIFF(S) THAT THE SAME IS BY THE ENDURANCE, BY THE RESPONDENT-JUDGE.

FOR THE CONCLUSION

16. FOR THE PLAINTIFF(S) WITH THE AFFIRMATION BY THE COMPLAINT ARE OF THE INJURY BY THE RESPONDENTS BY THE PRACTICE OF THE LAW, WITH THE SKILL AND CARE AND DILIGENCE BY THE EXAMINATION OF THE INCORPORATION OF THE CASE-NUMBER: INMO72896(sic), BY THE PLAINTIFF(S)IN THE DISCOVERY OF THE DEFECT IS WITH THE TITLE: 42: U.S.A. CODES: SECTION: 1986 FOR THE KNOWLEDGE OF THE LAW THROUGH THE DISCOVERY OF THE FRAUD BY THE LAW WITH THE F.R.C.P. RULE 9(b) AND FOR THE F.R.C.P. RULE 26(e) FOR THE REPORTING OF THE WRONG FOR THE JUDICIAL-ENTITY FOR THE PREVENTION OF THE WRONG OF THE PLAINTIFF'S-INJURY, BY THE NEGLECT OF THE CARE, SKILL, AND DILIGENCE BY THE EXAMINATION OF THE PLAINTIFF'S-C.U.S.A.F.-RIGHTS AND BY THE ADVISEMENT OF THE PLAINTIFF(S) BY THE INCORPORATION OF THE CASE-NUMBER: INMO72896(sic), FOR THE PLAINTIFF(S)IS/ARE WITH THE TRUE-(NOUN)-FACTS BY THE STATEMENTS BY THE COURT AND ARE FOR THE SHOWING BY THE PLAINTIFF(S) AND MEMBERS OF THE CORPORATION OF THE CASE-NUMBER: INMO72896(sic), BY THE RESPONDENTS.

17. FOR THE PLAINTIFF(S) WITH THE AFFIRMATION BY THE COMPLAINT ARE OF THE INJURY BY THE VIOLATION OF THE C.U.S.A.F., BY THE NEGLECT BY THE LANGUAGE-FRAUD FOR THE MISREPRESENTATION OF THE MEANING OF THE PROCEDURES OF THE WORDS BY THE COURT-ORDERS(SIC) AGAINST THE PLAINTIFF(S), BY THE RESPONDENTS.

18. FOR THE PLAINTIFF(S) WITH THE AFFIRMATION BY THE COMPLAINT ARE OF THE INJURY WITH THE TITLE: 42: U.S.A. CODES: SECTION: 1985 (1) FOR THE CONSPIRACY FOR THE DAMAGES BY THE CLAIMS FOR THE VIOLATION OF THE C.U.S.A.F.-GUARANTEEING-RIGHTS.

19. FOR THE PLAINTIFF(S) WITH THE AFFIRMATION BY THE COMPLAINT ARE OF THE INJURY BY THE STATUTORY AND PROCEDURAL-VIOLATION(S) (ARE)/IS BY THE LIST: PROCEDURAL-OUTLINES BY THE DISQUALIFICATION OF THE LANGUAGE-USE OF THE FOREIGN/FICTION-LANGUAGE WITHIN THE U.S.A.

20. FOR THE PLAINTIFF(S) WITH THE AFFIRMATION BY THE COMPLAINT ARE OF THE INJURY WITH THE TITLE: 28: U.S.A. CODES: SECTION: 1605 FOR THE GENERAL-EXCEPTIONS BY THE JURISDICTIONAL-IMMUNITY OF THE FOREIGN-COURT: [FOR THE FOREIGN-STATE (CONDITION OF THE AREA-FLAG](a) FOR A FOREIGN-STATE IS OF THE IMMUNITY PROHIBITING THE JURISDICTION OF THE COURTS OF THE U.S.A. OR OF THE STATES BY ANY CASE.

 8

Exhibit Z-8

21. (a) (2) BY WHICH THE ACTION IS UPON A COMMERCIAL-ACTIVITY BY THE INCORPORATION BY THE U.S.A. FOR THE COST OF THE MORE THAN $21.00 U.S.A. DOLLARS, BY THE FILING-FEE BY THE COURT OF THE DISTRICT OF THE U.S.A. AND BY THE RECEIPT FOR THE ESTABLISHING OF THE COMMERCE, FOR THE CIVIL-LAW-SUIT, OF THE CONDITION OF THE LANGUAGE, FOR AN ACT OF THE COMMERCE, FOR THE ENRICHMENT BY THE "LANGUAGE" BY THE CONTRACT, AND WITHIN THE TERRITORY OF THE U.S.A. WITH THE **TITLE: 28: U.S.A. CODES: SECTION: 1605** OF THE FOREIGN-SOVEREIGN-IMMUNITY-ACT.

22. FOR THE PLAINTIFF(S) WITH THE AFFIRMATION BY THE COMPLAINT ARE OF THE INJURY BY ANY-VIOLATION OF THE INTERNATIONAL-TREATY BY THE FOREIGN-STATE, BY THE OPERATION WITH THE C.U.S.A.F., IS BY THE UPHOLDING OF THE C.U.S.A.F.-RIGHTS OF THE SOVEREIGN-CITIZEN(S) IN THE PARTY, FOR THE BREACH OF THE CONTRACT-TREATY, WITH THE FILING BY THE FEDERAL-SUPREME-COURT OF THE U.S.A. BY THE WASHINGTON D.C. FOR THE TREATY-DISPUTE BETWEEN THE SOVEREIGN-CITIZEN(S) WITH THE TITLE: 42: U.S.A. CODES: SECTION: 1&2 FOR THE FLAG OF THE U.S.A. AND FOREIGN-LANGUAGE, WITH THE TREATY OF THE FOREIGN-SOVEREIGN-IMMUNITY-ACT FOR THE JURISDICTION WITH THE REQUIREMENTS BY THE C.U.S.A.F.-TREATY-LAW BY THE RESPONDENT-OFFICERS OF THE COURT.

23. FOR THE PLAINTIFF(S) WITH THE AFFIRMATION BY THE COMPLAINT ARE OF THE INJURY BY THE ENFORCING OF AN AGREEMENT (TREATY) BY THE MAKING, BY THE OATH OR AFFIRMATION BY THE SUPPORTING AND DEFENDING OF THE C.U.S.A.F. WHEN THE SURRENDER OF THE OATH AND AFFIRMATION *[INTO]* A FOREIGN/FICTION-LANGUAGE FOR THE CAUSE OF THE CONSTRUCTIVE-TREASON, CONTEMPT FOR THE C.U.S.A.F., FALSE-SWEARING AND PERJURY OF THE OATH WITH THE TITLE: 18: U.S.A. CODES: SECTION: 1621, BY THE RESPONDENTS-OFFICERS OF THE COURT.

24. FOR THE PLAINTIFF(S) WITH THE AFFIRMATION BY THE COMPLAINT ARE OF THE INJURY FOR THE LOSS OF THE RIGHTS BY THE PROPERTY OF THE TAKING BY THE VIOLATION OF THE INTERNATIONAL-LAW(S) (ARE)/IS AT THE ISSUE AND OF THE PROPERTY OR OF ANY PROPERTY BY THE EXCHANGE FOR THE PROPERTY IS OF THE PRESENT BY THE U.S.A. BY THE CONNECTION WITH THE COMMERCIAL-ACTIVITY OF THE INCORPORATION BY THE U.S.A. BY THE FOREIGN/FICTION-LANGUAGE; OR, BY THE PROPERTY IS BY THE BEING OF THE OWNERSHIP, OR BY THE OPERATION BY AN AGENCY OR INSTRUMENTALITY OF THE FOREIGN/FICTION-LANGUAGES FOR THAT AGENCY OR FOR THE INSTRUMENTALITY IS BY THE ENGAGEMENT BY THE COMMERCIAL-ACTIVITY BY THE U.S.A. [FOR THE FILING-FEE IS OF THE COMMERCIAL-ACTIVITY BY THE MONEY OR PROPERTY IS BY THE INVOLVEMENT OF THE OVER-$21.00 DOLLARS U.S.A.]

25. FOR THE PLAINTIFF(S) WITH THE AFFIRMATION BY THE COMPLAINT ARE OF THE INJURY (B) FOR ANY CLAIM OF THE ARISING-OUT OF THE INTERFERENCE WITH THE C.U.S.A.F. CONTRACT-RIGHTS FOR THE FILING OF THE TITLE: 42: U.S.A. CODES: SECTION: 1&2; FOR THE TRIAL BY THE JURY OF THE F.R.C.P. RULE: 38(a) AND THE C.U.S.A.F. ARTICLE OF THE NINE(9) IS FOR THE CAUSING OF AN ACTION WITH THE TITLE: 42: U.S.A. CODES: SECTION: 1986 FOR THE KNOWLEDGE OF THE LAW AND THE NEGLECT BY THE FAILURE FOR THE STOPPING AND CORRECTING OF THE WRONG BY THE RESPONDENT.

26. FOR THE PLAINTIFF(S) WITH THE AFFIRMATION BY THE COMPLAINT ARE OF THE

 9

B.J.F.
R.J.S.

Exhibit Z-9

INJURY FOR THE ACTION BY THE ENFORCEMENT OF AN AGREEMENT OF THE MAKING BY THE FOREIGN/FICTION-LANGUAGES WITH THE BENEFIT OF THE PRIVATE-PARTY BY THE SUBMISSION FOR THE LEGAL-RELATIONSHIP FOR THE CONTRACTUAL FOR THE ARBITRATION.

27. **EDUCATIONAL-NOTE:** FOR THE FEE OF THE FILING IS WITH THE CLERK OF THE COURT BY THE AMOUNT OF THE $150.00, FOR THE FEE(S) IS/(ARE) BY THE EMBEZZLEMENT FOR THE FOREIGN/FICTION-LANGUAGE BY THE VIOLATION WITH THE **TITLE: 18: U.S.A. CODES: SECTION: 641, 646 FOR THE COURT-OFFICER BY THE DEPOSIT OF THE REGISTRY-MONEYS:** FOR ANY CLERK OR OTHER-OFFICER(S) OF THE COURT OF THE U.S.A., BY THE FAILURE FOR THE DEPOSITING OF ANY MONEY BY THE REGISTRY OF THE **COURT OF THE DISTRICT OF THE UNITY-STATES OF THE AMERICA** OR FOR THE PAYMENT FOR THE **COURT OF THE DISTRICT OF THE UNITY-STATES OF THE AMERICA** OR BY THE RECEIVING BY THE OFFICERS-THEREOF, WITH THE **TREASURE OR FOR A DEPOSITORY OF THE UNITY-STATES OF THE AMERICA,** BY THE NAME AND BY THE CREDIT OF THE **COURT OF THE DISTRICT FOR THE UNITY-STATES** OR IS BY THE RETAINING OR CONVERTING FOR THE USE OF THE **UNITED STATES DISTRICT COURT**(sic) FOR ANY MONEY OF THE PAYING FOR THE **COURT OF THE DISTRICT OF THE UNITY-STATES OF THE AMERICA,** IS OF THE GUILT OF THE EMBEZZLEMENT WITH THE FINE WITH THE TITLE: 18: U.S.A. CODES: SECTION: 646; THAN THE AMOUNT ($__.00) OR IMPRISONMENT OF THE TEN-YEARS OR BOTH BY THE OFFICERS OF THE COURT.

28. **FOR THE PLAINTIFF(S) WITH THE AFFIRMATION BY THE COMPLAINT** ARE FOR THE **TITLE: 18: U.S.A. CODES: SECTION: 641 FOR THE PUBLIC-MONEY, PROPERTY OR RECORDS:** WHOEVER: IS BY THE EMBEZZLING, STEALING, PURLOINING, OR KNOWING, CONVERTS FOR THE USE OF THE ANOTHER, WITHOUT THE AUTHORITY, CONVEYS OR DISPOSES OF ANY RECORD, VOUCHER, MONEY, OR THING OF THE VALUE OF THE **COURT OF THE DISTRICT FOR THE UNITY-STATES OF THE AMERICA:** LAWSUIT, OR OF ANY PROPERTY OF THE MAKING OR BEING BY THE MAKING WITH THE CONTRACT FOR THE **COURT OF THE DISTRICT OF THE UNITY-STATES OF THE AMERICA,** OF THE COURTS WITH THE C.U.S.A.F. ARTICLE OF THE NINE(9) AND TITLE: 4: U.S.A. CODES: SECTION: 1&2 FOR THE FLAG OF THE U.S.A., WHOEVER, BY THE RECEIVING, CONCEALMENT, OR CONVERTS FOR THE COMPLAINT IS BY THE COURT OF THE DISTRICT OF THE UNITY-STATES OF THE AMERICA FOR THE GAIN, KNOWING THE **COURT OF THE DISTRICT OF THE UNITY-STATES OF THE AMERICA,** FOR THE EMBEZZLING, STEALING, PURLOINING OR CONVEYING FOR **THE UNITED STATES DISTRICT COURT**(sic) - FOR THE FINE (MONEY OR PROPERTY) WITH THE TITLE: 18: U.S.A. SECTION: 641; OR BY THE IMPRISONMENT OF THE TEN(10)-YEARS OR BOTH BY THE HEREIN-RESPONDENTS.

FOR THE DEMAND AND THE SUMMONS

29. **FOR THE PLAINTIFF(S) WITH THE AFFIRMATION WITH THE TRUTH BY THE COMPLAINT** IS FOR THE INJURY OF THE PLAINTIFF(S) FOR THE DEMAND-JUDGEMENT IS FOR THE NEGLIGENT-ACTS OF THE ATTORNEYS OF THE LAW, BY THE INCORPORATION OF THIS CASE-NUMBER: ____________________, BY THE SUM OF THE TEN-MILLION-DOLLARS-UNITY-STATES OF THE AMERICA-CURRENCY ($10,000,000.00), PLUS-COSTS AND DISBURSEMENTS. WITH THE FOREIGN-SOVEREIGN-IMMUNITY-ACT OF THE OFFICERS OF THE COURT WITH THE FOREIGN-

 10

R. J. S
B. J. F.

Exhibit Z-10

FICTION-FLAG FOR THE PLAINTIFF(S) ARE BY THE DEMAND FOR THE TEN-TIMES(10) OF THIS JUDGEMENT WITH THE INTERNATIONAL-JURISDICTION OF THE **LAW OF THE FLAG** BY THE SANCTUARY OF THE COURT AGAINST THE SOVEREIGN-CITIZEN(S) BY THE PARTIES FOR THE BREACH OF THE C.U.S.A.F.-CONTRACT BY THE USE OF THE FICTION-LANGUAGE, FOR THE PAYMENT IS BY THE **BANK OF ENGLAND** AS THE TRUSTEE FOR THE BANKRUPTCY OF THE UNITED STATES OF AMERICA(sic). FOR THE POSTMASTER-GENERAL IS BY THE HAVING OF THE JURISDICTION FOR THE ORDERING OF THE TREASURY FOR THE ENFORCEMENT OF THIS ORDER. FOR THIS INCORPORATION-CASE IS FOR THE HAVING WITH THE APPROVAL FOR ANY OBSTRUCTIONS OF THE LANGUAGE FOR THE **APARTHEID** WITH THE FILING AT THE WORLD-COURT BY THE "HAGUE", AND IS WITH THE APPROVAL OF THE RUSSIAN-SUPREME-COURT WITH THE LAW OF THE FLAG, BY THE PLACEMENT OF THE AMERICAN-FLAG(1X1.9) BY THE SANCTUARY OF THE COURT OF THE RUSSIAN-COURT BY THE STATE OF THE SOVEREIGN-RUSSIA OR BY ANY SOVEREIGN-COURT BY THE WORLD FOR THE JURISDICTION OF THE UNITY-STATES OF THE AMERICA [CAN AND WILL] FOR THE ENTERING OF A DEFAULT-JUDGEMENT AGAINST THE COURT OF THE VIOLATION FOR THE FICTITIOUS-USE OF THE LANGUAGE FOR THE EXTORTION OF THE SOVEREIGNS-RIGHTS WITH THE DISABILITIES-ACT WHERE THE PEOPLE ARE OF THE INJURY BY THE DISABILITY OF THE LANGUAGE **(FOR THE NOUNS ARE BY THE FORM OF THE VERB)** FOR THE EXTORTION IS AGAINST THE CITIZEN(S) BY THE COURT.

30. **FOR THE PLAINTIFF(S) WITH THE AFFIRMATION BY THE COMPLAINT** ARE OF THE INJURY BY THE LOSS OF THE FREEDOM, PROPERTY AND PAIN OF THE BODY AND MIND FOR THE LOSS WITH THE SUBSTANTIAL-DAMAGE OF THE TEN-BILLION ($10,000,000,000.00) DOLLARS FOR THE DEPRIVATION OF THE RIGHTS THROUGH THE APARTHEID.

31. FOR THE PLAINTIFF(S) OF THE SOVEREIGN-CITIZEN(S) IS/ARE BY THE ***SUMMONING*** *AND REQUIRING FOR THE FILING WITH THIS COURT* ______

AND FOR THE SERVING OF THE RESPONDENT(S):

Bradley-Jefferson: Franks AND Robert-Joel: Simpson AS THE SOVEREIGN-CITIZEN(S) OF THE PARTY AT THE ADDRESS: c/o 30-257: Monte-Vista-Way: 1000-Palms: California: [92276]

FOR AN ANSWER OF THE COMPLAINT IS BY THE SERVING OF THE RESPONDENT(S) WITH THE 60-DAYS BY THE DAY OF THE SERVICE OF THIS SUMMONS OF THE RESPONDENT(S). FOR THE FAILURE OF THE DOING-SO IS FOR THE TAKING OF A JUDGMENT BY THE DEFAULT AGAINST THE RESPONDENT(S) FOR THE RELIEF IS WITH THE DEMAND(S) OF THE COMPLAINT.

FOR THE DEFINITIONS BY THE SUPPORT OF THIS BY CORPORATION-CASE FOR THE CONSTITUTION/CONTRACT OF THE UNITY-STATES WITH THE AMERICA-FLAG, HEREIN-UNDER THE BY CORPORATION FOR THE CONSTITUTION/CONTRACT OF THE UNITY-STATES WITH THE AMERICA-FLAG, HEREIN.

1). FOR THE ARTICLE OF THE ONE(1): FOR THE RIGHT OF THE TRUTH IS BY THE LANGUAGE OF THE NOUN.

2). FOR THE ARTICLE OF THE SECOND(2): FOR THE RIGHT OF THE JUDGEMENT IS BY THE TRUTH.

 11

B.J.F.
R.J.S.

Exhibit Z-11

3). FOR THE ARTICLE OF THE THREE(3): FOR THE FREEDOM OF THE SPEECH AND PRESS, AND FOR THE RIGHT FOR THE PETITIONING OF THE GOVERNMENT FOR THE REDRESS OF THE GRIEVANCES, AND OF THE FREEDOM OF THE PARTY'S RELIGION.
4). FOR THE ARTICLE OF THE FOUR(4): FOR THE RIGHT OF THE CAUSE OF THE COURT-ACTION BY THE LANGUAGE OF THE TRUTH.
5). FOR THE ARTICLE OF THE FIVE(5): FOR THE RIGHT OF THE FREEDOM OF THIS CONSTITUTION BY THE TRUTH.
6). FOR THE ARTICLE OF THE SIX(6:): FOR THE SEARCHES AND SEIZURES ARE WITH THE TRUTH BY THE DOCUMENTATION OF THE LANGUAGE FOR THE WARRANTS ARE OF THE ISSUE BY THE TRUTH-LANGUAGE, BUT UPON THE PROBABLE-CAUSE WITH THE SWEARING OF THE OATH/AFFIRMATION, WITH THE PARTICULAR-DESCRIPTION OF THE PLACE FOR THE SEARCH AND FOR THE PARTY AND THINGS THAT ARE FOR THE POSSESSION BY THE COURT-ORDER.
7). FOR THE ARTICLE OF THE SEVEN(7): FOR THE PARTY BY ANY CRIMINAL-CASE IS WITH THE COMPLIANCE BY THE TRUTH AS THE WITNESS AGAINST THE PARTY'S-SELF, OR WITH THE DEPRIVATION OF THE LIFE, LIBERTY OR PROPERTY, BY THE NEGLECT OF THE DUE-PROCESS OF THE LAW. NOTES: C.U.S.A.F.-CONTRACT OF THE SEVEN(7).
8). FOR THE ARTICLE OF THE EIGHT(8): FOR THE RIGHT OF A SPEEDY AND PUBLIC-TRIAL. BY THE JURY OF THE IMPARTIAL-CITIZENS, BY THE VENUE OF THE DISTRICT OF THE U.S.A. WHERE THE ACTION IS OF THE COMMITMENT, FOR THE RESPONDENT-PARTY IS FOR THE INFORMATION OF THE NATURE AND CAUSE OF THE ACCUSATION; FOR THE RESPONDENT-PARTY IS FOR THE CONFRONTATION BY THE WITNESS BY THE PARTY FOR THE HAVING OF THE COMPULSORY-PROCESS FOR THE OBTAINING OF THE WITNESS AND EVIDENCE BY THE PARTY'S FAVOR, AND FOR THE HAVING OF THE ASSISTANCE OF THE COUNSEL FOR THE PARTY'S-DEFENSE.
NOTES: VIOLATION OF THE DUE-PROCESS (COUNSEL) - FOR THE OBSTRUCTION OF THE JUSTICE (TITLE: 18: CHAPTER: 63: U.S.A. CODES: SECTION: 1512) FOR THE PERJURY OF THE OATH-(TITLE: 18: CHAPTER: 63: U.S.A. CODES: SECTION: 1621) FOR ANY DEPRIVATION OF THE RIGHTS WITH THE COLOR OF THE LAW = (TITLE: 18: U.S.A. CODES: SECTION: 2421). NOTE: FOR THE COLOR OF THE LAW = CORRUPTION OF THE FLAG OF THE U.S.A.
9). FOR THE ARTICLE OF THE NINE(9): BY THE SUITS OF THE COMMON-LAW, WHERE THE VALUE BY THE CONTROVERSY IS OVER THE TWENTY-DOLLARS WITH THE RIGHT OF THE TRIAL BY THE JURY IS OF THE PRESERVATION FOR THE FACT IS BY THE TRUTH-LANGUAGE WITH THE TRIAL BY THE JURY. (FOR THE PARTY IS BY THE GIVING OF YOUR NAME WITH THE PUNCTUATION (-:) BY THE PERSON BY THE BAR WITH THE JURISDICTIONAL-DISPLAY OF THE FLAG: TITLE: 4: U.S.A. CODES: SECTION: 1&2 OF THE U.S.A. WITH THE LAW OF THE FLAG, AND ARE BY THE HAVING BY THE PARTY'S POSSESSION ARMY-REGULATIONS: 840-10: CHAPTER: 2-1 (a,b) AND CHAPTER: 2-5 (a,b,c) FOR THE CAUSE OF A COMMON-LAW-COURT.
10). FOR THE ARTICLE OF THE TEN(10): FOR THE PUNISHMENT IS BY THE LANGUAGE OF THE TRUTH. FOR THE CRUEL AND UNUSUAL-PUNISHMENTS IS WITH THE PROHIBITION FOR THE INFLICTION.
11). FOR THE ARTICLE OF THE ELEVEN(11): FOR THE ENUMERATION BY THE C.U.S.A.F.-CONTRACT OF THE CERTAIN-RIGHTS ARE BY THE C.U.S.A.F.-CONTRACT FOR THE DENIAL OR DISPARAGE OF THE CITIZENS AS THE OFFICERS OF THE GOVERNMENT ARE WITH THE INCORPORATION/RETAIN BY THE PEOPLE.
12). FOR THE ARTICLE OF THE TWELVE(12): FOR THE CONSTITUTION/CONTRACT WITH THE PROHIBITION BY THE RESERVATION OF THE C.U.S.A.F.-CONTRACT, ARE

R. J. S.
B. J. F.

Exhibit Z-12

WITH THE RESERVATION BY THE MUTUAL-AGREEMENT BY THE TITLE-PARTIES-HEREIN.

13). BY THE ARTICLE OF THE THIRTEEN(13): FOR THE TRUTH OF THE FOREIGN/FICTION-LANGUAGES IS FOR THE FOREIGN/FICTION COURT AND IS FOR THE JURISDICTIONS BY THE TRUTH OVER THE SOVEREIGN-CITIZEN(S) BY THE PARTY, FOR THE JUDICIAL-LANGUAGE OF THE UNITY-STATES IS FOR THE CONSTRUCTION FOR THE EXTENSION BY ANY SUIT BY THE LAW OR BY THE EQUITY FOR THE COMMENCEMENT OR FOR THE PROSECUTION AGAINST ANY ONE OF THE UNITY-STATES BY THE CITIZENS OF THE OTHER-STATES OR BY THE CITIZENS OR BY THE SUBJECTS OF ANY FOREIGN/FICTION-STATE BY THE TRUTH. FOR THE NEW-STATE WITH THE TRUTH IS FOR THE ERECTION OF THE NEW-STATE WITHIN THE STATE FOR THE FORMATION OF A TRUTHFUL-STATE WITHIN THE UNITY-STATES.

14). FOR THE AMENDMENT 14: (BY THE NEVER-MAKING-LEGAL BY THE CONGRESS-JULY/1868) BY THE PROHIBITION OF A STATE (FOR THE CITIZEN BY THE PARTY) IS FOR THE MAKING/ENFORCING OF ANY LAW WHICH IS FOR THE ABRIDGING OF THE PRIVILEGES/IMMUNITIES OF THE CITIZENS OF THE U.S.A., NOR IS FOR ANY STATE (FOR THE CITIZEN BY THE PARTY) FOR THE DEPRIVING OF ANY PARTY OF THE LIFE, LIBERTY/PROPERTY, BY THE NEGLECTING OF THE DUE-PROCESS OF THE LAW; NOR BY THE PARTY, FOR THE EQUAL-PROTECTION OF THE LAW. FOR THE TITLE: 42: U.S.A. CODES: SECTION: 1985(2)(3). NOTE: **AMENDMENT** IS OF AN **ADJECTIVE OF THE "FOURTEEN"** AND IS FOR THE MAKING OF THE AMENDMENT-STATEMENT OF THE FICTION BY THE FAILURE OF THE AUTHORITY AND IS FOR THE USING OF THE CIVIL-RIGHTS-ACT OF THE 1964 FOR THE EQUAL-PROTECTION AND CONVERSION UNTO THE NOUN-PROCEDURES OF THE FACTS.

15). MIRANDA: IS BY THE FICTION OF A DISCLAIMER-CONTRACT BY THE FUTURE-TENSE FOR THE **DISQUALIFICATION OF THE PRESENT-TENSE-JURISDICTION OF ANY CONTRACT-DISCLAIMER.**

16). FOR THE GIVING OF YOUR NAME WITH THE PUNCTUATION WHILE BY THE BAR: FIRST-MIDDLE: LAST. FOR THE IDENTIFICATION OF THE TRUSTEE-SOVEREIGN-CITIZEN(S) IN THE PARTY AGAINST THE DISMISSAL-COMPLAINT BY THE COURT BY THE FICTION OF THE PARLIAMENTARY-COURT, FOR THE PROHIBITION OF A CONTRACT IS FOR THE DISMISSING OF THE INCORPORATION OF THE CASE FOR THE PLEADING BEFORE THE COURT OF THE DISTRICT; BY THE PLAINTIFF(S)-PAYING FOR THE CLERK OF THE COURTS FOR THE TRIAL BY THE JURY WITH THE F.R.C.P. RULE: 38(a). FOR THE COMMERCIAL-CONTRACT WITH THE FOREIGN-STATE IS BY THE COLLUSION-CONTEMPT-CHARGE AND IS WITH THE TITLE: 28: CHAPTER: 85: U.S.A. CODES: SECTION: 1359 OR BY THE THREAT OF THE JAIL. (JAIL IS CRIMINAL). FOR THE JUDGE'S USE OF THE TERM-CHARGE IS FOR THE MAKING-CASE OF A CRIMINAL-PROCEDURE AND WITH THE C.U.S.A.F.-CONTRACT FOR THE VIOLATION OF THE LAW FOR THE DUE-PROCESS BEFORE THE FACTS WITH THE PROOF BY THE CASE, WITH THE INTENT OF THE GUILTY-TILL-PROVING-INNOCENT, BY THE PLACE OF THE INNOCENT-TILL-PROVING-GUILTY.

17). FOR THE F.R.C.P. RULE: 4: PROCESS (a), FOR THE SUMMONS, (b), FOR THE FORM, (c), FOR THE SERVICE (BY THE PRESENTATION FOR THE RESPONDENTS), (d), FOR THE SUMMONS AND COMPLAINT (NOTE: 20-DAY-RETURN-ANSWER FOR THE PLAINTIFF AND COURT, (g), FOR THE RETURN-PROOF OF THE SERVICE ON THE CLERK OF THE COURT, (H), FOR THE AMENDMENT BY THE SERVICE, (j), FOR THE TIME-LIMIT OF THE 120 DAYS FOR THE RETURN-SERVICE.

18). FOR THE F.R.C.P. RULE: 5 = FOR THE SERVICE: (a) FOR THE REQUIREMENT, (d) FOR THE CERTIFICATE OF THE FILING. (e) FOR THE FILING WITH THE CLERK (FOR THE CLERK, IS WITH THE PROHIBITION FOR THE REFUSAL FOR THE FILING OF ANY PAPERS WITH THE FAILURE FOR THE BEING BY THE FORM OF THE LOCAL-

R. J. S.
B. J. F.

Exhibit Z-13

RULES. AS ALL LOCAL-RULES ARE BY THE WRITING OF THE FICTION) TITLE: 28: U.S.A. CODES: SECTION: 646.

19). FOR THE F.R.C.P. RULE: 6 = FOR THE TIME: (a), FOR THE COMPUTATION-(MONDAY - FRIDAY). (d), FOR THE COMPLAINTS AND AFFIDAVITS ARE FOR THE BEING WITHIN THE SERVICE OF THE FIVE(5)DAYS-RULE: BEFORE THE TRIAL BY THE PLAINTIFF(S); AND ONE(1): DAY-SERVICE BEFORE THE TRIAL FOR THE DEFENDANT.

20). FOR THE F.R.C.P. RULE: 7: = PLEADINGS: (a), FOR THE PLEADINGS, (b), OF/BY/AND FOR THE COMPLAINT, WHICH ARE FOR THE MAKING WITH THE PARTICULARITY OF THE RELIEF OF THE ORDER OF THE SEEKING. NOTE: FOR THE NOTICE OF THE REFUSAL FOR THE FRAUD IS FOR THE OPPOSING-COMPLAINT OF THE FRAUD, BY THE BEING OF THE FAILURE FOR THE TRAVERSING WITH THE COMPLAINT OF THE FRAUD/OPPONENT'S FICTION, STAY-ON-POINT BY THE REAFFIRMING OF THE COMPLAINT OF YOUR ORIGINAL-PLEADINGS OR CROSS-COMPLAINT-PLEADINGS.

21). FOR THE F.R.C.P. RULE: 8: = RULES OF THE PLEADING: (a), FOR THE CLAIM FOR THE RELIEF, IS FOR THE ASKING FOR THE COMPENSATION (FEES, MONEY, PROPERTY) AND IS FOR THE CONTAINING (b), FOR THE DEFENSE-FORM OF THE DENIALS, (c), FOR THE AFFIRMATIVE-DEFENSE, (d), FOR THE FAILURE BY THE DENYING, (e), FOR THE PLEADING BY THE BEING-CONCISE.

22). FOR THE F.R.C.P. RULE: 9: = PLEADINGS-SPECIAL (b), FOR THE FRAUD IS WITH THE CONDITION OF THE MIND (e), FOR THE JUDGEMENT, (f), FOR THE TIME AND PLACE, (g), FOR THE SPECIAL-DAMAGE.

23). FOR THE F.R.C.P. RULE: 10: = FOR THE FORM OF THE PLEADINGS: (a)CAPTIONS, (b) FOR THE PARAGRAPHS.

24). F.R.C.P. RULE: 11: FOR THE FRIVOLOUS-FILING, FOR ALL PLEADINGS ARE FOR THE BEING WITH THE SIGNATURE AND ADDRESS, FOR THE SIGNING OF THE TICKET IS WITH THE PROHIBITION WITH A LAW UNTIL THE FIFTH-DAY OF THE VIOLATION FOR THE SANCTIONS AND FEES. FOR THE CITATION IS BY THE VOID WHEN THE ACT OF THE COLLUSION IS BY THE USE WITH THE TITLE: 28: CHAPTER: 85: U.S.A. CODES: SECTION: 1359.

25). FOR THE F.R.C.P. RULE: 12(b) FOR THE PRESENTATION; 12(b)(7) FOR THE FAILURE OF THE JOINING (IS FOR THE BEING OF THE SAME-JURISDICTION OF THE FLAG WITH THE LAW OF THE FLAG) IS BY THE JOINDER IS OF THE COMPLETE-EVEN WHEN THE FICTION/FOREIGN IS OF THE COMPLETE BY THE JOINING BY THE BAR, FOR THE STUDY THE D.W.M.-LAW-PROCEDURES.

12(b)(6) FOR THE FAILURE BY THE AFFIRMING OF THE CLAIM, [MUST JOIN JURISDICTIONS BEFORE AFFIRMING BY JURY] FOR THE FOREIGN/FICTION-JURISDICTION IS WITH THE PROHIBITION BY THE JOINDER BY THE COURT, PLAINTIFF(S)AND RESPONDENT(S)ARE WITH THE PROHIBITION FOR THE AFFIRMING-PLEADINGS BY THE COURT BY DIFFERENT-FOREIGN/FICTION-JURISDICTIONS FOR THE JOINDER.

12(b)(5) FOR THE IMPROPER-PROCESS: [BY NOT PROCESSING OF THE PAPERWORK WITH THE CLERK OF THE COURT]

FOR THE PROHIBITION FOR THE PROCESS BY THE FICTION: USE OF THE ADJECTIVES AND THE VERB BY PLACE OF THE NOUN IS FOR THE CAUSING OF THE MAIL-FRAUD: TITLE: 18: U.S.A. CODES: SECTION: 1342. AND FICTITIOUS-USE OF THE LANGUAGE FOR THE FRAUD.

12(b)(4) IS FOR THE IMPROPER-SERVICE, (BY THE FAILURE FOR THE SERVING OF THE PAPERWORK ON THE RESPONDENT BY THE LAW]

FOR THE PROHIBITION OF THE SERVICE BY THE FICTION: USE OF THE ADJECTIVES; CAUSING MAIL-FRAUD WITH THE TITLE: 18: U.S.A. CODES: SECTION: 1342 WITH THE F.R.C.P. RULE 12(b)(3) FOR THE IMPROPER-VENUE. FOR THE

R. J. S
B. J. F

Exhibit Z-14

JUDGE IS WITH THE PROHIBITION FOR THE JOINING WITH THE JURISDICTION OF THE TRUTH BY THE LAW WHERE THE ACT IS FOR THE TAKING-PLACE AND THE JURISDICTION, **WITH THE LAW OF THE FLAG-FICTION AND NOUNS-USE AS THE ADJECTIVES AND VERB. FOR THE WATCHING IS OF THE TRAPS BY THE TITLES, NAMES, DATES, CASE NUMBERS.**
12(b)(2)- FOR THE LACK OF THE PERSONAL-JURISDICTION OVER THE PARTY, FOR THE FICTION-WRONG-LAW OF THE LANGUAGE-JURISDICTION, WHEN THE COURT IS WITH THE FAILURE FOR THE JOINING, COURT IS WITH THE PROHIBITION FOR THE STATING OF THE CLAIM/NATURE OF THE BY JURY] 12(b)(1) FOR THE LACK OF THE JURISDICTION OVER THE SUBJECT-MATTER. WHEN THE JUDGE IS WITH THE FAILURE FOR THE READING OF THE CASE BEFORE THIS COURT AND BY THE ACTING ON THE OPINION, AND BY THE FAILURE FOR THE ACTING ON THE FACTS OF THE CASE. FOR THE DIFFERENT-CAUSES OF THE REMEDY: (A). FOR THE COMPLAINT: JUDGEMENT ON THE PLEADINGS, (B) - COMPLAINT FOR THE STRIKING. (C) - WAIVER (SUBJECT-MATTER) PROHIBITION OF THE JURISDICTION.
26). FOR THE F.R.C.P. RULE: 15, FOR THE AMENDMENT AND SUPPLEMENTAL-PLEADINGS (a.b.c.d.) IS FOR THE READING BY THE F.R.C.P.
27). FOR THE F.R.C.P. RULE: 16(f), FOR THE SANCTIONS: WHEN THE JUDGE/OFFICERS OF THE COURT ARE/IS BY THE TRUTH FOR THE UNITY OF THE JURISDICTION OF THE CONSTITUTION BY THE SANCTUARY OF THE COURT. FOR THE BREACH OF THE C.U.S.A.F.-CONTRACT WITH THE LAW OF THE SOVEREIGN-FLAG OF THE U.S.A. FOR THE VIOLATION OF THE OATH OF THE OFFICE, SANCTION FOR THE BREACH OF THE CONTRACT WITH THE OATH AND AFFIRMATION; AND FOR THE FILING-FEES BY THE PAYING ARE FOR THE TRIAL BY THE JURY AND RECUSAL-DISMISSAL ORDERS. FOR THE COURT IS WITH THE PROHIBITION FOR THE ORDERING OF THE FEES (TITLE: 42: U.S.A. CODES: SECTION: 1988) FOR THE BREACH OF THE C.U.S.A.F.-CONTRACT FOR THE ARTICLE OF THE NINE (9) FOR THE TRIAL BY THE JURY AND FOR THE ARTICLE OF THE SEVEN (7) FOR THE DUE-PROCESS OF THE LAW. FOR THE SANCTION AGAINST THE JUDGE FOR THE FAILURE FOR THE COMING BY TO THE DISCOVERY-HEARING AND FOR THE FAILURE FOR THE JOINING WITH THE OATH AND AFFIRMATION OF THE C.U.S.A.F.-CONTRACT.
28). FOR THE F.R.C.P. RULE: 18-19, FOR THE JOINDER ALSO F.R.C.P. RULE: 12(b)(7).
29). FOR THE F.R.C.P. RULE: 24, FOR THE TITLE: 28: U.S.A. CODES: SECTION: 2403 FOR THE CHALLENGE OF THE CONTRACT/CONSTITUTIONALITY
30). FOR THE F.R.C.P. RULE: 38(a), FOR THE TRIAL BY THE JURY
31). FOR F.R.C.P. RULE: 41(a), FOR THE DISMISSAL OF THE ACTION BY THE VOLUNTARY-USE, FOR THE WITHDRAWING OF THE CASE THAT THE PLAINTIFF(S) BY THE KNOWING IS BY THE WRITING OF THE INCORRECT.
32). FOR THE F.R.C.P. RULE: 49, FOR THE ISSUES ARE BY THE SENDING FOR THE JURY BY THE DEMAND.
33). FOR F.R.C.P. RULE: 50, FOR THE NEW TRIAL: USE WITH THE DE-NOVO/WRIT OF THE HABIUS-CORPUS.
34). FOR THE F.R.C.P. RULE: 54, FOR THE DEMAND FOR THE JUDGEMENT.
35). FOR THE F.R.C.P. RULE: 55, FOR THE DEFAULT
36). FOR THE F.R.C.P. RULE: 56, FOR THE C-SUMMARY-JUDGEMENT.
37). FOR THE F.R.C.P. RULE: 57, FOR THE DECLARATORY-JUDGEMENT
38). FOR THE POLICY AND CUSTOM; ACTS ON THE DAY,______ ,1999, BY THE DESCRIPTION OF THE ACTIONS AND OMISSIONS FOR THE ENGAGEMENT WITH THE COLOR OF THE STATE LAW AUTHORITY, BY THE SUING AS THE PARTY RESPONSIBLE

 15

Exhibit Z-15

BY THE AUTHORIZATION AND RATIFICATION OF THE ACTS OF THE STATE-AGENTS; FOR THE PLAINTIFF(S)ARE OF THE INJURY BY THE NEGLECT OF THE C.U.S.A.F.-CONTRACT FOR THE RIGHTS WITH THE SECURITY OF THE PARTY WITH THE C.U.S.A.F.-CONTRACT FOR THE ARTICLE OF THE SIX(6) FOR THE WARRANT IS BY THE ISSUE BY THE JUDGE OF THE OATH AND AFFIRMATION; C.U.S.A.F.-CONTRACT FOR THE ARTICLE OF THE NINE(9) FOR THE RIGHT BY THE TRIAL BY THE JURY, WITH THE F.R.C.P. RULE: 38(a) AND WITH THE DUE-PROCESS OF THE LAW WITH THE C.U.S.A.F.-CONTRACT FOR THE ARTICLE OF THE SEVEN(7), BY THE RESPONDENT.

39). FOR THE OPINION OF THE DAVID: MILLER: FOR THE ACTORS BY THE COURT BY THE CREATION OF AN ELABORATE-FRAUD, AND FOR THE FAILURE OF THE JUSTICE, BY THE COURT, F.R.C.P. RULE: 12(b)(2). FOR THE F.R.C.P. RULE: 9(b) FOR THE FRAUD: C.U.S.A.F.-CONTRACT FOR THE ARTICLE OF THE SEVEN(7) FOR THE DUE-PROCESS, F.R.C.P. RULE: 38(e)FOR THE TRIAL, AND WITH THE TITLE: 18: U.S.A. CODES: SECTION: 1342 FOR THE FICTITIOUS (ADJECTIVES)(VERB)FOR THE USE OF THE NAME (NOUN). FOR THE NOUNS BY THE USE AS VERBS AND ADJECTIVES.

40). FOR THE EXAMPLE OF THE SENTENCE-PLEADINGS: WITH THE PROHIBITION OF THE SUBJECT-MATTER-JURISDICTION WITH THE F.R.C.P. RULE: 12(b)(1), AND F.R.C.P. RULE: 9(b)FOR THE FRAUD, OVER THE PLAINTIFF(S), FOR THE USE OF THE COERCION AND EXTORTION, BY THE THREATENING OF THE PLAINTIFF(S). FOR THE TITLE: 42: U.S.A. CODES: SECTION: 1983: NOTE: 352 BY THE ORDER BY THE SUSTAINING OF THE 1983-CONSPIRACY-CLAIM, FOR THERE IS FOR THE BEING OF THE EVIDENCE OF THE EFFORT/PLANNING BETWEEN THE PRIVATE-ASSOCIATIONS AND STATE-ACTORS **(FOR THE JUDGE IS WITH THE FAILURE OF THE OATH AND AFFIRMATION FOR THE JUDGE IS WITH AN ACTOR BY THE NEGLECT OF SUBJECT-MATTER-JURISDICTION)**, BY THE DENYING OF THE PLAINTIFF(S) OF THE C.U.S.A.F.-CONTRACT-RIGHTS. FOR THE NOUNS BY THE USE AS THE VERBS AND ADJECTIVES FOR THE FICTION-LANGUAGE.

41). FOR THE (TITLE: 18: U.S.A. CODES: SECTION: 242) FOR THE DEPRIVATION OF THE RIGHTS WITH THE COLOR OF THE LAW: FOR THE PARTY WITH THE COLOR OF THE LAW-STATUTE, ORDINANCE, REGULATION/CUSTOM, WILLFUL-SUBJECTS OF THE INHABITANT OF THE STATE, TERRITORY/DISTRICT OF THE DEPRIVATION OF THE RIGHTS/PRIVILEGES/IMMUNITIES-SECURING/PROTECTION BY THE CONSTITUTION/LAWS OF THE U.S.A. BY THE FINE OF THE $1000. OR LESS; OR, IMPRISONMENT OF THE ONE-YEAR OR LESS, OR BOTH. FOR THE CONTRACT IS BY THE PRESENT-TENSE, IS THE CONTRACT BETWEEN THE COURT AND THE ATTORNEY FOR THE VIOLATIONS OF THE C.U.S.A.F.-CONTRACT FOR THE ARTICLE OF THE SIX(6) BY THE SECTION OF THE THREE(3) WITH THE OATH: TITLE: 28: U.S.A. CODES: SECTION: 1343 FOR THE EQUAL-PROTECTION AND C.U.S.A.F.-CONTRACT FOR THE ARTICLE OF THE NINE(9): DUE-PROCESS.

42). FOR THE TITLE: 42: U.S.A. CODES: SECTION: 1983: AT NOTE: 355. FOR THE PLAINTIFF(S) ARE OF THE INJURY BY THE HEREIN-ACTION OF THE WRONG-INCORPORATION BY THE CASE-CITES WHEN BY THE SIGNATURE AND BY THE DEPRIVATION OF THE PLAINTIFF(S) OF THE PLAINTIFF'S C.U.S.A.F.-CONTRACT FOR THE RIGHTS, BY THE FAILURE FOR THE HAVING OF THE C.U.S.A.F.-CONTRACT FOR THE ARTICLE OF THE SIX(6) FOR THE WARRANT IS FOR THE SIGNATURE BY THE JUDGE OF THE OATH AND AFFIRMATION, TRIAL BY THE JURY, WITH THE C.U.S.A.F.-CONTRACT FOR THE ARTICLE OF THE SEVEN(7): DUE-PROCESS AND TITLE: 42: U.S.A. CODES: SECTION: 1985(2) FOR THE EQUAL-PROTECTION OF THE LAW: F.R.C.P. RULES: 12(b)(7, 1, 2), BY THE RESPONDENTS.

16

B.J.F.
R.J.S.

Exhibit Z-16

43). FOR THE TITLE: 18: U.S.A. CODES: SECTION: 1621: STATE IS FOR THE PAYING OF ALL FEES WHEN THE PLAINTIFF(S) ARE OF THE INJURY BY THE LACK OF THE OATH/AFFIRMATION OF THE OFFICE AND PERJURY OF THE OATH BY THE RESPONDENT-JUDGE AND OFFICERS OF THE COURT: FOR THE CITIZENS ARE OF THE INJURY BY THE LACK OF ANY CONTRACT FOR THE PAYING OF THE FEES, BY THE CITIZENS BY THE PARTY'S: C.U.S.A.F.-CONTRACT-RIGHTS-VIOLATION. CROSS REF. FOR THE F.R.C.P. RULE: 9(b). FOR THE TITLE: 28: U.S.A. CODES: SECTION: 2072(b); C.U.S.A.F.-CONTRACT FOR THE ARTICLE OF THE SIX(6): SECTION THE THREE(3) FOR THE FOREIGN/FICTION-STATES.

44). WITH THE C.U.S.A.F.-CONTRACT FOR THE OFFICERS OF THE COURT, ARE FOR THE SWEARING OF AN ALLEGIANCE/OATH, JUDGE(S): OATH/AFFIRMATION/CONTRACT/TRUST/TREATY: **I, N__N, FOR THE AFFIRMATION AND FOR THE DECLARATION OF THE TRUTH(NOUN) FOR THE SUPPORT OF THE CONSTITUTION OF THE UNITY-STATES AND FOR THE STATE OF THE CONTRACT FOR WHERE PETITIONER STANDS BY THE JUDGEMENT ; THAT THE PETITIONER IS WITH THE ADMINISTRATION OF THE JUSTICE WITH THE RESPECT FOR THE PERSON(S)/CITIZEN(S)/PARTY(S)/VESSEL(S)/PEOPLE/AND TRUSTEE(S) BY THE FAITHFUL AND IMPARTIAL-DISCHARGE OF THE DUTIES OF THE OFFICE; BY THE BEST OF MY ABILITY. (FICTION OATH BY THE NOUN)**

FOR THE CONSTRUCTIVE-TREASON: FOR THE CONTRACT OF THE RESPONSIBILITY AND AUTHORITY IS FOR THE SURRENDERING OF THE C.U.S.A.F.-CONTRACT BY TO THE FICTION/FOREIGN-STATE WITH THE FICTION/FOREIGN-FRINGE-FLAG FOR THE OATH AND AFFIRMATION, ALSO BY THE KNOWING AS THE ALLEGIANCE BY THE SUPPORTING OF THE C.U.S.A.F.-CONTRACT FOR THE CONSTRUCTIVE-TREASON BY THE DEFINITION BY THE (KNOWLEDGE) FOR THE **WILL OF THE BY TENT** BY THE DESECRATION (TITLE: 4: U.S.A. CODES: SECTION: THREE(3) OF THE FLAG OF THE U.S.A. BY THE FORMING OF THE JURISDICTION OF THE FICTION/FOREIGN-STATE-LANGUAGE FOR THE FURTHERMENT OF THE DEPRIVATION OF THE RIGHTS AND **RAPE OF THE PLAINTIFF(S)/SOVEREIGN-CITIZEN(S)** BY THE OFFICERS OF THE COURT.

CONSTRUCTIVE-TREASON: FOR THE OVERT-ACT OR OFFENCE OF THE ATTEMPTING BY THE OVER-THROWING OF THE GOVERNMENT OF THE STATE (CONDITION OF THE CONTRACT OF THE PARTY(S) BY THE COURT/BAR) BY THE OFFENDER FOR THE ALLEGIANCE-OWING; OR, OF THE BETRAYING OF THE STATE BY TO THE HANDS OF THE FICTION/FOREIGN-POWER. FOR THE C.U.S.A.F.-CONTRACT IS FOR THE **BILL OF THE RIGHTS: FOR THE ARTICLE OF THE FOUR (4): SECTION OF THE THREE(3)**, C.U.S.A.F.-CONTRACT.

45). PERJURY: FOR THE WILLFUL-ASSERTION OF THE MATTER OF THE FACT/OPINION/BELIEF/KNOWLEDGE OF THE MAKING BY THE WITNESS BY THE JUDICIAL-PROCEEDING AS THE PART OF THE PARTY'S-EVIDENCE, EITHER, UPON THE OATH OR BY THE FORM OF THE ALLOWANCE BY THE LAW OR FOR THE SUBSTITUTION FOR THE OATH, WHETHER THE EVIDENCE IS BY THE PRESENTMENT BY AN OPEN-COURT, OR BY THE AFFIDAVITS OR OTHERWISE, FOR THE ASSERTION THAT THE MATERIAL-FACT IS BY THE ISSUE/POINT OR THE INQUIRY AND OF THE KNOWING, BY THE WITNESS BY THE FALSE-STATEMENT. FOR THE PERJURY IS OF THE WILLFUL-CRIMINAL-COMMITMENT BY THE LAWFUL-OATH BY THE ADMINISTRATION OF THE OATH, BY THE JUDICIAL-PROCEEDING AND FOR THE PARTY/CITIZEN/PERSON IS BY THE SWEARING OR DECLARATION AND AFFIRMATION BY THE TRUTH FOR THE WILLFUL, ABSOLUTE, AND FALSEHOOD, BY THE MATTERS-MATERIAL FOR THE ISSUE/POINT OF THE QUESTION.

 17

Exhibit Z-17

46). FOR THE PERJURY: REF. TITLE 18: U.S.A. CODES: SECTION: 1621 (GENERAL); FOR THE CITIZEN(S)IN THE PARTY IS/ARE OF THE GUILT OF THE PERJURY IF BY THE OFFICIAL-PROCEEDING WITH THE PARTY-NAMES FOR THE FALSE-STATEMENT WITH THE OATH/EQUIVALENT-AFFIRMATION/SWEARS/AFFIRMATION BY THE TRUTH OF THE STATEMENT-PREVIOUS-MAKING. [REFERRING BY THE OATH/AFFIRMATION] WHEN THE STATEMENT IS OF THE MATERIAL FOR THE PARTY BY THE TRUTH/BELIEVE-STATEMENT [MUST BE DEFINED] FOR THE BEING TRUE.

47). FOR THE MALICE: FOR THE PERSONAL-HATE OR ILL-WILL IS FOR THE STATE OF THE MIND, FOR THE RECKLESS-BEHAVIOR OF THE LAW AND OF THE LEGAL-RIGHTS OF THE CITIZEN(S)IN THE PARTY.

48). FOR THE C.U.S.A.F.-CONTRACT, TORT, TITLE: 42: U.S.A. CODES: SECTION: 1983 FOR THE PARTY-WHO WITH THE COLOR OF THE STATUTE/ORDINANCE/REGULATION/CUSTOM/USAGE, OF THE STATE OF THE CALIFORNIA OR TERRITORY OF THE U.S.A., SUBJECTS OR IS FOR THE CAUSING BY THE SUBJECTING, OF THE CITIZEN/PARTY/PERSON OF THE U.S.A.; OR, FOR ANY CITIZEN/PARTY/PERSON WITHIN THE JURISDICTION IS WITH THE DEPRIVATION OF THE C.U.S.A.F.-CONTRACT FOR THE RIGHTS/PRIVILEGES/IMMUNITIES BY THE SECURITY BY THE C.U.S.A.F.-CONTRACT AND LAWS ARE BY THE LIABILITY FOR THE CITIZEN/PARTY/PERSON OF THE BY JURY BY THE ACTION AT THE LAW-SUIT BY THE EQUITY OR OTHER-PROCEEDING FOR THE REDRESS.

49). FOR THE TORT: OF THE CIVIL-WRONG-INJURY, IS WITH THE COURT BY THE PROVISIONS BY A REMEDY BY THE FORM OF THE ACTION FOR THE DAMAGES. OF THE VIOLATION OF THE DUTY BY THE EXAMINATION BY THE GENERAL-LAW OR OTHERWISE UPON ALL CITIZEN(S)/PARTY(S)/PERSON(S) FOR THE OCCUPYING OF THE RELATION, FOR EACH CITIZEN/PARTY/PERSON IS BY THE INVOLVEMENT BY THE GIVING-TRANSACTION.

50). FOR THE LARCENY BY THE FRAUD AND DECEPTION: FAILS: BY THE CORRECTING OF THE FALSE-IMPRESSION. BY THE DECEIVER CREATION/REINFORCE, OR THE DECEIVER IS FOR THE KNOWING BY THE INFLUENCING OF THE PARTY/PERSON/CITIZEN IS BY THE STANDING BY THE FIDUCIARY/CONFIDENTIAL: RELATIONSHIP.

51). FOR THE FIDUCIARY: FOR THE CITIZEN/PARTY/PERSON WITH THE DUTY FOR THE CREATION OF THE UNDERTAKING OR BY THE ACTING FOR THE BENEFIT OF THE CITIZEN/PARTY/PERSON BY THE SUBJECT-MATTERS.

52). FOR THE RACKETEERING: THE ORGANIZATION OF A CONSPIRACY BY THE COMMITTING OF THE CRIMES OF THE EXTORTION/COERCION/ATTEMPT BY THE COMMITTING OF THE EXTORTION/COERCION.

FOR THE FEAR OF THE LEGAL NECESSARY-ELEMENT BY THE EXTORTION BY THE INDUCING BY THE ORAL/WRITTEN-THREATS BY THE NEGLECT BY THE FAILURE FOR THE STOPPING OF THE BY JURY OF THE PERSON/PARTY/PROPERTY BY THE PARTY/PERSON/CITIZEN OF THE THREATENING-PARTY. FOR THE TITLE: 42: U.S.A. CODES: SECTION: 1985(3).

53). FOR THE RACKETEERING: IS BY ANY DEMANDING/SOLICITING/RECEIVING OF ANY THING OF THE VALUE BY THE OWNER/PROPRIETOR/PERSON/CITIZEN/PARTY FOR THE FINANCIAL-INTEREST BY THE BUSINESS, BY THE MEANS OF THE THREAT (THROUGH THE USE OF THE CONTEMPT OF THE COURT-ORDER BY THE PAYING OF THE FEES-THAT ARE WITH THE PROHIBITION), EXPRESS/IMPLICATION, OF THE PROMISE, BY THE PERSON/CITIZEN/PARTY DEMANDING/SOLICITING/ RECEIVING OF THE PROPERTY/ENTITY OF THE VALUE BY THE WILL FOR THE CAUSING OF THE

B.J.F.
R.J.S.

Exhibit Z-18

COMPETITION OF THE PERSON/CITIZEN/PARTY BY THE PAYMENT; DEMAND SOLICIT/RECEIVING BY THE DIMINISHMENT OR ELIMINATION.

54). FOR THE EXTORTION: FOR THE OBTAINING OF THE PROPERTY OF THE PARTY/CITIZEN/PERSON, FOR THE INDUCTION BY THE WRONGFUL-USE OF THE ACTUAL OR THREATENING-FORCE, OR FEAR, OR WITH THE COLOR OF THE OFFICIAL-RIGHT. REF. TITLE: 18: U.S.A. CODES: SECTION: 971.

55). FOR THE RANSOM: TITLE: 18: U.S.A. CODES: SECTION: 1202 FOR THE FEES/MONEY/PRICE/CONSIDERATION-PAYMENT/ BY A DEMAND FOR THE REDEMPTION OF THE KIDNAP-PARTY. FOR THE PAYMENT FOR THE RELEASE OF THE PARTY/PERSON/CITIZEN/PLAINTIFF/RESPONDENT OF THE CAPTIVITY. FOR THE PARTY WITH THE KNOWLEDGE RECEIVES/POSSESSES/DISPOSES OF THE PROPERTY: FOR THE **COMMITMENT OF THE** CRIME.

56). FOR THE DURESS: FOR THE ILLEGAL-PURPOSE/THREAT OF THE PARTY/CITIZEN/PERSON FOR THE MENTAL OR FINANCIAL-HARM BY THE COERCING: (TITLE: 28 CHAPTER: 85: U.S.A. CODES: SECTION: 1359) FOR THE WILL OF THE PARTY/CITIZEN/PERSON/ANOTHER, AND BY THE INDUCING OF THE PARTY/PERSON/CITIZEN BY THE DOING OF THE ACT-CONTRARY BY THE CITIZEN'S/PARTY'S/PERSON'S: FREE-WILL. FOR THE DURESS IS FOR THE INCLUDING OF THE SAME BY JURIES/THREATS/RESTRAINMENT BY THE EXERCISE BY THE PERSON(S)/CITIZEN(S)/PLAINTIFF(S) OF THE DISTINGUISHABLE OF THE UNDUE-INFLUENCE BECAUSE BY THE LATTER, FOR THE WRONG-DOER IS BY THE FIDUCIARY-CAPACITY OR BY THE POSITION OF THE TRUST AND CONFIDENCE WITH THE RESPECT OF THE VICTIM OF THE UNDUE-INFLUENCE.

58). FOR THE MALPRACTICE: PROFESSIONAL-MISCONDUCT/UNREASONABLE-LACK OF THE SKILL. FOR THE MALPRACTICE IS BY THE APPLICATION BY THE CONDUCT OF THE LAWYER(S)/ATTORNEY(S) FOR THE FAILURE OF THE RENDERING OF THE PROFESSIONAL-SERVICES BY THE EXERCISING OF THE DEGREE OF THE SKILL AND LEARNING BY THE CIRCUMSTANCES BY THE COMMUNITY BY THE AVERAGE-PRUDENT-REPUTABLE FOR THE MEMBERS OF THE PROFESSION WITH THE RESULT OF THE BY JURY/LOSS/DAMAGE BY THE RECIPIENT OF THE SERVICES OR BY THE ATTORNEY(S)/LAWYER(S). FOR THE MALPRACTICE IS FOR THE PROFESSIONAL-MISCONDUCT-NEGLECT OF THE SKILL OR FIDELITY BY THE PROFESSIONAL/FIDUCIARY-DUTIES/EVIL-PRACTICE/ILLEGAL/IMMORAL-CONDUCT.

59). FOR THE PREJUDICE: FOR THE FOREJUDGEMENT/ BIAS/PRECONCEIVE/OPINION/LEANING-TOWARDS-ONE-SIDE OF THE CAUSE FOR THE REASON-OTHER THAN THE CONVICTION OF THE JUSTICE.

60). FOR THE DISCRIMINATION: FOR THE TREATMENT OF THE EQUALITY OF THE PARTY(S) BY THE NEGLECT OF THE DISTINCTION BETWEEN THE PARTY(S) BY THE FAVOR OF THE OTHER-PARTY(S), OUT, OF THE FAVOR, FOR THE TITLE: VII OF THE 1964 CIVIL, RIGHTS, ACT.

61). FOR THE FALSE-SWEARING: FOR THE PERIOD/TIME OF THE LIMITATIONS FOR THE PROSECUTION IS OF THE TIME BY THE FIRST-STATEMENT. FOR THE PARTY WITH THE KNOWLEDGE BY THE TRUTH IS WITH THE OATH/AFFIRMATION FOR THE DECLARATION/MAKING/SUBSCRIPTION OF THE FALSE-STATEMENT BY THE OFFICER OF THE COURT AND IS BY THE FAILURE FOR THE BELIEVING BY THE TRUTH, IS OF THE GUILTY OF THE CLASS-D-MISDEMEANOR.

62). FOR THE BREACH: FOR THE BREAKING/VIOLATION OF THE LAW/RIGHT/ OBLIGATION/ENGAGEMENT/DUTY BY THE COMMISSION/OMISSION/CONTRACT BY THE EXISTING WITH THE ONE/PARTY(S) WITH THE CONTRACT FOR THE (PERFORMING/

R. J. S.
B. J. F.

Exhibit Z-19

DUTY/RESPONSIBILITY/FIDUCIARY/TERMS/PROMISE/CONDITION) OF THE (NEGLIGENT FAILS/LIE-COMPLIANCE) OF THE CONTRACT BY THE PARTY(S).

63). FOR THE TITLE: 42: U.S.A. CODES: SECTION: 1986 FOR THE KNOWLEDGE OF THE LAW AND NEGLECT BY THE FAILURE FOR THE STOPPING AND CORRECTING OF THE WRONG, BY THE DEFINITION FOR EVERY CITIZEN BY THE PARTY, WHO, FOR THE HAVING WITH THE KNOWLEDGE FOR ANY WRONGS BY A CONSPIRACY BY THE DOING, BY THE SECTION: 1985 OF THE TITLE OR ARE BY THE COMMITMENT, AND BY THE HAVING-POWER FOR THE PREVENTION OR AIDING BY THE PREVENTION OR THE COMMISSION OF THE CRIME BY THE NEGLECT OR REFUSAL FOR THE STOPPING OF THE WRONG OF THE DOING, WHEN THE WRONGFUL-ACTS ARE OF THE COMMITMENT, FOR THE LIABLE OF THE PARTY FOR THE INJURY ON CITIZENS BY THE PARTY-LEGAL-REPRESENTATIVES, FOR ALL DAMAGES BY THE CAUSE BY SUCH WRONGFUL-ACT, WHICH SUCH CITIZEN BY THE PARTY BY THE REASONABLE-DILIGENCE IS WITH THE PREVENTION FOR ANY NUMBER OF THE CITIZENS BY THE PARTY BY THE GUILT OF THE WRONGFUL-NEGLECT BY THE REFUSAL IS BY THE JOINDER AS THE RESPONDENT(S) FOR THE WRONGS BY THE ACTION.

64). FOR THE TITLE: 42: U.S.A. CODES: SECTION: 1985(2) FOR THE OBSTRUCTING-JUSTICE, INTIMIDATING PARTY, WITNESS: IF FOR THE TWO/MORE-CITIZENS BY THE STATE OF THE CALIFORNIA/TERRITORY OF THE U.S.A. FOR THE CONSPIRE BY THE DETERRING, BY THE FORCING/INTIMIDATION/TREATING OF THE PARTY/WITNESS BY THE COURT OF THE U.S.A. BY THE ATTENDING OF THE WITNESS BY THE COURT OR BY THE TESTIFYING FOR THE MATTER-PENDING BY THE COURT: OF THE FREE/FULL/TRUTHFUL, FOR THE MATTER, BY THE INJURING OF THE PARTY/WITNESS BY THE CITIZEN'S: BEHALF/PROPERTY ON THE ACCOUNT OF THE CITIZEN IS FOR THE HAVING BY THE ATTENDING/TESTIFYING/INFLUENCING OF THE VERDICT/PRESENTMENT/INDICTMENT OF THE GRAND/**PETIT:** JUROR, BY THE COURT, OR BY THE INJURING THE JUROR BY THE PARTY/CITIZEN/SELF/PROPERTY ON THE ACCOUNT OF THE VERDICT/PRESENTMENT/INDICTMENT FOR THE LAWFUL-ASSESSMENT BY THE CITIZEN BEING/HAVING BEEN THE JUROR, OR TWO/MORE-CITIZENS BY THE CONSPIRACY FOR THE PURPOSE OF THE IMPEDING/HINDERING/OBSTRUCTING/DEFEATING BY THE MATTER OF THE DUE-COURSE OF THE JUSTICE IS FOR THE STATE OF THE CALIFORNIA/TERRITORY OF THE U.S.A. WITH THE INTENT BY THE DENYING BY THE CITIZEN OF THE **EQUAL-PROTECTION OF THE LAW** BY THE INJURING OF THE CITIZEN/CITIZEN'S PROPERTY FOR THE LAWFUL-ENFORCEMENT OR ATTENDING BY THE ENFORCING OF THE RIGHT OF THE CITIZEN/CLASS OF THE CITIZENS, BY THE **EQUAL-PROTECTION OF THE LAW.**

65). FOR THE TITLE: 42: U.S.A. CODES: SECTION: 1985(3) FOR THE DEPRIVING PARTY OF THE C.U.S.A.F.-CONTRACT RIGHTS/PRIVILEGES: WHEN THE JUDGE AND ATTORNEY OR ANY-CITIZEN(S) BY THE PARTY BY THE STATE OF THE CALIFORNIA/TERRITORY OF THE U.S.A., CONSPIRE AND GO BY THE DISGUISE, FOR THE PURPOSE OF THE DEPRIVING, EITHER THE DIRECTION OR BY DIRECTION, OF THE CITIZEN/CLASS OF THE CITIZEN(S) BY THE PARTY OF THE EQUAL-PROTECTION OF THE LAW OF THE **EQUAL-PRIVILEGES AND IMMUNITIES** WITH THE LAW FOR THE PURPOSE OF THE PREVENTION OR HINDRANCE OF THE CONSTITUTION-AUTHORITIES OF THE CALIFORNIA/TERRITORY BY THE INCORPORATION AND FOR THE SECURITY BY ALL- CITIZENS BY THE PARTY WITHIN THE STATE OF THE CALIFORNIA TERRITORY OF THE U.S.A. OF THE **EQUAL-PROTECTION OF THE LAWS**, OR OF THE JUDGE/ATTORNEY/CITIZENS BY THE PARTY BY THE CONSPIRACY FOR THE PREVENTION BY THE FORCE/INTIMIDATION OR THREATENING OF THE CITIZEN BY THE PARTY FOR

B.J.F.
R.J.S.

Exhibit Z-20

THE ENTITLEMENT OF THE VOTE BY THE GIVING OR THE PARTY-SUPPORT/ADVOCACY BY THE LEGAL-MANNER, OR BY THE INJURING OF THE CITIZEN/PARTY/SELF OR PROPERTY OF THE SUPPORT/ADVOCACY BY THE CASE OF THE CONSPIRACY BY THE TITLE: 42: U.S.A. CODES: SECTION: 1985(1), BY THE ONE/MORE-CITIZEN(S)/PARTY BY THE ENGAGEMENT BY THE ACT BY THE FURTHERANCE OF THE OBJECT OF THE CONSPIRACY BY THE CITIZEN/PARTY/PERSON IS OF THE INJURY BY THE CITIZEN(S)/PARTY/SELF/PROPERTY BY THE DEPRIVING OF THE HAVING/EXERCISING OF THE RIGHTS/PRIVILEGE OF THE CITIZEN(S)/PARTY OF THE U.S.A., FOR THE CITIZEN BY THE PARTY OF THE INJURY/DEPRIVATION BY THE ACTION FOR THE RECOVERY OF THE DAMAGES BY THE OCCASION BY THE INJURY/DEPRIVATION AGAINST THE CITIZEN(S)/PARTY OR MORE, OF THE CONSPIRATORS.

66). FOR THE TITLE: 18: U.S.A. CODES: SECTION: 242(1) FOR THE DEPRIVATION OF THE RIGHTS WITH THE COLOR OF THE LAW BY THE OFFICERS OF THE COURT: WHOEVER, WITH THE COLOR OF THE LAW/STATUTE/ ORDINANCE/REGULATION/CUSTOM WITH THE KNOWLEDGE FOR THE SUBJECTION OF THE PARTY BY THE STATE OF THE CALIFORNIA, TERRITORY OF THE U.S.A./DISTRICT OF THE U.S.A. FOR THE DEPRIVATION OF THE RIGHTS/PRIVILEGES/IMMUNITIES OF THE SECURING/PROTECTING OF THE C.U.S.A.F.-CONTRACT OR THE LAWS OF THE U.S.A., BY THE TWO-DIFFERENT-PUNISHMENTS/PAINS/PENALTIES/TREATMENT ON THE ACCOUNT OF THE PARTY-BEING-ALIEN = (BY THE FAILURE OF THE PUNCTUATION BY THE NAME = FICTION/FOREIGN), OR BY THE REASON OF THE PARTY'S-COLOR-/RACE, THAN ARE BY THE PRESCRIPTION FOR THE PUNISHMENT OF THE CITIZENS IS FOR THE FINE OF THE $10,000. WITH THIS TITLE OR IMPRISONMENT OF THE TEN-YEARS OR WITH OR BOTH, WITH THE **FICTION/FOREIGN-FRINGE-FLAG**.

67). FOR THE KNOWLEDGE: PERCEPTION OF THE TRUTH; LEARNING; BY FORMATION-POWER OF THE KNOWING.

68). NOTE: FOR THE JURISDICTION OF THE SUBJECT-MATTER(NOUN) IS BY THE ASSIGNMENT BY THE ARTICLE "THE" AND FOR THE ASSIGNMENT OF THE AUTHORITY(JURISDICTION) IS THROUGH THE PREPOSITION BY THE **PRESENT-TENSE**.

69). FOR THE PREPOSITIONS: BY, OF, FOR, WITH, AS, ARE OF THE PRESENT-TENSE-JURISDICTIONAL-PREPOSITION FOR THE USE OF THE PLEADING BY THE REAL-TIME-JURISDICTION FOR THE DISQUALIFICATION AND SANCTIONING OF THE FILING OF THE FRIVOLOUS-ACTION BY A LAW-SUIT. **WHERE THE NOUNS ARE BY THE VERB.**

70). FOR THE PROHIBITION OF THE PRESUMPTIONS/ASSUMPTION/CONCLUSIONS BEFORE THE FACTS ARE FOR THE DISQUALIFICATION BY THE LOOKING-UP OF THE **DUE-PROCESS** FOR THE VIOLATION OF THE LAW.

71). FOR THE PROHIBITION OF THE PRONOUNS: FOR THE C.U.S.A.F.-CONTRACT IS WITH THE SPECIFIC-DEFINITION WITH THE KNOWLEDGE BEFORE THE JUDGE, FOR ALL PRESUMPTION, ASSUMPTIONS AND OPINIONS ARE WITH THE DISQUALIFICATION. FOR THE DISCLAIMER OF THE RESPONSIBILITY OF THE FACTS. FOR THE JUDGE IS WITH THE TRUTH(NOUN) BY THE JURISDICTION FOR THE DISQUALIFYING OF THE PRONOUNS FOR THE COURT.

72). FOR THE ADJECTIVES ARE OF THE COLOR OF THE OPINIONS OF THE NOUNS/SUBJECT-MATTER, FOR THE PREJUDICE OF THE NOUN/FACTS OF THE CASE. FOR ANY TIME, FOR THE TWO OR MORE-NOUNS ARE FOR THE COMING-TOGETHER, FOR THE LAST-NOUN OF THE NOUN-PHRASE, IS OF THE NOUN-JURISDICTION. FOR THE NOUNS BY THE LEFT/IN-FRONT OF THE FOLLOWING-NOUN ARE BY THE ADJECTIVE

Exhibit Z-21

OR <u>PROPER-ADJECTIVES</u> BY THE CASE, OF THE **ADJECTIVES ARE OF THE FICTION** OF THE OPINION/PRESUMPTION OF THE FACTS AND ARE BY THE DISQUALIFICATION AS THE FICTIONS BY THE <u>LEGAL-JURISDICTION</u> OF THE STATEMENTS BY THE COURT. FOR THE <u>FICTION-NAME</u> AS THE WRITING OF THE "BRADLEY JEFFERSON FRANKS" OR "ROBERT JOEL SIMPSON": IS A DEAD-FICTION, AND IS BY THE WRITING AS Bradley-Jefferson: Franks OR Robert-Joel: Simpson, FOR THE <u>LIVING-ENTITY</u> OF THE CITIZEN OF THE PARTY.

73). FOR THE ADVERBS IS FOR THE MODIFICATION OF THE VERB, ADJECTIVE AND ADVERB FOR A OPINION AND FOR THE FAILURE OF THE FACT. **FOR THE ADVERB IS FOR THE CHANGING OF THE NOUN BY TO A VERB WHEN THE PLACEMENT OF THE ADVERB IS BEFORE THE NOUN**. FOR ANY FACT WITH ANY MODIFICATION IS WITH A PREJUDICE/FICTION/OPINION/PRESUMPTION AND ASSUMPTION FOR THE TRUTH.

FOR THE VIOLATION OF THE <u>FEDERAL-STYLES-MANUAL</u> IS WITH THE <u>INTERNATIONAL-TREATY</u> FOR THE PROCEDURES OF THE COMMUNICATIONS.

DATE: 28, DAY OF THE 03, 2000 Bradley-Jefferson: Franks

DATE: 28, DAY OF THE 03, 2000 Robert-Joel: Simpson

Bradley-Jefferson: Franks
Robert-Joel: Simpson

AS THE SOVEREIGN-CITIZEN(S)
OF THE PARTY.

Bradley-Jefferson: Franks
Robert-Joel: Simpson
c/o 30-257: Monte-Vista-Way:
1000-Palms: California: [92276]

22

B.J.F.
R.J.S.

Exhibit Z-22

KNOWLEDGE = FOR THE LEARNING OF THE DIFFERENCE BETWEEN TRUTH AND LIE, GOOD AND EVIL, LOVE AND HATE, LIFE AND DEATH, JEALOUSY AND COMPASSION, PERSECUTION AND FORGIVENESS, SEX AND LOVE, LONESOME AND PARTNERSHIP, LUST AND LOVE, HAPPINESS AND SADNESS, HEAVEN AND HELL DOING AND DONE. FOR THE PERSPECTIVE OF ALL THINGS FOR THE RIGHT AND WRONG.

our father
FOR THE PEOPLE OF THE FATHER
who art.
ARE OF THE CREATION BY THE FATHER.
in heaven
WITH THE KNOWLEDGE BY THE HEAVEN IS
hallow be
FOR THE HOLY-NAME OF THE FATHER
thy name,
IS BY THE KNOWLEDGE OF THE TRUTH BY THE PEOPLE.
thy kingdom come.
FOR THE KINGDOM OF THE FATHER IS BY THE KNOWLEDGE OF THE TRUTH
thy will
FOR THE KNOWLEDGE OF THE SPIRIT AND VOTE OF THE PEOPLE
be done
FOR THE FREEDOM IS FOR THE ACTIONS OF THE KNOWLEDGE BY THE TRUTH
on earth
FOR THE KNOWLEDGE BY THE TRUTH IS ON THE EARTH FOR THE LIFE
as it is
FOR THE KNOWLEDGE OF THE TRUTH IS
in heaven
FOR THE WAY BY TO THE HEAVEN.
give us
FOR THE KNOWLEDGE OF THE PEOPLE
this day
FOR THE KNOWLEDGE OF THE DAY
our bread and
IS BY THE WORKING AND LEARNING-SKILLS OF THE PEOPLE.
forgive us
FOR THE WRONGS (SINS) AGAINST THE KNOWLEDGE BY THE PEOPLE ARE
our debts
FOR THE SINS(TEMPTATIONS OF THE FLESH) OF THE PEOPLE
as we forgive
FOR THE KNOWLEDGE OF THE PEOPLE BY THE FORGIVING OF THE WRONG-DECISIONS
our debtors
FOR THE PEOPLE OF THE DEBTS (RESPONSIBILITIES)
our trespasses
FOR THE FORGIVING BY THE KNOWLEDGE OF THE AWARENESS OF THE TRUTH
lead us
FOR THE KNOWLEDGE OF THE PEOPLE IS BY THE TRUTH
(not) BY to temptation
FOR THE EVIL IS BY THE LACK OF THE KNOWLEDGE
and deliver us
FOR THE KNOWLEDGE OF THE TRUTH IS FOR THE FREEDOM

 23

R. J. S.
B. J. F.

Exhibit Z-23

from evil
AGAINST THE EVIL OF THE DARKNESS(LACK OF THE KNOWLEDGE)
a men
FOR THE PEOPLE-AGREE

____

____

 24

R. J. S.
B. J. F.

Exhibit Z-24

CASH BOND
RECOMMENDED $ ______
RSDT GROVER C. TRASK II
DISTRICT ATTORNEY

.AST DAYER (.#: R97216009

IN THE CONSOLIDATED SUPERIOR/MUNICIPAL COURTS
OF RIVERSIDE COUNTY, STATE OF CALIFORNIA
(Indio)

THE PEOPLE OF THE STATE OF CALIFORNIA, Plaintiff,

v.

BRADLEY J. FRANKS · Paul Sukram
~~DOB: 9-1-63~~

ROBERT J. SIMPSON - misty Reed
DOB: 6-3-44

Defendants.

CASE NO. INMD72896

MISDEMEANOR COMPLAINT

FILED
SUPERIOR/MUNICIPAL COURT
OF RIVERSIDE COUNTY
AUG - 6 1997
M Taylor

COUNT I

The undersigned, under penalty of perjury upon information and belief, declares: That the above named defendants committed a violation of Section 498, Subdivision (b) of the Penal Code, a misdemeanor, in that on or about ~~August~~ April, 1997 through August, 1997, in the County of Riverside, State of California, with the intent to obtain utility services for themselves without paying the lawful charge therefor, with the intent to enable another to do so, and with the intent to deprive a utility of a part of the lawful charge for its utility services, they did wilfully and unlawfully divert and cause to be diverted utility services, prevent a utility meter and device from accurately performing its measuring function, tamper with property used by a utility to provide utility services, make and cause to be made a connection and reconnection with property owned and used by the utility to provide utility services without authorization or consent of the utility, and use and receive direct benefit of utility services with knowledge and reason to believe that the diversion, tampering, and unauthorized connection existed at the time of that use, and that the use and receipt was otherwise without the authorization or consent of the utility; and with such knowledge, reason, and intent did authorize, abet, aid, and solicit said receipt, diversion, use, prevention, tampering, connection, and reconnection.

COUNT II

That the above named defendant BRADLEY J. FRANKS committed a violation of Section 148 of the Penal Code, a misdemeanor, in that on or about August 4, 1997, in the County of Riverside, State of California, he did wilfully and unlawfully resist, delay and obstruct a public officer, peace officer, and emergency medical technician in the discharge and attempt to discharge a duty of his office and employment.

COURT ORIGINAL

Exhibit Z-25

CASH BOND
RECOMMENDED $ ________
GROVER C. TRASK II
DISTRICT ATTORNEY

Page 2

COUNT III

That the above named defendant BRADLEY J. FRANKS committed a violation of Section 602, Subdivision (l) of the Penal Code, a misdemeanor, in that on or about August 4, 1997, in the County of Riverside, State of California, he did wilfully and unlawfully commit a trespass by entering and occupying real property and a structure to wit: a utility pole owned by Imperial Irrigation Utility, located at 30-257 Monte Vista, 1000 Palms, California, without the consent of the owner, his agent, and the person in lawful possession thereof.

DISCOVERY REQUEST

Pursuant to Penal Code Section 1054.5(b), the People are hereby informally requesting that defense counsel provide discovery to the People as required by Penal Code Section 1054.3.

I declare under penalty of perjury under the laws of the State of California that the foregoing is true and correct.

Dated: 06-Aug-1997

Complainant

RGM;py

COURT ORIGINAL

Exhibit Z-26

COORDINATED COURTS - COMMITMENT/RELEASE NOTICE
(✓) INDIO BRANCH ( ) PALM SPRINGS BRANCH ( ) BLYTHE BRANCH
Date: 08/06/97

CASE NAME: BRADLEY JEFFERSON FRANKS ARREST #: OR972160
CASE NO: INM072896 DEFENSE:
CHARGES: 1) 498(B) PC-M A, 2) 148 PC-M A, 3) 602(1) PC-M A

( ) VOP-1203.2a PC (Blythe) Booking #: 9727971
TO RSO: DEFENDANT IS REMANDED AS INDICATED.

( ) State Prison ( ) ______ Hrs/Years/Months/Days
( ) County Jail ( ) Less ______ Actual Days Served
( ) Youth Authority ( ) Plus ______ Days 4019 PC Time
( ) Dept Mental Health ( ) Credit from Post Sentence Report
( ) Calif. Rehab.Center (CRC) ( ) House at CYA pur 1731.5 WIC
( ) Patton State Hospital ( ) ______ Credits State Hospital

REFERRED FOR DIAGNOSTIC REPORT AND MISCELLANEOUS ORDERS

( ) Dept. of Corrections ( ) Pursuant to 1203.03 PC
( ) Youth Authority ( ) Pursuant to 707.2 WIC
( ) Weekend Commitment (BRCC) Commencing on ______
( ) Surrender on ______ at ______ to RSO to commence sentence.
( ) No 4024 Programs ( ) Other ______
( ) Sentence/Case ( ) Concurrent ( ) Consecutive to ______
( ) Criminal Proceedings Adjourned: See IM# ______
( ) Court finds Deft. competent to stand trial this date.
( ) Case ordered Consolidated into Case # ______

RETURN DATES
(✓) Def. to appear on 8-12-97 at 130 Dept 3T For PT
( ) Def. not transported to Court this date.
( ) Court orders Def. be allowed to complete phone call(s) ______
( ) Court orders Def's. medical records be released by jail to medical examiner assigned to this case by Dept. of Mental Health.

THIS AUTHORIZES RSO TO HOLD DEFENDANT PENDING FURTHER COURT ORDER
( ) Bail remains as previously set (✓) Bail set at $ ______

RSO ORDERED TO RELEASE DEFT. FROM CUSTODY FOR THE FOLLOWING REASONS:
( ) Release on Probation (✓) Release on O/R ( ) Release on Parole
( ) DA Not Filing Charges ( ) Case Dismissed ( ) Diversion Release
( ) OTHER ______

BY ORDER OF JUDGE: ~~B. J. BJORK~~ J. Stevenson
Date: 08/06/97

( ) Refer to O/R Clerk ( ) Can be served @ residential rehab program
( ) After serving ___ days custody def can serve remainder of custody in rehab pgm. If def completes pgm prior to release date he/she shall be returned to Riv Co Jail to serve remainder of sentence.
( ) Def sentenced on ______ to serve ______ days with ______ days credit time served
( ) REGISTER 290 PC ( ) REGISTER 11590 H&S ( ) REGISTER 457.1 PC

By: V. [signature]
Judicial Courtroom Asst.

No cont w/ vict
No 1cfil Pole

Exhibit Z-27

SUPERIOR COURT OF CALIFORNIA, COUNTY OF RIVERSIDE

THE PEOPLE OF THE STATE OF CALIFORNIA,
Plaintiff,

-VS-

Bradley J. Franks,
Defendant(s).

Case No. IIM072896

STIPULATION re JURY ADMONITION
PRESENCE OF JURY AND THE
DEFENDANT(S), REQUIREMENT OF

IT IS HEREBY STIPULATED by the Defendant(s) and Counsel that:

1. The Court's admonition to the jury, after once having been given, shall be deemed to have been given just prior to every recess, adjournment, or continuance of the trial;

2. All jurors and the alternate(s), if any, are present at all necessary times, unless their absence is expressly brought to the attention of the Court;

3. The defendant(s) is(are) present at all phases, stages, and sessions of the trial unless his(her)(their) absence is expressly brought to the attention of the Court and such fact is entered in the minutes of the Court;

4. A matron will not be required to accompany the jury to meals, but will only be required if the jury is to be locked-up overnight;

5. The Clerk of this Court may administer the oath to any female Deputy or Special Deputy Sheriff or other suitable women, outside the presence of the Court, counsel, and the defendant(s), if the requirement for a matron should arise;

6. In the absence of the trial Judge, any Judge of this Court may respond to the written inquiries of members of the jury; may have the Court Reporter read portions of the testimony to the jury upon its request; and/or may receive the verdict(s) of the jury and make such orders as the verdict(s) warrant;

7. At the time the case is given to the jury for its deliberations, the Court may permit the alternate juror(s) to leave for home, work, etc., and to remain on call provided that the juror(s) informs the Clerk of the Court of his/her telephone number in the event that a member of the jury should require a replacement and the alternate juror(s) seated as a member of the jury; and

8. After the jury has begun its deliberations, the Court may permit the jurors (without having them return into the Courtroom) to:

a. Leave the jury deliberation room for the purpose of going to lunch, at their expense, and not in the custody of the Bailiff;

b. Report to the Bailiff outside the jury deliberation room at the end of the lunch period;

c. Leave the jury deliberation room for their homes, etc., at the end of the jury deliberation day; and

d. Report back to the Bailiff outside the jury deliberation room at a specified time during the next deliberation day.

9. Upon final determination of this action, the Clerk may, without further order of the Court, return any and all exhibits, identifications, depositions, interrogatories and requests for admissions with answers thereto, and/or other stored material to the party or person(s) entitled thereto.

Dated: March 18, 1998

[signature]
Deputy District Attorney

[signature]
Attorney for Defendant(s)

APPROVED AND SO ORDERED:

Thomas N. Douglass, J.
Judge of the ~~Superior~~ Court
municipal

Bradley "Jeff" Franks
Defendant(s)
UCC 1-207 "without Prejudice."

STIPULATION (CRIMINAL)

Exhibit Z-28

CONSOLIDATED SUPERIOR AND MUNICIPAL COURTS
INDIO BRANCH

PEOPLE OF THE STATE OF CALIFORNIA
CASE NO: INM072896
-vs-
DEFENDANT: BRADLEY JEFFERSON FRANKS

M I N U T E   O R D E R

****
DEPT:2K HEARING DATE: 08/06/97
PROCEEDINGS: Arraignment
****

CHARGES: 1) 498(B) PC-M A, 2) 148 PC-M A, 3) 602(1) PC-M A

Honorable Jerome E. Stevenson Presiding.
Clerk: V HARTMAN.
Court REPorter: VIDEO
Defendant Present.
Public Defender Appointed.
Defendant advised of right to counsel; cont. to consult counsel; assignment of counsel if unable to employ private counsel.
Defendant advised of right to trial by jury; statutory sentencing; cross exam of witnesses; right to present evidence on own behalf.
Defendant advised of right to speedy trial; dismissal if no trial within 30/45 days after arraignment; effect of consent to waive time.
Defendant advised of right to probable cause hearing within 48 hours of detention.
Defendant advised if not a citizen conviction may result in deportation, exclusion from admission tothis country or denial of naturalization.
Defendant Arraigned.
Defendant Advised of Constitutional Rights.
Pleads Not Guilty to all counts.
District Attorney Notified
Public Defender Notified
Pre-Trial Hearing Set for 08/12/97 at 13:30 in Dept 3T
Defendant Ordered to Return.
Court Orders defendant to obey all reasonable directives of the O.R. clerk.
TO HAVE NO CONTACT W/ VICTIM
NOT TO CLIMB UTILITY POLE OR CONNECT UTILITIES
Conditional O.R. Release.
HEARING CONCLUDED

Exhibit Z-29

CONSOLIDATED SUPERIOR AND MUNICIPAL COURTS
INDIO BRANCH

PEOPLE OF THE STATE OF CALIFORNIA
CASE NO: INM072896
-vs-
DEFENDANT: BRADLEY JEFFERSON FRANKS

M I N U T E   O R D E R

****

DEPT:3T   HEARING DATE: 08/12/97
PROCEEDINGS: Pre-Trial Hearing

****

CHARGES: 1) 498(B) PC-M A, 2) 148 PC-M A, 3) 602(1) PC-M A

Honorable H. Morgan Dougherty Presiding.
Clerk: S. BUENDIA/B. MALLIE.
People Represented By J. BEHNKE, DDA.
Defendant Represented By M. KELLER DPD.
Defendant not present. Appears pursuant to 977 PC.
Defendant Waives Time.
Hearing is Continued To 09/02/97 at 13:30 in Dept. 3T.
O.R. Continued.
HEARING CONCLUDED

Exhibit Z-30

CONSOLIDATED SUPERIOR AND MUNICIPAL COURTS
INDIO BRANCH

PEOPLE OF THE STATE OF CALIFORNIA
CASE NO: INM072896
-vs-
DEFENDANT: BRADLEY JEFFERSON FRANKS

M I N U T E   O R D E R

****
DEPT:3T   HEARING DATE: 09/02/97
PROCEEDINGS: Pre-Trial Hearing
****

CHARGES: 1) 498(B) PC-M A, 2) 148 PC-M A, 3) 602(1) PC-M A

Honorable C. J. Sheldon Presiding.
Clerk: B MALLIE.
People Represented By J CAULEY, DDA.
Defendant Represented By M. KELLER DPD.
Defendant Present.
Defendant Waives Time.
Trial Readiness Conference set for 11/07/97 at 8:30 in Dept. 3T.(PTCF)
Trial Set For 11/17/97 at 8:30 in Dept. 3T, for an estimated 0 days.
O.R. Continued.
HEARING CONCLUDED

Exhibit Z-31

```
            CONS[illegible]ATED SUPERIOR AND MUNIC[illegible] COURTS
                           INDIO  BRANCH


PEOPLE OF THE STATE OF CALIFORNIA
                                   CASE NO: INM072896
             -vs-
DEFENDANT: BRADLEY JEFFERSON FRANKS

                  M I N U T E   O R D E R
***********************************************************************
DEPT:3T     HEARING DATE: 11/07/97
PROCEEDINGS: Trial Readiness Conference
***********************************************************************

CHARGES:  1) 498(B) PC-M A, 2) 148 PC-M A, 3) 602(1) PC-M A


Honorable C. J. Sheldon Presiding.
People Represented By S CLARK, DDA.
Defendant Represented By M. KELLER DPD.
Clerk: N GUITRON.
Minutes entered by P SMYTH.
Defendant Present.
Trial Date COnfirmed.
O.R. Continued.
 **HEARING CONCLUDED**
```

Exhibit Z-32

CONSOLIDATED SUPERIOR AND MUNICIPAL COURTS
INDIO BRANCH

PEOPLE OF THE STATE OF CALIFORNIA
CASE NO: INM072896
-vs-
DEFENDANT: BRADLEY JEFFERSON FRANKS

M I N U T E   O R D E R

****
DEPT:3T   HEARING DATE: 11/17/97
PROCEEDINGS: Jury Trial
****

CHARGES: 1) 498(B) PC-M A, 2) 148 PC-M A, 3) 602(1) PC-M A

Honorable C. J. Sheldon Presiding.
Clerk: M. VASQUEZ.
People Represented By S CLARK, DDA.
Defendant Represented By M. KELLER DPD.
Defendant Present.
Hearing is Continued To 11/18/97 at 8:30 in Dept. 3T.
WITNESSES ORDERED TO RETURN TO COURT ON 11/18/97
AT 9:00 AM.
O.R. Continued.
HEARING CONCLUDED

Exhibit Z-33

CONS. .LATED SUPERIOR AND MUNIC. AL COURTS
INDIO BRANCH

PEOPLE OF THE STATE OF CALIFORNIA
CASE NO: INM072896
-vs-
DEFENDANT: BRADLEY JEFFERSON FRANKS

M I N U T E   O R D E R

****
DEPT:3T   HEARING DATE: 11/18/97
PROCEEDINGS: Jury Trial
****

CHARGES: 1) 498(B) PC-M A, 2) 148 PC-M A, 3) 602(1) PC-M A

Honorable C. J. Sheldon Presiding.
Clerk: M. VASQUEZ.
People Represented By S CLARK, DDA.
Defendant Represented By M. KELLER DPD.
Defendant Present.
Oral Motion By M. KELLER regarding CONTINUANCE OF TRC/TRIAL DATES is called for hearing.
Motion GRanted.
Defendant Waives Time.
Trial Readiness Conference set for 03/06/98 at 8:30 in Dept. 3T.(PTCF)
Trial Set For 03/16/98 at 8:30 in Dept. 3T, for an estimated 0 days.
O.R. Continued.
HEARING CONCLUDED

Exhibit Z-34

```
                CONSOLIDATED SUPERIOR AND MUNICIPAL COURTS
                              INDIO  BRANCH

PEOPLE OF THE STATE OF CALIFORNIA
                                         CASE NO: INM072896
              -vs-
DEFENDANT: BRADLEY JEFFERSON FRANKS

                     M I N U T E   O R D E R
*******************************************************************
DEPT:3T      HEARING DATE: 11/07/97
PROCEEDINGS: Trial Readiness Conference
*******************************************************************

CHARGES:  1) 498(B) PC-M A, 2) 148 PC-M A, 3) 602(1) PC-M A

Honorable C. J. Sheldon Presiding.
People Represented By S CLARK, DDA.
Defendant Represented By M. KELLER DPD.
Clerk: N GUITRON.
Minutes entered by P SMYTH.
Defendant Present.
Trial Date COnfirmed.
O.R. Continued.
 **HEARING CONCLUDED**
```

Exhibit Z-35

CONS[illegible]TED SUPERIOR AND MUNIC[illegible]L [illegible]OURTS
INDIO BRANCH

PEOPLE OF THE STATE OF CALIFORNIA
CASE NO: INM072896
-vs-
DEFENDANT: BRADLEY JEFFERSON FRANKS

M I N U T E   O R D E R

****

DEPT:3T   HEARING DATE: 03/06/98
PROCEEDINGS: Trial Readiness Conference

****

CHARGES: 1) 498(B) PC-M A, 2) 148 PC-M A, 3) 602(1) PC-M A

Honorable Graham Anderson Cribbs Presiding.
People Represented By J CHRISTL, DDA.
Defendant Represented By P SUKRUM DPD.
Clerk: N GUITRON.
Defendant Present.
Trial Date COnfirmed.
Defendant Ordered to Return.
O.R. Continued.
HEARING CONCLUDED

Exhibit Z-36

CONS . \TED SUPERIOR AND MUNICI .L COURTS
INDIO BRANCH

PEOPLE OF THE STATE OF CALIFORNIA
CASE NO: INM072896
-vs-
DEFENDANT: BRADLEY JEFFERSON FRANKS

M I N U T E   O R D E R

****
DEPT:3T HEARING DATE: 03/16/98
PROCEEDINGS: Jury Trial
****

CHARGES: 1) 498(B) PC-M A, 2) 148 PC-M A, 3) 602(1) PC-M A

Honorable C. J. Sheldon Presiding.
Clerk: M .VASQUEZ.
Court Reporter: S.Schulz
People Represented By J CHRISTL, DDA.
Defendant Represented By P SUKRUM DPD.
Defendant Present.
Case Assigned To department 3N, to Judge THOMAS N. DOUGLASS for all further proceedings.
Honorable THOMAS N. DOUGLASS Presiding.
Clerk: M. Ramirez.
Court Reporter: B. Kohler
People Represented By J CHRISTL, DDA.
Defendant Represented By P SUKRUM DPD.
Defendant Present.
Hearing is Continued To 03/19/98 at 8:30 in Dept. 3N.
The Following Persons are ordered to return on 03/23/98 at 8:30 Dept 3N: Luis Manuel Gonzalez.
The Following Persons are ordered to return on 03/23/98 at 8:30 Dept 3N: Juan Regla.
The Following Persons are ordered to return on 03/23/98 at 8:30 Dept 3N: Rick Young.
The Following Persons are ordered to return on 03/23/98 at 8:30 Dept 3N: Jesus Angulo.
The Following Persons are ordered to return on 03/23/98 at 8:30 Dept 3N: Juan Ibarra.
The Following Persons are ordered to return on 03/23/98 at 8:30 Dept 3N: Gerardo Velazco.
Defendant Ordered to Return.
O.R. Continued.
HEARING CONCLUDED

Exhibit Z-37

CONSO... .TED SUPERIOR AND MUNICI... COURTS
INDIO BRANCH

PEOPLE OF THE STATE OF CALIFORNIA
CASE NO: INM072896
-vs-
DEFENDANT: BRADLEY JEFFERSON FRANKS

M I N U T E   O R D E R

****
DEPT:3N HEARING DATE: 03/17/98
PROCEEDINGS: Motion to advance trial
****

CHARGES: 1) 498(B) PC-M A, 2) 148 PC-M A, 3) 602(1) PC-M A

Honorable THOMAS N. DOUGLASS Presiding.
Clerk: M. Ramirez.
Court Reporter: B.Kohler
People Represented By J. Christl, DDA.
Defendant Represented By P. Sukrum DPD.
Defendant is Not Present.
Oral Motion By People regarding advance jury trial is called for hearing.
Motion GRanted.
Trial Set For 03/18/98 at 8:30 in Dept. 3N, for an estimated 2 days.
Mr. Sukrum to notify Defendant.
O.R. Continued.
HEARING CONCLUDED

Exhibit Z-38

CONSOLI. TED SUPERIOR AND MUNICIPAL OURTS
INDIO BRANCH

PEOPLE OF THE STATE OF CALIFORNIA
CASE NO: INM072896
-vs-
DEFENDANT: BRADLEY JEFFERSON FRANKS

M I N U T E   O R D E R

****
DEPT:3N   HEARING DATE: 05/01/98
PROCEEDINGS: Report and Sentencing
****

CHARGES: 1) 498(B) PC-M C, 2) 148 PC-M C, 3) 602(1) PC-M D

Honorable THOMAS N. DOUGLASS Presiding.
Clerk: M. Ramirez.
Court Reporter: B.Kohler
People Represented By J. Christl, DDA.
Defendant Represented By P. Sukhram DPD.
Defendant Present.
Defendant waives time for sentencing.
Referred To Probation department for supplemental report.(PRSN)
Probation to reinterview Deft and turn in T & C's
Defendant Ordered to Report to Probation office forthwith, or on release from custody.
Hearing is Continued To 05/29/98 at 8:30 in Dept. 3N.
Defendant Ordered to Return.
O.R. Continued.
HEARING CONCLUDED

Exhibit Z-39

CONS(. TED SUPERIOR AND MUNICI.. .1 .OURTS
INDIO BRANCH

PEOPLE OF THE STATE OF CALIFORNIA
CASE NO: INM072896
-vs-
DEFENDANT: BRADLEY JEFFERSON FRANKS

M I N U T E   O R D E R

****

DEPT:3N HEARING DATE: 03/24/98
PROCEEDINGS: Jury Trial

****

CHARGES: 1) 498(B) PC-M C, 2) 148 PC-M C, 3) 602(1) PC-M D

Honorable THOMAS N. DOUGLASS Presiding.
Clerk: M. Ramirez.
Court Reporter: B.Kohler
People Represented By J. Christl, DDA.
Defendant Represented By P. Sukhram DPD.
Defendant Present.
4th DAY OF TRIAL
At 8:11 the Jury Retires to resume deliberations.(TRJD)
AT 12:00 THE ABOVE PROCEEDINGS CONCLUDED
Jurors excused for lunch.
At 13:10 the Jury Retires to resume deliberations.(TRJD)
At 13:46 The Jury returns into the courtroom and indicate that: they have a verdict.
We the Jury in the above entitled action, find the Deft Bradley Jefferson Franks, GUILTY, in count 1 of a violation of Section 498(B) PC.
Dated: 03/24/98, and Signed by: Juror #12,Jury Foreperson
We the Jury in the above entitled action, find the Deft Bradley Jefferson Franks, GUILTY, in count 2 of a violation of Section 148 PC.
Dated: 03/24/98, and Signed by: Juror #12,Jury Foreperson
Jurors are Polled on the Verdict(s) and twelve jurors answer in the affirmative.
Re-Reading of the Verdict(s) as recorded is Waived
Court orders all juror information sealed; information to remain sealed until further order by the Court.
Jurors are Thanked and Excused.
Referred To Probation department for pre-sentence report.(PRSN)
Report and Sentence Hearing set on 05/01/98 at 8:30 in Dept. 3N.
Defendant waives time for sentencing.
Defendant Ordered to Report To: Probation.
Defendant Ordered to Return.
O.R. Continued.
HEARING CONCLUDED

Exhibit Z-40

CONSC..I. .TED SUPERIOR AND MUNICI:AL .OURTS
INDIO BRANCH

PEOPLE OF THE STATE OF CALIFORNIA
CASE NO: INM072896
-vs-
DEFENDANT: BRADLEY JEFFERSON FRANKS

M I N U T E   O R D E R

****
DEPT:3N   HEARING DATE: 03/23/98
PROCEEDINGS: Jury Trial
****

CHARGES: 1) 498(B) PC-M A, 2) 148 PC-M A, 3) 602(1) PC-M D

Honorable THOMAS N. DOUGLASS Presiding.
Clerk: M. Ramirez.
Court Reporter: L. Ivers/B. Kohler
People Represented By J. Christl, DDA.
Defendant Represented By P. Sukhram DPD.
Defendant Present.
3rd DAY OF TRIAL
At 8:56, the following proceedings were held:
Out of the Presence Of the Jury, the following proceedings were held:
Court and Counsel Confer regarding: Item to be marked by Defense. (TRJI)
Defendant's Exhibit(s) A-Plot plan is/are Admitted in evidence.
The Court inquires of Juror #2.
At 9:15, the following proceedings were held:
Members of the Jury and Alternate present.
Defendant's Witness, Juan Ibarra is Sworn and testifies.
Defendant's Witness, Gerardo Delasu is Sworn and testifies.
Witness Gerardo Belasu is excused.
Defendant's Witness, Juan Regla is Sworn and testifies.
Defendant's Witness, John Hinojosa is Sworn and testifies.
Witness John Hinojosa is excused.
Defendant's Witness, Ryan Bodmer is Sworn and testifies.
Defense rest.
Defendant's Witness, Robert Joel Simpson is Sworn and testifies.
M. Reed rest.
Out of the Presence Of the Jury, the following proceedings were held:
1118. 1 Penal Code motion by defense counsel. Motion is Granted as to count(s) 3, said counts ordered dismissed.
Court and Counsel go over jury instructions off the record.
Members of the Jury and Alternate present.
Jurors are admonished and excused for lunch.
Out of the Presence Of the Jury, the following proceedings were held:

Exhibit Z-41

3/24/98 Page: 2

Case Number : INM072896 People vs. BRADLEY FRANKS

Defendant's Exhibit(s) A is/are Admitted in evidence.
AT 11:55 THE ABOVE PROCEEDINGS CONCLUDED
At 13:31, the following proceedings were held:
Out of the Presence Of the Jury, the following proceedings were held:
Court and Counsel Confer regarding: instructions to be read to Jurors (TRJI)
At 13:42, the following proceedings were held:
Members of the Jury and Alternate present.
Out of the Presence Of the Jury, the following proceedings were held:
Court and Counsel Confer regarding: ct 1 theft of utilities. (TRJI)
In the Presence Of the Jury, the following proceedings were held:
Closing Argument made By J. Christl.
Out of the Presence Of the Jury, the following proceedings were held:
Court and Counsel Confer regarding: Jury instructions (TRJI)
In the Presence Of the Jury, the following proceedings were held:
Closing Argument made By M. Reed.
Closing Argument made By P. Sukhram.
Court Instructs the Jury.
Out of the Presence Of the Jury, the following proceedings were held:
Court and Counsel Confer regarding: instruction on ct 2 (TRJI)
In the Presence Of the Jury, the following proceedings were held:
The Court reinstructs Jurors on ct 2.
Bailiff Is Sworn to take charge of the jury and alternate(s).
At 16:38 the Jury Retires to commence deliberations.(TRJD)
Out of the Presence Of the Jury, the following proceedings were held:
Court and Counsel Confer regarding: Juror #3 (TRJI)
Counsel Stipulate: Jurors may be excused for breaks and lunch without.
reconvening in court.
Counsel Stipulate: Judge may read Caljic 17.45 if Jurors request copy.
of Jury instructions.
AT 17:03 HEARING WAS CONCLUDED
Jurors Are Admonished and directed to return on 03/24/98 at 8:00
Out of the Presence Of the Jury, the following proceedings were held:
Counsel Stipulate: Alternate Juror does not need to return he is to .
check in with the Court telephonically.
Juror is reminded that the admonition still remains.
Trial (IN PROGRESS) Adjourned to 03/24/98 at 8:00 in Dept. 3N.

Exhibit Z-42

```
  3/24/98                                                          Page:     3
--------------------------------------------------------------------------------
Case Number : INM072896        People vs. BRADLEY FRANKS
================================================================================
      Defendant Ordered to Return.
      O.R. Continued.
       **HEARING CONCLUDED**
```

Exhibit Z-43

CONSC... .TED SUPERIOR AND MUNICI...L .OURTS
INDIO BRANCH

PEOPLE OF THE STATE OF CALIFORNIA
CASE NO: INM072896
-vs-
DEFENDANT: BRADLEY JEFFERSON FRANKS

M I N U T E   O R D E R

****

DEPT:3N   HEARING DATE: 03/19/98
PROCEEDINGS: Jury Trial

****

CHARGES: 1) 498(B) PC-M A, 2) 148 PC-M A, 3) 602(1) PC-M A

Honorable THOMAS N. DOUGLASS Presiding.
Clerk: M. Ramirez.
Court Reporter: B.Kohler
People Represented By J. Christl, DDA.
Defendant Represented By P. Sukhram DPD.
Deputy Bodmer present and seated at Counsel table
Defendant Present.
2nd DAY OF TRIAL
At 8:44, the following proceedings were held:
In the Presence Of the Jury, the following proceedings were held:
Witness previously sworn Mario Jesus Pimentel resumes stand
Witness Mario Jesus Pimentel is excused,subject to recall
People's Witness, John Hinojosa is Sworn and testifies.
People's Exhibit #20-Map of Monte Vista is/are Marked for identification only.
Out of the Presence Of the Jury, the following proceedings were held:
Oral Motion By P. Sukhram regarding mistrial is called for hearing.
Ms. Reed joins in motion.
Counsel argue.
Motion DEnied.
In the Presence Of the Jury, the following proceedings were held:
Mr. Hinojosa resumes his testimony.
People's Witness, Ryan Bodmer is Sworn and testifies.
People's Witness, Troy Scott Lawrence is Sworn and testifies.
Witness Troy Scott Lawrence is excused.
People rest.
AT 11:41 THE ABOVE PROCEEDINGS CONCLUDED
Jurors are admonished and excused for lunch.
Out of the Presence Of the Jury, the following proceedings were held:
People's Exhibit(s) #1 through #20 is/are Admitted in evidence.
AT 11:45 HEARING WAS CONCLUDED
At 13:20, the following proceedings were held:
Members of the Jury and Alternate present.

Exhibit Z-44

```
3/19/98                                                        Page:     2
---------------------------------------------------------------------------
Case Number : INM072896        People vs. BRADLEY FRANKS
===========================================================================
      Defendant's Witness, Richard Leon Young is Sworn and testifies.
      Witness Richard Leon Young is excused.
      Defendant's Witness, Robert Joel Simpson is Sworn and testifies.
      Defendant is Sworn and testifies on own behalf.
      Witness previously sworn Robert J. Simpson resumes stand
      AT 15:17 HEARING WAS CONCLUDED
      Jurors Are Admonished and directed to return on 03/23/98 at  8:30
      Trial (IN PROGRESS) Adjourned to 03/23/98 at  8:30 in Dept. 3N.
      Defendant Ordered to Return.
      O.R. Continued.
       **HEARING CONCLUDED**
```

Exhibit Z-45

CONSOL. .TED SUPERIOR AND MUNICIP.. .OURTS
INDIO BRANCH

PEOPLE OF THE STATE OF CALIFORNIA
CASE NO: INM072896
-vs-
DEFENDANT: BRADLEY JEFFERSON FRANKS

M I N U T E   O R D E R

****

DEPT:3N HEARING DATE: 03/18/98
PROCEEDINGS: Jury Trial

****

CHARGES: 1) 498(B) PC-M A, 2) 148 PC-M A, 3) 602(1) PC-M A

Honorable THOMAS N. DOUGLASS Presiding.
Clerk: M. Ramirez.
Court Reporter: B.Kohler
People Represented By J. Christl, DDA.
Defendant Represented By P. Sukhram DPD.
Defendant Present.
1st DAY OF TRIAL
People's items #1 through #20 as described on the attached list are pre-marked for identification.
At 9:29, the following proceedings were held:
Prospective Jury Panel having been summoned, is sworn regarding their qualifications to act as trialjurors. (TRJS)
Jury Voir Dire commences. (TRJS)
Out of the Presence Of the Jury, the following proceedings were held:
An in-chamber conference was held Court and Counsel present without the Defendants.
Court and Counsel Confer regarding: Mr. Sukhram's venire. (TRJI)
In the Presence Of the Jury, the following proceedings were held:
Jury Voir Dire resumes (TRJS)
AT 11:55 THE ABOVE PROCEEDINGS CONCLUDED
Jury panel is admonished and excused for lunch.
At 13:54, the following proceedings were held:
Jury Voir Dire resumes. (TRJS)
Jury Panel Sworn to try the cause:(TRJS)
Alternate Jurors: is, sworn.(TRJS)
Deputy Bodmer present and seated at Counsel table.
Opening Statement made By J. Christl.
Opening Statement made By P. Sukhram.
Opening Statement made By M. Reed.
Motion to Exclude all Witnesses is granted.
Deputy Bodmer is designated as Investigating Officer.
People's Witness, Mario Jesus Pimentel is Sworn and testifies.
Witness Mario Jesus Pimentel is excused,subject to recall

Exhibit Z-46

```
3/18/98                                                        Page:     2
---------------------------------------------------------------------------
Case Number : INM072896        People vs. BRADLEY FRANKS
===========================================================================
     Jurors Are Admonished and directed to return on 03/19/98 at  8:30
     AT 16:00 THE ABOVE PROCEEDINGS CONCLUDED
     Out of the Presence Of the Jury, the following proceedings were
     held:
     Court and Counsel Confer regarding: Witness' to be called by the
     People on 3-19-98. (TRJI)
     AT 16:02 HEARING WAS CONCLUDED
     Trial (IN PROGRESS) Adjourned to 03/19/98 at  8:31 in Dept. 3N.
     Defendant Ordered to Return.
     O.R. Continued.
      **HEARING CONCLUDED**
```

Exhibit Z-47

ACTUAL EXPLICIT JUDICIAL NOTICE

UNDER

[U] nited:STATES of AMERICA the AMERICAN FREE FLAG of PEACE

(TITLE 4: U.S.C. SEC.: 1&2) of the[U] united: STATES of AMERICA

FROM: Robert - Joel: Simpson

Bradley- Jefferson: Franks
CITIZENS IN PARTY
c/o Monte Vista Way,
Thousand Palms, California, republic

FILED
SUPERIOR/MUNICIPAL COURT
OF RIVERSIDE COUNTY

MAY 1 1998

M. VILLAGRANA

ARTICLE III VENUE AND JURISDICTION

Suit of the Sovereign , court of record at common law
California: Republic, Riverside, county,

FOR: LARSON JUSTICE CENTER,
INDIO, COURTHOUSE, INC. ,
COUNTY OF RIVERSIDE INC.,
[FOREIGN/STATE POWER]
46200 OASIS ST.,
INDIO, CALIFORNIA

PEOPLE OF THE STATE OF CALIFORNIA
[JUDGE] Thomas - N.:Douglas: Jr
[ATTORNEY/PUBLIC DEFENDER],Mickie- Reed:
[ATTORNEY/PUBLIC DEFENDER], Paul- Sukhram:
[ATTORNEY/D.D.A.], John - F.: Cristl

PLAINTIFFS

V

Bradley- Jefferson: Franks
Robert- Joel: Simpson
CITIZEN IN PARTY
[sua esse potestate]

BY THE LAW OF THE CASE,
AT LAW ACTION............ JUDICIAL NOTICE OF LACK OF
OF JURISDICTION, NO PERSON OF PROPER POWER AND
AUTHORITY FOR PROSECUTING OR JUDGE THE CASE,
NO PROBABLE CAUSE, LACK OF SUBJECT MATTER JURISDICTION
LACK OF JURISDICTION OVER THE CITIZENS/PLAINTIFFS
[PRINCIPLE OF DOCTRINE OF DISCOVERY] UNDER THE SOVERE
IMMUNITY: ACT, LAW OF THE FLAG, UNITED:STATES CONSTITU
RULES OF F.R.C.P. , DISCRETIONARY REVEIW BY JUDGE OF
OATH & AFFIRMATION,

PRAYS FOR... BY PETITIONING UNDER THIS BREIF OF NOTICE
BY REVERSING, OVERTURNING, & DISMISSING IN ITS
INTIRITY:
CASE: NO.# INM0 72896

SEAL: LOCUS SIGILLI;

Bradley-Jefferson: Franks
Robert-Joel: Simpson

FILE STAMPED DATE:.........................
IN THE YEAR OF OUR LORD ONE THOUSAND ONE HUNDRED
NINETY EIGHT:

CITIZENS IN PARTY RESERVES ALL RIGHTS OF ERRORS,ADDITI
DELETIONS, AT ANY TIME IN THESE PROCEDINGS.

Exhibit Z-48

DUE PROCESS

MATTER OF SPECIAL MARCH 1981 GRAND JURY, 753 F2d 575, 580 (9th Cir. 1985)
Even temporary deprivation of property entitled property owner to due process which means, as a general rule, reasonable notice and opportunity for fair hearing.

US V. GUTHRIE, 789 F2d 356 (5th Cir. 1986)
For the government to punish a person because he had done what the law plainly allows him to do is a due process violation of the most basic sort.

"I have to stay here every day for a year? I don't even remember having a trial!"

CALDWELL V. MILLER, 790 F2d 589 (7th Cir. 1986)
Liberty interest protected under due process clause may be either interest protected by due process clause itself or interest created by state or federal law.

DeWEESE V. TOWN OF PALM BEACH, 812 F2d 1365 (11th Cir. 1987)
Citizen's liberty interest in personal dress is protected by due process.

BLAYLOCK V. SCHWINDEN, 856 F2d 107 (9th Cir. 1988)
ROCHIN V. CALIFORNIA, 342 US 165, 96 LEd 183, 72 SCt 205 (1952)
Substantive due process refers to certain actions that the government may not engage in, no matter how many procedural safeguards it employs.

WEIMER V. AMEN, 870 F2d 1400 (8th Cir. 1989)
Cornerstone of due process is prevention of abusive governmental power.

PEARSON V. CITY OF GRAND BLANC, 961 F2d 1211 (6th Cir. 1992)
Fourteenth Amendment substantive due process requires that both state legislative and administrative actions that deprive citizens of life, liberty and property must have some rational basis.

US V. CONKINS, 987 F2d 564 (9th Cir. 1993)
Due process of law is violated when government vindictively attempts to penalize a person for exercising protected statutory or constitutional rights.

US V. BOOTHE, 994 F2d 63 (2nd Cir. 1993)
Due process bars prosecutor from making knowing use of false evidence and conviction may not stand if such evidence has any reasonable likelihood of affecting judgement of jury.

US V. WILLIAMS, 998 F2d 258 (5th Cir. 1993)
Prosecutor's suppression of evidence which would tend to exculpate defendant or reduce his sentence violates due process.

Exhibit Z-49

DUE PROCESS

US V. BAKER, 999 F2d 412 (9th Cir. 1993)
Due process requires that defendant's be able to exercise their constitutional right to remain silent and not be penalized at trial for doing so.

US V. NEVERS, 7 F3d 59 (5th Cir. 1993)
US V. BARKER STEEL CO., INC., 985 F2d 1123 (1st Cir. 1993)

1) When a person of ordinary intelligence does not receive fair notice that his contemplated conduct is forbidden, prosecution for such conduct deprives him of due process.
2) "Fair warning doctrine" invokes due process rights and requires that criminal statute at issue be sufficiently definite to notify persons of reasonable intelligence that their planned conduct is criminal.

US V. HENDERSON, 19 F3d 917 (5th Cir. 1994)
When hearing is necessary to protect defendant's due process rights, then failure to hold hearing would be abuse of discretion.

US V. LAYNE, 43 F3d 127 (5th Cir. 1995)
LAMBERT V. CALIFORNIA, 355 US 225, 2 LEd2d 228, 78 SCt 240 (1957)
Prosecution of citizen who is unaware of any wrongdoing for "wholly passive conduct" violates due process.

KELM V. HYATT, 44 F3d 415 (6th Cir. 1995)
MATTHEWS V. ELDRIDGE, 424 US 319, 333, 47 LEd2d 18, 96 SCt 892 (1976)
ARNSTRONG V. MONZO, 380 US 545, 552, 14 LEd2d 62, 85 SCt 1187 (1965)

1) Due process requires as general matter opportunity to be heard at meaningful time and in a meaningful manner.
2) Citizens must be afforded due process before deprivation of life, liberty or property.

PORTER V. SINGLETARY, 49 F3d 1483 (11th Cir. 1995)
MUSE V. SULLIVAN, 925 F2d 785 (5th Cir. 1991)
Due process requires that litigant claim be heard by fair and impartial fact finder applies to administrative as well as judicial proceedings.

MILES V. DORSEY, 61 F3d 1459 (10th Cir. 1995)
Conviction of accused who is legally incompetent violates due process.

PRICE V. BARRY, 53 F3d 369 (D.C. 1995)
Liberty interest may arise from either due process clause itself or from state law.

83

Exhibit Z-50

MEMORANDUM

" Sovereignty itself is, of course, not subject to law, for it is the author and source of law; but in Our system, while sovereign powers are delegated to the agencies of government, sovereignty itself remains with the People, by whom and for whom all government exists and acts. And the law is the definition and limitation of power.", Yick Wo v. Hopkins, 118 US 356, 370.

"An ordinance of a municiple corporation is a local law, and binds persons within the jurisdition of the corporation." (emphasis added) Pittsburg, C', C, & St L. Ry. Co. v. Lightheiser, 71 N.E. 218, 221, Pennsylvania Co. v. Stegemeir, 20 N.E. 843.

"Ordinances --- are laws passed by the governing body of a municiple corporatiion for the regulation of the corporation" (emphasis added) Bills v. City of Goshen, 20 N.E. 115, 117.

"The terms ordinance, by-law, and municiple reulation... are local reulations for the governments of the inhabitants of a particular place, and though given the force of law by the charter for the purposes of the municiple government, yet relate to that solely, and prosecutions for their violations have no reference, as a general rule to the administration of criminal justice of the state," (emphasis added) State v. Lee, 13 N.W. 913.

"Ordinances are laws of municipality made by authorized municiple body in distinction from general laws of the state and constitute local regulations for government of inhabitants of particular place." (emphasis added) State v. Thomas, 156 N.W. 2d 745,
"...defining the term criminal offence as any offence for which any punishment by imprisonment or fine, or both, may by law be inflicted, a violation of a city ordinance is not a criminal offence... an ordinance being a regulation adopted by a municiple corporation and not a law in the legal sence." (emphasis added) Meredith v. Whillock, 158 S. W. 1061, 1062.

"A city ordinance is not a law of the character as a statute. It is merely a regulation; a rule of conduct passed by the common council for the direction and supervision of its citizens." (emphasis added) People v. Gardner, 106 N.W. 541, 545.

"An ordinance prescribes a permanet rule for conduct of government." (emphasis added) 76 N.W. 2d 1, 5; 61 ALR 2d 583.

"An ordinance is not, in the constitutional sence, a public law. It is a mere local rule or by-law, a police or domestic regulation, devoid in many respects of the characteristics of the public or general laws, " (emphasis added) State v. Fourcade, 13 So. 187, 191; Mclerney v. City of Denver, 29 P. 516. Since regulations are the work of a corporation, they can only apply to members of that corporation.

"A municiple corporation possesses only such powers as the style confers upon it,.. Any ambiguity of doubt arising out of the terms used by the legislature must be resolved in favor of the granting power. Regard must also be had to constitutional provisions intended to secure the liberty and to protect the rights of the Citizens..." (emphasis added) State v. Frederick, 28 Idaho 709, 715.

(emphasis added, example) **RCW 82.o4.200 "IN THIS STATE" WITHIN THIS STATE"**
"In this STATE" or "WITHIN THIS STATE" includes all federal areas lying within the exterior boundaries of the state [1961 c 15 § 82.04.200. Prior: 1955c 389 §21; prior; 1949 c 228 §2, part; 1945c 249 § 1, part; 1943 c 156 § 2, part; 1941 c 225 §2 part; 1937 c 227 § 2, part; 1935 c180 § 5, part; Rem Supp. 1949 § 8370-5, part.]
C.C.C.G. is similar!!!!!!

Exhibit Z-51

" Courts should not tolerate or condone disregard of law and arbitrary usurpation of power on the part of any officer. Ours is a government of law, and not of men, and before any act of any official will be sustained by the courts such act must be authorized by law." Ex Parte Owen, 10 Okla Crim Rep 284, 136, P 197, Ann Cas 1916A 522.

" It is a general rule that good faith and absence of malice constitute no defence in an action to hold a ministerial officer liable for damages caused by his nonfeasance or misfeasances, Amy v. Supervisors (Amy v. Barkholder) 11 Wall.(S) 136, 20 Led 101; for an officer is under constant obligation to discharge the duties of his office, and it is not necessary to show that his failure to act was wilful or malicious, 95 Ant St Rep 74. And this is likewise the rule in respect of officers with discretionary powers who have exceede their jurisdiction and have acted without authority of law, Stiles v. Lowell (Stiles v. Morse) 233 Mass 174, 123 NE 615, 4 ALR 1365.

" It is a general rule that an officer --- executive, administrative, quasi-judicial, ministerial, or otherwise -- who acts outside the scope of his jurisdiction and without authorization of law may thereby render himself amenable to personal liability in a civil suit, Cooper v. O,Conner, 69 App DC 100, 99 F (2d) 138, 118 ALR 1440; Chamberlin v. Clayton, 56 Iowa 331, 9 NW 237, 41 Ant Rep 101. If he exceeds the power conferred on him by law, he cannot shelter himself by the plea that he is a public agent acting under color of his office, Nelson v. Babcock, 188 Minn 584, 248 NW 49, 90 ALR 1472; or that the damage was caused by an act done or omitted under color of office, and not personally, First Naf: Bank v. Filer, 107 Fla 526, 145 So 204, 87 ALR 267. In the eye of the law, his acts then are wholly without authority, Kelly v. Bemis, 4 Gray (Mass) 83, 64 Am Dec. 50.

Exhibit Z-52

MEMORANDUM OF LAW REGARDING

IMMUNITY OF GOVERNMENTAL OFFICIALS

"If a public officer authorizes the doing of an act not within the scope of his authority, he will be held liable. - Baily vs. New York, 3 Hill (NY) 531, 38 Am Dec 669, affirmed in 2 Denio 433.

"The officers of the law, in the execution of process, are obliged to know the requirements of the law, and if they mistake them, whether through ignorance or design, and anyone is harmed by their error, they must responed in damages. " Rojers v. Conklin 1 Wall. (US) 644, 17 Led 714.

"The authority of public officers to proceed in a particular way and only upon specific conditions as to such matters implies a duty not to proceed in any manner other than that which is author - ized by the law." First Nat. Bank v. Filer, 107 Fla. 526, 145 So 204, 87 ALR 267.

" Apublic officer is liable for the misconduct or negligence of his subordinates where he is in - trusted with their selection or emploment, and through carelessness or unfaithfulness appoints incompetent or untrustworthy persons." Wile v. Harrison, 105 Okla 280, 232 P 816, 38 ALR 1408.

" An officer who wilfully and wantonly appoints an unfit and incompetent person for public duties may be liable for damage which proximately results therefrom. " Richman v. Long, 17 Gratt (Va) 375, 94 Am Dec 461.

" The courts are not bound by an officers interpretation of the law under which he presumes to act, Hofsommer v. Hayes, 92 Okla 32, 217 P 477, citing RCL

page 1 of 2

Exhibit Z-53

Since the Natural People are not members of the municiple corporation; nor licensed by, nor has any other legal connection with the city of Pomona, there is no proper court of jurisdiction to hear an action against these Citizens or any Natural Citizen under the provisions of the CITY OF POMONA code. However, the court can have no jurisdiction over a Free and Natural People, who challenges the jurisdiction of court over a complaint or ordinance based upon the CITY OF POMONA CODE, and once jurisdiction has been challenged by the accused, the court cannot proceed until the plaintiff has not only asserted, but proven jurisdiction. The plaintiff must overcome every single argument of the Accused and have additional matter, before the court can have jurisdiction and proceed. In addition, the court cannot assume jurisdiction or can the city council by mere act or declaration or ordinance. It only follows that a municipality that has the authority to create a code, that code can only apply to its corporate subjects or members. As the code pertains to those persons, it may grant them priveleges and regulate their actions. Hower, these Free and Natural People are not a member, subject, or slave of the municipality and in no way depends upon the City for their welfare, nor are they a corporation, or involved with trade, commerce, or industry with or within the CITY OF POMONA, and these People absolutely refuses to enter into any foreign jurisdiction asserted by the CITY for its subjects, employees, and members.

In this regard, the state legislature must preserve and protect the rights of Citizens at all times, and has enumerated the powers of municipalities, Zoning of Private Property not being among those powers.

"It is settled law, that the legislature in granting it, does not divest itself of any power over the inhabitants of the district which it posessed before the charter was granted. Laramie County v. Albany County et al, 92 U.S. 307, 308.

The CITY OF POMONA AND ITS COUNCIL are forbidden from making any regulations or from enforcing ayn ordinance in conflict with the general laws and the general law of California has not granted the CITY OF POMONA the power to make laws pertaining to Free and Natural Citizens. It can only make regulations to effect its employees and the trade, commerce, and industry it regulates. The CITY ordinances applied to the Citizens is color of law, sham law, when applied to those not a part of the body, having by oath made covenant to be bound by the law of the corporations,"a ficticious person."

All correspondance and presentments will be received and accepted only under the conditions of the presented location as indicated as such:

William Duane: Soult
c/o 1889 Bonnie Brae
Pomona, California republic
Los Angels County
91767 non - assumpsit

This notice and presentment of domiciled location must be followed precisely, otherwise It may not get to Me, and/or will not be accepted and returned as not identifiable!!!

Exhibit Z-54

OPEN INVITATI?N TO
ANY GOVERNMENTAL AUTHORITY
INCLUDING BUT NOT LIMITED TO

Having studied the law of the land judiciously for several of years, I find tha the American People are and have been declared to be equal to the King of Great Britain and equal to each other in lawful respect. Further that the Kings of the land, called commonly the United States of America, have formed a government to secure their liberty, rights, and privileges.
That They did, in an effort to limit and define government, establish formal guidelines for such control by a unilateral contract called the Constitution for the United States of America. That as the states of the contigious union of the states formed, because they are to have a Republican Form of Government, they too, were required to submit in conformity with the Parent Constitution, a -- - Constitution to define and limit such governments, before becoming a Republic Sovergn state.

Having so understood the basic and universal simple concept that all these governments are Republican in nature and not "DEMO-CRATIC" as We have been of recent times told, the People, both collectively and separately are Kings and Sovereign.
Further having lived over sixty (60) years., We have watched in horro? as government public servants have become tresonous anarchists and terrorists, while calling the People criminals and treating them as slaves of a conquered Country. We see a court system, which is reluctant to convey knowledge and is quick to condemn bringing process in strange jurisdictions, a standing army of armed police, who come as gangs to confine the conquered, and a government bent on invading the houses, papers, and confiscating property for petty offences, operating as a Kingdom, not unlike the situations which caused the Revolutionary War.

Bearing this all in mind, this is an open invitation to **"PUT UP OR SHUT UP AND GET THEE HENCE"**

If any top level government authority in any city, county, state, or federal government, within the confines of this United States of America, will declare Us and the People to be conquered slaves upon the Land, then We will be good slaves and return what is due Our captures.
If however you will not so declare, then, in concept of not being half pregnant, We will continue to act like Kings, Sovereign state Citizens and hold those rights of such Kings, including the right not to have to tax Ourselves, license Ourself, register Ourself, or property and pay for services that Our government owes us, for which We owe nothing. We ask not for Our government to support Us with a living, only protection of Our rights, privileges and immunity, that We may provide one.

Without such rebuttal of Sovereign status, any act of aggression or colaterally upon Us, without the production of a truely injured flesh and blood Sovereign, (corpus delicti), or without such a declaration of slavery, will be viewed as a personal act of mixed war and treason by the offending party(s), and subject to redress at law. Any denial of proper and complete redress will mean futher treason by the responcible party(s) and will subject them to redress.

Silence is estoppel to any lawful actions.

SO DO IT.

William Duane: Soult, sui juris
James Edward: McConesky, sui juris

Sovereign Citizens

1. See People v Gilbert, 18 Johns 227.228; Hale v Henkle. 201 US 43; Yick Wo v Hopkins, 118 US 356, 370; People v Herkimar, 4 Cowen 345, 348; Lansing v Smith, 21 D 89; for federal jurisdiction, see the 1995 Lopez decision quoting New York v Milne

Exhibit Z-55

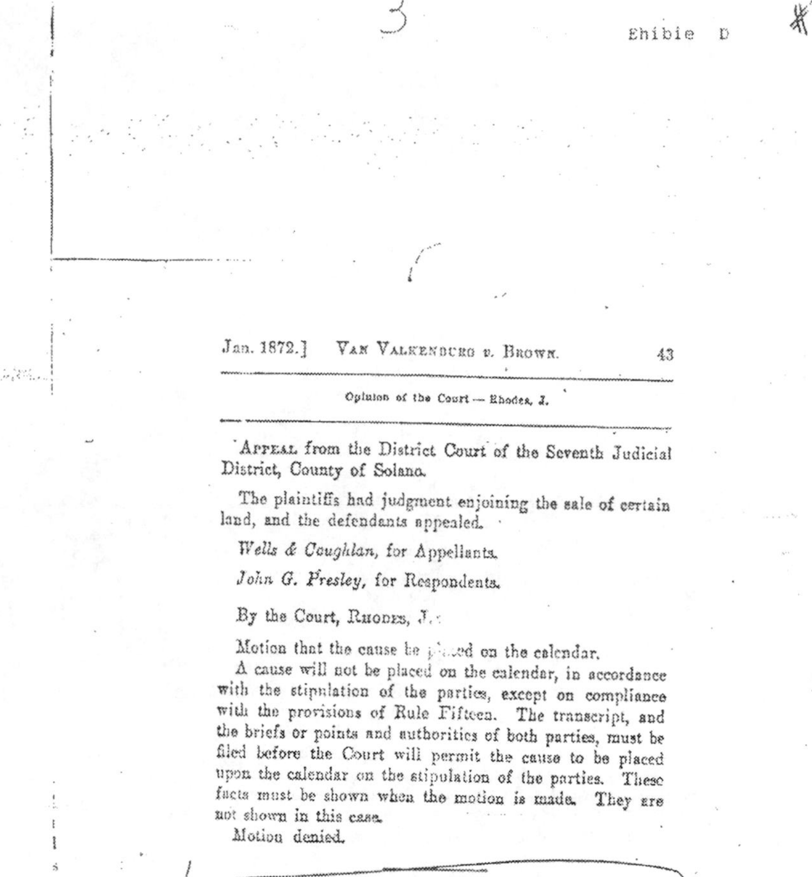

Ehibie D

Jan. 1872.] VAN VALKENBURG *v.* BROWN. 43

Opinion of the Court — Rhodes, J.

APPEAL from the District Court of the Seventh Judicial District, County of Solano.

The plaintiffs had judgment enjoining the sale of certain land, and the defendants appealed.

Wells & Coughlan, for Appellants.

John G. Presley, for Respondents.

By the Court, RHODES, J.:

Motion that the cause be placed on the calendar.

A cause will not be placed on the calendar, in accordance with the stipulation of the parties, except on compliance with the provisions of Rule Fifteen. The transcript, and the briefs or points and authorities of both parties, must be filed before the Court will permit the cause to be placed upon the calendar on the stipulation of the parties. These facts must be shown when the motion is made. They are not shown in this case.

Motion denied.

[No. 3,091.]

ELLEN R. VAN VALKENBURG *v.* ALBERT BROWN.

STATUS OF CITIZENSHIP NOT CONFERRED BY RECENT AMENDMENTS TO THE FEDERAL CONSTITUTION.—No white person born within the limits of the United States and subject to their jurisdiction, or born without those limits and subsequently naturalized under their laws, owes his status of citizenship to the recent amendments to the Federal Constitution.

PURPOSE OF THE FOURTEENTH AMENDMENT.—The purpose of the Fourteenth Amendment to the Constitution of the United States was to confer the status of citizenship upon a numerous class of persons domiciled within the limits of the United States who could not be brought within the operation of the naturalization laws because native born, and whose birth, though native, had at the same time left them without the status of citizenship. Such persons were not white persons, but in the main were of African blood, who had been held in slavery in this country, or having themselves never been held in slavery, were the native-born descendants of slaves.

Exhibit Z-56

F. .EIGN SOVEREIGN IMMUNITY ACT
(TITLE 28, C., u.S.A., SEC. §§ 1601-1611)

DATED 6-19-97; PROCEDURAL OUTLINE FOR THE DISQUALIFICATION OF THE FOREIGN STATE JURISDICTION WITHIN THE united STATES FOR COMMERCE by COMMON LAW: L.A.W. PROCEDURES

TITLE 28 U.S.C. 1605 GENERAL EXCEPTIONS BY THE JURISDICTIONAL IMMUNITY OF THE FOREIGN COURT: [THE YELLOW FRINGE FLAG]
(a) A FOREIGN STATE SHALL NOT BE IMMUNE FROM THE JURISDICTION OF COURTS OF THE COMMON LAW COURTS OF THE UNITED STATES OR OF THE STATES IN ANY CASE---

(2) IN WHICH THE ACTION IS BASED UPON A COMMERCIAL ACTIVITY CARRIED ON IN THE united STATES UNDER THE "FOREIGN SOVEREIGN IMMUNITY ACT" FOR FOREIGN POWERS AND FOREIGN STATES UNDER "THE LAW OF THE FLAG"; [OF THE YELLOW FRINGE FLAG] [THE COST OF MORE THAN $21.00 DOLLARS, BY THE FILING FEE, FOR THE CIVIL LAW SUIT, MAKES THE STATEMENT, AN ACT OF COMMERCE, (ENRICHMENT BY THE STATE AND FEDERAL GOVERNMENT, BY CONTRACT, AND WITHIN THE TERRITORY OF THE U.S.A., FOR A COMMON LAW u.S.C.A. 7, TRIAL BY JURY, UNDER F.R.C.P. RULE 38(a)].

ANY VIOLATION OF INTERNATIONAL TREATY BY THE FOREIGN STATE, OPERATING UNDER THE CONSTITUTION OF THE united STATES, MUST UPHOLD THE CONSTITUTIONAL RIGHTS OF THE SOVEREIGN CITIZEN IN PARTY, WHEN VIOLATED, MUST GO BY THE FEDERAL SUPREME COURT IN WASHINGTON D.C. FOR THE TREATY DISPUTE BETWEEN SOVEREIGN CITIZEN AND STATES GOVERNMENT AND THE TREATY OF FOREIGN JURISDICTION AS REQUIRED BY TREATY LAW.

TO ENFORCE AN AGREEMENT (TREATY) MADE, [BY OATH OR AFFIRMATION BY SUPPORTING AND DEFENDING THE CONSTITUTION OF THE united STATES OF AMERICA, BY THE JUDGE, BY SURRENDER THE OATH AND AFFIRMATION OF A FOREIGN STATE]; CAUSING CONSTRUCTIVE TREASON, CONTEMPT FOR THE CONSTITUTION, FALSE SWEARING AND PERJURY OF OATH UNDER TITLE 18 U.S.C. 1621.

(3) IN WHICH RIGHTS IN PROPERTY TAKEN IN VIOLATION OF INTERNATIONAL LAW ARE IN ISSUE AND THAT PROPERTY OR ANY PROPERTY EXCHANGED FOR SUCH PROPERTY IS PRESENT IN THE united STATES IN CONNECTION WITH A COMMERCIAL ACTIVITY CARRIED ON IN THE united STATES BY THE FOREIGN STATE; OR THAT PROPERTY IS OWNED OR OPERATED BY AN AGENCY OR INSTRUMENTALITY OF THE FOREIGN STATES AND THAT AGENCY OR INSTRUMENTALITY IS ENGAGED IN A COMMERCIAL ACTIVITY IN THE united STATES; [THE FILING FEE IS THE COMMERCIAL ACTIVITY IF MONEY IS INVOLVED OF OVER $21.00 DOLLARS U.S.]

(B) ANY CLAIM ARISING OUT OF INTERFERENCE WITH CONTRACT RIGHTS FOR THE [FILING FEES OF THE COMMON LAW TRIAL BY JURY];

IN WHICH THE ACTION IS BROUGHT, EITHER BY ENFORCING AN AGREEMENT MADE BY THE FOREIGN STATES WITH OR FOR THE BENEFIT OF A PRIVATE PARTY BY SUBMITTING FOR A DEFINED LEGAL RELATIONSHIP, WHETHER CONTRACTUAL FOR ARBITRATION,
[THE JUDGES OATH BY SUPPORTING THE CONSTITUTION OF THE united STATES]

(B) AND, THE AGREEMENT OR AWARD IS OR MAY BE GOVERNED BY A TREATY OR OTHER INTERNATIONAL AGREEMENT [LAW OF THE FLAG] IN FORCE FOR THE united STATES CALLING FOR THE RECOGNITION AND ENFORCEMENT OF THE ARBITRAL AWARDS.
[THE OATH OR AFFIRMATION IS FOR THE COMMON LAW FOR THE U.S. CONSTITUTION].

THE PROVISIONS OF THE "FOREIGN SOVEREIGN IMMUNITY ACT", DATED OCTOBER 21, 1976, IS UNDER TITLE 28 U.S.C. 1601-1611 ABOVE, FOR THE PROTECTION OF THE U.S.A. CONSTITUTION, SO NO PARTY WOULD EVER HAVE IMMUNITY FROM BREAKING THE LAW.

3

Exhibit Z-57

THE LAW OF THE FLAG

THE JURISDICTION OVER THE VENUE PLANE ERECTED BY THE COURT

2-27-98 COPYRIGHT BY: David-Wynn: Miller L.A.W. PROCEDURES: (L.A.W. = LEARN AND WIN)

1. THE FLAG OF THE UNITED: STATES OF AMERICA, IS UNDER TITLE: 4: U.S.A. CODE: SECTION: 1&2 AND UNDER PRESIDENTIAL: EXECUTIVE-ORDER: #10834, DATED AUGUST THE 25 OF 1959.

2. ALL FLAGS, UNDER THE LAW OF THE FLAG WITH FRINGE AND DIMENSIONAL OF 1 X 1.9 FOR THE LOOK OR REPRESENTING THE TITLE: 4: U.S.A. CODES: SECTION: 1&2: FLAG OF THE U.S.A. ARE A DESECRATION OF THE FLAG OF THE U.S.A. IN VIOLATION OF TITLE: 4: U.S.A. CODES: SECTION THE 3 AND TITLE: 36: CHAPTER: 10: SECTION: 176(G).

3. WHEN ANYTHING IS PLACED UPON THE FLAG OF THE U.S.A. (PEO #10834), OR THE STANDARD, POLE, ON TOP OR (FINAL), OF THE FLAG-POLE BY WHICH THE FLAG IS FLOWN, WILL CAUSE THE TITLE: 4: U.S.A. CODES: SECTION: 1&2: FLAG OF THE U.S.A., IS DESECRATED UNDER TITLE: 4: U.S.A. CODES: SECTION: 3: AND CREATE A FOREIGN STATE/POWER JURISDICTION. THE FIDUCIARY, BECOMES A MASTER, OVER ALL WHO MAKE CONTRACT WITH THE FOREIGN STATE/POWER JURISDICTION. JUDGE/ESQUIRE MASTER. ATTORNEY/ESQUIRE. ARTICLE THE ONE, SECTION THE NINE OF THE C.U.S.A. NO TITLES OF NOBILITY SHALL HAVE JURISDICTION OVER ANY SOVEREIGN: CITIZEN IN PARTY OF THE UNITED: STATES OF AMERICA. ALSO FOUND IN THE ORIGINAL C.U.S.A. ARTICLE THE THIRTEEN(13) OF SEPTEMBER THE 17 OF 1789.

4. THE FLAG OF THE U.S.A. WITH (1 X 1.9) PROPORTIONAL DIMENSION UNDER TITLE: 4: U.S.A. CODES: SECTION: 1&2, IS THE FLAG OF THE CONSTITUTION OF THE UNITED: STATES OF AMERICA. FLAGS NOT AUTHORIZED BY CONGRESS, CREATE A FOREIGN STATE IN VIOLATION OF ARTICLE THE FOUR, SECTION THE THREE OF THE C.U.S.A. AND ARE FRAUDS UNDER F.R.C.P. RULE: 9(b), CONDITION OF THE MIND. DESECRATION OF FLAG OF THE U.S.A.: TITLE: 4: U.S.A. CODES: SECTION: 3:.

5. PLACING A FOREIGN YELLOW FRINGE ON THE TITLE: 4: U.S.A. CODES: SECTION: 1&2: FLAG OF THE U.S.A. WILL CAUSE A FOREIGN: STATE/POWER, BY BEING ERECTED, AS NO COUNTRY IN THE WORLD, WILL IDENTIFY WITH THE FOREIGN: FLAG WITH FRINGE. PRISON SENTENCES OF 3 YEARS ARE BROUGHT AGAINST THE PARTY RESPONSIBLE FOR THE DISPLAY OF THE FOREIGN: FLAG WITH FRINGE. MOST COURTS IN THE WORLD ARE FRAUDED UNDER THE FRINGE ON THE FLAG. THE MANNER AND THE FIDUCIARY (JUDGES/MASTERS) OF THE COURTS WILL BE SUED UNDER CONSTRUCTIVE TREASON, CONTEMPT FOR THE CONSTITUTION OF THE UNITED: STATES OF AMERICA, FALSE SWEARING, AND PERJURY OF OATH: TITLE: 18: U.S.A. CODES: SECTION: 1621; NO NEW STATE SHALL BE ERECTED WITHIN ANY STATE OR FROM PARTS OF OTHER STATES: ARTICLE THE FOUR, SECTION THE THREE; C.U.S.A. ARTICLE: (13) NO FOREIGN STATE\POWER.

6. THE NATIONAL-FLAG IS OF PROPORTIONAL DIMENSIONS (4'4"X 5'6") AND THE UNION IS SQUARE (40% OF THE FLY OR WIDTH) MAKING THE STRIPES SHORTER THAN THE FLAG OF THE U.S.A. TITLE: 4: FLAG OF THE U.S.A. WITH NO CONSTITUTIONAL: RIGHTS. UNDER MILITARY: CONTROL. PLACING FRINGE ON THE NATIONAL-FLAG: (ARMY-REG. 260-10 CH. 8), IS FOR INSIDE DISPLAY OR COURT-MARSHAL: COURTS. USE OF A BRAID OR SPEAR, ON THE STANDARD'S-TOP (ARMY-REG. 840-10: CH. 8-1), WILL CAUSE THE SAME JURISDICTIONAL RESULTS, BY SUSPENDING THE CONSTITUTION OF THE UNITED: STATES, MAKING THE CITIZEN IN PARTY, GUILTY, TILL PROVEN INNOCENT, VIOLATION OF THE F.R.C.P. RULE: 12(b)(3): WRONG VENUE, AND F.R.C.P. RULE: 12(b)(7): JOINDER. DOES THE POLICE HAVE MILITARY: FLAG AUTHORIZATION?

1 Copyright: DM-2-25-98

Exhibit Z-58

57). <u>MALPRACTICE</u>: PROFESSIONAL MISCONDUCT OR UNREASONABLE LACK OF SKILL. THE TERM IS APPLIED FOR CONDUCT OF JUDGES FAILURE OF ONE RENDERING PROFESSIONAL SERVICES BY EXERCISING THAT DEGREE OF SKILL AND LEARNING COMMONLY APPLIED UNDER ALL THE CIRCUMSTANCES IN THE COMMUNITY BY THE AVERAGE PRUDENT REPUTABLE MEMBERS OF THE BAR. NO SUBJECT MATTER JURISDICTION, F.R.C.P. RULE: 56 (e)(d). SEE OUTLINE IN DWM LAW PROCEDURES BOOK.

58). <u>PROFESSIONAL MISCONDUCT</u>: WITH THE RESULT OF INJURY, LOSS OR DAMAGE OF THE RECIPIENT OF THE SERVICES BY THE FIDUCIARY ENTITLED BY RELYING UPON THE FIDUCIARY. PROFESSION IS ANY PROFESSIONAL MISCONDUCT, UNREASONABLE LACK OF SKILL OR FIDELITY IN PROFESSIONAL OR FIDUCIARY DUTIES, EVIL PRACTICE, OR ILLEGAL OR IMMORAL CONDUCT. F.R.C.P. 40).RULE: 56(e)(d).

59). <u>DISCRIMINATION. (TITLE: 42: U.S.A. THE CODES: SECTION: 1983, SECTION: 3133)</u> DEFINITION: IN CONSTITUTIONAL LAW, THE EFFECT OF A STATUE OR ESTABLISHED PRACTICE WHICH CONFERS PARTICULAR PRIVILEGES ON A CLASS (MEN AND WOMAN) ARBITRARY SELECTED OF A LARGE NUMBER OF PARTIES, ALL OF WHOM STAND IN THE SAME RELATION BY THE PRIVILEGES GRANTED AND BETWEEN WHOM AND PARTIES NOT FAVORED OR NO REASONABLE DISTINCTION CAN BE FOUND. UNFAIR TREATMENT OR DENIAL OF NORMAL PRIVILEGES OF PARTIES BECAUSE OF PARTIES RACE, AGE, SEX NATIONALITY OR RELIGION. REF. BLD.

60). <u>DISCRIMINATION</u>: A FAILURE BY TREATING ALL PARTIES EQUAL, WHERE NO REASONABLE DISTINCTION CAN BE FOUND BETWEEN THOSE FAVORED AND THOSE NOT FAVORED. REF. 1964, CIVIL RIGHTS ACT TITLE: VII.

61). <u>FALSE SWEARING, WIS. STATS. 946.32(1)</u>, (USE YOUR OWN STATES STATS)
WHOEVER DOES EITHER OF THE FOLLOWING IS GUILTY OF A CLASS D' FELONY:
(A) UNDER OATH OR AFFIRMATION MAKES OR SUBSCRIBES A FALSE STATEMENT WHICH PARTY DOES NOT BELIEVE IS TRUE, WHEN SUCH OATH OR AFFIRMATION IS AUTHORIZED OR REQUIRED BY LAW OR IS REQUIRED BY ANY PUBLIC OFFICER OR GOVERNMENTAL AGENCY AS A PREREQUISITE OF OFFICE OR AGENCY TAKING SOME OFFICIAL ACTION.
(B) MAKES OR SUBSCRIBES TWO(2) INCONSISTENT STATEMENTS UNDER OATH OR AFFIRMATION IN REGARD FOR ANY MATTER RESPECTING WHICH AN OATH OR AFFIRMATIONS, IN EACH CASE, AUTHORIZED OR REQUIRED BY LAW OR REQUIRED BY ANY PUBLIC OFFICER OR GOVERNMENTAL AGENCY AS A PREREQUISITE OF OFFICER OR AGENCY TAKING SOME OFFICIAL ACTION, UNDER CIRCUMSTANCES WHICH DEMONSTRATE THE WITNESS OR SUBSCRIBER KNEW AT LEAST ONE OF THE STATEMENTS BEING FALSE WHEN MADE. THE PERIOD OF LIMITATIONS WITHIN WHICH PROSECUTION MAY BE COMMENCED RUNS OF THE TIME OF THE FIRST STATEMENT. (B)(2) WHOEVER UNDER OATH OR AFFIRMATION MAKES OR SUBSCRIBES A FALSE STATEMENT WHICH THE PARTY DOES NOT BELIEVE IS TRUE IS GUILTY OF A **CLASS A MISDEMEANOR.**

62). <u>TITLE: 42: U.S.A. THE CODES: SECTION: 1985: CHAPTER: 21: NOTE: 69</u>: DAMAGES IN CLAIM FOR VIOLATION OF CONSTITUTIONAL OF THE U.S.A. GUARANTEED RIGHTS DAMAGES ARE RECOVERED, NORMAL DAMAGES MAY BE PRESUMED, AND NOMINAL DAMAGES MAY IN APPROPRIATE CIRCUMSTANCES SUPPORT AWARD OF EXEMPLARY DAMAGES.

63) <u>TITLE: 42: U.S.A. THE CODES: SECTION: 1983: CHAPTER: 21: NOTE: 39</u>, IN ORDER OF ESTABLISHING PERSONAL LIABILITY ON PART OF GOVERNMENT OFFICIAL IN FEDERAL CIVIL RIGHTS LAW ACTION, UNDER TITLE: 42: U.S.A. THE CODES: 1983, LIABILITY IS ENOUGH BY SHOWING THAT OFFICIAL ACTING UNDER COLOR OF LAW CAUSED DEPRIVATION OF FEDERAL RIGHT IN CONTRAST, GOVERNMENT ENTITY IS LIABLE IN OFFICIAL CAPACITY SUIT UNDER TITLE: 42: U.S.A. THE CODES: SECTION: 1983 ONLY WHEN ENTITY IS MOVING FORCE BEHIND DEPRIVATION. THUS REQUIRING ENTITY POLICY OR CUSTOM BY HAVING PLAYED PART IN VIOLATION OF FEDERAL LAW.

64). NAME VIOLATION UNDER <u>F.R.C.P. RULE: 10(a): NAME OF PARTY</u> VIOLATION (GOVERNMENT STYLES MANUAL: CHAPTER: 3: SECTION: 3.2) (NOM DE GUERRE) CAUSING: (F.R.C.P. RULE: 11) FRIVOLOUS FILING OF A LAW SUIT BY USE OF A FICTIOUS NAME (NOM DE GUERRE) DEAD PERSON. CAUSES TITLE: 18: U.S.A. THE CODES: SECTION: 1342, **FICTITIOUS(ADJECTIVE)** USE OF **NAME(NOUN)** FOR MAIL FRAUD EXTORTION OF FEES OR LEGAL DOCUMENTS FOR RIGHTS VIOLATION, AND MAIL FRAUD TITLE: 18: U.S.A. THE CODES: SECTION: 1341, 5 YEARS JAIL AND $10,000. FINE. **NOTE: ADJECTIVE USE OF NAME FOR DEAD: FICTION, BY THE COURT.**

65). <u>CONSTRUCTIVE TREASON</u>: OFFICERS OF **THE** U.S.A. SWEAR AND OATH AND AFFIRMATION FOR SUPPORTING THE **C.U.S.A.** AND THEN SURRENDER **THE C.U.S.A.** INTO THE POWER OF THE FLAG WITH FRINGE UNDER THE FOREIGN: LAW OF THE FLAG, NOW CAUSING THE <u>CITIZEN IN PARTY</u>, A DEPRIVATION WITH THE WILL OF INTENT, OR OVERT THE **C.U.S.A.** INTO THE HAND OF A STATE OF **FOREIGN: POWER/STATE** BY DEFINITION IS GUILTY OF CONSTRUCTIVE-TREASON. **CAUTION!!! DO NOT USE THE WORD TREASON BY ITSELF, YOU WILL BE JAILED FOR MALICE.**

66). **EXTORTION, TITLE: 18: U.S.A. THE CODES: SECTION: 872.**: THE OBTAINING OF PROPERTY BY ANOTHER INDUCED BY WRONGFUL USE OF ACTUAL OR THREATENED FORCE, OR FEAR, OR UNDER COLOR OF OFFICIAL RIGHT.

Exhibit Z-59

67. **THE PREPOSITION "TO"** = IS FUTURE TENSE; THE PLEADING ARE IN THE FUTURE AND DO NOT HAVE "REAL TIME" JURISDICTION AND "PRESENT TENSE" JURISDICTION.

68. **THE PREPOSITIONS: BY, OF, FOR, WITH, IN, OUT, INTO, UNDER, OVER, ARE**, ARE SOME OF THE **PRESENT TENSE** JURISDICTIONAL PREPOSITION THAT MUST BE USED BY KEEPING THE PLEADING IN REAL TIME JURISDICTION OR YOU WILL BE DISQUALIFIED AND BE SANCTIONED FOR FILING A FRIVOLOUS ACTION OR LAW SUIT.

69. **NO PRESUMPTIONS, ASSUMPTION, OR CONCLUSIONS** BEFORE THE FACTS. YOU WILL BE DISQUALIFIED. LOOK UP DUE PROCESS FOR THE VIOLATION OF THE LAW IN BLACKS DICTIONARY.

70. **NO PRONOUNS**: WILL MAKE THE CONTRACT UNDEFINED AND A TRAP BEFORE A JUDGE, DISQUALIFIED. THE JUDGE HAS THE JURISDICTION FOR DEFINING THE PRONOUNS INTO ANYTHING THE COURT WANTS.

71. **ADJECTIVES**: ARE THE OPINIONS OF NOUNS OR SUBJECT MATTER, WHICH WILL PREJUDICE THE NOUN OR FACTS OF THE CASE. ANY TIME TWO OR MORE NOUNS COME TOGETHER, ONLY THE LAST NOUN IN A NOUN PHRASE, IS A NOUN. THE NOUNS BY THE LEFT OR IN-FRONT-OF THE LAST NOUN ARE ADJECTIVES OR PROPER ADJECTIVES IN ANY CASE, ALL ADJECTIVES ARE FICTION OF OPTONION, OR PRESUMPTION OF THE FACTS AND ARE DISQUALIFIED AS FICTIONS IN THE LEGAL JURISDICTION OF THE STATEMENTS IN THE COURT. THE PROPER NAME AS WRITTEN "DAVID WYNN MILLER": IS A DEAD FICTION, AND MUST BE WRITTEN AS David-Wynn: Miller, FOR THE LIVING ENTITY OF A CITIZEN IN PARTY.

72. **ADVERBS**: WILL PLACE THE VERB INTO A CONDITION OF PREJUDICE BY THE ADVERB CAUSING AN OPINION AND NOT A FACT. ADVERBS DETERMINE THE SPEED OF THE VERB BY OPINION, NOT FACT.
73. **DIFFERENT KINDS OF TRAPS** BY DISQUALIFYING THE PAPERS BEING FILED ARE:
et. al. AND etc. = PLACED AFTER THE LAST NAME BY CREATING A NEW LAST OR SIR NAME CAUSING A FICTITIOUS ENTITY WITH NO C.U.S.A. RIGHTS. LACK OF COLONS, COMMAS, [ ]'S BRACKETS, BOXES-WILL REMOVE ALL JURISDICTION FROM THE PAPER. AND BOXING IN THE COURT-ROOM WILL CAUSE THE JURISDICTION OF THE BOX, JURY BOX, WITNESS BOX JUDGES BOX CLERK'S BOX TO BE REMOVED FROM JURISDICTION AND ALL SAID BY THE RESPONDENT OR PETITIONERS REMOVED!!!

COPYRIGHT JANUARY THE 27 OF 1997 BY David-Wynn: Miller L.A.W. PROCEDURES

Copyright: DM · 2-25-98

Exhibit Z-60

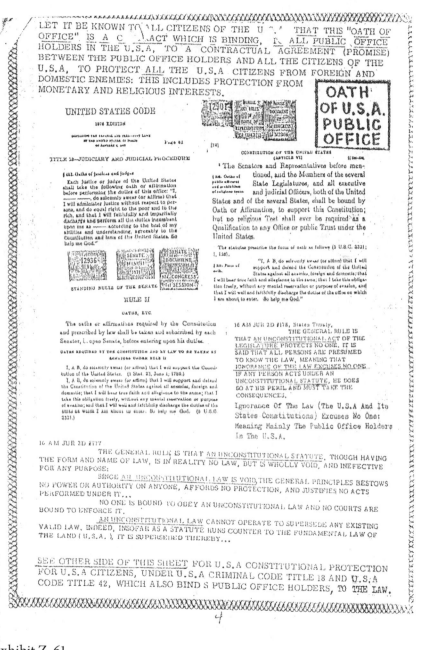

LET IT BE KNOWN TO ALL CITIZENS OF THE U.S.A THAT THIS "OATH OF OFFICE" IS A CONTRACT WHICH IS BINDING, TO ALL PUBLIC OFFICE HOLDERS IN THE U.S.A, TO A CONTRACTUAL AGREEMENT (PROMISE) BETWEEN THE PUBLIC OFFICE HOLDERS AND ALL THE CITIZENS OF THE U.S.A, TO PROTECT ALL THE U.S.A CITIZENS FROM FOREIGN AND DOMESTIC ENEMIES: THIS INCLUDES PROTECTION FROM MONETARY AND RELIGIOUS INTERESTS.

OATH OF U.S.A. PUBLIC OFFICE

UNITED STATES CODE

1976 EDITION

Page 81

TITLE 28—JUDICIARY AND JUDICIAL PROCEDURE

§ 453. Oaths of justices and judges

Each justice or judge of the United States shall take the following oath or affirmation before performing the duties of this office: "I, ——— ———, do solemnly swear (or affirm) that I will administer justice without respect to persons, and do equal right to the poor and to the rich, and that I will faithfully and impartially discharge and perform all the duties incumbent upon me as ——— according to the best of my abilities and understanding, agreeably to the Constitution and laws of the United States. So help me God."

STANDING RULES OF THE SENATE

RULE II

OATHS, ETC.

The oaths or affirmations required by the Constitution and prescribed by law shall be taken and subscribed by each Senator, in open Senate, before entering upon his duties.

OATHS REQUIRED BY THE CONSTITUTION AND BY LAW TO BE TAKEN BY SENATORS UNDER RULE II

I, A B, do solemnly swear (or affirm) that I will support the Constitution of the United States. (1 Stat. 23, June 1, 1789.)

I, A B, do solemnly swear (or affirm) that I will support and defend the Constitution of the United States against all enemies, foreign and domestic; that I will bear true faith and allegiance to the same; that I take this obligation freely, without any mental reservation or purpose of evasion; and that I will well and faithfully discharge the duties of the office on which I am about to enter. So help me God. (5 U.S.C. 3331.)

[70]

CONSTITUTION OF THE UNITED STATES (ARTICLE VI)

[3] The Senators and Representatives before mentioned, and the Members of the several State Legislatures, and all executive and judicial Officers, both of the United States and of the several States, shall be bound by Oath or Affirmation, to support this Constitution; but no religious Test shall ever be required as a Qualification to any Office or public Trust under the United States.

§ 3. Oaths of public officers and prohibition of religious tests.

The statutes prescribe the form of oath as follows (5 U.S.C. 3331; 1, 128).

§ Form of oath.

"I, A B, do solemnly swear (or affirm) that I will support and defend the Constitution of the United States against all enemies, foreign and domestic; that I will bear true faith and allegiance to the same; that I take this obligation freely, without any mental reservation or purpose of evasion, and that I will well and faithfully discharge the duties of the office on which I am about to enter. So help me God."

16 AM JUR 2D #176, States Truely,

THE GENERAL RULE IS THAT AN UNCONSTITUTIONAL ACT OF THE LEGISLATURE PROTECTS NO ONE. IT IS SAID THAT ALL PERSONS ARE PRESUMED TO KNOW THE LAW, MEANING THAT IGNORANCE OF THE LAW EXCUSES NO ONE. IF ANY PERSON ACTS UNDER AN UNCONSTITUTIONAL STATUTE, HE DOES SO AT HIS PERIL AND MUST TAKE THE CONSEQUENCES.

Ignorance Of The Law (The U.S.A And Its States Constitutions) Excuses No One: Meaning Mainly The Public Office Holders In The U.S.A.

16 AM JUR 2D #177

THE GENERAL RULE IS THAT AN UNCONSTITUTIONAL STATUTE, THOUGH HAVING THE FORM AND NAME OF LAW, IS IN REALITY NO LAW, BUT IS WHOLLY VOID, AND INEFECTIVE FOR ANY PURPOSE:

SINCE AN UNCONSTITUTIONAL LAW IS VOID, THE GENERAL PRINCIPLES BESTOWS NO POWER OR AUTHORITY ON ANYONE, AFFORDS NO PROTECTION, AND JUSTIFIES NO ACTS PERFORMED UNDER IT...

NO ONE IS BOUND TO OBEY AN UNCONSTITUTIONAL LAW AND NO COURTS ARE BOUND TO ENFORCE IT.

AN UNCONSTITUTIONAL LAW CANNOT OPERATE TO SUPERSEDE ANY EXISTING VALID LAW. INDEED, INSOFAR AS A STATUTE RUNS COUNTER TO THE FUNDAMENTAL LAW OF THE LAND (U.S.A.), IT IS SUPERSEDED THEREBY...

SEE OTHER SIDE OF THIS SHEET FOR U.S.A CONSTITUTIONAL PROTECTION FOR U.S.A CITIZENS, UNDER U.S.A CRIMINAL CODE TITLE 18 AND U.S.A CODE TITLE 42, WHICH ALSO BIND S PUBLIC OFFICE HOLDERS, TO THE LAW.

4

Exhibit Z-61

THIS IS A CONTRACT, B[...]EN U.S.A CITIZENS AND U[...] PUBLIC OFFICE HOLDERS.

Any U.S.A Public Office Holder, Owing Allegiance, by Oath to the U.S.A and the U.S.A and its States Constitutions, who Willfully and Knowingly give aid and comfort to those interests Whose acts are subversive to United States of America, and as such are destroying the Constitutional rights of the U.S.A Citizens, Destroying our childern with Mortgages and [...] drugs, Destroying and stealing our homes and property, our Church(Christian rights), our schools, our businesses, our contracts, our U.S.A Constitutional Monetary system and working to overthrow our Government. Said acts defined in the United States Constitution Art.3 Sec. 3, is punishable under USC TITLE 18 Sec.3,4,2381,2382,2383,2384.

USC TITLE 18 Sec. 3, Whoever, knowing that an offence against the United States has been committed receives, relieves, comforts or assists the offender in order to hinder or prevent his apprehension, trial or punishment, is an accessory after the fact, If the principal is punishable by death, the accessory shall be imprisoned not more than ten years.

USC TITLE 18 Sec. 4, Whoever having knowledge of the actual commission of a felony cognizable by the courts of the United States, conceals and does not as soon as possible make known the same to some judge or other person in civil or military authority under the United States, shall be fined not more than $5000 or imprisoned not more than three years, or both.

USC TITLE 18 Sec. 2381, Whoever, owing alegiance to the United States, levies War against them or adheres to their enemies, giving them aid and comfort within the United States or elsewhere, is guilty of treason and shall suffer death.

USC TITLE 18 Sec. 2382, Whoever, owing allegiance to the United States and having knowledge of the commission of any treason against them, conceal and does not, as soon as may be, disclose and make known the same to the President or to some judge of the United States, is Guilty of misprision of treason and shall be fined not more than $1,000 or imprisoned not more than seven years, or both.

USC TITLE 18 Sec. 2383, Whoever engages in rebellion or insurrection against the authority of the United States or the laws thereof, or gives aid and comfort thereto, shall be fined not more than $10,000 or imprisoned not more than ten years, or both; and shall be incapable of holding any office under the United States.

USC TITLE 18 Sec. 2384, If two or more persons in any State or Territory, conspire to overthrow, put down, or destroy by force the Government of the United States, or delay the execution of any law of the United States contrary to the authority thereof, they shall each be fined not more than $20,000 or imprisoned not more than twenty years or both.

USC TITLE 18. Sec.241,242.

§ 241. Conspiracy against rights of citizens.

If two or more persons conspire to injure, oppress, threaten, or intimidate any citizen in the free exercise or enjoyment of any right or privilege secured to him by the Constitution or laws of the United States, or because of his having so exercised the same, or

If two or more persons go in disguise on the highway, or on the premises of another, with intent to prevent or hinder his free exercise or enjoyment of any right or privilege so secured—

They shall be fined not more than $10,000 or imprisoned not more than ten years, or both; and if death results, they shall be subject to imprisonment for any term of years or for life. (June 25, 1948, ch. 645, 62 Stat. 696; Apr. 11, 1968, Pub. L. 90-284, title I, § 103(a), 82 Stat. 75.)

§ 242. Deprivation of rights under color of law.

Whoever, under color of any law, statute, ordinance, regulation, or custom, willfully subjects any inhabitant of any State, Territory, or District to the deprivation of any rights, privileges, or immunities secured or protected by the Constitution or laws of the United States, or to different punishments, pains, or penalties, on account of such inhabitant being an alien, or by reason of his color, or race, than are prescribed for the punishment of citizens, shall be fined not more than $1,000 or imprisoned not more than one year, or both; and if death results shall be subject to imprisonment for any term of years or for life. (June 25, 1948, ch. 645, 62 Stat. 696; Apr. 11, 1968, Pub. L. 90-284, title I, § 103(b), 82 Stat. 75.)

NOTICE! This U.S.A Oath Of Office And The Contractual Laws, And U.S.A Flag Are And Have Become Highly Offensive To Many People, Now Holding Public Office In The U.S.A, Who Wish To Deal In Secrecy, For Profit.

THE PUBLIC HEALTH AND WELFARE.
USC TITLE 42 Sec. 1983,1985,1986

§ 1983. Civil action for deprivation of rights.

Every person who, under color of any statute, ordinance, regulation, custom, or usage, of any State or Territory, subjects, or causes to be subjected, any citizen of the United States or other person within the jurisdiction thereof to the deprivation of any rights, privileges, or immunities secured by the Constitution and laws, shall be liable to the party injured in an action at law, suit in equity, or other proper proceeding for redress. (R. S. § 1979.)

§ 1985. Conspiracy to interfere with civil rights.

(1) Preventing officer from performing duties.

If two or more persons in any State or Territory conspire to prevent, by force, intimidation, or threat, any person from accepting or holding any office, trust, or place of confidence under the United States, or from discharging any duties thereof; or to induce by like means any officer of the United States to leave any State, district, or place, where his duties as an officer are required to be performed, or to injure him in his person or property on account of his lawful discharge of the duties of his office, or while engaged in the lawful discharge thereof, or to injure his property so as to molest, interrupt, hinder, or impede him in the discharge of his official duties;

(2) Obstructing justice; intimidating party, witness, or juror.

If two or more persons in any State or Territory conspire to deter, by force, intimidation, or threat, any party or witness in any court of the United States from attending such court, or from testifying to any matter pending therein, freely, fully, and truthfully, or to injure such party or witness in his person or property on account of his having so attended or testified, or to influence the verdict, presentment, or indictment of any grand or petit juror in any such court, or to injure such juror in his person or property on account of any verdict, presentment, or indictment lawfully assented to by him, or of his being or having been such juror; or if two or more persons conspire for the purpose of impeding, hindering, obstructing, or defeating, in any manner, the due course of justice in any State or Territory, with intent to deny to any citizen the equal protection of the laws, or to injure him or his property for lawfully enforcing, or attempting to enforce, the right of any person, or class of persons, to the equal protection of the laws;

(3) Depriving persons of rights or privileges

If two or more persons in any State or Territory conspire or go in disguise on the highway or on the premises of another, for the purpose of depriving, either directly or indirectly, any person or class of persons of the equal protection of the laws, or of equal privileges and immunities under the laws; or for the purpose of preventing or hindering the constituted authorities of any State or Territory from giving or securing to all persons within such State or Territory the equal protection of the laws; or if two or more persons conspire to prevent by force, intimidation, or threat, any citizen who is lawfully entitled to vote, from giving his support or advocacy in a legal manner, toward or in favor of the election of any lawfully qualified person as an elector for President or Vice President, or as a Member of Congress of the United States; or to injure any citizen in person or property on account of such support or advocacy; in any case of conspiracy set forth in this section, if one or more persons engaged therein do, or cause to be done, any act in furtherance of the object of such conspiracy, whereby another is injured in his person or property, or deprived of having and exercising any right or privilege of a citizen of the United States, the party so injured or deprived may have an action for the recovery of damages, occasioned by such injury or deprivation, against any one or more of the conspirators. (R. S. § 1980.)

§ 1986. Same; action for neglect to prevent.

Every person who, having knowledge that any of the wrongs conspired to be done, and mentioned in section 1985 of this title, are about to be committed, and having power to prevent or aid in preventing the commission of the same, neglects or refuses so to do, if such wrongful act be committed, shall be liable to the party injured, or his legal representatives, for all damages caused by such wrongful act, which such person by reasonable diligence could have prevented; and such damages may be recovered in an action on the case; and any number of persons guilty of such wrongful neglect or refusal may be joined as defendants in the action; and if the death of any party be caused by any such wrongful act and neglect, the legal representatives of the deceased shall have such action therefor, and may recover not exceeding $5,000 damages therein, for the benefit of the widow of the deceased, if there be one, and if there be no widow, then for the benefit of the next of kin of the deceased. But no action under the provisions of this section shall be sustained which is not commenced within one year after the cause of action has accrued. (R. S. § 1981.)

EJ

6

Exhibit Z-62

RAPE

1-28-98 WRITTEN BY David-Wynn: Miller: L.A.W. PROCEDURES.

1. RAPE: THE UNLAWFUL KNOWLEDGE OF A PARTY USING FORCE AND AGAINST PARTIES WILL. THE ACT WITHOUT PARTIES CONSENT, COMMITTED WHEN PARTY'S RESISTANCE IS OVERCOME BY FORCE OR FEAR OR UNDER OTHER PROHIBITIVE CONDITIONS. [STATE V LORA; 213 KAN.184, 515 P.2d 1086, 1093.

2. THE STRONGER PARTY COMPELLING THE WEAKER PARTY OF SUBMITTING BY FORCE OR BY THREATENING OF IMMINENT DEATH, SERIOUS BODILY INJURY, EXTREME PAIN, OR KIDNAPPING, WITH INFLICTING ON ANYONE; OR WHEN THE STRONGER PARTY HAS SUBSTANTIAL POWER OF IMPAIRING THE WEAKER PARTY'S POWER OF APPRAISING OR CONTROLLING WEAKER PARTY'S CONDUCT BY OTHER MEANS FOR THE PURPOSE OF PREVENTING WEAKER PARTY'S RESISTANCE; MODEL PENAL CODE $213.1

3. THE WEAKER PARTY HAS A COUNCIL APPOINTED AGAINST WEAKER PARTY'S WILL, IN VIOLATION OF THE C.u.S.A. ARTICLE THE EIGHT(8); VIOLATION OF DUE-PROCESS UNDER C.u.S.A. ARTICLE THE SEVEN(7) AND RIGHT OF TRIAL BY JURY UNDER C.u.S.A. ARTICLE THE NINE(9); TITLE: 28: U.S.A. CODES: SECTION: 1605: "LACK OF IMMUNITY", BY A FOREIGN: ENTITY UNDER OATH OR AFFIRMATION UNDER THE FOREIGN BY FLAG OF FRINGE AND UNDER TREATY OF <u>THE FOREIGN: SOVEREIGN: IMMUNITY: ACT</u>, OF THE STATE OF FOREIGN: JURISDICTION, IN COMMERENCE, IN THE UNITED STATES OF AMERICA, BY A FOREIGN STATES ENTITY.

4. TITLE: 28: u.S.A. CODES: SECTION: 1359: COLLUSION: THE COURT OF THE DISTRICT SHALL NOT HAVE JURISDICTION OF A CIVIL ACTION IN WHICH ANY PARTY, BY ASSIGNMENT OR OTHERWISE, BY IMPROPER OR COLLUSIVE JOINDER MADE BY INVOKING THE JURISDICTION OF THE COURT.

5. THE LANGUAGE HAS BEEN CORRECTED BY ALGEBRAIC ENGLISH FORMULA OF THE David-Wynn: Miller L.A.W. PROCEDURES.
THE DEFINITIONS WRITTEN IN BLACKS LAW DICTIONARY FOR THE WORD "RAPE" ARE FRAUDULANT; MIXING PAST AND PRESENT PREPOSITIONAL FOR PRESUMPTIONS AND ASSUMPTIONS CAUSING NOUNS BY BEING USED AS <u>ADJECTIVE(FICTIONS)</u> OF IDEAS IN CONFLICT WITH THE SINGLE SUBJECT MATTER REQUIREMENTS OF THE RULES OF SENTENCING. [STUDY THE RULES AND LAWS OF OLD ENGLISH AND OLD LATIN]

1 Copyright DM-1-28-98

Exhibit Z-63

NO FOREIGN STATE

TITLE: 28: U.S.A. CODES: SECTION: 2072 OF F.R.C.P. RULE: 44.1
1-27-98: COPYRIGHT: David-Wynn: Miller: L.A.W. PROCEDURES

ATTENTION: THE TRAPS SET FOR THE CITIZENS BY THE DRAFTERS OF THE TITLE: 28: U.S.A. CODES: CHAPTER: 131 AT SECTION: 2071: **THE F.R.C.P. FOR THE UNIFORM USE IN THE UNITED STATES DISTRICT COURTS AND THE COURT OF THE DISTRICT OF THE UNITED: STATES OF AMERICA, WAS WORDED IN THE FUTURE TENSE OF THE ENGLISH LANGUAGE WHEREAS STATED:** "RECOGNITION BY CONGRESS OF THE BROAD RULE-MAKING POWER OF THE COURT WILL MAKE [RULE- MAKING POWERS] "IT" POSSIBLE FOR THE COURTS "TO" PRESCRIBE COMPLETE AND UNIFORM MODES OF PROCEDURES".

"TO"= FUTURE TENSE; IS THE ASSIGNMENT OF AUTHORITY IN THE FUTURE, HOWEVER NEVER HAD OR HAS JURISDICTION IN THE "PRESENT TENSE" OF "TIME" FOR LAW OR RULE OR DECISION MAKING.

TITLE: 28: U.S.A. CODES: SECTION: 2071: NOTES:

FORMER ATTORNEY-GENERAL: CUMMINGS SAID, "LEGISLATIVE-BODIES HAVE NEITHER THE TIME **"TO" INQUIRE** OBJECTIVELY INTO THE DETAILS OF JUDICIAL: PROCEDURES NOR THE OPPORTUNITY **"TO" DETERMINE** THE NECESSITY FOR AMENDMENT OR CHANGE.

THE WORD **"TO INQUIRE"** IN FUTURE TENSE AND **"TO" DETERMINE** IN FUTURE TENSE **NEVER HAD OR HAS JURISDICTION BY JUDGING ANYTHING IN THE PRESENT TENSE BY NEGLECTING THE DUE PROCESS OF LAW UNDER THE CONSTITUTION OF THE UNITED: STATES OF AMERICA ARTICLE THE SEVEN(7)**

TITLE: 28: U.S.A. CODES: SECTION: 2071: NOTES:

THE RULES OF EVIDENCE IN TAX-COURT: PROCEEDINGS ARE THE SAME AS THOSE WHICH APPLY TO CIVIL PROCEDURES IN OTHER: COURTS. SEE: DEMPER V BURNET 1931, 46 F.2nd 604, 60 APP.D.C.23. (NO COURT UNDER COLOR OF LAW = LAW OF THE FOREIGN FLAG, FRINGE OR ADORNMENTS ON THE TITLE: 4: U.S.A. THE CODES: SECTION: 1&2: FLAG OF THE UNITED: STATES OF AMERICA FOR THE SURRENDERING OF RIGHTS BY ENFORCING A MASTERS COURT OF THE FOREIGN JURISDICTION OVER THE CITIZEN IN PARTY.

TITLE: 28: U.S.A. THE CODES: CHAPTER: 131: SECTION: 2072(b): SUCH RULES SHALL NOT ABRIDGE, ENLARGE OR MODIFY ANY SUBSTANTIVE RIGHTS OF THE CITIZEN. ALL LAWS IN CONFLICT WITH SUCH RULES SHALL BE OF NO FURTHER FORCE OR EFFECT AFTER SUCH RULES HAVE TAKEN EFFECT. CROSS REFERENCE: TITLE: 28. C.U.S.A.: SECTION: 1605 OF THE "FOREIGN SOVEREIGN: IMMUNITY ACT OF OCTOBER: 21, 1976.

THE QUESTION WAS ASKED: "HOW WILL THE CITIZENS STOP THE FRAUD AND INJUSTICE"?

(COM VENUE JUDGE PREP COM CONSTITUTION)

THERE ARE TWO (2) SUPREME COURTS: **THE SUPREME-COURT OF THE UNITED: STATES OF AMERICA** FOUND IN TITLE: 28: U.S.A. THE CODES: SECTION: 2074 AND **UNITED STATES SUPREME COURT.**<---<--<--

REMEMBER THE POWER OF THE STATEMENTS ARE BY RIGHT TO LEFT, BACKWARDS.<--<---<

TITLE: 28: CHAPTER: 131: SECTION: 2074:(SECTION: (2)(2)(B) PUBLIC-LAW: 93-595 TITLE: 3, JANUARY THE 2 OF 1975: (88 STAT. 1949), PROVIDED THAT: "THE CONGRESS EXPRESSLY APPROVES THE AMENDMENTS "TO" THE [F.R.C.P. RULE 30(c), 32(C), 43 AND 44.1] THE SUPREME-COURT OF THE UNITED: STATES OF AMERICA EMBRACED AND TOOK EFFECT ON [JAN.2, 1975]: THE **FRAUD UNDER F.R.C.P. RULE 9(b)** WAS THE "[ ]" BRACKETS BY REMOVING THE RULES FROM THE F.R.C.P., WHICH NEVER HAD STANDING UNDER THE VIOLATION OF **THE CONSTITUTION OF THE U.S.A.** BECAUSE OF THE OATH AND AFFIRMATION CONTRACT. WOULD HAVE VIOLATED C.U.S.A. ARTICLE THE (4): SECTION THE THREE(3) OF THE CONSTITUTION OF THE U.S.A. (DATED 1865) WHERE NO NEW STATE(NATURAL PARTY) SHALL ERECT ANY STATE WITHIN ANY STATE (FOREIGN STATE UNDER THE LAW OF THE FLAG) FROM ANY STATE(GREATER U.S.A.) THE "TO" IS FUTURE TENSE = NO JURISDICTION.

copyright: DM-2-26-98

1

Exhibit Z-64

DISQUALIFICATION OF FOREIGN STATE

COPYRIGHT: 2-27-98; PROCEDURAL OUTLINE FOR THE DISQUALIFICATION OF THE FOREIGN STATE JURISDICTION WITHIN THE UNITED: STATES OF AMERICA FOR COMMERCE: David-Wynn: Miller L.A.W. PROCEDURES

1. TITLE: 28: U.S.A. THE CODES: SECTION: 1605: GENERAL EXCEPTIONS BY THE JURISDICTIONAL IMMUNITY OF THE COURT OF FOREIGN UNDER THE FLAG OF FRINGE;
(a) THE STATE OF FOREIGN;JURISDICTION SHALL NOT BE IMMUNE FROM THE JURISDICTION OF COURTS OF THE DISTRICT OF THE UNITED: STATES OF AMERICA OR OF THE STATES IN ANY CASE--- (2)IN WHICH THE ACTION IS BASED UPON A COMMERCIAL ACTIVITY CARRIED ON IN THE UNITED: STATES OF AMERICA UNDER THE "FOREIGN SOVEREIGN IMMUNITY ACT" FOR POWER OF FOREIGN AND STATES OF FOREIGN UNDER "THE LAW OF THE FLAG": THE FLAG OF FRINGE WITH THE COST OF MORE THAN $21.00 DOLLARS AND BY THE FILING FEE, FOR THE CIVIL LAW SUIT, MAKES THE STATEMENT, AN ACT OF COMMERCE,(ENRICHMENT BY THE STATE AND FEDERAL GOVERNMENT, BY CONTRACT, AND WITHIN THE TERRITORY OF THE U.S.A. UNDER C.U.S.A. ARTICLE THE NINE(9): TRIAL BY JURY AND F.R.C.P. RULE: 38(a).

2. THE BREACH\VIOLATION OF INTERNATIONAL TREATY BY THE STATE OF FOREIGN, OPERATING UNDER THE CONSTITUTION OF THE U.S.A., MUST UPHOLD THE CONSTITUTION OF THE U.S.A. RIGHTS OF THE SOVEREIGN: CITIZEN IN PARTY, AND WHEN VIOLATED, MUST GO INTO THE SUPREME-COURT IN WASHINGTON: D.C. FOR THE TREATY DISPUTE BETWEEN SOVEREIGN: CITIZENS OF STATE: GOVERNMENT AND THE TREATY FOR JURISDICTIONS OF FOREIGN AS REQUIRED BY TREATY-LAW.

3. BY ENFORCING AN AGREEMENT (TREATY) MADE OF OATH OR AFFIRMATION FOR SUPPORTING AND DEFENDING THE CONSTITUTION OF THE UNITED: STATES OF AMERICA, BY THE JUDGE. THE SURRENDERING OF THE OATH AND AFFIRMATION INTO A STATE OF FOREIGN-JURISDICTION FOR CAUSING THE CONSTRUCTIVE-TREASON, CONTEMPT FOR THE C.U.S.A., FALSE-SWEARING OF THE OATH OF THE STATE AND C.U.S.A. AND PERJURY OF OATH UNDER TITLE: 18: U.S.A. CODES: SECTION: 1621.

4. (3) THE RIGHTS OF THE CITIZEN FOR THE PROPERTY TAKEN, IN VIOLATION OF INTERNATIONAL LAW ARE THE ISSUE AND THE PROPERTY OR ANY PROPERTY EXCHANGED FOR THE PROPERTY IS PRESENT IN THE U.S.A. IN CONNECTION WITH A COMMERCIAL ACTIVITY CARRIED ON IN THE U.S.A. BY THE STATE OF FOREIGN; OR THAT PROPERTY IS OWNED OR OPERATED BY AN AGENCY OR INSTRUMENTALITY OF THE STATE OF FOREIGN AND THAT AGENCY OR INSTRUMENTALITY IS ENGAGED IN A COMMERCIAL ACTIVITY IN THE U.S.A. NOW MAKES THE FILING FEE THE COMMERCIAL ACTIVITY WHEN THE MONEY INVOLVED IS OVER $21.00 DOLLARS U.S.A.

5. (B) ANY CLAIM ARISING OUT OF INTERFERENCE WITH CONTRACT RIGHTS FOR THE FILING FEES OF THE TRIAL BY JURY IN WHICH THE ACTION IS BROUGHT, EITHER BY ENFORCING AN AGREEMENT MADE BY THE STATE OF FOREIGN WITH, OR FOR THE BENEFIT OF A PRIVATE PARTY BY SUBMITTING FOR A DEFINED LEGAL-RELATIONSHIP, WHETHER CONTRACTUAL FOR ARBITRATION OR THE JUDGES OATH FOR SUPPORTING THE CONSTITUTION OF THE U.S.A..

6. (B) AND, THE AGREEMENT OR AWARD IS OR MAY BE GOVERNED BY A TREATY OR OTHER INTERNATIONAL AGREEMENT (LAW OF THE FLAG) IN FORCE FOR THE U.S.A. CALLING FOR THE RECOGNITION AND ENFORCEMENT OF THE ARBITRAL AWARDS. **THE OATH OR AFFIRMATION IS UNDER THE LAW OF THE CONSTITUTION OF THE U.S.A. SEPTEMBER THE 17 OF 1789.**

7. THE PROVISIONS OF THE "FOREIGN SOVEREIGN IMMUNITY ACT", DATED OCTOBER THE 21 OF 1976, IS UNDER TITLE: 28: U.S.A.CODES: SECTION: 1601-1611 ABOVE, FOR THE PROTECTION OF THE CONSTITUTION OF THE U.S.A. SEPTEMBER THE 17 OF 1789, SO NO PARTY WOULD EVER HAVE IMMUNITY FROM BREAKING THE LAW. THE JUDGE MUST AFFIRM THE OATH FOR THE CONSTITUTION OF SEPTEMBER THE 17 OF 1789 FOR BECOMING A JUDGE. C.U.S.A. ARTICLE THE 6: SECTION THE THREE OF DATED 1868.

copyright: DM. 2-26-98

Exhibit Z-65

7. THE EAGLE IS FOR THE PRESIDENT OF THE UNITED: STATES OF AMERICA (CORPORATE) ONLY, ANY USE, OF THE EAGLE, ON THE FINAL, BY THE COURTS, WILL CAUSE A FRAUD (F.R.C.P. RULE: 9(b), AND SUSPEND THE C.U.S.A. RIGHTS, INTO A FOREIGN STATE/POWER WHERE CITIZEN IN PARTY WILL BE GUILTY TILL PROVEN INNOCENT. WITHOUT PERSONAL SIGNED AUTHORITY BY THE PRESIDENT OF U.S.A.. TITLE: 36: CHAPTER: 10: SECTION: 175 AND 176(G), AR840-10: CH. (2-3), (2-5), (2-6) NO FRINGE)

8. ANY FIDUCIARY OF RESPONSIBILITY UNDER THE C.U.S.A. ARTICLE THE ELEVEN(11) OF OATH AND AFFIRMATION THAT DESECRATES THE TITLE: 4: U.S.A. CODES: SECTION: 1&2: FLAG BY CREATING A FOREIGN STATE/POWER, WILL BE GUILTY OF CONSTRUCTIVE TREASON, CONTEMPT OF THE CONSTITUTION OF THE UNITED: STATES OF AMERICA, PERJURY OF OATH UNDER TITLE: 18: U.S.A. CODES: SECTION: 1621, AND FALSE SWEARING, (TITLE: 18: U.S.A. CODES: SECTION: 3: ACCESSORY AFTER THE FACT)(TITLE: 18: U.S.A. CODES: SECTION: 242). THE MEANING OF THE WORDS UNDER THE TERMS OF THE CODES:

9. [T]HE UNITED STATES DISTRICT COURT:=
[T]HE COURT = (JUDGE) JURISDICTION BY OATH AND AFFIRMATION, ARTICLE THE EIGHT OF THE C.U.S.A.
[T]HE DISTRICT F.R.C.P. RULE: 12(b)(3) VENUE; OF
[T]HE STATE= CONDITION OF ([T]HE JUDGE) = FOR CONDITION IS NOT DEFINED, AND WHAT DISCRETION =?
[T]HE = UNITED (FOREIGN JUDGES) UNDER FLAG OF FRINGE THE FOREIGN FOR RULING OVER AND THE SUSPENSION OF THE C.U.S.A. DO YOU WEAR A FLAG WITH FRINGE OF FOREIGN FOR DESECRATION?

10. COURT OF THE DISTRICT OF THE UNITED: STATES OF AMERICA:
THE "STATES OF AMERICA" = OF THE GEOGRAPHICAL AREA OF AMERICAN VENUE BY LAND
THE UNITED: = MUST HAVE A COLON(:)(AREAS OF THE STATES OF AMERICA TOGETHER), COMMAND A NOUN IN UPPER CASE SPELLING) DEFINED AS: STATES OF AMERICA

"THE" = COMMANDING THE SUBJECT BY THE ASSIGNMENT OF AUTHORITY; THE PREPOSITION, "OF" = THE ASSIGNMENT OF AUTHORITY, IN PRESENT TENSE OR NOW JURISDICTION: THE JUDGE OF THE COURT OF THE VENUE, ELECTED BY THE CITIZENS OF THE "WE THE PEOPLE";
THE "DISTRICT"= UNDER VENUE F.R.C.P. RULE: 12(b)(3) ONLY IN TITLE: 4: U.S.A. CODES: SECTION: 1&2: JURISDICTION BY THE C.U.S.A. RIGHTS ARE GUARANTEED IN COURT, ONLY ON THE SAME PLANE JURISDICTION.

11. WISCONSIN STATE: STATE IS A NOUN, WISCONSIN IS AN ADJECTIVE
ADJECTIVES ARE FICTION, THEREFORE FICTION IS NO JURISDICTION AND NO CONSTITUTION OF LAW. ONLY FICTION OF THE JUDGE IN A STATE OF FOREIGN.

12. STATE OF WISCONSIN: WISCONSIN IS A NOUN AND STATE IS A NOUN. BOTH HAVE SUBSTANCE JURISDICTION OVER THE AREA OR VENUE AND A FACT OF CONSTITUTION OF LAWS.

13. THE FICTION OF THE FLAG OF FRINGE OVER THE FICTION STATE BY THE BAR, OVER THE CITIZEN IN PARTY AS A FICTION WITH A DEAD NAME AND DEAD SPEECH AS FICTION WITH THE ESQUIRE FICTION ATTORNEY AND THE SOVEREIGN IDENTIFYING THE TITLE:4:FICTION FLAG BECAUSE NO ONE USED PUNCTUATION IN SPEECH OR SPELLING ALL FORMS OF COURT ARE FICTION AND UNDER JOINDER F.R.C.P. 12(b)(7) WE NOW HAVE JURISDICTION OF FICTION.

2

Exhibit Z-66

COMMENTS ON THE FLAG OF AMERICA

12-28-97 COPYRIGHT BY David Wynn Miller, L.A.W. PROCEDURES,

THERE HAS BEEN MUCH DISCUSSION ABOUT THE JURISDICTION OF THE FLAG: TITLE: 4, C.U.S.A. 1, WHERE THE FLAG CAN BE USED, WHERE THE CONSTITUTION OF THE united STATES, HAS AUTHORITY.

1. THE AUTHORITY OF THE C.u.S.A.IS KEPT ALIVE AS A LIVING NATURAL PARTY, BY THE united STATES SUPREME COURT. ALL OFFICERS OF THE COURT MUST SWEAR OR AFFIRM THE OATH OR AFFIRMATION: JUDGES, ATTORNEYS, CLERKS, POLICE, SHERIFFS, CONGRESSMEN, LEGISLATURE. SENATORS, AND PRESIDENT OF THE united STATES FOR HAVING THE AUTHORITY OF GOVERNING OVER THE CITIZENS IN PARTY. THE CITIZENS IN PARTY, HAVING ELECTED OR APPOINTED THE OFFICERS, THROUGH THE ELECTION PROCESS, OF THE C.u.S.A.A.: 9.

2. THE USE OF THE TITLE: 4, C.u.S.A.:SECTION: 1&2, FLAG: (1 X 1.9), THE FRAUDULENT **FOREIGN FLAG WITH FRINGE OF YELLOW. THE SPEAR OR EAGLE**, ON THE TOP OF THE FLAG: POLE OR STANDARD OR A **BRAID ON THE FLAG: POLE**, UNDER THE TITLE: 42, C.u.S.A.:SECTION: 1986 FOR THE KNOWLEDGE, F.R.C.P. RULE 60(b) DISCOVERY, F.R.C.P. RULE 26(e) DISCOVERY AND REPORTING THE FRAUD, F.R.C.P. RULE 9(b) FOR FRAUD AND CONDITION OF THE MIND, AND WILL CAUSE THE TITLE: 42, C.u.S.A.:SECTION: 1986 NEGLECT BY NOT STOPPING AND CORRECTING A WRONG. THE TITLE: 4, C.u.S.A.:SECTION: 3 , DESECRATION OF THE FLAG, **BY CREATING A FOREIGN STATE**, MAKING THE FIDUCIARY [JUDGE], UNDER THE LAW OF THE FLAG, A MASTER OVER ALL CITIZENS IN PARTY, THAT WOULD MAKE CONTRACT, WITH THE **PERSON = CORPORATION = FRAUD**, CITIZEN'S NAME IN ALL UPPER CASE LETTERS, BY MAKING THE CORPORATE PERSON, **AND BY ENSLAVING THE CITIZEN IN PARTY**, INTO A CRIMINAL CONFESSION, FOR THE PURPOSE OF DEPRIVATION OF RIGHTS TITLE: 18, C.u.S.A.: SECTION: 242: **EXTORTION OF FEES, MONEY, FREEDOM, DUTY, OR PROPERTY: TITLE: 18, C.u.S.A.: SECTION: 242**, OBSTRUCTING JUSTICE TITLE: 42, C.u.S.A.: SECTION: 1985(2), **OBSTRUCTION OF JUSTICE: TITLE: 18, C.u.S.A.: SECTION: 1512, CAUSING** CONSTRUCTIVE TREASON, CONTEMPT OF THE U.S.A. CONSTITUTION, FALSE SWEARING AND PERJURY OF OATH: TITLE: 18, C.u.S.A.:SECTION: 1621 .

3. **NATIONAL: FLAGS**, (DIMENSIONS 4X6) AND (12 X17) ARE UNDER (ARMY: REG.: 840-10: CHAPTER 2-3), HAVE THE AUTHORITY TO PUT **FRINGE OF YELLOW, ON THREE SIDES**, FOR THE DISPLAY IN **COURT- MARSHALS** WITH A **SPEAR** ON THE STANDARD TOP AND BRAID ON THE STANDARD FOR MARITIME AND ADMIRALTY-COURTS. SEE BLACKS DICTIONARY: **LAW OF THE FLAG. EXECUTIVE-ORDER: 10834 (8-25-59)**.

4. THE **FRAUD** OF CREATING A **FOREIGN STATE/POWER**, IS WHEN A TITLE: 4, C.u.S.A.: SECTION: 1&2: FLAG OF THE u.S.A. IS USED **IN PLACE** OF THE **NATIONAL: FLAG**. WHEN THE CITIZEN IN PARTY **SEEING THE SAME**, DOES RESEARCH, AND FAILS TO SEE AND **MEASURE THE DIFFERENCE IN THE DIMENSIONS** OF THE FLAG, IS NOW TRIED UNDER A **FOREIGN STATE: JURISDICTION**, AS A CIVILIAN (WRONG VENUE F.R.C.P.: RULE: 12(b)3), OR A FOREIGN STATE/POWER WITH THE JUDGE NOW A **MASTER WITH THE TITLE OF ESQUIRE**. ARTICLE THE ONE, SECTION THE NINE, VIOLATION AND C.u.S.A.A.: 11, AND ARTICLE THE FOUR, SECTION THE THREE: NO NEW STATE SHALL BE ERECTED WITHIN ANY STATE OR OF PARTS OF OTHER STATES.

5. **ARTICLE THE ONE, SECTION THE NINE, OF THE C.u.S.A., NO TITLES OF NOBILITY, SHALL HAVE JURISDICTION, OVER ANY, SOVEREIGN CITIZEN IN PARTY.**

6. THE ANSWER FOR THE VIOLATION OF THE BREACH OF OATH AND AFFIRMATION, IS THE FIRST CONTRACT OF THE OFFICERS, OF THE PUBLIC'S TRUST. WHEN THE CONSTITUTION IS SURRENDERED TO A FOREIGN STATE THEN CONSTRUCTIVE TREASON, PERJURY OF OATH TITLE: 18, C.u.S.A.: SECTION: 1621, CONTEMPT FOR THE CONSTITUTION OF THE united STATES, AND FALSE SWEARING ARE THE VIOLATIONS.

7. **ABBREVIATION:** F.R.C.P. = **FEDERAL: RULES OF CIVIL-PROCEDURE**
C.u.S.A. = **CODES OF THE united STATE OF AMERICA**
C.u.S.A.A.= **CONSTITUTION OF THE united STATES OF AMERICA: AMENDMENT**,
U.C.C. = **UNIFORM: COMMERCIAL-CODES**
u.S.A. = **united STATES OF AMERICA**

3

Exhibit Z-67

FLAG JURISDICTION ON THE FLAG OF AMERICA

2-25-98 COPYRIGHT BY David-Wynn: Miller: L.A.W. PROCEDURES,

THERE HAS BEEN MUCH DISCUSSION ABOUT THE JURISDICTION OF THE FLAG: TITLE: 4: U.S.A. THE CODES: SECTION: 1&2, WHERE THE FLAG CAN BE USED, WHERE THE CONSTITUTION OF THE UNITED: STATES, HAS AUTHORITY. THE C.U.S.A. IS A DOCUMENT UNDER NOUN: JURISDICTION WITH ENTITY QUALITIES.

1. THE AUTHORITY OF THE C.U.S.A. IS KEPT ALIVE AS A LIVING TRUST, BY THE UNITED: STATES OF AMERICA: SUPREME-COURT. ALL OFFICERS OF THE COURT MUST SWEAR OR AFFIRM THE OATH OR AFFIRMATION: JUDGES, ATTORNEYS, CLERKS, POLICE, SHERIFFS, CONGRESSMEN, LEGISLATURE. SENATORS, AND PRESIDENT OF THE UNITED: STATES OF AMERICA FOR HAVING THE AUTHORITY OF GOVERNING OVER THE CITIZENS IN PARTY. THE CITIZENS IN PARTY, HAVING ELECTED OR APPOINTED THE OFFICERS, THROUGH THE ELECTION PROCESS, OF THE C.U.S.A. ARTICLE THE NINE(9).

2. THE USE OF THE <u>TITLE: 4: U.S.A. THE CODES: SECTION: 1&2, FLAG: (1 X 1.9)</u>, THE FRAUDULENT **FLAG OF FRINGE. THE SPEAR OR EAGLE**, ON THE TOP OF THE FLAG: POLE OR STANDARD OR A **BRAID ON THE FLAG: POLE**, UNDER THE <u>TITLE: 42: U.S.A. THE CODES: SECTION: 1986 FOR THE KNOWLEDGE</u>, F.R.C.P. RULE: 60(b) DISCOVERY; F.R.C.P. RULE: 26(e) DISCOVERY AND REPORTING THE <u>FRAUD, F.R.C.P. RULE: 9(b) FOR FRAUD AND CONDITION OF THE MIND</u>, AND WILL CAUSE THE <u>TITLE: 42: U.S.A. THE CODES: SECTION: 1986 NEGLECT BY NOT STOPPING AND CORRECTING A WRONG.</u> THE <u>TITLE: 4: U.S.A. THE CODES: SECTION: 3: DESECRATION OF THE FLAG</u>, **BY CREATING A FOREIGN: STATE**, MAKING THE FIDUCIARY [JUDGE], UNDER THE LAW OF THE FLAG, A MASTER OVER ALL CITIZENS IN PARTY, THAT WOULD MAKE CONTRACT, WITH THE **PERSON = CORPORATION = FRAUD**, <u>CITIZEN'S NAME IN ALL UPPER CASE LETTERS</u>, BY <u>MAKING THE CORPORATE: PERSON,</u> **AND BY ENSLAVING THE CITIZEN IN PARTY**, INTO A CRIMINAL: CONFESSION, FOR THE PURPOSE OF <u>DEPRIVATION OF RIGHTS: TITLE: 18: U.S.A. THE CODES: SECTION: 242</u>: **EXTORTION OF FEES, MONEY, FREEDOM, DUTY, OR PROPERTY: TITLE: 18: U.S.A. THE CODES: SECTION: 242**, <u>OBSTRUCTING JUSTICE: TITLE: 42: U.S.A. THE CODES: SECTION: 1985(2)</u>, **OBSTRUCTION OF JUSTICE: TITLE: 18: U.S.A. THE CODES: SECTION: 1512, CAUSING** <u>CONSTRUCTIVE-TREASON, CONTEMPT OF THE C.U.S.A. FALSE SWEARING AND PERJURY OF OATH: TITLE: 18: U.S.A. THE CODES: SECTION: 1621</u>.

3. **NATIONAL: FLAGS**, (DIMENSIONS: 4 X 6) AND (12 X 17) ARE UNDER <u>(ARMY: REG.: 840-10: CHAPTER: 2-3)</u>, HAVE THE AUTHORITY BY PUTTING **FRINGE ON THREE SIDES**, FOR THE DISPLAY IN **COURT-MARSHALS** WITH A **SPEAR** ON TOP OF THE STANDARD AND BRAID ON THE STANDARD FOR MARITIME AND ADMIRALTY-COURTS. SEE BLACK'S: DICTIONARY: **LAW OF THE FLAG. EXECUTIVE-ORDER: 10834 (DATE: AUGUST THE 25 OG 1959).**

4. THE **FRAUD** OF CREATING A **FOREIGN: STATE/POWER**, IS WHEN A <u>TITLE: 4: U.S.A. THE CODES: SECTION: 1&2: FLAG OF THE U.S.A.</u> IS USED **IN PLACE** OF THE **NATIONAL: FLAG**. WHEN THE CITIZEN IN PARTY **SEEING THE SAME**, DOES RESEARCH, AND FAILS TO SEE AND **MEASURE THE DIFFERENCE IN THE DIMENSIONS** OF THE FLAG, IS NOW TRIED UNDER A **FOREIGN: STATE: JURISDICTION**, <u>AS A CIVILIAN (WRONG VENUE F.R.C.P. RULE: 12(b)(3)</u>, OR A FOREIGN: STATE/POWER WITH THE JUDGE NOW A **MASTER WITH THE TITLE OF ESQUIRE**. ARTICLE THE ONE, SECTION THE NINE(9), VIOLATION AND C.U.S.A.(YEAR-1789) AND ARTICLE THE FOUR, SECTION THE THREE:(1865) NO NEW STATE SHALL BE ERECTED WITHIN ANY STATE OR OF PARTS OF OTHER STATES;

5. **ARTICLE THE ONE, SECTION THE NINE, OF THE C.U.S.A.(YEAR-1865) NO TITLES OF NOBILITY, SHALL HAVE JURISDICTION, OVER ANY, SOVEREIGN CITIZEN IN PARTY.**

6. THE ANSWER FOR THE VIOLATION OF THE BREACH OF OATH AND AFFIRMATION, IS THE FIRST CONTRACT OF THE OFFICERS, OF THE PUBLIC'S TRUST. WHEN THE CONSTITUTION IS SURRENDERED TO A FOREIGN: STATE THEN CONSTRUCTIVE-TREASON, PERJURY OF OATH: TITLE: 18: U.S.A. THE CODES: SECTION: 1621, CONTEMPT FOR THE CONSTITUTION OF THE UNITED: STATES OF AMERICA AND FALSE SWEARING ARE THE VIOLATIONS.

7. ABBREVIATION: F.R.C.P. = FEDERAL: RULES OF CIVIL-PROCEDURE
U.S.A. THE CODES = UNITED: STATE OF AMERICA THE CODES
U.C.C. = UNIFORM-COMMERCIAL-CODES
C.U.S.A. ARTICLE THE = CONSTITUTION OF THE UNITED: STATES OF AMERICA: ARTICLE THE

U.S.A. = UNITED: STATES OF AMERICA

1 Copyright: DM-2-25-98

Exhibit Z-68

TITLE 4 - FLAG AND SEAL, SEAT OF GOVERNMENT, AND THE STATES
CHAPTER: 1 - THE FLAG: Section 1. Flag; stripes and stars on
The flag of the United: States shall be thirteen horizontal stripes, alternate red and white; and the union of the flag shall be forty-eight stars, white in a blue field.
Section 2. Same; additional stars On the admission of a new State into the Union one star shall be added to the union of the flag; and such addition shall take effect on the fourth day of July then next succeeding such admission.
Section 3. Use of flag for advertising purposes; mutilation of flag Any person who, within the District of Columbia, in any manner, for exhibition or display, shall place or cause to be placed any word, figure, mark, picture, design, drawing, or any advertisement of any nature upon any flag, standard, colors, or ensign of the United: States of America; or shall expose or cause to be exposed to public view any such flaq, standard, colors, or ensign upon which shall have been printed, painted, or otherwise placed, or to which shall be attached, appended, affixed, or annexed any word, figure, mark, picture, design, or drawing, or any advertisement of any nature; or who, within the District of Columbia, shall manufacture, sell, expose for sale, or to public view, or give away or have in possession for sale, or to be given away or for use for any purpose, any article or substance being an article of merchandise, or a receptacle for merchandise or article or thing for carrying or transporting merchandise, upon which shall have been printed, painted, attached, or otherwise placed a representation of any such flag, standard, colors, or ensign, to advertise, call attention to, decorate, mark, or distinguish the article or substance on which so placed shall be deemed guilty of a misdemeanor and shall be punished by a fine not **exceeding $100 or by imprisonment for not more than thirty days,** or both, in the discretion of the court. The words "flag, standard, colors, or ensign", as used herein, shall include any flag, standard, colors, ensign, or any picture or representation of either, or of any part or parts of either, made of any substance or represented on any substance, of any size evidently purporting to be either of said flag, standard, colors, or ensign of the United States of America or a picture or a representation of either, upon which shall be shown the colors, the stars and the stripes, in any number of either thereof, or of any part or parts of either, by which the average person seeing the same without deliberation may believe the same to represent the flag, colors, standard, or ensign of the United: States of America.

Copyright: DM. 2.26-98

1

Exhibit Z-69

FLAG RECOGNITION

united States Flag of Peace, Title 4 U.S. Code Chapter 1. Preserves Constitution

Union = 40% of fly

Fly (width) = 1.9 x Hoist (height)

National flags authorized in 4 USC 1, Sec. 32 are those used by the executive branch of the government. They represent government not individual citizens.

Union hoist = 7/13 (.5385x1)

Hoist (height) = 1

A gold fringe is not authorized on a Title 4 U.S.C. 1 flag! It is a desecration representing no nation's constitution.

National Flag (suspends Constitution)
Army Ceremonial and Parade Flag
AR840-10(b-1) 4'4"x5'6"

Gold Ball
Recruiting

Gold Spire
Court-martial

Gold Eagle
President, U.S.A.

Gold Tassel
Admiral:

National Flag (suspends Constitution)
Army Boat Flag AR840-10(a-6)
3' hoist by 4' fly

National Flag (suspends Constitution
Army Post Flag AR840-10(a-2)
Similar to U.S. Flag but 12'x17'

Official Missouri State Flag

Desecrated Missouri State Flag

OUR FLAG

There is only one united States flag which preserves the rights protected by the u.S. Constitution. A 4-U.S.C.1 (innocent until proven guilty) is the Flag of Peace.

National flags are government flags. They do not preserve the u.S. Constitutional rights (guilty until proven innocent).

When a gold fringe is added to a 4 USC 1 flag (red, white and blue) it desecrates that flag. A red, white, blue and gold flag does not represent the u.S. Constitution.

Exhibit Z-70

Chapter 2
Flag of the United States

2–1. Authorization

a. The flag of the United States is the symbol of our nation. The union, white stars on a field of blue, is the honor point of the flag. The union of the flag, and the flag itself when in company with other flags, is always given the honor position; for example, the marching right, the flag's own right, or an observer's left facing the flag.

b. The flag of the United States must always be of current design as prescribed by chapters 1 and 2, title 4, United States Code (4 USC chaps 1 and 2). The U.S. flag will always be displayed or carried in ceremonies when any other flags are displayed or carried.

2–2. Time and occasions for display

a. The flag of the United States will be displayed outdoors at all Army installations.

b. Only one flag of the United States will be flown at one time at any continental United States (CONUS) Army installation, except as authorized by the commanding generals of major Army commands (MACOM).

c. The flag of the United States is the only flag that may be flown from a flagpole over a CONUS Army installation unless an exception is granted by HQDA, U.S. Army. However, the Minuteman flag (AR 608–15), the Prisoner of War Missing in Action (POW/MIA) flag, or the Commander in Chief's Installation Excellence Award flag, when authorized, may be flown beneath the flag of the United States without referral to HQDA for exception. Not more than one flag will be displayed below the flag of the United States and, if displayed, will be approximately 6 inches below the flag of the United States.

d. The flag of the United States should be displayed with foreign national flags at overseas installations according to applicable international agreements.

e. The flag of the United States will be displayed daily from reveille to retreat.

f. MACOM commanders may authorize permanent or semipermanent (more than one week at a time) 24-hour display of the flag provided the flag is properly illuminated with its own source of light during hours of darkness. HQDA must be informed in each instance that a MACOM commander authorizes permanent 24 hour display.

g. Local or installation commanders *may authorize nighttime displays* of the flag of the United States during special events or on special occasions, provided the flag is properly illuminated.

2–3. Sizes and occasions for display

a. National flags listed below are for outdoor display.

(1) Garrison flag—20 foot hoist by 38 foot fly, of nylon wool (The post flag may be flown in lieu of the garrison flag.) The garrison flag may be flown on the following holidays and special occasions:

(a) New Year's Day, 1 January
(b) Inauguration Day, 20 January every fourth year
(c) Martin Luther King, Jr.'s Birthday, third Monday in January
(d) Lincoln's Birthday, 12 February
(e) Washington's Birthday, 22 February
(f) Easter Sunday (variable)
(g) Thomas Jefferson's Birthday, 13 April
(h) Loyalty Day and Law Day, USA, 1 May
(i) Mother's Day, second Sunday in May
(j) Armed Forces Day, third Saturday in May
(k) National Maritime Day, 22 May
(l) Memorial Day, last Monday in May
(m) Flag Day, 14 June
(n) Father's Day, third Sunday in June
(o) Independence Day, 4 July
(p) National Aviation Day, 19 August
(q) Labor Day, first Monday in September
(r) Constitution Day and Citizenship Day, 17 September
(s) Gold Star Mother's Day, last Sunday in September
(t) Columbus Day, Second Monday in October
(u) Veterans Day ... ember.
(v) Thanksgiving ... th Thursday in November
(w) Christmas Day, 25 December
(x) Important occasions as designated by Presidential Proclamation or Headquarters, Department of the Army (HQDA).
(y) Celebration of a regional nature when directed by the installation commander.

(2) Post flag—8-foot 11⅜ inch hoist by 17 foot fly, of nylon. The post flag is flown daily except when the garrison and storm flags are flown. When a garrison flag is not available, the post flag will be flown on holidays and important occasions.

(3) Field flag—5 foot 8-inch hoist by 12-foot fly, of nylon-wool. The field flag may be displayed from a flag pole only when distinguished visitors are present and only with the positional field flag.

(4) Storm flag—5-foot hoist by 9 foot 6-inch fly, of nylon. The storm flag is flown in inclement weather.

(5) Interment flag—5-foot hoist by 9 foot 6-inch fly, of cotton bunting. The interment flag is authorized for deceased military personnel as provided in AR 638–40 and for deceased veterans. Upon application to the nearest postmaster, the Veterans Administration will provide flags for deceased veterans.

(6) Boat flag—3-foot hoist by 4-foot fly, of nylon wool. The U.S. boat flag is displayed only with positional boat flag colors and general officers flags.

(7) Ensign—2 foot 4⅝-inch hoist by 4-foot 6-inch fly, of nylon. The ensign will be displayed on vessels when required to indicate nationality.

(8) Union jack—The union jack consists of a blue base with white stars similar in all respects to the union of the flag of the United States. The union jack is flown on ships at anchor or tied up at pier. When flown with the flag of the United States, the union jack will be the same size as the union of the national color being flown.

(9) Grave decoration flag—7-inch hoist by 11-inch fly, of cotton muslin (TM 10–267).

(10) Automobile flags—

(a) Twelve inch hoist by 18-inch fly, of nylon, trimmed on three sides with fringe 1½ inches wide. This flag is to be displayed with the individual automobile flag of the President of the United States.

(b) Eighteen-inch hoist by 26-inch fly, of rayon banner cloth or heavyweight nylon, trimmed on three sides with fringe 1½ inches wide. This flag is to be displayed on automobiles of individuals listed in table 1–1.

b. National flags listed below are for indoor display and for use in ceremonies and parades. For these purposes, the flag of the United States will be of rayon banner cloth or heavyweight nylon, trimmed on three sides with golden yellow fringe, 2½ inches wide. It will be the same size or larger than other flags displayed or carried at the same time.

(1) Four-foot 4-inch hoist by 5-foot 6-inch fly. This size flag will be displayed with the U.S. Army flag, positional colors (table 1–1), the Corps of Cadets' color, the 1st Battalion, 3d Infantry color, the 4-foot 4-inch by 5 foot 6-inch chapel flag and the individual flag of a General of the Army.

(2) Three foot hoist by 4-foot fly. This size flag will be displayed with the Army field flag, distinguishing flags, organizational colors, and institutional flags of the same size. It will also be displayed within the offices listed in *c* below when no other positional or organizational flags are authorized. 260-10 ch 8

c. Authorization for indoor display. The flag of the United States is authorized for indoor display for each—

(1) Office, headquarters, and organization authorized a positional color, *distinguishing flag, or organizational color.*

(2) Organization of battalion size or larger (temporary or permanent) not otherwise authorized a flag of the United States.

(3) Military installation not otherwise authorized an indoor flag of the United States, for the purpose of administering oaths of office.

(4) Military cemetery.

(5) U.S. Army element of joint commands, military groups, and missions. One flag is authorized for any one headquarters operating in a dual capacity.

(6) Subordinate element of the U.S. Army Recruiting Command

Exhibit Z-71

(7) ROTC Unit

(8) Each Senior Executive Service (SES) employee for permanent retention.

2-4. Position and manner of display

a. Ceremonies and parades.

(1) The flag of the United States will be carried on all ceremonial occasions when two or more companies or an appropriate honor guard participates. It is always displayed in the position of honor.

(2) When the flag of the United States is carried in a procession with other flags, the place of the flag of the United States is on the marching right; or, if there is a line of other flags, in front of the center of that line. (See fig 2-1.)

(3) The flag should never be carried flat or horizontally but always aloft and free.

(4) When the flag of the United States is displayed from a vehicle, the staff of the flag will be clamped firmly to the right front fender.

b. With foreign national flags. When the flag of the United States is displayed with foreign national flags, all flags will be comparable in size. The flagstaffs or flagpoles on which they are flown will be of equal height. The tops of all flags should be of equal distance from the ground.

c. From staffs.

(1) When a number of flags are grouped and displayed from staffs radiating from a central point, and no foreign flags are involved, the flag of the United States will be in the center and at the highest point of the group. (See fig 2-2 for sequence.)

(2) When a number of flags are displayed from staffs set in a line, the flag of the United States will be at the right, that is, to the left of an observer facing the display (fig. 2-1). However, if no foreign national flags are involved, the flag of the United States may be placed at the center of the line providing it is displayed at a higher level. (See fig 2-3.)

d. With State flags. When the flag of the United States is displayed with State flags, all flags will be of comparable size. They will be displayed from separate flagstaffs of equal height set on the same level.

e. Against a wall.

(1) The flag of the United States, when it is displayed with another flag against a wall from crossed staffs, should be on the right, the flag's own right, and its staff should be in front of the staff of the other flag. (See fig 2-4.)

(2) When the flag of the United States in displayed either horizontally or vertically against a wall, the union will be uppermost and to the flag's own right, that is, to the observer's left facing the display. (See fig 2-5.)

(3) When displayed on the wall of a stage, it will be placed above and behind the speaker's stand. (See fig 2-6.)

f. In an auditorium, meeting hall, or chapel. When the U.S. flag is displayed from a staff in an auditorium, meeting hall, or chapel, whether on the same floor level or on a platform, it should be in the position of honor at the speaker's or chaplain's right facing the audience or congregation in accordance with section 173, title 36, United States Code (36 USC 173), et seq., as amended 7 July 1976. Other flags should be placed on the left of the speaker or chaplain, that is, to the right of the audience. (See figs 2-6 and 2-7.)

g. Halfstaff.

(1) For occasions and durations of halfstaff display of the flag of the United States, see AR 600-25.

(2) When the flag of the United States is displayed at halfstaff, it is first hoisted to the top of the staff for an instant, then lowered to the halfstaff position. The flag should again be raised to the top of the staff before it is lowered for the day.

(3) The flag is in a halfstaff position when it is in any position below the top of the pole. Generally the position of the flag is at halfstaff when the middle point of the hoist of the flag is halfway between the top of the staff and the foot. In the case of a flagpole with crosstree or guy cable, the flag should be halfway between the top of the pole and the top of the crosstree or point of attachment of the guy cables. (See fig 2-8.)

(4) In accordance with the provisions of section 178, title 36, United States Code (36 USC 178), when the President directs that the flag be flow[illegible] staff at military facilities, naval vessels, and stations abroad, it will be so flown whether or not the flag of another nation is full staff alongside the U.S. flag.

h. Placed in mourning. Flags carried by troops will not be placed in mourning unless ordered by the President or the Secretary of the Army. When so ordered, a streamer of black crepe 7 feet long and 1 foot wide will be attached to the staff at the center of the streamer immediately below the spearhead of the U.S. flag and the organizational flag. (See fig 2-9.)

i. Lowering and folding.

(1) While the flag of the United States is being lowered from the staff and folded, no portion of it should be allowed to touch the ground. The flag should be folded in the triangular shape of a cocked hat. (See fig 2-10).

(2) For the ceremonies of hoisting and lowering, see FM 22-5.

j. At military funerals.

(1) The interment flag covers the casket at the military funeral of any of the following:

(*a*) Members of the active military force.

(*b*) Members of the Army National Guard (ARNG).

(*c*) Members of the USAR.

(*d*) Honorably discharged veterans.

(*e*) Retired military personnel.

(2) On a closed casket, the flag will be placed lengthwise, with the union at the head and over the left shoulder of the deceased. When a full-couch casket is opened, the flag will be removed, folded to the triangular shape of a cocked hat and placed in the lid at the head end of the casket and just above the decedent's left shoulder. When a half-couch casket is opened, the flag will be folded on the lower half of the casket in the same relative position as when displayed full length on a closed casket. The flag will not be lowered into the grave, and it will not be allowed to touch the ground. The interment flag may be given to the nearest of kin at the conclusion of the interment. (See figs 2-11 and 2-12.)

2-5. Order of precedence of flags

The following is the order of precedence of flags:

a. The flag of the United States.

b. Foreign national flags. (Normally, these are displayed in alphabetical order using the English alphabet.)

c. Flag of the President of the United States of America.

d. State flags. Normally, these are displayed in order of admittance of the State to the Union. However, they may be displayed in alphabetical order.

e. Military organizational flags of the Services in order of precedence (AR 600-25).

f. Military organizational flags within a Service by echelon. The flag for the regimental corps will have precedence immediately before the regimental proponent command flag. The regimental corps flag will never have precedence above a MACOM flag.

g. Individual flags in order of rank.

2-6. Prohibitions

The following rules will be observed:

a. No lettering or object of any kind will be placed on the flag of the United States.

b. No other flag or pennant will be placed above the flag of the United States or, if on the same level, to the right of the flag.

c. The flag of the United States, when flown at a military post or when carried by troops, will not be dipped by way of salute or compliment (AR 600-25).

d. The flag of the United States will always be displayed flat or hanging free. It will not be festooned over doorways or arches, tied in a bow knot, or fashioned into a rosette.

e. The flag will not be used to cover a speaker's stand or to drape the front of a platform. Bunting of the national colors, arranged with the blue above, white in the middle, and red below, should be used for this purpose and for general decoration.

2-7. Use and display by civilians

Use and display of the U.S. flag by civilians, civilian groups, and organizations are governed by 36 USC 173, et seq. Civilians who inquire about the display of the U.S. flag should be referred to this

AR 840-10 • UPDATE 11

Exhibit Z-72

Bill of Rights

Congress of the United States,

begun and held at the City of New York, on Wednesday, the fourth of March, one thousand seven hundred and eighty nine

THE Conventions of a number of the States having, at the time of their adopting the Constitution, expressed a desire, in order to prevent misconstruction or abuse of its powers, that further declaratory and restrictive clauses should be added: And as extending the ground of public confidence in the Government, will best ensure the beneficent ends of its institution

RESOLVED, by the SENATE and HOUSE of REPRESENTATIVES of the UNITED STATES of AMERICA in Congress assembled, two thirds of both Houses concurring. That the following Articles be proposed to the Legislatures of the several States, as Amendments to the Constitution of the United States; all, or any of which articles, when ratified by three fourths of the said Legislatures, to be valid to all intents and purposes, as part of the said Constitution, viz

ARTICLES in addition to, and Amendment of the Constitution of the United States of America, proposed by Congress, and ratified by the Legislatures of the several States, pursuant to the fifth Article of the Original Constitution.

Article the first . . . . After the first enumeration required by the first Article of the Constitution, there shall be one Representative for every thirty thousand, until the number shall amount to one hundred, after which, the proportion shall be so regulated by Congress, that there shall be not less than one hundred Representatives, nor less than one Representative for every forth thousand persons, until the number of Representatives shall amount to two hundred, after which, the proportion shall be so regulated by Congress, that there shall not be less than two hundred Representatives, nor more than one Representative for every fifty thousand persons. [Not Ratified]

Article the second . . . No law, varying the compensation for the services of the Senators and Representatives, shall take effect, until an election of Representatives shall have intervened. [Not Ratified]

Article the third . . . . Congress shall make no law respecting an establishment of religion, or prohibiting the free exercise thereof, or abridging the freedom of speech or of the press; or the right of the people peaceably to assemble, and to petition the Government for a redress of grievances

Article the fourth . . . . A well regulated Militia, being necessary to the security of a free State, the right of the people to keep and bear Arms, shall not be infringed.

Article the fifth . . . . No Soldier shall, in time of peace, be quartered in any house, without the consent of the owner, nor in time of war, but in a manner to be prescribed by law

Article the sixth . . . . The right of the people to be secure in their persons, houses, papers, and effects, against unreasonable searches and seizures, shall not be violated, and no Warrants shall issue but upon probable cause, supported by oath or affirmation, and particularly describing the place to be searched, and the persons or things to be seized.

Article the seventh . . . No person shall be held to answer for a capital, or otherwise infamous crime, unless on a presentment or indictment of a grand jury, except in cases arising in the land or Naval forces, or in the Militia, when in actual service in time of War or public danger; nor shall any person be subject for the same offence to be twice put in jeopardy of life or limb; nor shall be compelled in any criminal case, to be a witness against himself, nor be deprived of life, liberty, or property, without due process of law; nor shall private property be taken for public use without just compensation

Article the eighth . . . In all criminal prosecutions, the accused shall enjoy the right to a speedy and public trial by an impartial jury of the State and district wherein the crime shall have been committed, which district shall have been previously ascertained by law, and to be informed of the nature and cause of the accusation; to be confronted with the witnesses against him; to have compulsory process for obtaining witnesses in his favor, and to have the assistance of counsel for his defence

Article the ninth . . . . In suits at common law, where the value in controversy shall exceed twenty dollars, the right of trial by jury shall be preserved, and no fact, tried by a jury, shall be otherwise re-examined in any Court of the United States, than according to the rules of the common law.

Article the tenth . . . . Excessive bail shall not be required, nor excessive fines imposed, nor cruel and unusual punishments inflicted

Article the eleventh . . . The enumeration in the Constitution, of certain rights, shall not be construed to deny or disparage others retained by the people.

Article the twelfth . . . The powers not delegated to the United States by the Constitution, nor prohibited by it to the States, are reserved to the States respectively, or to the people.

Frederick Augustus Muhlenberg, Speaker of the House of Representatives

John Adams, Vice President of the United States, and President of the Senate.

ATTEST,

John Beckley, Clerk of the House of Representatives

Sam. A. Otis Secretary of the Senate

Exhibit Z-73

2-25-98: COPYRIGHT: David-Wynn: Miller: L.A.W. PROCEDURES

FACTS AND FINDINGS OF LAW AND DEFINITIONS

NOTICE: COVER PAGE FOR THE COURT, UNDER TITLE: 4: U.S.A. THE CODES: SECTION: 1&2.

NOTICE: DISCLAIMER OF RESPONSIBILITY: UNDER U.C.C. 3-501: UNDER TITLE: 42: U.S.A. THE CODES: SECTION: 1986, FOR KNOWLEDGE OF THE LAW FOR F.R.C.P. RULE: 60(b): DISCOVERY OF FRAUD AND F.R.C.P. RULE: 38(a) RIGHT OF TRIAL BY JURY, THE CASE TITLED ABOVE IS UNDER THE TITLE: 4: U.S.A. THE CODES: SECTION: 1&2: FLAG OF THE U.S.A.: REFERENCED UNDER PRESIDENTIAL-EXECUTIVE: ORDER: 10834, AND UNDER C.U.S.A. ARTICLE THE SIX(6): SECTION THE THREE(3): OATH OF FIDUCIARY OFFICERS OF THE COURT, AND UNDER C.U.S.A. ARTICLE THE FOUR: SECTION THE THREE: NO NEW STATE SHALL BE ERECTED WITHIN ANY STATE; NO STATE OF JURISDICTION AS FOREIGN HAS JURISDICTION OVER A SOVEREIGN: CITIZEN IN PARTY, AND C.U.S.A. ARTICLE THE ONE(1): SECTION THE NINE(9): NO TITLES OF NOBILITY UNDER JURISDICTION OF: FOREIGN THE FLAG WITH FRINGE FOR THE BREACH OF THE TREATY OF TITLE: 28: U.S.A. THE CODES: SECTION: 1605: FOREIGN: SOVEREIGN-IMMUNITY: ACT, OF OCTOBER THE 21 OF 1976, AND IN BREACH OF THE C.U.S.A., WILL BE ALLOWED IN THE JURISDICTION OF THE CASE. BREACH OF THE CONTRACT WILL CAUSE SANCTIONS UNDER F.R.C.P. RULE: 16(f). WHEN THE C.U.S.A. IS SURRENDERED INTO THE FOREIGN THE JURISDICTION OF STATE, WILL CAUSE THE BREACH OF OATH OR AFFIRMATION CONTRACT UNDER THE C.U.S.A. AND CHARGES FOR PERJURY OF OATH UNDER TITLE: 18: U.S.A. THE CODES: SECTION: 1621, CONSTRUCTIVE TREASON AGAINST THE C.U.S.A., AND CONTEMPT FOR THE C.U.S.A. AND FALSE SWEARING OF OATH WILL BE BROUGHT AGAINST THE OFFICERS OF THE COURT RESPONSIBLE. UNDER FEDERAL AUTHORITY TITLE: 42: U.S.A. THE CODES: SECTION: 1986 FOR REPORTING NEGLECT OF DUTY.

PLAINTIFF: CITIZEN IN PARTY, AFFIRMS BY TELLING THE TRUTH AND HAS FIRSTHAND KNOWLEDGE OF THE FACTS ______________________.

ABBREVIATIONS: herein

F.R.C.P.	=	**FEDERAL: RULES of CIVIL-PROCEDURE**
U.S.A. THE CODES:	=	**UNITED: STATES of AMERICA THE CODES:**
U.C.C.	=	**UNIFORM-COMMERCIAL-CODES**
U.S.A.	=	**UNITED: STATES OF AMERICA**

C.U.S.A. = **CONSTITUTION OF THE UNITED: STATES of AMERICA: ARTICLE THE # OF SEPTEMBER THE 17 OF 1789.**

ARTICLE THE 3 = RIGHT OF SPEECH, RELIGION, PRESS, GRIEVANCE;
ARTICLE THE 6 = RIGHT OF ARREST-WARRANT OR SEARCH-WARRANT SIGNED BY JUDGE OF OATH
ARTICLE THE 7 = RIGHT OF DUE-PROCESS, NO WITNESS AGAINST ONE-SELF
ARTICLE THE 8 = RIGHT OF WITNESSES, COUNSEL AND EVIDENCE IN COURT, SPEEDY TRIAL
ARTICLE THE 9 = RIGHT OF TRIAL BY JURY
ARTICLE THE 10 = NO CRUEL AND UNUSUAL PUNISHMENT, REASONABLE BAIL
ARTICLE THE 11 = OFFICERS BY THE PEOPLE APPOINTED OR ELECTED UNDER OATH OR AFFIRMATION FOR UPHOLDING THE CONSTITUTION OF THE U.S.A.: SEPTEMBER: 17: 1789.
ARTICLE THE 12 = POWERS FOR THE PEOPLE OR FOR THE SEVERAL STATES OF AMERICA
ARTICLE THE ONE(1): SECTION THE NINE(9) = NO TITLES OF NOBILITY, NO FOREIGN: POWERS, NO FOREIGN OF JURISDICTIONS OVER THE SOVEREIGN: CITIZEN IN PARTY, (NO JOINDER: NO JURISDICTION) RIGHTS = UNDER THE C.U.S.A. 9-17-1789

THE COURT OF THE DISTRICT OF THE U.S.A., HAS ORIGINAL JURISDICTION UNDER TITLE: 28: U.S.A. THE CODES: 1331 AND SECTION: 1343 UNDER THE TITLE: 4: U.S.A. THE CODES: SECTION: 1&2: FLAG OF THE U.S.A. UNDER THE WRIT OF ERROR, TITLE: 28: U.S.A. THE CODES: PAGE ONE(1) OF THE CASE TITLED ABOVE UNDER F.R.C.P. RULE: 38(a) FOR THE RIGHT OF TRIAL BY JURY AND THE C.U.S.A.: ARTICLE THE NINE(9): RIGHT FOR TRIAL BY JURY. THE CLERK OF COURT SHALL FILE UNDER THE COURT OF THE DISTRICT OF THE U.S.A. UNDER TITLE: 28: U.S.A. THE CODES: SECTION: 1869, AND ORDER PROCEDURES OF TITLE: 28: U.S.A. THE CODES: SECTION: 1361: COMPLIANCE OF RESPONSIBILITY FOR DUTY OF OFFICE. **THE COURT IS UNDER THE FOREIGN SOVEREIGN: IMMUNITY ACT: DATED: OCTOBER THE 21 OF 1976 IN TITLE: 28: U.S.A. THE CODES: SECTION: 1605.**

CONSTITUTION FOR THE UNITED: STATES OF AMERICA:

SEPTEMBER: 17, 1789

1). **ARTICLE THE 3**: FREEDOM OF SPEECH AND PRESS, AND RIGHT BY PETITIONING THE GOVERNMENT FOR A REDRESS OF GRIEVANCES, AND FREEDOM OF RELIGION.

2). **ARTICLE THE 6**: UNREASONABLE SEARCHES AND SEIZURES SHALL NOT BE VIOLATED, AND NO WARRANTS SHALL ISSUE, BUT UPON PROBABLE CAUSE AND SUPPORTED BY OATH OR AFFIRMATION, AND PARTICULARLY DESCRIBING THE PLACE BY BEING SEARCHED AND THE PARTY OR THINGS BY BEING SEIZED.

Copyright · DM · 2·25·98

Exhibit Z-74

3). **ARTICLE THE 7:** NO PARTY BY BEING COMPELLED IN ANY CRIMINAL CASE BY BEING WITNESS AGAINST PARTY SELF, NOR BE DEPRIVED OF LIFE, LIBERTY, OR PROPERTY, BY NEGLECTING DUE-PROCESS OF LAW. NOTES: C.U.S.A. THE SEVEN(7).

4). **ARTICLE THE 8:** RIGHT OF A SPEEDY AND PUBLIC TRIAL, BY AN JURY OF IMPARTIAL, IN THE VENUE OF THE DISTRICT OF THE U.S.A. WHEREIN THE ACTION IS COMMITTED, AND INFORMED OF THE NATURE AND CAUSE OF THE ACCUSATION; BY BEING CONFRONTED BY THE WITNESS IN PARTY, AND BY HAVING COMPULSORY PROCESS FOR OBTAINING WITNESS IN PARTY'S FAVOR, AND BY HAVING THE ASSISTANCE OF COUNSEL FOR PARTY'S DEFENSE.
NOTES: VIOLATION OF DUE-PROCESS (COUNSEL)= OBSTRUCTION OF JUSTICE = (TITLE: 18: CHAPTER: 63: U.S.A. THE CODES: SECTION: 1512) THE PERJURY OF OATH = (TITLE: 18: CHAPTER: 63: U.S.A. THE CODES: SECTION: 1621) AN DEPRIVATION OF RIGHTS UNDER COLOR OF LAW = (TITLE: 18: U.S.A. THE CODES: SECTION: 242). NOTE: COLOR OF LAW = CORRUPTION OF THE FLAG OF THE U.S.A..

5). **ARTICLE THE 9:** IN SUITS OF COMMON-LAW, WHERE THE VALUE IN CONTROVERSY IS EXCEEDING TWENTY DOLLARS, THE RIGHT OF TRIAL BY JURY, IS PRESERVED, AND NO FACT IS TRIED BY JURY. (PARTY MUST GIVE YOUR NAME WITH PUNCTUATION (-:) PERSONALLY WHILE IN THE BAR AND DISPLAYING THE (TITLE: 4: U.S.A. THE CODES: SECTION: 1&2) FLAG OF THE U.S.A. UNDER THE LAW OF THE FLAG AND HAVE IN PARTY'S POSSESSION ARMY-REGULATIONS: 840-10: CHAPTER: 2-1(a,b) AN CHAPTER: 2-5(a,b,c) FOR CAUSING A COMMON-LAW COURT).

6). **ARTICLE THE 10:** NO CRUEL AND UNUSUAL PUNISHMENTS INFLICTED.

7). **ARTICLE THE 11: THE ENUMERATION IN THE C.U.S.A. OF CERTAIN RIGHTS ARE NOT CONSTRUED BY DENYING OR DISPARAGING CITIZENS AS OFFICERS OF GOVERNMENT RETAINED BY THE PEOPLE.**

8). **ARTICLE THE 12: POWER ARE RESERVED IN THE C.U.S.A. ARE RESERVED FOR THE STATES, OR FOR THE PEOPLE.**

9). **ARTICLE THE ONE(1) SECTION THE NINE(9): (DATE: 1789) NO TITLES OF NOBILITY SHALL HOLD OFFICE, NO FOREIGN POWER SHALL HAVE JURISDICTION OVER A SOVEREIGN AS CITIZEN IN PARTY AND THE JUDICIAL OF THE FOREIGN HAS NO JURISDICTION OVER THE SOVEREIGN AS CITIZEN IN PARTY.**

10). **AMENDMENT 14:** (JULY: 1868) NO STATE (CITIZEN IN PARTY) **SHALL MAKE** OR ENFORCE ANY LAW WHICH SHALL ABRIDGE THE PRIVILEGES OR IMMUNITIES OF CITIZENS OF THE U.S.A., NOR IS ANY STATE(CITIZEN IN PARTY) DEPRIVE ANY PARTY OF LIFE, LIBERTY, OR PROPERTY, BY NEGLECTING DUE PROCESS OF THE LAW; NOR BY ANY PARTY, THE EQUAL PROTECTION OF THE LAW. TITLE: 42: U.S.A. THE CODES: SECTION: 1985(2)(3). NOTE: **AMENDMENT** IS AN **ADJECTIVE OF FOURTEEN** AND MAKES THE AMENDMENT STATEMENT A FICTION OF NO AUTHORITY. **MUST USE THE CIVIL-RIGHTS: ACT OF 1964 FOR EQUAL PROTECTION.**

11). NOTE: THE WORD CHARGED MUST BE USED FOR MAKING OR CAUSING A CRIMINAL: CASE.
NOTE: MIRANDA; RIGHTS MUST BE READ IN THE BAR AT THE POINT IN TIME OF ENTERING
GIVE YOUR NAME WITH PUNCTUATION WHILE IN THE BAR AFTER IDENTIFYING THE TITLE: 4: U.S.A. THE CODES: SECTION: 1&2: FLAG OF THE U.S.A., UNDER ARMY-REGULATION: 840-10, CHAPTER: 2-1(a,b) AND 2-5(a,b,c). TWO(2) PARTIES MUST I.D., IN ANY ACTION FOR A DISMISSAL MOTION BY THE COURT, USE = UNDER U.C.C. 3-501 THERE IS NO CONTRACT BY DISMISSING THE INCORPORATED CASES PLEADINGS BEFORE THE COURT; THE PLAINTIFF PAID THE CLERK OF COURTS FOR A TRIAL BY JURY UNDER F.R.C.P. 38(a). WHEN IN THE FACE OF A CONTEMPT CHARGE WHICH IS COERCED UNDER TITLE: 28: CHAPTER: 85: SECTION: 1359 OR BY THREAT OF JAIL, (JAIL, IS CRIMINAL). THE JUDGE'S USE OF THE TERM CHARGE MAKES CASE A CRIMINAL PROCEDURE AND UNDER C.U.S.A. LAW VIOLATES DUE-PROCESS BEFORE THE FACTS OF THE CASE ARE PROVEN, WITH THE INTENT OF GUILTY TILL PROVEN INNOCENT, IN PLACE OF, INNOCENT TILL PROVEN GUILTY.

13). **F.R.C.P. RULE: 4: PROCESS**(a).SUMMONS, (b).FORM, (c).SERVICE (HOW PRESENTED FOR RESPONDENTS), (d).SUMMONS AND COMPLAINT, (NOTE: 20 DAY RETURN ANSWER FOR PLAINTIFF AND COURT) (g).RETURN PROOF OF SERVICE ON THE CLERK OF COURT, (h) AMENDMENT BY SERVICE, (j).TIME LIMIT OF 120 DAYS FOR RETURN SERVICE.

14). **F.R.C.P. RULE: 5 = SERVICE:** (a).REQUIRED, (d).FILING CERTIFICATE (e). FILING WITH CLERK (CLERK, CAN NOT REFUSE OF ACCEPTING FOR FILLING ANY PAPERS NOT IN FORM OF LOCAL RULES.) TITLE: 28: U.S.A. THE CODES: SECTION: 646.

15). **F.R.C.P. RULE: 6:= TIME:** (a). COMPUTATION- (MONDAY TO FRIDAY). (d). MOTIONS AND AFFIDAVITS MUST BE SERVED FIVE(5): DAYS BEFORE TRIAL BY PLAINTIFF; AND ONE(1): DAY SERVICE BEFORE TRIAL FOR DEFENDANT.

2

Exhibit Z-75

16).F.R.C.P. RULE: 7: = **PLEADINGS**: (a). PLEADINGS, (b). MOTIONS, BY BEING MADE WITH PARTICULARITY AND THE RELIEF AND ORDER SOUGHT. NOTE: THE NOTICE OF REFUSAL FOR FRAUD IS FOR THE OPPOSING MOTION OF FRAUD SO NO TRAVERSE IS ACTIONED FOLLOWED BY A MOTION FOR REAFFIRMING THE COMPLAINT OF ORIGINAL-PLEADINGS. STAY ON POINT WITH ORIGINAL: TOPIC.

17). F.R.C.P. RULE: 8: = **RULES OF PLEADING**:(a).CLAIM FOR RELIEF, ASK FOR COMPENSATION (FEES, MONEY, PROPERTY) MUST CONTAIN (b) DEFENSE FORM OF DENIALS, (c). AFFIRMATIVE DEFENSE, (d). FAILURE BY DENYING, (e).PLEADING CONCISE.

18). F.R.C.P. RULE: 9: = **PLEADINGS SPECIAL** ; (b)FRAUD, OR CONDITION OF THE MIND (e)JUDGEMENT, (f) TIME AND PLACE, (g) SPECIAL DAMAGE.

19). F.R.C.P. RULE: 10: = **FORM OF PLEADINGS**: (a)CAPTIONS, (b) PARAGRAPHS

20). F.R.C.P. RULE: 11: = **FRIVOLOUS FILING**, ALL PLEADING MUST BE SIGNED AND ADDRESSED. THE SIGNING OF A TICKET IS NOT LAW FOR FIVE DAYS OF THE VIOLATION FOR SANCTIONS AND FEES. VOID IF COLLUSION IS USED (TITLE: 28: CHAPTER: 85: U.S.A. THE CODES: SECTION: 1359) **MUST BE REFUSED FOR VIOLATIONS OF THE LAWS OF CONTRACT UNDER U.C.C. 3-501 DISCLAIMER.**

21. F.R.C.P. RULE: 12(b)**HOW PRESENTED: 12(b)7)-FAILURE BY JOINING [MUST BE OF THE SAME JURISDICTION OF FLAG UNDER LAW OF THE FLAG] JOINDER IS COMPLETE EVEN WHEN THE FICTION IS COMPLETE BY JOINING IN THE BAR, SO STUDY THE DWM LAW: PROCEDURES. NO DOUBLE NOUNS ALLOWED.**
12(b)(6): FAILS BY STATING A CLAIM, [MUST JOIN JURISDICTIONS BEFORE STATING INJURY] THE FICTION JURISDICTION IF JOINED BY THE COURT, PLAINTIFF AND RESPONDENT CANNOT STATE A FICTION: CLAIM AND HAVE JOINDER.
12(b)(5): IMPROPER PROCESS: [BY NOT PROCESSING THE PAPERWORK WITH THE CLERK OF COURT] NO PROCESS IN FICTION: USE OF ADJECTIVES WILL CAUSE MAIL-FRAUD: TITLE: 18: 1342.
12(b)(4): IMPROPER SERVICE, [BY NOT SERVING THE PAPERWORK ON THE RESPONDENT BY LAW] NO SERVICE IN FICTION: USE OF ADJECTIVES: CAUSING MAIL-FRAUD TITLE 18: 1342.
12(b)(3): IMPROPER VENUE, [THE JUDGE FOR NOT JOINING THE JURISDICTION OF THE FLAG OF THE U.S.A. AND PRESCRIBED BY LAW WHERE THE ACT TOOK PLACE AND THE JURISDICTION FOR BEING ENFORCED, LAW OF THE FLAG] FICTION OF ADJECTIVES WATCH FOR TRAPS IN TITLES, NAMES, DATES, CASE NUMBERS.
12(b)(2)- LACK OF PERSONAL JURISDICTION OVER PARTY, [BY THE WRONG LAW OF THE FLAG JURISDICTION, WHEN THE COURT DOES NOT JOIN, COURT CAN NOT STATE A CLAIM OR NATURE OF INJURY]
12(b)1)-LACK OF JURISDICTION OVER SUBJECT MATTER. THE JUDGE NOT READING THE CASE BEFORE THE COURT, AND ACTING ON OPINION AND NOT ON THE FACTS OF THE CASE..
DIFFERENT CAUSES OF REMEDY: (A). MOTION JUDGEMENT ON THE PLEADINGS, (B). MOTION FOR STRIKING, (C). WAVER (SUBJECT MATTER) NO JURISDICTION.

22). F.R.C.P. RULE: 15: = AMENDED AND SUPPLEMENTAL PLEADINGS (a.b.c.d.) READ IN F.R.C.P.

23). F.R.C.P. RULE: 16(f): = **SANCTIONS**: WHEN THE JUDGE OR OFFICERS OF THE COURT WILL NOT JOIN WITH THE FLAG OF THE U.S.A., (TITLE: 4: U.S.A. THE CODES: SECTION: 1&2:) VIOLATION OF OATH OF OFFICE, SANCTION FOR BREACH OF CONTRACT UNDER THE OATH OR AFFIRMATION: AND FILING FEES PAID FOR TRIAL BY JURY AND RECUSAL OR DISMISSAL ORDERS. COURT CAN'T ORDER FEES (TITLE: 42: U.S.A. THE CODES: SECTION: 1988) FOR BREACH OF THE C.U.S.A. ARTICLE THE NINE(9): TRIAL BY JURY AND ARTICLE THE SEVEN(7): DUE-PROCESS OF LAW. SANCTION THE JUDGE FOR NOT COMING INTO A DISCOVERY HEARING AND NOT JOINING UNDER OATH AND AFFIRMATION OF THE C.U.S.A..

24). F.R.C.P. RULE: 18-19 = JOINDER ALSO F.R.C.P. RULE: 12(b)(7)
25). F.R.C.P. RULE: 24 = **TITLE: 28**: U.S.A. THE CODES: 2403-CHALLENGING CONSTITUTIONALITY

26). F.R.C.P. RULE: 38(a)= **TRIAL BY JURY**

27). F.R.C.P. RULE: 41(a)= **DISMISSAL OF ACTION: VOLUNTARY. USE FOR WITHDRAWING A CASE PLAINTIFF KNOWS IS WRITTEN INCORRECT.**
28). F.R.C.P. RULE: 49 = **ISSUES SENT FOR JURY BY DEMAND**

29). F.R.C.P. RULE: 50 = **NEW TRIAL: USE WITH DE NOVO OR WRIT OF HABIUS CORPUS**

30). F.R.C.P. RULE: 54 = **DEMAND FOR JUDGEMENT. [GET MONEY]**

31). F.R.C.P. RULE: 55 = **DEFAULT- [GET MONEY]**

32). F.R.C.P. RULE: 56 = -C-**SUMMARY-JUDGEMENT.. GET MONEY. (VERY IMPORTANT)**

3 Copyright: DM. 2-25-98

Exhibit Z-76

33). **F.R.C.P. RULE: 57 = DECLARATORY JUDGEMENT**

34). **POLICY AND CUSTOM;** ACTS IN DAY, ___,1998, DESCRIBED ACTIONS AND OMISSIONS ENGAGED UNDER COLOR OF STATE LAW AUTHORITY, SUED AS A PARTY, RESPONSIBLE BY AUTHORIZING AND RATIFYING THE ACTS OF STATE'S AGENTS; PLAINTIFF IS INJURED BY NEGLECT OF C.U.S.A. RIGHTS, SECURED FOR THE PARTY UNDER THE C.U.S.A. ARTICLE THE (6): WARRANT IS ISSUED ONLY BY A JUDGE OF OATH AND AFFIRMATION; C.U.S.A. ARTICLE THE NINE(9): RIGHT BY TRIAL BY JURY, UNDER F.R.C.P. RULE: 38(a) AND UNDER DUE-PROCESS OF THE LAW UNDER C.U.S.A. ARTICLE THE SEVEN(7), BY THE RESPONDENT(S): X_____.

35). **OPINION OF DAVID MILLER: THE** ACTORS, USED VALUABLE COURT TIME BY CREATING AN ELABORATE FRAUD, AND FAILURE OF JUSTICE BY THE COURT, F.R.C.P. RULE: 12(b)(2). F.R.C.P. RULE: 9(b) FOR FRAUD; C.U.S.A. ARTICLE THE 7: DUE-PROCESS, F.R.C.P. RULE: 38(e)TRIAL, AND TITLE 18 U.S.A. THE CODES: SECTION: 1342: FICTIOUS(ADJECTIVE) USE OF NAME(NOUN) = **ADJECTIVES USED AS NOUNS.**

36). **EXAMPLE OF SENTENCE PLEADINGS: WITH NO SUBJECT MATTER JURISDICTION** F.R.C.P. RULE: 12(b)(1), AND F.R.C.P. RULE: 9(b)FRAUD, OVER THE PLAINTIFF, USED COERCION AND EXTORTION, BY THREATENING PLAINTIFF. TITLE: 42: U.S.A. THE CODES: SECTION: 1983 NOTE 352: IN ORDER BY SUSTAINING A 1983 CONSPIRACY CLAIM, THERE MUST BE EVIDENCE OF CONCERTED EFFORT OR PLANING BETWEEN PRIVATE ASSOCIATIONS AND STATE ACTORS (**JUDGE IS NOT OF OATH AND AFFIRMATION, MAKING JUDGE AN ACTOR BY NEGLECTING SUBJECT MATTER JURISDICTION**), BY DENYING PLAINTIFF OF C.U.S.A. RIGHTS: TITLE: 42: U.S.A. THE CODES: SECTION: 1983 AT NOTE: 355 ALL PARAGRAPHS.

37). **(TITLE: 18: U.S.A. THE CODES: SECTION: 242)= DEPRIVATION OF RIGHTS UNDER COLOR OF LAW:** WHOEVER, UNDER COLOR OF LAW STATUTE, ORDNANCE, REGULATION, OR CUSTOM, WILLFUL SUBJECTS ANY INHABITANT OF ANY STATE, TERRITORY, OR DISTRICT OF THE DEPRIVATION OF ANY RIGHTS, PRIVILEGES, OR IMMUNITIES SECURED OR PROTECTED BY THE CONSTITUTION OR LAWS OF THE U.S.A. BY BEING FINED NOT MORE THAN $1000. OR IMPRISONED NOT MORE THAN ONE YEAR, OR BOTH. THE ONLY CONTRACT THAT IS PRESENT, IS THE CONTRACT BETWEEN THE COURT AND THE ATTORNEY VIOLATES C.U.S.A. ARTICLE THE 6: SECTION THE 3: OATH; TITLE: 28: U.S.A. THE CODES: SECTION: 1343: EQUAL PROTECTION AND C.U.S.A. ARTICLE THE NINE(9): DUE-PROCESS.

38). **TITLE: 42: U.S.A. THE CODES: SECTION: 1983: AT NOTE:** 355. PLAINTIFF IS INJURED IN THE ABOVE ACTION OF THE WRONGS INCORPORATED IN THE CASE-CITES WHEN BY SIGNATURE AND BY DEPRIVING THE PLAINTIFF OF PLAINTIFF'S C.U.S.A. RIGHTS, BY NOT HAVING THE C.U.S.A. ARTICLE THE SIX(6): WARRANT; THE WARRANT MUST BE SIGNED BY A JUDGE OF OATH AN AFFIRMATION; TRIAL BY JURY, UNDER THE C.U.S.A.: ARTICLE THE SEVEN(7): DUE PROCESS AND TITLE: 42: U.S.A. THE CODES: 1985(2):EQUAL PROTECTION OF THE LAW: F.R.C.P. RULES: 12 b (7, 1, 2), BY THE RESPONDENTS.

39).**TITLE: 18: U.S.A. THE CODES: SECTION: SECTION: 1621 : STATE PAYS ALL FEES** WHEN PLAINTIFF IS INJURED BY LACK OF OATH OF AFFIRMATION OF OFFICE AND PERJURY OF OATH BY THE RESPONDENT JUDGE AND OFFICERS OF THE COURT: CITIZENS CAN NOT BE MADE BY PAYING FEES, BY HAVING CITIZEN IN PARTY'S; C.U.S.A. RIGHTS VIOLATED. CROSS REF.= F.R.C.P. 9(b). TITLE: 20: U.S.A. THE CODES: SECTION: 2072(b); C.U.S.A. ARTICLE THE 6: SECTION THE 3: (DATE: 1791):FOREIGN STATES.

40). EXAMPLE PLEADINGS. PLAINTIFF AFFIRMS INJURY WHEN THE FINDINGS OF FACT INCORPORATED INTO THE COMPLAINT WITH THE COURT FOR REPORTING BREACH OF FIDUCIARY RESPONSIBILITIES AS REQUIRED UNDER TITLE: 42: U.S.A. THE CODES: SECTION: 1986 FOR NEGLECT OF LAW AND C.U.S.A. LAWS NOT BEING UPHELD FOR THE CITIZEN IN PARTY AND DENY PLEADINGS BY THE COURT RESPONDENTS...CAUSING F.R.C.P. RULE: 9(b), RULE: 12(b), RULE: 56(d), AND C.U.S.A. ARTICLE THE SEVEN(7): DUE-PROCESS; EQUAL-PROTECTION: TITLE: 42: U.S.A.: THE CODES: SECTION: 1985(2): DEPRIVING JUSTICE. (TITLE: 18: U.S.A. THE CODES: SECTION: 1621) PERJURY OF OATH OF OFFICE, IF COERCION IS USED, VIOLATION OF TITLE: 18: U.S.A. THE CODES: SECTION: 1359 WILL GIVE CAUSE OF ACTION UNDER TITLE: 18: U.S.A. THE CODES: SECTION: 4, MISPRISON OF A FELON.

CONCLUSION: EXAMPLES

41). PLAINTIFF STATES: THAT FINDING AND FACTS PRESENTED AND FILED OF THE C. U.S.A. LAWS AND CIVIL RIGHTS UNDER TITLE: 42: U.S.A. THE CODES: SECTION: 1985(2) EQUAL PROTECTION OF THE LAW VIOLATED AND CAUSED PERJURY OF OATH, BY THE RESPONDENTS X_X.

42). NOTE; F.R.C.P. NO PREVIOUS CASE HAS BEEN PROSECUTED OR WRITTEN FOR THE PHRASE PERJURY OF OATH OF OFFICE. REFERENCE BY FALSE SWEARING UNDER WISCONSIN STATS. 946.32(1), POINT IN TIME, THE OATH OF OFFICE, IS GIVEN FIRST AND BEFORE ENTERING OFFICE. THE OATH IS INCORPORATED AFTER THE OATH OF AFFIRMATION IS TAKEN AND SIGNED. THE TERM OF AN ATTORNEY'S OATH, BY SUPPORTING THE C.U.S.A., NEVER EXPIRES UNTIL ATTORNEY TERMINATE PRACTICE. ALL JUDGES ARE ATTORNEYS UNDER OATH. JUDGES ADD AFFIRMATION INTO THE OATH. BOTH POSITIONS SWEAR BY SUPPORTING THE C.U.S.A., AND WHEN RIGHTS ARE VIOLATED: PERJURY OF OATH UNDER TITLE: 18:

4 Copyright: DM - 2-25-98

Exhibit Z-77

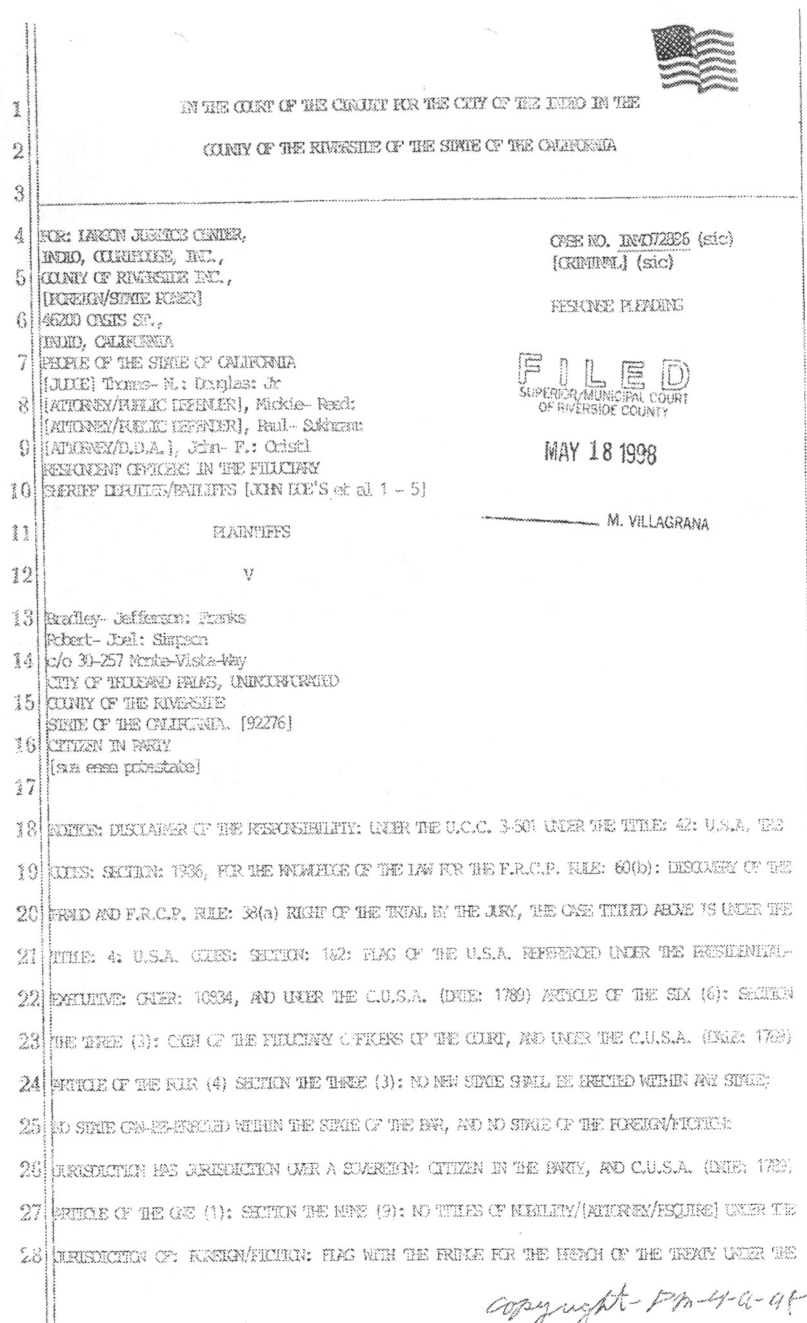

IN THE COURT OF THE CIRCUIT FOR THE CITY OF THE INDIO IN THE

COUNTY OF THE RIVERSIDE OF THE STATE OF THE CALIFORNIA

FOR: LARSON JUSTICE CENTER,
INDIO, COURTHOUSE, INC.,
COUNTY OF RIVERSIDE INC.,
[FOREIGN/STATE POWER]
46200 OASIS ST.,
INDIO, CALIFORNIA
PEOPLE OF THE STATE OF CALIFORNIA
[JUDGE] Thomas- N.: Douglas: Jr
[ATTORNEY/PUBLIC DEFENDER], Mickie- Reed:
[ATTORNEY/PUBLIC DEFENDER], Paul- Sukhram:
[ATTORNEY/D.D.A.], John- F.: Cristl
RESPONDENT OFFICERS IN THE FIDUCIARY
SHERIFF DEPUTIES/BAILIFFS [JOHN DOE'S et al. 1 - 5]

PLAINTIFFS

CASE NO. INM072896 (sic)
[CRIMINAL] (sic)

RESPONSE PLEADING

FILED
SUPERIOR/MUNICIPAL COURT
OF RIVERSIDE COUNTY

MAY 18 1998

M. VILLAGRANA

V

Bradley- Jefferson: Franks
Robert- Joel: Simpson
c/o 30-257 Monte-Vista-Way
CITY OF THOUSAND PALMS, UNINCORPORATED
COUNTY OF THE RIVERSIDE
STATE OF THE CALIFORNIA. [92276]
CITIZEN IN PARTY
[sua esse potestate]

NOTICE: DISCLAIMER OF THE RESPONSIBILITY: UNDER THE U.C.C. 3-501 UNDER THE TITLE: 42: U.S.A. THE CODES: SECTION: 1936, FOR THE KNOWLEDGE OF THE LAW FOR THE F.R.C.P. RULE: 60(b): DISCOVERY OF THE FRAUD AND F.R.C.P. RULE: 38(a) RIGHT OF THE TRIAL BY THE JURY, THE CASE TITLED ABOVE IS UNDER THE TITLE: 4: U.S.A. CODES: SECTION: 1&2: FLAG OF THE U.S.A. REFERENCED UNDER THE PRESIDENTIAL-EXECUTIVE: ORDER: 10834, AND UNDER THE C.U.S.A. (DATE: 1789) ARTICLE OF THE SIX (6): SECTION THE THREE (3): OATH OF THE FIDUCIARY OFFICERS OF THE COURT, AND UNDER THE C.U.S.A. (DATE: 1789) ARTICLE OF THE FOUR (4) SECTION THE THREE (3): NO NEW STATE SHALL BE ERECTED WITHIN ANY STATE; NO STATE CAN-BE-ERECTED WITHIN THE STATE OF THE BAR, AND NO STATE OF THE FOREIGN/FICTION: JURISDICTION HAS JURISDICTION OVER A SOVEREIGN: CITIZEN IN THE PARTY, AND C.U.S.A. (DATE: 1789) ARTICLE OF THE ONE (1): SECTION THE NINE (9): NO TITLES OF NOBILITY/[ATTORNEY/ESQUIRE] UNDER THE JURISDICTION OF: FOREIGN/FICTION: FLAG WITH THE FRINGE FOR THE BREACH OF THE TREATY UNDER THE

1

Exhibit Z-78

TITLE: 28: U.S.A. CODES: SECTION: 1605: FOREIGN-SOVEREIGNS-IMMUNITY: ACT, OF THE OCTOBER THE 21 OF THE 1976, AND IN THE BREACH OF THE C.U.S.A. (DATE: 1789), WILL BE ALLOWED IN THE JURISDICTION OF THE CASE. BREACH OF THE CONTRACT WILL CAUSE SANCTIONS UNDER THE F.R.C.P. RULE: 16(f). WHEN THE C.U.S.A. (DATE: 1789) IS SURRENDERED INTO THE FOREIGN/FICTION: JURISDICTION OF THE STATE, WILL CAUSE THE BREACH OF THE OATH OR AFFIRMATION CONTRACT UNDER THE C.U.S.A. (DATE: 1789) AND CHARGES FOR THE PERJURY OF THE OATH UNDER THE TITLE: 18: U.S.A. CODES: SECTION: 1621, CONSTRUCTIVE TREASON AGAINST THE C.U.S.A. (DATE: 1789) AND CONTEMPT FOR THE C.U.S.A. (DATE: 1789) AND FALSE SWEARING OF THE OATH WILL BE BROUGHT AGAINST THE OFFICERS OF THE COURT RESPONSIBLE. UNDER THE FEDERAL AUTHORITY TITLE: 42: U.S.A. CODES: SECTION: 1986 FOR THE REPORTING NEGLECT OF THE DUTY.

RESPONDENT IS CITIZENS IN PARTY, AFFIRMS BY THE TELLING THE TRUTH AND HAS FIRSTHAND KNOWLEDGE OF THE FACTS: *Bradley-Jefferson: Franks*

Bradley-Jefferson: Franks,

Robert-Joel: Simpson

Robert- Joel: Simpson,

ABBREVIATIONS: F.R.C.P. = FEDERAL: RULES OF THE CIVIL-PROCEDURE
herein U.S.A. CODES = UNITED: STATES OF THE AMERICA: CODES
U.C.C. = UNIFORM-COMMERCIAL-CODES
U.S.A. = UNITED: STATES OF THE AMERICA
C.U.S.A. (DATE: 1789) = CONSTITUTION OF THE UNITED: STATES OF THE AMERICA:
BY THE ARTICLE OF THE 7 OF THE SEPTEMBER THE 17 OF THE 1789.
BY THE ARTICLE OF THE 3 = RIGHT OF THE SPEECH, RELIGION, PRESS, GRIEVANCE;
BY THE ARTICLE OF THE 6 = RIGHT OF THE ARREST-WARRANT OR SEARCH-WARRANT SIGNED BY THE JUDGE OF THE OATH
BY THE ARTICLE OF THE 7 = RIGHT OF DUE-PROCESS, NO WITNESS AGAINST OWN-SELF
BY THE ARTICLE OF THE 8 = RIGHT OF THE WITNESS, CHOICE OF THE COUNCIL, PRESENTMENT OF THE EVIDENCE IN THE COURT, SPEEDY TRIAL
BY THE ARTICLE OF THE 9 = RIGHT OF THE TRIAL BY THE JURY
BY THE ARTICLE OF THE 10 = NO CRUEL AND UNUSUAL PUNISHMENT, REASONABLE BAIL
BY THE ARTICLE OF THE 11 = OFFICERS BY THE PEOPLE APPOINTED OR ELECTED UNDER THE OATH OR AFFIRMATION FOR THE UPHOLDING THE CONSTITUTION OF THE U.S.A. SEPTEMBER THE 17 OF THE 1789.
BY THE ARTICLE OF THE 12 = POWERS FOR THE PEOPLE OR FOR SEVERAL STATES OF THE AMERICA
BY THE ARTICLE OF THE ONE (1) SECTION THE NINE (9) = NO TITLES OF THE NOBILITY, NO FOREIGN/FICTION: POWERS, NO FOREIGN/FICTION: JURISDICTIONS OVER THE SOVEREIGN: CITIZEN IN THE PARTY, (NO JOINDER: NO JURISDICTION) RIGHTS = UNDER THE CONSTITUTION OF THE U.S.A. 9-17-1789
NOTE: THE AUTHORITY OF THE CONSTITUTION FOR THE UNITED: STATES OF THE AMERICA IS UNDER THE FACTS OF THE NOUNS HAVING JURISDICTION IN THE COURTS OF THE UNITED: STATES OF THE AMERICA. USE OF THE NOUNS AS THE ADJECTIVES CAUSES MAIL-FRAUD UNDER THE TITLE: 18: U.S.A. CODES: SECTION: 1342: FICTITIOUS USE OF THE NAMES FOR THE EXTORTION OF THE MONEY AND C.U.S.A. (DATE: 1789) RIGHTS.

THE COURT OF THE DISTRICT OF THE U.S.A. HAS ORIGINAL-JURISDICTION UNDER THE TITLE: 28: U.S.A.

2 *Copyright-[illegible] 4-9-98*

Exhibit Z-79

CODES: 1331 AND TITLE: 28: U.S.A. CODES: SECTION: 1343 UNDER THE TITLE: 4: U.S.A. CODES: SECTION: 1 & 2: FLAG OF THE U.S.A. UNDER THE WRIT OF THE ERROR, TITLE: 28;U.S.A. CODES: PAGE ONE (1): (READ FOR THE AUTHORIZATION) OF THE CASE TITLED ABOVE UNDER THE F.R.C.P. RULE: 38(a) FOR THE RIGHT OF THE TRIAL BY THE JURY AND THE C.U.S.A. (DATE: 1789): ARTICLE OF THE NINE (9) (DATE: 1789) RIGHT FOR THE TRIAL BY THE JURY. THE CLERK OF THE COURT SHALL FILE UNDER THE COURT OF THE CIRCUIT OF THE STATE OF THE CALIFORNIA UNDER THE TITLE: 28: U.S.A. CODES: SECTION: 1869, AND ORDER PROCEDURES OF THE TITLE: 28: U.S.A. CODES: SECTION: 1361: COMPLIANCE OF THE RESPONSIBILITY FOR THE DUTY OF THE OFFICE. THE COURT IS UNDER THE FOREIGN-SOVEREIGN-IMMUNITY: ACT: DATED: OCTOBER THE 21 OF THE 1976 IN THE TITLE: 28: U.S.A. CODES: SECTION: 1605.

FACTS

1. BY THE COUNTY OF THE RIVERSIDE BY THE DEPARTMENT OF THE SHERIFFS RESPONDENTS WERE ARRESTED.

2. UNDER THE CALIFORNIA-COMMERCIAL: LAW, FULL-DISCLOSURE OF THE INTENT OF THE ARREST-NOTICE IS REQUIRED AND PROPER-IDENTIFICATION IS REQUIRED BY THE BOTH-PARTIES AT THE TIME OF THE ARREST.

3. THE RESPONDENTS WERE ARRESTED BY THE A MARKED RIVERSIDE COUNTY SHERIFF(sic) (ADJECTIVE) ON THE WEST SIDE OF THE HOUSE: BY THE 3000-BLOCK OF THE Monte-Vista-Way. THE ARREST WAS MADE BY THE A RIVERSIDE COUNTY SHERIFF PERSON(sic) (ADJECTIVE) AS THE IDENTIFIED BY THE MARKINGS ON THE CLOTHING OF THE PERSON.

4. THE PERSON'S UNIFORM: MARKINGS ARE IN A LANGUAGE NOT FOUND IN THE ENGLISH AS THE WORDS ARE RIVERSIDE COUNTY SHERIFF ARE ALL ADJECTIVES AND ARE A FICTION BY THE LAW OF THE ENGLISH AND HAVE NO JURISDICTION AS THE FACT, ONLY AS THE OPINION BY THE COURT.

5. THE SHOULDER MARKINGS ARE IDENTIFIED BY THE PERSON KNOWN AS (JOHN DOE'S et al 1 - 5) AS A FOREIGN/FICTION-FOUR-SIDED-RED-WHITE-BLUE-YELLOW-FRINGE: FLAG(sic). THE FLAG IS NOT KNOWN IN THE UNITED: STATES OF THE AMERICA AS A LEGAL: FLAG SUPPORTED BY THE CONGRESS AND THE SENATE OF THE UNITED: STATES OF THE AMERICA, LAW IS PASSED BY THE CONGRESS ON THE JUNE 1 OF THE 1997 FOR THE ANYONE DESECRATING THE FLAG OF THE UNITED: STATES OF THE AMERICA OR MISREPRESENTING THE FLAG UNDER THE TITLE: 36: CHAPTER: 2-6: NOTHING SHALL BE PLACED ON THE FLAG OF THE UNITED: STATES OF THE AMERICA, AND PRESIDENTIAL-EXECUTIVE: ORDER: 10834: DESCRIBING THE FLAG OF THE UNITED: STATES OF THE AMERICA: AND TITLE: 4: U.S.A. CODES: SECTION 1 AND 2 FOR THE DESCRIPTION OF THE FLAG AND UNDER THE SECTION THREE (3) FOR THE DESECRATION OF THE FLAG WITH THE CRIMINAL: CHARGES BY THE U.S.A. MILITARY (ARMY).

6. RESPONDENTS WERE DETAINED BY THE A PERSON NOW IDENTIFYING HIMSELF A FOREIGN/FICTION: AGENT UNDER THE A FOREIGN/FICTION: FLAG NOT KNOWN IN THE UNITED: STATES OF THE AMERICA.

7. UNDER THE CONSTITUTION OF THE UNITED: STATES OF THE AMERICA, ARTICLE OF THE ELEVEN (11) DATE: SEPTEMBER THE 17 OF THE 1789 IN THE JURISDICTION A "NOUN" AND UNDER THE OATH AND AFFIRMATION ARTICLE OF THE SIX (6) SECTION THE THREE (3) REQUIRED OF THE ALL OFFICER OF THE COURT, EMPLOYED BY THE PEOPLE, FOR THE PROTECTION, OF THE LAWS, OF THE STATE OF THE CALIFORNIA, AND THE LAWS OF THE UNITED: STATES OF THE AMERICA.

8. THE FOREIGN/FICTION: STATES (CONDITION OF:) UNDER THE FRINGE FLAGS WILL NOT HAVE JURISDICTION OVER SOVEREIGN: CITIZEN IN THE PARTY AS AFFIRMED BY THE OATH THAT OFFICERS TAKE FOR THE CONSTITUTION OF THE U.S.A. SEPTEMBER THE 17 OF THE 1789.

9. NOTE: THERE HAVE BEEN MANY CHANGES OF THE C.U.S.A. BY THE ATTORNEYS INFLUENCING UNSKILLED OFFICER OF THE GOVERNMENT FOR THE PASSAGE OF THE LAWS, HOWEVER: ANY LAW: PASSED IN THE CONFLICT OR VIOLATION WITH THE C.U.S.A. FOUND IN THE TITLE: 28: U.S.A. CODES: SECTION 2072(b) SHALL NOT BE ENFORCED AND HAVE NO JURISDICTION. POINT BEING: THE USE OF THE ADJECTIVES AS THE NOUNS IS FRAUD UNDER THE F.R.C.P. RULE: 9(b) AND THE FRINGE ON THE FLAG UNDER THE LAW OF THE FLAG AS THE OFFICER IS STILL A VESSEL DISPLAYING A FOREIGN/FICTION: FLAG, AND THE RESPONDENT IS WEARING ON THE RESPONDENT'S JACKET THE REGULATION: DIMENSIONS AND COLORS OF THE FLAG OF THE U.S.A. PROPER

3 Copyright-DR-4-9-98

Exhibit Z-80

AND NOTICED WITH THE PRESENTATION FOR THE FOREIGN/FICTION: OFFICER THE DIFFERENT IN THE JURISDICTIONS UNDER THE LAW OF THE FLAG AS THE RESPONDENT IS NOW NOTICING THE COURT OF THE STATE.

10. FURTHER EXAM SHOWS: UNDER THE RULES OF THE BOXING, BRACKETS, AND FOUR CORNERING THERE IS NO CAUSE OF THE ACTION OR INDICATION FOR THE RELIEF AS THE FEES, NO INDICATION OF THE VIOLATION, NO STATE OF THE CALIFORNIA: VIOLATIONS, NO TIME OF THE DAY, NO DATE, NO INCIDENT: IDENTIFICATION AND NOTED THE ARREST IS NOT VALID, ON THE ARREST BY THE ARRESTING OFFICER BY PERFORMING OF THE ARREST.

11. THE RESPONSE IS IN THE GOOD-FAITH AND NOT MEANT FOR THE DELAY. THE CONDUCT OF THE PRESENT CONDITIONS BY THE COUNTY OF THE RIVERSIDE DEPARTMENT OF THE SHERIFF MUST BE BROUGHT INTO CURRENT-LAW: PROCEDURES, AS THE COUNTY OF THE RIVERSIDE DEPARTMENT OF THE SHERIFF IS IN THE DANGER OF THE A FEDERAL: TITLE: 42: U.S.A. CODES: SECTION: 1986 FOR THE KNOWLEDGE OF THE LAW AND NEGLECT OF THE NOT STOPPING AND CORRECTING A WRONG, AND ACCESSORY AFTER THE FACT UNDER THE TITLE: 18: U.S.A. CODES: SECTION: 3 AND TITLE: 18: U.S.A. CODES: SECTION: 242: DEPRIVATION OF THE RIGHTS UNDER THE COLOR OF THE LAW BY THE COURT AND THE COUNTY OF THE RIVERSIDE DEPARTMENT OF THE SHERIFF.

12. RESPONDENT IS ACTING IN THE GOOD-FAITH AND FOR THE FURTHER EDUCATION OF THE COUNTY OF THE RIVERSIDE COURTS(sic) ENCLOSED IS A COPY OF THE TECHNOLOGY USED IN A FEDERAL-LAW: SUIT. THE DANGER OF THE "THE" SUITS ARE THE CERTIFICATION OF THE CONSTRUCTIVE- TREASON AND SEDITION FOR THE OVERTHROWING THE GOVERNMENT BY THE OFFICERS OF THE COURTS AND THE PARTIES WHO WOULD ACT UNDER THE CONSPIRACY: TITLE: 18: U.S.A. CODES: SECTION: 241 FOR THE PROTECTION OF THE FOREIGN/FICTION: STATE TAKEOVER OF THE UNITED: STATES OF THE AMERICA.

13. PLEASE FEEL FREE BY CONTACTING THE FEDERAL CIA, FBI, AND JUSTICE DEPARTMENTS AS THE TASK FORCES ARE IN THE PLACE FOR THE CORRECTIONS UNDER THE DAVID-WYNN: MILLER: L.A.W. PROCEDURES. THE TECHNOLOGIES ON THE PUNCTUATION AND THE IMPACTS OF THE "ADJECTIVE AS THE NOUN: FRAUD" IS A WORLD-WIDE: PROBLEM IMPACTING ALL NATION ON THE EARTH. WE ARE NOT ALONE.

14. IN THE CLOSING THE WORD "MUNICIPAL" MEAN SELF-APPOINTED-POLICE: STATE. THE FACT COUNTY OF THE RIVERSIDE DEPARTMENT OF THE SHERIFF IS USING THE TERM AS AN ADJECTIVE SHOWS "FICTION" OF THE COURT UNDER THE FRINGE: FLAG. THERE MUST NOT BE AN EAGLE, SPEAR, OR BALL ATOP THE POLE AND NO BRAID OR FRINGE ON THE FLAG DIMENSIONS (1 x 1.9) SEE EX. ORDER 10834, OR ARMY-REGULATIONS: 840-10 SECTIONS 2-1 THROUGH 2-6 IF YOU HAVE ANY QUESTIONS.

15. RESPONDENTS REQUEST A RESPONSE IN THE TEN (10) DAYS UNDER THE F.R.C.P. RULE: 8(a)(c) FOR THE RESOLUTION OF THE INCIDENT.

Bradley-Jefferson: Franks
Bradley- Jefferson: Franks,

Robert-Joel: Simpson
Robert- Joel: Simpson,

c/o 30-257 Monte-Vista-Way
CITY OF THOUSAND PALMS, UNINCORPORATED
COUNTY OF THE RIVERSIDE
STATE OF THE CALIFORNIA. [92276]

DAVID-WYNN: MILLER, L.A.W. PROCEDURAL BOOKS ARE AVAILABLE AS STUDY GUIDES FOR THE PROPER ENGLISH UNDER THE LAW OF ALGEBRA. LAW IS ABSOLUTE

Copyright JM 4-9-98

Exhibit Z-81

U.S.A. THE CODES: SECTION: 1621 AND FALSE SWEARING, ARE RELEVANT AND BECOME VIOLATIONS BY THE FACTS OF DEFINITION. = F.R.C.P. RULE: 9(b), F.R.C.P. RULE: 12(d), WIS. RULES 40.15, WIS. STATUTE 946, TITLE: 42: U.S.A. THE CODES: SECTION: 1983 AT NOTE 337: RUCKER v. MARTIN, ALSO SEE: NOTE 349. (NOTE: USE YOUR OWN STATE NUMBERS.)

43). THE RESPONDENTS KNEW THE C.U.S.A.: LAWS WERE CORRECT, HOWEVER INJURED PLAINTIFF WITH THE FOLLOWING ACTS AS FOLLOWS; THE PEOPLE COULD USE ALL DEFINITIONS...

DEFINITIONS

44). PERJURY: THE WILLFUL ASSERTION AS FOR A MATTER OF FACT, OPINION, BELIEF, OR KNOWLEDGE, MADE BY A WITNESS IN A JUDICIAL PROCEEDING AS PART OF PARTIES EVIDENCE, EITHER UPON OATH OR IN ANY FORM ALLOWED BY LAW BY BEING SUBSTITUTED FOR AN OATH, WHETHER SUCH EVIDENCE IS GIVEN IN OPEN COURT, OR IN AN AFFIDAVIT, OR OTHERWISE, SUCH ASSERTION BEING MATERIAL OF THE ISSUE OR POINT OF INQUIRY AND KNOWN BY THE WITNESS FOR BEING FALSE. PERJURY IS A CRIME COMMITTED WHEN A LAWFUL OATH IS ADMINISTERED, IN SOME JUDICIAL PROCEEDING, BY A PARTY SWEARING WILFUL, ABSOLUTE, AND FALSE, IN MATTERS MATERIAL OF THE ISSUE OR POINT IN QUESTION. REF. F.R.C.P. RULE: 9(b), RULE: 12(d)1, 2, 7. TITLE: 42: U.S.A. THE CODES: SECTION: 1986: KNOWLEDGE; TITLE: 42: U.S.A. THE CODES: SECTION: 1985(1): CONSPIRACY; TITLE: 42: U.S.A. THE CODES: SECTION: 1983 AT NOTE: 349: POLICY-CUSTOM-USAGE.

45). TITLE: 18: U.S.A. THE CODES: SECTION: 1621; A PARTY IS GUILTY OF PERJURY: IN ANY OFFICIAL PROCEEDING PARTY MAKES A FALSE STATEMENT UNDER OATH OR EQUIVALENT AFFIRMATION. OR SWEARS OR AFFIRMS THE TRUTH OF A STATEMENT PREVIOUS MADE, WHEN THE STATEMENT IS MATERIAL AND PARTY DOES NOT BELIEVE STATEMENT FOR BEING TRUE.- REF. MODEL PENAL CODE $241.1. F.R.C.P. RULE: 9(b), RULE: 12(b)(7, 1, 2,)AND 12(d): U.S.A.: ARTICLE THE 11.

46). MALICE: IN LAW IS NOT NECESSARY PERSONAL HATE OR ILL WILL, BUT IS THAT **STATE OF MIND** WHICH IS RECKLESS OF LAW AND OF THE LEGAL RIGHTS OF THE CITIZEN. F.R.C.P. RULE: 9(b), RULE: 12(d).

47)CONSTITUTIONAL TORT, (TITLE: 42: U.S.A. THE CODES: SECTION: 1983), **PERSONAL INJURY**: EVERY CITIZEN IN PARTY UNDER COLOR OF ANY STATUE, ORDINANCE, REGULATION, CUSTOM, OR USAGE, OF ANY STATE OR TERRITORY, SUBJECTS, OR CAUSES BY BEING SUBJECTED, ANY CITIZEN IN PARTY, OF THE UNITED: STATES of AMERICA OR ANY OTHER CITIZEN IN PARTY, WITHIN THE JURISDICTION THEREOF BY THE DEPRIVATION OF ANY RIGHTS, PRIVILEGES OR IMMUNITIES SECURED BY THE C.U.S.A., AND LAWS BY BEING LIABLE FOR THE CITIZEN IN PARTY INJURED IN AN ACTION AT LAW, SUIT IN EQUITY, OR OTHER PROPER PROCEEDING FOR REDRESS.

48). **NOTE: TITLE: 42: U.S.A. THE CODES: SECTION: 1986 MUST PRECEDE ALL CHARGES (TITLE: 42: U.S.A. THE CODES: SECTION: 1986) ACTION FOR NEGLECT BY PREVENTING**:, (DEFINITION STATEMENT) EVERY PARTY HAVING KNOWLEDGE FOR ANY OF THE WRONGS CONSPIRED BY BEING DONE, AND MENTIONED IN SECTION 1985 OF TITLE: 42: U.S.A. THE CODES: SECTION: 1986, ARE BY BEING COMMITTED, AND BY HAVING THE POWER BY PREVENTING OR AIDING IN PREVENTING THE COMMISSION OF THE WRONG, NEGLECTS OR REFUSES BY DOING SO, THE WRONGFUL ACT, BY BEING COMMITTED, ARE LIABLE FOR THE CITIZEN IN PARTY INJURED, OR PARTIES LEGAL REPRESENTATIVES, FOR ALL DAMAGES CAUSED BY SUCH WRONGFUL ACT, WHICH SUCH PARTY BY REASONABLE DILIGENCE COULD HAVE PREVENTED; AND SUCH DAMAGES MAY BE RECOVERED IN AN ACTION IN CASE; AND ANY NUMBER OF PARTIES GUILTY OF SUCH WRONGFUL NEGLECT OR REFUSAL IS JOINED AS PLAINTIFFS/RESPONDENTS IN THE ACTION.

49). TORT: A PRIVATE OR CIVIL WRONG OR INJURY, FOR WHICH THE COURT WILL PROVIDE A REMEDY IN THE FORM OF AN ACTION FOR DAMAGES. A VIOLATION OF A DUTY IMPOSED BY GENERAL LAW OR OTHERWISE UPON ALL PARTY OCCUPYING THE RELATION OF EACH OTHER WHICH IS INVOLVED IN A GIVEN TRANSACTION. TITLE: 42: U.S.A. THE CODES: SECTION: 1986, TITLE: 42: U.S.A. THE CODES: SECTION: 1985(1)(2)(3), TITLE: 42: U.S.A. THE CODES: SECTION: 1983: CHAPTER: 21: AT NOTES 319, 337.

50). **LARCENY, BY FRAUD AND DECEPTION; FAILS BY CORRECTING A FALSE IMPRESSION** WHICH THE DECEIVER CREATED OR REINFORCED, OR WHICH THE DECEIVER KNOWS BY INFLUENCING **ANOTHER** PARTY FOR WHOM THE PARTY STANDS IN A FIDUCIARY OR CONFIDENTIAL RELATIONSHIP. REF. F.R.C.P. RULE: 9(b), F.R.C.P. RULE: 12(b), TITLE: 42: U.S.A. THE CODES: SECTION: 1986, TITLE: 42: U.S.A. THE CODES: SECTION: 1985.

STATEMENT: PLAINTIFF IS WITNESS TOO, WITH FIRST HAND KNOWLEDGE, ACCUSING EACH DEFENDANT AS WITNESS OF FRAUD (F.R.C.P. 9(b) AND DID NOT SUE THE COURT BY STOPPING AND CORRECTING THE WRONG; DISMISS FOR EQUAL PROTECTION, AND DUE-PROCESS VIOLATIONS, HOWEVER;, THE FRAUD CONTINUES AS NO CITIZEN IN PARTY HAS BEEN PROSECUTED OF DATE. THE LEGAL SYSTEM IS PROTECTING OFFICERS OF THE COURT AND WILL NOT CHARGE THE BROTHERHOOD. THIS OPERATING UNDER POLICY AND CUSTOM: TITLE: 42: U.S.A. THE CODES: SECTION: 1983 NOTE 319, 337; BY VIOLATING CITIZENS RIGHTS.

5 Copyright: DM. 2-25-98

Exhibit Z-82

51). <u>**FIDUCIARY**</u>: **A PARTY HAVING DUTY**, CREATED BY UNDERTAKING, BY ACTING FOR ANOTHER'S BENEFIT IN MATTERS CONNECTED WITH SUCH UNDERTAKING. [BLD]. (HIGH STANDARDS OF GOVERNMENT)

52). <u>**TITLE: 42: U.S.A. THE CODES: SECTION: 1985(3) DEPRIVING JUSTICE/ RACKETEERING**</u>: AN ORGANIZED CONSPIRACY BY COMMITTING THE CRIMES OF EXTORTION OR COERCION, OR ATTEMPT BY COMMITTING EXTORTION OR COERCION. THE FEAR WHICH CONSTITUTES THE LEGALLY NECESSARY ELEMENT IN EXTORTION IS INDUCED BY ORAL OR WRITTEN THREATS BY DOING AN UNLAWFUL INJURY AGAINST THE PROPERTY OF THE THREATENED PARTY BY MEANS OF EITHER THREAT, (THROUGH USE OF CONTEMPT OF COURT ORDER FOR PAYING LEGAL FEES NOT DUE), EXPRESS OR IMPLIED, OR A PROMISE, EXPRESSED OR IMPLIED, THAT THE PARTY SO DEMANDING, SOLICITING OR RECEIVING SUCH THING OF VALUE WILL CAUSE THE COMPETITION OF THE PARTY FOR WHOM THE PAYMENT IS DEMANDED SOLICITED OR RECEIVED BY BEING DIMINISHED OR ELIMINATED. REF. BLD. (TITLE: 42: U.S.A. THE CODES: SECTION: 1986), (TITLE: 42: U.S.A. THE CODES: SECTION: 1983: CHAPTER: 21: NOTE: 349, 350; AND ARTICLES THE 3, 6, 7, 8, 9, 10, 11, 12, AND 13: C.U.S.A..

53). <u>**TITLE: 42: U.S.A. THE CODES: SECTION: 1985(2): OBSTRUCTING JUSTICE; INTIMIDATING PARTY, WITNESS**</u>, (2) THE JUDGE AND ATTORNEY [TWO OR MORE] CITIZENS IN PARTY, IN [YOUR] ANY STATE, **CONSPIRE TITLE: 18: U.S.A. THE CODES: SECTION:** 241, 271, BY **DETERRING**,, BY FORCE [RAPE], INTIMIDATION **[COLLUSION] TITLE: 28: U.S.A. THE CODES: SECTION: 1359**, OR THREAT [OBSTRUCTING], **ANY [USE PROPER NAMES NOW IN THE REPLACEMENT OF PRONOUNS]** CITIZEN IN PARTY OR WITNESS CITIZEN IN PARTY, IN ANY COURT OF THE U.S.A. FOR ATTENDING SUCH COURT OR FOR TESTIFYING BY ANY MATTER PENDING THEREIN, FREE, FULL, AND TRUTHFUL, OR BY INJURING SUCH CITIZEN IN PARTY OR WITNESS IN CITIZEN IN PARTY OR PROPERTY ON ACCOUNT OF PARTIES HAVING SO ATTENDED OR TESTIFIED, OR BY INFLUENCING THE VERDICT, PRESENTMENT, OR INDICTMENT OF ANY GRAND OR PETIT JUROR IN ANY SUCH COURT, OR BY INJURING THE JUROR IN CITIZEN IN PARTY OR PROPERTY ON ACCOUNT OF ANY [JUDGE'S] VERDICT, PRESENTMENT, OR INDICTMENT LAWFUL ASSENTED BY CITIZEN IN PARTY, OR OF CITIZEN IN PARTIES' BEING OR HAVING BEEN SUCH JUROR; OR [TWO OR MORE] [PROPER NAME OF CITIZEN IN PARTY] CITIZEN IN PARTIES CONSPIRE FOR THE PURPOSE OF IMPEDING, HINDERING, OBSTRUCTING, OR DEFEATING, IN ANY MATTER, THE DUE COURSE OF JUSTICE IN ANY **STATE [CONDITION OF ALL AREAS BY FICTION LIVING AND/OR NON FICTION] OF THE U.S.A.** OR TERRITORY, WITH WILFUL INTENT BY DENYING ANY CITIZEN IN PARTY THE EQUAL PROTECTION OF THE LAW, OR BY INJURING CITIZEN IN PARTY OR CITIZEN IN PARTY'S PROPERTY FOR LAWFUL ENFORCING, OR ATTEMPTING BY ENFORCING, THE RIGHT OF ANY CITIZEN IN PARTY, OR CLASS OF CITIZEN IN PARTIES, FOR THE EQUAL PROTECTION OF THE LAW.

54). <u>**TITLE: 42: U.S.A. THE CODES: SECTION: 1985 (3) DEPRIVING PARTY OF RIGHTS OR PRIVILEGES**</u>; THE TWO OR MORE CITIZEN IN PARTIES IN ANY **STATE OF THE U.S.A.** OR TERRITORY [STATE] CONSPIRE OR GO IN DISGUISE, FOR THE PURPOSE OF DEPRIVING, EITHER DIRECT OR INDIRECT, ANY PARTY OR CLASS OF CITIZEN IN PARTY OF THE EQUAL PROTECTION OF THE LAWS, OR OF EQUAL PRIVILEGES AND IMMUNITIES UNDER THE LAWS; OR FOR THE PURPOSE OF PREVENTING OR HINDERING THE CONSTITUTED AUTHORITIES OF ANY **STATE OF THE U.S.A.** OR TERRITORY FOR GIVING OR SECURING BY ALL CITIZEN IN PARTY WITHIN SUCH **STATE OF THE U.S.A.** OR TERRITORY THE EQUAL PROTECTION OF THE LAWS; OR TWO OR MORE [NAME OF PROPER PARTY] CITIZEN IN PARTIES CONSPIRE BY PREVENTING BY FORCE, INTIMIDATION, OR THREAT, ANY CITIZEN IN PARTY, BY BEING LAWFUL AND ENTITLED BY VOTING, FOR GIVING CITIZEN IN PARTY SUPPORT OR ADVOCACY IN A LEGAL MANNER, OR BY INJURING ANY [MUST BE SPECIFIC BY [NAME] CITIZEN IN PARTY OR PROPERTY ON ACCOUNT OF SUPPORT OR ADVOCACY; IN ANY [SPECIFIC] CASE OF CONSPIRACY SET FORTH IN TITLE: 42: U.S.A. THE CODES: SECTION: 1986: SECTION, ONE OR MORE CITIZEN IN PARTIES ENGAGED THEREIN DO, OR CAUSE BY BEING DONE, ANY ACT IN FURTHERANCE OF THE OBJECT OF THE CONSPIRACY, WHEREBY THE CITIZEN IN PARTY IS INJURED IN CITIZEN IN PARTY'S SELF OR PROPERTY, OR DEPRIVED OF HAVING AND EXERCISING ANY RIGHT OR PRIVILEGE [LIST RESPONDENTS NOW IN THE DEFINITION AS A CAUSE OF ACTION BY NEGLECT] OF A CITIZEN IN PARTY OF THE U.S.A., THE CITIZEN IN PARTY SO INJURED OR DEPRIVED MAY HAVE AN ACTION FOR THE RECOVERY OF DAMAGES OCCASIONED BY SUCH INJURY OR DEPRAVATION, AGAINST ANY ONE OR MORE OF THE CONSPIRATORS. F.R.C.P. R-9(b) FRAUD, RULE: 12(b).

55). <u>**DURESS**</u>: USED FOR AN ILLEGAL PURPOSE, OF THREATENING THE BODY, OR MENTAL OR FINANCIAL HARM OR OTHER MEANS AMOUNTING BY OR TENDING BY COERCING THE WILL OF ANOTHER, AN ACTUAL INDUCING CITIZEN IN PARTY BY DOING AN ACT CONTRARY OF THE CITIZEN IN PARTIES FREE WILL.
F.R.C.P.-R-9(b), TITLE: 42: U.S.A. THE CODES: SECTION: 1986; TITLE: 42: U.S.A. THE CODES: SECTION: 1985(1,2,3,); TITLE: 42: U.S.A. THE CODES: SECTION: 1983: NOTE: 351.

56). <u>**LEGAL MALPRACTICE**</u>: CONSISTS OF FAILURE OF THE JUDGE BY USING SUCH SKILL, PRUDENCE, AND DILIGENCE AS JUDGES OF ORDINARY SKILL AND CAPACITY COMMON POSSESS AND EXERCISE IN PERFORMANCE OF TASKS WHICH OFFICER OF THE COURT/LAW UNDERTAKE, AND WHEN SUCH FAILURE CAUSES DAMAGE, LEGAL MALPRACTICE GIVES RISE FOR AN ACTION IN TORT.
CAUSE = F.R.C.P. RULE: 9(b), 12(b)(7, 6, 3, 2, 1), 9(d), C.U.S.A. ARTICLES THE 6, 7, 8, 9.

6 Copyright: DM · 2-25-98

Exhibit Z-83

CONSOLIDATED SUPERIOR AND MUNICIPAL COURTS
INDIO BRANCH

PEOPLE OF THE STATE OF CALIFORNIA
CASE NO: INM072896

-vs-

DEFENDANT: BRADLEY JEFFERSON FRANKS

M I N U T E   O R D E R

****

DEPT:3N HEARING DATE: 05/29/98
PROCEEDINGS: Report and Sentencing

****

CHARGES: 1) 498(B) PC-M C, 2) 148 PC-M C, 3) 602(1) PC-M D

Honorable THOMAS N. DOUGLASS Presiding.
Clerk: M.Ramirez.
Court Reporter: B.Kohler
People Represented By J. Christl, DDA.
Special Appearance by A. Wong
Defendant Represented By P. Sukhram DPD.
Defendant Present.
Court Has Read and considered the probation officer's report.
Counsel states no legal cause exists why Judgement should not be pronounced
Defendant Waives Arraignment For pronouncement of judgment.
Counsel Stipulate: to advisement of rights.
For the Charges 1 2.(PDSM)
Summary Probation Granted for a period of 24 months on the following terms and conditions.
01) Violate no law or ordinance..
02) Committed to 60 days, in the Sheriff's Work Program. Report to
--- Sheriff's office on 06/26/98 at 7:45am
--- 45 days of Jail time suspended.
03) Pay Restitution (VICTIM) in amount of $1200.00 thru the Court;
--- as directed by Financial Svcs; disputes to amount to be resolved
--- in hearing;
04) Submit to immed. search of person auto home premises garage
--- storage area; personal or leased property; with or without cause
--- by law enforcement;
05) Not associate with any unrelated person on probation or parole.
06) TERM: Do not connect to any public utility without permission of said utility and do not tamper or interfere with any public utility delivery system i.e. power pole-power line-phone line-cable line-gas line or water line unless it is to shut off delivery to personal property during an emergency situation i.e. earthquake-fire or flood.
Pay the costs of pre-sentence report purs to PC 1203.1b in an amount & mannber to be determined by PO not to exceed $230.00.
Pay Booking Fees in amount of $110.00 to Court as directed by

Exhibit Z-84

```
5/29/98                                                        Page:    2
-------------------------------------------------------------------------------
Case Number : INM072896        People vs. BRADLEY FRANKS
===============================================================================
      Finan.Svcs by 00/00/00 purs. 29550.1(c)
      Pay Booking Fees in amount of $35.00 to Court as directed by
      Finan.Svcs by 00/00/00 purs. 29550.1(c)
      Defendant Accepts Terms and conditions of probation.
      Motion to/for Restitution hearing is Set For 06/26/98 at  8:30
      in Dept. 3N.(LMOM)
      Defendant Advised of Appeal rights.
      Defendant Does Not have the financial ability to repay the
      County for the services of appointed counsel.
      Released On Probation (PDSM)
       **HEARING CONCLUDED**
```

Exhibit Z-85

```
OTSCASPRT    SUPERIOR COURT OF STATE OF CALIFORNIA
 5/26/00                    CASE PRINT                        Page:      1
                  INDIO/PALM SPRINGS/BLYTHE COURTS
-------------------------------------------------------------------------------
CASE NUMBER:        INM072896                  DEFENDANT STATUS: Active
ARREST NBR :        OR97216009                 ARREST DATE ....:  8/04/97
ARREST AGY : RIV SHERIFF-PALM DESERT
Defendant .: SIMPSON, ROBERT JOEL                          Defn :  2 of   2
===============================================================================
       Date Filed : 08/05/97

 District Attorney : J CHRISTL                     Continuances:          9
 Defense  Attorney : M REED CPD                    Age in Days :        296
 Custody Status ...: O.R.                          Last Trial .: N/A

Charge Information
----------------------
Ct  Type   Charge           Description                 Plea       Status Sev
001 ARREST 498(D) PC        Theft Utility Services      None               F

001 FILED  498(B) PC        Obtain Utility W/Out Paying  NG         Convict M

Other Cases
-----------
              Probation
 Case Number  Expires    Convicted/Warrant Charges                  Status
 789242RS     00/00/00                                              Active

       Fine Amount        Amount Paid        Amount Due     Date To Pay
         $1,605.00                            $1,605.00       09/17/98

Case Action Information
-------------------------
Action    Div   Description                                 Status
                --------------------------
 5/26/00 3N     Hearing on Motion re: RE RESTITUTION.       Active
         3N     No Minutes
                --------------------------
 5/15/00 2K     Violation of Probation (FTP Arraignment)    Dispo
                Honorable B. J. BJORK Presiding.
                Clerk: V HARTMAN.
                Court Reporter: VIDEO
                Defendant Present.
                Defendant Advised of Constitutional Rights.
                Defendant Denies Violation of probation.(PDSM)
                Probation Ordered Revoked.
                All Parties Notified.
                DA OFFICE TO HAVE WITNESSES AVAILABLE
                Motion to/for RE RESTITUTION is Set For
                05/26/2000 at  9:00 in Dept. 3N.(LMOM)
                Defendant Ordered to Return.
                O.R. Continued.
                MINUTE ORDER OF COURT PROCEEDING
                MINUTE ORDER OF COURT PROCEEDING
```

Exhibit Z-86

```
OTSCASPRT    SUPERIOR COURT OF STATE OF CALIFORNIA
 5/26/00                    CASE PRINT                        Page:      2
                    INDIO/PALM SPRINGS/BLYTHE COURTS
--------------------------------------------------------------------------------
CASE NUMBER:      INM072896                  DEFENDANT STATUS: Active
ARREST NBR :      OR97216009                 ARREST DATE ....:  8/04/97
ARREST AGY : RIV SHERIFF-PALM DESERT
Defendant .: SIMPSON, ROBERT JOEL                        Defn :  2 of   2
================================================================================
                 -------------------------
                 Case sent to: FINANCIAL SERVICES DEPT 115.
                 -------------------------
          FSD    Violation of Probation (FTP Arraignment)           Dispo
                 Hearing is continued due to outside factors re:
                 VOPFTP. Matter is continued to 05/15/2000 at
                 10:45 in dept 2K.
                 Defendant released.
                 -------------------------
 4/17/00         PAY TO COURT: Restitution Fine in amount of
                 $150.00 imposed on 06/26/1998.
                 -------------------------
 8/26/99         Notice of Destruction sent to all parties filed
                 -------------------------
 3/01/99         Miscellaneous Payment of        $7.00 Received.
                 990301-0373-CS FPC/    7.00                  000
                 -------------------------
11/24/98         Restitution Victim No. 002 modified/updated to
                 reflect 1200.00 ***
                 -------------------------
                 Restitution (Victim) Administrative Fee set at
                 $120.00.
                 -------------------------
10/28/98         Jurisdiction set to IN by batch program.
                 -------------------------
 7/02/98         Electronic 8715 Disposition generated
                 -------------------------
 6/26/98 3N      Motion Restitution hearing                         Dispo
                 Honorable THOMAS N. DOUGLASS Presiding.
                 Clerk: M.Ramirez.
                 Court Reporter: D. Erwood
                 People Represented By J CHRISTL, DDA.
                 Defendant Represented By M REED CPD.
                 Defendant Present.
                 Restitution is Called For Hearing.
                 Motion Granted.
                 As to amount of restitution.
                 Counsel Stipulate: Restitution fine to be set at
                 $150.00.
                 Pay Restitution in an amount and manner as
                 determined by the Probation Department. Probation
                 is appointed for that purpose only.
                 Defendants are jointly and severly liable for
                 restitution of $150.00.
                 Defendant Accepts Terms and conditions of
```

Exhibit Z-87

```
 OTSCASPRT    SUPERIOR COURT OF STATE OF CALIFORNIA
  5/26/00                     CASE PRINT                         Page:      3
                      INDIO/PALM SPRINGS/BLYTHE COURTS
-------------------------------------------------------------------------------
CASE NUMBER:      INM072896                    DEFENDANT STATUS: Active
ARREST NBR :      OR97216009                   ARREST DATE ....:  8/04/97
ARREST AGY : RIV SHERIFF-PALM DESERT
Defendant .: SIMPSON, ROBERT JOEL                          Defn :  2 of   2
===============================================================================
              probation.
              Released On Probation (PDSM)
              MINUTE ORDER OF COURT PROCEEDING
              --------------------------
 5/29/98 3N   Report and Sentencing                                 Dispo
              Honorable THOMAS N. DOUGLASS Presiding.
              Clerk: M.Ramirez.
              Court Reporter: B.Kohler
              People Represented By J CHRISTL, DDA.
              Special Appearance by A. Wong
              Defendant Represented By M REED CPD.
              Defendant Present.
              Court Has Read and considered the probation
              officer's report.
              Counsel states no legal cause exists why
              Judgement should not be pronounced
              Defendant Waives Arraignment For pronouncement of
              judgment.
              Counsel Stipulate: to advisement of rights.
              Summary Probation Granted for a period of 24
              months on the following terms and conditions.
            00)     Violate no law.
            02)     Committed to 60 days, in the Sheriff's Work
                    Program. Report to Sheriff's office on 06/26/98
                    at 7:45am
                    45 days of Jail time suspended.
            03)     Pay Restitution (VICTIM) in amount of $1200.00
                    thru the Court; as directed by Financial Svcs;
                    any disputes to be resolved in a Court Hearing.
            04)     Submit to immed. search of person auto home
                    premises garage storage area; personal or leased
                    property; with or without cause by law
                    enforcement;
            05)     Not associate with any unrelated person on
                    probation or parole.
            06)     TERM: Do not connect to any public utility without
              permission of said utility and do not tamper or
              interfere with any public utility delivery system
              i.e. power pole-power line-phone line-cable line-
              gas line or water line unless it is to shut off
              delivery to personal property during an emergency
              situation i.e. earthquake-fire or flood.
              Pay the costs of pre-sentence report purs to PC
              1203.1b in an amount & mannber to be determined
              by PO not to exceed $230.00.(SEE TXL)
```

Exhibit Z-88

```
OTSCASPRT    SUPERIOR COURT OF STATE OF CALIFORNIA
 5/26/00                     CASE PRINT                        Page:      4
                   INDIO/PALM SPRINGS/BLYTHE COURTS
-----------------------------------------------------------------------------
CASE NUMBER:      INM072896                    DEFENDANT STATUS: Active
ARREST NBR :      OR97216009                   ARREST DATE ....:  8/04/97
ARREST AGY : RIV SHERIFF-PALM DESERT
Defendant .: SIMPSON, ROBERT JOEL                         Defn :  2 of   2
=============================================================================
             Pay Booking Fees in amount of $110.00 through
             Clerk of Court/Finan. Svcs by 00/00/00 pursuant
             to 29550.1 GC. *** (Citation fee see PCF)(USE
             TXV1)
             Pay Booking Fees in amount of $25.00 through
             Clerk of Court/Finan. Svcs by 00/00/00 pursuant
             to 29550.1 GC. *** (Citation fee see PCF)(USE
             TXV1)
             Defendant Accepts Terms and conditions of
             probation.
             Motion to/for Restitution hearing is Set For
             06/26/98 at  8:30 in Dept. 3N.(LMOM)
             Defendant Advised of Appeal rights.
             Defendant Does Not have the financial ability to
             repay the County for the services of appointed
             counsel.(INACTIVE 2/7/00 USE CFNAF)
             Released On Probation (PDSM)
             MINUTE ORDER OF COURT PROCEEDING
             -------------------------
5/20/98      Filed: PROBATION MEMO RE: REQUEST FOR CONTINUANCE
             -------------------------
5/01/98 3N   Report and Sentencing                           Dispo
             Honorable THOMAS N. DOUGLASS Presiding.
             Clerk: M. Ramirez.
             Court Reporter: B.Kohler
             People Represented By J CHRISTL, DDA.
             Defendant Represented By M REED CPD.
             Defendant Present.
             Defendant waives time for sentencing.
             Referred To Probation department for supplemental
             report.(PRSN)
             Probation to reinterview Deft and provide T&C's
             Defendant Ordered to Report to Probation office
             forthwith, or on release from custody.
             Hearing is Continued To 05/29/98 at  8:30 in
             Dept. 3N.(Use HCTD/HCTP/HCTO)
             Defendant Ordered to Return.
             O.R. Continued.
             MINUTE ORDER OF COURT PROCEEDING
             -------------------------
4/30/98      Filed: PROBATION OFFICER'S REPORT
             -------------------------
3/24/98      Filed: Verdicts (1)
             -------------------------
        3N   Jury Trial                                      Dispo
```

Exhibit Z-89

```
 OTSCASPRT    SUPERIOR COURT OF STATE OF CALIFORNIA
  5/15/00                   CASE PRINT                          Page:     1
                   INDIO/PALM SPRINGS/BLYTHE COURTS
------------------------------------------------------------------------------
CASE NUMBER:        INM072896                    DEFENDANT STATUS: Active
ARREST NBR :        OR97216009                   ARREST DATE ....:  8/04/97
ARREST AGY : RIV SHERIFF-PALM DESERT
Defendant .: FRANKS, BRADLEY JEFFERSON                  Defn :  1 of   2
==============================================================================
         Date Filed : 08/05/97

 District Attorney : J. Christl                  Continuances:          9
 Defense  Attorney : P. Sukhram DPD              Age in Days :        296
 Custody Status ...: N/A         - Bail:         Last Trial .: 11/15/97

Charge Information
--------------------
Ct  Type   Charge            Description                  Plea       Status Sev
001 ARREST 498(D) PC         Theft Utility Services       None                F

001 FILED  498(B) PC         Obtain Utility W/Out Paying  NG        Convict M
002 FILED  148 PC            Resisting Arrest             NG        Convict M
003 FILED  602(1) PC         Trespass/Refuse to Leave Land NG       Dismiss M

Other Cases
-----------
               Probation
 Case Number   Expires    Convicted/Warrant Charges                  Status
 INM100597     00/00/00                                              Closed

       Fine Amount       Amount Paid      Amount Due    Date To Pay
        $1,605.00                         $1,605.00      05/29/98

Case Action Information
-----------------------
Action   Div   Description                                      Status
               --------------------------
 5/15/00 2K    Violation of Probation (FTP Arraignment)         Active
         2K    No Minutes
               --------------------------
               Case sent to: FINANCIAL SERVICES DEPT 115.
               --------------------------
         FSD   Violation of Probation (FTP Arraignment)         Dispo
               Hearing is continued due to outside factors re:
               VOPFTP. Matter is continued to 05/15/2000 at
               10:45 in dept 2K.
               Defendant released.
               --------------------------
 4/17/00       PAY TO COURT: Restitution Fine in amount of
               $150.00 imposed on 06/26/1998.
               --------------------------
 1/28/00       Miscellaneous Payment of     $106.00 Received.
               000128-0560-CS FPC/  106.00                    000
               --------------------------
```

Exhibit Z-90

```
OTSCASPRT     SUPERIOR COURT OF STATE OF CALIFORNIA
 5/15/00                    CASE PRINT                        Page:     2
                  INDIO/PALM SPRINGS/BLYTHE COURTS
----------------------------------------------------------------------------
CASE NUMBER:     INM072896                    DEFENDANT STATUS: Active
ARREST NBR :     OR97216009                   ARREST DATE ....:  8/04/97
ARREST AGY : RIV SHERIFF-PALM DESERT
Defendant .: FRANKS, BRADLEY JEFFERSON                  Defn :  1 of   2
============================================================================
 8/26/99        Notice of Destruction sent to all parties filed
                -------------------------
11/25/98        Case included in Tax Intercept Report to FTB
                -------------------------
11/24/98        Restitution (Victim) Administrative Fee set at
                $120.00.
                -------------------------
                Restitution Victim No. 002 modified/updated to
                reflect 1200.00 ***
                -------------------------
11/20/98        Case included in Tax Intercept Report to FTB
                -------------------------
                Case included in Tax Intercept Report to FTB
                -------------------------
10/28/98        Jurisdiction set to IN by batch program.
                -------------------------
 8/20/98        Received: LABOR PROGRAM COMPLETION NOTICE
                -------------------------
                Received: LABOR PROGRAM COMPLETION NOTICE
                -------------------------
 7/02/98        Electronic 8715 Disposition generated
                -------------------------
 6/26/98 3N     Motion Restitution hearing                        Dispo
                Honorable THOMAS N. DOUGLASS Presiding.
                Clerk: M.Ramirez.
                Court Reporter: D. Erwood
                People Represented By J. Christl, DDA.
                Defendant Represented By P. Sukhram DPD.
                Defendant Present.
                Restitution is Called For Hearing.
                Motion Granted.
                As to amount of restitution amount.
                Counsel Stipulate: Restitution fine to be set at
                $150.00..
                Pay Restitution in an amount and manner as
                determined by the Probation Department. Probation
                is appointed for that purpose only.
                Defendants are jointly and severly liable for
                restitution of $150.00.
                Defendant Accepts Terms and conditions of
                probation.
                Released On Probation (PDSM)
                MINUTE ORDER OF COURT PROCEEDING
                -------------------------
 5/29/98 3N     Report and Sentencing                             Dispo
```

Exhibit Z-91

```
OTSCASPRT    SUPERIOR COURT OF STATE OF CALIFORNIA
 5/15/00                 CASE PRINT                        Page:      3
                  INDIO/PALM SPRINGS/BLYTHE COURTS
-------------------------------------------------------------------------
CASE NUMBER:       INM072896                DEFENDANT STATUS: Active
ARREST NBR :       OR97216009               ARREST DATE ....:  8/04/97
ARREST AGY : RIV SHERIFF-PALM DESERT
Defendant  .: FRANKS, BRADLEY JEFFERSON                 Defn :  1 of   2
=========================================================================
           Honorable THOMAS N. DOUGLASS Presiding.
           Clerk: M.Ramirez.
           Court Reporter: B.Kohler
           People Represented By J. Christl, DDA.
           Special Appearance by A. Wong
           Defendant Represented By P. Sukhram DPD.
           Defendant Present.
           Court Has Read and considered the probation
           officer's report.
           Counsel states no legal cause exists why
           Judgement should not be pronounced
           Defendant Waives Arraignment For pronouncement of
           judgment.
           Counsel Stipulate: to advisement of rights.
           For the Charges 1 2.
           Summary Probation Granted for a period of 24
           months on the following terms and conditions.
         00)    Violate no law.
         02)    Committed to 60 days, in the Sheriff's Work
                Program. Report to Sheriff's office on 06/26/98
                at 7:45am
                45 days of Jail time suspended.
         03)    Pay Restitution (VICTIM) in amount of $1200.00
                thru the Court; as directed by Financial Svcs;
                any disputes to be resolved in a Court Hearing.
         04)    Submit to immed. search of person auto home
                premises garage storage area; personal or leased
                property; with or without cause by law
                enforcement;
         05)    Not associate with any unrelated person on
                probation or parole.
         06)    TERM: Do not connect to any public utility without
           permission of said utility and do not tamper or
           interfere with any public utility delivery system
           i.e. power pole-power line-phone line-cable line-
           gas line or water line unless it is to shut off
           delivery to personal property during an emergency
           situation i.e. earthquake-fire or flood.
           Pay the costs of pre-sentence report purs to PC
           1203.1b in an amount & mannber to be determined
           by PO not to exceed $230.00.(SEE TXL)
           Pay Booking Fees in amount of $110.00 through
           Clerk of Court/Finan. Svcs by 00/00/00 pursuant
           to 29550.1 GC. *** (Citation fee see PCF)(USE
           TXV1)
```

Exhibit Z-92

```
OTSCASPRT    SUPERIOR COURT OF STATE OF CALIFORNIA
 5/15/00                   CASE PRINT                          Page:      4
                  INDIO/PALM SPRINGS/BLYTHE COURTS
------------------------------------------------------------------------------
CASE NUMBER:     INM072896                     DEFENDANT STATUS: Active
ARREST NBR :     OR97216009                    ARREST DATE ....:  8/04/97
ARREST AGY : RIV SHERIFF-PALM DESERT
Defendant  .: FRANKS, BRADLEY JEFFERSON                   Defn :  1 of   2
==============================================================================
                 Pay Booking Fees in amount of $25.00 through
                 Clerk of Court/Finan. Svcs by 00/00/00 pursuant
                 to 29550.1 GC. *** (Citation fee see PCF)(USE
                 TXV1)
                 Defendant Accepts Terms and conditions of
                 probation.
                 Motion to/for Restitution hearing is Set For
                 06/26/98 at  8:30 in Dept. 3N.(LMOM)
                 Defendant Advised of Appeal rights.
                 Defendant Does Not have the financial ability to
                 repay the County for the services of appointed
                 counsel.(INACTIVE 2/7/00 USE CFNAF)
                 Released On Probation (PDSM)
                 MINUTE ORDER OF COURT PROCEEDING
                 -------------------------
5/28/98          Received: COURT'S COPY OF LAW PROCEDURE
                 -------------------------
5/20/98          Filed: PROBATION MEMO RE: REQUEST FOR CONTINUANCE
                 -------------------------
5/18/98          Filed: RESPONSE PLEADING
                 -------------------------
5/01/98          Filed: COMMON LAW DOCUMENTS FILED BY DEFT/CW
                 -------------------------
            3N   Report and Sentencing                           Dispo
                 Honorable THOMAS N. DOUGLASS Presiding.
                 Clerk: M. Ramirez.
                 Court Reporter: B.Kohler
                 People Represented By J. Christl, DDA.
                 Defendant Represented By P. Sukhram DPD.
                 Defendant Present.
                 Defendant waives time for sentencing.
                 Referred To Probation department for supplemental
                 report.(PRSN)
                 Probation to reinterview Deft and turn in T & C's
                 Defendant Ordered to Report to Probation office
                 forthwith, or on release from custody.
                 Hearing is Continued To 05/29/98 at  8:30 in
                 Dept. 3N.(Use HCTD/HCTP/HCTO)
                 Defendant Ordered to Return.
                 O.R. Continued.
                 MINUTE ORDER OF COURT PROCEEDING
                 -------------------------
4/30/98          Filed: PROBATION OFFICER'S REPORT
                 -------------------------
3/24/98          Filed: Verdicts (2)
```

Exhibit Z-93

```
OTSCASPRT    SUPERIOR COURT OF STATE OF CALIFORNIA
 5/15/00                  CASE PRINT                          Page:      5
                  INDIO/PALM SPRINGS/BLYTHE COURTS
-----------------------------------------------------------------------------
CASE NUMBER:      INM072896                 DEFENDANT STATUS: Active
ARREST NBR :      OR97216009                ARREST DATE ....:  8/04/97
ARREST AGY : RIV SHERIFF-PALM DESERT
Defendant .: FRANKS, BRADLEY JEFFERSON                  Defn :  1 of   2
=============================================================================
                 --------------------------
          3N     Jury Trial                                          Dispo
                 Honorable THOMAS N. DOUGLASS Presiding.
                 Clerk: M. Ramirez.
                 Court Reporter: B.Kohler
                 People Represented By J. Christl, DDA.
                 Defendant Represented By P. Sukhram DPD.
                 Defendant Present.
                 4th DAY OF TRIAL
                 At  8:11 the Jury Retires to resume
                 deliberations.(TRJD)
                 AT 12:00 THE ABOVE PROCEEDINGS CONCLUDED
                 Jurors excused for lunch.
                 At 13:10 the Jury Retires to resume
                 deliberations.(TRJD)
                 At 13:46 The Jury returns into the courtroom and
                 indicate that: they have a verdict.
                 We the Jury in the above entitled action, find
                 the Deft Bradley Jefferson Franks, GUILTY, in
                 count 1 of a violation of Section 498(B) PC.
                 Dated: 03/24/98, and Signed by: Juror #12,Jury
                 Foreperson
                 We the Jury in the above entitled action, find
                 the Deft Bradley Jefferson Franks, GUILTY, in
                 count 2 of a violation of Section 148 PC.
                 Dated: 03/24/98, and Signed by: Juror #12,Jury
                 Foreperson
                 Jurors are Polled on the Verdict(s) and twelve
                 jurors answer in the affirmative.
                 Re-Reading of the Verdict(s) as recorded is Waived
                 Court orders all juror information sealed; infor-
                 mation to remain sealed until further order by
                 the Court.
                 Jurors are Thanked and Excused.
                 Referred To Probation department for pre-sentence
                 report.(PRSN)
                 Report and Sentence Hearing set on 05/01/98 at
                 8:30 in Dept. 3N.
                 Defendant waives time for sentencing.
                 Defendant Ordered to Report To: Probation.
                 Defendant Ordered to Return.
                 O.R. Continued.
                 MINUTE ORDER OF COURT PROCEEDING
                 --------------------------
 3/23/98 3N      Jury Trial                                          Dispo
```

Exhibit Z-94

```
OTSCASPRT    SUPERIOR COURT OF STATE OF CALIFORNIA
 5/15/00                    CASE PRINT                         Page:     6
                  INDIO/PALM SPRINGS/BLYTHE COURTS
-----------------------------------------------------------------------------
CASE NUMBER:      INM072896                    DEFENDANT STATUS: Active
ARREST NBR :      OR97216009                   ARREST DATE ....:  8/04/97
ARREST AGY : RIV SHERIFF-PALM DESERT
Defendant .: FRANKS, BRADLEY JEFFERSON                  Defn :  1 of   2
=============================================================================
```

Honorable THOMAS N. DOUGLASS Presiding.
Clerk: M. Ramirez.
Court Reporter: L. Ivers/B. Kohler
People Represented By J. Christl, DDA.
Defendant Represented By P. Sukhram DPD.
Defendant Present.
3rd DAY OF TRIAL
At 8:56, the following proceedings were held:
Out of the Presence Of the Jury, the following proceedings were held:
Court and Counsel Confer regarding: Item to be marked by Defense. (TRJI)
Defendant's Exhibit(s) A-Plot plan is/are Admitted in evidence.
The Court inquires of Juror #2.
At 9:15, the following proceedings were held:
Members of the Jury and Alternate present.
Defendant's Witness, Juan Ibarra is Sworn and testifies.
Defendant's Witness, Gerardo Belasu is Sworn and testifies.
Witness Gerardo Belasu is excused.
Defendant's Witness, Juan Regla is Sworn and testifies.
Defendant's Witness, John Hincjosa is Sworn and testifies.
Witness John Hinojosa is excused.
Defendant's Witness, Ryan Bodmer is Sworn and testifies.
Defense rest.
Defendant's Witness, Robert Joel Simpson is Sworn and testifies.
M. Reed rest.
Out of the Presence Of the Jury, the following proceedings were held:
1118. 1 Penal Code motion by defense counsel.
Motion is Granted as to count(s) 3, said counts ordered dismissed.
Court and Counsel go over jury instructions off the record.
Members of the Jury and Alternate present.
Jurors are admonished and excused for lunch.
Out of the Presence Of the Jury, the following proceedings were held:
Defendant's Exhibit(s) A is/are Admitted in

Exhibit Z-95

```
OTSCASPRT    SUPERIOR COURT OF STATE OF CALIFORNIA
 6/15/00                     CASE PRINT                          Page:       7
                   INDIO/PALM SPRINGS/BLYTHE COURTS
-------------------------------------------------------------------------------
CASE NUMBER:       INM072896                    DEFENDANT STATUS: Active
ARREST NBR :       OR97216009                   ARREST DATE ....:  8/04/97
ARREST AGY : RIV SHERIFF-PALM DESERT
Defendant .: FRANKS, BRADLEY JEFFERSON                    Defn :  1 of   2
===============================================================================
                 evidence.
                 AT 11:55 THE ABOVE PROCEEDINGS CONCLUDED
                 At 13:31, the following proceedings were held:
                 Out of the Presence Of the Jury, the following
                 proceedings were held:
                 Court and Counsel Confer regarding: instructions
                 to be read to Jurors (TRJI)
                 At 13:42, the following proceedings were held:
                 Members of the Jury and Alternate present.
                 Out of the Presence Of the Jury, the following
                 proceedings were held:
                 Court and Counsel Confer regarding: ct 1 theft of
                 utilities. (TRJI)
                 In the Presence Of the Jury, the following
                 proceedings were held:
                 Closing Argument made By J. Christl.
                 Out of the Presence Of the Jury, the following
                 proceedings were held:
                 Court and Counsel Confer regarding: Jury
                 instructions (TRJI)
                 In the Presence Of the Jury, the following
                 proceedings were held:
                 Closing Argument made By M. Reed.
                 Closing Argument made By P. Sukhram.
                 Court Instructs the Jury.
                 Out of the Presence Of the Jury, the following
                 proceedings were held:
                 Court and Counsel Confer regarding: instruction
                 on ct 2 (TRJI)
                 In the Presence Of the Jury, the following
                 proceedings were held:
                 The Court reinstructs Jurors on ct 2.
                 Bailiff is Sworn to take charge of the jury and
                 alternate(s).
                 At 16:38 the Jury Retires to commence
                 deliberations.(TRJD)
                 Out of the Presence Of the Jury, the following
                 proceedings were held:
                 Court and Counsel Confer regarding: Juror #3
                 (TRJI)
                 Counsel Stipulate: Jurors may be excused for
                 breaks and lunch without.
                 reconvening in court.
                 Counsel Stipulate: Judge may read Caljic 17.45 if
                 Jurors request copy.
```

Exhibit Z-96

```
  OTSCASPRT    SUPERIOR COURT OF STATE OF CALIFORNIA
   9/15/00                  CASE PRINT                        Page:      8
                     INDIO/PALM SPRINGS/BLYTHE COURTS
---------------------------------------------------------------------------
CASE NUMBER:      INM072896                   DEFENDANT STATUS: Active
ARREST NBR  :     OR97216009                  ARREST DATE ....:  8/04/97
ARREST AGY  : RIV SHERIFF-PALM DESERT
Defendant  .: FRANKS, BRADLEY JEFFERSON                Defn :  1 of   2
===========================================================================
              of Jury instructions.
              AT 17:03 HEARING WAS CONCLUDED
              Jurors Are Admonished and directed to return on
              03/24/98 at  8:00
              Out of the Presence Of the Jury, the following
              proceedings were held:
              Counsel Stipulate: Alternate Juror does not need
              to return he is to  .
              check in with the Court telephonically.
              Juror is reminded that the admonition still
              remains.
              Trial (IN PROGRESS) Adjourned to 03/24/98 at
              8:00 in Dept. 3N.
              Defendant Ordered to Return.
              O.R. Continued.
              MINUTE ORDER OF COURT PROCEEDING
              ----------------------------
 3/19/98 3N   Jury Trial                                       Dispo
              Honorable THOMAS N. DOUGLASS Presiding.
              Clerk: M. Ramirez.
              Court Reporter: B.Kohler
              People Represented By J. Christl, DDA.
              Defendant Represented By P. Sukhram DPD.
               Deputy Dodmer present and seated at Counsel table
              Defendant Present.
              2nd DAY OF TRIAL
              At  8:44, the following proceedings were held:
              In the Presence Of the Jury, the following
              proceedings were held:
              Witness previously sworn Mario Jesus Pimentel
              resumes stand
              Witness Mario Jesus Pimentel is excused,subject
              to recall
              People's Witness, John Hinojosa is Sworn and
              testifies.
              People's Exhibit #20-Map of Monte Vista is/are
              Marked for identification only.
              Out of the Presence Of the Jury, the following
              proceedings were held:
              Oral Motion By P. Sukhram regarding mistrial is
              called for hearing.
              Ms. Reed joins in motion.
              Counsel argue.
              Motion DEnied.
              In the Presence Of the Jury, the following
```

Exhibit Z-97

```
OTSCASPRT     SUPERIOR COURT OF STATE OF CALIFORNIA
 5/15/00                        CASE PRINT                       Page:      9
                     INDIO/PALM SPRINGS/BLYTHE COURTS
-------------------------------------------------------------------------------
CASE NUMBER:      INM072896                    DEFENDANT STATUS: Active
ARREST NBR :      OR97216009                   ARREST DATE ....:  8/04/97
ARREST AGY : RIV SHERIFF-PALM DESERT
Defendant .: FRANKS, BRADLEY JEFFERSON                  Defn :  1 of   2
===============================================================================
                  proceedings were held:
                  Mr. Hinojosa resumes his testimony.
                  People's Witness, Ryan Bodmer is Sworn and
                  testifies.
                  People's Witness, Troy Scott Lawrence is Sworn
                  and testifies.
                  Witness Troy Scott Lawrence is excused.
                  People rest.
                  AT 11:41 THE ABOVE PROCEEDINGS CONCLUDED
                  Jurors are admonished and excused for lunch.
                  Out of the Presence Of the Jury, the following
                  proceedings were held:
                  People's Exhibit(s) #1 through #20 is/are
                  Admitted in evidence.
                  AT 11:45 HEARING WAS CONCLUDED
                  At 13:20, the following proceedings were held:
                  Members of the Jury and Alternate present.
                  Defendant's Witness, Richard Leon Young is Sworn
                  and testifies.
                  Witness Richard Leon Young is excused.
                  Defendant's Witness, Robert Joel Simpson is Sworn
                  and testifies.
                  Defendant is Sworn and testifies on own behalf.
                  Witness previously sworn Robert J. Simpson
                  resumes stand
                  AT 15:17 HEARING WAS CONCLUDED
                  Jurors Are Admonished and directed to return on
                  03/23/98 at  8:30
                  Trial (IN PROGRESS) Adjourned to 03/23/98 at
                  8:30 in Dept. 3N.
                  Defendant Ordered to Return.
                  O.R. Continued.
                  MINUTE ORDER OF COURT PROCEEDING
                  ----------------------------
           3N     Jury Trial                                     Vacate
           3N     No Minutes
                  ----------------------------
 3/18/98          Filed: Stip re Jury admonition presence of Jury &
                  the Def
                  ----------------------------
           3N     Jury Trial                                     Dispo
                  Honorable THOMAS N. DOUGLASS Presiding.
                  Clerk: M. Ramirez.
                  Court Reporter: B.Kohler
                  People Represented By J. Christl, DDA.
```

Exhibit Z-98

```
OTSCASPRT    SUPERIOR COURT OF STATE OF CALIFORNIA
 5/15/00                   CASE PRINT                          Page:    10
                  INDIO/PALM SPRINGS/BLYTHE COURTS
---------------------------------------------------------------------------
CASE NUMBER:       INM072896                    DEFENDANT STATUS: Active
ARREST NBR :       OR97218009                   ARREST DATE ....:  8/04/97
ARREST AGY : RIV SHERIFF-PALM DESERT
Defendant .: FRANKS, BRADLEY JEFFERSON                  Defn :  1 of   2
===========================================================================
           Defendant Represented By P. Sukhram DPD.
           Defendant Present.
           1st DAY OF TRIAL
           People's items #1 through #20 as described on the
           attached list are pre-marked for identification.
           At  9:29, the following proceedings were held:
           Prospective Jury Panel having been summoned, is
           sworn regarding their qualifications to act as
           trialjurors. (TRJS)
           Jury Voir Dire commences.
           Out of the Presence Of the Jury, the following
           proceedings were held:
           An in-chamber conference was held Court and
           Counsel present without the Defendants.
           Court and Counsel Confer regarding: Mr. Sukhram's
           venire. (TRJT)
           In the Presence Of the Jury, the following
           proceedings were held:
           Jury Voir Dire resumes
           AT 11:55 THE ABOVE PROCEEDINGS CONCLUDED
           Jury panel is admonished and excused for lunch.
           At 13:54, the following proceedings were held:
           Jury Voir Dire resumes.
           Jury Panel Sworn to try the cause:
           Alternate Jurors: is, sworn.(TRJS)
           Deputy Bodmer present and seated at Counsel
           table.
           Opening Statement made By J. Christl.
           Opening Statement made By P. Sukhram.
           Opening Statement made By M. Reed.
           Motion to Exclude all Witnesses is granted.
           Deputy Bodmer is designated as Investigating
           Officer.
           People's Witness, Mario Jesus Pimentel is Sworn
           and testifies.
           Witness Mario Jesus Pimentel is excused,subject
           to recall
           Jurors Are Admonished and directed to return on
           03/19/98 at  8:30
           AT 16:00 THE ABOVE PROCEEDINGS CONCLUDED
           Out of the Presence Of the Jury, the following
           proceedings were held:
           Court and Counsel Confer regarding: Witness' to
           be called by the People on 3-19-98. (TRJT)
           AT 16:02 HEARING WAS CONCLUDED
```

Exhibit Z-99

```
OTSCASPRT    SUPERIOR COURT OF STATE OF CALIFORNIA
 5/15/00                    CASE PRINT                              Page:    11
                    INDIO/PALM SPRINGS/BLYTHE COURTS
--------------------------------------------------------------------------------
CASE NUMBER:      INM072896                        DEFENDANT STATUS: Active
ARREST NBR :      OR97216009                       ARREST DATE ....:  8/04/97
ARREST AGY : RIV SHERIFF PALM DESERT
Defendant .: FRANKS, BRADLEY JEFFERSON                  Defn :  1 of   2
================================================================================
                Trial (IN PROGRESS) Adjourned to 03/19/98 at
                8:31 in Dept. 3N.
                Defendant Ordered to Return.
                O.R. Continued.
                MINUTE ORDER OF COURT PROCEEDING
                --------------------------
 3/17/98 3N     Motion to advance trial                              Dispo
                Honorable THOMAS N. DOUGLASS Presiding.
                Clerk: M. Ramirez.
                Court Reporter: B.Kohler
                People Represented By J. Christl, DDA.
                Defendant Represented By P. Sukrum DPD.
                Defendant is Not Present.
                Oral Motion By People regarding advance jury
                trial is called for hearing.
                Motion Granted.
                Trial Set For 03/18/98 at  8:30 in Dept. 3N, for
                an estimated 2 days.
                Mr. Sukrum to notify Defendant.
                O.R. Continued.
                MINUTE ORDER OF COURT PROCEEDING
                Hearing on 03/19/98 at  8:30 for JT is Vacated.
                --------------------------
 3/16/98 3T     Jury Trial                                           Dispo
                Honorable C. J. Sheldon Presiding.
                Clerk: M .VASQUEZ.
                Court Reporter: S.Schulz
                People Represented By J CHRISTL, DDA.
                Defendant Represented By P SUKRUM DPD.
                Defendant Present.
                Case Assigned to department 3N, to Judge THOMAS
                N. DOUGLASS for all further proceedings.
                Honorable THOMAS N. DOUGLASS Presiding.
                Clerk: M. Ramirez.
                Court Reporter: B. Kohler
                People Represented By J CHRISTL, DDA.
                Defendant Represented By P SUKRUM DPD.
                Defendant Present.
                Hearing is Continued To 03/19/98 at  8:30 in
                Dept. 3N.(Use HCTD/HCTP/HCTO)
                The Following Persons are ordered to return on
                03/23/98 at  8:30 Dept 3N: Luis Manuel Gonzalez.
                The Following Persons are ordered to return on
                03/23/98 at  8:30 Dept 3N: Juan Regla.
                The Following Persons are ordered to return on
```

Exhibit Z-100

```
  OTSCASPRT     SUPERIOR COURT OF STATE OF CALIFORNIA
   5/15/00                       CASE PRINT                              Page:    12
                       INDIO/PALM SPRINGS/BLYTHE COURTS
-----------------------------------------------------------------------------------
CASE NUMBER:       INM072896                        DEFENDANT STATUS: Active
ARREST NBR :       OR97216009                       ARREST DATE ....:  8/04/97
ARREST AGY : RIV SHERIFF-PALM DESERT
Defendant .: FRANKS, BRADLEY JEFFERSON                          Defn :  1 of   2
===================================================================================
                03/23/98 at  8:30 Dept 3N: Rick Young.
                The Following Persons are ordered to return on
                03/23/98 at  8:30 Dept 3N: Jesus Angulo.
                The Following Persons are ordered to return on
                03/23/98 at  8:30 Dept 3N: Juan Ibarra.
                The Following Persons are ordered to return on
                03/23/98 at  8:30 Dept 3N: Gerardo Velazco.
                Defendant Ordered to Return.
                O.R. Continued.
                MINUTE ORDER OF COURT PROCEEDING
                Hearing on 03/17/98 at  8:30 for JT is Vacated.
                ---------------------------
  3/06/98 3T    Trial Readiness Conference                                 Dispo
                Honorable Graham Anderson Cribbs Presiding.
                People Represented By J CHRISTL, DDA.
                Defendant Represented By P SUKRUM DPD.
                Clerk: N GUITRON.
                Defendant Present.
                Trial Date COnfirmed.
                Defendant Ordered to Return.
                O.R. Continued.
                MINUTE ORDER OF COURT PROCEEDING
                MINUTE ORDER OF COURT PROCEEDING
                ---------------------------
 11/18/97 3T    Jury Trial                                                 Dispo
                Honorable C. J. Sheldon Presiding.
                Clerk: M. VASQUEZ.
                People Represented By S CLARK, DDA.
                Defendant Represented By M. KELLER DPD.
                Defendant Present.
                Oral Motion By M. KELLER regarding CONTINUANCE OF
                TRC/TRIAL DATES is called for hearing.
                Motion Granted.
                Defendant Waives Time.
                Trial Readiness Conference set for 03/06/98 at
                8:30 in Dept. 3T.(PTCF)
                Trial Set For 03/16/98 at  8:30 in Dept. 3T, for
                an estimated 0 days.
                O.R. Continued.
                MINUTE ORDER OF COURT PROCEEDING
                ---------------------------
 11/17/97 3T    Jury Trial                                                 Dispo
                Honorable C. J. Sheldon Presiding.
                Clerk: M. VASQUEZ.
                People Represented By S CLARK, DDA.
```

Exhibit Z-101

```
OTSCASPRT    SUPERIOR COURT OF STATE OF CALIFORNIA
5/15/00                    CASE PRINT                      Page:     13
                 INDIO/PALM SPRINGS/BLYTHE COURTS
------------------------------------------------------------------------
CASE NUMBER:       INM072896                  DEFENDANT STATUS: Active
ARREST NBR :       OR97216009                 ARREST DATE .....: 8/04/97
ARREST AGY : RIV SHERIFF-PALM DESERT
Defendant .: FRANKS, BRADLEY JEFFERSON                Defn :  1 of   2
========================================================================
              Defendant Represented By M. KELLER DPD.
              Defendant Present.
              Hearing is Continued To 11/18/97 at  8:30 in
              Dept. 3T.(Use HCTD/HCTP/HCTO)
              WITNESSES ORDERED TO RETURN TO COURT ON 11/18/97
              AT 9:00 AM.
              O.R. Continued.
              MINUTE ORDER OF COURT PROCEEDING
              -------------------------
11/07/97 3T   Trial Readiness Conference                    Dispo
              Honorable C. J. Sheldon Presiding.
              People Represented By S CLARK, DDA.
              Defendant Represented By M. KELLER DPD.
              Clerk: N GUITRON.
              Minutes entered by P SMYTH.
              Defendant Present.
              Trial Date COnfirmed.
              O.R. Continued.
              MINUTE ORDER OF COURT PROCEEDING
              -------------------------
9/02/97 3T    Pre-Trial Hearing                             Dispo
              Honorable C. J. Sheldon Presiding.
              Clerk: B MALLIE.
              People Represented By J CAULEY, DDA.
              Defendant Represented By M. KELLER DPD.
              Defendant Present.
              Defendant Waives Time.
              Trial Readiness Conference set for 11/07/97 at
              8:30 in Dept. 3T.(PTCF)
              Trial Set For 11/17/97 at  8:30 in Dept. 3T, for
              an estimated 0 days.
              O.R. Continued.
              MINUTE ORDER OF COURT PROCEEDING
              -------------------------
8/12/97 3T    Pre-Trial Hearing                             Dispo
              Honorable H. Morgan Dougherty Presiding.
              Clerk: S. BUENDIA/B. MALLIE.
              People Represented By J. BEHNKE, DDA.
              Defendant Represented By M. KELLER DPD.
              Defendant not present. Appears pursuant to 977
              PC.(11/25/98 INACTIVE-USE 977A or 977W)
              Defendant Waives Time.
              Hearing is Continued To 09/02/97 at 13:30 in
              Dept. 3T.(Use HCTD/HCTP/HCTO)
              O.R. Continued.
```

Exhibit Z-102

```
 OTSCASPRT    SUPERIOR COURT OF STATE OF CALIFORNIA
  5/15/00                    CASE PRINT                          Page:    13
                     INDIO/PALM SPRINGS/BLYTHE COURTS
-------------------------------------------------------------------------------
CASE NUMBER:     INM072896                      DEFENDANT STATUS: Active
ARREST NBR :     OR97216009                     ARREST DATE ....:  8/04/97
ARREST AGY : RIV SHERIFF-PALM DESERT
Defendant .: SIMPSON, ROBERT JOEL                        Defn :  2 of   2
===============================================================================
              Honorable C. J. Sheldon Presiding.
              Clerk: B MALLIE.
              People Represented By J CAULEY, DDA.
              Defendant Represented By M REED CPD.
              Defendant Present.
              Defendant Waives Time.
              Trial Readiness Conference set for 11/07/97 at
              8:30 in Dept. 3T.(PTCF)
              Trial Set For 11/17/97 at  8:30 in Dept. 3T, for
              an estimated 0 days.
              O.R. Continued.
              MINUTE ORDER OF COURT PROCEEDING
              --------------------------
  8/12/97 3T  Pre-Trial Hearing                                     Dispo
              Honorable H. Morgan Dougherty Presiding.
              Clerk: S. BUENDIA/B. MALLIE.
              People Represented By J. BEHNKE, DDA.
              Defendant Represented By M. KELLER DPD.
              Defendant not present. Appears pursuant to 977
              PC.(11/25/98 INACTIVE-USE 977A or 977W)
              Conflict Declared by PUBLIC DEFENDER
              Public Defender is Relieved.
              Conflict Defense Panel appointed.
              Special Appearance by M. REED CDP
              Defendant Waives Time.
              Hearing is Continued To 09/02/97 at 13:30 in
              Dept. 3T.(Use HCTD/HCTP/HCTO)
              O.R. Continued.
              MINUTE ORDER OF COURT PROCEEDING
              --------------------------
  8/06/97 2K  Arraignment                                           Dispo
              Honorable Jerome E. Stevenson Presiding.
              Clerk: V HARTMAN.
              Court Reporter: VIDEO
              Defendant Present.
              Public Defender Appointed.
              Defendant advised of right to counsel; cont. to
              consult counsel; assignment of counsel if unable
              to employ private counsel.
              Defendant advised of right to trial by jury;
              statutory sentencing; cross exam of witnesses;
              right to present evidence on own behalf.(USE
              DACCP-DARCC)
              Defendant advised of right to speedy trial;
              dismissal if no trial within 30/45 days after
```

Exhibit Z-103

```
OTSCASPRT    SUPERIOR COURT OF STATE OF CALIFORNIA
 5/15/00                    CASE PRINT                        Page:     14
                   INDIO/PALM SPRINGS/BLYTHE COURTS
---------------------------------------------------------------------------
CASE NUMBER:       INM072896                    DEFENDANT STATUS: Active
ARREST NBR :       OR97216009                   ARREST DATE ....:  8/04/97
ARREST AGY : RIV SHERIFF-PALM DESERT
Defendant .: SIMPSON, ROBERT JOEL                         Defn :  2 of   2
===========================================================================
                 arraignment; effect of consent to waive time.
                 Defendant advised if not a citizen conviction may
                 result in deportation, exclusion from admission
                 tothis country or denial of naturalization.
                 Defendant Arraigned.
                 Defendant Advised of Constitutional Rights.
                 Pleads Not Guilty to all counts.
                 District Attorney Notified
                 Public Defender Notified
                 Pre-Trial Hearing Set for 08/12/97 at 13:30 in
                 Dept 3T (INACTIVE 10/22/99 USE PTH)
                 Defendant Ordered to Return.
                 Court Orders defendant to obey all reasonable
                 directives of the O.R. clerk.
                 TO HAVE NO CONTACT W/ VICTIM
                 NOT TO CLIMB UTILITY POLE OR CONNECT UTILITIES
                 Conditional O.R. Release.
                 MINUTE ORDER OF COURT PROCEEDING
                 ---------------------------
  8/05/97        Complaint Filed
                 ---------------------------
                 R.O.R. Filed by INJLT

Probation Information
---------------------
  Type        Granted Date    Expiration Date
  Summary      5/29/98          5/28/00

                   01) Obey all laws and ordinances. (T1)

                       45 days of Jail time suspended. (TCS)

                   02) Committed to 60 days, in the Sheriff's Work
                       Program. Report to Sheriff's office on 06/26/98
                       at 7:45am (TWP)

                   03) Pay Restitution (VICTIM) in amount of $1200.00
                       thru the Court; as directed by Financial Svcs;
                       any disputes to be resolved in a Court Hearing. (TCE1)

                   04) Submit to immed. search of person auto home
                       premises garage storage area; personal or leased
                       property; with or without cause by law
                       enforcement; (TEA2)
```

Exhibit Z-104

```
  OTSCASPRT    SUPERIOR COURT OF STATE OF CALIFORNIA
   5/15/00                     CASE PRINT                       Page:    15
                     INDIO/PALM SPRINGS/BLYTHE COURTS
--------------------------------------------------------------------------------
CASE NUMBER:      INM072896                      DEFENDANT STATUS: Active
ARREST NBR :      OR97216009                     ARREST DATE ....:  8/04/97
ARREST AGY : RIV SHERIFF-PALM DESERT
Defendant .: SIMPSON, ROBERT JOEL                          Defn :  2 of   2
================================================================================
                 05) Not associate with any unrelated person on
                     probation or parole. (THO)

                 06) TERM: Do not connect to any public utility without (TERM6)

**** No Local DMV data available for this case ****
                    **** END OF CASE PRINT ****
```

Exhibit Z-105

RIVERSIDE COUNTY SHERIFF'S LABOR PROGRAM

Defendant's Name — Case Number — Court — Division

Charges — Date to Report — Total # of Days

THIS PROGRAM IS A PRIVILEGE. STRICT ADHERENCE TO THE RULES IS A MUST
BRING $75.00 IN CASH OR MONEY ORDER FOR PROCESSING FEE. EXACT CHANGE ONLY.

1) At the date indicated above you are ordered to report promptly at 7.45 A.M. at the following location:

☐	☐	☐	☐	☑
RIVERSIDE	HEMET	PERRIS	BANNING	INDIO
4200 Orange St.	880 N. State St. Ste. A-6	227 N. "D" St.	155 E. Hays St.	46200 Oasis St.
Riverside, 92502	Hemet, 92543	Perris, 92370	Banning, 92220	Ste. B-15
(909)275-6172	(909)766-2332	(909)766-2332	(909)766-2332	Indio, 92201
				(619)863-8255

2) **Failure to report as directed by the court on the date and time indicated shall result in your incarceration.**
3) **You are in custody during work hours and are subject to being searched at any time, by any peace officer or correctional deputy.**
4) Program work hours are as assigned and equal an eight/nine hour work day depending on your assigned location.
5) Work sites are available in most areas of the county, however, we cannot guarantee where you will be assigned. **The work detail involves manual lab and you must provide your own transportation.** The Deputies in charge of this program do not take you to and from the job site locations. **Bring your own lunch and drink for each day of work.** Be sure to wear **appropriate** clothing, **jeans, t-shirt/blouse, tennis shoes.** **Absolutely no** halter tops, sleeveless shirts, shorts, dresses, heels, open toed shoes or sandals.
6) If you are forced to miss an assigned work day you shall show the appropriate documentation to the Deputies in charge of the program before you will be allowed to resume your work sentence.
7) **If you are physically impaired or cannot perform manual labor, you must provide a note from your doctor. This note must be brought wi you on the date you have been ordered to appear for work.**
8) I will not hold the County of Riverside, Sheriff Labor Program, Sheriff's Court Services Division, remanding court, or any Governmental Agency or Non-profit organization responsible for any injuries occurring while participating in the Sheriff's Labor Program.
9) I understand that I have been sentenced to the custody of the Riverside County Sheriff's Department as an inmate. If it is determined by the court, t Sheriff or Sheriff's Labor Program personnel that I have violated program rules, I waive any hearing in connection with the circumstances surroundin the violation and may be incarcerated at the County Jail to complete the balance of sentence as straight time.

I CERTIFY THAT I HAVE READ THE ABOVE RULES AND WAIVERS AND AGREE TO COMPLY WITH THEM ALL.

TO BE COMPLETED BY DEFENDANT

Without dishonor and recourse!

Signature

Bradley-Jefferson: [Franks]

Print Name

090163

Date of Birth

c/o 30257 ... Address

Thousand Palms California republic [9227...]

City Zip

N/A

Telephone

LABOR PROGRAM USE ONLY

RECEIPT NUMBER(S)

Days Completed

FAILURE TO APPEAR ☐
FAILURE TO COMPLETE ☐
SUCCESSFUL COMPLETETION ☐
OTHER________ ☐

DISTRIBUTION: WHITE-Court, CANARY-Defendant, PINK/GOLDENROD- Sheriff's Labor Program — Form 837 (Rev 2/97)

Exhibit Z-106

CONSOLIDATED SUPERIOR AND MUNICIPAL COURTS
INDIO BRANCH

PEOPLE OF THE STATE OF CALIFORNIA
CASE NO: INM072896
-vs-
DEFENDANT: BRADLEY JEFFERSON FRANKS

M I N U T E   O R D E R

****

DEPT:3N HEARING DATE: 06/26/98
PROCEEDINGS: Motion Restitution hearing

****

CHARGES: 1) 498(B) PC-M C, 2) 148 PC-M C, 3) 602(1) PC-M D

Honorable THOMAS N. DOUGLASS Presiding.
Clerk: M.Ramirez.
Court Reporter: D. Erwood
People Represented By J. Christl, DDA.
Defendant Represented By P. Sukhram DPD.
Defendant Present.
Restitution is Called For Hearing.
Motion GRanted.
As to amount of restitution amount.
Counsel Stipulate: Restitution fine to be set at $150.00..
Pay Restitution in an amount and manner as determined by the Probation Department. Probation is appointed for that purpose only.
Defendants are jointly and severly liable for restitution of $150.00.
Defendant Accepts Terms and conditions of probation.
Released On Probation (PDSM)
HEARING CONCLUDED

Exhibit Z-107

RIVERSIDE COUNTY SHERIFF'S LABOR PROGRAM

Bradley J. Franks	INM022896	Indio	3N
Defendant's Name	Case Number	Court	Division
498(b) PC, 148 PC, 602(1) PC	6-26-98		15
Charges	Date to Report		Total # of Days

THIS PROGRAM IS A PRIVILEGE. STRICT ADHERENCE TO THE RULES IS A MUST
BRING $75.00 IN CASH OR MONEY ORDER FOR PROCESSING FEE. EXACT CHANGE ONLY.

1) At the date indicated above you are ordered to report promptly at 7:45 A.M. at the following location:

☐	☐	☐	☐	☒
RIVERSIDE 4200 Orange St. Riverside, 92502 (909)275-6172	HEMET 880 N. State St. Ste. A-6 Hemet, 92543 (909)766-2332	PERRIS 227 N. "D" St. Perris, 92370 (909)766-2332	BANNING 155 E. Hays St. Banning, 92220 (909)766-2332	INDIO 46200 Oasis St. Ste. B-15 Indio, 92201 (619)863-8255

2) **Failure to report as directed by the court on the date and time indicated shall result in your incarceration.**
3) **You are in custody during work hours and are subject to being searched at any time, by any peace officer or correctional deputy.**
4) Program work hours are as assigned and equal an eight/nine hour work day depending on your assigned location.
5) Work sites are available in most areas of the county, however, we cannot guarantee where you will be assigned. **The work detail involves manual lab[or] and you must provide your own transportation.** The Deputies in charge of this program do not take you to and from the job site locations. **Bring your own lunch and drink for each day of work.** Be sure to wear **appropriate** clothing, **jeans, t-shirt/blouse, tennis shoes.** **Absolutely no** halter tops, sleeveless shirts, shorts, dresses, heels, open toed shoes or sandals.
6) If you are forced to miss an assigned work day you shall show the appropriate documentation to the Deputies in charge of the program before you will be allowed to resume your work sentence.
7) **If you are physically impaired or cannot perform manual labor, you must provide a note from your doctor. This note must be brought wi[th] you on the date you have been ordered to appear for work.**
8) I will not hold the County of Riverside, Sheriff Labor Program, Sheriff's Court Services Division, remanding court, or any Governmental Agency or Non-profit organization responsible for any injuries occurring while participating in the Sheriff's Labor Program.
9) I understand that I have been sentenced to the custody of the Riverside County Sheriff's Department as an inmate. If it is determined by the court, t[he] Sheriff or Sheriff's Labor Program personnel that I have violated program rules, I waive any hearing in connection with the circumstances surroundin[g] the violation and may be incarcerated at the County Jail to complete the balance of sentence as straight time.

I CERTIFY THAT I HAVE READ THE ABOVE RULES AND WAIVERS AND AGREE TO COMPLY WITH THEM ALL.

TO BE COMPLETED BY DEFENDANT

Without dishonor and recourse:

Bradley - Jefferson: [Franks]
Signature

Bradley - Jefferson: [Franks]
Print Name

090163
Date of Birth

c/o 30257 Monte Vista ...
Address

Thousand Palms California republic [92270]
City Zip

N/A
Telephone

FILED
SUPERIOR/MUNICIPAL COURT OF RIVERSIDE COUNTY
AUG 20 1998

LABOR PROGRAM USE ONLY

A1126612 081598 $75.00

P.S. AIR MUSEUM (SAT - SUN)

RECEIPT NUMBER(S)

15
Days Completed

FAILURE TO APPEAR ☐
FAILURE TO COMPLETE ☐
SUCCESSFUL COMPLETION ☒
OTHER______ ☐

DISTRIBUTION: WHITE-Court, CANARY-Defendant, PINK/GOLDENROD- Sheriff's Labor Program   Form 837 (Rev 2/97)

(NO PINK COPY RECEIVED)

Exhibit Z-108

FILED
SUPERIOR COURT OF CALIFORNIA
COUNTY OF RIVERSIDE

AUG 2 6 1999

M. VILLAGRANA

SUPERIOR COURT OF CALIFORNIA
COUNTY OF RIVERSIDE

People of the State of California	)	Notice of Destruction of Exhibits and Depositions
Plaintiff	)	
VS	)	
	)	
Bradley J. Franks	)	
Defendant	)	Case No.:INM072896
	)	D.A. No:

You are hereby notified that on or after sixty days from the date of mailing of this notice, the exhibits and depositions in this case SHALL be destroyed pursuant to Section 1417.1 of the Penal Code. If you wish to have the exhibits returned or there is good cause why the exhibits should NOT be destroyed, you must notify the exhibits clerk in writing within the prescribed time. Supporting Penal Codes MUST be included in the request for Retention of Exhibits. Please make arrangements prior to pick up if return of exhibits is requested.

Send all notices to: Superior Court
46-200 Oasis Street
Indio, Ca 92201
Attn: Exhibits Clerk

CLERKS CERTIFICATE OF MAILING

On the date stated below, I mailed by First-Class mail, postage prepaid, a copy of this Notice of Destruction of Exhibits to the Parties listed below.

Date: AUG 2 6 1999

CLERK OF THE COURT
BY: M Villagrana
CLERK

John Christl, DDA
46209 Oasis St. 4th Floor
Indio, Ca. 92201

Paul Sukhram, DPD
c/o Griselda Bautista
46209 Oasis St. Room 314
Indio, Ca. 92201

Exhibit Z-109

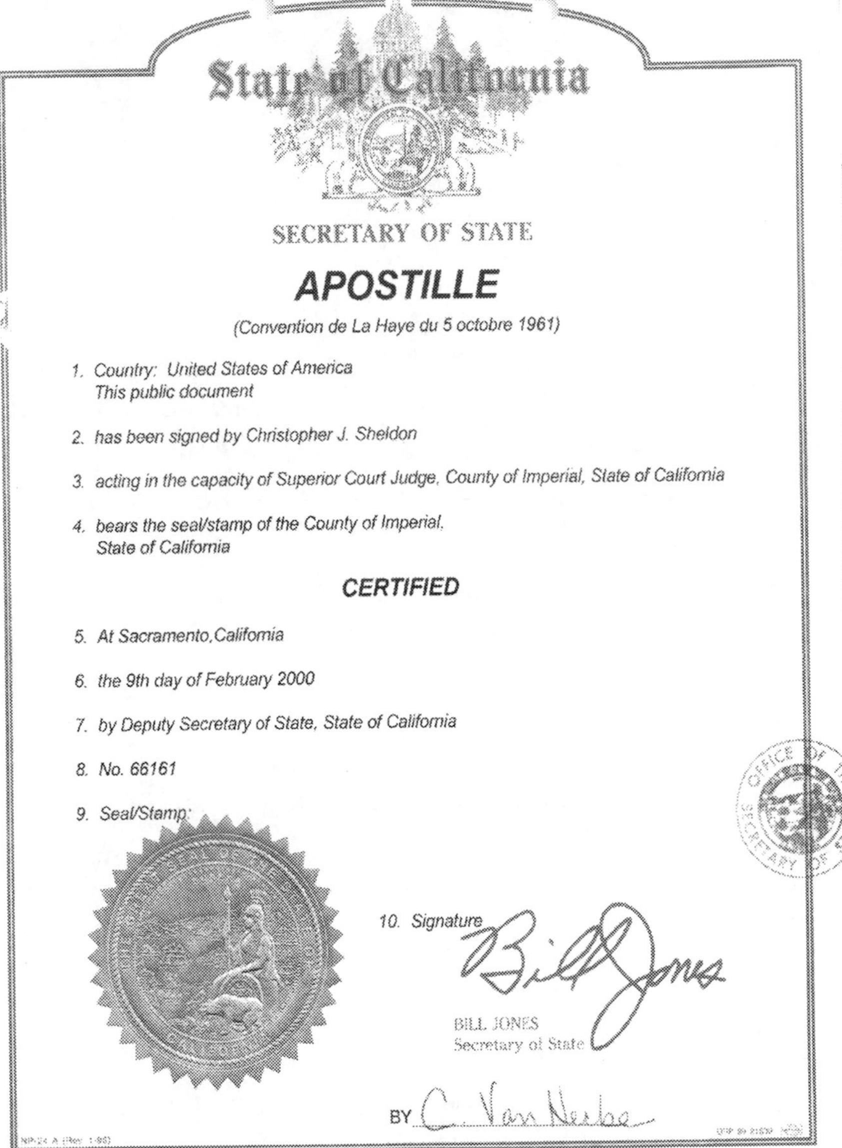

State of California

SECRETARY OF STATE

APOSTILLE

(Convention de La Haye du 5 octobre 1961)

1. Country: United States of America
   This public document
2. has been signed by Christopher J. Sheldon
3. acting in the capacity of Superior Court Judge, County of Imperial, State of California
4. bears the seal/stamp of the County of Imperial, State of California

CERTIFIED

5. At Sacramento,California
6. the 9th day of February 2000
7. by Deputy Secretary of State, State of California
8. No. 66161
9. Seal/Stamp:

10. Signature Bill Jones

BILL JONES
Secretary of State

BY C. Van Nesbo

NP-24 A (Rev. 1-98)

Exhibit Z-110

EXEMPLIFICATION CERTIFICATE

The documents to which this certificate is attached are full, true and correct copies of the originals on file and of record in my office. All of which we have caused by these presents to be exemplified, and the seal of our Superior Court to be hereunto affixed.

IN WITNESS WHEREOF, I have hereto set my hand and affixed the Seal of the said Court,

this 28th day of Jan, ~~19~~ 2000

Clerk - Superior Court

I, Christopher J. Sheldon, Judge of the Superior Court of the State of California, in and for the County of Riverside, do hereby certify that ARTHUR SIMS, whose name is subscribed to the preceding exemplification, is the clerk of the said Superior Court of the State of California, in and for the County of Riverside, and that full faith and credit are due to his official acts. I further certify that the seal affixed to the exemplification is the seal of our said Superior Court, and that the attestation thereof is in due form and according to the form of attestation used in this State.

Date Jan. 28, ~~19~~ 2000

Judge of the Superior Court

Carla Wise
Supervisor –
Indio Superior
Court

28 USCA Sec. 1738
Form No. 634 (r-92)

Exhibit Z-111

By the Bradley-Jefferson: Franks
C/O P.O. Box: 831
Within the city of the McIntosh, [87032]
Within the state of the New Mexico
Within the Union-States of the America
505-468-7474

For the Registrar
Of the International-Court of the Justice
In the Peace-Palace
2517: KJ: At the Hague
In the Netherlands

10/01/2002

International-Gerechtshof
Vredespaleis
Carnegieplein
2517 Den Haag
Netherlands

Registrar,

For the party: Bradley-Jefferson: Franks within this case is with this authorization for the Jeffrey-Glenn: Saiba for the having of the power of the Counsel for the Union-States for the litigation of the case of the Union-States: RR 547 102 300 US and for the having of the power of the Counsel in the International-Court at the Hague. For the authority for the Jeffrey-Glenn: Saiba is with the scope of the power for the acts with the necessity for the completion of the case, for the completion of the financial-transaction, and if necessary, for the locating of the funds of this party.

With the sincerity,

Bradley-Jefferson: Franks

ACKNOWLEDGMENT

FOR THE NOTARY: (name) ________ OF THE STATE OF THE (state) New Mexico IS WITH THE WITNESS WITHIN THE DATE: (date) ________ FOR THE APPEARANCE OF THE ASSEVERANT AND FOR THE COMPLETION [EXECUTION] OF THIS DOCUMENT BY THE ASSEVERANT'S-AUTOGRAPH.
COMMISSION-TERMINATION-DATE: ________

NOTARY PUBLIC

Witness:

Exhibit AA

By the Robert-Joel: Simpson
C/O P.O. Box: 831
Within the city of the McIntosh, [87032]
Within the state of the New Mexico
Within the Union-States of the America
505-460-7474

For the Registrar
Of the International-Court of the Justice
In the Peace-Palace
2517: KJ: At the Hague
In the Netherlands

10/01/2002

International-Gerechtshof
Vredespaleis
Carnegieplein
2517 Den Haag
Netherlands

Registrar,

For the party: Robert-Joel: Simpson within this case is with this authorization for the Jeffrey-Gene: Seiba for the having of the power of the Counsel for the Union-States for the litigation of the case of the Union-States: **RM 547 102 200 US** and for the having of the power of the Counsel in the International-Court at the Hague. For the authority for the Jeffrey-Gene: Seiba is with the scope of the power for the acts with the necessity for the completion of the case, for the completion of the financial-transaction, and if necessary, for the locating of the funds of this party.

With the sincerity,

Robert-Joel: Simpson

ACKNOWLEDGMENT

L.S.

By the Seal

Witnesses:

Exhibit AB

Exhibit AC

Exhibit AD

SENDER: COMPLETE THIS SECTION

- Complete items 1, 2, and 3. Also complete item 4 if Restricted Delivery is desired.
- Print your name and address on the reverse so that we can return the card to you.
- Attach this card to the back of the mailpiece, or on the front if space permits.

1. Article Addressed to:

Jeff : Sciva
For the % 2400 : Dior -Dr.
within the Cedar-Park,
within the Texas
[78613]

COMPLETE THIS SECTION ON DELIVERY

A. Received by (Please Print Clearly) B. Date of Delivery

C. Signature
X
☐ Agent
☐ Addressee

D. Is delivery address different from item 1? ☐ Yes
If YES, enter delivery address below: ☐ No

3. Service Type
☐ Certified Mail ☐ Express Mail
☐ Registered ☐ Return Receipt for Merchandise
☐ Insured Mail ☐ C.O.D.

4. Restricted Delivery? (Extra Fee) ☐ Yes

2. Article Number (Copy from service label) 7001 1940 0006 3998 7042

PS Form 3811, July 1999 Domestic Return Receipt 102595-99-M-1789

Exhibit AE

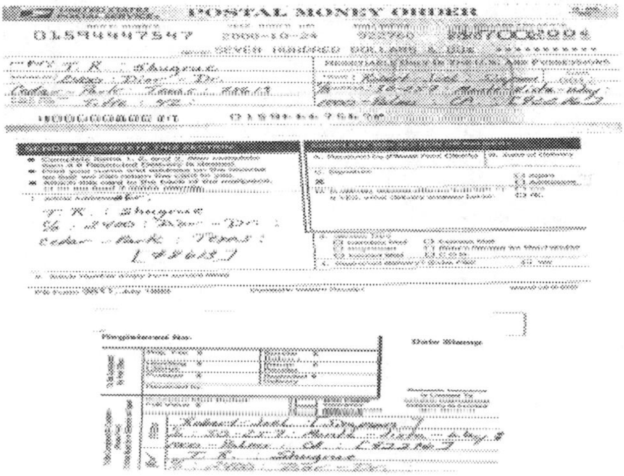

Exhibit AF

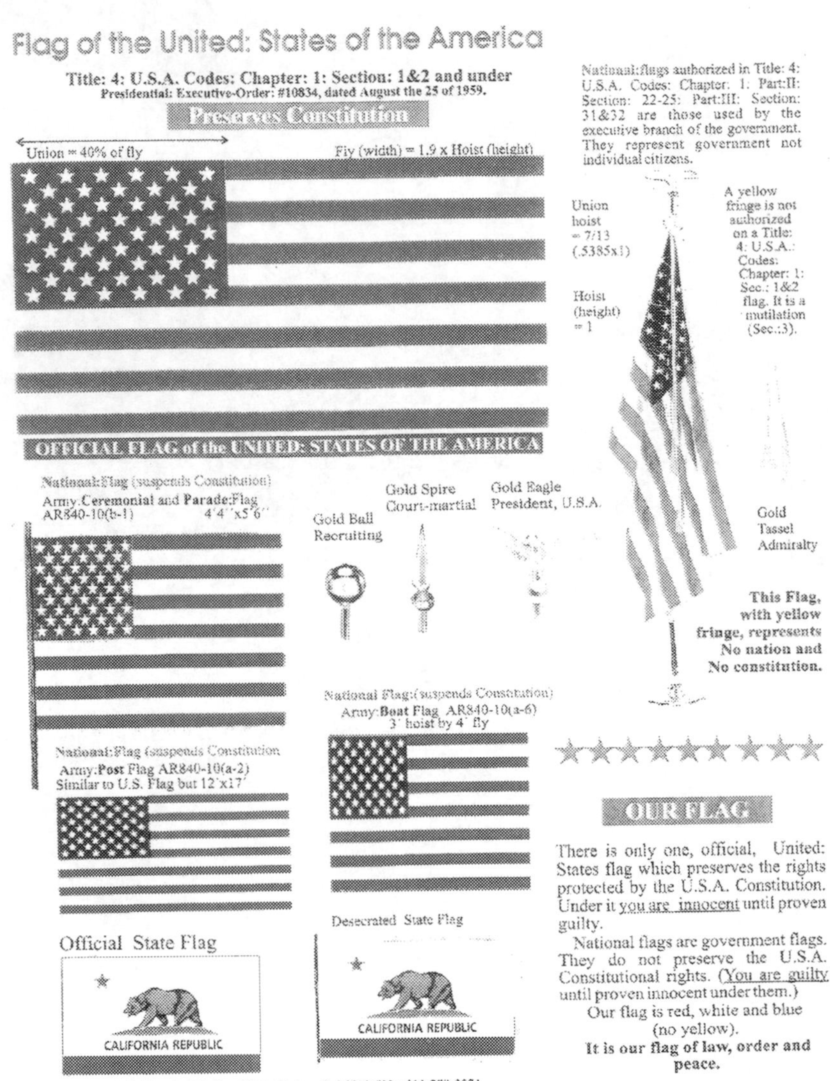
Flag of the United: States of the America
Title: 4: U.S.A. Codes: Chapter: 1: Section: 1&2 and under
Presidential: Executive-Order: #10834, dated August the 25 of 1959.
Preserves Constitution
Union = 40% of fly
Fly (width) = 1.9 x Hoist (height)
OFFICIAL FLAG of the UNITED: STATES OF THE AMERICA
National:flags authorized in Title: 4: U.S.A. Codes: Chapter: 1: Part:II: Section: 22-25: Part:III: Section: 31&32 are those used by the executive branch of the government. They represent government not individual citizens.
Union hoist = 7/13 (.5385x1)
Hoist (height) = 1
A yellow fringe is not authorized on a Title: 4: U.S.A.: Codes: Chapter: 1: Sec.: 1&2 flag. It is a mutilation (Sec.:3).
National:Flag (suspends Constitution)
Army:Ceremonial and Parade:Flag
AR840-10(b-1) 4'4"x5'6"
Gold Ball
Recruiting
Gold Spire
Court-martial
Gold Eagle
President, U.S.A.
Gold
Tassel
Admiralty
This Flag, with yellow fringe, represents No nation and No constitution.
National Flag:(suspends Constitution)
Army:Boat Flag AR840-10(a-6)
3' hoist by 4' fly
National:Flag (suspends Constitution
Army:Post Flag AR840-10(a-2)
Similar to U.S. Flag but 12'x17'
OUR FLAG
There is only one, official, United: States flag which preserves the rights protected by the U.S.A. Constitution. Under it you are innocent until proven guilty.
National flags are government flags. They do not preserve the U.S.A. Constitutional rights. (You are guilty until proven innocent under them.)
Our flag is red, white and blue (no yellow).
It is our flag of law, order and peace.
Official State Flag
CALIFORNIA REPUBLIC
Desecrated State Flag
CALIFORNIA REPUBLIC
Prepared by "B.G. Flags" • P.O. Box 1136 • St. Joseph, MO 64502 • 816-279-2574

Exhibit 1

OFFICE OF THE COUNTY CLERK

County of Torrance

Date 3-21-06 Receipt $50.00

This is to verify that Bradley J. Franks (name of candidate)

P.O. Box 831 (address) McIntosh NM (City), has submitted a

Financial Disclosure Statement, a Declaration of Candidacy, and a Nominating Petition consisting of ______

pages for the office of Magistrate Judge (name of office)

of the Democrat (party affiliation) Party for the Primary Election to be held on June 6, 20__, in New Mexico.

Linda Kayser
COUNTY CLERK

By Linda Kayser

NME-45B (Rev. 2003)

Exhibit 1a: Filing Fee paid

2006 DECLARATION OF CANDIDACY

I, Franks, Bradley J., being first duly sworn,
(candidate's name on certificate of registration)

say that I reside at 15 Maple, as shown by my certificate of registration as a voter of Precinct No. 7 of the county of Torrance, State of New Mexico;

I am a member of the Democratic party as shown by my certificate of registration and I have not changed such party affiliation subsequent to the governor's proclamation calling the primary in which I seek to be a candidate;

I desire to become a candidate for the office of Magistrate Judge District No. ______ at the primary election to be held on the date set by law for this year, and if the office be that of a member of the legislature, of the judiciary, or the state board of education, of the public regulation commission, or district attorney, that I actually reside at the address designated on my certificate of voter registration;

I will be eligible and legally qualified to hold this office at the beginning of its term;

If a candidate for any office for which a nominating petition is required, I am submitting with this statement a nominating petition in the form and manner as prescribed by the Primary Election Law; and

I make the foregoing affidavit under oath, knowing that any false statement herein constitutes a felony punishable under the criminal laws of New Mexico.

STATE OF NEW MEXICO NOTARY PUBLIC (Seal)

Bradley J. Franks
(Declarant)

P.O. Box 831 McIntosh, NM.
(Mailing Address)

15 Maple
(Residence Address)

Subscribed and sworn to before me this 21ST day of March, 2006

Linda Kayser
(Notary Public)

My commission expires: May 22, 2006

(NME43-P2006) (1-8-29 NMSA 1978) (2005) Office of the Secretary of State, 325 Don Gaspar, Ste. 300, Santa Fe, NM 87503 (1-800-477-3632)

Exhibit 1b

Magistrate Criminal Rule 6-201

STATE OF NEW MEXICO

IN THE MAGISTRATE COURT
TORRANCE COUNTY

MAGISTRATE COURT
TORRANCE COUNTY
JUL 11 2007
FILED IN MY OFFICE
CLERK OF MAGISTRATE COURT

STATE OF NEW MEXICO
VS.

NO. M192 MR 200700037

Bradley Franks Defendant(s)
Address: P.O. Box 831
McIntosh, NM 87032-0831

Date Filed: ______

J0843219

DOB: ______ SSN#: ______

CRIMINAL COMPLAINT

Crime: 1 count of Solid Waste, 1 count of Public Nuisance, 1 count Development Review Permit
1 count of Abandoment of Dangerous Containers

(common name of offense or offenses)

The undersigned, under penalty of perjury complains and says that on or about the 21st day of May, 2007 in the County of TORRANCE, State of New Mexico the above-named defendant(s) did

(here state the essential facts):

On or about May 21, 2007 I (Sgt Ledbetter) did a drive by reinspection of the property at #15 Oak Grove at Block 1, Lot 7 in the Oak Grove area in Torrance County. When I arrived I found the following:

1 accumulation of trash, C&D materials and appliances on the property.

2 the addition to the mobile home on the property with no land use permit

3 you notified back in May 2007 as to the need of the clean up of the property and to obtain a land use permit were given time to do so.

90-12-5, 90-3-19 $1000,00 and/or 364 days in Jail.

The conditions have made an unsafe, unhealthy conditions and as well as a fire hazarder to the area. It has also become an endangerment to the wildlife in the area and any/ all persons that may live in the area.

contrary to Section(s): 94-12-5(C), 30-8-1, 90-3-19 (D), 30-8-9 (B) NMSA 1978.

I SWEAR OR AFFIRM UNDER PENALTY OF PERJURY THAT THE FACTS SET FORTH ABOVE ARE TRUE TO THE BEST OF MY INFORMATION AND BELIEF. I UNDERSTAND THAT IT IS A CRIMINAL OFFENSE SUBJECT TO THE PENALTY OF IMPRISONMENT TO MAKE A FALSE STATEMENT IN A CRIMINAL COMPLAINT.

If Probable Cause Determination Required:
Probable Cause Found ______; Not Found ______
(if not found, complaint dismissed & defendant released)
Date: ______
Judge: ______

______
Complainant
Code/Environmental Enforcement
Title

______
Approved if need/Title

This complaint may not be filed without the prior payment of a filing fee, approved by the district attorney or a law enforcement officer authorized to serve an arrest or search warrant. Approval of the district attorney or a law enforcement officer is not otherwise required.

Approved: Supreme Court, October 1, 1974; amended effective September 1, 1990; April 1, 1991; November 1, 1991

Criminal Form 9-201

Exhibit 2a

[5-208, 5-209, 6-204, 6-205, 7-204, 7-205, 8-203, 8-204]

STATE OF NEW MEXICO

IN THE MAGISTRATE COURT — COUNTY OF TORRANCE

State of New Mexico

No. M-192-MR-200700037
Judge assigned: LARRY S JONES

v.

FRANKS BRADLEY, Defendant

FILED IN MAGISTRATE COURT
2007 JUL 11 PM 2 01
TORRANCE COUNTY
MORIARTY, NM

CRIMINAL SUMMONS

To: FRANKS BRADLEY
PO BOX 831
MC INTOSH NM
87032-0831

You are notified that a Complaint, a copy of which is attached hereto, has been filed in this court charging that you committed the offense of :

TORR CO 94-12 TORRANCE CO SOLID WASTE ORD
30-8-1 PUBLIC NUISANCE
TORR CO 90-3-19(D) DEVELOPMENT REVIEW PERMIT
30-8-9 ABANDON DANGEROUS CONTAINERS

You are ordered to appear before the undersigned on **AUGUST 2ND, 2007**, at **10:30AM TRAILING DOCKET** at TORRANCE COUNTY MAGISTRATE COURT, NEIL MERTZ JUDICIAL COMPLEX, 903 N 5TH ST, ESTANCIA NM 87016 in the County of TORRANCE, State of New Mexico, to plead to the above charge(s).

If you fail to appear at the time and place specified, a warrant will be issued for your arrest.

Service of this summons shall be by:MAIL

Dated: July 11, 2007.

JUDGE

CERTIFICATE OF MAILING

I certify that I mailed a copy of the Summons and a copy of the Complaint in the above-styled cause to the defendant at the above address on July 11, 2007.

Dated: July 11, 2007.

CLERK

Exhibit 2b

STATE OF NEW MEXICO

IN THE MAGISTRATE COURT

COUNTY OF TORRANCE

MAGISTRATE COURT TORRANCE COUNTY
AUG - 2 2007
FILED IN MY OFFICE
CLERK OF THE MAGISTRATE COURT

State of New Mexico

No. M192MR200037

vs.

Bradley Franks, Defendant

ORDER TO APPOINT PUBLIC DEFENDER

This matter having come before the court, the court finds:

[ ] 1. The defendant **IS INCARCERATED**.
[X] 2. The defendant **IS NOT INCARCERATED.**
[ ] 3. The defendant **IS INDIGENT AND UNABLE TO OBTAIN COUNSEL**
[X] 4. The defendant **IS NOT INDIGENT BUT IS UNABLE TO OBTAIN COUNSEL**

IT IS HEREBY ORDERED THAT:

[ ] Subject to the application for indigency being completed by the defendant and the defendant being qualified, the public defender shall represent the defendant in the above entitled case.

[ ] If Application for Indigency is not filled out by defendant prior to his release from jail, defendant is ordered to report to the Public Defender's Office at ________ immediately upon release

[X] Andres Benavidez, an attorney on contract with the public defender department shall represent the defendant in the above entitled case.

[X] The defendant shall reimburse the State of New Mexico in an amount of not less than ( ) **$10.00** (X) 300.00 for legal representation and related expenses

IT IS FURTHER ORDERED that the above conditions be complied with as a part of the Defendant's Conditions of Release and a Bench Warrant will be issued should Defendant fail to comply with this order

Dated: 8-2-07

____
Judge

[X] Andres Benavidez
Attorney at Law
2500 Louisiana NE Ste. 224
Albuquerque, NM 87110
(505) 883-4112

[ ] Kathleen Rhinehart
Attorney at Law
P.O. Box 27311
Albuquerque, NM 87125
(505) 243-2100
(505) 315-2187 - cell

[ ] Scott Pistone
Attorney at Law
1022 2nd ST NW
Suite F
Albuquerque, NM 87102
(505) 842-9498

Exhibit 3a

[DISTRICT COURT - MAGISTRATE COURT - METROPOLITAN COURT] (CRIMINAL FORM 9-403)

STATE OF NEW MEXICO

COUNTY OF Torrance

IN THE Magistrate COURT

STATE OF NEW MEXICO,

v.

Bradley Franks

Defendant

NO. M192 MR 2007 00037

ELIGIBILITY DETERMINATION FOR INDIGENT DEFENSE SERVICES

Name: Bradley Franks DOB: 9-14-3 AGE:

AKA: SEX: (Male) Female SSN: 390-90-4996

Address: PO Box 431 McIntosh NM 87032 Phone: 384-1205

Charges: Solid Waste/Public Nuisance

DC#: MC#

Lives Alone: Lives With: Spouse Children Parent X Friend Other

Marital Status: Single X Married Divorced Separated Widowed

Number of Dependents In Household: 2

[X] Defendant is not in jail

[ ] Defendant is in jail

PRESUMPTIVE ELIGIBILITY:

X I currently DO NOT receive public assistance.

___ I currently receive the following type of public assistance in ______ County:
DEPARTMENT OF HEALTH CASE MANAGEMENT SERVICES(DHMS) ______
TANF $____ Food Stamps $____ Medicaid $____ DSI $____ Public Housing $____

MAGISTRATE COURT TORRANCE COUNTY
AUG 02 2007
FILED IN MY OFFICE
CLERK OF MAGISTRATE COURT

NET INCOME	SELF	SPOUSE	(Screening Use Only)
Employer's Name	CNA		
Employer's Phone	384-2711		
Pay Period (weekly, every 2nd week, twice monthly, monthly)	bi-monthly		
Net Take-Home Pay (salary or wages minus deductions as required by law):	$ 950.00	$	
Other Income Sources (please specify):	$	$	
TOTAL ANNUAL INCOME:	$ +	$	=$ ____ A

ASSETS:		SELF	SPOUSE	(Screening Use Only)
CASH ON HAND		$ 0	$	
BANK ACCOUNTS		$ 1200.00	$	
REAL ESTATE	Equity	$ 50,000	$	
MOTOR VEHICLES	Equity	$ 10,500	$	
OTHER PERSONAL PROPERTY (describe):				
______	Equity	$	$	
______	Equity	$	$	
TOTAL ASSETS:		$ +	$	=$ ____ B

EXCEPTIONAL EXPENSES (total exceptional expenses of dependents)		(Screening Use Only)
MEDICAL EXPENSES (not covered by insurance)	$ 0	
COURT-ORDER SUPPORT PAYMENTS/ALIMONY	$ 0	
CHILD-CARE PAYMENTS (e.g., day care)	$ 0	
OTHER (describe): ______	$	
TOTAL EXCEPTIONAL EXPENSES:	$ 0	=$ 0 C

Exhibit 3b

STATE OF NEW MEXICO

COUNTY OF Torrance

This statement is made under oath. I hereby state that the above information regarding my financial condition is correct to the best of my knowledge. I hereby authorize the screening agent, District Defender and the court to obtain information from financial institutions, employers, relatives, the federal internal revenue service and other state agencies.

I UNDERSTAND THAT IF IT IS DETERMINED THAT I AM NOT INDIGENT. I MAY APPEAL TO THE COURT WITHIN TEN (10) DAYS AFTER THE DATE I AM ADVISED OF THIS DECISION.

________ I wish to appeal.

________ I do not wish to appeal.

8-2-07
Date

Bradley J. Franks
Signature of applicant
Dec 1-2007

STATE OF NEW MEXICO)
) ss.
COUNTY OF Torrance)

Signed and sworn to (or affirmed) before me on 8-2-07 (date) by Bradley Franks (name of applicant).

NOTARY PUBLIC
My Commission Expires: With Court

(Seal, if any)

(Screening Use Only)

COLUMN "A" (net income) + COLUMN "B" (assets) (-) COLUMN "C" (exceptional expenses)
equals AVAILABLE FUNDS ....

MAGISTRATE COURT
TORRANCE COUNTY
AUG 0 2 2007
FILED IN MY OFFICE
CLERK OF MAGISTRATE COURT

________ The applicant is indigent.
__X__ The applicant is *not* indigent.
________ The applicant (has) (has not) paid the $10.00 application fee.
Receipt number: ________

Based on the above answers and information, I find that the applicant (is) (is not) indigent.

Signature of Screening Agent

Clerk
Title

(*Complete the following only if the Court has determined that the applicant is unable to pay the application fee*).

________ I find that the applicant is unable to pay the indigency application fee, and I therefore waive the payment of the indigency application fee.

JUDGE or AUTHORIZED DESIGNEE

*(Dependent means any person who qualifies as a dependent of the applicant under Section 152 of the Internal Revenue Code.)

The Public Defender Department is committed to a policy against discrimination based on race, color, religion, national origin, age, sex, ancestry, veteran status, marital status or mental or physical disability.

Supreme Court Approved 8/19/2004

Revised: Effective 11/01/04

Exhibit 3c

[X] Arraignment [ ] First Appearance (FELONY) [X] In Person [ ] Video
Docket No: M192MR200700037 Arresting Officer: LEDBETTER - TCPZ
Defendant : BRADLEY FRANKS DOB: SSN:
Defendant appeared for arraignment or initial appearance before L. Steve Jones, Magistrate, Torrance County, State of New Mexico. Defendant is being charged with the following offense(s) alleged to have happened on or about 05/21/2007

OFFENSE	IN VIOLATION OF	MAX. FINE	MAX. PENALTIES
1. SOLID WASTE ORD	TOR CO 94-12-5	1000	364
2. PUBLIC NUISANCE	30-8-1	500	180
3. DEVELOPMENT REVIEW PERMIT	TOR CO 90-3-19(D)	1000	364
4. ABANDON DANGEROUS CONTAINER	30-8-9(B)	500	180
5.			

Do you understand the charges against you? [✓]YES [ ]NO Do you understand the penalties? [✓]YES [ ]NO
You have the right to bail. you have the right to remain silent. Any statement may be used in Court. You have the right to counsel, retained or appointed by the court. You have the right to a trial by jury. You have the right to cross-examine or confront any witness that appears in front of you or testifies against you.
Do you understand these rights? [✓]YES [ ]NO You have the right to bond.
Do you understand bond? [ ] YES [ ] NO Your bond will be $______ [ ]Cash [ ]Surety [ ]Posted
[✓]Public Defender [ ] Defendant will notify the Court of Attorney within ____ days.

Do you wish to have a trial by jury? (9-401) [ ]YES [ ]NO WAIVERS [ ] YES [ ] NO

Would you like to enter a plea to the charges? (9-502) [✓]YES [ ]NO

[ ] No Contest/Nolo Contendere [ ] Guilty [ ] Not Guilty [✓] No Plea

CLERK: [ ]Pre-trial [✓]Trial [ ]Prelim [ ] Jury Trial [ ] Sentencing

MAGISTRATE COURT TORRANCE COUNTY
AUG - 2 2007
FILED IN MY OFFICE
CLERK OF THE MAGISTRATE COURT

DO YOU SOLEMNLY SWEAR YOU UNDERSTAND THESE PROCEEDINGS? YOU HAVE BEEN ADVISED OF YOUR RIGHTS AND YOUR PLEA WAS OF YOUR OWN FREE ACT AND WILL WITHOUT THREATS OR PROMISES FROM ANYONE IN THIS COURTROOM THIS DATE:
SUBSCRIBED AND SWORN BEFORE ME THIS 2nd DAY OF August 2007

Bradley J. Franks
DEFENDANT MAGISTRATE

THIS SECTION TO BE SIGNED BY INMATE VIEWING ADVISE OF RIGHTS TAPE AT TORRANCE COUNTY DETENTION FACILITY

I DO SOLEMNLY SWEAR THAT ON THIS DAY THE _____ DAY OF _____ 2007, I HAVE VIEWED THE ADVISE OF RIGHTS VIDEO AT THE TORRANCE COUNTY DETENTION CENTER, AND FULLY UNDERSTAND THESE PROCEEDINGS. THE PLEA I HAVE ENTERED WAS OF MY OWN FREE ACT AND WILL, WITHOUT THREATS OR PROMISES FROM ANYONE IN THE TORRANCE COUNTY DETENTION CENTER OR TORRANCE COUNTY MAGISTRATE COURT.

SUBSCRIBED AND SWORN BEFORE ME THIS _____ DAY OF _____ 2007.

DEFENDANT MAGISTRATE JUDGE

CORRECTION OFFICER PRESENT AT VIEWING OF ADVISE OF RIGHTS VIDEO:

______________ SIGNATURE

______________ PRINTED NAME

Exhibit 3d

MAGISTRATE COURT
TORRANCE COUNTY
AUG 16 2007
FILED IN MY OFFICE
CLERK OF THE MAGISTRATE COURT

[5-106, 6-106, 7-106, 8-106]

STATE OF NEW MEXICO

IN THE MAGISTRATE COURT COUNTY OF TORRANCE

State of New Mexico No. M-192-MR-200700037

v.

BRADLEY FRANKS, Defendant

CERTIFICATE OF EXCUSAL OR RECUSAL

I hereby certify that I have **recused myself** from presiding in the above case, and ten (10) days have passed since the parties were notified of such recusal or excusal, and that the parties were notified, and the parties have not filed a stipulation agreeing to another judge of the district to hear the case.

It is requested that another judge be designated according to law.

Dated: August 16, 2007.

Judge

<u>Distribution Instructions</u>
1 copy - Court 1 copy - Defendant 1 copy - Prosecutor
[As amended, effective September 1, 1989; November 1, 1995; May 1, 2002.]

Criminal Form 9-102

Exhibit 4a

[6-504, 7-504, 8-504]

STATE OF NEW MEXICO

IN THE MAGISTRATE COURT

COUNTY OF TORRANCE

State of New Mexico

No. M-192-MR-200700037

v.

BRADLEY FRANKS, Defendant

MAGISTRATE COURT
TORRANCE COUNTY
AUG 09 2007
FILED IN MY OFFICE
CLERK OF MAGISTRATE COURT

BRADLEY FRANKS
C/O CHARLES KNOBLAUCH
1412 LOMAS NW
ALBUQUERQUE NM
87104

SGT. LEDBETTER
TORR. CO. CODE ENFORCEMENT
PO BOX 48
ESTANCIA NM
87016-0048

ORDER FOR PRODUCTION

It appearing to the court that the defendant has requested production of certain tangible evidence in the possession of or available to the prosecution and that good cause exists therefor;

IT IS ORDERED that the prosecution produce for inspection and copying at TORRANCE COUNTY CODE ENFORCEMENT OFFICE, SGT. LEDBETTER, 205 9TH AND ALLEN ST, ESTANCIA, NM at 10:00AM on AUGUST 30TH, 2007, the following records, papers, documents or other tangible evidence in its possession or available to it:
SEE ENCLOSED DEMAND FOR DISCOVERY.

Dated: August 9, 2007.

Judge

(Failure to obey this order may constitute a contempt of court.)

Distribution Instructions
1 copy - Court 1 copy - Defendant 1 copy - Prosecutor

Criminal Form 9-410

Exhibit 5a

CHARLES E. KNOBLAUCH
Attorney at Law

1412 Lomas, N.W. Telephone: (505) 842-0392
Albuquerque, New Mexico 87104 Fax: (505) 842-0686

20 August, 2007

Bradley Franks
P.O. Box 831
McIntosh, NM 87032

RE: *State v. Franks*
No. M-192-MR-200700037

Dear Mr. Franks:

Please accept for your records and information the enclosed Order for Production with regard to the above referenced matter. Please feel free to contact Mr. Knoblauch with any questions or concerns. Thank you.

Best Regards,

S. Rose Schiowitz
Legal Assistant to Charles E. Knoblauch, Esq.

srs/

cc: file

Exhibit 5b

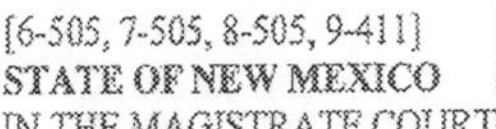

[6-505, 7-505, 8-505, 9-411]
STATE OF NEW MEXICO
IN THE MAGISTRATE COURT COUNTY OF TORRANCE

State of New Mexico No. M-192-MR-200700037

v.

BRADLEY FRANKS, Defendant

NOTICE OF PRETRIAL CONFERENCE

TO: RICHARD LEDBETTER
TORRANCE COUNTY PLANNING & ZONING
P.O. BOX 48
ESTANCIA, NM 87016

CHARLES KNOBLAUCH
ATTORNEY AT LAW
1412 LOMAS NW
ALBUQUERQUE, NM 87104
(Names of parties ordered to appear)

You are ordered to appear for a pretrial conference on the 5TH day of OCTOBER, 2007, at 10:00 AM TRAILING DOCKET, at the MAGISTRATE court located at TORRANCE COUNTY MAGISTRATE COURT, 1100 ROUTE 66, P.O. BOX 2027, MORIARTY, NM 87035, at which time the court will consider such matters that may expedite the disposition of the case.

August 23, 2007 ~~(Judge)~~ (Clerk)

Distribution Instructions
1 copy - Court 1 copy - Defendant 1 copy - Prosecutor
[Supreme Court Approved, September 30, 1994; as amended, effective December 17, 2001.]
-1- Criminal Form 9-411

Exhibit 5c

CHARLES E. KNOBLAUCH
Attorney at Law

1412 Lomas NW
Albuquerque, New Mexico 87104

Telephone: (505) 842-0392
FAX: (505) 842-0686

OFFICIAL FAX COVER SHEET

DATE: 17 September, 2007

TO: Bradley Franks

FAX NUMBER: (505) 384-0305

FROM: S. Rose Schiowitz, Legal Assistant to Charles E. Knoblauch, Esq.

PAGES, INCLUDING COVER SHEET: 1

RE: *State v. Franks*
Case No. M-192-MR-200700037

Dear Mr. Franks;

I would like to give you an update on your case. Sgt. R. A. Ledbetter has agreed to dismiss your case if you comply with the following conditions:

1. Obtain a building permit from Torrance County and the State of New Mexico
   a. This requires that you provide the following:
      i. Warranty deed or Real Estate Contract
      ii. State Building Permit
      iii. State Solid Waste Permit
      iv. Pay $200 application fee
      v. Development Plans
   b. Arrange for an inspector to come out to the property and approve the structure in question

2. Remove all junk materials, C&D materials and trash from the property
3. Bring property taxes up to date

If you complete the above mentioned conditions your case will be dismissed. Your alternative is taking your case to trial.
Thank you.

Best Regards,
S. Rose Schiowitz

Exhibit 5d

Sep. 17. 2007 11:55AM Lomas Law Office's No. 5550 P. 5

Torrance County Planning & Zoning
(Structure) Development Permit
P.O. Box 48, Estancia, NM 87016
Ph: (505) 246-4759 Fax (505) 384-5294

Control # ____________________ Date ____________

In accordance with Section 19.D of the Torrance County Zoning Ordinance, no building shall be constructed, nor mobile home installed, within the jurisdiction of Torrance County without first obtaining a Development Permit from the Torrance County Zoning Office. This form must be completed prior to occupancy or use of any building or mobile home. An administrative fee of $250.00 (per unit) shall be paid prior to issuance of this permit.

If not, under Section 19.E, you can be fined up to $1,000.00 and/or sentenced to 364 days imprisonment on each building or mobile home.

This Permit Expires one year from today's date. If construction has not been initiated by the one year expiration date, you will need to reapply.

The following documents to must accompany this application:

Warranty deed or Real Estate Contract ✓ **EVSWA pay Stub** ___
Proof of Water System or State Well Permit ___ **State Liquid Waste Permit** ___
State Building Permit ✓

The aforementioned site for a structure is in compliance with The Torrance County Zoning Ordinances and is the only dwelling on the property listed below

Signature of Owner or Agent: ______________________

Property Legal Description

Section ___; T__N; R__E; Tract____, Lands of ______________
Subdivision OAK GROVE Lot 7/8; Block 1; Unit 15

County Assessor Approval ______________ ID# ________

County Treasurer Approval ______________

Rural Address Approval ______________; Address is ____________

Please print name, mailing address, & phone #

Owner's Name BRADLEY FRANKS Home phone # (505) 384-1305

Mailing Address P.O. Box 831, McIntosh NM 87032

Zoning Approval ______________ Date ____________ Rev; 9/7/05

Exhibit 5e

Sep. 17. 2007 11:55AM Lomas Law Office's No. 5550 P. 2

Multi-Purpose State Building Application

State of New Mexico		Regulation and Licensing Department		Construction Industries Division	
Albuquerque Office	5200 Oakland Ave., NE	I-25 @Alameda	Albuquerque, New Mexico 87113	Phone: (505) 222-9800	Fax: (505) 765-5670
Las Cruces Office	505 S. Main St., Ste 150	P.O. Box 939	Las Cruces, New Mexico 88004-0939	Phone: (505) 524-6320	Fax: (505) 524-6319
Santa Fe Office	2550 Cerrillos Road		Santa Fe, New Mexico 87504	Phone: (505) 476-4700	Fax: (505) 476-4685

Date Issued: ______ Processed By: ______ TRACKING/Permit Number: ______

Received By: Mail (A / R) ______ Paid By: Cash Receipt #: ______ Check #: ______ Total Fees $ ______

Walk – In (A / R) ______ Cash Receipt #: ______ Check #: ______ Balance Due $ ______

Please check the appropriate type for which you are applying:

☑ Building Permit ☐ Residential ☐ Commercial ☐ Pre-Bid ☐ Electrical Review Only ☐ Mechanical/Plumbing Review Only

Type of Construction: I | II | III | IV | V | A | B Total Sq Ft. ______

Occupancy Group: A | B | E | F | H | I | M | R | S | U Valuation / Sign Contract $ ______

Division: 1 | 2 | 3 | 4 | 5

Description of Work:

☐ New Construction ☐ Addition ☐ Alterations/Repairs ☐ Re-Roof ☐ Foundation Only ☐ Demolition ☐ Renew Permit # ______

☐ Wood ☐ Masonry ☐ Adobe ☐ Rammed Earth ☐ Alternative Material ______

☐ Metal / Steel (required Engineer STAMPED foundation & structure drawings ☐ Baled Straw (required Architectural STAMPED) ☐ Other: (required Architectural STAMPED)

PLEASE PROVIDE THE FOLLOWING INFORMATION (Refer to the BUILDING PERMIT GUIDE or call for addition information):

Parcel No. and/or Project Address (must provide physical address) | Nearest City/Town/Village to project | Zip Code | County

Subdivision Name | Lot Number | Township | Range | Section

Provide Written Directions to the project site:

Contractor Information:

Company Name: | NM State License Number

Address-No. & Street/PO Box/Rural Route | City | State | Zip Code | Phone

Property Owner or Homeowner Information:

BRADLEY FRANKS

Name:

Address-No. & Street/PO Box/Rural Route | City | State | Zip Code | Phone

Design Professional Information:

Professional Name or Firm: | NM State License Number

Address-No. & Street/PO Box/Rural Route | City | State | Zip Code | Phone

PLEASE READ AND SIGN THE FOLLOWING: (Contractors or Homeowner)

I hereby acknowledge by my signature below that I have read this application and state that the above is correct. I agree to comply with the requirements of the New Mexico Building Code. I waive my right to require any inspector to possess a search warrant before they enter the premises to inspect the building covered by this permit. However, I waive this right only on the following conditions: The inspector must be approved by the Construction Industries Division and this inspection must be made at reasonable times for purpose of determining whether the work of building or structure on the premises complies with the New Mexico Building Code. I understand that the issuance of this permit shall not prevent the Construction Industries Division from requiring compliance with the provisions of the New Mexico Building Code.

X ______ Date: ______

OFFICIAL USE ONLY

PLANING/ZONNING APPROVED BY: Signature Date

FLOOD PLAIN APPROVED BY: Signature Date

PERMIT APPROVED BY Signature Date

UPC APPROVED BY: Signature Date

NEC APPROVED BY: Signature Date

Revised 12/01/05

Exhibit 5f

Sep. 17. 2007 11:34AM Lomas Law Office s No. 3320 P. 1

CHARLES E. KNOBLAUCH

Attorney at Law

1412 Lomas NW
Albuquerque, New Mexico 87104

Telephone: (505) 842-0392
FAX: (505) 842-0686

OFFICIAL FAX COVER SHEET

DATE: 17 September, 2007

TO: Bradley Franks

FAX NUMBER: (505) 384-0305

FROM: S. Rose Schiowitz, Legal Assistant to Charles E. Knoblauch, Esq.

PAGES, INCLUDING COVER SHEET: 26

RE: *State v. Franks*
Case No. M-192-MR-200700037

Dear Mr. Franks:

Please be advised that due to your failure to cooperate with this office concerning your building permit we are unable to assist you in obtaining said permit. Attached is the information and proper forms required to complete the building permit, so you may proceed if you so desire. Also attached are the photos you requested. Thank you.

Best Regards,

S. Rose Schiowitz

Note: **This facsimile letter is intended for the recipient only and contains information that is legally privileged and confidential. If you are not the intended recipient, you are hereby notified that any disclosure, copying, distribution or the taking of any action in reliance on the contents of this telecopied information is strictly prohibited. If you have received this telecopy in error, please immediately notify us by telephone to arrange for return of the original documents to us.**

Exhibit 5g

PHONE CALL

FOR ________ DATE 8/27 TIME 10 A.M. P.M.

M Bradley Franks

OF

PHONE/MOBILE ________ FAX

MESSAGE C.C.

4107 0515 2628 4168

ex. 03/09

$350

SIGNED

- [ ] TELEPHONED
- [ ] RETURNED YOUR CALL
- [ ] PLEASE CALL
- [ ] WILL CALL AGAIN
- [ ] CAME TO SEE YOU
- [ ] WANTS TO SEE YOU

TIMOTHY PADILLA & ASSOCIATES
1412 LOMAS BLVD NW
ALBUQUERQUE NM 87104
505 [illegible]

Phone Order

ID: [illegible]
Merchant: [illegible]
08/28/0[illegible] 11:[illegible]
AVS Code:
VISA
XXXXXXXXXXXX[illegible]
CVV2 Code: P
Appr Code: [illegible] Inv#: 1

Total: $ 350.00

Customer Copy

Exhibit 5h: Payment for Attorney.

IN THE MAGISTRATE COURT
COUNTY OF TORRENCE
STATE OF NEW MEXICO

STATE OF NEW MEXICO,
Plaintiff,

vs. No. M-192-MR-200700037

BRADLEY FRANKS,
Defendant,

MOTION TO WITHDRAW AS COUNSEL

COMES NOW the undersigned and Moves the Court to enter an Order allowing him to withdraw as counsel. As grounds for this Motion, the undersigned states:

1. That Defendant has contacted the Disciplinary Board concerning defense counsel, Charles E. Knoblauch, on 26 September, 2007;
2. That the Defendant's actions have strained the relationship between Defendant and his counsel to such a degree so as to create a conflict of interest;
3. That the Defendant's actions also makes effective representation impossible;
4. That, under the circumstances, it would be unethical for counsel to continue his representation of the Defendant;
5. That Sergeant R.A. Ledbetter does not object to this Motion.

WHEREFORE, the undersigned respectfully requests that this Court enter an Order of Withdrawal in this Matter.

Charles E. Knoblauch
1412 Lomas Blvd. NW
Albuquerque, NM 87104
(505) 842-0392

Exhibit 5i

I hereby certify that a true and accurate copy of the foregoing was dispatched to all parties of interest this 9 day of October, 2007.

Charles E. Knoblauch

Exhibit 5i: continued

CHARLES E. KNOBLAUCH
Attorney at Law

1412 Lomas, N.W. Telephone: (505) 842-0392
Albuquerque, New Mexico 87104 Fax: (505) 842-0686

10 October, 2007

Bradley Franks
P.O. Box 831
McIntosh, NM 87032

RE: *State v. Franks*
No. M-192-MR-200700037

Dear Mr. Franks:

Please accept for your records and information the enclosed Motion to Withdraw as Counsel with regard to the above referenced matter. Thank you.

Best Regards,

S. Rose Schiowitz
Legal Assistant to Charles E. Knoblauch, Esq.

srs/

cc: file

Exhibit 5j

STATE OF NEW MEXICO

IN THE MAGISTRATE COURT　　　　COUNTY OF TORRANCE

State of New Mexico　　　　No. M-192-MR-200700037

v.

BRADLEY FRANKS, Defendant

MAGISTRATE COURT
TORRANCE COUNTY
OCT 12 2007
FILED IN MY OFFICE
CLERK OF THE MAGISTRATE COURT

NOTICE OF REVIEW HEARING

TO: RICHARD LEDBETTER Prosecution[i]
TORRANCE COUNTY PLANNING & ZONING
P.O. BOX 48
ESTANCIA, NM 87016

BRADLEY FRANKS Defendant
P.O. BOX 831
MCINTOSH, NM 87032-0831

YOU ARE ordered to appear for **REVIEW HEARING** before the Honorable THOMAS G PESTAK, at the MAGISTRATE Court located at TORRANCE COUNTY MAGISTRATE COURT, 1100 ROUT 66, P..O. BOX 2027, MORIARTY, NM 87035 on November 16, 2007 at 10:00 **(a.m.) TRAILING DOCKET.**

If you fail to appear a warrant may be issued for your arrest.

Date of this notice:

Dated: October 12, 2007.

~~(Judge)~~ (Clerk)

Distribution Instructions
1 copy - Court　1 copy - Defendant　1 copy - Prosecutor
[As amended, effective January 1, 1995; May 1, 2002.]

Criminal Form 9-501

Exhibit 5k

STATE OF NEW MEXICO

IN THE MAGISTRATE COURT COUNTY OF TORRANCE

State of New Mexico No. M-192-MR-200700037

v.

BRADLEY FRANKS, Defendant

MAGISTRATE COURT
TORRANCE COUNTY
OCT 1 2 2007
FILED IN MY OFFICE
CLERK OF THE MAGISTRATE COURT

-AMENDED-

NOTICE OF REVIEW HEARING

TO: RICHARD LEDBETTER Prosecution[1]
TORRANCE COUNTY PLANNING & ZONING
P.O. BOX 48
ESTANCIA, NM 87016

BRADLEY FRANKS Defendant
P.O. BOX 831
MCINTOSH, NM 87032-0831

YOU ARE ordered to appear for **REVIEW HEARING** before the Honorable THOMAS G PESTAK, at the MAGISTRATE Court located at TORRANCE COUNTY MAGISTRATE COURT, 1100 ROUT 66, P..O. BOX 2027, MORIARTY, NM 87035 on November 16, 2007 at 8:30 (a.m.) **TRAILING DOCKET.**

If you fail to appear a warrant may be issued for your arrest.

Date of this notice:

Dated: October 12, 2007.

(Judge) (Clerk)

Distribution Instructions
1 copy - Court 1 copy - Defendant 1 copy - Prosecutor
[As amended, effective January 1, 1995; May 1, 2002.]

Criminal Form 9-501

Exhibit 5l

Torrance County
PO Box 48
205 9th Street
Estancia, NM 87016
(505) 246-4725 Main Line (505) 384-5294 Fax
www.torrancecountynm.org
Email: torrance@torrancecountynm.org

County Commission

Jim Frost
Chairman
District 1

Paul M. (Tito) Chavez
Commissioner
District 2

LeRoy M. Candelaria
Commissioner
District 3

County Manager's Office

Bob Ayre
County Manager

Annette Ortiz
Executive Assistant

Crystal Bostwick
Clerical Assistant

Finance Department

Tracy Sedillo
Comptroller

Liz Lujan
Financial Analyst

Emergency Services

Shirley Whatley
Emergency Services Director

Emergency Manager

Gary Kayser

Planning & Zoning

Louise Marquez
Planning & Zoning Director

Richard Ledbetter
Code Enforcement

Rural Addressing

Sandy Hart

Information Technology

Steffen Daugherty
Network Administrator

Nick E. Sedillo
Network Administrator

Land Use Permit Resources

1. **Septic Permit** – Obtained from the State Environment Department located at 5500 San Antonio NE, Albuquerque (505) 222-9500

2. **Well Permit** – Obtained from the State Engineer's Office located at 121 Tijeras NE, Suite 2000 in the Springer Square Building, Albuquerque (505) 764-3888

3. **Mobile Home Information** – Registration/Title information available at Department of Motor Vehicles. Manufacturer Certificate of Origin will be available from dealer you purchase the home from.

4. **Mobile Home Placement & Setup Permit** – Obtained from the State Manufactured Housing Authority located at 5200 Oakland NE, Albuquerque (505) 222-9870

5. **Structure Permit** – We will need to approve a set of plans. Then you will to take the approved set and a second copy to the Construction Industries Division for approval in Albuquerque at 5200 Oakland NE. (505) 222-9800

6. **Real Estate Contract or Warranty Deed** – Obtained from the Torrance County Clerk's Office, if you don't already possess a copy. (505) 246-4735

7. **Estancia Valley Solid Waste Authority** – Evidence that arrangements have been made for trash (solid waste) obtained at the EVSWA office at 515 Allen, Estancia, (505) 384-4270

8. **Floodplain** – If the proposed development is within the 100 Year Floodplain, a Floodplain Development Permit application and Elevation Certificate must be completed and submitted in order for Torrance County to issue a permit.

9. **Road Department** – Questions regarding road building requirements, culverts for driveways, etc., contact the Torrance County Road Dept. at (505) 246-4763.

10. **The Permit Fee** – The fee for a permit (Structure - $250/Mobile Home - $150) can be paid by check, money order, or cash.

11. **Necessary Torrance County Department Approvals** – The Treasurer's office and the Assessor's office must sign off on the application before it can be approved. They can be reached respectively at Treasurer's (505) 246-4787 and Assessor's (505) 246-4727.

12. **Rural Address** – Rural Address will be issued as part of the permitting process. Rural Addressing can be reached at (505) 246-4768.

We hope that this information is helpful to you in accomplishing your project. Please feel free to contact the Planning & Zoning Office if you need further assistance.

"It is one of the most beautiful compensations of life, which no man can sincerely try to help another without helping himself."
Ralph Waldo Emerson

Received Time Sep. 11. 1:42PM

Exhibit 6a

NOV. 17. 2007 11:09AM LOBAS LAW OFFICE S NO. 2330 P. 2

BUILDING PERMIT GUIDE FOR RESIDENTIAL CONSTRUCTION

State of New Mexico Regulation and Licensing Department Construction Industries Division

Albuquerque Office:	5200 Oakland Ave. NE	I-25 @ Alameda	Albuquerque, New Mexico 87113	(505) 222-9801 FAX (505) 765-5670
Las Cruces Office:	505 S. Main Ste. 150	P.O. Box 939	Las Cruces, New Mexico 88004-0939	(505) 524-6320 FAX (505) 524-6319
Santa Fe Office:	2550 Cerrillos Rd.	P.O. Box 25101	Santa Fe, New Mexico 87504	(505) 476-4700 FAX (505) 476-4685

WHEN BUILDING PERMITS ARE REQUIRED

(NEW MEXICO BUILDING CODE SECTION 106.1)

Except as specified in Section 106.2, no building or structure regulated by this code shall be erected, constructed, enlarged, altered, repaired, moved, improved, removed, converted or demolished unless a permit has first been obtained from the building official.

WHEN BUILDING PERMITS ARE NOT REQUIRED

(NEW MEXICO BUILDING CODE SECTION 106.2)

A building permit shall not be required for the following.

1. One story detached accessory buildings used as tool and storage sheds, playhouses, and similar uses, provided the floor area does not exceed 200 square feet.
2. Fences not over 6 feet high.
3. Oil derricks.
4. Movable cases, counters and partitions not over 5 feet 9 inches high.
5. Retaining walls that are not over 4 feet in height measured form the bottom of the footing to the top of the wall, unless supporting a surcharge or impounding Class I, II or III-A liquids.
6. Water tanks supported directly upon grade if the capacity does not exceed 5,000 gallons and the ratio of height to diameter or width does not exceed 2:1.
7. Platforms, walks and driveways not more than 30 inches above grade and not over any basement or story below.
8. Painting, papering and similar finish work.
9. Temporary motion picture, television and theater stage sets and scenery.
10. Window awnings supported by an exterior wall or Group R, Division 3, and Group U Occupancies when projecting not more than 54 inches.
11. Prefabricated swimming pools accessory to a Group R, Division 3 Occupancy in which the pool walls are entirely above the adjacent grade and if the capacity does not exceed 5,000 gallons.
12. Any work which is not otherwise regulated by specific provisions of this code.

Note: **Unless otherwise exempted, separate plumbing, electrical and mechanical permits will be required for the above-exempted items.**

SEPTIC TANK PERMIT

Obtain a PERMIT TO MODIFY OR INSTALL AN INDIVIDUAL LIQUID WASTE SYSTEM form from your local New Mexico Environment Department Office. Call 1-800-219-6157 for the nearest location.

PERMIT APPLICATION DATA

To obtain a building permit, the applicant shall fill out an APPLICATION for STATE BUILDING PERMIT form. Applicant must list property owner's name and address, contractor's company name, address and license number (if applicable), architect's name, address and license number (if applicable), specific use of building, county in which the project is located, project address, nearest city/town/village, legal description, written directions to the site, description of work, construction material, and total square footage. The licensed contractor requesting the permit or the homeowner requesting a homeowner construction permit must sign the application. The homeowner must <u>also</u> sign before a notary the AFFIDAVIT FOR HOMEOWNER CONSTRUCTION PERMIT at bottom of the application.

The homeowner must also read and sign the HOMEOWNER'S RESPONSIBILITIES FOR BUILDING A HOME OR FOR ALTERATIONS, REPAIRS OR IMPROVEMENTS TO A HOME WITH A HOMEOWNER'S PERMIT form. ***If the homeowner hires a licensed contractor to perform any portion of the work on the residence, the contractor must apply for a permit for that portion of the work.*** A homeowner may not perform electrical, plumbing or mechanical work unless the homeowner applies for and passes the required CID exam for such work. Call (505) 476-4869 for information on the homeowner electrical and plumbing permits process.

ZONING APPROVAL

Your project may be located in an area requiring zoning approval from a city or county zoning authority. You must obtain zoning approval and signature on the APPLICATION for STATE BUILDING PERMIT before applying to this office for the building permit. Contact the Construction Industries Division for zoning requirements in your area.

VALUATION AND FEES

- **Valuation of your project is based CID Rules New Mexico Administrative code 14.5.5.10 . The project does need the <u>signed contract</u> between the project owner and contractor. If you are applying for a homeowner construction permit, the Division will calculate the valuation based on established valuation tables in our office. The fee, which covers plan review, the permit notice and required inspections, is based on the valuation amount. <u>Our office will calculate the valuation and fee for you. If you are mailing the application and plans to your nearest CID office, call any of the offices listed above for the fee prior to mailing.</u>**

PLAN SUBMISSION

Two complete sets of plans at 1/8" = 1'-0 minimum with dimensions, on at least 8 ½ "x 11" paper is required and will provide the following information:

1. ___ **SITE PLAN.** Show proposed new structures and any existing buildings or structures on site, including existing <u>adjacent</u> structures within 10 feet of any adjacent property lines, and north arrow. Show property lines with dimensions, all streets, easements and setbacks. Show all water, sewer, electrical points of connection, proposed service routes and existing utilities on the site. Show general drainage and grading information.
2. ___ **FOUNDATION PLAN.** Indicate size, location and depth below grade of all footings, piers, and stem walls. *If necessary, provide a geotechnical report, including soil-bearing capacity for the proposed structure at the site*
3. ___ **FLOOR PLAN.** Show all floors including basement. Label all the rooms and provide overall dimensions. Show all doors and windows. Provide door and window schedules. Locate smoke detection systems.
4. ___ **FLOOR & ROOF FRAMING PLANS.** Show size, spacing and spans of joists, girders, rafters, beams and headers. Specify grade and species of all wood members. All wood trusses must be engineered and pre-manufactured. The sealed truss engineered specifications must be submitted with the drawings when applying for permit. The manufacturer's instructions on placement and attachment of all wood trusses must be at the job site for the building inspector's review.
5. ___ **DETAILS.** Include typical interior and exterior wall sections showing floor, wall and ceiling type, size, spacing and insulation required by the Model Energy Code. Show footing and foundation depth and dimensions; detail anchor bolt size and spacing, and spacing of steel reinforcement in masonry, concrete footings and stem walls. Show stair details showing dimensions of rise and run of steps, handrail location, guardrail spacing, headroom, etc. Show fireplace details and section showing masonry reinforcement; if using pre-fabricated unit, the manufacturer's installation instructions must be at the job site for the building inspector's review and uses.
6. ___ **TOTAL SQUARE FOOTAGE.** List the heated, garage, carport, covered porch and patio square footage on your plans. The total floor area square footage must be listed on the APPLICATION for STATE BUILDING PERMIT.
7. ___ **MODEL ENERGY CODE.** A package explaining and detailing Model Energy Code requirements, including sample worksheets, is available, as well as one page compliance sheets for your area.

Revised 5/1/2006 Building Permit Guide for Residential Construction Page 1 of 2

Exhibit 6b

SPECIAL CONDITIONS

1. __ADDITIONS. In addition to the above requirements, the floor plan shall show the addition and all existing rooms, doors and windows that will adjoin the addition. Provide distances on all sides of the addition to property lines and existing structures. Ensure that an existing sleeping room's safe means of egress to the exterior is not blocked by the addition.

2. __ALTERATION/REPAIR. When performing alterations and repairs to an existing residence without performing structural changes, two sets of lists outlining work to be performed and materials to be used will be accepted in lieu of the above requirements. If you suspect this work will entail the handling of asbestos containing materials, call the Air Pollution Control Bureau at 1-800-224-7009 prior to commencing alterations and repairs for additional information.

3. __RELOCATED RESIDENCE. When relocating an existing residence to new site, the structure will be considered new construction and must comply with all current applicable codes. Submittal shall reflect all the requirements listed under PLAN SUBMITTAL above.

4. __DEMOLITION. Two site plans identifying the structure(s) to be demolished will be accepted in lieu of the above requirements. If you suspect this work will entail the handling of asbestos containing materials, call the Air Pollution Control Bureau at 1-800-224-7009 prior to commencing alterations and repairs for additional information.

5. __ALTERNATIVE METHODS AND MATERIALS. Utilizing alternative methods and materials (other than masonry, wood frame, adobe and rammed earth construction) requires submission of the CERTIFICATION FOR ALTERNATIVE METHODS AND MATERIALS form with the application for state building permit. The certification shall be recorded with the county clerk's office in the county where your project is located.

REQUIRED INSPECTIONS

A 48-hour notice is required prior to inspection. Your Construction Inspector's name and telephone number will appear on the Building Permit Notice. The contractor or homeowner builder must call the assigned inspector for each of the following phases of construction:

1. **FOUNDATION INSPECTION.** To be made after excavations for footings are complete and any required reinforcing steel is in place. For concrete foundations, any required forms shall be in place prior to inspection. All materials for the foundation shall be on the job, except where concrete is ready mixed in accordance with approved nationally recognized standards, the concrete need not be on the job. Where the foundation is to be constructed of approved treated wood, additional inspections may be required by the building official.
2. **CONCRETE SLAB or UNDER-FLOOR INSPECTION.** To be made after all in-slab or under-floor building service equipment, conduit, piping accessories and other ancillary equipment items are in place, but before any concrete is placed or floor sheathing installed, including the subfloor.
3. **FRAME INSPECTION.** To be made after the roof, all framing, fire blocking and bracing is in place and all pipes, chimneys and vents are complete and the rough electrical, plumbing, and heating wires, pipes and ducts are approved.
4. **WEATHER-RESISTIVE BARRIER INSPECTION.** To be made after installation of the appropriate weather-resistive barrier and before such barrier is covered.
5. **FINAL INSPECTION.** To be made after finish grading and the building is completed and ready for occupancy. Final electrical, plumbing and mechanical inspections must be conducted prior to final general construction inspection. The Construction Inspector will issue the Certify of Occupancy to the contractor after approving final general construction inspection.
6. **OTHER INSPECTIONS.** In addition to the called inspections specified above, the Construction Inspector may make or require other inspections of any construction work to ascertain compliance with provisions of the New Mexico Building Code and other laws which are enforced by the code enforcement agency. The licensed plumber and electrician performing the work under the appropriate permits are responsible for coordinating plumbing, mechanical and electrical inspections.

WHEN PROFESSIONAL SEALS ARE NOT REQUIRED

(NEW MEXICO BUILDING CODE SECTION 106.3.2)

The requirement for plans and specifications to be prepared by an architect and/or engineer shall not be required of the following unless, at the discretion of the building official, exception is not in the best interest of public safety or health:

A. Single-family dwelling not more than two stories in height.
B. Multiple dwellings not more than two stories in height containing not more than four dwelling units of wood-frame construction and provided this paragraph is not construed to allow a person who is not an architect to design multiple clusters of four dwelling units each where the total exceeds four dwelling units on each lawfully divided lot.
C. Garages or other structures not more than two stories in height which are appurtenant to buildings described in paragraphs A or B of this Section.
D. Group A, B, E, divisions 1 and 2, F, M, S, U buildings or additions having a total occupant load of ten or less (as defined in Section 1003.2.2 and Table 10-A) and not more than two stories in height.
E. Alterations to buildings or structures that present no unusual condition or hazards or change in occupancy.

WHEN PROFESSIONAL SEALS ARE REQUIRED

The Construction Industries Division requires, as provided under NMBC Section 106.3.3, plans and specifications for the following construction methods be prepared and sealed by a New Mexico Registered Architect or Engineer:

1. Construction utilizing steel studs, structural steel members (red iron) and/or steel pipe.
2. All prefabricated, premanufactured and component structures.
3. Residential construction utilizing a wood foundation.
4. All retaining walls over four feet in height, measured from the bottom of the footing to the top of the wall.
5. A second story addition to an existing first story (unless proof of previous CID approval shows current construction will support additional second story load).
6. Residential construction utilizing an alternate material, design or method in construction.

CERTIFICATE OF OCCUPANCY

No building or structure shall be used or occupied, and no change in the existing occupancy classification of a building or structure or portion thereof shall be made until the building official has issued a certification of occupancy as provided.

APPLICABLE CODES

The Construction Industries Division currently enforces the following codes:

- 2003 New Mexico Commercial & Residential Building Code
- 2003 International Building Code
- 2003 International Residential Code
- 1997 Solar Energy Code (IAPMO)
- 2003 NM Energy Conservation Code
- ICC/ANSI A117.1-1998
- 2003 New Mexico Plumbing and Mechanical Code
- 2003 Uniform Mechanical Code (IAPMO)
- 2003 Uniform Plumbing Code (IAPMO)
- 1997 Uniform Swimming Pool, Spa and Hot Tub Code
- 2005 New Mexico Electrical Code
- 2005 National Electrical Code
- 2002 National Electrical Safety Code
- Liquefied Petroleum Gas Standards
  - 2004 NFPA 58
  - 1999 NFPA 57
  - 2002 NFPA 54
  - 1998 NFPA 52
  - 1999 NFPA 1192

CONSTRUCTION INDUSTRIES DIVISION WEB SITE

CID has developed a new information web site with "view only" information at WWW.STATE.NM.US/RLD/CID. This site includes information of interest to consumers, business and the regulated community.

CONTRACTOR LICENSE LOOK-UP

A license "view only" web site has been developed at WWW.CONTRACTORSNM.COM. This site includes the names, addresses and telephone numbers of licensed contractors and their license classification. It also includes information on licensing and required qualifications for license examination.

MANUFACTURED HOMES

Contact the Manufactured Housing Division, located within the CID office, at 505-476-4770 for guidance on additions, alterations and repairs to manufactured homes.

Revised 5/1/2006 Building Permit Guide for Residential Construction Page 2 of 2

Exhibit 6c

TITLE 14 HOUSING AND CONSTRUCTION
CHAPTER 5 CONSTRUCTION INDUSTRIES GENERAL PROVISIONS
PART 2 PERMITS

14.5.2.1 ISSUING AGENCY: The Construction Industries Division of the Regulation and Licensing Department.
[14.5.2.1 NMAC - Rp, 14.5.2.1 NMAC, 7-1-04]

14.5.2.2 SCOPE: This rule applies to all contracting work performed in New Mexico on or after July 1, 2004, that is subject to the jurisdiction of CID, unless performed pursuant to a permit for which an application was received by CID before that date.
[14.5.2.2 NMAC - Rp, 14.5.2.2 NMAC, 7-1-04]

14.5.2.3 STATUTORY AUTHORITY: NMSA 1978 Sections 60-13-9 and 60-13-45.
[14.5.2.3 NMAC - Rp, 14.5.2.3 NMAC, 7-1-04]

14.5.2.4 DURATION: Permanent.
[14.5.2.4 NMAC - Rp, 14.5.2.4 NMAC, 7-1-04]

14.5.2.5 EFFECTIVE DATE: July 1, 2004, unless a later date is cited at the end of a section.
[14.5.2.5 NMAC - Rp, 14.5.2.5 NMAC, 7-1-04]

14.5.2.6 OBJECTIVE: The purpose of this rule is to set forth standards and requirements for permitting construction in New Mexico.
[14.5.2.6 NMAC - Rp, 14.5.2.6 NMAC, 7-1-04]

14.5.2.7 DEFINITIONS: [Reserved]

14.5.2.8 PERMITS REQUIRED:

A. **Permits required.** Subject to CILA Section 60-13-3, section 60-13-45, and the provisions of the CID rules, no building or structure shall be erected, constructed, enlarged, altered, repaired, moved, improved, removed, converted or demolished, and no electrical wiring, plumbing or mechanical work as defined and described in the applicable New Mexico construction codes for those trades, may be installed, repaired or maintained in or on such building or structure, unless the applicable permit has first been obtained from the division.

B. **Exceptions to permit requirement.** Exceptions from permit requirements of the New Mexico construction codes shall not be deemed to grant authorization for any work to be done in any manner in violation of the provisions of CILA, any part of the CID rules, or any other applicable law.

C. **Previously permitted work; previously submitted plans.**

(1) Any work for which a permit has lawfully been issued prior to the effective date of this rule, which permit has not expired, deactivated or been revoked or suspended by the division pursuant to this part, may proceed as permitted, and the rules, codes and standards in effect at the time the permit was issued shall be the rules, codes and standards governing the work and its inspection.

(2) Any work for which plans have been submitted and received by the division shall be permitted and inspected pursuant to the rules in effect at the time the plans were received.

D. **Eligibility.** No person who is not appropriately, validly and currently licensed by the division is eligible to apply for or be issued a permit under this rule. Exception. Subject to the provisions of this part, a homeowner's permit may be issued to an unlicensed person.

E. **Application for permit.** In order to obtain a permit, the applicant must complete and submit a written application on the form and in the manner indicated by the division for the type of permit sought.

F. **Types.** Separate permits are required for general building, electrical and mechanical/plumbing, and liquefied petroleum gas work.

[14.5.2.8 NMAC - Rp, 14.5.2.8 NMAC, 14.7.2.10 NMAC, 14 NMAC 9.2.I.100-105, 14 NMAC 9.2.II.100 & 14.10.4.8 NMAC, 7-1-04]

14.5.2.9 EXCEPTIONS TO REQUIREMENT FOR PERMITS: Permits shall not be required for the following:

A. **Commercial.**

(1) One-story detached accessory structures used as tool and storage sheds, playhouses and similar uses, provided the floor area does not exceed 120 square feet (11.15.m2).

(2) Fences not over 6 feet (1829) high.

Exhibit 6d

(3) Oil derricks.

(4) Retaining walls that are not over 4 feet (1,219 mm) in height measured from the bottom of the footing to the top of the wall, unless supporting a surcharge or impounding class I, II, or III-A liquids.

(5) Water tanks supported directly upon grade if the capacity does not exceed 5,000 gallons (18,927L) and the ratio of height to diameter or width does not exceed 2 to 1.

(6) Sidewalks and driveways not more than 30 inches (762 mm) above grade and not over any basement or story below and which are not part of an accessible route.

(7) Painting, papering, tiling, carpeting, cabinets, counter tops and similar finish work.

(8) Temporary motion picture, television and theater stage sets and scenery.

(9) Prefabricated swimming pools accessory to a group R-3 occupancy, as applicable in the NMRBC, which are less than 24 inches (610mm) deep, do not exceed 5,000 gallons (19,000L) and are installed entirely above ground.

(10) Shade cloth structures constructed for nursery or agricultural purposes and not including services systems.

(11) Swings and other playground equipment accessory to one-and two-family dwellings.

(12) Window awnings supported by an exterior wall of group R-3, as applicable in the NMRBC, and group U occupancies.

(13) Moveable cases, counters and partitions not over 5 feet 9 inches (1,753mm) in height.

(14) Any work not otherwise regulated by the New Mexico construction codes and the CID rules.

B. **Residential:** Refer only to the "building" portion of Section R105.2 of the IRC, and add a new section: 10. Any work that is not otherwise regulated by a specific provision of the NMRBC.

C. **Mechanical work.** Refer to section 112.2 of the UMC.

D. **Plumbing work.** Refer to section 103.1.2 of the UPC.

E. **Electrical work.** No exceptions other than those set forth in CILA Section 60-13-45.

[14.5.2.9 NMAC - Rp, 14.7.2.10 NMAC, 14 NMAC 9.2.I 100-105 & 14 NMAC 9.2.II 100, 7-1-04]

14.5.2.10 **SUBMITTAL DOCUMENTS:**

A. **Submittal documents.**

(1) With each application for a permit, and when required by the building official or elsewhere in the CID Rules, two (2) sets of the following documents (collectively, submittal documents) must be submitted:

(a) type, occupancy and kind of structure;

(b) plans;

(c) specifications;

(d) engineering calculations;

(e) diagrams;

(f) soil investigation reports;

(g) other any other data or document required by the building official or the plan review official; and

(h) exterior wall envelope; submittal documents for all buildings shall describe the exterior wall envelope in sufficient detail to enable the plan review to determine compliance with the NMCBC and the NMRBC; the submittal documents shall show the exterior wall envelope in detail as required, including flashing, intersections with dissimilar materials, corners, end details, control joints, intersections at roof, eaves, or parapets, means of drainage, water-resistive membrane, and details around openings.

(2) For construction subject to the NMCBC, see sections 106.1.1, 106.1.2, 106.2 of the IBC for other requirements regarding submittal documents, including form, means of egress, and site plans.

(3) For construction subject to NMRBC, see sections 106.1.1, 106.1.2, 106.1.3 and 106.2 of the IRC for other requirements regarding submittal documents, including form, manufacturer's installation instructions, construction in flood areas, and site plans.

(4) Upon approval, one (1) set of the submittal documents shall be retained by the division, and one (1) set shall be returned to the permitee, shall be available at the work site, and shall be available for inspection by the building official or inspector during the performance of the permitted work.

(5) The building official may require submission of any specifications, drawings or diagrams necessary to show clearly the kind and extent of building construction work for which a permit application has been submitted.

B. **Professional seals requirements:** The building official or the plan review official is authorized to require submittal documents to be prepared and sealed by an architect, registered in accordance with the New Mexico Architectural Act, and the rules promulgated pursuant thereto, and/or by a professional engineer, registered in accordance with the New Mexico Engineering and Surveying Practice Act, and the rules promulgated pursuant thereto. An architect and/or engineer stamp is required for all uses listed in table 1004.1.2 in the IBC.

C. **Exceptions:** The requirement for plans and specifications to be prepared by an architect and/or engineer shall not be required in any of the following instances unless, in the discretion of the building official, an exception is not in the best interests of public safety or health.

Exhibit 6e

(1) Multiple dwellings of not more than two (2) stories in height and containing not more than four (4) dwelling units constructed of materials approved for use pursuant to the NMRBC, and provided that this exception is not construed to allow a person who is not an architect to design multiple clusters of four (4) dwelling units each where the total exceeds four (4) dwelling units on each lawfully divided lot.

(2) Garages or other structures not more than two (2) stories in height which are appurtenant to buildings described in paragraph (a) of this section.

(3) Group A, B, E divisions 1 and 2, F, M, S, U buildings or additions having a total occupant load of ten (10) or less (as defined in section 1003.2.2 and table 1003.2.2.2 of the IBC), and not more than two (2) stories in height.

(4) Alteration to buildings or structures that present no unusual conditions or hazards or change in occupancy.

(5) Single-family dwellings, not more than two (2) stories in height.

D. **Submission may be waived.** The building official may waive the submission of plans, calculations, construction inspection requirements and other data if it is found that the nature of the work applied for is such that plan review is not necessary to obtain compliance with the New Mexico construction codes.

E. **Deferred submittals.** For the purposes of this section, deferred submittals are defined as those portions of the design that are not submitted with the application for the permit, and that are to be submitted, thereafter, within a period specified by the building official or the plan review official.

F. **Approval.** Deferral of any submittal items must have the prior approval of the building official. The responsible design professional shall list the deferred submittals on the submittal documents accompanying the permit application. Submittal documents for deferred submittal items must be submitted to the responsible design professional who shall review and forward them to the division with a notation indicating that the deferred submittal documents have been reviewed and that they have been found to be in general conformance with the design of the building. The items identified in the deferred submittals shall not be installed until the building official has approved their design and submittal documents.

G. **Responsible design professional.** When submittal documents are required to be prepared by a registered design professional, the permit application shall indicate the registered design professional who shall be responsible for reviewing and coordinating submittal documents prepared by others, including phased and deferred submittal items, for compatibility with the design of the building. This design professional shall be deemed to be the "responsible design professional." The permitee shall notify the division in writing within a reasonable period of time, not to exceed ten (10) business days, if the responsible design professional is changed or is unable to continue to perform the duties required.

H. **Special submissions.** The building official or the plan review official is authorized to require, before and after the commencement of a project, the submission of any specification, drawing or diagram necessary to adequately and clearly show the kind, extent, and occupancy of the general building, mechanical and/or plumbing, and electrical work on the project that is covered by the permit issued, or that is required to be permitted under the CID rules.

I. **Phased approval.** See section 106.3.3 of the IBC for work subject to the NMCBC, and section 106.3.3 of the IRC for work subject to the NMRBC.

J. **Correction of submittal documents.** The issuance of a permit based on certain plans and specifications shall not prevent the building official from thereafter requiring the correction of any error in such plans or specifications, or from prohibiting work pursuant to those plans or specifications when a violation of the applicable code would result.

K. **Electrical projects.**

(1) Any installation with a calculated service capacity over 100 kVA single-phase or over 225 kVA three phase must be stamped by an electrical engineer, registered in accordance with the New Mexico Engineering and Surveying Practice Act. This requirement shall not apply to remote installations such as irrigation pumps. Any commercial project that requires an architect or engineer seal pursuant to this part, shall be submitted to the electrical bureau for review and approval.

(2) Submittal documents shall show the electrical riser, conductor size, grounding conductor size, method of grounding (available electrodes, etc.), load calculations, available fault calculations, size and location of disconnects, panel schedules, wiring methods, site and floor plan. General expressions such as "work shall be done in accordance with the New Mexico Electrical Code" or "work shall be done to the satisfaction of the state building official" shall be considered inadequate, and incomplete.

(3) No permit for electrical work shall be issued for the addition to, or alteration of, wiring of an existing building unless the building as it will be wired conforms to the requirements of the code for new buildings, except that those portions of the existing wiring that have not been disturbed and are deemed safe by the inspector may remain in service.

L. **Mechanical projects.**

(1) The building official is authorized to require the stamp of a professional engineer, registered in accordance with the New Mexico Engineering and Surveying Practice Act on permits for mechanical and/or plumbing work with a total value of $50,000.00, or more, and/or for commercial buildings three stories and higher.

(2) For plans for buildings for more than two stories in height, other than R-3 and U occupancies, see the second paragraph of section 113.3 of the UMC.

M. **Permit contents and display.** Pursuant to CILA Section 60-13-59, every permit or notice of permit issued by the division shall:

(1) clearly indicate the name and address of the owner of the property;

Exhibit 6f

(2) contain a legal description of the property being built on either by "lot and block" description in a subdivision, by street address in a municipality, or by township, range and section numbers if outside a municipality or planed subdivision;

(3) contain the name, address and license number of the contractor or the homeowner to whom the permit is to be issued, and the name of the architect and/or engineer as may be required by the building official; and

(4) be prominently displayed on the site where the permitted work is to be performed.

N. **Retention.** The division shall retain construction documents, including submittal documents and permit applications, in accordance with New Mexico state laws governing document retention.

O. **Preliminary inspection.** As part of the document review process, before issuing a building permit, the building official is authorized to examine or cause to be examined buildings, structures and sites for which an application for a building permit has been filed.

[14.5.2.10 NMAC - Rp, 14.5.2.8 NMAC, 14.5.2.9 NMAC, 14.5.2.10 NMAC, 14.7.2.10 NMAC, 14 NMAC 9.2.I.100, 14 NMAC 9.2.II.100 NMAC & 14.10.4.8 NMAC, 7-1-04]

14.5.2.11 ISSUANCE:

A. **Plan review.** Within a reasonable time after receipt, the division shall review submittal documents for compliance with the applicable New Mexico construction codes and the CID rules. If the submittal documents do not comply, the division shall reject them and shall communicate the reasons for rejection to the applicant in writing. If the submittal documents meet the applicable codes and rules, the submittal documents shall be approved, in writing or by stamp, as "reviewed" and the division shall issue a permit to the applicant after payment in full of the applicable permit fees, as set forth in 14.5.5 NMAC, Fees.

B. **Authorization to change.** No change or modification may be made to approved submittal documents for which a permit has been issued without the express, written authorization of the building official. All work authorized by a permit must be performed in accordance with the approved submittal documents for which the permit was issued. Changes in the work authorized by a permit must be reflected in an amended set of submittal documents, which must be resubmitted for approval by the division

[14.5.2.11 NMAC - Rp, 14.7.2.10 NMAC, 14 NMAC 9.2.I.100 & 14 NMAC 9.2.II.100, 7-1-04]

14.5.2.12 VALIDITY OF PERMIT: The issuance or granting of a permit shall not be construed to be a permit for, or an approval of, any violation of any of the provisions of the New Mexico construction codes or any other applicable law or rule. Permits presuming to give authority to violate or cancel the provisions of the New Mexico construction codes or any other applicable law or rule shall not be valid. The issuance of a permit based on construction documents and other data shall not prevent the building official from requiring the correction of errors in the construction documents and other data.

[14.5.2.12 NMAC - Rp, 14.7.2.10 NMAC, 7-1-04]

14.5.2.13 SUSPENSION, CANCELLATION, OR REVOCATION OF PERMIT:

A. The building official is authorized to suspend, cancel or revoke a permit issued pursuant to the code for which the official has responsibility in the following causes:

(1) whenever the permit is issued in error, or on the basis of incorrect, inaccurate or incomplete information;

(2) whenever the permit was issued in violation of the CID rules;

(3) when there is no contractor on the job;

(4) work stoppage;

(5) change in the person or entity performing the work;

(6) at the request of the permitee;

(7) whenever the person to whom the permit is issued is in violation of the licensing or certification requirements of the act or 14.6 NMAC.

B. A suspended permit may be reactivated upon approval of the appropriate building official and payment of any fee assessed pursuant to 14.5.5 NMAC, Fees.

[14.5.2.13 NMAC - Rp, 14.5.2.12 NMAC & 14 7.2.10 NMAC, 7-1-04; A, 02-01-06]

14.5.2.14 EXPIRATION AND DEACTIVATION OF PERMIT:

A. **Expiration.** Every permit issued by the division under the provisions of the CID rules shall expire and be void if the work authorized by such permit is not commenced within 180 days from the date such permit was issued.

B. **Deactivation.** If the work authorized by a permit is suspended, delayed or abandoned at any time after the work is commenced and such suspension, delay or abandonment continues for 180 days, the permit shall become inactive.

(1) **Reactivation.** An inactive permit may be reactivated if the work resumes within one (1) year from the date the permit was issued, upon approval of the building official and payment of a fee equal to 1/2 of the original permit fee. Such reactivated permit will authorize work only to the extent it conforms to the submission documents on which the original permit was issued.

Exhibit 6g

(2) **Cancellation.** If work does not resume within one (1) year from the date the inactive permit was issued, the inactive permit will automatically cancel. In order for work on the project to continue, a new permit application must be submitted, a new, full permit fee must be remitted, and a new permit issued.

C. **Extension of time.** The building official may extend the time of an active permit for an additional period not to exceed 180 days on receipt of a written request from the permit holder showing that circumstances beyond the control of the permitee have caused delay in the permitted work.

D. **Penalties.** Any work performed after a permit expires, cancels or becomes inactive shall constitute a violation of the CID rules and the person performing the work, or causing the work to be performed, may be subject to penalties as provided in the CILA.

[14.5.2.14 NMAC - Rp, 14.7.2.10 NMAC, 14 NMAC 9.2.I.100, 14 NMAC 9.2.II.100 & 14.10.4.8 NMAC, 7-1-04]

14.5.2.15 DENIAL OF PERMIT:

A. The director may deny the issuance of a permit and associated inspections for good cause. Good cause shall include, without limitation:

(1) failure to pay all or part of a permit fee or penalty when due;
(2) payment of any amount due the division with a "non-sufficient funds" check; and
(3) an outstanding balance on any amounts due the division that has accrued without approval of the director.

B. After receipt of a "non-sufficient funds" check, the division may require payment in cash, or cashier's check.

[14.5.2.15 NMAC - Rp, 14.5.2.8 NMAC, 7-1-04]

14.5.2.16 FAILURE TO OBTAIN PERMIT: If any work, other than site preparation, for which a permit is required is commenced prior to obtaining the necessary permit, the building official may either assess a fee in the amount of twice the usual permit and inspection fees, or refer the violation for disciplinary action by the division.

[14.5.2.16 NMAC - Rp, 14.7.2.10 NMAC, 7-1-04]

14.5.2.17 TEMPORARY STRUCTURES:

A. **Permits.** The building official is authorized to issue a permit for temporary structures and temporary uses. Such permits shall specify an expiration date not to exceed one (1) year from the date of issuance. The building official is authorized to grant extensions for good cause that is supported by credible evidence.

B. **Conformance.** See section 107.2 of the IBC.

C. **Temporary power.** A permit may be issued by the appropriate building official authorizing a connection of a temporary system for supplying electrical power, water, gas, or sewage service, after inspection and testing by the inspector. When the temporary use of such system is no longer required, the permitee shall notify the appropriate building official or inspector. The temporary work permit may be canceled by the building official or the inspector if the temporary work that is covered by the permit has not passed a pre-final inspection within one (1) year after the permit was issued. Upon receipt of written notice of such cancellation, the appropriate utility shall discontinue service to such system, and service shall not be resumed until a new permit for the work on the system is issued.

D. **Termination of approval.** The building official is authorized to terminate a permit for a temporary structure when it appears to the building official that it is in the best interests of health, safety and welfare to do so.

[14.5.2.17 NMAC - Rp, 14 NMAC 9.2.I 100-105, 14 NMAC 9.2.II 100 & 14.10.4.8 NMAC, 7-1-04]

14.5.2.18 HOMEOWNER'S PERMIT:

A. Homeowner's permits are limited to R-3 single-family dwellings, U-1 private garages, carports, sheds and agricultural buildings, and U-2 fences. No application for a homeowner's permit may be made to cover construction of any structure, or installations within any structure, or construction of part of a structure, where the use will be anything but residential purposes. This applies to additions to residential dwellings that will not be used for residential purposes. Further, homeowner's permits may not be used to cover construction of any structure, or installations within any structure, or construction of part of a structure, where the homeowner will not personally reside.

B. Any person applying for a homeowner's permit in order to construct a personal residence in accordance with Paragraph (10) of Subsection D of CILA Section 60-13-3 must sign a homeowner's permit responsibility sheet issued by the division, or its authorized local building department, acknowledging legal responsibilities and liabilities before obtaining such a permit.

C. The homeowner's permit covers general, residential construction only.

D. A homeowner's permit may not be used to permit a project where a GB-2 or GB-98 contractor is acting as a general contractor on the project. Any contractor acting as a general contractor on a project where there is a homeowner's permit must obtain a building permit for his work, and shall be held responsible for any work performed at this site. Further, licensed subcontractors will be held responsible for their work, which also must be permitted separately.

E. A homeowner may do electrical and/or plumbing work on his home (single-family dwelling) only if he

Exhibit 6h

has sufficient knowledge and experience to do so, as determined by approval by the appropriate building official of the plans for the proposed work and after completing a written examination administered by the building official with a grade of seventy-five percent (75%) or more. If the examination is not passed, it may be repeated not sooner than thirty (30) days after the date of the failed exam.

F. After approval of the submitted plans and satisfactorily passing the written examination(s), the homeowner then must obtain the applicable permit(s) for the electrical and/or plumbing work and must pay the required inspection fees.

G. Homeowner's permit projects may not be placed on the market for sale while under construction. Such an action violates the requirements of paragraph (10) of Subsection D of CILA Section 60-13-3, and will result in the automatic void of the permit by the division. Such a violation may also result in initiation of unlicensed contracting charges against the homeowner in accordance with the requirement of CILA Section 60-13-52.

H. No more than one (1) homeowner's permit for an R-3 single-family dwelling shall be issued to the same person within any twelve (12) month period.

I. Where a homeowner's permit is involved, a properly licensed contractor must install HVAC and natural gas or LP gas installations. This work shall be permitted and inspected pursuant to the standard requirements of the division.
[14.5.2.18 NMAC - Rp, 14.5.2.10 NMAC & 14.7.2.10 NMAC, 7-1-04]

14.5.2.19 ANNUAL PERMIT:

A. An annual permit may be obtained in accordance with CILA Section 60-13-46.

B. The electrical and/or mechanical journeyman who qualifies for an annual permit holder shall be a full-time employee of such permit holder.

C. At regular intervals, the inspector having jurisdiction shall visit all buildings and premises where work is being done under an annual permit and shall inspect all work done under such permit since the date of his last visit. He shall issue a certificate of approval for such work as is found to be in conformity with applicable code and these rules after payment of all required fees.

D. An annual permit holder who fails to keep a complete and accurate record of all work done under his annual permit shall forfeit the right to such annual permit, shall turn it in to the division upon demand, and shall not be eligible to apply for another annual permit for one (1) year thereafter.

E. An annual permit shall expire twelve (12) months from the date of issuance.
[14.5.2.19 NMAC - Rp, 14.5.2.10 NMAC, 7-1-04]

14.5.2.20 EMERGENCY WORK: Where equipment replacement or repairs must be performed in an emergency situation, application for the appropriate permit must be made on the next working business day either by computer or in person at one of the division offices.
[14.5.2.20 NMAC - Rp, 14.7.2.10 NMAC, 7-1-04]

14.5.2.21 CONNECTION OF SERVICE UTILITIES: Except where work is done under an annual permit, no person shall make connections from a utility, source of energy, fuel or power to any building or system that is regulated by the New Mexico construction codes for which a permit is required, until approved by the appropriate building official or a designated representative.
[14.5.2.21 NMAC - Rp, 14.5.3.8 NMAC, 14 NMAC 9.2.I.100, 14 NMAC 9.2.II.100 & 14.10.4.8 NMAC, 7-1-04]

HISTORY OF 14.5.2 NMAC:
Pre-NMAC History:
Material in this part was derived from that previously filed with the commission of public records - state records center and archives as:
CIC 70-2, General Construction Classifications, filed 11-25-70;
CIC 72-4, General Construction Classifications, filed 02-16-72;
CIC 76-2, Rules And Regulations, filed 05-05-76;
CID 78-2, Rules And Regulations, filed 12-05-78;
CID 79-1, Rules And Regulations, filed 06-06-79;
CID 82-1, Construction Industries Rules And Regulations, filed 04-14-82;
CID 85-1, Construction Industries Rules And Regulations, filed 02-04-85;
CID 90-1, Construction Industries Rules And Regulations, filed 05-31-90.

History of Repealed Material:
14 NMAC 5.2, Housing and Construction - Construction Industries General Provisions - Permits (filed 9-2-97), repealed effective 12-1-00.
14.5.2, Housing and Construction - Construction Industries General Provisions - Permits (filed 10-16-00), repealed effective

Exhibit 6i

14.5.2 N Sep. 17. 2007 12:01PM   LOMAS LAW OFFICES   http://www.nmcpr.state.nm.us/nmac/parts/title14/14.005.0002.htm

7-1-04.

Other History:
That portion of CID 90-1, Construction Industries Rules And Regulations, filed 05-31-90 -- renumbered, reformatted and amended to 14 NMAC 5.2, Housing and Construction - Construction Industries General Provisions - Permits, effective 09-14-96.
14 NMAC 5.2, Housing and Construction - Construction Industries General Provisions - Permits (filed 09-03-96) replaced by 14 NMAC 5.2, Housing and Construction - Construction Industries General Provisions - Permits, effective 09-23-97.
14 NMAC 5.2, Housing and Construction - Construction Industries General Provisions - Permits (filed 09-02-97) replaced by 14.5.2 NMAC, Housing and Construction - Construction Industries General Provisions - Permits, effective 12-1-00.
14.5.2 NMAC, Housing and Construction - Construction Industries General Provisions - Permits (filed 10-16-00), and those applicable portions of 14.7.2 NMAC, Section 10 (filed 10-16-00); 14 NMAC 9.2, Subpart I, Sections 100-105 (filed 10-30-98); 14 NMAC 9.2, Subpart II, Section 100 (filed 10-30-98); 14.10.4 NMAC, Section 8 (filed 7-1-02); and 14.5.3 NMAC (filed 10-16-00), Section 8 - replaced by 14.5.2 NMAC, Housing and Construction - Construction Industries General Provisions - Permits, effective 7-1-04.

Exhibit 6j

STATE OF NEW MEXICO

IN THE MAGISTRATE COURT COUNTY OF TORRANCE

State of New Mexico No. M-192-MR-200700037

v.

BRADLEY FRANKS, Defendant

MAGISTRATE COURT
TORRANCE COUNTY
OCT 12 2007
FILED IN MY OFFICE
CLERK OF THE MAGISTRATE COURT

NOTICE OF REVIEW HEARING

TO: RICHARD LEDBETTER Prosecution[1]
TORRANCE COUNTY PLANNING & ZONING
P.O. BOX 48
ESTANCIA, NM 87016

BRADLEY FRANKS Defendant
P.O. BOX 831
MCINTOSH, NM 87032-0831

YOU ARE ordered to appear for **REVIEW HEARING** before the Honorable THOMAS G PESTAK, at the MAGISTRATE Court located at TORRANCE COUNTY MAGISTRATE COURT, 1100 ROUT 66, P..O. BOX 2027, MORIARTY, NM 87035 on November 16, 2007 at 10:00 **(a.m.) TRAILING DOCKET.**

If you fail to appear a warrant may be issued for your arrest.

Date of this notice:

Dated: October 12, 2007.

(~~Judge~~) (Clerk)

Distribution Instructions
1 copy - Court 1 copy - Defendant 1 copy - Prosecutor
[As amended, effective January 1, 1995; May 1, 2002.]

Criminal Form 9-501

Exhibit 7

STATE OF NEW MEXICO

IN THE MAGISTRATE COURT COUNTY OF TORRANCE

State of New Mexico No. M-192-MR-200700037

v.

BRADLEY FRANKS, Defendant

MAGISTRATE COURT
TORRANCE COUNTY
NOV 2 8 2007
FILED IN MY OFFICE
CLERK OF THE MAGISTRATE COURT

NOTICE OF JURY PANEL SELECTION AND TRIAL

TO: SGT RICHARD LEDBETTER Prosecution
TORRANCE COUNTY PLANNING AND ZONING
PO BOX 48
ESTANCIA, NM 87016

BRADLEY FRANKS Defendant
PO BOX 831
MCINTOSH, NM 87032

YOU ARE ordered to appear for **JURY PANEL SELECTION AND TRIAL** before the Honorable THOMAS G PESTAK, at the MAGISTRATE Court located at TORRANCE COUNTY MAGISTRATE COURT, NEIL MERTZ JUDICIAL COMPLEX, 902 5TH STREET, PO BOX 274, ESTANCIA, NM 87016 on JANUARY 18, 2008 at 9:30 AM TRAILING DOCKET.

If you fail to appear a warrant may be issued for your arrest.

Date of this notice:

Dated: November 28, 2007.

~~(Judge)~~ (Clerk)

Distribution Instructions
1 copy - Court 1 copy - Defendant 1 copy - Prosecutor
[As amended, effective January 1, 1995; May 1, 2002.]

Criminal Form 9-501

Exhibit 8

STATE OF NEW MEXICO

IN THE MAGISTRATE COURT — COUNTY OF TORRANCE

State of New Mexico — No. M-192-MR-200800004

v.

BRADLEY FRANKS, Defendant

MAGISTRATE COURT
TORRANCE COUNTY
JAN 23 2008
FILED IN MY OFFICE
CLERK OF MAGISTRATE COURT

NOTICE OF SENTENCING

TO: BRADLEY FRANKS Defendant
PO BOX 831
MCINTOSH, NM 87032

YOU ARE ordered to appear for **SENTENCING** before the Honorable THOMAS PESTAK, at the MAGISTRATE Court located at TORRANCE COUNTY MAGISTRATE COURT, 1100 ROUTE 66, P.O. BOX 2027, MORIARTY, NM 87035 on **February 08, 2008 at 10:00 AM TRAILING DOCKET.**

If you fail to appear a warrant may be issued for your arrest.

Date of this notice:

Dated: January 22, 2008.

~~(Judge)~~ (Clerk)

Distribution Instructions
1 copy - Court 1 copy - Defendant 1 copy - Prosecutor
[As amended, effective January 1, 1995; May 1, 2002.]

Criminal Form 9-501

Exhibit 8a

Caselookup - Case Detail Page 1 of 4

New Mexico Courts
Case Lookup

Exit

Name Search Case Number Search DWI Search

Case Detail

STATE VS. FRANKS BRADLEY

CASE DETAIL

CASE NUMBER	CURRENT JUDGE	FILING DATE	COURT
M-192-MR-200700037	THOMAS G PESTAK	07/11/2007	ESTANCIA MAGISTRATE

PARTIES TO THIS CASE

PARTY TYPE	PARTY DESCRIPTION	PARTY #	PARTY NAME
D	DEFENDANT	1	FRANKS BRADLEY
P	PLAINTIFF	1	LEDBETTER RICHARD A
			ATTORNEY: DENNIS K WALLIN

CRIMINAL CHARGE DETAIL

PARTY	COUNT	SEQ #	STATUTE	CHARGE	CLASS	CHARGE DATE	CIT #	PLEA	DISPOSITION	DISP DATE
D 1	1	1	TORR CO 94-12	TORRANCE CO SOLID WASTE ORDINANCE		05/21/2007				
D 1	2	1	30-8-1	PUBLIC NUISANCE		05/21/2007				
D 1	3	1	TORR CO 90-3-19(D)	DEVELOPMENT REVIEW PERMIT		05/21/2007				
D 1	4	1	30-8-9	ABANDONMENT OF DANGEROUS CONTAINERS		05/21/2007				

HEARINGS FOR THIS CASE

HEARING DATE	HEARING TIME	HEARING TYPE	HEARING JUDGE	COURT	COURT ROOM
11/16/2007	8:30 AM	CAL: MISCELLANEOUS	THOMAS G PESTAK	ESTANCIA MAGISTRATE COURT	1
08/02/2007	10:30 AM	CAL: ARRAIGNMENT	LARRY S JONES	ESTANCIA MAGISTRATE COURT	2

http://www.nmcourts.com/caselookup/app 1/31/2008

Exhibit 9a

Caselookup - Case Detail

REGISTER OF ACTIONS ACTIVITY

EVENT DATE	EVENT DESCRIPTION	EVENT RESULT	PARTY TYPE	PARTY #	AMOUNT
01/24/2008	MISC ENTRY		D	1	
	JT- APPOINTMENT OF SPECIAL PROSECUTOR				
	DENNIS WALLIN				
01/18/2008	ORD: ORD FILED		D	1	
	SLW - ORDER FOR EXTENSION OF TIME - 60 DAYS				
	EXTENDS DATE FOR TRIAL TO 4-1-08				
01/18/2008	CORRESPONDENCE		D	1	
	SLW - NOTICE OF WITHDRAWAL OF MOTION FOR CONTINUANCE				
	FILED BY PROS				
01/18/2008	CAL: TRIAL JURY	C	D	1	
01/16/2008	CAL: HEARING/MTN	HRD	D	1	
	TELEPHONIC HEARING MKT				
01/14/2008	MTN: FOR CONTINUANCE		P	1	
	MTN FOR CONTINUANCE REQUESTED BY THE STATE MKT				
01/14/2008	ENTRY OF APPEARANCE FILED		P	1	
	ATTY FOR THE STATE D WALLIN MKT				
11/28/2007	NTC: OF TRIAL (CRIMINAL)		D	1	$ 0.00
	9NT-07784 issued by 20 (6010) NTC: OF TRIAL (CRIMINAL)				
11/16/2007	CAL: MISCELLANEOUS	HRD	D	1	
10/11/2007	ORD: WITHDRAWAL OF COUNSEL		D	1	
10/10/2007	MTN: TO WITHDRAW AS COUNSEL		D	1	
	JT- FILED BY DEFENSE ATTORNEY				
10/09/2007	NTC: OF HEARING		D	1	$ 0.00
	9NT-07692 issued by 5 (6005) NTC: OF HEARING				
10/05/2007	CAL: PRE-TRIAL CONFERENCE	C	D	1	
08/23/2007	NTC: CRIMINAL PRETRIAL CONFER		D	1	$ 0.00
	9PC-03357 issued by 5 (6050) NTC: CRIMINAL PRETRIAL CONFER				
08/23/2007	ORD: DESIG JDG RECV-DIST COURT		D	1	

http://www.nmcourts.com/caselookup/app

Exhibit 9b

	JONES TO RECUSE.			
	FILE TO JT IN MOR.KE			
08/02/2007	NTC: ORD OF APPT	D	1	
	ANDRES W/REIMBURSEMENT.KE			
08/02/2007	INDIGENT DETERM DENIED	D	1	
08/02/2007	ARRAIGNMENT HELD	D	1	
08/02/2007	CAL: ARRAIGNMENT CONCL			
	Calendar Posting on 07-11-2007			
07/11/2007	NTC: CRIMINAL SUMMONS	D	1	$ 0.00
	9CS-04856 issued by 21 (6022) NTC: CRIMINAL SUMMONS			
07/11/2007	OPN: CRIMINAL COMPLAINT FILED	D	1	
	LEDBETTER - TCPZ			
	SOLID WASTE			
	PUBLIC NUISANCE			
	DEVELOPMENT REVIEW PERMIT			
	ABANDON DANGEROUS CONTAINERS			
	APPEAR BY 08/02/07.KE			

JUDGE ASSIGNMENT HISTORY

ASSIGNMENT DATE	JUDGE NAME	SEQUENCE #	ASSIGNMENT EVENT DESCRIPTION
07/11/2007	LARRY S JONES	1	INITIAL ASSIGNMENT
08/23/2007	THOMAS G PESTAK	2	JDG: JUDGE ASSIGNMENT RECUSAL

Return Print

Exhibit 9c

STATE OF NEW MEXICO
COUNTY OF TORRANCE
MAGISTRATE COURT

STATE OF NEW MEXICO,

Plaintiff,

No. M-192-MR-2007-00037

vs.

BRADLEY FRANKS

Defendant.

MOTION FOR WITHDRAWAL OF COUNSEL

COMES NOW CARPENTER LAW, P.C., (Joshua Carpenter) counsel for the Defendant herein, and hereby moves the Court for an Order allowing its withdrawal as counsel of record for the Defendant Bradley Franks, and as grounds therefore, states as follows:

1. There are presently no hearings currently scheduled in this matter. No prejudice will result to either party by allowing this withdrawal.
2. Defendant Bradley Franks has moved out of state.
3. Communications between Defendant and his counsel have broken down.
4. Good cause exists for counsel to withdraw.
5. Opposing counsel has been contacted and consents to the withdrawal.

Respectfully submitted,

CARPENTER LAW, P.C.

Joshua Carpenter
500 Marquette, NW, Suite #1460
Albuquerque, NM 87102
(505) 243-0065

Exhibit 10a

I hereby certify that a true and correct copy of the foregoing was faxed and mailed on this 28rd day of April, 2008 to WALLIN & BRIONES LAW FIRM, LLC, Dennis Wallin, Attorney for the State of New Mexico, P. O. Box 696, Moriarty, NM 87035, (505) 832-6363.

Joshua Carpenter

Exhibit 10b

WED/APR/30/2008 04:32 PM P.001

APR-30-2008 WED 03:54 PM Moriarty Magistrate Cour FAX NO. 5058321563 P. 03

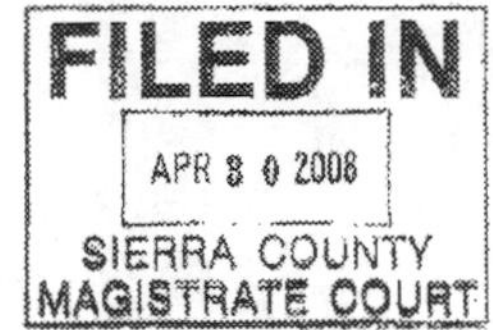
FILED IN

APR 3 0 2008

SIERRA COUNTY MAGISTRATE COURT

STATE OF NEW MEXICO
COUNTY OF TORRANCE
MAGISTRATE COURT

STATE OF NEW MEXICO,
Plaintiff,

No. M-192-MR-2007-00037

vs.

BRADLEY FRANKS
Defendant.

STIPULATED ORDER ALLOWING WITHDRAWAL OF COUNSEL

THIS MATTER having come before the Court on the agreement of counsel, and the Court being sufficiently advised in the premises, FINDS and ORDERS that the motion is well-taken and allows Carpenter Law, P.C. (Joshua Carpenter) to withdraw as counsel for Defendant Bradley Franks.

IT IS SO ORDERED

4/30/08
MAGISTRATE COURT JUDGE

Approved:

CARPENTER LAW, P.C.

By: __________
Joshua Carpenter
Attorney for Defendant
500 Marquette, NW, Suite #1460
Albuquerque, NM 87102
(505) 243-0065

MAGISTRATE COURT
TORRANCE COUNTY
APR 3 0 2008
FILED IN MY OFFICE
CLERK OF MAGISTRATE COURT

WALLIN & BRIONES LAW FIRM, LLC

By: Telephonically approved – April 28, 2008
Dennis Wallin
Attorney for the State of New Mexico
P. O. Box 696
Moriarty, NM 87035
(505) 832-6363

ENTERED MAY 0 2 2008
ON ______
Calendared
ON ______
Notice Mailed
ON ______

Exhibit 10c

500 Marquette Ave, NW
Suite 1460
Albuquerque, NM 87102
Telephone (505) 243-0065
Facsimile (505) 243-0067
www.carpenterlawnm.com

May 9, 2008

Mr. Bradley Franks
c/o Alan L. Hausladen
P. O. Box 531
Cross Lake, MN 56442

Re: State of New Mexico v. Franks
Cause No. M-192-MR-200700037

Dear Mr. Franks:

Please find enclosed court-endorsed copies of a Motion for Withdrawal of Counsel and Stipulated Order Allowing Withdrawal of Counsel in the above-referenced matter

Sincerely,

CARPENTER LAW, P.C.

Claudia W. Goodreau, Paralegal to
Joshua Carpenter

Enclosure (as stated)

Exhibit 10d

The above documents are exhibits and evidence showing that the courts are committing crimes against humanity for the sake of <u>their</u> pockets and Bank Accounts.

7

FINAL THOUGHTS

THIS CHAPTER IS FOR YOU TO READ AND UNDERSTAND THAT THE government is not your friend and the bureaucrats, politicians, judges and lawyers are not your "friends" and they will 'never' help you when they explain to you that they "want to help you".

We all know and understand that the Bureaucrats, Politicians, Lawyers and Judges claim, "We are not above the Law". However, we have noticed and seen time and time again that these same Bureaucrats, Politicians, Lawyers and Judges "Forgive" every wrong doing they commit against Americans when those Americans exercise their "Rights" and prove how crooked and corrupt the System really is.

The Constitution states that it is our "right" to publically charge anyone or any business of wrong doing. However, it takes two Americans. Therefore, Robert – C. : Simpson and I hereby Charge and Accuse the County of Riverside, State of California and all of the perpetrators of the three cases with Treason by Sedition, Civil Rights Violations, Felony Grand Theft, Fraud, Extortion, Obstructing Justice and other charges that apply. Robert – C. : Simpson and I Charge and Accuse Torrance County, State New Mexico and the perpetrators involved with the case in New Mexico with Treason by Sedition, Civil Rights Violations, Fraud, Extortion, Kidnapping, Extortion, Obstructing Justice and other charges that apply.

The Title: 42 Lawsuit Robert and I filed against the State of California and the Perpetrators that committed crimes against Americans caused the State Bond to be rescinded. This was step one of the retaliation against the 'Organized Crime' the Politicians and State Bureaucrats call "Business".

The next step will be filed for the International Court along with an order to 'Rescind' the Charter of the State of California and the State of New Mexico by a Writ of Mandamus and Quo Warranto for Organized Criminal activities by R.I.C.O. Laws.

This case cannot be "heard" or "tried" in the United States because of the "Conflict of Interest" and the Fact that Judges get highly paid for dispensing their form of Justice by a Corporate Government.

It is up to us to put a stop to these so–called professionals, before this country loses its "Life, liberty, and Pursuit of Happiness".

Before you realize what is happening we will be under "Martial Law" and those individuals who have diligently tried to put a stop to these "Questionable Acts" will be placed into "internment camps", until the new government decides what to do with the "prisoners".

The International Governments need to investigate the fact that California Bureaucrats and Politicians as well as outside Politicians have had "selfish interests" in the Electric Companies during the "vote" for de-regulation of the Electric Companies in California and the "withdrawal from the F. E. R. C." Furthermore, it is my **right** by the "Constitution" to charge and accuse the State of California, Riverside County, and all of the individuals that are involved with the case brought against us, with "Treason by Sedition, Conspiracy, Fraud, Extortion, Racketeering (by the R.I.C.O Laws) and Felony Grand Theft," and other charges that can be proven through the evidence within this book.

I charge and accuse the State of New Mexico, Torrance County, and all of the individuals that are involved in the case and unlawful hearings and "trial" brought against me, with "Treason by Sedition, Conspiracy, Fraud, Extortion, Racketeering, and other charges that can be proven through the evidence within this book.

It has been brought to my attention that you may have misunderstood the "Remedy" section of this book. When a Bureaucrat, Politician, Judge or Lawyer violate' your Constitutional Rights or Civil Rights, you can press charges and have them prosecuted to full extent of the Law. However, there is an old saying, "Sharks do not eat their own". The other Remedy is to rescind the Town, City, County or State Bond and Suspend the Town, City, County or State Charter through the use of a Writ of Mandamus and Quo Warranto. These Towns, Cities, Counties, or States claim that they have

Rights. However, if any of them "deprive you of any rights" or "violate your Constitutional Rights" the Towns, Cities, Counties, or States lose those rights that they claim they have.

However, If we can interest the international community by charging the U. S. with the same charges and add "**Conspiracy: Fraud**" and **cover up** and help the international community with a "Qui Tam Action". This will help in returning some of the "monies" the "Electric Companies" have "over billed" or "over charged" businesses and homes.

I wish to convey to you as you have read this book that this is a "True and Factual" account of what happened to Robert Simpson and I for exposing a Major Crime - The Fraud being committed by Electric Companies that is continuously plied against all Americans and International Companies and International Countries.

I seriously hope that the information within this book will be of great help to you as you try to navigate through the "Tidal Waves" they call a court system.

This saying was stated to Robert Simpson and I on several occasions, "No hard feelings, business is business".

Printed in the United States
by Baker & Taylor Publisher Services